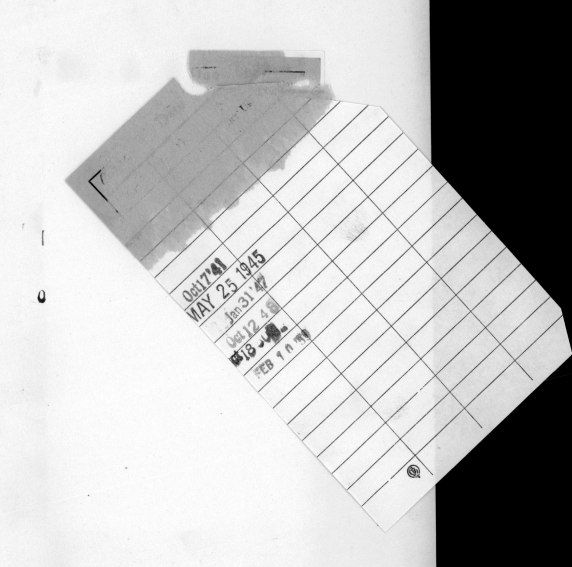

THE GREAT
CULTURAL TRADITIONS

《‹-《‹-››-››

Volume II
THE CLASSICAL EMPIRES

THE GREAT
CULTURAL TRADITIONS

The Foundations of Civilization

IN TWO VOLUMES

❮❮❮·❮❮❮·❯❯❯·❯❯❯

Volume I
THE ANCIENT CITIES

The beginnings of cultural developments among preliterate men, the transmission of their achievements among early literate men, and the organization of the traditional structures of behavior, feeling, and thought in the ancient cities of the Near East, Asia, and Europe.

Volume II
THE CLASSICAL EMPIRES

The ancient Asiatic and European urban cultures in their imperial phase and decline, the interactions among them, and the reorientation of their cultural traditions under the influence of the displacement of their carrying populations.

VICTORS AND VICTIMS

This relief from a Sarcophagus of the Roman Imperial Age suggests that the classical
empires were established by violence and supported by exploitation, notwithstanding
whatever benevolence their ruling classes displayed.

THE GREAT CULTURAL TRADITIONS

The Foundations of Civilization

≪≪-≪≪-≫≫-≫≫

VOLUME II
THE CLASSICAL EMPIRES

by RALPH TURNER, PH.D.

FIRST EDITION

McGRAW-HILL BOOK COMPANY, INC.
NEW YORK AND LONDON
1941

THE GREAT CULTURAL TRADITIONS

THE MAPLE PRESS COMPANY, YORK, PA.

PREFACE

≪≪-≪≪-≫≫-≫≫

Me thought I was a billow in the crowd
Of Common Men, that stream without a shore,
That ocean which at once is deaf and loud.
—SHELLEY.

If the first volume of this work expressed a point of view toward history and its study, it should be made clear at the beginning of the second volume that this point of view implies an attitude toward the social order. This attitude arises from the conviction that the norm for studying and interpreting a culture is the pervasive condition of life among the great body of the population that carries a culture. The significance of this attitude for the treatment of cultural developments in the period of the classical empires is great indeed, for in that period the emotional reactions of the great bodies of carrying populations to the distresses that pervaded their lives became the primary factor in cultural development. For this reason the reorientations of the fundamental urban cultural traditions that were shaped in the period of the classical empires were not so much the products of innovations as they were the results of the regrouping of traits and patterns in conformity with the emotional reactions of the masses, and for this reason, also, the reorientations were primarily religious in content and in tone.

The moving of the great body of a population that carries a cultural tradition to the center of attention of the historian and social analyst has significance in the present age of imperial conflict, revolutionary strife, and cultural disorganization, for it points to that factor which may be decisive for further cultural development, *viz.*, the new circumstances that organize the lives of the great bodies of men and women now carrying the cultural traditions persisting from the ancient period discussed in this volume. Common men, again, are the decisive social factor in the development of culture.

The classical empires were undemocratic organizations, *i.e.*, they embodied an institutional structure and a correlative complex of social attitudes which maintained a special interest at the expense of common well-being. And in this effort, they either coerced opinion or frustrated the advancement and diffusion of knowledge. Indeed, it should be recognized that an undemocratic social order must ultimately either suppress facts or distort them or become intolerant of conviction shaped in terms of them, for if the utilization of these facts in a service of common well-being cannot be achieved without endangering the entrenched special interest, an active resistance to their full utilization will be organized. Only a democracy can face facts for what they are and use them for the most complete achievement of well-being that they make possible. Unfortunately the duty to face facts too easily becomes the right to distort them and the right of free and full discussion, without the moral responsibility that asserts the common interest and the intellectual integrity which declares the facts as they are fully known, become merely the right to organize a propaganda.

The period of the classical empires culminated in an age of economic decline and social disorder; the present age—confused and turbulent—will do no better if it fails to make intellectual integrity the support of liberty and common well-being the goal of democracy.

If it is indicated in the sections of this book, as the author hopes it is, that arrangements of historical data and their interpretation, *i.e.*, knowledge and judgments, serve social functions, the reader who derives from this knowledge the willingness to ask, "Who assembled these facts?" "What was his purpose?" and "How did his purpose affect his judgment?" has won the beginnings of the intelligent action which a democracy demands. Finally, inasmuch as many prevailing judgments are transmitted interpretations of human experience long since past, it may be that a knowledge of their origins and the function they first served will be useful in evaluating them under the changed conditions of present life. This knowledge may also reveal that competition among special interests for the sanction of tradition is a primary aspect of politics. If to determine which ideas are to be transmitted from the past is to fix a present social order, as the recurring struggle to edit history suggests, the beginning of liberty is the capacity to evaluate the transmission. Freedom and whatever well-being it serves arose in the life that is the subject matter of history; to maintain them as they are is impossible, for, as life changes, they can endure only by development. To save democracy it is necessary to develop it—with knowledge, with moral responsibility, and with intellectual integrity—and to each of these the study of history has something to contribute.

RALPH TURNER.

WASHINGTON, D. C.,
June, 1941.

CONTENTS

⋘-⋘-⋙-⋙

PART THREE

The Interaction of the Traditional Asiatic and European Urban Cultures

CONCLUSION

The Rise and Decline of the Traditional Urban Cultures of Asia and Europe

ILLUSTRATIONS

❮❮❮-❮❮❮-❯❯❯-❯❯❯

MAPS, CHRONOLOGICAL CHARTS, AND DIAGRAMS

≪←≪←≫→≫→

xv

Part Three

THE INTERACTION OF THE TRADITIONAL ASIATIC AND EUROPEAN URBAN CULTURES

Chapter XI

THE MACEDONIAN EMPIRE AND THE MINGLING OF GREEK AND ASIATIC CULTURAL MATERIALS

〰〰〰〰

Each of the Asiatic and European urban culture areas became a center of imperialistic expansion, and in the course of time great empires arose. In a sense the Persians, who threatened the Greeks, were the heirs of the ancient-oriental imperialism, and through them many elements of this imperialism were transmitted to the other Asiatic and European urban culture areas. But the forces of imperialism, regardless of the forms under which they were organized, had origin in the new urban cultures, which set up an economic penetration of neighboring lands and led to the rise of new peoples in these lands. Thus the expansion of the areas within which urban centers exercised control was accompanied by constant warfare until unification brought the organization of the great empires and periods of internal peace. The Persian advance was a factor in the developments in Greece which culminated in the Macedonian conquest of the ancient-oriental lands and Iran; these movements, in turn, stimulated imperial activities in India and central Asia. At the western and eastern ends of the urban culture belt Rome and China rose to imperial greatness mainly by the forces their own urban cultures generated.

The political outcome of these several developments was an age of great empires, reaching its height in the first and second centuries after Christ, when Rome's dominion extended to the Tigris-Euphrates valley and China's power rested on the Oxus. The Parthian and Kushan empires divided the rule over Iran and northwestern India.[1]

By that time, too, cultural influences from each of the urban culture areas had contributed something to the life of every other

[1] See map facing p. 664.

602

area. In this interaction Greek influences were most significant, for they reached more lands and in greater variety than materials from the other urban cultures. For this reason the period of Macedonian imperialism—the fourth, third, and second centuries B.C., or the "Hellenistic age"—was especially important in the history of both Asiatic and European urban cultures. On the one hand it carried Greek materials far and wide; on the other hand it brought together materials from different centers of urban culture, stimulating new developments. In the main the effects of the diffusion of Greek materials and the new developments fed by the mingling of cultural materials were at their height in the age of the great empires.

THE MACEDONIAN EMPIRE AND THE HELLENISTIC KINGDOMS

At the opening of the Hellenistic age the Greek people were sacrificed to the particularism of the city-states; at its close the Greek people survived mainly as ruling groups in a cosmopolitan society from which issued the developments that gave enduring form to the Western cultural tradition. And its distinctive element as known to later times in Christianity—a social universalism transcending all nationalities—was the creation of this cosmopolitan society.[1]

THE MACEDONIANS.

The Macedonians held lands—a coastal plain and long mountain valleys—between the Aegean Sea and the Danube River from Thessaly to the Hellespont. The Greeks, whose cities dotted the northern coast of the Aegean Sea, looked upon them as barbarians, but actually the two peoples were racially akin and spoke related tongues. The Macedonian polity developed from tribalism to a centralized monarchy largely as a result of contacts with the Athenians, who, early in the fifth century B.C., began to draw from Macedonian forests the timber and pitch so necessary

[1] For brief discussions of the various aspects of the Hellenistic age see J. B. Bury *et al.*, *The Hellenistic Age* (1923); W. W. Tarn, *Hellenistic Civilization* (1927).

The standard history of the Greek expansion is A. Bouche-Leclercq's translation of J. G. Droysen's German work under the title *Histoire de l'Hellénisme* (2 vols., 1883–1885). Other histories of the Hellenistic age are *The Cambridge Ancient History*, Vol. 6, *Macedon 401–301 B.C.* (1933); Max Cary, *The Legacy of Alexander: A history of the Greek world from 323 to 146 B.C.* (1932); Pierre Jouguet, *Macedonian Imperialism and the Hellenization of the East* (1932); Julius Kaerst, *Geschichte des Hellenismus* (2 vols., 1936); and Robert Cohen, *La Grèce et l'Hellénisation du monde antique* (1934).

for the maintenance of their fleet. To protect this traffic the Athenians began the practice of dealing with a single clan, and ultimately its leader became king. Greek philosophers, poets, and artists followed merchants to his court, giving it a veneer of refinement, and soon the Macedonian nobles adopted Greek names. The capital, Pella, was a well-fortified city from which the king's rule spread over the other clans. The social base of Macedonian power was a hardy peasantry; its leaders were landowners who formed a warlike aristocracy. The army, organized on Greek lines, was kept continuously on a war footing.

Macedonia rose to imperial dominion over the politically disorganized Greek cities, but the main force of its imperialism, if the army is excepted, was derived from Greek culture and directed by Greeks.

The Failure of the Greeks to Achieve National Unity.

In spite of its democracy, Athens failed to catch the vision of a Greece united on a democratic basis.[1] The law of 451 B.C., which, by limiting citizenship to men tracing descent from citizen ancestors on both sides, closed the citizen body, not only stopped the assimilations of the metics, or resident aliens, who were the life-blood of the commerce upon which the wealth of the city rested, but also, by denying citizenship to the Greeks of the tribute-paying cities of the empire, prevented the evolution of the empire into a unified state. These policies drove the aristocracies of the tribute-paying cities into the arms of Sparta, which everywhere supported oligarchy against democracy. The political antagonism of the two greatest Greek cities was complicated by the commercial rivalry of Athens and Corinth. Athenian commercial policies had irritated other cities, too, and Sparta, jealous of Athenian power, was quick to court their favor.

The clash of Athens and Sparta came finally in the Peloponnesian War which, lasting from 431 to 404 B.C., proved to be national suicide.[2] Stupid leadership, factional strife, and treachery weakened each contestant in turn. Sparta's success was finally due to Persian subsidies, which enabled it to build a fleet and break Athens's sea power. The Macedonians were half-hearted allies of Athens during the struggle. But Sparta's victory did not lead

[1] See M. L. W. Laistner, *A History of the Greek World from 479 to 323 B.C.* (1936); Gustave Glotz, *La Grèce au IVᵉ siecle: La lutte pour l'hégémonie* (404–336) (1936).

[2] B. W. Henderson, *The Great War between Athens and Sparta: A companion to the military history of Thucydides* (1927).

to peace in Greece. The oligarchies which it restored irritated the partisans of democracy, and the tribute which it collected from the cities of central Greece, as well as from maritime cities formerly subject to Athens, was very heavy.

Sparta betrayed the Greek national feeling by surrendering the Ionian cities to Persia in order to obtain support for its dominance in European Greece. Also, because success bred corruption, the commanders of garrisons in the tribute-paying cities lost their military virtues 'and became venal. Spartan power was finally broken by the cities of central Greece, which under the leadership of Thebes and its brilliant commander, Epaminondas (*ca.* 418– 362 B.C.), overthrew a Spartan garrison, defeated a Spartan army in the field, and then invaded the Peloponnesus, where the long-suppressed Messenians were released from Spartan overlordship.

The defeat of Sparta destroyed the last hope of Greek unification. New cities rose to power, and new leagues were formed, but always particularism triumphed. Wars between the cities were incessant, and the old menace of Persian conquest reappeared.

In the fourth century B.C. economic changes greatly disturbed the relations of the social classes. Industry and commerce expanded, but mining and agriculture declined. The use of money spread. The rich grew wealthier and the poor more numerous. Slavery increased. Professional politicians managed the governments; appealing to the poorer citizens, they found the best claim for support to be the denunciation of the rich. Revolutions were recurrent. When the democratic party gained power, the richer citizens were burdened with excessive taxation; when the aristocratic party triumphed, the poor were oppressed. The citizens lost the military spirit, and mercenary armies led by professional generals supplanted the traditional militia. The cities sheltered a drifting population of exiles, foreigners, mercenaries, and adventurers whose chief need was money and who stooped to any employment to get it. Political chaos was accompanied by social and moral anarchy.[1]

This social world nurtured an individualism unrestrained by any feeling of national patriotism and undirected by any principle of social justice. For citizens, always a limited body in every city, there was the effort to maintain a political, social, and economic equality at the expense of the state. For the mixed population without political rights there was only the quest of wealth,

[1] On social and economic conditions during the fourth century B.C. see H. W. Parke, *Greek Mercenary Soldiers* (1933), pp. 227 *ff.*

and to its pursuit they gave all their energies. The Greek city-states, having sacrificed national unity to the preservation of local autonomy, finally fell before the Macedonian conqueror, who opened to their citizens and residents a new world in which to realize to the fullest degree the individualism which the city-states had nourished. As individualists the Greeks lost the social cohesiveness necessary for group survival, but they gained a motivation powerful enough to transform the world into which their conqueror led them. It was not an accident that in the fourth century B.C. the universally popular Greek deity was Tyche, or Fortune.

THE ADVANCE OF MACEDONIA: PHILIP II AND ALEXANDER THE GREAT.

Under Philip II (*ca.* 359–336 B.C.), who completed the unification of the clans, the Macedonians advanced on the warring Greek cities. Part of his early life was spent at Thebes, where he learned military tactics and the use of the siege engines which the Greeks had developed. His intervention in Greece was originally inspired by a desire to head an attack on the Persians, who, as ever, were interfering in Greek politics. But the pretext for his intervention was the request of the oracle of Delphi for aid in recovering treasure and lands that the Phocians had seized. The Athenians, led by the great orator Demosthenes (*ca.* 383–322 B.C.), who dyed eloquence with invective and exaggeration, raised a citizen army against the invader, and Persia, fearing his success, poured money into the Greek resistance. But eloquence, valor, and money failed before superior arms. Philip II triumphed in the battle of Chaeronea in 338 B.C. An assassin's knife struck him down before he could turn his arms against Persia in an expedition to Asia.

To Philip's son, known even in his own day as Alexander the Great (*ca.* 336–323 B.C.), fell the leadership of the invasion of Asia. Disorders in Europe, which were put down by a rapid campaign to the Danube River and the siege and destruction of Thebes, delayed his departure until 334 B.C.; then, with a well-disciplined and well-supplied army of some thirty-five thousand men, he set out on the great adventure. The main body of the army consisted of infantrymen, drawn from the Macedonian peasantry; armed with eighteen-foot pikes they went into battle in solid ranks, eight deep. When directed toward a weak point in an enemy's lines, this formation—the *phalanx*—was almost always successful in breaking through. A heavy-armed cavalry, recruited

ALEXANDER

Alexander's career had its roots in Greece, from which the Macedonians borrowed their urban culture, and his enduring achievement was the diffusion of Greek urban culture throughout the ancient-oriental lands.

from the aristocracy, supported the infantry, usually on the flanks; they carried swords and lances. Light-armed cavalry and numerous bowmen filled in between these forces. Throughout the years of campaigning that took the army from the Hellespont to the Indus River, Alexander never lost its affection.

In 334 B.C. Alexander liberated the Greek cities of Asia Minor and occupied Sardis, the old capital of Lydia. In 333 B.C. he moved along the southern coast of Asia Minor and occupied Syria and Phoenicia, where the resistance of Tyre necessitated a long siege.

THE MACEDONIAN EMPIRE c. 320 B.C.

In the next year the priests and people of Egypt received him as a liberator. These campaigns had been directed chiefly toward the capture of the bases from which the Persian fleet threatened Greece and the line of communications from Macedonia to Asia. Finally, in 331 B.C., Alexander struck directly at the Persian emperor and broke his power in the battle of Gaugamela near Nineveh; in the next year be destroyed the Persian royal palace and seized the Persian hoard of precious metals. The following campaigns in Iran, Turkestan, and India (*ca.* 330–326 B.C.) had little lasting political consequence, but economically and culturally they established permanent contacts between the Mediterranean Basin and central Asia and India.

To rule these vast conquests Alexander ascended the Persian throne as the "king of the world." The satrapies were placed under new appointees, both Macedonians and Iranians, who, deprived of the right of keeping mercenary soldiers and coining money, became merely administrative officials. The central government was carried on by a council of ten bodyguards, which served not only as a general staff but also as a kind of ministry. The court became Persian in organization and etiquette, at least so far as such practices could be imposed upon the Macedonians and Greeks. It seems impossible to ascertain exactly the policies which Alexander meant to apply in the development of his empire.

Certainly he envisioned the fusion of the Europeans and Asiatics, a movement he initiated by bringing about intermarriages between his veterans and oriental women. But more important was the practice of founding cities of the Greek type. During the campaigns in Asia, Alexander established some seventy cities, and his successors increased their number to almost three hundred. These cities, to which came a steady stream of Greek colonists—mostly men—were not so much garrisons as they were centers of the economic activity that the new political situation fostered. Organized on the Greek model, the cities were ruled by an elected assembly, council, and magistrates, and, like their Greek counterparts, their influence generally extended into the surrounding country. Of course the growth of these cities did not destroy the older political units or practices, but it did set down in the traditional oriental polity a communal organization which released somewhat the energies of the people. Less destructive than most of the other great conquerors of history, Alexander gave to subject peoples an opportunity for new developments.[1]

THE HELLENISTIC KINGDOMS.

Alexander's death in 323 B.C. put an end to whatever designs he had for integrating the diverse lands into a strongly centralized state, for his generals immediately fell to quarreling and then to fighting. The struggles of these successors, known as the Diadochi, lasted almost half a century; when a new system of states finally appeared, at its center stood monarchies ruled by lines of kings founded by the successful generals among them. In Egypt the Ptolemies, heirs of Lagus, one of Alexander's favorite commanders, reigned. Syria, Babylonia, and part of Asia Minor fell to Seleucus, a Macedonian nobleman; his heirs, the Seleucids, ruled with varying fortunes until Rome became supreme in the east in the first century B.C. Antiochus III (223–187 B.C.), known as "the Great," followed the footsteps of Alexander across Iran to India. The Antigonids, chosen by the army, as all Macedonian kings had been, won control of most of the European territories. The founder of the line, Antigonus the one-eyed (382–301 B.C.), was a half-brother and a favorite general of Alexander. He fought long and desperately for the imperial throne.

[1] On Alexander the Great see D. C. Hogarth, *Philip and Alexander of Macedon* (1897); T. A. Dodge, *Alexander the Great* (2 vols., 1918); V. Wilcken, *Alexander the Great* (1932); H. Beive, *Das Alexanderreich* (1926); Victor Ehrenberg, *Alexander and the Greeks* (1938); Lewis W. Cummings, *Alexander the Great* (1940).

EASTERN MEDITERRANEAN LANDS c. 280 B.C.

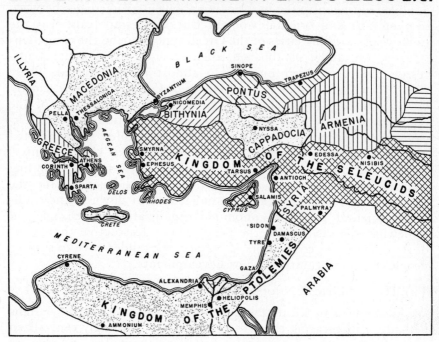

Around these kingdoms clustered almost a dozen smaller monarchies, such as Epirus, Bithynia, Pergamum, Pontus, Parthia, and Bactria. In Greece many of the city-states recovered their independence and formed leagues for mutual protection, but the old internal antagonisms were not abated. Wars, conspiracies, and sometimes insurrections gave little peace to the peoples of these states.[1]

The Social and Economic Aspects of the Hellenistic Age.

The main economic achievement of Macedonian imperialism was the formation of a world market, which, centering in the new monarchies, touched at its outer rim western Africa, western Europe, the Danubian and Russian plains, central Asia, India, Arabia, and the eastern coasts of Africa as far south as Somaliland.[2]

---

[1] See *The Cambridge Ancient History,* Vol. 7, *The Hellenistic Monarchies and the Rise of Rome* (1928); E. R. Bevan, *A History of Egypt under the Ptolemaic Dynasty* (1927); E. R. Bevan, *The House of Seleucus* (2 vols., 1902).

[2] For economic developments of the Hellenistic Age see Fritz M. Heichelheim, *Wirtschaftsgeschichte des Altertums* . . . (2 vols., 1938); *The Cambridge Ancient History,* Vol. 8,

Its greatest entrepôts were Alexandria in Egypt, Antioch in Syria, and Rhodes off the southwestern tip of Asia Minor. Alexandria was the center of a traffic which brought Indian, Arabian, and African wares into the Mediterranean Basin; likewise local agricultural and industrial products were exchanged for the goods of northern lands. In the first century B.C. a sea-borne commerce began to flow with the monsoon winds back and forth between the Red Sea and India. Antioch was the terminus of routes from India, central Asia, and Iran, as well as those which, coming by way of the new metropolis of the Tigris-Euphrates valley, Seleucia, carried the commerce that once had belonged to Babylon. Rhodes was the center of reshipping from eastern Mediterranean ports to Egypt, Greece, Rome, Carthage, and Gaul. In Asia Minor Ephesus succeeded Miletus as the chief port. Among the Greek cities Corinth alone held its old position. In Italy the rise of Puteoli on the Bay of Naples signalized the transfer of local commercial leadership from Greek to Roman hands.

1. *The New Means of Transportation.* General improvements in transportation aided the development of this wide market. The great Persian roads were extended—a protected road led into Asia as far as The Pamirs, and the Egyptian desert tracks, especially from the Nile to the Red Sea, were policed and provided with shelters. About the eastern Mediterranean many seaports, even the small ones, were equipped with sea walls and lagoons for safe anchorage, while the greatest of them were marked with lighthouses. Shipping began to lose its seasonal character, and vessels become larger. The average Hellenistic ship seems to have carried a cargo of about two hundred and fifty tons. Inland river traffic was facilitated by the building of canals at various places. Land traffic was still slow and dangerous. The ass and the mule, which now became common, were the chief pack animals, but horse trains were coming into use. Camels were introduced for desert transport.

2. *The Spread of Money Economy in the Hellenistic Age.* Not the least important factor in this economic expansion was the dissipation of the Persian hoard of precious metals, which amounted to between 170,000 and 180,000 talents, equivalent today, perhaps, to almost two billion dollars. When it is realized that Athens

Rome and the Mediterranean 218–133 *B.C.* (1930), Chap. XX, "Rhodes, Delos, and Hellenistic Commerce"; M. I. Rostovtzeff, "Commerce of Ptolemaic Egypt," *Journal of Economic and Business History*, Vol. 4 (1932), pp. 728–769; M. I. Rostovtzeff, "The Hellenistic World and Its Economic Development," *American Historical Review*, Vol. 41 (1936), pp. 231–252.

dominated Greece with a treasure (not including gold and silver vessels) of nine thousand talents, the importance of this influx of gold and silver can at least be guessed. Part of the vast sum was given outright to the Macedonian soldiers; other parts, in amounts up to ten thousand talents, went to Greek cities to finance rebuilding projects, and still other parts were spent on public works, such as the restoration of the Mesopotamian irrigation system. The effect of this sudden influx of precious metal was intensified by the increased production of copper and iron due to the introduction of the techniques of mining and smelting of the old urban areas into new regions. In fact, a greater change in the available supplies of metals and in the values of the metals in relation to one another occurred than at any time since the original diffusion of ironworking. Notable results of these changes were a freer use of the precious metals in the arts and a decline in the interest rate.

The use of money, which until Alexander's time was slight in the ancient-oriental lands, spread rapidly. Mints were set up at Tyre and Sidon in the fourth century B.C., and the Ptolemies gave Egypt its first monetary system. There was little difference between the three monetary standards—the Attic, the Phoenician, and the Asiatic—and the Greek drachma soon became an international coin.

Many of the bankers of the age were money-changers. Frequently, it seems, they received deposits and made loans, either on goods or on the credit of municipal governments. They did not know either the check or the bill of exchange, but they did use book accounts and the banker's order for the transfer of funds. Interest rates varied from 6 to 12 per cent. Most of the banking was still carried on by temples. Egypt created a state bank. Rhodes was the chief international financial center. The organization of business enterprises took on characteristics which seem modern. Partnerships were common, and companies, although not of the joint-stock variety, appeared. As the practice of collecting taxes in money spread, two new elements of public finance developed: (1) tax farming and (2) municipal borrowing. The enterprisers who farmed taxes bought the right to collect the yearly taxes of a city or a province for a fixed sum; this practice allowed a government to anticipate its yearly revenue. Most of the early municipal borrowing was occasioned by the need to meet some exceptional expenditure; commonly the loans only anticipated taxes levied to meet the expenditures. Tax farmers profited by the difference between what they paid and what they collected; sometimes the governments permitted them to keep only a percentage of the excess collections.

3. *Hellenistic Industry, Agriculture, and Commerce.* Neither commerce nor industry nor agriculture underwent any great change in technique or organization during the Hellenistic expansion of business.

The chief commercial developments were the growth of the long distance trade and the rise of an active retail trade in the cities. A regular caravan traffic moved between the markets of Syria and Mesopotamia and the new cities of central Asia, to which came, first, the products of India and, at the end of the age, the exports of China. The penetration of the Danube valley and the lands north of the Black Sea went on without interruption. Like the western Mediterranean lands, these areas furnished raw materials—grain, horses, timber, tar, pitch, iron, and copper—to the urban centers. Egypt supported its military power by importing these commodities from Italy, Sicily, and Carthage, sending in payment linen, glass, papyrus, ointments, and perfumes. This commerce was an important factor in the rise of new centers of production and, consequently, new centers of power in the western Mediterranean area. Direct trade between Egypt and Rome was opened early in the third century B.C. Egypt also developed a regular trade with southern Arabia, eastern Africa, and India. Among the products it obtained from India were war elephants. From this far-flung traffic the cities received the wares that filled their numerous shops. Oriental fabrics, rugs, spices, and perfumes became common articles of luxury. At the same time, because the populations of the cities increased, the trade in grain, oil, and wine expanded, especially in Egypt, which became a source of foodstuffs for most of the eastern Mediterranean lands.

The increased supplies of raw materials supported a general industrial advance. Iron, copper, and silver became more plentiful, and petroleum, known as naphtha, found its way into the market. Silver plate supplanted fine pottery, but the demand for containers for wine gave rise to an expansion of the manufacture of common grades. The spread of literacy stimulated the making of papyrus in the Nile Delta. The chief textile-producing areas were Syria and Asia Minor. Gold cloth was produced at Antioch. Miletus kept its long-established position as a producer of fine woolens. Linen and cotton were introduced into Greece for the first time in the fourth century B.C. About this time, also,

carpets, rugs, and tapestries began to find their way from Mesopotamia and Iran to the West. Corinth developed a high-grade
bronze industry, and Pergamum introduced the manufacture of
parchment.

Alexandria was the center of the industrial, as well as the
commercial, world; in its shops there was a "fever of work."
The chief products were glass, textiles, perfumes, ointments,
and metals. The Greek or the Hellenized-oriental merchant and
the Greek manufacturer were the leaders of this expansion of
enterprise; they took over the Babylonian business system,
utilized and improved the technical processes of the East, and
adapted their wares to the demands of the market. The Hellenistic
age was the greatest period of "business" before modern times.

More progress was made in agriculture than in commerce
and industry. Throughout the valleys of Asia Minor the growing
of wheat and barley became common, and husbandry spread
over the uplands. The plantation system of cultivating the olive
and the grape was introduced into Egypt, and the production
of fine wines began in Babylonia, Persia, and even India. Syria
and Egypt became horse-breeding countries; in the Nile valley
special tenants of the Ptolemies cared for great herds of cattle
and horses. The ordinary peasant, it seems, owned only goats;
only the richer peasants possessed asses. Neither the Greeks nor
their Hellenistic successors kept the cow for dairy purposes;
cattle were valuable chiefly for meat and hides. The ox was the
universal draft animal. The Hellenistic age was probably the
first "horse age," for it saw not only the appearance of chariot
racing as a widespread popular amusement but also the general
keeping of horses by the well to do. Cereal cultivation was improved
by the introduction of manuring and crop rotation. Orchards and
vineyards were given systematic care. And fodder plants and
grasses were added to the older field crops.

Agricultural advances were most rapid in Egypt, where the
Ptolemies, masters of the land, undertook to direct a general
improvement. Special strains of seeds were selected. Reclamation
projects created strips of pasturage outside the grain lands bordering each bank of the Nile. The Faiyum irrigation project alone
created about five hundred square miles of arable land.[1] Ordinary
tillage was carried on in a two-year rotation of wheat and vegetables. Vineyards and olive orchards were given special care.

[1] See A. E. R. Book, "Irrigation and Population in the Fayum," *Geographical Review*,
Vol. 16 (1926), pp. 353–364.

Husbandry was improved by the importation of Greek herdsmen. As a result of these developments the Egyptian countryside took on the aspects that endured almost without change until the early nineteenth century.

Not the least notable feature of the Hellenistic agricultural advance was the transformation into villagers of the nomads who had long held the hill countries bordering the Fertile Crescent.

4. *The Multiplication of Cities and the Changing Class Structure of the Hellenistic Age.* The entire eastern Mediterranean area, as well as the ancient-oriental lands and the arable districts of Iran and central Asia became more or less well settled, the cities multiplied in number and increased in size, and everywhere, except perhaps in Greece, where soil exhaustion and military depredations led to a decline, the population seems to have grown. On the whole the military activities of the age were not destructive of orderly economic and social life. Although the Hellenization of cities in Asia Minor began before the rise of Macedonia, the planting of colonies by Alexander and his successors was the chief factor in the spread the Greek municipal pattern into Asia and Africa. The growth of commerce gave some of the new cities economic importance, notably Alexandria in Egypt and Seleucia in Mesopotamia. But they never became Greek in character, although they possessed Greek institutions. At first they were the residences of the new ruling class; later they became the homes of mixed oriental and Greek populations. Most of the Greeks who migrated were men, and they commonly married native women. After the middle of the secondary century B.C. it was impossible in many cities to tell a man's nationality from his name, so general had the mixing of the nationalities become. Under the stimulus of intensified commercial activity the traditional hostility to trade disappeared, so that these new cities, more than their predecessors, were milieus that engendered a secular outlook on the world.[1]

The increase of wealth fostered, of course, the growth of a luxury greater than any known before. Pomp and extravagant show became normal aspects of the court life of the ruling dynasties. The well to do generally set new standards of ostentatious consumption in food, raiment, housing, furniture, and equipages. Gold and silver plate graced banquets at which only rare and

[1] On Hellenistic urban life see W. S. Ferguson, *Hellenistic Athens* (1911); P. Roussel, *Delos* (1925); E. S. Borchier, *A Short History of Antioch* (1921); C. Torr, *Rhodes in Ancient Times* (1885) and A. H. M. Jones, *The Cities of the Eastern Roman Provinces* (1939).

costly foods were served. Gaudy uniforms for soldiers added color to all occasions. Fine public buildings, decorated with colored marbles and set in well-planted gardens, graced the cities. Landscape gardening rose to the dignity of an art. And costly festivals and games multiplied in all the cities.

The growth of luxury and the development of a secular outlook together led to an intensification of the antagonisms between the social classes. The gap between the peasant-village masses and the urban groups widened. The new ruling class, alien in origin in the new Asiatic monarchies, because it was recruited from the soldiers of the Macedonian armies and Greek adventurers, supplanted the native military and priest classes. The old Iranian nobility was almost completely destroyed, and the Zoroastrian priests were forced to find safety in the villages. The Egyptian priest class, after one attempt to recover its lost authority and wealth, became a satisfied state-supported caste. Throughout Syria, Asia Minor, and Mesopotamia local priesthoods were allowed to retain many lands. In Palestine the Hebrew priesthood continued to rule. The new ruling class, which, although enjoying income from land, was distinctly urban, was composed mainly of high-ranking military commanders, bureaucrats, and rich merchants whose great wealth opened the doors of officialdom. A small middle class of well-to-do industrial and agricultural enterprisers and traders shared in the economic advance, if not in the political advantages, that the possession of wealth gave. As time went on the line between the well to do and the poor coincided more and more with the line between the governing and the governed.

The masses suffered greatly, for the new wealth did not filter down to them. About the opening of the third century B.C. the cost of living increased, wheat becoming twice, common wine two and a half times, and oil three and a half times as dear as they had been before the dissipation of the Persian hoard of precious metals. In the second century B.C. prices moved toward their former levels, but conditions for the masses improved very little. Among the peasant villagers free landowners, although still numerous, became fewer, while serfs and slaves increased in numbers. Every man without property tended to fall into serfdom, and the principle of hereditary employment was applied to urban craftsmen as well as to agricultural workers. At the same time the system of cultivating large estates with slave labor became well established. The rural masses, who lived at or near the subsistence level, produced with their own labor the few industrial products they consumed. Only the rich and well to do of the cities provided a market for industrial products; this limited demand largely determined the character of manufacturing.

Besides the governing class the chief urban groups were the free artisans, the proletariat of unskilled laborers, and slaves. Among the craftsmen life became increasingly difficult. Masons, carpenters, and smiths earned barely enough to support a wife; wages were low and employment irregular. Strikes and disputes were frequent. To escape the burden of a growing family, parents commonly exposed children beyond the number of two. The evidence suggests that many working-class families restricted their children to two sons. More than one daughter was seldom reared. Over every man who labored independently hung the menace of debt and the threat of enslavement, for creditors generally had the right to claim the persons of their debtors. The urban proletariat was composed of freemen who had lost their occupations; to meet their bare needs the cities introduced the practices of furnishing free food and amusements. At Samos, where these practices seem first to have become well established, they were maintained by a fund raised from gifts by the rich. Other cities soon made them part of the burden supported by taxation.

The extension of slavery into agriculture was only a phase of the general expansion of forced labor. Temples, kings, and rich financiers kept gangs of slaves. Mining was almost exclusively a slave-worked industry. And many of the small industrial shops were manned by slaves. The slave trade was probably the richest branch of commerce. After the decline of Athens its center shifted to Delos and in the second century b.c. to Rhodes. In the course of this shift the Cilicians supplanted the Athenians as the chief slave traders. The Black Sea coasts and the hinterlands of Syria and Palestine were the main sources of supply. In Egypt, where complete descriptions of slaves were given when title of ownership passed from hand to hand, a tax was levied on such transactions—a fact which proves that they were sufficiently numerous to make possible the collection of considerable sums—and a systematic effort was made to catch and return runaways.

Admiration for the economic advances of the Hellenistic age should not obscure the fact that life for peasants and urban workers probably became less secure.

5. *Hellenistic Revolutionary Movements.* The growing insecurity of life engendered a spirit of revolution which in Greece,

even as early as the fourth century B.C., was strong enough to fill the well to do with dread.[1] Aristotle recorded this attitude of the well to do in the statement "I will be the enemy of the people, and will continue to inflict as much damage upon them as possible." Athenian jurymen took an oath not to vote to cancel debts or to redivide the land. And one of the reasons for the success of Macedonia in Greece was the support given to Philip II by the well to do. He forbade the division of lands or the liberation of slaves by revolution.

The economic developments of the Hellenistic age intensified the revolutionary spirit, especially in the Greek cities which retained their traditional regimes. In 297 B.C. Ephesus was forced to declare a moratorium on all debts. At least four other debtors' revolts occurred in the Aegean Islands before the middle of the third century B.C. In 244 B.C. the revolutionary movement spread to Sparta, where, the Lycurgan constitution having decayed, the possession of the land was in the hands of about seven hundred Spartiates. Agis IV (*ca.* 244–240 B.C.) undertook reforms that would have given lands to over four thousand *perioikoi;* with the support of a section of the well to do whose interests were favored by the cancellation of mortgages he released debtors from their burdens and proposed a bill for the redistribution of lands. His royal colleague held up the reforms, and his enemies contrived his judicial murder. Cleomenes III (*ca.* 235–221 B.C.), who had been converted to the reform program by his wife, the widow of Agis, abolished the ephorate and carried the reforms, enfranchising about four thousand new citizens. Military successes following the reforms recovered for Sparta the domination of the Peloponnesus. But the struggle between the classes went on. In 207 B.C. another revolutionary outbreak brought the intervention of Rome, whose protection the well to do welcomed. In the second century B.C. there were debtors' revolts in Boeotia and several abortive peasant uprisings in Egypt.

The revolutionary element in Hellenistic society was confined largely to the Greek cities, where the poor citizens, debtors, slaves, and a few philosophers supported a fourfold program of reform: (1) the confiscation of the property of the well to do; (2) the cancellation of debts; (3) the redivision of the land; and (4) the liberation of slaves. A few of the philosophers envisioned, it seems, a communistic society.

[1] See Max Beer, *Social Struggles in Antiquity* (1922); Richard von Pöhlmann, *Geschichte der Sozialen Frage und des Sozialismus in der antiken Welt* (3d ed., 2 vols., 1925).

The clearest picture of the revolutionary goal was set forth in a work said to have been written by a certain Iambulus who was believed to have traveled to India sometime in the third century B.C. While in that country he visited an island in the Indian Ocean where men, so he reported, were equal in every respect, even in wisdom. Economic production was directed by small councils, each member working and sharing equally with all others. The high productivity of the tropical island made slavery unnecessary. And every man was eligible to hold any office in the state. Although the voyage of Iambulus to India cannot be established, there is no doubt that ideas of economic, political, and social equality similar to those ascribed to him circulated in the Hellenistic revolutionary circles. They knew this ideal social order as the "sun city," and it remained the goal of revolutionary movements until the last of them were broken up by the Romans in the first century B.C.

6. *The Persistence of the Traditional Economy during the Hellenistic Age.* In spite of the economic advance of Hellenistic times, the traditional economy persisted everywhere. Tillage and husbandry underwent no improvements that disturbed the ancient ways of the peasantry. There were no important technical innovations in manufacturing. Money did not circulate outside the cities, except perhaps in Egypt and Syria. The new commerce and industry served the well to do, not the urban poor or the peasant villagers. Even in the cities the crafts were practiced in small shops more than in large establishments. There was no mass production. The spread of the estate system in agriculture was probably the most important development in economic organization, and it was accompanied by a further decline of free labor. The accumulation of capital, although considerable, was checked by the policies of the kings and the dangers from the urban mobs; it took form more in hoards than in investments. The unit of economic organization was still the household, where economic self-sufficiency was the mode, and each local area was able to live almost completely to itself.

THE ORIENTAL MONARCHY IN THE WESTERN CULTURAL TRADITION.

Under the social and economic conditions described in the preceding paragraphs the Hellenistic kings struggled to consolidate their power. Except in Greece, where clashes of the urban social classes were continuous, this consolidation was achieved with the aid of the new ruling class, and its outcome was a highly centralized absolute monarchy, having Egyptian, Assyrian, Persian, and Greek elements.[1]

The central organ of the Hellenistic monarchy was the kingship. Greek hero worship united with the oriental conception of the divine king to create the practice of deifying rulers. Thus the Hellenistic kings, regardless of their antecedents, became divine, and their power was regarded as having a supernatural basis. The king and the state were one. Actually, however, the royal authority functioned through the new ruling class of Macedonians, immigrant Greeks, and Hellenized orientals, who not only held an overwhelming proportion of the wealth but also monopolized the offices in the civil and military hierarchies. Very few representatives of the old ruling groups were left in any responsible military or financial positions. But the traditional systems of local government were generally preserved, and through them native officials administered native law. The king's agents stood alongside these officials, policing the villages and collecting the royal revenues. The natives retained the ancient right of direct petition to the king, who was, it seems, normally attentive to popular appeals. The privileged groups lived under a combination of Greek and oriental law. The despotism of the Hellenistic king, whose power was absolute and irresponsible, was enlightened, for he governed generally with an eye to increasing his wealth as well as extending his dominion. The kingdom was quite as much an estate as a state.

Egypt is the leading example of a Hellenistic polity, and from it, through Rome, passed the traditions which influenced later Western monarchism.[2] The Ptolemies, having won power by

[1] On the antecedents of the Hellenistic monarchy see Calvin W. McEwan, *The Oriental Origin of the Hellenistic Kingship* (The Oriental Institute, Studies in Ancient-Oriental Civilization, No. 13, 1934).

[2] On the Egyptian monarchy see E. R. Bevan, *A History of Egypt under the Ptolemaic Monarchy* (1927), pp. 132–188; also W. L. Westermann, "The Ptolemies and the Welfare of Their Subjects," *American Historical Review*, Vol. 43 (1938), pp. 270–287; M. I. Rostovtzeff, "The Foundations of Social and Economic Life in Hellenistic Times," *Journal of Egyptian Archaeology*, Vol. 6 (1920), pp. 161–171. Rostovtzeff summarizes the regime as follows: "Everything was for the State and through the State, nothing for the individual, except the mere possibility of a grey existence which saved the worker from starvation. Nowhere in the whole evolution of mankind can be found so far-reaching and so systematic limitations as those which applied to private property in Ptolemaic Egypt." Rostovtzeff inclines to the view that the Greeks merely elaborated the core of the regime inherited from Egyptian practices. For a discussion of the Egyptian imperial regimentation of economic activities see p. 296.

On the wide influence of the Hellenistic state-controlled economy see Fritz M. Heichelheim, *Wirtschaftsgeschichte des Altertums* . . . (2 vols., 1938), Vol. I, pp. 647 ff.

force of arms, accepted from the Egyptian priest class the traditional consecration of the pharaohs and ascended the throne as
the sons of Re. As the heirs of the pharaohs the Ptolemies possessed
Egypt as their own private property. They were heads of the navy,
the army, the civil government, and the priesthood. Little is
known about Ptolemaic sea power. Only a few garrisons, settled
as tenants on royal lands, were necessary to hold the country.
A regular army, chiefly of Greek mercenaries, was maintained
around the court. Service in such armies provided a means of
escape from the economic distress that afflicted the Greek homeland. The civil government was also manned mostly by Greeks;
it was headed by a chief minister and the *dioecetes*, a minister of
imperial finance. The representatives of the dioecetes, mostly
scribes, surveyed the crops in each village and kept the tax rolls.
The ancient nomarchs stood between these agents of the monarch
and the people. The favoritism which permeated the civil administration imposed extra burdens upon the people. The priesthood,
having become hereditary, was satisfied to retain its popularity
with the people at the expense of its political power; the temples
were ruled by priestly councils under the supervision of royal
agents.

The most remarkable feature of the Ptolemaic regime was the
economic administration—"the new system of planned economy,"
it has been called—which turned Egypt into a gigantic wealth-
producing machine. All land was "the king's inheritance." It
was managed partly as great estates, which, if not held directly
by the king, were in the hands of royal tenants who were members
of the civil and military hierarchies, and partly as small holdings
by ordinary peasants. The temple lands were supervised by royal
agents. The authority of the king's financial agents extended
everywhere. They prescribed the crops to be planted, determined
the acreage, fixed rotations, and provided the seed. The planting
of orchards and their care were strictly supervised. The great
herds of cattle, horses, goats, and sheep were accurately enumerated and closely guarded. Fees were paid to landlords for
growing fodder plants. Even the breeders of geese and pigs were
subject to regulation. The production of honey was a state monopoly. And one-fourth of every catch of fish went to the state.
The fellahin, whose names were enrolled on the tax registers,
were not allowed to leave their villages from plowing time till
harvest; also they were subject to forced labor at any time and for
any project. They were not, however, absolutely bound to the

land. In every village the king maintained a granary to receive taxes in kind and a bank to receive the various dues paid in money. Both foreign and local trade, as well as the chief industries, were royal monopolies. The state carried on foreign commerce, but most of the local trade was in the hands of licensees, who paid a direct tax to the treasury. Manufacturers of olive oil, wine, beer, textiles, papyrus, perfumes, glass, dyes, and metals operated under a licensing system. Certain crops, such as grain and oil, were purchased by the government at fixed prices and retailed under its exclusive control. The export of grain was highly profitable. It is a fair conclusion that every economic transaction paid at least one, and sometimes several, profits to the royal treasury, for many indirect, as well as direct, taxes were levied. The entire population, except the members of the civil, ecclesiastical, and military hierarchies, *i.e.*, the ruling classes, paid a poll tax.

In the Seleucid kingdom the same principles were followed as in Egypt, but they were much modified in practice by the survival of the Persian system of local administration. A unified land register was established. Land was held mostly by royal tenants, temples, and cities. The cities, organized as Greek municipalities, generally gave freedom to the peasants; the royal and temple estates were cultivated by serfs who were bought and sold with the land. The temples held many slaves and prostitutes; the latter were recruited among the daughters of the peasants. Mines and forests were the property of the king. Direct and indirect taxation also followed Egyptian lines. The ordinary levy, lighter than in Egypt, was one-tenth of the harvest. Much of the royal revenue was collected in kind, and the king was a great corn merchant. The Seleucids, although they improved the Tigris-Euphrates irrigation system, seem never to have become as rich as the Ptolemies.

Under Greek and Macedonian leadership the traditional urban social pyramid developed toward a complete political centralization, a caste system, and a regimented economy. Political power, social prestige, and the possession of wealth were concentrated in the hands of small ruling groups. These groups were everywhere distinguished more by economic and political privileges than by racial and national unity. Outside Egypt the members of these groups generally enjoyed the privileges of municipal self-government on the Greek model. The professions and occupations tended to become hereditary, so that most forms of labor approached the status of serfdom. Political power was largely concerned with the management of production and distribution, and income was determined largely by social and political privilege. The masses, rooted in the village and the low intellectual tradition, were powerless to resist the demands which the new regime imposed upon them. In Egypt the fellahin, continuously prophesying the downfall of the Ptolemies, could do no more than call for supernatural relief. And few sparks of humanitarianism enlightened the self-interest that motivated the ruling groups. But self-interest did temper their greed. The Hellenistic monarchy was the mature form of the exploitive state; it was, indeed, a planned exploitation.

THE DIFFUSION AND ELABORATION OF GREEK CULTURE IN THE HELLENISTIC AGE

The influence of the penetration of Asia upon Greek culture was immediate and far-reaching. The Greeks became interested in Egypt, Ethiopia, Phoenicia, Babylonia, Parthia, Bactria, and India, and wrote accounts of them. Although some knowledge of Palestine seems to have spread among the Greeks in the fourth century B.C., little was learned about the Jewish people and their religion until two centuries later.

In general the influence of Asiatic culture on the Greeks was exerted by orientals who made Greek their literary language. The Hebrew religious books were translated into Greek in the middle of the third century B.C. by Alexandrian Jews who had forgotten literary Hebrew. Under the patronage of the Seleucids a considerable body of cuneiform learning was revived. The tradition of Marduk was rendered in verse, and Sumerian hymns became popular. Babylonian astrological and astronomical concepts were made available to the Hellenistic world by Berossos (fl. *ca.* 280 B.C.), who also wrote a history of Babylonia in Greek. A great body of omenology also moved west about this time. Since much Egyptian learning had passed to Greece in the sixth and fifth centuries B.C., Egypt had less to contribute to the new intellectual development than Babylonia. Manethon (fl. *ca.* 300–275 B.C.) produced in Greek the three-volume work *Annals of Egypt* which long furnished all that was known of Egyptian chronology. In Egypt the Greek infiltration stimulated a popular literary revival whose products were rendered in the simplified cursive script known as the demotic; it was based upon popular speech, not upon the ancient priestly literary language. Inscriptions in hieroglyphic, demotic, and Greek (such as that found on the Rosetta stone, which led to the deciphering of the hieroglyphic writings) were made at this time. Although Persian learning was suppressed by the Seleucids because of its nationalistic spirit, the Zoroastrian teachings slowly became known in the West, influencing Hebrew as well as Greek thought. The extent of Indian influence in the West during the Hellenistic age cannot be determined. Asoka[1] sent to Mesopotamia a Buddhist mission whose fate is unknown, and late in the first century B.C. a Buddhist monk, it is said, committed suicide in Athens. Probably a general diffusion of Indian ideas occurred more through the commercial intercourse that converged at Alexandria than through the activities of Buddhist missionaries. Not many Greek travelers seem to have reached India and returned.

The social changes of the Hellenistic age—widespread travel, the growth of cities, and the disturbance of the traditional class structure—awakened new interests among the intellectuals and presented new experiences both to them and to the generality of the population. Travel and the expansion of commerce made the ports centers of an active cultural interaction, so that it is not at all surprising that the chief intellectual figures of the age came from new cities where strange lands, peoples, religions, customs, animals, and plants first became known. The growth of cities also brought more and more persons under the influence of a stimulating social process. Throughout Asia Minor, Syria, and Babylonia the spread of Greek municipal organization introduced the theater, the gymnasium, the school, and public festivals, giving a new tone to city life. The impact of this development may have been felt somewhat by the peasant villagers of these countries. Even more important, perhaps, was the shock to traditional social controls and attitudes by the economic contrasts which appeared as a result of the growth of wealth and its unequal distribution. The rich acquired new tastes and habits, while the poor were not able to maintain even their traditional mode of life. The new economic conditions disturbed the established routines of life in many ways and, as a result, raised many questions about the caprices of fortune, the evils of worldly existence, and the right way of life. Under these circumstances more and more people became eager to accept beliefs that offered any solace for their misfortunes.

The effects of this cultural interaction and these social forces were not uniform throughout the Greek world. Athens, still the center of learning to which most eyes looked, held fast to the traditions of its great age. But intellectual and artistic leadership

[1] See p. 744.

slowly passed to new centers—Ephesus, Pergamum, Antioch, and, above all, Alexandria—where new facts were assembled and new ideas advanced in a spirit that was both tolerant and curious.[1] Increasingly, as time went on, the Hellenized orientals replaced the European Greeks as the carriers of the Hellenic cultural tradition.

LITERATE LEARNING AND LITERATURE IN THE HELLENISTIC AGE.

Although the expansion of commerce strengthened the secular tendency in Greek culture, in the end Asiatic religious materials combined with the emotions stirred by the growing economic insecurity of the age to give religious beliefs a new appeal. Much of the cultural development of the Hellenistic age can be understood only when it is realized that for a time both the secular and the religious tendencies of Greek culture were strengthened.

1. *The Spread of Literacy and the Growth of Intellectual Institutions.* The diffusion of a knowledge of writing, particularly among the urban population, and the evolution of institutions devoted to the advancement and preservation of learning, were very important factors in Hellenistic intellectual development. Recent studies of literacy in Alexandria have indicated that perhaps about as many as half of the population could read and write Greek. Undoubtedly the percentage was not as high in cities like Antioch and Pergamum, for almost all Egyptian political, military, commercial, and literary activities were concentrated in Alexandria. At any rate, it seems clear that the ruling groups of the Hellenistic kingdoms were generally educated and that many merchants, soldiers, and artisans had a knowledge of writing sufficient for practical purposes. The growth of the book trade is another evidence of the spread of literacy. Two reading publics appeared—the highly educated, whose interests were scholarly and philosophical, and the popular, whose interests were essentially recreational and religious. Commercial publication was a profitable business; the work of duplicating manuscripts was largely done by educated slaves. The works of Homer were the "best sellers" of the age. The oriental peoples, including the Jews outside Palestine, frequently mastered Greek, for almost all scholarship and literary efforts were confined to the Greek tongue.

[1] See H. T. Bell, "Alexandria," *Journal of Egyptian Archaeology*, Vol. 13 (1927), p. 173: "From the first Alexandria seemed destined for its rôle of a melting-pot in which East and West, Greece and Egypt and Asia and countries yet hardly known, could meet and contribute their several quotas to a hybrid culture. . . . "

Secular intellectual institutions appeared in every important Hellenistic city. Chief among them was the theater, where new as well as classical plays were performed. Many municipal school systems were established on the Athenian model. When the Athenians abolished military training for youths, they substituted a literary and philosophical education which they entrusted to publicly chosen teachers. These schools, of course, were open only to the sons of citizens. The institutions of higher learning were patterned after the schools founded by Plato and Aristotle, *i.e.*, the Academy and the Lyceum. The Academy was devoted to the study of mathematics, philosophy, and rhetoric. The Lyceum taught philosophy, logic, literature, and science. When these schools declined, new schools, the Porch of the Stoics and the Grove of the Epicureans (the names were taken from places of meeting), superseded them. The Alexandrian library, founded about 285 B.C. by Ptolemy I, was modeled on Aristotle's Lyceum. There is a wide divergence in the views of the number of works in the library. They seem to have been in two collections, a greater and a lesser; perhaps in the first century B.C. they numbered together well over 500,000 works. These works were mostly rolls of papyrus; perhaps a few of them were made of the new materials, parchment and vellum, manufactured at Pergamum. The ordinary papyrus roll was about ten inches wide and thirty-five feet long. The writing was arranged in narrow columns which could be read as the manuscript was unrolled. The museum connected with the library was a "round table for learned men" who were supported by the state. The scholars were chiefly interested in literary and scientific pursuits. The halls of the museum housed numerous collections of specimens of plants, animals, and fish.[1] Probably no provision was made for teaching. The library at Pergamum contained about 200,000 rolls. Other libraries were collected at Athens, Antioch, Tarsus, and a few other centers of learning.

On the whole, it seems, the content of education did not keep pace with the growth of knowledge or the development of literature. The textbooks became stereotyped, old unedited texts survived long after the librarians had produced more authoritative versions of the standard authors, and many new writers never found places in the classrooms. In all but the greatest schools the sciences, except geometry, were almost entirely neglected, and rhetoric, the leading subject, soon began to take on those degenerate characteristics which ultimately stultified intellectual initia-

[1] G. H. Bushnell, "The Alexandrian Library," *Antiquity*, Vol. 2 (1928), pp. 196–204.

tive. The early attempts to produce "artistic prose" degenerated into the making of fine phrases, the playing on words, the elaboration of antitheses, and the construction of balanced clauses. The "Asianic style," as prose characterized by the foregoing devices has been called, was especially popular among Hellenized orientals and Asiatic Greeks. More fatal still to the general diffusion of knowledge was the divergence of the literary language from the speech of the people; in compensation, however, a modified Greek tongue was formed—the *Koinē*—which became the language of popular literature and propaganda and, later, of the New Testament. It was the product of the commercial and industrial towns. Attic Greek, the language of classical Hellenic literature, survived only in the schools.

But more important for the spread of new beliefs and knowledge among the masses than these educational institutions was the multiplication of wandering scholars, half philosopher and half quack, who recited poetry, told stories, made prophecies, explained omens, read the stars, and taught strange philosophical doctrines and religious beliefs. In the libraries thrived "literary scholars," who wrote books about books; in the streets stalked seers and charlatans, who, quite as important for the future development of Western culture as their erudite contemporaries, instructed the people without books.

2. *Hellenistic Literature.* In the last period of Hellenic greatness—the fourth century B.C.—many of the tendencies that were to become more and more prominent in Hellenistic times appeared. Literacy spread. The reading public grew. And new interests found literary expression.

The critical political position of Athens inspired her leaders to flights of speech still recognized as the greatest of orations. Isocrates (*ca.* 436–338 B.C.) and Demosthenes (*ca.* 384–322 B.C.) stand foremost among the founders of oratory as a literary art. Isocrates, who after 390 B.C. became the leading teacher of rhetoric in Athens, was not himself an orator. He composed speeches for others to give or read. His studied and elaborated style included elements such as the balance of clauses in antithesis, the use of clauses of the same length, the use of words of the same sound at the same positions in different clauses, and the refusal to place a word beginning with a vowel after a word ending in a vowel. In unskillful hands, it is evident, a style characterized by these practices could become highly artificial, and in time this was its effect. Demosthenes relied on clarity of thought, vivid imagery, "invented quotes," and figures of speech for his effects, which were enhanced by the vehemence and sincerity of his presentation. Isocrates gave oratory a place in classical education; Demosthenes made political oratory a part of literature.

Other developments in line with changing social conditions, especially after Athens took the lead in substituting literary and philosophical studies for military exercises in the education of youths, were a further growth of the book trade and a multiplication of the number of authors.[1] Counting the authors of scientific and philosophical works, the names of eleven hundred Hellenistic literary figures have been preserved. They include exponents of every sort of literary learning and expression. Poets, good and bad, contrived verses, some on the principle of making the mere arrangement of words form the picture of an object. Critics argued over the placing of accents and the length of epic poems. Epigrammatists vied with one another in making wit sharp and brief:

> A viper stung a Cappadocian's hide,
> And poisoned by his blood that instant died.

The cosmopolitanism of the age was the prime factor in bringing about a great development of grammatical and philological learning.

The chief centers of philological study were in the libraries at Alexandria and Pergamun, where scholars had ample opportunity to investigate the texts of the older authors and the language of living men. Zenodotus (*ca.* 325–234 B.C.), the first librarian of the Alexandrian library, arranged Homer's works in books. Aristophanes of Byzantium (*ca.* 257–180 B.C.), also a librarian at Alexandria, was the greatest philologist of the age. In addition to improving accentuation and punctuation, he prepared new editions of Homer and Hesiod and collected the works of Pindar, Euripides, and Aristophanes. Aristarchus (*ca.* 220–145 B.C.), a successor at the Alexandrian library, produced the Homeric text which subsequent times have generally regarded as authoritative. He was one of the first grammarians to recognize the parts of speech. Many current

[1] On Hellenistic literary developments see *The Cambridge Ancient History* Vol. 7, *The Hellenistic Monarchies and the Rise of Rome* (1928), Chap. VIII, "Alexandrine Literature"; J. E. Sandys, *A History of Classical Scholarship* (3d ed., 3 vols., 1921), Vol. I, *From the Sixth Century B.C. to the End of the Middle Ages;* F. A. Wright, *A History of Later Greek Literature from the Death of Alexander in 323 B.C. to the Death of Justinian in 565 A.D.* (1932); Alfred Korte, *Hellenistic Poetry* (1929); H. J. Rose, *A Handbook of Greek Literature from Homer to the Age of Lucian* (1934).

grammatical terms, such as "genitive," "accusative," and "infinitive," are derived from Latin mistranslations of his terms. His was the leading grammatical work for thirteen centuries. Crates of Mallos (fl. *ca.* 170 B.C.) wrote the first formal grammar. The philologists also produced commentaries upon most of the Hellenic writers. The literary scholar, as an intellectual type, was a Hellenistic creation.

The creative works of Hellenistic authors were less distinctive, although more varied, than those of their Hellenic predecessors. Parodies were common and plagiarizing was universal. To steal a line was merely to compliment its author. The poets, who wrote almost exclusively for court audiences, were confronted with the impossible task of surpassing the great Ionian bards and Athenian dramatists, and of course they failed. Apollonius Rhodius (fl. *ca.* 194 B.C.), an Alexandrian scholar, produced the last Greek epic, the *Argonautica*, which retold the story of Jason's quest for the Golden Fleece.[1] Its best passages deal with Medea's mad love for the hero. Callimachus (*ca.* 310–245 B.C.) adapted the old legends to the times. His idylls were masterpieces of polished verse and, although lacking in poetic fire, were neither sentimental nor rhetorical. The most original poet of the age was Theocritus (fl. *ca.* 270 B.C.), who created the pastoral idyll, a poetic rendering of peasant life, a sweet love of nature, and a feeling for the beauty of the landscape; he gave lasting meaning to the word "idyllic." He has had many imitators but no superiors; of Hellenistic poetic works, his alone have become classic. Menander (*ca.* 342–291 B.C.) developed the New Comedy, a five-act play in dialogue without a chorus. His work reflected the morality of the new-rich. Some of his lines, such as "Whom the gods love die young," have become proverbs.[2] Herondas (fl. *ca.* 240 B.C.) was master of the mime, a comic song sketching all sorts of persons in a variety of moods. He was a representative of that trend which freed the actor from the mask, making facial expression a part of his art, and brought women to the stage. In the third century B.C. the actors, released from the performance of military service and the payment of taxes, were organized in guilds and allowed to go from city to city; their movements were an important factor in the dissemination of the classical drama throughout the Mediterranean Basin.

Among Hellenistic poems the *Phaenomena* of Aratus of Soli (fl. *ca.* 275 B.C.) is notable, not because of literary merit but because

---

[1] R. C. Seaton, *Apollonius Rhodius, The Argonautica* (1921).
[2] F. G. Allison, *Menander, The Principal Fragments* (1930).

it was a precedent for the poetic treatment of scientific and pseudoscientific subjects which became popular in late Roman times.

Prose was the typical literary product of the Hellenistic age. Scientists, philosophers, historians, biographers, and fictionists found it the ready medium for the communication of ideas and the rendering of narrative. Practically every section of the old Greek world found a chronicler and, as previously noted, so also did the chief countries of the East; the age also invented the historical study of philosophy, literature, mathematics, physics, and geography. Most of the information now existing about Hellenic authors has survived in such Hellenistic works. Standard collections of biographies, including the lives of philosophers, artists, and poets, as well as generals and rulers, were also compiled. The autobiographies of the age have been lost. Prose fiction originated as a parasite on history—a kind of narrative of startling episodes and marvels. Tales of travel to strange lands and of adventure became generally popular, but brief accounts of political intrigue, battles, banquets, moral delinquencies, and gossip mongering won easy audiences. The love romance was created and the muckraking exposé invented. Stories of the demimonde vied with the maxims of "teetotalers" for popularity.

One motif of the Hellenistic age—the legend of Alexander—worked its way into the literature of every country from the Indian to the Atlantic Ocean. Originally rendered about the opening of the fourth century B.C., it described the career of the great hero of the age, combining episodes from the "Epic of Gilgamesh" with stories of Greek heroes and bits of history and fiction in a narrative of war and adventure in strange lands. Today modern versions of the legend can be read in French, English, Spanish, Flemish, Dutch, Danish, Swedish, Icelandic, and Bohemian; six or seven German poets have treated the motif. In the Ethiopian version Alexander was portrayed as a Christian saint.

What Hellenistic literary works lacked in high feeling and enthusiasm for life they made up in accurate observation and sound expression of the gentler emotions—humor, pity, and conviviality. They were almost completely secular in outlook; only a few philosophic poets, chiefly Stoics, continued the traditional hymnology. The epigram, the moral precept, and the maxim summarizing tersely some aspect of life were the best products of an age that knew both the disturbing effects of an economic revolution and the exciting experience of a cultural uprooting.

By the courtesy of the University of Pennsylvania Museum

AN UNKNOWN GREEK GODDESS

This head of an unknown Greek goddess is an excellent example of the finest qualities of Hellenistic sculpture. Life in the fullest sense had come at last to the classical type. Because she is unknown, the goddess symbolizes well the ideal to which every heir of the Greeks aspires but does not attain.

THE ARTS IN THE HELLENISTIC AGE.

Generally, the same influences that affected literature found expression in the arts; these lost the classical ideality and became realistic and analytical, presenting life in moments of action and as bits of emotion rather than with a feeling for the whole of it.

1. *Hellenistic Sculpture.* Lysippus (fl. *ca.* 375–300 B.C.), the last great Greek sculptor, exercised a strong influence upon Hellenistic sculpture; he rendered men not as they are known or thought to be but as they appear to the eye—in other words, from a secular and realistic point of view. Athenian sculptors long maintained an excellence in portraiture. Corinth became the center of the manufacture of copies of classical figures which were widely popular. Three schools developed outside Greece. At

Pergamum an exceedingly high quality of craftsmanship was achieved; its greatest work was the "Altar of Zeus" on the Pergamene acropolis. This remarkable relief shows the struggles of gods and giants. In the third century B.C., as a result of an invasion of the Celts, the old theme of struggle between the barbarians and Greeks was revived; figures representative of this revival are the "Dying Gaul" and the "Gaul Killing His Wife." They expressed violent emotion, torture, and pain. The influence of Lysippus was particularly strong at Rhodes. Rhodian sculptors developed the group, used on the ancient Sumerian seals, as a motif; the best known example is the "Laocoön," showing the destruction of a priest and his two sons by a serpent sent by the gods. The "Victory of Samothrace," a winged female figure riding the prow of a wave-tossed ship, was a Rhodian product. The "Venus of Milo," whose author is unknown, perhaps the best-known Hellenistic statue, is a fine example of the free treatment of the female figure that Hellenistic artists achieved. Many examples of the Venus motif, which was popular throughout classical times, have survived. The Alexandrian school was inferior to those of Pergamum and Rhodes; it introduced the allegorical figure. The diversified interests of Hellenistic sculptors is exemplified in their treatment of children, of old men and women in humorous moods, and of diverse racial types. There was no loss of technical skill in sculpturing until toward the end of the age, but the classical conception of the beautiful seems to have become clouded somewhat earlier.[1]

The most notable achievement of the Hellenistic sculptors was the representation of the motion of the human body, not merely in position but as the play of muscles and bones.

   2. *Hellenistic Architecture.* The increase of wealth and its concentration in the hands of a small urban-dwelling class, the founding of new cities, and the rise of dynasties eager for pomp and power made the fourth, third, and second centuries B.C. a great age of architecture; it was, in fact, the first age in which building was not almost entirely limited to the main political and religious centers. With the construction of lighthouses, sea walls, and ports architecture entered directly into the service of commerce. Few new building materials were used, and no distinctive departures in style were introduced. Construction, characterized chiefly by technical skill and traditional design, was distinguished only by size and ornamentation.

[1] See A. W. Lawrence, *Later Greek Sculpture and Its Influence on East and West* (1927), and G. Dickins, *Hellenistic Sculpture* (1920).

Statuary was used in profusion and painting with both taste and skill. The arch was increasingly employed. Hermogenes (fl. *ca.* 150 B.C.), it seems, introduced certain modifications of the Ionic order that influenced Roman and early modern European architecture. The elaboration of the Corinthian order from the Ionic exemplifies the growth of a taste for ostentation. The Doric order was used infrequently. The chief buildings were temples (fewer in number than in Hellenic times), palaces, libraries and gymnasiums, banquet halls, pavilions, hippodromes, and theaters. The theater underwent a significant evolution. Its general design still followed the classical model of auditorium, orchestral circle, and skene (a rectangular structure closing the space between the ends of the semicircular auditorium; the word is the source of the "scene"), but the auditorium was built with its lower and upper tiers of seats at different slopes, the orchestra was connected by passages with the extremities of the skene, and the proscenium, a narrow, flat-topped structure, was run around the skene, fronting the orchestra. At first the proscenium served merely as a background for actors in the orchestra; later, when actors began to appear on its roof, it became the stage. The luxurious private residences of the well to do were built around square courtyards; this style, probably developed from a Sumerian prototype, was well suited to the subtropical climate. In the second century B.C. the round court, bordered with columns, appeared. Painting—sometimes to imitate marble, at other times to represent gardens—was the chief form of interior decoration. The Ptolemies occasionally built in the Egyptian style. A hypostyle hall—the large rectangular-roofed building—was built at Miletus in 210 B.C.; two sides were enclosed by walls and two by pillars. The Roman basilica, or law court, was derived, it seems, from this structure. Traces of oriental decorative styles, such as sculptured bases for columns and animal figures, began to appear toward the close of the Hellenistic age.[1]

The chessboard city plan originated by Hippodamus for the Athenian Piraeus was widely adopted in the laying out of new cities. In Asia, where fortifications were necessary, walls, penetrated by several gates, enclosed the cities. Large cities were frequently built in walled sections, each laid out on the rectangular plan. Great care was taken to provide an adequate supply of water, and when possible the entire city was often, for sanitary reasons, built

[1] Theodore Fyfe, *Hellenistic Architecture* (1930); S. B. Butler, *Hellenistic Architecture in Syria* (1917).

on a southern slope open to the wind. In fact, city planning, for both artistic and utilitarian purposes, was first widely practiced in the Hellenistic age.

3. *Hellenistic Painting.* Painting was a highly developed and widespread art. Great wall paintings in architectural settings were the most common; representatives of these paintings are best known from imitations of Greek originals found at Pompeii and Herculaneum.[1] The chief colors employed were white, olive green, pale green, pale lilac, pink, chestnut red, and several shades of brown. Backgrounds were almost universally rendered in scarlet. Most of the motifs were taken from mythology, but the secular tendency of the age brought such simple subjects as peaches and jugs, bits of landscapes, and ordinary people in familiar moods. Timomachus (fl. *ca.* second century B.C.), the last important Greek painter, excelled in depicting qualities of personality and scenes of emotional stresses. The portrait paintings of the Hellenistic age are known from seventy-eight pictures recovered from Faiyum mummy cases of Roman times. These portraits, both male and female, have a remarkable feeling of life.[2]

The distinctive achievements of Hellenistic painters were the mastery of perspective and the development of composition by grouping figures.

4. *The Hellenistic Minor Arts.* The decline of pottery making continued as the skill and artistry of metalworking increased. Jewelry in both gold and silver was richly elaborated. Coins and metals reached a new degree of excellence. And metal objects were commonly embellished with inlaid gems. Vase painting seems to have ceased some time in the first century B.C. The manufacture of terra-cotta figurines was a popular industry; the best of them were artistically executed copies of statues. The laying of mosaics, improved as a result of the expansion of building, was one of the chief decorative arts.

Music, which was widely appreciated, featured public festivals and athletic carnivals. The water organ was introduced about 80 B.C.

SCIENCE IN THE HELLENISTIC AGE.

The secular tendencies which gave peculiar quality to Hellenistic literature and art received their chief expression in the

[1] See p. 968.
[2] See Mary H. Swindler, *Ancient Painting from the Earliest Times to the Period of Christian Art* (1929); J. D. Beazeley and Bernard Ashmole, *Greek Sculpture and Painting* (1932).

sciences. No new intellectual methods were developed, but investigation was differentiated from speculation; and system making, *i.e.*, philosophizing about nature as a whole, was given up in favor of limited and specialized inquiries. The sciences still overlapped, and investigators commonly made contributions to more than one subject. Alexandria became the capital of an international world of science. Connected with its famous museum, where at one time or another most of the scientists of the age worked, were an astronomical observatory and the first combined research and teaching medical school; in them Greek and Babylonian scientific learning were fused. Plato's influence was dominant in mathematics; Aristotle's genius lighted the way of investigators in the other sciences. But Hellenistic science was probably as much oriental as it was Greek.[1]

1. *Hellenistic Mathematics.* Mathematics held its traditional position as the foremost science, and its method was still entirely deductive.[2] Eudoxus (*ca.* 408–355 B.C.) worked out a theory of proportions and applied the method of exhaustion to the computation of the volume of various solids, including the pyramid and the sphere. The volumes of spheres, he discovered, were to one another as the cubes of their radii. Euclid (fl. *ca.* 300 B.C.), trained, like Eudoxus, at Plato's Academy, wrote the first integrated mathematical treatise, the *Elements of Geometry*. Its thirteen books dealt with 465 propositions. The chief quality of the work, which remained the best known of all mathematical works until A.D. 1800, was its lucidity of exposition. Euclid drew together the propositions worked out by his predecessors and related them to a few axioms which he, like other Greeks, regarded as "self-evident truths." Apollonius of Perga (fl. *ca.* 247–205 B.C.) wrote a great book, containing 387 propositions, on the geometry of cones and conic sections; he introduced such terms as "ellipse," "parabola," and "hyperbola." Hipparchus (*ca.* 160–125 B.C.), who was famous as an astronomer, invented plane and spherical trigonometry. Heron (fl. *ca.* 50 B.C.), known chiefly for his inventions, seems to have worked out simple algebraic propositions, producing formulas for several areas and volumes. He also made approximations of the

---

[1] See George Sarton, "The Unity and Diversity of the Mediterranean World," *Osiris*, Vol. 2 (1936), pp. 429–430. On the general history of science in the Hellenistic age see *The Cambridge Ancient History*, Vol. 7, *The Hellenistic Monarchies and the Rise of Rome* (1928), Chap. IX, "Hellenistic Science and Mathematics"; Arnold Reymond, *History of the Sciences in Greco-Roman Antiquity* (1927); J. L. Heiberg, *Geschichte der Mathematik und Naturwissenschaften im Altertum* (1925).

[2] See T. L. Heath, *A History of Greek Mathematics* (1921).

By the courtesy of Bryan Holme

THE TOWER OF THE WINDS
(For descriptive legend see opposite page)

square roots of numbers that were not squares. The Hellenistic mathematicians, although they elaborated Hellenic beginnings, were creative thinkers in their own right, probably the greatest of their time.

There is no evidence to indicate that in the Hellenistic age mathematical theory was generally applied in engineering and architecture more than it had been in Hellenic times.

2. *Hellenistic Astronomy.* The Hellenistic astronomers not only greatly advanced the detailed knowledge of the universe but also produced two enduring theories of its structure.[1] Heraclides of Pontus (*ca.* 388–315 B.C.) asserted that the earth rotates on its axis once in twenty-four hours; he also held that the planets Venus and Mercury revolve around the sun. To explain the seeming motion of the sun around the earth and the movement of these planets he invented the theory of epicycles, which declared that planets move in circular orbits that are carried in another orbit around the earth.[2] Aristarchus (*ca.* 310–230 B.C.) developed the heliocentric theory of the universe. The sun, he said, is fixed and the earth and the planets revolve around it. He also worked out by geometrical deduction a scheme of heavenly sizes and distances. His estimate of the distance from the earth to the moon was fairly accurate. He also advanced the view, daring for the time, that the sun is much larger than the earth. Hipparchus elaborated the geocentric theory of the universe which became the leading astronomical view of late classical times and the Middle Ages. He adapted the theory of epicycles to the explanation of the movement of the planets, moon, and sun, which he arranged in a definite order about the earth as a center. Drawing upon Babylonian materials, which had become available in Greek translation in the second century B.C., he worked out the precession of the equinoxes, estimated the length of the year to within six minutes of its true period, and made a catalogue of 1,080 stars. He was the first mathematician and astronomer to adapt the Babylonian system of 360° to a circle for the purpose of observation. He is said to have

[1] T. L. Heath, *Greek Astronomy* (1932); T. L. Heath, *Aristarchus of Samos* (1913); Pierre Duhem, *Le système du monde; histoire des doctrines cosmologiques de Platon à Copernic* (5 vols., 1913–1917).

[2] See p. 972 for an illustration of the theory of epicycles.

THE TOWER OF THE WINDS

This beautiful building survives from Athens of the first century B.C. Its instruments— a waterclock, a sundial, and a weather vane—suggest the observation of natural phenomena which was the highest achievement of science in classical times.

invented an early form of the astrolabe. Aristarchus also contrived some scientific instruments.

3. *Hellenistic Medicine.* Medicine, like astronomy, advanced in detailed knowledge but suffered from controversy over rival theories. Anatomy became an important field of study because the philosophical doctrine that diseases center in the internal organs stimulated the practice of dissecting human bodies. Dissection began at Alexandria in the third century B.C. and continued until the second century after Christ. But it was opposed at all times, partly because of the fear of dead bodies, which the Greeks shared with their contemporaries, and partly because of religious prejudices.[1] Herophilus (fl. *ca.* 300 B.C.), known as the "father of anatomy," made the first public systematic dissections of the human body. He differentiated between the nerves and tendons and between the cerebellum and the cerebrum. He studied the arteries, the veins, the retina, the liver, the digestive tract, the salivary glands, and the genital organs. He gave the name "duodenum" to the upper portion of the intestines. He located the lungs as the seat of pneumonia. He paid great attention to the pulse and invented a device for measuring its rate. On the basis of these anatomical studies he developed a theory of four forces controlling the body: nourishment, which was directed through the liver; heat, through the heart; perceiving, through the nerves; and thinking, through the brain. But he held to the Hippocratic humoral theory of disease and relied chiefly on vegetable drugs for cures, having special faith in the therapeutic value of white hemlock.

Erasistratus (fl. *ca.* 290 B.C.), the rival of Herophilus, is known as the "father of physiology." He rejected the humoral in favor of the *pneuma* theory of health and disease. The blood flowed in the veins, nourishing the body. The pneuma was an invisible vital substance. In the lungs the air became the vital spirit, one form of the pneuma; it circulated in the arteries, which, after death, were always found empty. Upon reaching the brain the vital spirit became the animal spirit, another kind of pneuma, which was distributed through the body by the nerves. Erasistratus thought that the nerves were hollow, like the arteries. In normal

---

[1] Ludwig Edelstein, "The Development of Greek Anatomy," *Bulletin of the Institute of Medical History*, Vol. 3 (1935), pp. 235–248. On Hellenistic medicine see Charles Singer, *Greek Biology and Greek Medicine* (1922); Charles Singer, *The Evolution of Anatomy* (1925); Alfred E. Cohn, "The Development of the Harveian Circulation," *Annals of Medical History*, Vol. 1 (1929), pp. 16–136.

health pressure in the arteries prevented blood from flowing through channels which were believed to connect the veins and the arteries; any disturbance that brought blood from the veins to the arteries was regarded as a cause of disease. It is evident that the new knowledge of the circulatory system derived from anatomical studies was used in the elaboration of this theory. Erasistratus distinguished between the motor and sensory nerves, described the convolutions of the brain, and invented the names which the valves of the heart now bear. The heart, he believed, regulated the pressure that kept the blood from flowing from the veins into the arteries. In the treatment of disease he relied chiefly on simple remedies, diet, and exercise; he repudiated the use of drugs and bloodletting. Eudemus of Alexandria (fl. *ca.* 250 B.C.), a follower of Erasistratus, first drew the distinction between therapeutics and preventive medicine.

The rivalry of Herophilus and Erasistratus, both of whom worked at the museum, was exceedingly bitter, and its effects contributed somewhat to the decline of medicine toward the close of the Hellenistic age.

4. *Hellenistic Zoology and Botany.* There was a wide extension of the knowledge of the fauna and flora of Asia and Africa in the Hellenistic age. The elephant, the rhinoceros, the tiger, the giraffe, the leopard, the peacock, the parrot, and the guinea fowl became known. And many new plants were introduced, chiefly as sources of drugs. Zoos and botanical gardens were established in Alexandria and Athens, and greenhouses were popular among the wealthy. Theophrastus of Eresos, Lesbos (*ca.* 372–287 B.C.), who succeeded Aristotle as head of the Lyceum, is known as the "founder of botany" because he wrote the first scientific work in Western culture on botany. He drew together old information with the new data brought back by Alexander's expedition to India. He made no contribution to the systematization of his subject, failing to develop either a method of classifying plants or a scientific nomenclature. Although somewhat skeptical of charms, he did not renounce the belief in the occult influence of plants. He held that changes occur in plants automatically.[1]

5. *Hellenistic Geography.* The Hellenistic age was particularly favorable to the growth of geographical knowledge. Alexander's

[1] See Lynn Thorndike, "Disputed Dates, Civilization and Climate, and Traces of Magic in the Scientific Treatise ascribed to Theophrastus," in Charles Singer and Henry E. Sigerist, editors, *Essays on the History of Medicine Presented to Karl Sudhoff* (1924), pp. 73–85.

expedition gave detailed information about Asia as far east as The Himalaya and the upper Indus valley. About 330 B.C. Pytheas of Massilia voyaged along the Atlantic coast of Europe; he brought back the first accurate knowledge of Britain and wrote a treatise on the ocean. Eratosthenes (*ca.* 276–196 B.C.), the first systematic geographer, had a clear view of the inhabited world from the Atlantic to the Indian Ocean. He knew that a great mountain ridge extended from Anatolia to the headwaters of the Indus River, considered the oceans to be one body of water, and believed the tides of the Atlantic and Indian oceans to be connected. He calculated the circumference of the earth at 24,000 miles, only slightly less than its true figure. Mathematical geography began with Dicaearchus of Messina, Sicily (fl. *ca.* 300 B.C.), who measured the height of mountains in Greece and projected, if he did not make, a map on the principle of measured distance. However, the true founder of mathematical geography was Hipparchus, the astronomer, who invented the system of latitudinal and longitudinal location of position on the earth's surface; as a base meridian he took a line through the Fortunate Islands, now generally identified as the Canary Islands. Crates, the grammarian, seems to have made the first terrestrial globe. Posidonius of Apamea in Syria (*ca.* 135–51 B.C.) put together a huge collection of geographical knowledge and lore. He invented the now well-known system of five zones, made a good guess at the existence of the tropical desert belt, preserved the legend of the lost land of Atlantis, vaguely conceived an earthquake area that included the Mediterranean region, and reduced considerably Eratosthenes' estimate of the circumference of the earth. This error played some part in forming Columbus's conviction that it was possible to reach Asia by a relatively short westward voyage.

Hellenistic geographers made almost no advance in the interpretation of geological phenomena.[1]

6. *Hellenistic Physics and Engineering.* Archimedes of Syracuse (*ca.* 287–212 B.C.) was the most creative thinker—a mathematician, a physicist, and a technician—among the Hellenistic scientists. He first united deductive mathematics with scientific observation and technology. In mathematics his main achievements were the computation of the volumes of irregular solids, an exceedingly close approximation of the value of π, the invention

[1] See R. E. Dickinson and O. J. R. Howarth, *History of Geography* (1933); H. F. Tozer, *A History of Ancient Geography* (1934); E. H. Warmington, *Greek Geography* (1932); and Max Cary and E. H. Warmington, *The Ancient Explorers* (1929).

By the courtesy of the Metropolitan Museum of Art

ARCHIMEDES

Archimedes laid the theoretical foundations of engineering. Almost alone among classical thinkers he carried speculative inquiry into the solution of technological problems.

of a terminology for numbers of any magnitude, and the discovery of the ratio of the volume of a cylinder to the volume of an inscribed sphere. He created the science of hydrostatics by discovering the relative density of substances suspended in liquids; this discovery is now usually known as the principle of specific gravity. And he founded scientific mechanics by deducting from the common knowledge of the lever, which had been in use for centuries, and geometrical propositions, the principles of the lever's operation. His chief inventions were the compound pulley, the endless screw, which was soon widely used in irrigation and the drainage of mines, and the burning mirror. He also made a planetarium moved by water.

The practical tendencies which characterized Archimedes' thought were evident in the work of at least two other Hellenistic scientists. Ctesibios (fl. *ca.* 200 B.C.) is said to have invented a force pump, a water-clock, and a catapult worked by compressed air. Heron of Alexandria (fl. *ca.* 50 B.C.) not only wrote about mechanics but also applied his knowledge; he is credited with having invented the siphon, the water level, useful in land surveying, a slot machine, and a cyclometer for measuring the distance traveled by a wheeled vehicle. He was also interested in the phenomena of light, about which he wrote a book. He described clearly what he called the "five simple machines"—the lever, the wheel and axle, the pulley, the wedge, and the screw—and wheels geared to one another so as to transmit power. In the main the Hellenistic engineers worked at the problem of directing and transmitting mechanical power rather than at that of creating it. In the time of Heron the word "mechanics" meant the lifting of heavy weights.[1]

Throughout preliterate, ancient-oriental, and Greek times matter-of-fact knowledge, largely embodied in technology, grew independently of scientific investigation and speculation, for it belonged almost exclusively to the low intellectual tradition. When the Hellenistic scientists gave up system making for specific inquiries about nature, they almost arrived at the position of applying the results of their inquiries in useful ways. Apparently this arrival was on the point of occurring in both medicine and technology, more so in the latter than in the former. Indeed, the approximate assimilation of science into technology must be recognized not only as the high point in the development of Hellenistic secular thought but also as a critical point in the intellectual evolution of mankind; the human mind, for the first time in history, was on the point of consciously investigating nature in order to win knowledge useful for the control of nature. The bare enumeration of the mechanical appliances of the time—the lever, the pulley, the screw, the crank, the pegged wheel, and the windlass—indicates that only one thing was lacking for the achievement of such a control, namely, a source of mechanical power. And the

[1] On Hellenistic technological developments see A. P. Usher, *A History of Mechanical Inventions* (1929); Hugh P. Vowles, *The Quest for Power* . . . (1931); Hugh P. Vowles, "Early Evolution of Power Engineering," *Isis*, Vol. 17 (1932), pp. 412–420; A. Vierendael, *Esquisse d'une histoire de la technique* (2 vols., 1921); T. L. Heath, editor, *Works of Archimedes* (1897). For the general development of technology see Ludwig Darmstaedters, *Handbuch zur Geschichte der Naturwissenschaften und der Technik* (2d ed., rev., 1908).

technicians of the age were near the solution of this problem, for they knew the power of falling water, the force of air pressure, and the energy of expanding steam. But they never took the grand step. Why? The answer to this question can be found, it seems, partly in the tendencies which produced the characteristic philosophical and religious products of the age and partly in the economic situation, which failed to give the necessary stimulus to scientific and technological innovation.[1]

PHILOSOPHY IN THE HELLENISTIC AGE.

The Hellenic philosophers constructed their systems under the relatively stable conditions of the city-state, which, although often disturbed by factional strife, showed no signs of disruption; for them there were elements of certainty in social life.[2] But as economic distress deepened and Macedonia became more menacing, men, regardless of status, were impelled to consider more and more the problems of individual and social existence. The subsequent events of the Hellenistic age only reinforced this original impulse, for with the advent of the social problem and the rise of the new monarchies the old solutions of the problem of the relations of individuals to one another and to their in-group, if they could determine which was their in-group, no longer held good. In other words men were uprooted, *i.e.*, released from old social controls and loyalties, confronted with new demands, set new goals, and menaced with new dangers. When uncertainty is the normal fact in almost every significant phase of existence, how should a man live? Was Fortune—Tyche—the only deity? Was there a justice? What was the right way of life? The strain of social criticism which ran from the Sophists through Socrates into the new age provided the immediate departure for the consideration of these new questions by literate intellectuals. Thus the chief philosophical interest of the Hellenistic age was ethical rather than cosmological or metaphysical or epistemological. At least five important ethical schools arose in the course of the development of this interest.

[1] See M. I. Rostovtzeff, "The Hellenistic World and Its Economic Development," *American Historical Review*, Vol. 41 (1936), p. 252.

[2] See Eduard Zeller, *Outlines of the History of Greek Philosophy* (14th ed., 1931), pp. 207–209; *The Cambridge Ancient History*, Vol. 7, *The Hellenistic Monarchies and the Rise of Rome* (1928) Chap. VI, "Athens." On the Hellenistic philosophies see also Paul E. More, *Hellenistic Philosophies* (1923); Arthur O. Lovejoy and others, *A Documentary History of Primitivism and Related Ideas* (1935); H. L. Leisegang, *Hellenistische Philosophie von Aristoteles bis Plotin* (1923); Richard von Pöhlmann, *Geschichte der Sozialen Frage und des Sozialismus in der antiken Welt* (3d ed., 2 vols., 1925).

1. *The Cynics.* The founder of Cynicism was Antisthenes (*ca.* 450–366 B.C.), a pupil of Socrates, sometimes known as "the Thracian," and most of his original followers were foreigners in Athens from Thrace, Asia Minor, and Phoenicia.[1] In fact, Cynicism can be best understood as the philosophy of men who did not "belong"; this means that Cynicism reflected the feelings of noncitizens, foreigners (metics), and slaves. And its appeal throughout late classical times was chiefly to "uprooted" men.

The Cynics directed a bitter attack against the institutions and social values of the aristocratic city-state. They denounced its government. They repudiated its loyalties. And they mocked its typical citizen, the aristocratic gentleman who was proud of his athletic prowess, learning, and refinement. When the Cynics argued that true freedom is freedom from the tyranny of desires, they really meant that the quest of social prestige, political power, wealth, ostentatious pleasures, and intellectual refinements—the values of the ruling body of citizens—was impossible for foreigners, the poor, and the workers.

To the established order of values the Cynics opposed the "simple life"—conceived in terms of Orphic asceticism, Thracian primitivism, and the deprivations suffered by the poor. Why, they asked, should a freeman need a valet, when a slave can get along without one? Why, they argued, should a man wish to be rich, when he cannot use most of his possessions? When they praised austerity, poverty, rude manners, unconventional behavior, sharpness of the tongue, and the honest presentation of unadorned thought, they merely declared the values which the foreigner, the poor, and the worker already possessed. To the exclusive city-state they opposed a democratic cosmopolis including the entire civilized world. To a subtle intellectualism they opposed a severe regard for only those facts knowable through the senses. They glorified physical work and for the first time in history raised doubts as to the value of decorative and meditative learning; in fact, they called upon intellectuals to see themselves as workers and dispossessed.

In the Cynic Utopia, as described by Diogenes of Sinope (*ca.* 412–323 B.C.), no private property existed, women were possessed in common, and children were cared for in public institutions. Diogenes, who was the son of a banker, favored a currency of sheep knucklebones, which, since there were just eight to a sheep, could

[1] See article "Cynics" in the *Encyclopaedia of the Social Sciences*; also Farrand Sayre, *Diogenes of Sinope: A study of Greek cynicism* (1938).

be increased only by breeding, *i.e.*, by the production of actual commodities. This novel idea was proposed as a cure for the irresponsible manipulation of the coinage which contributed so much to the economic disorders of the time. The full realization of the Cynic ideal would have taken form in a universal republic in which labor, physical and intellectual alike, no longer subverted to the support of idleness and luxury, would have been pleasurable as a form of social service.

Cynicism was in fact little more than a form of individual and social defeatism. Its leading exponents were merely street-corner orators, pamphleteers, and wandering teachers who prided themselves on their unkempt persons and sharp tongues. In declaring virtue to consist of rising above desires, they sublimated dirtiness, deprivation, and distemper, for their asceticism was valuable not as a means of moral purification but for its own sake. And they taught no rule of individual life but the acceptance of fate: "What the good man has to do is to play well any part with which Fortune may invest him. You have been shipwrecked; very well, give a fine rendering of the part 'Shipwrecked Man.'" Their social influence was unimportant, for they added nothing to the growing body of scientific knowledge and organized no propaganda for social change. And their doctrines that poverty is virtuous and that differences of wealth and social position have no moral consequences have never contributed either to the humanizing of the powerful and well to do or to the amelioration of the lot of the poor and underprivileged. For its own age Cynicism begot only a "shiftless resignation"; for later times it revealed the futility of founding a program of social amelioration merely on the criticism, however just, of a corrupt social order.

2. *The Cyrenaics.* Aristippus of Cyrene (*ca.* 435–356 B.C.), the founder of the Cyrenaic school, was a pupil of Socrates, a representative of the Athenian ruling class, the owner of several estates, and a frequenter of the banquets of the rich and powerful. His teachings reflected the environment in which he moved.[1]

The leading Cyrenaic doctrine, that pleasure in all forms is good and always to be preferred to pain, was grounded in an interpretation of nature which saw every living thing tending to avoid pain and obtain pleasure. Pleasure was understood not as absence of pain but as an active state of feeling which could be stimulated. The aim of life was, therefore, the satisfaction of desires through induced gratifications. Since each man could know

[1] See article "Cyrenaics" in the *Encyclopaedia of the Social Sciences*.

only his own sensations, for so the Cyrenaics held, all pleasures were necessarily individual. No pleasure was to be shunned as evil in itself; only those that left a bad aftereffect were to be avoided. And mental pleasures, although they never distressed, were no better than bodily pleasures. When describing pleasure, the Cyrenaics always contrasted it with labor or drudgery, which the Cynics idealized; practically, this contrast, together with their doctrine that pleasure is to be found in the "flattery of the senses," meant a life of ostentatious consumption, luxury with or without refinement, and above all no work.

The concentration upon the individual pursuit of pleasure necessarily gave the Cyrenaics a limited social outlook. They advocated obedience to all laws as a means of avoiding pain; practically this meant the full acceptance of the existing social order, which, as a matter of fact, they declared to be good. But they were antipatriotic on the grounds that a wise man would not sacrifice himself in the service of an interest not his own. The Cyrenaics did not understand the social nature of man, neither comprehending the individual's need for social sympathy nor recognizing the satisfactions derived from altruistic action. They were not able to compute the value of such action in the pleasure-pain calculus. They looked upon religion as a means of keeping the masses quiet. But also they valued dialectic as a means of breaking down superstition. They denied the validity of science on the grounds that the physical world is incomprehensible. And they valued education chiefly as the means of forming habits that would restrain the pursuit of pleasures having evil aftereffects. Probably their most noteworthy social contribution was the doctrine that criminals should be re-educated rather than punished. Finally they seem to have taken the view that sensations are relative, giving pleasure at one time and pain at another. Practically, this meant that they did not become the advocates of standardized gratifications but sought an elaboration of pleasure, and, from time to time, even its redefinition; they were, therefore, at least by implication, the advocates of a kind of progress.

To an ethics of the type taught by the Cyrenaics is given the designation *hedonism*. In worst form hedonism begets merely a selfish pursuit of sensual gratification; in best form it promotes the diffusion of physical well-being under canons of aristocratic good taste. Unfortunately it establishes no sense of social responsibility to prevent individual excesses from frustrating the diffusion.

Hedonism justifies those who possess the pleasant things of life in making the most of their possession.

3. *The Skeptics.* Pyrrho (*ca.* 360–270 B.C.), who went to India with Alexander, studied, it is said, under the Hindu rishis and the Persian Magi; when he returned to Greece he founded a philosophy which soon won the adherence of Plato's Academy.[1] Its central doctrine was that man can know nothing as a certainty either through the senses or by reason. Such a doctrine was no doubt easily derived from a comparison of Indian doctrines, Magian teachings, and Hellenic speculations. Like Antisthenes and Aristippus, Pyrrho was chiefly interested in achieving happiness for the individual. From the doctrine that knowledge is impossible, he developed the theory that pain and disappointment arose because men, making false judgments, became deluded and sought false ends. Therefore to achieve happiness it was only necessary to repress these unwarranted desires and to restrain unfounded enthusiasms. This meant maintaining a mental calm; passive and imperturbable, the wise man, affecting humility, avoided physical exertion, emotional excitement, and mental stress. Above all he did not allow material objects and conditions to engross his attention. This idea was in line with Plato's idealism.

The Skeptics erected intellectual criticism into a moral discipline. They foreswore speculation and abhorred dogmatism. They demolished the theories of opponents, holding fast to nothing that could not be proved as fact. It is interesting to note in this connection that the great physicians of Alexandria were influenced by this position of the Skeptics to concentrate attention upon the study of actual specimens of human anatomy and disease. The Skeptics were early apostles of the scientific spirit; unfortunately the doctrine of "suspended judgment" supported, then as now, a quietism that left custom dominant in social affairs. The Skeptics produced neither a social criticism nor a social program; they were the advocates of a Greek version of the Indian ideal of renunciation, both in speculation and in practice.[2] They appealed chiefly to literate intellectuals and artists whose feeling of uncertainty was compensated by a sense of their superiority to the struggling crowd. The crowd, of course, lived on, pursuing ends that, when ultimately realized, left no place for Skeptics of any kind. Knowledge may not be possible, but faith is.

[1] See Eduard Zeller, *Stoics, Epicureans, and Sceptics* (1880).
[2] See Leon Robin, *Greek Thought and the Origin of the Scientific Spirit* (1928), pp. 318–319.

4. *The Stoics.* The Stoic school was founded at Athens by Zeno (*ca.* 336–264 B.C.), a Hellenized Phoenician from Cyprus, and its chief masters during the third century B.C. were from Asia, where Stoicism quickly spread—to Ephesus, Tarsus, Antioch, Seleucia, and Alexandria.[1]

The fundamental Stoic doctrine, based upon the conception of design in nature, was that the universe is rational. This rationality was a manifestation of the Deity—the supreme reasoner—who, as the all-wise heart of the universe, governed nature and men under law. The universe, therefore, was fundamentally good. Because man was endowed with a spark of the divine fire—a soul, he had contact with reality; thus, in fact, he was a microcosm, *i.e.*, a little universe, and as such could live in harmony with the great universe —the macrocosm.

Stoic ethics was developed in terms of this theory of the nature of the universe and man. Man's duty was to live according to the law which God had planted in nature; through his rational soul, man could know this law and, if he so willed, could follow it. This meant that man, acting under a self-imposed duty, accepted the world as he found it and himself in it, seeking the natural goods: self-preservation, the propagation of the species, health, long life, and perfection in body and mind. The Stoic ideal was the *sage*, *i.e.*, the wise man who, through wisdom, realized in his behavior the four virtues, courage, prudence, justice, and temperance, and avoided the four vices, fear, discontent, greed, and enthusiasm. If one were born noble and gained wealth and reputation he should accept his good fortune; if he suffered loss and deprivation his duty was to "carry on." To withdraw from the world was a form of cowardice. The Stoic believed in doing the world's work as it came to him, in facing the hazards of life bravely, and in enduring both pains and joys without emotional stress. Men were born immoral but with a capacity to become moral, and moral growth was the essential proof of a man's worth.

Zeno described an ideal republic, which his chief followers, Cleanthes (*ca.* 301–232 B.C.) and Chrysippus (*ca.* 280–208 B.C.), elaborated. They conceived mankind as one great city living in harmony under divine law. The members of this city were bound together by love, which meant to them mutual sympathy through reason, and formed a universal brotherhood. On the one hand this ideal involved the abandonment of racial and class distinctions.

[1] See article "Stoics" in the *Encyclopaedia of the Social Sciences.* See also R. D. Hicks, *Stoics and Epicureans* (1910); H. C. Pearson, *The Fragments of Zeno and Cleanthes* (1891).

By the courtesy of the Metropolitan Museum of Art

ZENO

Zeno, the founder of Stoicism, came from Citium, a Phoenician city in Cyprus. Stoicism may be regarded as the product of the first contact between the Semitic and Hellenic cultural traditions. As time passed, more and more Semitic elements found places in the Stoic faith.

In this connection it is interesting to note that the geographer Eratosthenes refused to divide mankind into Greeks and barbarians and slave and free. On the other hand this ideal accepted the institutions of the state, private property, and slavery as parts of the natural order of society. Notwithstanding its cosmopolitanism, Stoicism was in no sense a philosophy of social reform; it agreed with Cynicism that poverty is virtuous.

The intellectual outlook of Stoicism was in harmony with its individual and social ideals, for it accepted both science and religion. Science was a knowledge of nature obtained through reason; when remembered, it was merely recalled inborn knowledge. Science was chiefly useful as the basis of morality. These ideas, it can readily be seen, were derivatives from the teachings of Socrates and Plato. The Stoics had little conception of scientific research as carried out under Aristotle's stimulation. Cleanthes denounced the heliocentric theory of the universe as blasphemy. The dominant religious mood of Stoicism was reverence for nature: "There is one Motherland, stranger, in which we all dwell, and that is the Cosmos: there is one Father of whom we are all begotten, and He is the void." But the belief in the traditional gods was maintained; by allegorical interpretation they were identified with natural processes. Babylonian astrology was readily accepted because its doctrine that human destiny can be read in the heavens fitted in well with the conception that man lives under natural law in a universe divinely guided. The Stoics taught a teleological interpretation of the universe. But they made little of the life of the soul after death. The soul was chiefly important as the means to the knowledge by which life on earth was ordered. They believed that social distinctions reflected the varying degrees with which individual souls obtained knowledge.

Intellectually Stoicism was a Greek philosophy suffused with an emotional attraction to the Deity; socially it was the product of Hellenized orientals; practically it justified the social conformity which the new age demanded of those who had its responsibilities as well as its privileges.

5. *The Epicureans.* Epicurus (*ca.* 341–270 B.C.) settled in Athens about 306 B.C. and founded an association of brothers, or friends.[1] Both men and women were admitted, the sole qualification for membership being a knowledge of reading. Similar organizations soon appeared in other Greek cities, and later they spread throughout the Hellenistic world. After the death of the founder the members of the brotherhoods from time to time celebrated a common meal in his honor.

The fundamental Epicurean teaching was that pleasure is the beginning and end of life. This doctrine was developed in accordance with a physical interpretation of nature derived from the atomists. The universe was a fortuitous aggregation of atoms; gods

[1] See Cyril Bailey, *Epicurus* (1926); Cyril Bailey, *The Greek Atomists and Epicurus* (1928); and W. Wade, *Epicureanism* (1880).

EPICURUS

The philosophy of Epicurus found adherents throughout Greco-Roman times—being, in fact, the last of the classical ethical philosophies to disappear when Christianity spread among the Mediterranean peoples.

existed but, by virtue of their perfection, took no part in human affairs; the body was the house of the soul; all knowledge was derived from sensation; and sensation was the sole criterion of pleasure and pain. Knowledge was not an end in itself, but merely a means to the maintenance of the soul's state of pleasure. This state existed when the soul was tranquil. To maintain this calm, it was necessary to satisfy desires in different ways. Desires were divided into three classes: (1) those neither natural nor necessary, (2) those natural but not necessary, and (3) those natural and necessary. To yield to a desire in the first class brought greater annoyance than pleasure. Desires of the second class were valuable because of their rarity; to cultivate them sparingly was to become refined. Desires of the third class should always be satisfied within the limitations of nature. No pleasure in itself was evil; only as it caused pain was it evil. The chief obstacle to happiness was a feeling of insecurity induced by fears of social disapproval, the gods, and life after death. In the atomic physics the Epicureans found release from the fear of the gods and life after death; they escaped from the fear of social disapproval by withdrawing from society. Their brotherhoods were closed circles whose members shirked the duties of the state, escaped the excitement of public life, and felt no sense of responsibility for social evils. The prevailing mood of the brotherhoods was friendliness, cultivated not for its own sake but for the advantage of the individual. The most important means of winning happiness was the acquisition of friends.

The Epicurean wise man was a mild ascetic who considered himself above the law and beyond social demands. He sought pleasure in restraint and happiness in communal meditation. He had no interest in science except as it justified the self-centered life of pleasure. His belief that language embodied natural knowledge sustained an interest in literary expression. He fought heroically against magic, divination, and astrology as fear-arousing superstitions. He accepted poverty cheerfully. He desired no wealth beyond the requirements of nature—a vague requirement when it is remembered that he abhorred labor. (The Epicureans were generally the well to do.) He sought seclusion in the faith that a natural satisfaction of the desires in congenial company was the best existence possible for men. And he upheld the dignity of man as a personality, making the purely human sentiment of friendship the supreme value.

Intellectually Epicureanism was little more than a fusion of Cyrenaicism and Skepticism; socially it was the work of literate intellectuals who lacked the qualities for an active life in a world becoming increasingly unstable.

6. *The Central Elements of the Hellenistic Ethical Philosophies.* A comparative view of Hellenistic ethical philosophies reveals that generally they turned away from the secular world, failing either to investigate its institutions or to demand its reorganization. Least of all did they embody any understanding of the relation of social institutions or science or technology to the conditions of human life. In Hellenic times philosophy and natural

science had been closely associated—had been, in fact, one body of thought; in Hellenistic times they parted company—science to wither after a brief flowering, philosophy to bloom unchecked by any body of facts.

The Hellenistic ethical philosophers deplored the evils and distresses of life, mocking them or enduring them with fortitude or denying them or fleeing from them. And whatever ideal they set before men, it was to be realized only in an individual morality, for which, indeed, they recognized no social purpose. They repudiated the traditional racial and class distinctions in the name of cosmopolitanism. But generally social change went on without their cooperation or understanding. Not one advocated a significant social reform; not one aroused an enthusiasm for welldoing; not one inculcated a genuine humanitarian feeling; and not one praised laughter. The revolutionary movement among the poor, the debtors, and the slaves burned itself out, receiving only the casual approval of a few Cynics and Stoics. The Hellenistic philosophers conceived happiness not as a matter of doing things but as a matter of receiving things. Chiefly they found virtue in passivity. Certainly they had a right to fear power, for in their world power meant only irresponsible exploitation. Although they either repudiated or modified the traditional religion, they relied upon feeling rather than upon logic in their own arguments. They talked much of knowledge. But to them it meant more nearly an intuitive faith than inference from an ordered body of observed data. They were generally strangers to the scientific spirit, and they failed to keep in touch with the growth of scientific knowledge. In fact, as it has been well observed, Cynicism, Stoicism, and Epicureanism—the enduring Hellenistic philosophies—belong properly to religious history.[1]

RELIGION IN THE HELLENISTIC AGE.

The disintegration of the city-state and the spread of economic distress, which impelled the consideration of ethical questions, also stimulated religious change. As insecurity increased men sought new refuges, *i.e.*, psychological compensations for their irritations, and new reasons for having hopes. The spread of literacy necessarily brought men from the low intellectual tradition into contact not only with the high intellectual tradition but also with the current literate treatment of the problems of the age, and the results were: (1) the new literates carried materials from

[1] See Gilbert Murray, *The Five Stages of Greek Religion* (1925), p. 17.

the low intellectual tradition into the field of literate learning, and (2) they tended to select from the high intellectual tradition the materials which fitted their backgrounds and current needs. By the very nature of these circumstances the emotional elements of thought were deepened. Among the illiterate masses set in the low intellectual tradition the disturbance of the normal routine of life only stirred their fundamental primitive mentality. Furthermore, when literate intellectuals appealed to the illiterate masses, they necessarily spoke in terms which could be understood, and these terms were fixed, of course, by (1) the primitive mentality and (2) the current psychological needs of the illiterate masses. These circumstances gave religious beliefs and feelings wide opportunities for development. Whereas those who possessed literate learning could discuss the problems of the age philosophically and escape from its distresses either by withdrawing from society or by setting up beliefs which gave a psychological compensation for their irritations, the illiterate masses, having no means of flight from insecurity, could think of the problems it brought them in the only terms they knew—religious.[1]

The widespread cultural interaction of the age also nourished the religious growth which had its roots in the prevailing psychological disturbance, because it brought the Hellenistic low and high intellectual traditions into contact with the ancient-oriental low and high intellectual traditions. The low intellectual traditions, different in detail, were fundamentally primitive; the Greek high intellectual tradition was mainly philosophical, while the oriental high intellectual tradition was chiefly systematized superstition. Clearly, when these several traditions were mingled, religious materials outweighed all others.

---

[1] "It is worth remembering that the best seed-ground for superstition is a society in which the fortunes of men seem to bear practically no relation to their merits and efforts. A stable and well-governed society does tend, speaking roughly, to ensure that the Virtuous Apprentice shall succeed in life, while the Wicked and Idle Apprentice fails. And in such a society people tend to lay stress on the reasonable or visible chain of causation. But in a country suffering from earthquakes or pestilences, in a court governed by the whim of a despot, in a district which is habitually the seat of war between alien armies, the ordinary virtues of diligence, honesty, and kindness seem to be of little avail. The only way to escape destruction is to win the favour of the prevailing powers, take the side of the strongest invader, flatter the despot, placate the Fate or Fortune or angry god that is sending the earthquake or the pestilence. The Hellenistic period pretty certainly falls in some degree under all of these categories." Reprinted from Gilbert Murray, *Five Stages of Greek Religion* (1929), pp. 164–165: by permission of Columbia University Press, New York. On religion in the Hellenistic age see also E. R. Bevan, *Later Greek Religion* (1927); Richard Reitzenstein, *Die Hellenistischen Mysterienreligionen* (1920); Hugo Gressmann, *Die Hellenistische Gestirnreligion* (1925).

1. *The Social Basis of Hellenistic Religious Developments.*
The social circumstances of the mingling of Western and Eastern
cultural materials favored a deepening of religious feeling. When
the Greek cults spread into the East they attracted members
almost exclusively from the ruling classes; there is no example
of a Hellenic cult displacing an oriental religion among the masses.
Among Hellenized orientals, who retained many elements of their
traditional cultures, there occurred an assimilation not only of
Hellenic religious beliefs but also of the main Hellenic and Hellenistic philosophical conceptions. In this connection it is well to
remember that both Platonism and Aristotelianism emphasized
the role of deity and soul in the universal scheme of things; there
was, in fact, an affinity between many Hellenic philosophical
conceptions and the oriental religions. It is probably not incorrect
to see Stoicism as the offspring of this affinity. Among the literate
Greeks oriental materials, except the pseudo science of astrology,
had little appeal, but they found in astrology a confirmation of the
philosophical theory of order in nature. When Greek and oriental
cults met, although they found adherents among all classes, they
were popular chiefly among the sailors, workers, and merchants
of the ports and industrial towns. These groups consisted mainly
of "uprooted" men and women. The role of women in religious
development cannot be dismissed lightly, for upon them always
has fallen the full burden of insecurity, particularly upon the
women of displaced social groups. The new cults which appeared
in the eastern cities seem to have been especially popular among
women. When the oriental cults began to spread into western
Mediterranean lands, even as early as the close of the fourth
century B.C. (no oriental cult made real headway in the West
until the second century B.C.), the chief channel of diffusion was
among the sailors, workers, and merchants of the port towns, *i.e.*,
among those groups whose members, because they were distressed
economically, because they carried primitive beliefs, and because
they had become recently somewhat acquainted with literate
materials, were most likely to accept new religious ideas.

There were no serious obstacles to religious growth in any
social group of the Hellenistic age, and in many groups circumstances were extremely favorable to such growth. Although the
Stoics and the Epicureans opposed superstition, they accepted,
on the grounds that mankind had always believed in gods, the
existence of spiritual beings. The only issue between them and
the adherents of the various cults was the relation of gods and

men. The Epicureans, fortified with atomic physics, denied that the gods played any part in human affairs. But the Stoics, convinced of the forethought of the divine mind, soon became devotees of astrology as a means of obtaining knowledge of that forethought and accepted, as a result, innumerable superstitions. It is a mistake to believe that philosophical or scientific criticism was sufficiently widespread to prevent the acceptance of any belief that might have popular appeal. Indeed, it is probable that the leading ideas of Platonism, Aristotelianism, and Skepticism were no more familiar to the average Hellenistic urban dweller or peasant villager than the quantum theory now is to the denizens of New York or of the Ozark Mountains, or for that matter to the members of chambers of commerce and university clubs.

There was little or no intolerance of one religion by another, except among the Jews, who were powerless to do anything but resist the corruption of their own faith. The tolerant attitude of the age was a significant influence in the diffusion and the syncretism, *i.e.*, the growing together, of the various cults. The few cases of religious strife which occurred had their origin chiefly in priestly quarrels or political intrigues.

When the fall of the city-state discredited the traditional gods, they became mere abstractions. Zeus ended his career as the primal stuff of which all spiritual beings were believed to be made. And the new worship of divine kings was largely a formal ritualism; the people had no enthusiasm for it and felt it no obstacle to the worship of other gods. Indeed, the chief religious problem of the age was concerned not with the struggle of a true god with false gods but with the finding of a god—any god—that offered some salvation to uprooted men and women.

The first effect of the new circumstances upon the growth of religion was to spread the worship of Fortune and Chance. Fortune was sometimes described as a lovely goddess, who, blindfolded and standing on a marble ball, rolled this way and that about the market place, distributing favors to whomsoever she touched. Chance was conceived as a sinister figure whose special domain was the sublunary world inhabited by men. Human worth, effort, or need mattered not at all, Fortune and Chance everything; their wide popularity only testified to the prevailing insecurity of life.

2. *The Spread of the Mystery Religious.* Far more important than the worship of Fortune was the growth and spread of the mysteries which promised immortality beyond the grave. The

mysteries of Dionysos spread to Asia and Egypt, where, identified with many deities, he met other "redeemers"—Attis, the consort of Cybele, the Phrygian Earth Mother, and Mithra, the Persian intermediary between men and Ahura Mazda, and Serapis, a Graeco-Egyptian Osiris, and his consort Isis, the Mother Goddess of the ancient Osiris cult.[1] The central belief in the cults of these redeeming gods was that through communion with them men gained a *knowledge* which saved them from sin and gave aid in obtaining immortality. The mysteries were pervaded with the same feeling of human weakness that characterized the worship of Fortune and Chance. Their general pattern was no different from their forerunners of Hellenic times, but each, it seems, underwent considerable elaboration.[2] All sorts of miracles, healings, virgin births, exorcisms, and superstitions clung to them, and their complicated rituals aroused every emotion, from sensuality to intense spiritual longing.[3]

The mysteries of Serapis and Isis, which penetrated all parts of the Aegean world, were products of a syncretism of Greek and Egyptian beliefs.[4] Serapis—invented by Ptolemy I, so the story goes—seems to have been an assimilation of the Egyptian bull-god, Apis, who was identified with Osiris, with Pluto, the Greek god of the underworld. In the character of Osiris, Serapis was a life-giving deity; his communicants engraved on their tombs the prayer, "May Osiris give you drink of the refreshing water (*i.e.,* immortality)." At Alexandria he was represented by a famous blue statue, in Greek style, with eyes of inlaid gems. Admission to the cult was by initiation, which involved praying, fasting, washing in a sacred laver, and an entrance—as in a dream—into the holy presence of the god. After the initiation, which was conceived as a rebirth, the communicant wore a symbolical ring, prayed to Serapis for help in time of need, joined from time to time in a sacramental meal, had the priests make sacrifices for him, and looked forward to a state of immortal bliss. Isis was even more popular than Serapis. Her statues, also in Greek style,

---

[1] Sterling Dow, "The Egyptian Cults in Athens," *Harvard Theological Review*, Vol. 30 (1937), pp. 183–232.

[2] See page 548.

[3] See Samuel Angus, *The Mystery-Religions and Christianity* (1925).

[4] See T. A. Brady, "*The Reception of the Egyptian Cults by the Greeks* (330–30 *B.C.*)" *University of Missouri Studies*, Vol. 10 (1935), p. 17: "As the Egyptian gradually takes over the Greek cult-types of Isis, the Greeks gradually adopt much of the Egyptian ritual. The result of this process is a Hellenistic deity—neither Greek nor Egyptian." Courtesy of the University of Missouri Press.

were representations of a young matron, often carrying the infant Horus in her arms; as the special patroness of sailors, the bene-factress of women, and the friend of all men, she became univer-sally popular. The sentiments that clustered round her were similar to those which Christians later attached to the Virgin Mary. Like the traditional religion, the cults of Serapis and Isis were sacerdotal, *i.e.*, ministered by a priest class. These priests lived a semimonastic life in the temples, wore special robes, abstained from drinking wine and eating flesh, uttered numerous prayers, presided over the sacramental meals, and inculcated the doctrine of their faith. Both the Egyptian and the Greek languages were used in the temple services.

The mystery cults, which were organized as sacred brother-hoods recognizing no racial, national, or class lines, were con-trolled by priestly colleges. Apparently these colleges were never consolidated in an inclusive order. All members were equal before the "redeemer"; only the cult distinction between priests and communicants was recognized. Hundreds of these associations sprang up after the opening of the third century B.C., providing not only an opportunity for the expression of religious faith but also a focus of social sympathy in the new cosmopolitan world. They had no political aims. Few of the brotherhoods, it seems, numbered more than a hundred members.

3. *The Impact of Astrology upon Hellenistic Thought.* Astrology struck the literate Greek world as a new disease falls upon some remote island people. The Babylonian pseudo science, which first became known in the Greek world about the opening of the fourth century B.C., penetrated practically all fields of learning in the third century B.C.[1] Its chief sponsor Berossos was a neo-Babylonian scholar. The appeal of astrology to educated Western men arose chiefly from the fact that it provided an integrating principle for their science, philosophy, and religion. Scientific discovery had revealed an orderly universe. Philosophical specula-tion had made human reason supreme. And religious faith had declared the gods good. But the times were out of joint, men suffered, and Fortune reigned. Astrology gave a higher unity to these phenomena. Above the gods was a *necessity*, which, revealed in the orderly movements of the heavenly bodies, determined the affairs of men. These bodies, universally believed to be deities, were merely manifestations of the divine ethereal fire, and man's soul was a spark of the same divine element. Thus man, the micro-

[1] See Franz Cumont, *Astrology and Religion among the Greeks and Romans* (1912).

cosm, moved with the universe, the macrocosm. And the course of the movement was to be read in the heavens. The divine mind, which ordered nature, could be known by men.

As this conception of the universe and man was elaborated by Hellenistic thinkers, it became more and more encrusted with superstitions. The planets were identified with the Greek gods, who, as interpreters of the divine mind, were the immediate rulers of the world. The Babylonian notions about the magic character of the number 7 were mingled with Greek ideas. The seven Greek vowels became the signs of the planets, and prayers—no more than gibberish—were concocted by putting them together in unintelligible combinations. The seven-day week began to win acceptance. The wonders of the world, the ages of man, the gates of hell, the deadly sins, and the heavens were said to be seven in number. Casting horoscopes became an honorable profession. Cities adopted stars as their guardians. And men looked forward to immortal bliss in a heaven among the stars, where, in a state of holy intoxication, souls, free from bodily passions, contemplated the beauty of the heavens, listened—enraptured—to the music of the spheres, and satisfied their insatiable desire for a knowledge of deity.

Hipparchus, the greatest astronomer of the age, believed that the stars were the chief manifestation of the divine fire. The Stoics, who held that the soul was a spark of divine fire, immediately accepted the doctrine that men's fates were fixed by the stars. Only their belief that the divine mind was moral held them back from a complete surrender to the new superstition. The opposition of the Epicureans was unable to prevent its spread. The synthesis of oriental beliefs and Hellenistic learning was achieved by Posidonius. He was versed in astrology and demonology as well as in Pythagoreanism, Platonism, Aristotelianism, and Stoicism. The leading principle of his synthesis was the doctrine that God, the divine fire, pervades all nature as a vital force. His geographical system, previously noted, was developed in order to illustrate this belief. Man, he said, was the bridge between the earthly and heavenly worlds. In his work *On Heroes and Demons* he explained that human souls, like all vital forces, originate in the sun, come to the earth by way of the moon, and, after death, dwell in the space between the earth and the moon. As a corollary of this last notion, he believed that intercourse with departed souls was possible. The divine was manifested in earthly affairs by both omens and prophecy. Man could approach the divine reality in sleep and in ecstasy. The creation of the world and its beings had occurred in a process of emanation from the divine being.

The significance of Posidonius in the development of thought in Hellenistic and Roman times should be emphasized. He was the last important thinker before the rise of Rome, and his school at Rhodes was the center from which Hellenistic ideas were widely disseminated among the Romans. If he regarded man as a bridge between the earthly and the heavenly, he should be seen as the span between systems of thought having a worldly orientation and systems of thought having an otherworldly orientation:

> With his acceptance of bodiless souls, heroes, and demons, Posidonius stands on the border line of the two tendencies which we have followed throughout the history of Greek philosophy—the monistic and the dualistic. He smoothed the path for the revival of the latter tendency and unnoticed changed philosophy into theosophy.[1]

4. *The Philosophical Element in Hellenistic Religions.* If the Hellenic thinkers rose from a religious to a philosophical conception of the universe, the Hellenistic thinkers lifted religion to the level of a philosophy. This was a development, rather than a shift, of outlook. If they grasped more firmly the view that the universe is a unity, they also asserted more vigorously the supremacy of deity. If they depreciated the human body more, they also emphasized the human soul more. If they conceived earthly evil more deeply, they also aspired more ardently to a heavenly bliss. If they pursued knowledge more diversely, they also demanded of knowledge a fuller revelation of God. If they felt all mankind to be one, they also gave a higher worth to individuality and personality. If they lacked faith in human strength and good intention, they also had a firmer belief in a divine saving power. If they conceived man in a cosmic setting, they also saw in him nothing less than the cosmos itself. If they multiplied ritual, practiced magic, and cast horoscopes, they also felt a poignant yearning for the goodness which, in spite of all evidence to the contrary in the suffering of the age, they believed to be at the heart of the universe. If they cultivated science, they also developed allegory which showed in verse, ritual, and language, indeed in

---

[1] Eduard Zeller, *Outlines of the History of Greek Philosophy* (13th ed., 1931), p. 252. By permission of Harcourt, Brace and Company, Inc., New York. On Posidonius see also Richard Reitzenstein, *Die Hellenistischen Mysterienreligionen: Ihre Gundlagen und Wirkung* (1910); J. R. Mattingly, "Cosmogony and Stereometry in Posidonian Physics," *Osiris*, Vol. 2 (1938), pp. 558–583.

the whole universe, the hidden meanings that proclaimed the wish fathering their thought:

> Naught e'er comes to pass on earth apart from thee, O God,
> Nor in the sacred pole of ether above nor in the deep,
> Save all the sin men do with folly cursed.

5. *The Survival of Priest Classes in the Hellenistic Age.* The development of formal elements—priests, rituals, and symbols—kept pace with the elaboration of the other aspects of religion. As previously noted, the mystery cults were ministered by priestly colleges. In Egypt the ancient priest class preserved its privileged position, presenting to the other Mediterranean lands an example of the integration of religion with economic, political, and social institutions.[1] Every government maintained an official cult with special priests. Individual prophets taught divine knowledge to any who would listen, and of listeners there usually were many. The magic of priests, it was everywhere believed, was necessary for the achievement of the supreme goal—heavenly life.

THE SIGNIFICANCE OF THE HELLENISTIC AGE IN THE GENERAL DEVELOPMENT OF CULTURAL TRADITIONS

The centuries immediately following Alexander's conquests of the ancient-oriental lands were one of the most important of all periods in the development of cultural traditions, Western and Eastern alike.

For the Western world these centuries began a social and cultural interaction that gave a lasting quality to its life. In this interaction, although Greek materials were dominant, oriental traits blended with them, affecting political and economic organization, the arts, the sciences, the philosophies, and especially the religions. But if Greek materials were uppermost, men of oriental origin became increasingly prominent, at least in every field of intellectual activity, and in the end the achievements which survived were theirs rather than those of the true Greeks:

There is a quarter of the eastern Mediterranean which has been singularly fertile in the history of thought. Place yourself, in time, in the four centuries from 300 B.C. to A.D. 100: place yourself, in space, on the island of Cyprus, and look northward to Cilicia, eastward to northern

---

[1] On the survival of the Egyptian priest class, which should be understood as having special significance for the evolution of the Christian priest class, see Walter Otto, *Priester und Tempel in Hellenistischen Ägypten: Ein Beitrag zur Kulturgeschichte des Hellenismus* (2 vols., 1905).

Syria, and south-eastward to Phoenicia; and then so placed and so looking, you will find a constellation of many stars. From Citium in Cyprus came Zeno, a Hellenized Phoenician . . . who founded the Stoic school. From Soli, in Cilicia, to the north, came Chrysippus, the systematizer of Stoicism. From the neighboring city of Tarsus came Zeno the Second, the successor to Chrysippus as master of the Porch; and from Tarsus there also came a Hellenized Hebrew . . . whom we call St. Paul and who visited Athens three and a half centuries after the Hellenized Phoenician from Cyprus, and preached in terms of the Stoic philosophy, as it is recorded in the Acts of the Apostles, in the midst of Mars' Hill. . . . Let us now turn eastward, to the mainland of northern Syria, and here we shall find, in the city of Apamea, the birth place of the great Posidonius, who lived from 135 to 51 B.C. and was the teacher of Cicero and Caesar and the friend of Pompey—the man who reconciled Stoicism to Platonism, and perhaps also to Oriental ideas which were indigenous to northern Syria or had come travelling up the Euphrates from farther east: the man who did most to make the general world of thought into which Christianity was born.[1]

Closely connected with the cultural interaction of which these men were products was the spread of literacy among new groups, especially the free craftsmen of the towns. That their speech—the *Koinē*—became more and more widely used as the vehicle of learning is full evidence of their significance in cultural development. Their rise to literacy was itself a primary factor shaping cultural development, for not only did it release abilities long locked in the low intellectual tradition but also it meant that the emotional and daimonistic elements of the mentality of the masses would find new expression in literate forms. These circumstances gave support everywhere to ethical and religious movements. At the same time they tended to concentrate the study of the sciences in a few places, far removed from the currents of popular thought. The failure of the Hellenistic thinkers to create a scientific technology left the new literates, as well as the illiterate masses, in the old routines of labor so that, except as they were disturbed by new conditions of economic exchange and social intercourse, their lives went on as in the past. For this reason religious rather than scientific developments became increasingly important as time went on.

The new concepts of the Hellenistic age—"world empire," "civilized world," "humanity," and "concord"—were mainly expressions of the growing feeling of unity to which the widened

[1] Ernest Barker, "Some Foreign Influences in Greek Thought," *Greece & Rome*, Vol. 5 (1935), p. 2.

social intercourse gave support. In the fourth century B.C., when it was declared that the differences between men were not the distinctions between Greeks and barbarians but those between good and bad men, was established the emotional basis of the separation of the City of God from the City of the Devil proclaimed by the great Christian thinkers seven centuries later. The Hellenistic religious movements contributed to this evolution, and the mingling of cultural materials from every local area of the ancient Near East and the lands of the Mediterranean Basin ensured that its product would be ultimately a cosmopolitan culture embodying ethical values that had origin in the distresses of uprooted common men. The Hellenistic age shaped the emotional fixations that gave in succeeding centuries the order of importance to the patterns of the Western cultural tradition.

The Hellenistic age also opened a new phase in the history of Eastern cultural traditions. In Asia Minor Greek influence became paramount, the native languages actually disappearing. In Palestine Hebrew culture faced a new danger to its survival. In Syria and Mesopotamia a veneer of Greek culture spread over the urban populations. In Armenia, Iran, and Bactria Greek luxury, manners, amusements, and coinage were adapted to the needs of the local dynasties. The impact of Hellenism upon India is difficult to judge. Some Greek military and astronomical terms entered its language. Some of the early images of Buddha were conceived in the pattern of Apollo, and the style of execution in drapery, pose, and expression was Greek. Perhaps Indian temple architecture was influenced by Hellenic models. Coins were struck in imitation of Greek pieces. And Greek dialogue seems to have set the pattern of Hindu philosophical discussion. From Bactria and India Greek influence carried the vine, decorative motifs, a style of statuary, and probably coinage to China. It seems, too, that the Greek influence finally reached Japan. In Africa some elements of Hellenism filtered to Ethiopia. However, nowhere in Asia, except in Asia Minor, did Hellenic culture affect the life of the peasant-village masses. At best the Hellenized sections of the population were only tiny islands in the masses, who held fast to their traditional cultures. In Iran and India these masses became in time the support of native reactions to Hellenism which, in fact, gave their traditional cultures a new firmness.[1]

---

[1] See Pierre Jouguet, *Macedonian Imperialism* (1932), p. 390. See also Eduard Meyer, *Blüte und Niedergang des Hellenismus in Asien* (1925); M. I. Rostovtzeff, "L'Hellénisme en Mésopotamie," *Scientia*, Vol. 53 (1933), pp. 110–124.

What Asiatic influences moved westward in the wake of the Macedonian conquests? To this question no certain answers can be given. From Mesopotamia came astronomical lore and astrology. From Iran Zoroastrian ideas flowed into the mingling of cultures. And the contact of Greek and Hebrew ideas was decisive for the future of the Western cultural tradition. But what came west from the countries beyond Iran? A few Hellenistic men are credited with having visited India, but there is little direct evidence that anything they learned there entered significantly into Western thought. Probably, it may be surmised, Indian thought penetrated Egypt, chiefly through commercial channels, and stimulated there the development of the many varieties of religious beliefs and modes of living for which Egypt became famous in Roman times. However, it should be emphasized that Egypt assimilated whatever materials it received from the East into its own religiosity, which, although commonly disregarded, was an important cultural influence in both Hellenistic and Roman times. Nothing, it seems, reached Western lands from China in the Hellenistic age.

In the Hellenistic age the West and East met and, although neither imposed a cultural dominance on the other, each became more like the other. Also it is not wrong to recognize that the Hellenistic age gave outlines to European, north African, and Asiatic culture areas which remained little changed until modern times.

Chapter XII

THE CONSOLIDATION OF THE IRANIAN AND HEBREW CULTURAL TRADITIONS

≪≪≪-≪≪≪-≫≫≫-≫≫

Imperialism has important cultural results for its victims as well as its victors. If to the victors it brings *élan*, new wealth, and a flood of out-group cultural materials, to victims it brings a disorganization of life which, if it persists for a sufficiently long period of time, is likely to disintegrate their cultural tradition. But this extreme result occurs infrequently. Commonly the results of the very different circumstances for victor and victim are quite alike so far as cultural development is concerned. In each case the fundamental cultural tradition is affected by new social conditions among the carrying populations—a circumstance which contributes to a cultural reorientation, *i.e.*, a change in outlook on life—and by out-group cultural materials which are assimilated into the fundamental tradition in terms of the new outlook. Inasmuch as the disturbance of the traditional modes of life intensifies the emotional attachment to them, the new rendering of the fundamental tradition embodying these effects of imperialism has a resistance to further change which makes almost certain its persistence through any future circumstance that does not destroy its carrying population. A cultural tradition whose elements are so well established and tightly knit together that they yield only slightly either to the force of new social conditions or to the impact of external contacts may be said to be *consolidated;* the normal cultural effect of imperial action is—ultimately—to consolidate the cultural traditions it touches.

THE IRANIAN CULTURAL TRADITION: MAZDAISM

For about three centuries after the Macedonian conquest Iranian culture was carried by the native Iranian peasantry and a dispersed Zoroastrian priesthood. When Iran recovered political independence, first under the Parthians and later under the

Sassanian Persians, the Iranian cultural tradition was reconstituted and rendered in an enduring form—Mazdaism—which embodied Greek and Indian, as well as Iranian, materials. The Zoroastrian priesthood took the lead in the work.

EMPIRES AND CONQUERORS IN IRAN.

The first Persian empire, ruled by the Achaemenian Dynasty, against which Alexander led the Greek counterattack, had arisen on the ruins of the ancient-oriental urban culture, and its political regime, into which Zoroastrianism entered deeply, was the channel through which many elements of the ancient-oriental monarchy flowed into the traditional Asiatic and European cultures. Under the second Persian empire, founded by the Sassanian Dynasty, Mazdaism became a cultural influence not only in Iran but also in neighboring lands, both east and west.

1. *Iran under the Achaemenian Dynasty, ca.* 559–330 *B.C.* As previously noted, Cyrus and his successors extended Persian rule from the Danube to the Indus and from the Nile to the Oxus, and gave this vast territory a unified government.[1] But following the attempts of Darius and Xerxes to conquer Greece, the regime slowly weakened. The nobility, the backbone of the state, lost military prowess as luxury sapped its strength. The influence of the Iranian priesthood steadily increased. And intrigues continually disturbed the imperial court. More important, however, than these normal factors of disintegration in the oriental monarchy was the fundamental circumstance that no advance of trade, industry, or science gave new economic and social support to the state.

The Persians were the ruling nation among conquered peoples they regarded as slaves. In other words, the Persian in-group succeeded to the position ordinarily held by the military and priestly classes of an urban culture. Its members, forming the nucleus of the imperial army, paid no taxes but made gifts to the king, while he, in turn, rewarded them yearly with portions of the tribute paid by the conquered peoples. The Persians were not governed as part of the empire but as an Iranian tribe; in fact, the members of the Achaemenian Dynasty were merely the leaders of the dominant clan of this tribe.

The Persian empire was, therefore, an oriental monarchy adapted to the government of diverse peoples. But whereas the Babylonians and Assyrians had attempted to pacify their domin-

[1] See p. 361.

ions by transporting conquered peoples from their homelands to distant parts of the empire, thereby making them dependent on the imperial overlord, Cyrus and Darius gave up this practice and, along with it, the ancient custom of carrying the gods of conquered nations to the imperial capital. Thus Cyrus allowed the Hebrews to return from Babylon to Palestine and to take with them the sacred vessels of the cult of Yahweh. Conquered peoples were allowed to keep their own religions, customs, laws, and local governments. Captured cities were not destroyed, defeated populations were not decimated, except as punishment for rebellion, and overthrown ruling houses, save in rare cases, were not maltreated. Only two obligations were imposed on subjected peoples: (1) to pay a fixed tribute and (2) to furnish a military levy.

To enforce these obligations Darius established an imperial administration. The emperor, who took the title "King of Kings," held supreme power under Ahura Mazda. At the head of the administration was the commander of the royal bodyguard, the "ten thousand immortals," who served as a kind of vizier. The heads of the noble families who had stood with Darius against Gaumata, the Magian rebel, formed a royal council. "Law bearers" and scribes—a civil bureaucracy—performed the detailed work of government. An elaborate spy system, headed by an official known as the "eye of the king," watched everyone and everything. The conquered lands were divided into some twenty districts; over these ruled satraps, whose chief duties were to collect tribute and enforce the military levy. Associated with each satrap, although independent of his authority, were two other royal officials: a secretary, who kept the king informed, and a general, who commanded the Persian garrison stationed at the capital of the satrapy. This division of authority in the satrapies was a device to prevent rebellion. The heads of local noble families and the commanders of the Persian garrisons held prominent positions in the courts of the satraps. Each year representatives of the "eye of the king" inspected the satrapies; they did not follow a fixed schedule in their tours. A system of imperial posts made possible the easy transmission of news and orders between the imperial court and the provincial capitals. A royal road, protected by fortified posts and serviced by courier stations, ran from Sardis in Lydia to Susa, where it connected with the ancient route that led from Elam to Parsa. The distance—over fifteen hundred miles —from Sardis to Susa, which would take a pedestrian three months to cover, was made by couriers in two weeks.

All imperial officials, as well as the imperial garrisons, were supported by the imperial treasury. The chief sources of revenue were payments in kind levied on the twenty satrapies in various amounts. The tax paid by the peasant was based on an exact measure of land, but differences in fertility modified the rate, which varied from one-tenth to one-half of the yearly product. Crops were not harvested until the tax gatherer was ready to take the state's share. Some of the satrapies paid in kind. Babylonia supplied food for one-third of the army and the imperial court. Egypt furnished grain for 120,000 men. Media was a source of horses, mules, and sheep. From provinces, especially northwestern India, where the precious metals were mined, taxes were collected in gold and silver, and in the course of time the king accumulated a colossal hoard. He alone minted gold coins. Satraps and generals were permitted to mint silver coins. Since the satraps did not receive fixed salaries, they took advantage of their power to collect taxes and tribute in order to enrich themselves.

The army was the weakest pillar, although the main one, of the empire. It consisted of a Persian and Median core, mainly cavalry probably numbering not more than fifty thousand warriors, and the levies of conquered peoples. These levies—the infantry— when assembled in large numbers were dangerous to their Persian masters, who frequently found it necessary to drive them to battle with the lash. Although the nobles were trained as officers in special schools, the Persians fought more as nomads than as a disciplined urban people.

The Western tradition of regal splendor descended from Assyria by way of the Persian court. The king wore robes of purple, a golden tiara set with brilliantly colored gems, a golden girdle, and heavy golden ear rings, bracelets, and chains; his sartorial elegance was completed with curled beard and hair, oiled and heavily perfumed. On state occasions he sat on an elaborately wrought throne, behind which stood an attendant with a flyflap. His domestic life was spent in the harem, where concubines shared his favor with legitimate wives. His chief amusement was the hunt. The succession was hereditary, but the first son did not have a prior claim over other sons; the son chosen by the royal father from among all of his male offspring ascended the throne as his successor. Sisters of the king were not given as wives to foreign kings; they were commonly married to their royal brothers. Harem intrigues were a normal aspect of imperial politics.

The Achaemenian Dynasty ruled according to the Zoroastrian ideal of justice; on his tomb Darius boasted, "Right I have loved, and Wrong I have not loved. My will was that no injustice should be done to any widow or orphan. . . . I strictly punished the liar but him who labored I well rewarded." The administration of justice was in the hands of appointed judges. Bribe-taking judges were executed, and their tanned skins were stretched over the benches upon which their successors sat. The king held absolute power of life and death over every subject. For minor crimes the usual punishment was flogging. For treason, rape, murder, and displeasing the king the punishment was death, sometimes preceded by mutilation. Common modes of execution were throwing into hot ashes, burying alive, flaying, crucifying, and impaling. Rebels were subjected to especially horrible cruelties. The laws of the Medes and Persians, although notoriously severe, were not more so than other ancient codes.

From the point of view of the Persian king, the Zoroastrian ideal of making the world better ordered meant making the Achaemenian regime more secure.

2. *Iran under Macedonian Rule.* In 330 B.C., when the Achaemenian Dynasty fell under the swift blows of Alexander the Great, Iran passed under foreign rule which lasted for several centuries. Alexander, although he despoiled the Achaemenian ruler, burning his palaces and seizing his hoard of jewels and gold, adopted his court ceremonials and costumes; this action seems to have been part of a policy that aimed to bring about the fusion of the Macedonian and Iranian ruling groups. The marriage of Iranian women to Macedonian officers was the basic element of this policy. But it was short-lived, for Alexander's successors were soon too busy fighting among themselves to promote it. However, the interaction between Greek and Iranian cultures, once begun, was continuous until both cultures were merged with new traditions at the opening of the middle ages.

At Alexander's death Iran fell to Seleucus (*ca.* 305–280 B.C.), whose successors held part of southwestern Asia until shortly before the middle of the first century B.C.[1] Although the Seleucids fought continuously for Syria, their power rested on the great satrapies of the Achaemenian empire—Babylonia, Susiana, Persia, and Media. Seleucia, not Antioch, was the capital of these satrapies. Like Alexander, the Seleucids promoted the Hellenization of

[1] See p. 609.

Iran by founding cities, but except for a short period of military success by Antiochus III (*ca.* 223–187 B.C.) their power, especially over the eastern satrapies, was shadowy. Wars in the west for the control of Syria and Asia Minor and against nomadic invaders from central Asia prevented the Seleucids from unifying Iran.

In central Asia Bactria broke away from the Seleucid monarchy shortly before the middle of the third century B.C. Its culture and kings and many of its inhabitants were Greek. Recent archaeological discoveries have proved for the first time that Greek architectural techniques and motifs were known in Bactria. How this island of Hellenic culture in central Asia developed is not exactly known. The fertile Oxus valley supported a rich agriculture, and the routes that led in one direction to China and in another to India were the channels of a trade which, during the second and first centuries B.C., was bringing China and southwestern Asia ever closer together. The campaigns of the Bactrian kings in Chinese Turkestan and northwestern India may have had as an objective the extension of control over these routes. One of the results of these campaigns was the introduction of nickel, probably from China, into the Bactrian coinage. The significance of Bactria, through which eastern Asiatic influences moved westward and Iranian and Mediterranean influences passed eastward, although only vaguely indicated in surviving materials, must have been very great. Its incorporation in the Kushan empire[1] about 126 B.C. probably increased rather than lessened this significance.[2]

3. *Iran under the Parthian Empire, 250 B.C.–A.D. 224.* About the time Bactria won independence a nomadic people—the Parnae—from central Asia established a kingdom in north central Iran and from its chief province, Parthava, took the name Parthian. As a ruling group they seized the land but did not disturb the local culture. Their main settlements, like Hecatompylos (the word means hundred-towered), their capital, the location of which is now unknown, seem to have been walled cities and castles. Their leaders absorbed the Greek veneer of the Iranian nobility, adopted Persian political methods, and maintained a firm control over the trade from central Asia to the Mediterranean lands. Their revenues were drawn from a duty on silk, tribute from cities, and payments in kind from the peasants. But they never developed a centralized state. The royal bodyguard was the only standing army. They depended on a feudal levy of horse-

[1] See p. 752.
[2] See W. W. Tarn, *The Greeks in Bactria and India* (1938).

By the courtesy of the Aerial Survey of the Oriental Institute, Mary-Helen Warden Foundation. Photograph by Dr. Erich F. Schmidt

A PARTHIAN STRONGHOLD

This mountain top—Takht-i-Suleiman—is located in Atropatene, about 140 miles southeast of Lake Urmia. Most of the ruins are remains of the fortified capital where the Parthian kings maintained their wives and children. The wall, originally 16 feet thick and 45 feet high, was three-quarters of a mile in circumference. It was strengthened by 27 bastions. Only two narrow gates led to the barracks, storehouses, temples, and palaces within the walls. The lake—the most remarkable feature of the site—is fed continually by fresh-water streams.

In 36 B.C. when Mark Antony audaciously attacked the stronghold without siege engines, the Parthian cavalry harried his legions, destroyed his transport, and forced him to retreat. This defeat checked Rome's eastward expansion.

men and mercenaries (also horsemen) for their main fighting force. Plundering and raiding both inside and outside the borders of their kingdom were continuous. There is some evidence indicating that the Greek drama and, perhaps, bits of Greek philosophy were known at the Parthian court.

Parthian power was at its height in the second and first centuries before Christ when, although attacks by the Turki peoples and the Yuet Chi weakened them in central Asia and eastern Iran, they advanced westward. First, after defeating the Seleucids, they reached the Tigris River, and then, after destroying a Roman army under Crassus in 53 B.C. and defeating Antonius in 36 B.C.,[1] they occupied Mesopotamia as far north as the great bend in the Euphrates River.[2] Parthian success against the Romans was due to the fact that their mobile horsemen could never be brought to battle by the legions, which, because of their numbers, were difficult to provision in arid Mesopotamia. After wars over Armenia early in the first century A.D., the Romans and the Parthians came to terms and maintained peace along the Euphrates border for over a half century. However, in the second century war broke out again, and Trajan, the Roman emperor, captured Seleucia-Ctesiphon. His death brought the campaign to an abrupt end.

The Parthians never controlled all of Iran. In areas away from the trade routes from Mesopotamia to central Asia, local Iranian kings and princes, although they sometimes acknowledged the overlordship of the Parthians, generally ruled without imperial interference. The effect of this policy was to strengthen the feudal element, *i.e.*, the landed nobility, in the Iranian social structure. The wars of the Parthians, it should be noted, seem to have disorganized agricultural production in parts of Mesopotamia and Iran and to have caused a loss of population.[3]

4. *The Revival of the Persian Empire under the Sassanian Dynasty, 226–651.* The Persian imperial tradition survived especially in Atropatene, a priestly state east of Lake Urmia, and in Persia, where the local king, who had a connection with the Iranian priesthood, also claimed descent from the Achaemenian Dynasty. Early in the third century, when Parthian power weakened, the Persian king, Ardashir I (226–240), revolted and, with the close cooperation of the Mazdean priests, re-established the Persian empire; he was the founder of the Sassanian Dynasty.[4] His successors, among whom the greatest were Shapur II (309–379) and Anoshirwan (531–579), successfully fought the Romans, the Arabs, the Huns, and the Turks and raised Persia again to the position of a world power. Under Anoshirwan the imperial capital, Ctesiphon, on the Tigris River, rivaled in magnificence

[1] See p. 885.

[2] See map, The Great Empires, Early Second Century A.D., facing p. 912.

[3] On the history of the Parthians see Neilson C. Debevoise, *A Political History of Parthia* (1938).

[4] On the Persian empire under the Sassanian Dynasty see Arthur Christensen, *L'Iran sous les Sassanides* (1936).

any other city in the world. The power of the Sassanian Dynasty was based on the traditional influences in Iranian culture and the new urban forces that had arisen with the growth of trade; both supported a policy of political centralization.

The central administration, organized on Achaemenian lines, was headed by a vizier and carried on by a bureaucracy whose members were drawn mainly from the great families that surrounded the royal house. In the provinces satraps ruled, and the system of royal couriers was re-established. The core of the army was a heavily armed cavalry drawn mainly from the lower nobility; supporting it, besides a light-armed infantry, were a force of fighting elephants and well-organized siege trains. The elephant force was organized on the Indian model, the siege trains on the Roman. The imperial court was a center of flamboyant luxury and political intrigue, where eunuchs and harem favorites, as well as generals and viziers, exerted influence on imperial policies. Only the highest nobles and court favorites ever saw the king, the masses never. Foreigners who visited the court paid their respects to a golden image of him.

5. *The Economic and Social Organization of the Persian Empire under the Sassanian Dynasty.* The economic base of the revived Persian empire was threefold: (1) an intensive agriculture, especially on the Tigris-Euphrates flood plain, (2) a spread of the metal and textile industries through the Iranian cities, and (3) the control of the overland trade with China. As under the Achaemenian Dynasty, imperial policy favored agriculture. Old irrigation works were restored and new ones constructed. Villages were rebuilt. Poor men were given land, seed, and cattle. Prisoners of war were settled in various places in order to introduce new crops. Ardashir I declared the principle of this policy: "There can be no power without an army, no army without money, no money without agriculture, and no agriculture without justice." The expansion of industry was promoted by contacts with India and, especially, Syria, which was probably the most advanced industrial area in the world. Iranian commerce flowed over the ancient routes of southwestern Asia. Nisibis was the center of intercourse with the west. From Ctesiphon routes led to the Persian Gulf and to India, to Susa and southern Iran, and to central Asia and China.

Between 455 and 513 ten missions passed between northern China and Persia. Besides silk, the main products sent west by the Chinese were iron, jade, and bamboo; in the Iranian cities they purchased varnishes, tapestries, the woven stuffs of Syria, precious stones, corals, pearls, and narcotics. Indian, as well as Chinese, merchants frequented the Mesopotamian fairs in the fifth century. The Chinese records of visits to Ctesiphon, which describe its magnificence and the productivity of the surrounding agricultural lands, confirm the testimony of other sources about the economic prosperity of the revived Persian empire.

The social developments of Parthian and Sassanian times moved steadily toward a caste system. In Sassanian times the kings ordered each class to look at the class below it, so that the king alone viewed the whole social structure. The Parthian feudalism, as noted, strengthened the landed aristocrats, and the early Sassanian emperors did not interfere with their power or break up their estates. They remained, as they had been in Achaemenian times, the backbone of the state. Their purity of blood was protected by registration of their descent in national archives, and their social distinction was preserved by regulations of their mounts, arms, clothes, houses, gardens, women, and domestic servants. Under the Parthians the Zoroastrian priests had retained their influence but had not become a favored class; chief among the measures of Ardashir I was the elevation of this priestly group to a privileged position. Admission of talented persons to the privileged orders was possible only after an inquest by a priestly body. Men who acquired great wealth, exhibited remarkable bravery in battle, or displayed high achievement in art and learning were sometimes so elevated by the king.

Among the lower social classes were the merchants, the craftsmen, the slaves, and the peasants. The first three groups, relatively few in number, were, it seems, mostly foreigners. The merchants were probably exempt from military service. The peasants of course were, as ever, mainly native Iranians, except in the Tigris-Euphrates valley. The declaration of Ardashir I that there could be no agriculture without justice does not seem to have been followed in practice, for the peasants were badly treated. They were attached to the land, liable to forced labor as well as military service, and defenseless against the exactions and cruelties of their masters, the landed aristocrats. They were, in fact, the private slaves of the owners of the great estates. Strict legal regulations governed the use of irrigation canals, the tending of sheep, the care of dogs. Urban workers were subjected to treatment no less harsh.

These conditions finally gave rise to a revolutionary movement, which, as in other urban cultures, was closely connected with

THE PERSIAN EMPIRE c. A.D. 500

religious heresy, in this case, Mazdakism.[1] The aim of the revolutionary leaders was to establish the communistic ownership and use of land, cattle, and women.

Anoshirwan's fame rests partly upon the suppression of this movement and partly upon the reform of the irregularities which caused it. The reforms, it is fair to note, were initiated by his predecessor, Kavadh I (*ca.* 485–531), who sympathized, at least during the early part of his reign, with the revolutionaries. On the basis of a new land survey the amounts paid on fields sown to wheat and barley, planted to lucerne and rice, and kept as vineyards, olive and date orchards, and palm groves were fixed. Only the tax on sown land was collected in kind; the tax on orchards and vineyards was paid in money. All other crops were tax exempt; more important than this exemption as a stimulus to production was the freedom of choice which the peasant was allowed to exercise in selecting his crops. As a consequence of this freedom of choice by the peasants, a large staff of tax gatherers was necessary in order to make a yearly estimate of the sown land and to determine exemptions. Appeals to judges from the findings of the tax gatherers were allowed. Priests had final authority over the land survey. When taxes fell in arrears they were generally remitted. A poll tax was levied on all males between the ages of twenty and fifty except nobles, dignitaries, soldiers, priests, government employees, servants, and invalids. Four classes, each having a

[1] See p. 688.

From FRIEDRICH SARRE, *Die Kunst des Alten Persien* (1922) *B. Cassirer, Berlin*

A PERSIAN SILKEN FABRIC

The design, woven into the fabric, which dates from the sixth century, shows the Sassanian king on a lion hunt. The control of the trade in silk between China and the Mediterranean Basin was an important stake in the imperial struggles of the Parthians, Kushans, and Persians.

different capacity to pay, were established for those liable to this personal tax. In order to facilitate the collection of taxes, payment in installments—three a year—was permitted.[1]

Anoshirwan decreed that no change was ever to be made in the rates and ordered that those who violated them should be severely punished. These measures, which pacified the peasantry, were accompanied by orders that increased the military burdens of the lower nobility and reconstituted the families among the higher nobility whose male members had been killed in war. The effect of this legislation was to consolidate the class structure which Iranian economic development had produced. The peasants were settled in their occupation and obligations. The nobles were established according to ranks and duties. And the priests were fixed in a hierarchy which, even more than the feudal structure, was the support of the ruling dynasty.

THE TRANSFORMATION OF IRANIAN LITERATE LEARNING.

The destruction of the Achaemenian court undoubtedly dispersed the earlier carriers of Iranian learning, for the Zoroastrian literature disappeared early in the Hellenistic age; in Parthian times, however, Iranian learning revived, and under the Sassanian Dynasty it became a factor in the development of both Eastern and Western cultures.

1. *The Formation of the Zend-Avesta, the Sacred Book of Mazdaism.* The Parthians adopted a philhellenic attitude, but their Asiatic origin turned attention to native beliefs. They were not hostile to the Zoroastrian priesthood, and, under Vologases I (*ca.* A.D. 51–77), the reconstruction of the ancient literature was begun. It was not completed until Sassanian times, probably in the reign of Shapur II. The Zend-Avesta, as these writings are called, was the "sum of knowledge" of the restored Zoroastrian cult, Mazdaism. Besides theological and liturgical sections, it included material dealing with legal, philosophical, and scientific matters. Although this literature never became as complex as the Jewish Talmud, it was developed, it seems, somewhat in the same manner, *i.e.*, by commentaries upon the ancient teachings. Of this book, which in Sassanian times was regarded as the source of all right teachings, only about one-quarter has survived.

---

[1] Mostafa Khan Fateh, "Taxation in Persia: A synopsis from early times to the conquest of the Mongols," *Bulletin of the School of Oriental Studies* (London Institution), Vol. 4 (1926–1928), pp. 723–743.

The script of revived Iranian learning is known as Pahlavi; it was an adaptation of Aramaic symbols, many of them abbreviated and grouped as single signs, to the writing of the Persian language. To the eye it seems quite unlike Persian, but, when pronounced, it sounds like Persian. In Sassanian times the Greek script, which the Parthians had used along with Pahlavi, completely disappeared.

2. *Secular Literature and Learning in Sassanian Times.* Besides the renderings of the ancient Zoroastrian teachings embodied in the Zend-Avesta, Pahlavi literature consisted of commentaries upon these texts, religious treatises, and secular works. Only eleven secular works of the Sassanian period have survived. Chief among them are the *Deeds of Ardashir*, an account of the career of the first Sassanian emperor, and the *Tale of Anoshirwan and His Page*, a statement of the great emperor's humane feeling. In his reign a record of the Persian kings was compiled which became the basis of the later Persian epic, the *Shah Nama*. Other secular works dealt with the Iranian cities and the game of chess. The bulk of Pahlavi literature was undoubtedly much greater than these few surviving works indicate.[1]

Iranian science was derived almost entirely from foreign sources. Medicine, it may be believed, was studied by the Zoroastrian priests. For every disease, they held, the supreme deity had provided a plant that would "put it to sleep." Besides drugs the priests recognized dietary, surgical, and ritualistic treatments as having therapeutic value. They conceived that sickness and sin were closely related and strove to give health to the soul as well as to the body. They paid close attention to methods of diagnosis and, it is said, used convicted criminals for purposes of medical observation. The scientific interests of the Zoroastrian priests extended certainly to astronomy or, more properly, astrology and geography. The height of Iranian scientific learning came in Anoshirwan's reign, when the famous medical school Jundishapur flourished. The date of the founding of this school and its location are not exactly known.

It rose to prominence toward the end of the fifth century after Christ, when the Nestorian Christians, expelled from the Eastern Roman Empire, carried to it Syrian renderings of Greco-Roman scientific and philosophical works. Chief among these renderings were translations of Greek medical works, including

[1] See Edward G. Browne, *A Literary History of Persia* (4 vols., 1929), especially Vol. 1.

those of Galen. A digest of Aristotle's logic, in Pahlavi, was prepared at the school, and some parts of Plato, probably in Neoplatonic dress, were known. Jewish, Hindu, and Buddhistic intellectual materials also found their way into Persia in Anoshirwan's reign. The Hebrew Psalms were translated into Pahlavi. Somewhere in eastern Iran translations of a Buddhist romance and the famous Hindu collection of stories, the *Panchatantra*, were also made.[1] This collection, which was extremely popular in Iran, later moved westward, as did also other elements of Hindu learning, especially medical lore. Persia in Sassanian times was far more important for the transmitting and fusing of alien bodies of learning than for creative achievements.

Iranian learning was almost exclusively the possession of the privileged classes. Probably the merchants were able to read, write, and count sufficiently for the purpose of trade but the peasants were completely illiterate. The higher nobles, it seems, were given a rigorous training. At five years of age they began the exercise of arms and the study of reading and writing. At fifteen years of age they were instructed in the dogmas of the national cult. When they reached twenty, having studied literature, history, oratory, music, and gastronomics, they were admitted, after a strict examination, to full membership in the order of knights. The education of the lower nobles consisted almost entirely of military exercises. The training of the priesthood seems to have been carried on in the ancient manner of teacher and disciple. An official known as the "master of priestly instruction" was stationed at the imperial court. The priests possessed and maintained a monopoly over all forms of learning, except those deemed useful to the knights.

The Development of Religion in the Persian Empire.

Just as Alexander the Great's conquests opened a new period of cultural diffusion and assimilation in eastern Mediterranean lands, so they affected Asia from Mesopotamia to India. In Bactria and eastern Iran Indian beliefs became known, and Iranian ideas penetrated northwestern India, where they played a part in shaping Mahayana Buddhism. In Mesopotamia cultural interaction hardly less intense than that in Syria and Egypt developed, while in Armenia, Pontus, Cappadocia, and neighboring areas Greek and Iranian ideas met. Everywhere cultural interaction occurred, it

[1] See p. 765.

may be believed, in the presence of primitive beliefs which, due to disturbed social conditions, found opportunities to mingle with ideas from the urban cultures.[1]

1. *Religious Currents in Iran in Macedonian and Parthian Times.* As an imperial people the Persians, in contrast to the Hebrews, whose religion developed as a mode of preserving national identity, were inclined to see their gods in the pantheons of other peoples. Thus they came to consider Ahura Mazda, the Greek Zeus, and the Babylonian Bel as comparable supreme beings. This kind of belief facilitated the spread of foreign gods among the Iranians and made easy the amalgamation of Iranian gods with the deities of foreign peoples; also it allowed native Iranian folk beliefs to rise to new importance. The general result of the mingling of Greek and Iranian beliefs was to weaken the positions of Semitic gods in the pantheons of southwestern Asia.

Among the native gods who advanced, the most important were Anahita and Mithra. Originally Anahita was the goddess of springs in the Oxus valley; in time she became a matronly being having the powers and traits of the ancient fertility goddess whom the Semitic peoples knew as Ishtar. Mithra, an old Aryan god of light, who had been relegated by Zoroaster to a secondary position in the cult of Ahura Mazda, or Ormazd, became prominent as an intermediary between men and the supreme being; in this role he was the protector of warriors, the defender of the truth, the genius of prosperity, the lord of the pastures and the rolling countryside, the preserver of contracts, and the defender of souls against attacks by daimons. Mithra was, in fact, the personal guardian of men and the earth that Ahura Mazda had created. In Babylonia he became the peer of Shamash. In the lands deeply touched by Hellenic culture he became a salvation god similar to those of the mystery cults. The mystery cult, it should be noted, was completely foreign to Iranian culture.

Greek and Babylonian intellectual influences stimulated theological speculation among the Iranian priests; its chief product was Zervanism, a monotheistic rendering of Zoroastrian ideas. Beyond Ormazd and Ahriman, the good and evil gods of Mazdaism, who were the active agents in the world process, was the supreme being, Zervan, or "boundless time," who ordered the universe and fixed the destinies of men; in these activities, it should be emphasized, he played no direct part in human affairs. Like the supreme

---

[1] On religious developments in Iranian culture see O. G. von Wesendonk, *Das Weltbild der Iranier* (1933).

being of the Greek philosopher, he was the unchanging and un-
moving principle of universal order. One of his sons, Ahura Mazda
or Ormazd, was born of faith; the other, Ahriman, was born of
doubt. Between them went on a struggle for the rule of the world.
Zervan, who had willed this struggle, gave it four periods, each
lasting three thousand years. This conception of the universal
conflict between good and evil was the result of astrological
influences which emphasized the movements of the stars, conceived
as heavenly beings, through time. In late Parthian times and for a
long period of Sassanian rule Zervanism seems to have been the
dominant Iranian theology.

2. *Mazdaism: the State Cult of the Sassanian Empire.* Besides
restoring the lands, privileges, and titles of the ancient priests,
Ardashir I, so legend ran, called a council whose members chose a
supreme pontiff, the *mobadhan mobadh* of the priestly hierarchy,
and this individual, after taking an opiate, slept for several days
and awoke to dictate the faith of Ormazd. This story, which supported the claim that the Sassanians, with the aid of the priests,
had restored the true faith, obscures the fact that Zervanism was
long a rival of the traditional dualism.

The religion of Ormazd triumphed, it seems, only after a
religious reaction of uncertain origin; probably it arose as national
feeling became hostile to foreign cults. This hostility, evident in
Ardashir I's persecution of the Jews, was turned against the
Christians when, after Constantine, they were sympathetic with
the Roman state, against which the Sassanians made long and
bitter war. Intolerance was more a political than a religious fact
in the Sassanian state. The advance of the Mazdean cult was also
bound up with the struggles of the classes which culminated in
Anoshirwan's reforms, for only in his reign did Mazdaism finally
triumph over all rivals. In fact, it is probably more correct to see
the development of Mazdaism as the advance of a priest class
than as a purely religious growth.

In Parthian times the traditional priests did not form a closely
knit body, except perhaps in Atropatene, which, as previously
noted, was associated with the advent of the Sassanian Dynasty.
Whereas, although there may have been a high priest at the
court, the priests were organized only about local shrines. In
Sassanian times, probably on the basis of Ardashir I's favors, the
ancient local priesthoods were consolidated in a national hierarchy.
At its head stood the mobadhan mobadh, who directed ecclesiastical affairs, the persecution of heretics, and the moral instruction of

the people. In each district there was a mobadh, charged with the religious care of the people and the supervision of the lower clergy and the temple priests who tended the sacred fires. Theologians seem to have been responsible to an official attached to the mobadhan mobadh.

Besides the secular functions connected with the judicial administration and, especially, the collection of taxes as decreed by Anoshirwan, this hierarchy had three main tasks:[1] (1) to guide and counsel the king in order that justice might prevail; (2) to perform the rituals that gave order to society, particularly those connected with births, marriages, and deaths and with the feasts, which, it should be noted, had origin in the yearly routine of agriculture; and (3) to keep individuals from falling into sin, *i.e.*, to aid them in the fight against the daimons. The supreme power of the Sassanian priesthood rested on its right to reject an aspirant to the throne; if it did not have the power to elect the king, it at least had the power to reject a candidate for the kingship. As the one who crowned the king, the mobadhan mobadh was the first dignitary of the imperial court. Astrological forecasting was an important element in the priestly counsel to the kings. In the performance of rituals the priests presided over the important events in the lives of individuals and the nation, giving divine support in times of greatest need. And finally, as the religious guides of individuals, they were the earthly leaders of men in the cosmic struggle between Ormazd and Ahriman.

The power of the Mazdean hierarchy rested, theoretically, on the possession of right knowledge of the spiritual overworld; actually it was organized in an intellectual supremacy which had three main supports: (1) the Zend-Avesta as the "sum of knowledge," (2) a control of moral instruction, and (3) an inquisition which hunted down and condemned heretics. Among the surviving portions of the Zend-Avesta the most considerable fragment is the *Vendidad*, or "Law against the Demons" which sets forth the purifications, expiations, and penances to be made or imposed by the priests; this priestly code was the fundamental law, civil and criminal as well as religious, of the Sassanian state. The educational control of the population began with the children, who, when they reached the age of six, were taught the proper prayers. Sometime in the reign of Shapur II a prayer book—the Khorda-Avesta—containing the prayers to be said to the sun,

[1] On the organization and activities of the Mazdean church, see Arthur Christensen, *L'Iran sous les Sassanides* (1936), pp. 110–117.

moon, fire, and water was compiled; it was undoubtedly the guide of popular worship. Besides inculcating orthodoxy by moral instruction, the hierarchy protected orthodoxy by suppressing heretics; its first commandment was: "Hunt down heresy." After a year's imprisonment, heretics who refused to recant were executed. Inasmuch as no king could be crowned without the assent of the mobadhan mobadh and no law went into force without his consent, it appears that the Mazdean heirarchy was the dominant group in the Sassanian empire; as a self-ruling body it was, indeed, a state within a state.

In the theology of the Mazdean hierarchy Ahura Mazda became Ormazd, an all powerful and omniscient but faraway deity who, as the spirit of light and wisdom, carried on the cosmic struggle with Ahriman, the daimon of darkness and evil. Associated with Ormazd in this struggle were Six Immortal Beneficents. But the commander of men was Mithra, the ancient Aryan god of light, who was the mediator between men and Ormazd. Mithra, prayed to as the sun, illuminated the earth and nourished plants and animals. Anahita, the goddess of springs, presided over the procreative process and guarded the king's palace. Numerous archangels ruled over aspects of nature and fought against the daimons. Natural elements such as water, fire, and land were venerated. Fire was worshiped in five different forms. Beef urine was more efficacious for purification than water; water was useful only to quench thirst and to nourish plants. Many of the Mazdean rites were derived from the ancient Iranian peasant religion, as were also the six great seasonal feasts. The New Year celebration, which lasted five days, was the greatest holiday. The Iranians used a calendar of twelve months of thirty days each; the five days of the New Year celebration were added to complete the year.

The eschatology of the Mazdean cult reflected the influence that produced Zervanism. The universe was to endure through twelve thousand years, divided into four periods of three thousand years. In the first period Ormazd and Ahriman remained tranquil, and light and darkness were unmixed. At its end Ahriman awoke with a desire to blot out light, and Ormazd foresaw the creation of the universe and man and the struggle with Ahriman for the control of their destiny. In the second period, while Ahriman, paralyzed by the fear of defeat, fell into darkness, Ormazd created the world, the primordial bull, and the primordial giant, the prototype of man. Ahriman finally attacked these creations with a multitude of insects and reptiles. Ormazd defended them by building great ramparts in the sky. In an attack on these ramparts Ahriman killed the bull and the giant, but their seed fell to earth and from them sprang animals, plants, and men. Thus began the third period of the mixture of light and darkness and the earthly struggle of good to escape from evil. In this struggle men joined with Ormazd to fight the evil. Those who followed the good way crossed, after death, the bridge of judgment—*Tchinvat*—to paradise. Those who followed the evil way fell off the bridge into hell. Those whose good and bad deeds weighed equally in the balance remained, until the final resurrection, in an intermediary place.

At the beginning of the fourth period Zoroaster appeared to instruct men, and at the end of each thousand years of this period another savior was born. At the birth of the last savior the final combat between Ormazd and Ahriman began. All men, as well as the heroes and monsters of legendary history, were resurrected. A comet struck the earth, which was consumed by fire. From it the metals flowed in a white torrent, and all men crossed the fiery stream. For the good it was like cold milk, and it purified them. The evil perished, falling into eternal darkness. After these events the earth became tranquil and was enlarged so that it extended to heaven. Men never grew older than forty, and children remained always young. Relatives were united. Thus the cosmic struggle culminated in the "grand renewal" of life, and men entered into the joys of heaven.

The social and ethical teachings of Mazdaism, which were completely Zoroastrian, gave support to an agrarian order ruled over by the prince and the priest. In the Zend-Avesta, Ahura Mazda or Ormazd was addressed as "Creator of settlements supplied with creatures, righteous one"; "the most excellent thing in the world," it was said, "was to have a prince and a priest." Labor at agriculture was praised as the torture of the daimons, and men were urged to be physically strong:

> There is no strength in those who do not eat,
> Neither for vigorous righteousness,
> Nor for vigorous husbandry,
> Nor for vigorous begetting of sons.
> For by eating all living things exist; without eating they must die.

Dwarfishness, deformity, monstrous teeth, and leprosy were condemned as marks of Ahriman. In the eyes of Ormazd self-mortification was sinful, and sacred virginity irreligious. Along with bodily strength, honor, fair dealing, bravery, and truthfulness were praised. The punishment for breaking a verbal contract was three hundred lashes. Wrongdoers were commonly set at useful labor, such as killing snakes, building bridges, and digging irrigation ditches. The ancient mutilations inflicted on criminals were modified so that those so punished were not made unfit for work. Lastly, it should be noted, peace and prosperity rested on divine sanction, and if distress so great that the king could not deal with it appeared, then the priests could intervene to dethrone him, either by ejection or by murder, and to elevate another.[1]

3. *Manichaeism.* Under the influence of Indian and Hellenistic ideas, especially Gnosticism,[2] Mani (*ca.* 216–274) developed from Zoroastrianism a religion of salvation. Born of high rank, he early acquired a knowledge of the many beliefs of Babylonia, and before he began to teach he added to this knowledge by traveling to India. Each country, he said, had its prophet—India Buddha, Iran Zoroaster, the West Jesus, and Babylonia Mani. He did not recognize Moses as a prophet. His aim was to reveal the true faith by making clear to all sectarians the truth that was in other beliefs as well as in their own. Mani, it can be seen, applied in the interpretation of the many religions which had become known to the Iranians their tendency to see the gods of their religion in the pantheons of other peoples.

At the base of his religious system was the Zoroastrian dualism of light and darkness. Originally, he said, the Father of Grandeur, or Zervan, lived in a paradise of light completely apart from the King of Darkness. But after a time the King of Darkness attacked the paradise of light. As a defense the Father of Grandeur created two beings, the Mother of Life and Primal Man, or Ormazd. Together with the Father of Grandeur, they formed the original trinity. The Mother of Life bore Primal Man five sons—the ether, the breeze, light, water, and fire—and with them he went out to fight the King of Darkness. But the evil one, bearing the consuming flame, scorching heat, darkness, smoke, and murky water, prevailed. Thus the elements of light were mixed with the elements of darkness. Then the Father of Grandeur, in order to rescue Primal Man from the suffering caused by this mixing, created the Soul of Light, who in turn created the Grand Architect, and he, in turn,

---

[1] On this power of the Mazdean hierarchy, see Arthur Christensen, *L'Iran sous les Sassanides* (1936), pp. 257–261.

[2] See p. 999.

called forth the Living Spirit. These three beings formed a second trinity. The Living Spirit then begot five sons, and with them attacked the King of Darkness, rescued Primal Man, and slew the archons of the King of Darkness. Then Zervan, acting through the spirits, created the visible universe. From the skins of the slain archons the Mother of Light made the sky, from their flesh the lands, and from their bones the mountains. In all, eight worlds were created. The sun and moon were made from the pure light won back from the King of Darkness. From the sparkling material that remained the stars were formed. The sun, moon, Milky Way, and zodiac were set in motion in order to help win the light still imprisoned by the King of Darkness; on earth the three wheels— fire, air, and water—contributed to this liberation. To give protection to the universe the Father of Grandeur then called forth Mithra as God of the World of Light. He dwelt in the sun. He and the Grand Architect constructed a new prison for the daimons. Then, arousing the sensual desire of the daimons chained in the sky, he brought into being, from the light thus released, the plants and animals of the land and sea. Finally from a daimonic pair were born Adam and Eve, the parents of humanity. Then Jesus (created by Mithra, the Mother of Life, Primal Man, and the Living Spirit) was sent to reveal to men their condition; symbolizing the suffering of light enchained in darkness, Jesus was the guide of men to paradise.

In the Manichaean theology the universe was regarded as the means of liberating the divine light from the imprisoning darkness. When a bit of light, as a human soul, escaped from darkness, it rose as a pillar of glory to the moon, then to the sun, and finally to paradise, where dwelt the Father of Grandeur.

Upon these doctrines Mani founded a well-organized sect having two grades of members: (1) the "elect," who aspired to a pure life, and (2) the "hearers" or "combatants."

The elect practiced a severe morality, based partly on Indian and partly on Christian customs and beliefs. They abstained from sexual intercourse and refused to take life, even to the point of not picking a flower or an ear of corn. When they ate they protested their sinlessness in the prayer, "I have neither reaped, nor ground, nor pressed, nor cast into the oven. All these things another has done and brought thee [*i.e.*, the food] to me. I am free from fault." They neither ate flesh nor drank wine. Water, they believed, was so holy that they used it only to drink, not to bathe. They were not permitted to acquire property or possess clothes for longer than a year or food for longer than a day. Their worldly duty was to exhort men to live a pure life; by prayers they got the sins of "hearers" forgiven.

Hearers—the ordinary members—remained at their usual pursuits. They married, ate flesh, and drank wine. Individuals were not permitted to eat the flesh of an animal they had killed. Their duty was to nourish the elect by making gifts to them. All believers were required to pay a tenth of their income to the elect. Hearers fasted seven days each month and prayed four times in every twenty-four hours. In each prayer the individual prostrated himself twelve times. The giving of alms, also required of each hearer, was regulated by prohibitions which forbade giving water and bread to nonbelievers. To do so, it was held, involved injury to light. Clothes and money could be given without injury. After death the hearers went through a long period of purification before entering paradise. The nonbelievers wandered over the earth after death and finally perished in the conflagration which, lasting 1,458 years, completed the redemption of light from darkness.

The Manichaean church was organized as a hierarchy. Twelve apostles, headed by a thirteenth chosen by the twelve, ruled over seventy-two bishops, who in turn supervised the local presbyters and deacons presiding over the local congregations of "hearers." The head of the hierarchy resided in Babylonia. The chief agents of dissemination of the cult were traveling missionaries. The Manichaean church neither administered sacraments nor aspired to worldly power; it sought only to teach the way to moral perfection. But in spite of its peacefulness it won the hatred of the Mazdean priesthood, by which, as a result, it was from time to time persecuted. Mani himself was executed, his body flayed, and the skin stuffed with straw; his followers were finally driven from the Sassanian empire.

Manichaeism spread from Persia into central Asia and the Mediterranean lands. In central Asia its writings, which were made in the Syriac alphabet, were rendered in the language of Sogdiana and gave birth to the system of writing used by central Asiatic peoples. Documents pertaining to the religion have been found recently in eastern Turkestan. In the Mediterranean lands Manichaeism won considerable following in the fourth century A.D. and contributed somewhat to the strengthening of the ascetic elements of Christianity.[1]

[1] A. V. William Jackson, *Researches in Manichaeism* (1932), pp. 19–20: "As a faith Manichaeism no longer exists and was always regarded by other creeds as a heresy, particu-

4. *Mazdakism.* Just as Manichaeism was the product of contacts between Iranians and foreign peoples, so Mazdakism was a
religious expression of the conflict of interests among the classes
of the Iranian social structure, for it was the heresy which gave
doctrinal support to the revolutionary movement of the late fifth
and early sixth centuries. Mazdak (*ca.* 480–528), it seems, was not
the original teacher of the heresy; he was the man of action who
tried to give it social expression. Although presented as a renova-
tion of Mazdaism, Mazdakism was probably derived from Western
ideas, particularly Christian and Gnostic. From Christianity or
the Hellenistic ethical philosophers came the doctrine of primitive
equality among men; from Gnosticism came an allegorical interpretation of the Zend-Avesta, which gave the sanction of tradition
to that idea.

The Mazdakites held that the purification of the world sought
by the Manichaeans was incomplete. In addition to the purification
of the individual by ascetic practices, which they accepted, they
desired a purification of the social order. Evil, they said, did not
exist because of Ahriman but because the universe was ruled by
chance. To triumph over it, the removal of its immediate cause
among men was necessary. This cause was inequality of fortune—
a product of chance. From this source came five things—jealousy,
hate, vengeance, need, and covetousness—to turn men away from
righteousness. The argument for equality rested on the proposition
that God had placed the means of subsistence on earth for all of his
servants. Thus water, fire, pastures, and women should be owned
in common. Mutual assistance was the ideal of individual and social
behavior. Hospitality was a universal obligation. No one should
cause pain to another. All killing was forbidden, and enemies
should be treated kindly.

As previously noted, the insurrectionary movement which
developed in terms of these doctrines was rooted in the exploitation
of the peasants by the nobles. The immediate cause of the outbreak
seems to have been a famine, which revealed in a strong light the
great inequalities that existed. A famine, it should be understood,
always had this effect, for the ruling classes used their power to

larly because of its eclectic character. But it was a veritable religion and exercised an influence, for more than a thousand years, upon the lives of countless numbers of devoted
followers, inspired by the ideals and high principles of its Founder, whom they accounted
divine, and the example of whose martyr death they were led to emulate at the time and
in after ages." By permission of the Columbia University Press. See also F. C. Burkitt,
The Religion of the Manichees (1925); P. Alfaric, *Les écritures manichéenes* (2 vols., 1918–
1919).

take from the peasants as much of their normal payments as possible. When Kavadh I attempted to lessen the tax burden, he was driven from the throne (498) by a palace revolution of Mazdean clergy and high nobles. The peasants seized land, cattle, and women, destroyed when possible the evidences of their obligations to the priests and the nobles, and transformed the villages into communistic communities. Soon in these villages men did not know their children and children did not know their father. Mazdak proclaimed the struggle as the final conflict between light and darkness; after Kavadh I escaped from prison and fled, it seems to have developed into a contest over the throne. The Mazdakites put forward a candidate, and the coalition of priests and princes resisted him. The Mazdakites also undertook to displace the Mazdean clergy. Meanwhile the peasants seized more and more property. Finally Kavadh I returned (501), probably with foreign aid. His reaccession to the throne was followed by the suppression of the peasants. Their leaders were murdered— Mazdak among them—their literature destroyed, and thousands of them slaughtered. The Christians in Persia joined the Mazdeans in opposing the heretical peasants.

Anoshirwan's reforms were accompanied, it seems, by the religious reaction which purged the Zend-Avesta of passages giving support to Zervanism and the heresies that sprang from it. At any rate, shortly after the accession of Anoshirwan, aristocracy and orthodoxy again were supreme in Iran.

Iranian Art.

Except for the ruins of the royal palaces and tombs at Pasargadae and Persepolis, little remains of the art of the Archaemenian period. It was a dynastic rather than a national art, designed to glorify the king and based largely upon Assyrian forms and practices. Walls were built of mud bricks. Stone was used for foundations, reinforcements at corners, doorways, and pillars. The Persian pillar was remarkably slender and always fluted. The base was shaped like an inverted bell; the capital was rectangular and heavily decorated with kneeling bulls and floral motifs. At Persepolis, built by Darius I, color was used profusely throughout the Palace. The main room of this structure was a large rectangular hall, whose wooden roof was supported by many columns. A monumental double stairway, placed flat against a wall, was a notable feature of this palace; above it were representations in colored brick of the royal guards. The Persians used sculpture in relief with considerable skill. The chief motifs were royal personages, lions, bulls, and rampant monsters.

In Xerxes' reign Greek influence began to produce a greater delicacy of treatment of motifs, a freer use of color, and a refinement of the massive construction; these tendencies continued in Hellenistic and Parthian times.

In Sassanian times the best elements of the ancient Iranian artistic tradition and influences from the Mediterranean lands and India were drawn together. The chief buildings were still royal palaces on an oblong pattern. They were built of burned bricks and hewn stones, with barrel-vaulted roofs and domes. Cornices, pilasters, niches, and arcades were skillfully adapted for decorative purposes. In statuary the best Iranian products were monumental reliefs, some of which, although cut on a huge scale, were done with great skill and realism, such, for example, as the one showing the capture of the Roman emperor Valerian by Shapur I. Paintings in imitation of Buddhist frescoes adorned the walls of palaces. Evidences of rich vestments in the representations of the king and the court retinue testify to the existence of the textile arts, which probably had their greatest expression in the tapestries, rugs, and draperies for which Iran was in later times to become world-famous. The art of rugmaking seems to have originated in central Asia. Probably the Iranians learned many things about dyeing and textile working from India. Motifs for the decorative arts were taken from animals, plants, and geometry. In metalworking great skill was shown in rendering animal motifs; in fact, the Sassanian artists synthesized the animal art of the Assyrians, Scythians, and Parthians and refined it somewhat with Greek influences. Through their hands the "animal in action" became a unifying motif in the art of all Asia outside of India. A conventionalized landscape motif, probably taken over from India, was also transmitted by them to central Asia and China.

The Persians did not interpret the life of Zoroaster in art as did the Buddhists the career of Buddha and the Christians the career of Jesus. Although Ahura Mazda was represented on royal monuments, the worship of the deity in the form of light prevented the development of religious sculpture of the human form. The chief motifs of Iranian religious art—birds in flight, doves sipping water, a pair of wings, vines, and a tree with buds at the ends of its branches—symbolized heaven; they were rendered with delicacy and grace. The Manichaeans produced the earliest known miniature portraits and illuminated manuscripts.

The Significance of Iranian Culture.

Under Achaemenian rule the ancient-oriental lands were politically united, and an orderly and continuous flow of commercial and social intercourse for the first time passed through them. On the east this intercourse touched India and central Asia; on the west it reached the Mediterranean lands, to which it brought rich gifts. Under Macedonian and Parthian rule this intercourse increased and even spread to far-off China. In Sassanian times commercial intercourse with China was strengthened by the exchange of political missions. Thus the Persian empire forged the links between the Eastern and Western worlds which remained unbroken until early modern times.

Although serving as the cultural intermediary between the East and the West, Iran preserved its cultural independence. Iranians generally became neither Greeks nor Indians; they did not regard either culture as their own. Zoroastrian ideas, however rendered, possessed a fundamental vitality, particularly as they opposed a world optimism to the pessimism that dominated Indian thought from the first and triumphed ultimately in the West in Christianity. And Iranian art, reflecting the peculiarities of Iranian nature, retained its identity, although it was enriched by foreign techniques. When the Sassanian empire, after having been assailed by the Turks, fell before the Arabs (642), Iranian culture was submerged under Islam, and, except for survival in India among the Parsees, descendants of Persian refugees, the Avestan religion was broken up. But many of its elements, notably the dualistic character of the universe, the ethical struggle in human life, and the cosmic denouement of the conflict between light and darkness, had already entered deeply into Judaism, Christianity, and Islam. The Persians, moreover, because they became the chief instructors of the Arabs in the arts, philosophy, and literature, did not lose their culture, nor did its wide influence cease. It spread into central Asia, even to China, and filtered westward to Europe. Persian was spoken throughout southwestern and central Asia, much as English is now spoken on the European continent; it was the language of merchants, travelers, and pilgrims. The Chinese horsemen and the Teutonic knights adopted the arms of the Sassanian nobles. The Saxons in England produced inlaid work on Iranian models, and the Chinese adapted Persian landscape motifs to their own artistic purposes.

By the courtesy of the University of Pennsylvania Museum and Dr. Erich F. Schmidt, The Oriental Institute, University of Chicago

A MOUND AT DAMGHAN, PERSIA

This mound is probably the remains of a Sassanian castle of the fourth or fifth century. Similar structures are known to have existed along the northern frontier of the Sassanian empire from the Caspian Sea to the Hindu Kush Mountains. Damghan is about fifty miles south of the eastern end of the Caspian Sea, near where many authorities believe Hecatompylos, the capital of the Parthian empire, was located. The castle, together with the heavy arms and armor of the Sassanian knight, became characteristic elements of medieval military patterns in both Europe and Asia.

THE HEBREW CULTURAL TRADITION: JUDAISM

After the Greek penetration of the ancient-oriental lands the Semitic cultural tradition was carried almost exclusively by Aramaic-speaking peoples; this was true of the Hebrew rendering, and the natives of Mesopotamia called themselves Aramaeans. When the Parthians destroyed Seleucia in 154, the Greek influence disappeared in the Tigris-Euphrates valley, and with the rise of the Sassanian Dynasty Iranian materials spread westward rapidly. As a result the ancient-oriental lands recovered their cultural independence, and local cultures rooted in the ancient Semitic tradition appeared. One, known as the Syriac, had its center at Edessa; its language was a form of Aramaic and its religion a form of Christianity.[1] Around the southern edges of the Fertile Crescent developments began that culminated in the Arabic rendering of the Semitic tradition—Islam. And in Babylonia and Palestine there took place a consolidation of the Hebrew cultural tradition. The language of the chief literary product of this consolidation—the Babylonian Talmud—was, it should be noted, Aramaic. The recovery of independence for new growth by the Semitic culture area was one of the most important developments of late Greco-Roman times.[2]

The form of the consolidated Hebrew cultural tradition was a rigid structure of belief and custom—the religion of Judaism. The derivation of the word "Judaism" from a Latin word signifying a quarter of a town where the Jews lived suggests the social experience—a close community life among foreigners—which contributed so much to the consolidation.

THE HEBREWS UNDER PERSIAN, HELLENISTIC, AND ROMAN RULERS.

Although conqueror after conqueror crushed the political aspirations of the Hebrew state, it always arose again until at last it perished in insurrectionary movements that swept the Hebrews from Palestine; since the second century the Jews have lived as they live now—a scattered people in foreign lands whose rulers have never been at a loss for excuses to persecute them. The complex of prejudices that have clustered about the Jews in modern times dates, at least in part, from the circumstances of their final dispersion in the Roman Empire.[3]

1. *The Rise of the Hebrew Priestly State under Persian Rule.* When Cyrus overthrew the Neo-Babylonian kingdom, he proclaimed as his divine mission the rebuilding of the Temple in Jerusalem, and under his friendly rule Zerubbabel, heir of the House of David, led a few refugees back to Palestine, where, together with other refugees returned from Egypt, they formed the nucleus of a Hebrew satrapy in the Persian empire. Persian policy, of course, allowed them to follow their own law and keep their own religion.

---

[1] See pp. 1116, 1137.

[2] On the recovery of the cultural independence of the Semitic culture area see J. J. Saunders, "The Orient and the Graeco-Roman World before Islam," *History*, Vol. 25 (n.s., 1940), pp. 161–170.

[3] For the general history of the Hebrews in these times see Salo Wittmayer Baron, *A Social and Religious History of the Jews* (3 vols., 1937), and A. Schlatter, *Geschichte Israels von Alexander dem Grossen bis Hadrian* (1925).

Difficulties soon engulfed this "sacred remnant" which, it was believed, had survived Yahweh's purification of the nation. Zerubbabel, who began the rebuilding of the Temple, was displaced as the leader of the community by the high priest of the Temple; with Zerubbabel's fall the Davidic line came to an inglorious end. Social and religious troubles compounded with political difficulties. The rich again oppressed the poor. The returned exiles and refugees quarreled with the native peasants, with the neighboring Arab nomads, and with the Samaritans. The Samaritans, a people descended from the colonists planted by the Assyrians around Samaria, the ancient capital of Israel, claimed to be the ten lost tribes of Israel; ultimately they became a Hebrew sect and maintained a shrine that rivaled the Temple in Jerusalem. In fact, until reinforcements reached Jerusalem from Babylonia the returned exiles and refugees formed little more than a camp in the midst of ruins.

The leaders of the new Babylonian contingent were Nehemiah (fl. *ca.* 444 B.C.) and Ezra (fl. *ca.* 397 B.C.).[1] Nehemiah, who held a high position in the Persian court, labored for twelve years in rebuilding the city and inculcating the law. Ezra continued his work, particularly in teaching the law to the people. Jewish men were forced to abandon their non-Jewish wives and children. As a result of their work the priests, because political life was no longer possible, became the exclusive administrators of the law, and the observance of the national cult became the single means of preserving the in-group. Nehemiah taught that separation from the heathen was the chief test of piety. Ezra declared that the rigorous observance of the law was the sole rule for righteous living. The theory of this regime was promulgated in a final rendering of the in-group tradition—the Torah, or "teaching," now the first five books of the Old Testament. It received further elaboration in the Book of Kings:

This new history began with the majestic story of creation in which the all-powerful God of the universe, by his spoken word, brought order and light out of chaos and darkness. A beneficent being, he found his creation all very good for man's abode and then he entered upon a Sabbath of rest. . . . This noble account of creation, that culminated in the conception of the Sabbath as an institution observed by God himself, was followed by a barren genealogy of ten antediluvians. The genealogy

---

[1] See Theodore H. Robinson and W. O. E. Oesterley, *A History of Israel* (1932), Vol. 2, p. 112.

served as a connection between the creation and an account of the flood culminating in a covenant between God and Noah.

There follows a genealogy of the sons of Noah which is continued, in the line of Shem, down to Abram. A very brief account of Abram's migration leads up to the covenant of circumcision and the birth of Isaac, with whom a covenant is to be established. Thus the priestly historians, writing in Babylonia, conceived of the covenant relation with God as having long antedated the meeting at Sinai.

These writers also thought of the most elaborate details of ecclesiastical organization and sacrificial worship as formulated in the wilderness by Moses, so that they placed the great law codes in their narrative of the time of Moses. All of this is quite contrary to the older histories of Israel and the express testimony of the eighth-century prophets.[1]

Thus the prophetic teaching, since political defeat had destroyed the Messianic monarchy, was institutionalized in a purely religious structure: the nation became a church, and with this development the Hebrew religion became the religion of the book whose first and final commandment was: "The Law is King."

With the disappearance of secular rulers, the priesthood became the dominant social group. At its head stood the high priest of the Temple. The rank and file of the priesthood were ranged in twenty-four divisions, which rotated, one officiating each week, in the performance of the Temple rituals. At the great festivals the entire priesthood assembled. When the exiles returned from Babylon one in ten of the population was a temple official. The religious law provided so amply for the support of the priesthood that its members drew to themselves a substantial portion of the national production. This appropriation of the economic surplus was achieved, it should be remembered, entirely by the inculcation of religious feeling which made the payment of the Temple dues a matter of individual conscience.[2] As time went on the control of the priesthood, and with it, of course, political supremacy in the state, became centered in a "great council of elders," the Sanhedrin —an aristocratic institution. Probably at no time was this body ever without lay members, nobles and scholars, who, although aristocratic, did not see eye to eye with the priests; the administration of government, certainly, was performed by individuals from the lay aristocratic families.

[1] H. T. Fowler, *The Origin and Growth of the Hebrew Religion* (1916), pp. 145–146. By permission of the University of Chicago Press, Chicago.

[2] See T. G. Soares, *The Social Institutions and Ideals of the Bible* (1915), p. 127; also Edwyn Bevan, *Jerusalem under the High Priests* (1904), p. 9.

Under the priestly state the chief social institutions were the family, the fundamental economic and religious unit, and the synagogue, where the people gathered for instruction in the law. As a religious body the nation was a brotherhood of equals under Yahweh. This ideal of Judaism was a heritage from the primitive Semitic clansmen, which because of the diverse social experiences of the nation had become more rather than less meaningful. From the strong feeling of in-group exclusiveness arose the concepts "One Nation," "One God," and "One Law"; also in the name of in-group unity social justice was defined as removal of the abuses which originated in the formation of classes within the in-group. During the period in which these ideas of in-group life were evolving, the role of the individual, especially in religious behavior, was continually being reshaped, for such individual behavior was conceived to have a direct bearing upon the fate of the in-group. Thus the frustration of the in-group interest was paralleled by the growth of the individual's sense of sin. The ideal man of Judaism was, therefore, a pious, God-fearing man who, obeying God's commands, dealt justly with his fellow men in order that the nation as a whole might achieve the purpose God had set for it. And this purpose was the creation of the perfect social order—the Hebrew Utopia—in which, through moral leadership, the Hebrew nation ruled over all other nations, giving them peace, prosperity, and justice under the command of the One—universal and just— God. The "New Jerusalem" was envisioned as the "temple city" of the "Kingdom of God."

However, under priestly rule the nation became a plutocracy whose members—priests, administrative officials, and rich merchants—ruled over the urban poor and the peasants. The failure of the priesthood to achieve the social justice for which the great eighth-century B.C. prophets had cried was eloquently described in the Book of Job, composed near the end of the fifth century B.C.:

> Men remove boundaries;
> They steal flocks and pasture them;
> They lead away the ass of the fatherless;
> They take as a pledge the ox of the widow;
> They turn aside the needy from the way;
> Moreover the needy of the land hide themselves.
>
> Indeed, like wild-asses in the wilderness,
> They go forth to their work, seeking for food;
> The steppe furnishes them bread for their children.

They make harvest in the field by night;
And they glean the vineyard of the wicked.
Naked they pass the night without clothing,
And they have no covering against the cold.
They are drenched by the rain from the mountains,
And for the lack of refuge they cleave to the rocks;
They snatch the fatherless from the breast,
And they take the infant of the poor for security.
Naked they go about, without clothing,
And hungry, they carry sheaves.
Within walls they make oil;
They tread the wine-presses, but are thirsty.
From the city the dying groan,
And those who are wounded call for help;
But God does not hear their prayer.[1]

2. *The Hebrews in the Hellenistic Age: the Maccabees.* When Alexander the Great swept through Syria and Palestine in 332 B.C.—like a leopard with the wings of an eagle, the Hebrews said— the Greeks and the Hebrews came into direct contact for the first time; for the Hebrews the relation meant only another phase of the old struggle to preserve their cultural identity. During the third century B.C., when the Ptolemies of Egypt ruled Palestine, the Greek influence was weak. But after 198 B.C., when the king of Syria seized the country, Hellenization began in earnest. Its greatest exponent was Antiochus IV (*ca.* 175–164 B.C.), who chose for himself the designation—it was an insult to Hebrew religious feelings—"Epiphanes," *i.e.*, "the god made manifest." He met the Hebrew resistance to Hellenization with persecution, sacking the Temple, forbidding the observance of the national rituals, and executing those caught with a copy of the Torah in their possession. He was supported by some of the Hebrews, mainly rich merchants and time-serving priests, who were called *Letzim*, or Hellenizers. Among them was a certain Jason, who had the high priest of the Temple deposed, usurped his office, and used the treasure of the Temple to build a Greek gymnasium. And he permitted pigs to be sacrificed to Zeus on altars dedicated to Yahweh.

Led by the *Hasidim*, or "pious ones," who forbade all intercourse with the Greeks, the great body of the common people held fast to the old rituals and the law, and soon they found in the priest Mattathias and his five sons men who would carry the fight

[1] *The Bible: An American translation*, p. 847, Job 24: 2–12. By permission of the University of Chicago Press, Chicago.

to the enemies of their faith. From the designation "Maccabaeus," *i.e.*, "the hammerer," given to Judas, the third son, who recruited an army and defeated one Syrian general after another, the family became known as the Maccabees. Judas was leader of the Jews from 165 to 160 B.C., and for almost a century and three-quarters his name was the rallying cry of all Jewish patriots. The family is also known as the Hasmonaeans, from the name of a grandfather of Mattathias.[1]

But from the first, although victory was with their arms, the Maccabees were uncertain of their position. Both domestic and foreign dangers surrounded them. Judas irritated the Hasidim by proclaiming that it was not contrary to the Torah for a Jew to defend himself in warfare on the Sabbath, and Jonathan, his successor, increased the religious hostility by taking the office of high priest. Military and political expediency dictated both acts, but they alienated the approval of those parts of the nation whose support was necessary if Maccabean rule was to be secure. Simon, the last of the sons of Mattathias, won the recognition of independence from Syria about 142 B.C. and became the first Hasmonaean king. The high priestship and the kingship were both declared hereditary in his line, a Jewish coinage was issued, and a new era was dated from the beginning of his reign. The entanglement in foreign difficulties dated from the time of Judas, who had negotiated a treaty with Rome guaranteeing him the protection of that great Western power. For a time the Maccabees played successfully the dangerous international game, capturing cities, converting their populations at the point of the sword, and keeping an eye out for commercial advantage; but ultimately internal discord united with external intrigue to drag them to destruction.

Although the Maccabees failed to win the approval of those who transmitted the religious tradition from their time to later centuries, they gave the Hebrew nation a last flare of political hope. Palestine became a state again, and the prophecies of world leadership uttered by the Prophets seemed to be on the point of fulfillment. And this expectancy aroused political feelings to a high pitch of excitement: patriotism flamed. Except for the Maccabees the Hebrew people and their religion would probably have been swept into the fusion of Hellenistic and oriental cultures which

---

[1] On the Maccabees see Shailer Mathews, *A History of New Testament Times in Palestine* (175 *B.C.–A.D.* 70) (rev. ed., 1933); H. F. Henderson, *The Age of the Maccabees* (1907); C. R. Conder, *Judas Maccabaeus and the Jewish War of Independence* (1878); and A. W. Streane, *The Age of the Maccabees* (1898).

was organizing all Mediterranean life in a more or less uniform cosmopolitanism.

3. *The Hebrews under Roman Rule.* The Romans first came to Palestine in the course of Pompey's campaign to pacify the East.[1] Originally they were concerned with suppressing the nomads of northern Arabia, who were continually raiding the caravans from Mesopotamia, but they soon became involved in the intrigues of the Maccabean aspirants to the throne, who were willing to make almost any kind of deal in order to gain support. The result was that Pompey's legions besieged Jerusalem; when it fell after a seige of two years—65–63 B.C.—Maccabean power ceased to be an important factor in Jewish life. The Temple was captured, the Maccabean heir was left with only the high priestship, territories were stripped from his domain, and thousands of his subjects were sold into slavery.

After Pompey's legions came Caesar's, and then Cassius's. For Cassius, who needed money, Herod (*ca.* 37–4 B.C.), the "Edomite slave," as the Jews called him, sold some thirty thousand persons into slavery; this and other services to the Romans won him the kingship. His reign was a period of turmoil and terror.[2] Hezekiah the Galilean raised an insurrection in which many perished. Herod levied harsh taxes and confiscated properties at will, and those who resisted were sought out by spies and punished by mercenaries. Like Pompey and Caesar, he undertook to destroy the last remnant of the Hasmonaean line. For the Jews he was the "incarnation of evil"; the youth were especially bitter against him. It is worth noting that Galilee, the center of the most violent opposition to political and religious repression, was a relatively prosperous land whose mixed peasant population held a simple faith undisturbed by philosophical speculations or learned contentions. Its willingness to resort to violence had been nurtured by a long experience in brigandage.

At Herod's death insurrection flamed again. Judas, the son of Hezekiah the Galilean, terrorized northern Palestine. Another rebel spread disorder through Judea. And still another declared himself king. In Crete, Melos, and even Rome the Jews gave support to a fraudulent Maccabean claimant to the throne. Finally the conservative Jewish leaders, facing the fact that Roman power was dominant, asked for direct Roman rule, and A.D. 6 a Roman procurator was sent to Palestine. The Sanhedrin, however,

[1] See p. 883.
[2] A. H. M. Jones, *The Herods of Judea* (1938).

enforced the Jewish law in domestic affairs. The high priest was appointed by the procurator.

Under direct Roman rule the country did not quiet down. The procurators, of whom Pilate—in Palestine for ten years, A.D. 26–36—is the most notorious, were unprincipled and cruel. The legions occupied the Temple. Tax farmers plundered the country. And the spirit of insurrection persisted. "Holy wars" in which fanatics rushed joyously to martyrdom kept the land in turmoil. A brief restoration of the Herodian line did not abate the disorder. There was famine in Judea, murder in the Temple, and rioting in the cities. And the procurators, who returned in A.D. 44, were unable to halt the revolutionary outbreaks. In A.D. 67 they culminated in the "great rebellion," which ended with the destruction of the Jewish state. When Jerusalem fell, A.D. 70, it was razed and declared an accursed city, the Temple was demolished, and thousands were sold into slavery—thousands more having died during the siege. Many of those sold into slavery perished, fighting wild animals in the arenas of Antioch and other cities.

The "great rebellion" was the beginning rather than the end of the Jewish struggle for freedom. With the destruction of the Temple, the religious center of the nation, the spirit of insurrection passed from Palestine to the Jews of the eastern Mediterranean lands. From 118 to 120 a revolt swept Cyprus—Salamis was burned —Cyrenaica, Egypt, and Mesopotamia. In Cyprus and Cyrenaica perhaps as many as a hundred thousand Greeks and Romans were killed. The destruction of life in Cyrenaica was so great that the country had to be recolonized. The Romans finally put down the uprisings.

From the failure of this revolt the Jews learned that organization, as well as courage, was necessary if Roman rule was to be cast off, and they began at once to prepare for a future opportunity. In the mountainous districts of Judea the caves were made into forts and connected with subterranean passages. Infantry and cavalry forces were created. And plans to rebuild the Temple were made. Bar Kocheba, the leader of the movement, who was hailed by some of the Jewish religious teachers as the heaven-sent liberator, aroused the Jews outside of Palestine and sought the assistance of the Parthians, the deadly enemies of the Romans. His success was sufficiently great to make the outbreak of 132–135 appear to the Romans like a universal insurrection.

. . . All Judaea had been stirred up, and the Jews everywhere were showing signs of disturbance, were gathering together, and giving evidence of great hostility to the Romans, partly by secret and partly by overt acts; many outside nations, too, were joining them through eagerness for gain, and the whole earth, one might almost say, was being stirred up over the matter.

To meet the crisis the emperor Hadrian sent Severus, Rome's ablest general, from Britain to Palestine.

Severus did not venture to attack his opponents in the open at any one point, in view of their numbers and their desperation, but by intercepting small groups, thanks to the number of his soldiers and his under-officers, and by depriving them of food and shutting them up, he was able, rather slowly, to be sure, but with comparatively little danger, to crush, exhaust and exterminate them. Very few of them in fact survived. Fifty of their most important outposts and nine hundred and eighty-five of their most famous villages were razed to the ground. Five hundred and eighty thousand men were slain in the various raids and battles, and the number of those that perished by famine, disease and fire was past finding out. Thus nearly the whole of Judaea was made desolate, a result of which the people had had forewarning before the war. For the tomb of Solomon, which the Jews regard as an object of veneration, fell to pieces of itself and collapsed, and many wolves and hyenas rushed howling into their cities.[1]

To the Jews the collapse of Solomon's pillar seemed to be a sign that the nation was utterly lost. And Roman persecution promised to fulfill the omen. The Jews were forbidden to enter Jerusalem, and the reading of the Torah was proscribed. In order to save themselves the Jews were permitted by their religious leaders to violate all the sacred laws except those against idolatry, incest, and murder.

The causes of these continued disturbances were far from simple. Jewish religious feeling, fed by the exclusiveness of Yahwism and the hope of a divinely sent leader—a Messiah—who would achieve the Jewish political domination of the world, was undoubtedly at the root of the fierce patriotism which drove generation after generation to revolt. In an age which everywhere brought rising religious feelings, it was almost certain that these tendencies of the Jewish faith would find expression. Roman arrogance, greed, and brutality also played their part. But the Roman leaders, from Caesar on, recognized the right of the Jews to practice their national faith and, in fact, gave them a special religious status, including the right of local self-government of their

[1] *Dio's Roman History*, Book LXIX.

religious communities.[1] The difficulties faced by the procurators in
Palestine were practically insoluble, for the Jews gave their religious practices a political significance which, of course, the procurators could not recognize. There can be no doubt that the
contemporary view of the Jews as a "stiff-necked" people was
correct.

But behind the religious and political difficulties was an
intolerable economic situation and an internal social crisis.[2]
Palestine had never been a rich land, and continuous political
disorder impoverished it further. The Jews resisted even the
Herodian and Roman efforts at economic rehabilitation. The
cultivation of the date palm, it may be noted, was begun in
the Jordan valley in the last century before Christ. Taxation, both
priestly and imperial, was excessive. Under the Roman procurators,
it has been estimated, between 30 and 40 per cent of the national
income was taken by taxes. These burdens fell heaviest on the
poor. The priests never found a reason to lessen the dues paid
to the Temple, and each Roman administrator added a special
bit to the financial load of the country. Priestly cupidity and
imperial greed consumed the nation like a fever.

It would be a mistake, however, to see these evils as merely
setting the Jews against the Romans; actually the Jews were
divided and at war with one another. "The masses lived in dismal
poverty."[3] The daughters of Israel, it was said, were made ugly by
poverty. The poor, the destitute, the unemployed, and the landless
hated and, then, attacked the wealthy farmers, the great landlords, the rich merchants, and the usurious bankers. The brigands,
who took the lead in every insurrection, were recruited from the
ranks of the dispossessed. The conservative leaders who made
the requests for Roman rule were from the ranks of the well to do.
The failure to achieve the social justice taught by the Prophets
was as much a cause of disorder as the frustration of national
political ambitions. The murder and thievery of the insurrections
were directed quite as much against the well-to-do Jews as the
Romans, and the punishment for insurrection imposed by Rome
always fell most harshly on the poor. Poverty and want were the
great evils. From them issued hate, intolerance, fanaticism, and—

---

[1] See E. G. Hardy, *Christianity and the Roman Government: A study in imperial administration* (1925); V. Chapot, *The Roman World* (1928).

[2] See Salo Wittmayer Baron, *A Social and Religious History of the Jews* (3 vols., 1937),
Vol. 1, pp. 191–207.

[3] *Ibid.*, p. 195.

counterweighting these—religious hope; and calamity after calamity only intensified them.[1]

THE DIASPORA: THE DISPERSION OF THE JEWS.

Since almost every aspect of imperialism contributed to an uprooting of peoples, the Jews were progressively dispersed. Enslavements and deportations carried many out of the homeland. The profits of trade and the need of employment drew others away, especially to the eastern Mediterranean cities. Some enlisted in the mercenary armies of the rival kings; the Jews were known everywhere as good soldiers. Others fled from persecution and the dangers of internal disorder. Once the Jews had left Palestine, they went wherever opportunities led, and in the widening social intercourse of Rome's imperial age these paths were ever more extended.

There is little evidence for the existence of Jews outside of Palestine, except in Babylonia and Egypt, before Alexander the Great, but after his time they spread rapidly. In the third century B.C. a permanent Jewish population developed in Alexandria; in the first Christian century it held two of the five districts of the city. Also in the third century B.C. migration from Babylonia to Asia Minor scattered Jews from Cilicia to the coasts of the Black

---

[1] Frederick C. Grant, *The Economic Background of the Gospels* (1926), p. 106–107: " . . . There is an intimate connexion between crushing oppression, which leads to despair of the present, and the hopes of men for divine intervention, for the judgement to come (first of all, upon their oppressors), and a golden age in the future. This is proved by the form which eschatological speculation took in Judaism. It was no accident that apocalyptists dreamed of the world to come under the figure of a banquet, a Messianic feast, a time of rejoicing and plenty, of freedom and prosperity, with the hungry filled and the mournful and disheartened comforted. Or that they placed in the forefront of their vision, in times of acute political distress, a divine intervention and chastisement of their enemies. Or that the more spiritual guides and interpreters of the common hope, men who realized that their 'hope was laid up in heaven', and that the consummation lay in another world than this— that these men retained the crude symbolism of the political-economic dream which fired the hearts of the poor and oppressed, giving it a higher interpretation. The *forms* taken by this expectation were no accident; one of the surest of psychological laws, the very one that governs all dreams of the hungry and persecuted, of all persons with repressed desires—the prisoner's dream of deliverance, the fever-stricken man's vision of cooling waters, the famine sufferer's dream of bread—rendered inevitable their choice of imagery. And in our Lord's time the people were not only hungry for bread, and restless under the political restraints of the Roman occupation; they were yearning for the actual realization and establishment of the first premise of their priestly religion, the theocracy, the *regnum dei in terra*, the actual, tangible, visible manifestation of God's supreme power upon earth and the conformation of this world's affairs to His divine and perfect will. This premise was not yet actually realized. The Kingdom of God had not yet 'come.' And the longer it remained unrealized, the more vividly, it seems, were its coming and the consequences of its coming pictured." By permission of the Oxford University Press, New York.

Black Star. Photograph by Z. KLUGER

THE SITE OF THE TEMPLE, JERUSALEM

(For descriptive legend see opposite page)

Sea. At the same time a steady flow from Palestine to Syria began. Perhaps the outward movements were at their height from Pompey's intervention to the fall of the Temple. Then the Jews became numerous in the coastal cities from Cyrenaica to the Ionian coast of Asia Minor and on the islands of Cyprus, Rhodes, and Melos. In the western Mediterranean, except for a large number in Rome, they seem first to have gone to lands once held by Carthage. The disastrous insurrections of the late first and the early second century merely completed the dispersion which these earlier movements had promoted. In the early fourth century the Jews became prominent in Spain, and at its end they were found in the Rhine valley. At the same time, under the favorable rule of the Sassanians, they penetrated Iran.

In the high period of Roman prosperity, *i.e.*, in the second Christian century, perhaps one out of every ten persons in the Roman Empire was a Jew, in other words, about seven million in a population of seventy million. Perhaps another million Jews lived in Mesopotamia outside the area of Roman rule. In the third century, when the total population of the empire declined, the number of Jews, although it decreased, did not decrease proportionately to the whole population.

In the course of the Dispersion the Jews changed their economic and social positions. Originally they had been a pastoral people, then they became peasants, and finally they were almost entirely urban dwellers, engaged in industry and trade. The transition from agriculture to urban callings was first made in Alexandria. In the first century the Jews became important as craftsmen in the linen, silk, metal, and glass industries, and as shopkeepers; for centuries after this time they were more prominent in petty trade than in long-distance commerce. About this time, too, they entered the moneylending and banking businesses. After the second century agriculture is seldom mentioned in Jewish records. The Jews were concentrated in the lower middle classes and in the freedmen section of the working class. Inasmuch as the third century crisis impoverished large sections of the urban population, the economic conditions of the Jews undoubtedly became worse as time went on.

THE SITE OF THE TEMPLE, JERUSALEM

On the site, now occupied by the mosque, was situated the Temple, the shrine of Yahweh, from the time of Solomon to the day of Herod. When Jesus lived, the Temple was on an adjoining site. The Temple was finally destroyed by the Romans in A.D. 70. The buildings in the foreground are in the old Mohammedan part of the present city.

Hostility to the Jews appeared among the gentile populations of the eastern Mediterranean commercial cities almost as early as Jewish groups were permanently established among them. Massacres occurred in Alexandria and Damascus in the first century B.C. There were many sources of gentile antipathy. The Jews remained aliens, kept to themselves, and took pride in aloofness; except in economic dealings they had few contacts with gentiles. They took a superior, if not intolerant, attitude toward the religions of other peoples, and during the period of most rapid dispersion they aggressively proselyted from other faiths. When they became concentrated in the lower middle and working classes, they suffered under those attitudes in Greco-Roman culture which disapproved of trade and labor. And the bitter struggles for liberation, in which the Jews mingled religious hopes and political aspirations, left a heritage of hate and suspicion among both Jews and gentiles. Persecution kept alive every animosity. From these feelings and attitudes was compounded the prejudice which the Christians, for religious reasons peculiarly their own, intensified as they became more numerous and rose to power in the state.

For pagans and Christians alike, then, the Jews became the human symbol of those emotions which, because they sustained in-group loyalties, also embodied out-group antipathies. This was the root of the anti-Semitic feeling which persisted in the Western cultural tradition after Greco-Roman times. It is worth noting, whenever the Western cultural tradition has been disturbed, even by forces having no relation to the Jews or their position in Western life, this feeling has always run violently. A resurgence of anti-Semitism is, in fact, an important symptom of cultural change in the Western world.

HEBREW LITERATE LEARNING: THE BIBLE AND THE TORAH.

The exile in Babylonia was an important period not only in the development of Hebrew religious ideas but also in the evolution of Hebrew literate learning. There is little reason to believe that a knowledge of reading and writing was widespread among the pre-exilic Hebrews, even among the priests. But in Babylonia the practice of Judaism without the performance of the national rituals set up a tendency that, in making for a wider acquaintanceship with the sacred writings among the common Hebrews, led to a slow spread of literacy, and after the Exile this tendency continued. The dispersion of the Jews continually strengthened it. The result was twofold. On the one hand it produced the Sopherim, or scribes, who were expert in the study and exposition of the law. Such scholars appear to have existed as early as the time of Ezra. On the other hand the gathering of the people for reading and instruction became more and more common.

Because the formation of the priestly state concentrated the performance of the national rituals in the Temple, popular religious study increased, especially when the Hellenization policy of Syria stirred up the people. After the beginning of the second century B.C. the scribes increased steadily in number and importance, and the popular meeting for religious instruction evolved into the synagogue, the enduring institution of worship. Sometime in this period, probably, the synagogues became places where reading and writing were taught to the children also.

During the disorders which brought the destruction of the Temple, the scribes founded schools where rabbis, or masters, expounded the law and from which disciples spread their ideas among the people. When the destruction of the Temple dispersed the priesthood, religious leadership passed to these scholars, and they quickly seized its opportunities. The great rabbinical schools which gave Judaism its enduring form appeared in the first Christian century. A century later the scholars—the doctors of the law—had won both prestige and authority, and they had no competitors as the leaders of the nation.

When Nehemiah and Ezra made Judaism a religion of the "Book," it began an evolution which inevitably begot an elaboration of literate learning, and the social and political circumstances of national survival threw into the hands of the masters of this learning the task of preserving the national cultural tradition. Thus in a more significant way than any other religion in the Western world Judaism produced scholars and nurtured intellectual pursuits. Among the common people there spread only that amount of literate learning necessary for the functioning of the rabbis, but it was enough to make the Jews more literate than any people among whom they lived.

1. *The Formation of the "Book": the Bible.* The formation of the Bible was the outcome of literary, as well as religious, developments, and, like every other aspect of Hebrew culture, was deeply affected by the history of the nation.[1]

---

[1] On the formation of the Bible see I. G. Matthews, *Old Testament Life and Literature* (1934); Max L. Margolis, *The Hebrew Scriptures in the Making* (1915); G. B. Gray, *A Critical Introduction to the Old Testament* (1913); J. A. Brewer, *Literature of the Old Testament* (1924); S. R. Driver, *Introduction to the Literature of the Old Testament* (10th rev. ed., 1900);

From the early period of migrations came war songs, proverbs, and oracles, the typical products of a people acquiring a knowledge of writing for the first time. During the reign of David and his successors poems, historical narratives, and simple law codes, which became the fundamental elements in the sacred writings, appeared. These materials were woven together in different ways. The ninth and eighth centuries B.C. produced from them the Yahwist and Elohist documents which formed the core of the Bible. In fact after the eighth century B.C. Hebrew literary development consisted mainly of reorienting the ideas in these compilations in terms of new social experiences. The greatest effort of this kind was made by the Prophets whose works came finally to stand alongside the earlier works as one of the three sections of the Hebrew Bible. The Exile weakened the belief that Yahweh spoke continually to His people in new revelations; the result was that although literary activity continued, the writings were less likely to be regarded as divinely inspired.

By the time of Ezra (the opening of the fourth century B.C.) the five books ascribed to Moses—Genesis, Exodus, Leviticus, Numbers, and Deuteronomy—were fixed as the highest authority of Judaism. The canon of the Prophets, *i.e.*, the expounders of the law, consisting of the Books of Joshua, Judges, First and Second Samuel, and First and Second Kings (the Former Prophets), and the Books of Isaiah, Jeremiah, Ezekiel, and the Twelve, including Amos, Hosea, and others (the Latter Prophets), was fixed by the opening of the second century B.C. From the diverse literary products of the Maccabean age a third section of the Bible known as the Writings was formed; it included the Book of Daniel, Psalms, Proverbs, the Book of Job, the Canticles, Ruth, Lamentations, Ecclesiastes, Esther, Ezra, Nehemiah, and Chronicles. In all, the Hebrew Bible contained twenty-eight books; the final canon was fixed by a council of rabbis held at Jamnia about A.D. 100.

A group of works finally excluded from the Hebrew sacred writings at this time is particularly important for the study of the religious ideas of the Maccabean period and the succeeding revolutionary age.[1]

Laura Wild, *Literary Guide to the Old Testament* (1922); J. M. Smith, *The Old Testament: An American translation* (1927); and R. H. Charles, *Apocrypha and Pseudepigrapha* (1913).

For a list of the books of the Old Testament in the order of their composition see Evelyn W. Hippisley, "The Old Testament Chronologically Arranged," in W. L. Wardle, *The History and Religion of Israel* (1936), following p. 228.

[1] See pp. 713, 717.

2. *The Hebrew Law: the Torah.* Like the Bible as a whole, the law, or as it was known in final form, the Torah, was the product of a long development. Contemporary scholars recognize several different documents as marking significant phases of its growth.[1]

Some scholars regard the statement of the commandments in Exodus, Chapter 20, as the original law, while others consider the commandments in Exodus, Chapter 34, verses 14–26, to be just as old, if not older. The Book of the Covenant (Exod. 20: 22– 23: 23) was a simple code, suited to an agricultural society; its two divisions, religious and civil, were similar in many ways to Hammurabi's code, but the provisions were in the main less complex. In Deuteronomy the written law for the first time superseded custom as the rule of life. Nine chapters at the end of the Book of Ezekiel defined the functions of the priest class. The Law of Holiness (Lev. 17—26) emphasized moral as contrasted with ritualistic law. Toward the end of the fifth century B.C. the priestly and ritualistic laws were brought together in the Priestly Code which Ezra made the basis of his teachings, and sometime in the fourth century B.C. the Law of Holiness was united with it. Perhaps as late as 350 B.C. the several important renderings of the law—the Ten Commandments, the Book of the Covenant, Deuteronomy, the Law of Holiness, and the Priestly Code—were united in a single compilation which, for subsequent generations, was regarded as the complete law—the Torah.

The crediting of the authorship of this compilation to Moses was only a way of giving to it the sanction of tradition. It was regarded as the absolute and unquestioned word of God, and so satisfied was Yahweh with His work that, it was believed, He spent the Sabbath reading its sections.

Viewed as a historical development, the Hebrew law is an amalgamation of the codes of nomadic and peasant peoples, adapted in some ways to the needs of an urban social order. In certain phases of development it was influenced by the Babylonian civil law; in other phases the Egyptian social outlook seems to have been important. But through every phase of development it retained the character of an in-group code; the retention of the distinction between aliens and Hebrews was full evidence of its

[1] On the Hebrew law see W. L. Wardle, *Israel and Babylon* (1925); C. H. W. Johns, *The Relation between the Laws of Babylonia and the Laws of the Hebrew People* (2d ed., 1917); H. S. Linchfield, *Relation of Jewish to Babylonian Law* (1919); Rudolf Kittel, *The Religion of the People of Israel* (1925); Leo Baeck, *The Essence of Judaism* (1936); William Roseneau, *Jewish Ceremonials, Institutions, and Customs* (3d rev. ed., 1925); and C. F. Kent, *Israel's Laws and Legal Precedents from the Days of Moses to the Closing of the Legal Canon* (1907).

primitive orientation. At base, of course, Hebrew law differed little from all primitive in-group codes, for the commandments, except as they established the exclusive worship of Yahweh, duplicated the chief moral precepts of other primitive peoples. Its distinguishing quality was the religious motivation of every provision. The laws of other primitive and ancient-oriental peoples were divinely inspired; Hebrew law not only was divinely given but also served a divine purpose. It was the guide for a behavior pleasing to a God who could not be served except by its observance. Fundamentally, however, the religiosity of the law was necessitated by the social circumstances which, because they had destroyed Hebrew political institutions, permitted in-group survival only under religious controls.

The Hebrew code embodied three main classes of provisions: (1) those pertaining to worship, (2) those defining the functions of the priests, and (3) those regulating individual behavior and social relations.

The first class fixed the rules of sacrifices, the observation of the Sabbath, and the great national festivals and defined the "unclean," *i.e.*, those who were defiled in the sight of God. Rules for the purification of the unclean formed a significant portion of this group of provisions. Diet, sexual intercourse, and the treatment of lepers were regulated on a strictly religious basis. Idolatry, tattooing, and omenology were absolutely prohibited, as was also the trimming of the beard. The effect of these provisions as a whole was to bring the life of the in-group under a thoroughgoing ritualism.

The second class of provisions fixed the membership of the priesthood, formalized the installation of priests, laid down the rule of "holy living," and established the claims of the Temple and its ministrants on the economy; in theory this priesthood mediated between the nation and God by carrying on the ritual of the national cult. Central in this class of provisions were those which distinguished the temple priests (by designating them the descendants of Aaron, brother of Moses) from the Levitical priests brought into the temples from local shrines.

The third class of provisions, bearing on the main aspects of daily life, dealt with the family, crime, war, property, business, slaves, and the poor. The family was organized as a patriarchate. The degrees of relation within which marriage was permissible were strictly defined. All criminal cases were to be heard by recognized judges. No man was to be convicted on the testimony of one witness. A father was not to be responsible for the crimes of his son, and vice versa. The chief rule of punishment was the *lex talionis*—an eye for an eye and a tooth for a tooth; hanging, stoning, and burning were prescribed forms of execution for certain crimes. The body of a hanged criminal was to be taken down before sunset. The inhabitants of a besieged city, if it surrendered without resistance, were to pay tribute; if it resisted, the males were to be killed and the children and women taken captive. After a month of mourning, a captive woman could be taken in marriage by her Hebrew captor.

The nomadic Hebrew tribes originally held lands in common. When they settled in Canaan private ownership in tillable land appeared; under the monarchy private property was fully recognized. But vestiges of the communal system remained, for pastures seem to have continued to be held in common and the crops of each seventh year may have belonged to the group as a whole. The law of inheritance gave the eldest son a double portion of his father's property; the general rule of the law of inheritance was to hold property together in the family. Trade was recognized as a normal activity. The use of just weights and measures was required. Usury might be charged to the alien but not to the native; in other words, on the basis of in-group interest a dual economic morality was permitted. The widow's garment and the millstone could not be pledged for debt. No man could enter a house in order to seize his pledge. Slaves were to be purchased only from foreigners. The native debtor was to be treated not as a slave but as a hired laborer. An escaped slave could become the slave of the man with whom he found refuge. When a slave was freed, he was to be provided with funds so that he could undertake to make his own living. A master could beat his slave "almost to death." Hired laborers were to be paid at the end of each working day. No owner of a field or vineyard was to gather all the grain or the grapes; the gleanings belonged to the poor, the widows, the orphans, and the resident aliens. Aliens were permitted to consume the carcasses of animals dying from disease or by accident. The deaf and the blind were not to be subjected to harsh treatment. The sick were treated as unclean; in fact, the Hebrews never arrived at any theory of disease other than that ailments were punishment for sins.

As long as the Hebrews possessed a state the power of government stood behind the priesthood in enforcing the law. Judges sat at the gates of the cities to hear cases between individuals, and the Sanhedrin dealt with major offenders. Capital punishment was inflicted on murderers, adulterers, harlots, and blasphemers.

Treason and apostasy were identical, and both were punishable with death. Minor violations of the code were regarded as sins in the sight of God, and for each violation a sin offering was prescribed as a means of expiation.

The Hebrews conceived their religious duty to be the leading of this life according to this law. It was the function of the scholars of the law not only to instruct the people in the word of the law but also to inculcate in them that spirit of obedience which satisfied God. The law, although ultimately spun out in a multitude of interpretations, was the living content of Judaism.

Because the Hebrews understood individual suffering and social distress as evidences of God's displeasure, it was inevitable that the disorganization of life brought by the imperial age should provoke a religious crisis in which the observance of the law was the foremost issue. Affecting the crisis also were the religious ideas which appeared as the result of the contacts of the Hebrew with surrounding cultures.

THE IMPACT OF HELLENIC CULTURE ON JUDAISM.

From these contacts, especially with Persian and Greek culture, innovations arose which gave Judaism an almost completely new intellectual orientation. It ceased to be the simple and naive faith it had been among the pre-exilic Hebrews and became philosophical and syncretic like the other religions affected by Hellenistic and Greco-Roman cultural developments. The law remained its unique element.[1]

1. *The Fusion of Greek and Hebrew Learning.* Recent archaeological discoveries have revealed that the Greek and Hebrew cultures were in contact in Egypt as early as the sixth century B.C., and there, as the Alexandrine Jewish population grew, the contact became closer. Because this population lost its native tongue and spoke Greek, the prejudice against rendering the sacred writings in any language except Hebrew broke down; the result was a Greek translation known, from the legend that it was the work of seventy scholars, as the Septuagint. The Torah was translated first, then the Prophets, and finally the Writings; among the last were some of those works which were excluded from the canon at Jamnia.

[1] On Judaism in the Hellenistic age see Adam C. Welsh, *Post-Exilic Judaism* (1935); T. K. Cheyne, *Jewish Religious Life after the Exile* (1915); Archibald Duff, *A History of the Religion of Judaism 500 to 200 B.C.* (1927); Nahun Levison, *The Jewish Background of Christianity: A manual of the political, religious, social and literary life of the Jews from 586 B.C. to A.D. 1* (1932); and Meyer Waxman, *A History of Jewish Literature from the close of the Bible to our own days* (2 vols., 1938).

The first translations were made under the supervision of Alexandrine Jewish priests; the last were private undertakings. Probably the work of translation extended from early in the third to late in the second century B.C. The making of the Septuagint was the primary step in the blending of Greek and Hebrew ideas, for it gave to the Greek world for the first time a full view of Hebrew beliefs.

However, this blending was not to be exclusively the work of Greeks who became acquainted with Hebrew beliefs, for soon Hebrews began to assimilate Greek ideas. Probably by the second century B.C. most educated Hebrews, even in Palestine, knew Greek, and many of them wrote it. The Book of Ecclesiastes, which was admitted to the Hebrew canon only after long contention, was written about 200 B.C.; except for its last chapter, which repudiates worldly ideals, the book is an account of a man who found life pleasurable in the Epicurean manner. He viewed the universe in Greek terms, as a vast orderly machine without a purpose. And God, he inclined to believe, was indifferent to human suffering. The author of the *Wisdom of Solomon*, composed in Egypt (*ca.* 100–50 B.C.) in pure Greek, argued that the Hebrew Prophets were superior to the Greek philosophers but set forth the Platonic rather than the Genesis account of creation, as well as many Stoic ideas. The general effect of Greek learning upon Hebrew scholars was to impel them to find in the Bible philosophical as well as religious ideas and to raise questions about God's relation to the world and men. How, they asked, if God is transcendent, can He intervene in worldly affairs? How, in the face of the fact, can it be argued that the divine government of the world is moral? If God cares for the individual soul, how can He abandon it at death? In the first century B.C. such questions received wide attention among the Hebrews.[1]

Among educated Hebrews, especially outside of Palestine, the need, therefore, to bring Jewish thought into harmony with Greek philosophy became steadily greater. About 150 B.C. Aristobulus of Alexandria wrote the *Laws of Moses* to prove that the Greek philosophers had drawn their doctrines from the Hebrew sacred books; he began the allegorical interpretation of the Old Testament. About the same time another writer explained that the Greeks had borrowed writing from the Phoenicians, who had

[1] See H. K. Booth, *The Bridge between the Testaments; A survey of the life and literature of the period of connections* (1929); R. H. Charles, *Religious Development between the Old and New Testaments* (1914); F. C. Burkitt, *Jewish and Christian Apocalypses* (1914).

learned it from the Hebrews; he also asserted that Moses, who he said was the actual inventor of writing, was the source of all Egyptian wisdom.

Somewhat later Philo (*ca.* 30 B.C.–A.D. 50) blended Hebrew religious thought and Greek philosophy. He claimed for his work, which contained many references to Pythagorean, Platonic, and Stoic ideas, the authority of revelation. Opposed to the world of being, divinity, and ideas there was, he said, the world of lifeless matter. The human body was the prison of the soul; at death the soul was liberated. Man's duty was to live so as to keep the soul pure; ascetic practices, meditation, and an inward worship were the chief means of achieving purity. Between God and man were numerous intermediaries. Chief among them was the *Logos*, divine reason, which gave order to material chaos; angels and daimons were lesser intermediaries constantly passing between the material and the spiritual world. The Greek heroes were identical with the angels of Moses; Plato, he said, was "most holy." Inspiration came to men in the state of frenzy, for then the divine voice struck the soul like a musician playing a lyre. Philo held to the prophetic conception of the mission of the Hebrew nation and looked for the sudden coming of a "man of war" who would bring universal peace.

By resorting to allegorical interpretations of both Hebrew and Greek writings, Philo fused Hebrew monotheism with Platonic idealism, but the synthesis, because it was religious rather than philosophical in outlook, was more Hebraic than Greek in quality.[1]

Josephus (*ca.* A.D. 37–95), whose religious and political career touched almost every phase of Jewish life in the first Christian century, was also an exemplar of the fusion of Greek and Hebrew learning; his works, *The Jewish War*, an account of the "great rebellion," and *The Jewish Antiquities*, a survey of Jewish history from the creation to the outbreak of the rebellion, were done in the Greek, not the Hebrew, style.[2]

2. *The Elaboration of Hebrew Religious Ideas in the Hellenistic Age.* It may be safely asserted that few, if any, new ideas appeared in Judaism as a result of contacts with foreign cultures, but that

---

[1] See N. D. Bentwich, *Philo-Judaeus of Alexandria* (1910); F. H. Colson, *Philo, with an English translation* (1929); E. Bréhier, *Les Idées philosophiques et religeuses de Philon d'Alexandrie* (2 ed., revue, 1925); and Edmund Stein, *Die allegorische Exegese des Philo aus Alexandrien* (1929).

[2] N. D. Bentwich, *Josephus* (1914); F. J. Foakes-Jackson, *Josephus and the Jews: The religion and history of the Jews as explained by Flavius Josephus* (1930); H. St. John, *Josephus, the Man and the Historian* (1929).

many old ideas, especially vague ones expressed by the Prophets, were given new forms and added emphasis. These ideas were developed mainly in a new type of literature which set forth visions of the future; apocalyptic works, of which the Book of Daniel, included in the Hebrew canon, and the apocryphal Book of Enoch are the best examples, were a typical product of the Maccabean age. They reached a height of popularity early in the revolutionary period. The tendency of thought they expressed made Judaism a religion quite like the others that spread widely in Hellenistic times.[1]

The Jewish conception of God was refined under the influence of Persian and Greek ideas. He became more transcendent and spiritual and less anthropomorphic. Although still the national God, He was also the sublime ruler of the universe. As the Father of all mankind, as well as the Jews, He was still close to men, loving them with an infinite kindness. The ancient Jewish feeling toward Yahweh persisted in the refusal to pronounce God's name.

As God became transcendent, the Jews, following both Persian and Greek precedents, developed the belief in intermediaries as the agents of His will among men. Supreme among these agents was the Word, or Wisdom,—in Philo's thought the Logos—which gave the universe a rational government. Around the divine throne was an angelic host whose members served as messengers of God, conveying revelations to men, and as officers of the divine government. At their head stood the archangels. Michael, the prince of the angels, was the patron and avenger of Israel; he had given the law to the "chosen people." Gabriel, the "revealing angel," was the supreme judge. Uriel watched over the earth and the underworld. Raphael presented the prayers of the faithful to God. To the original archangels—six in number—the rabbis of the revolutionary period added seventy others as the guardians of the various nations. The cherubim were the winged spirits of the storm; the seraphim were the dazzling lightning strokes; together they personified the thunderstorm in which God rode to judgment. The ophannim were angelic princes of the celestial court where a vast host—six hundred and forty thousand—of angels continually

---

[1] For general treatments of social and religious developments in late Hellenistic and early Roman times among the Jews see Charles Guignebert, *The Jewish World in the Time of Jesus* (1939); Charles F. Jean, *Le Milieu biblique avant Jésus-Christ* (1923); Emil Schürer, *Geschichte des jüdischen Volkes im Zeitalter Jesu Christi* (4 vols., 4th ed., 1909); Joseph Klausner, *Jesus of Nazareth: His life, times, and teaching* (1927); Thomas Walker, *Hebrew Religion between the Testaments: An exposition of the Judaism of the home of Jesus* (1937).

chanted, "Holy, Holy, Holy." Under Persian influence the conception of a host of devils took form. The story of the fallen angels who became the leaders of the evil spirits first appeared in the Book of Enoch. Satan, king of the evil daimons, seduced men to sin against God; his minions, both male and female, tormented and tempted men. Some they made ill. To others they brought bad luck. They lurked in desolate spots and deserted houses, always seeking a chance to attack the unwary. It should be realized that the life of the Jews in Greco-Roman times went on in the presence of a "threatening cloud of hostile spirits," and they thought of the struggle between good and evil as a war between the angels and the evil daimons.[1]

Man's position in a universe so organized and governed was extremely difficult. God had bestowed life upon him both as a body and as a soul. But the tendency of the flesh was to sin, and the soul, although immortal, was so entangled that escape without God's help was impossible. Originally the Hebrews had believed in a shadowy underworld, Sheol, somewhat like the Babylonian Arallu, to which all men went. But in late Hellenistic times the views of the other world became sharper. Sheol was identified with Gehenna, a valley southwest of Jerusalem, where refuse and garbage were burned. Hell was conceived in Persian terms as the House of Lies; heaven as the House of Song. In the apocalyptic literature heaven was developed into seven ascending abodes of the blessed, which later Jewish speculation described in great detail. As these views of hell and heaven developed, Sheol became an intermediate place where men waited for final judgment. This notion corresponded closely with the subsequent Christian belief in purgatory. Part and parcel of these views was, of course, the idea that the soul survives after death. In the Maccabean age the doctrine of the resurrection of the soul spread from the Alexandrine Jews to Palestine, where it quickly attained popularity. Persian and Greek ideas, as well as certain ideas developed by the Prophets, gave force to the belief; as a corollary it was held that life in the other world brought reward or punishment for life on earth.

It should be understood that the Jews did not emphasize the resurrection of the individual so much as they did the resurrection of mankind as part of the divine plan of salvation. In this emphasis, which was transmitted to Christianity, they were more in accord with Iranian than with Greek ideas.

[1] H. K. Booth, *The Bridge between the Testaments: A survey of life and literature between the Old and New Testaments* (1929); W. O. E. Oesterley, *The Age of Transition* (1937).

The Jewish expectation of a divine savior arose out of the continual frustration of political ambitions and the distresses of the people, who sought, as a result, a religious escape from misery.[1] Under the influence of the Iranian doctrine of intermediaries and the Greek concept "savior-god," this expectancy gave rise to the belief in the Messiah. Among the Prophets the Messianic hope was limited to a divine restoration of the nation under an ideal king; in the Maccabean age and later the hope was bound up with the moral regeneration and ultimate salvation of mankind. Throughout the revolutionary age these beliefs became more and more popular, and the hope they nourished intensified the spirit of revolt. In fact, so strong was the influence of the Messianic hope, it would not be improper to designate the Jewish struggles for liberation in the first and second centuries as the "Messianic revolutions." The Messiah, it was believed, would come in the midst of wars, famines, plagues, and other calamities. The wicked would form a universal coalition against him, but they would be defeated. Then from a celestial city, descended from on high, the Messiah would rule the regenerated earth in a true golden age to last for a thousand years. At its end the dead would be resurrected, the wicked and the righteous would be separated, and eternity would begin. The Jews were somewhat uncertain as to the character of the final judgment.

The beliefs described in the foregoing paragraphs reached a height of popularity in the middle of the last century B.C. and persisted until the second Christian century. They were discussed in the schools, proclaimed in public, and argued in the dark places where conspiracies were formed and insurrections plotted. There can be no understanding of the milieu from which Christianity emerged without close attention to the economic misery and political aspirations and the religious ideas which were their intellectual companions. Unfortunately the actions which, together, they motivated were disastrous to the Jewish nation.

3. *The Fundamental Opposition of Hebrew and Hellenic Culture.* The impact of Hellenic culture upon the Hebrews was, thus, both intellectual and social. Undoubtedly the Messianic idea, the belief in future rewards and punishments, and the conception of life as a moral struggle were strengthened by contact with Greek religious and philosophical thought. More important, however, for the

---

[1] J. H. Greenstone, *The Messiah Idea in Jewish History* (1906). See also T. H. Grindley, *Religious Thought in Palestine in the Time of Jesus Christ* (1931); H. Silver, *A History of Messianic Speculation in Israel from the First to the Seventeenth Century* (1927).

future of Judaism than this effect was the intensification of the separatist tendency of the Hebrew nation, which was the chief social result of the clash of the two cultures. They were, indeed, too unlike to blend. The Greeks lived under city-states with many forms of government, the Hebrews in a single theocratic state. The Greeks believed in many gods, the Hebrews in One God. The Greek philosophers taught contradictory ethical principles; the Hebrew Prophets proclaimed a single moral law. The Greeks enjoyed worldly life, exalted physical strength and beauty, and found pleasure in art and intellectual pursuits; the Hebrews bore worldly life as a burden of suffering, sought moral purity, and made piety the goal of intellectual effort. The Greeks discovered the best and the worst that urban culture produces; the Hebrews, failing to achieve the political ambition generated in urban culture, repudiated its artistic and intellectual achievements in favor of a religious orientation of life which opposed the simple code of the nomad and the peasant to the diversity of moral practices of urban life.

Neither the Greek nor the Jew successfully dealt with the problem of exploitation inherent in urban societies. The Greeks accepted it, chiefly on the grounds that since men's souls had different qualities the class structure was an order having a basis in the real world of ideas; the Hebrews abhorred the injustices of urban culture but found no escape from them except in the advent of a supernatural savior.

THE JEWISH PARTIES AND SECTS IN THE REVOLUTIONARY PERIOD, 65 B.C.–A.D. 135.

As social distress and political frustration deepened under Roman rule and religious ideas were elaborated, parties embodying different attitudes and beliefs appeared among the Jews; and each party attempted, at least, to hold to a line of action which it believed was best for the nation. After the Hellenizers were killed off or passed into the throng of Hellenized orientals in the eastern Mediterranean cities, there were four well-defined groups among the Jews in Palestine, and at least the first three of them, as enumerated below, had supporters among the Jews of the Diaspora. In the main the parties represented fundamental social divisions in the nation.[1]

[1] See Eduard Meyer, *Ursprung und Anfänge des Christentums* (3 vols., 1921–1923); G. F. Moore, *Judaism in the First Centuries of the Christian Era* (3 vols., 1925–1927);

1. *The Sadducees.* The Sadducees were drawn from the wealthy and conservative section of the nation, being mainly well-to-do farmers, priests, and officials closely bound into the Jerusalem aristocracy. They had played a significant part in the struggle against Syria and were the leaders of the nation under the Maccabees. But after Pompey's intervention they became steadily weaker. They sought to preserve the state, with which, in fact, they identified the Temple; as political conditions became worse they advocated accepting Roman overlordship rather than inviting disaster by a resort to violence. They were opposed to the religious innovations, especially the doctrines of the immortality of the soul and the resurrection, the belief in angels and daimons, and the expectancy of a Messiah. They opposed this expectancy because it disturbed law and order. They held fast to the law but objected to the emphasis upon those parts of it which separated the Hebrews further from other people. It is said that they recognized only the Torah as the word of God.

2. *The Pharisees.* The Pharisees were drawn mainly from the middle-class townsmen—"polished city plebeians";[1] although strong in the synagogues, where, it may be believed they originated, they were mainly laymen until there sprang from their ranks the rabbis, who succeeded to the leadership of the nation.

As indicated by their name, which meant "the separated ones," they believed in strict adherence to the law. "The beginning of wisdom," they said, "is the fear of the Lord." In contrast to the Sadducees, they accepted the oral law as well as the Torah. But they also accepted many of the popular religious beliefs. They were ardent advocates of the doctrines of the immortality of the soul and the resurrection. They contributed much to the elaboration of angelology and daimonology. They joined in the

---

S. Zeitlin, *The History of the Second Jewish Commonwealth* (1933); Moriz Friedländer, *Die Religiösen Bewegungen innerhalb Judentums im Zeitalter Jesu* (1905).

[1] See W. O. E. Oesterley, *The Age of Transition* (1937), p. 123; also Louis Finkelstein, "The Pharisees: Their Origin and Philosophy," *Harvard Theological Review*, Vol. 22 (1929), p. 231: "It is curious that, from among the many foreign ideas which the Persians and Greeks brought to Jerusalem, only the notions of resurrection of the dead, the immortality of the soul, and the belief in angels and evil spirits should have been definitely accepted by the Pharisees. Upon analysis we shall find that these selected doctrines were especially expressive of the individualist point of view. In view of the close association of individualism with the conditions that make for urban life this is important. It furnishes additional corroboration of our basic hypothesis that the Pharisees were originally an urban group."

On the general history of the Pharisees see Louis Finkelstein, *The Pharisees: The sociological background of their faith* (2 vols., 1938); R. Travers Hertford, *The Pharisees* (1924); H. Loewe, *The Contact of Pharisaism with Other Cultures* (1937).

expectancy of a Messiah, but were inclined to believe that his advent would not be sudden. As advocates of religion in daily life, they elaborated rituals and prayers and developed considerably a charitable work that gave aid to the sick, the young, captives in war, and the aged. By the second century they held as dogma the beliefs in the resurrection of the body, the everlasting condemnation of the wicked, and the eternal joyousness of the life of the saved. They regarded the afflictions of the righteous as evidence of God's love and the prosperity of sinners as the lure that led them to greater punishment. As middle-class men they stood for and ultimately carried into effect certain modifications of the law. The master, they held, was not liable for damages perpetrated by a slave. Debts owed to a court of law were still valid after the seventh year, when debts to individuals were canceled. They took and gave interest. Married women were protected in certain financial rights. The slave was declared to be a person. Along with these modifications of the interpretation of the law went a softening of the disapprovals on trade and business.

During the wars of the Maccabees the Pharisees had been valiant soldiers, but as internal strife developed under Roman rule they tended to withdraw from politics. In fact, it was their representatives who requested Pompey to set aside the last Maccabean ruler and, later, went to Rome to ask for direct Roman rule. As long as religious independence was maintained, they saw no reason to take up arms; in fact, because the patriotic ideal provoked so much disorder they came ultimately to regard the state as an evil. They preferred law and order under Roman rule to revolutionary action that involved social conflict among the Jews. By strict adherence to the law they felt that the essentials of the traditional faith were preserved; the fate of the nation, they believed, could be safely left to God.

3. *The Zealots.* The Zealots, or "patriots," came from all ranks of society, though their strength undoubtedly lay in the peasantry and the urban working classes. Galilee has been called the cradle of zealotism,[1] a fact which suggests the strength of patriotism among the peasants; the close similarity of the Zealots to the Pharisees in religious outlook points to a distinct urban element in the party. Its distinguishing characteristic was the practice of resorting to violence in order to maintain religious and political freedom, for one without the other they regarded as useless. The Romans called them "robbers" and "knife throwers";

[1] Joseph Klausner, *Jesus of Nazareth: His life, times, and teaching* (1927), p. 153.

as conditions grew worse in Palestine they undoubtedly became the brigands who continually disturbed the country. After A.D. 6 they were, it seems, the chief instigators of the rebellions. They looked upon the payment of the Roman poll tax as a mark of slavery. Like the Pharisees, they adhered strictly to the law; but they were far more hopeful of the immediate coming of the Messiah—a king of the Davidic line—who, leading the nation in a "holy war," would raise the Hebrews to the overlordship of the nations. It is probably not an error to see the apocalyptic literature of the first Christian century as the propaganda of this most patriotic of the Jewish parties.

4. *The Essenes.* The Essenes—a minority of not more than four thousand persons—were passivists, who withdrew from the political, economic, and religious life of the nation. Avoiding the towns, they dwelt in small communities at the edge of the desert or on barren and rocky wastes. They wore white garments and ate the simplest foods. When an individual became a member of the sect he surrendered his property to the community and took a vow of celibacy. Thus members had to be recruited continually by conversion or by the adoption of orphan children. Only manual occupations were followed; slavery was condemned. Every community was governed by a leader, and the individual was free only to perform acts of mercy. The aim of religious life, which was highly ritualistic, was to establish a "perfect communion with God." Many practices, such as bathing only in cold water, were designed to purify the soul; magical rites and exorcisms were commonly performed. The Essenes studied medicine—chiefly magic, of course—in order to minister to the sick and the needy. At death, according to their belief, the soul, which had been imprisoned in the body, escaped and, if life on earth had been pure, went to an island of happiness beyond the sea. But if life on earth had been wicked, it went to a place of everlasting torment under the earth.

As to the sources of Essenic beliefs, some authorities find evidences of Buddhistic influence and others note Pythagorean and Orphic elements; it seems, however, that the main inspiration of the Essenes was a world-weariness induced by the economic misery and political disorders of the late Maccabean age. They are heard of for the first time just before the end of the second century B.C. It is probable that they represented the continuation of that strain of religious thought in Hebrew culture which had never found the customary piety sufficiently rigorous; foreign ideas and great social distress induced the extreme expression found in Essenic ideas and practices.

In summary, it may be said that these parties represent four typical reactions to a disturbed social order. The Sadducees said, "Accept the situation so that we may enjoy what we have." The Pharisees accepted the situation in the hope that it might become better. The Zealots held that the situation was so bad that nothing, even the loss of life itself, could be worse. The Essenes agreed with this view but rejected its conclusion in favor of complete negative action. Because the Hebrews could think only in religious terms, they gave each of these positions a religious orientation.

THE FINAL RENDERING OF JUDAISM: THE TALMUD.

The economic and political disturbances of the Maccabean and revolutionary ages constituted a process of social selection that was all-important in determining the form in which Judaism was finally rendered. The Sadducean aristocrats, always a small group, probably disappeared before the destruction of the Temple. The Essenes, because of their manner of living, were not able to perpetuate their views without a constant stream of new recruits, and after the rise of Christianity many who might have become Essenes probably accepted the new faith. The leaders of the Zealots were killed and the rank and file dispersed during the insurrections. When the Pharisees abandoned political action in favor of a religious quietism under the Torah, they took the step that guaranteed survival, and their prominence in the urban middle and working classes, which came to be the main elements of the dispersed nation, favored the growth of their influence. It was, therefore, the Pharisaic interpretation of Judaism which survived the revolutionary period. The outlines of this interpretation have been sketched previously; here it is necessary only to note the course of its evolution and the forms into which it was cast.

1. *The Mishnah.* The basis of the Pharisaic interpretation was, of course, the Torah, but by its side developed an authoritative oral tradition known as the Mishnah. The roots of this oral tradition were deep in the period following Ezra; perhaps its original creators were a group of scholars called the "men of the great synagogue." Toward the end of the third century B.C., a body of priests, including the high priests (and lay scholars) known as the "Great Assembly," closed the canon of the Prophets, created the Sanhedrin, and adopted prayers for use in the syna-

gogue. Following these developments the scribes, who composed commentaries on the law, not new books, became the chief carriers of the Hebrew religious tradition.[1] In the Maccabean age this tradition, still oral, of course, was elaborated by the Pharisees. These teachings had two aspects. The Mishnah was the statement of the law; the Midrash was the explanation of the law according to Biblical verses.[2]

In the middle of the first century B.C. two great teachers, Shammai and Hillel, founded schools which had great influence on the development of the oral tradition. Shammai emphasized the importance of ceremonials in daily life. Hillel (fl. *ca.* 40 B.C.– A.D. 1), a Babylonian Jew, who came to Palestine to study the Scriptures, remained to become a "prince of the Sanhedrin" and the "greatest of the Pharisees." It was said that he understood the languages of all men, all animals, and all daimons. He laid down the fundamental rules for interpreting Scripture which the great rabbis of succeeding centuries followed; according to these rules every word and accent was important in an understanding of the divine law. His ethical views expressed clearly the Pharisaic conviction that religion—the living law—should serve life; they may be judged from the following precepts:

Do not unto others that which thou wouldst not have done unto thee. Here lieth the first principle of the Torah; the rest is but the explanation thereof.

My abasement is my exaltation.

Judge not thy neighbor till thou standest in his place.

Man should be so clean as not to offend his guest.

Say not I will repent when I have leisure, for you may never have leisure.

Separate not thyself from the congregation.

From him flowed a love of peace, a kindness, a patience, a charity, and a moral optimism—indeed, a faith in divine justice—which

[1] See Louis Finkelstein, "The Oldest Midrash: Pre-Rabbinic Ideals and Teachings in Passover Haggadah," *The Harvard Theological Review*, Vol. 31 (1938), pp. 291–317.

[2] On the rise of Rabbinical Judaism see R. Travers Hertford, *Talmud and Apocrypha: A comparative study of the Jewish ethical teachings in the rabbinical literature and non-rabbinical sources in the early centuries* (1933); Ben Zion Bokser, *Pharisaic Judaism in Transition* (1935); J. Bonsirven, *Le Judaisme Palestinien au temps de Jésus-Christ* (2 vols., 1934–1935); G. F. Moore, *Judaism in the First Centuries of the Christian Era* (3 vols., 1925–1927); Gershom Rader, *The Jewish Spiritual Heroes* (3 vols., 1939); and Nathan Drazin, *History of Jewish Education from 515 B.C.E. to 220 C.E.* (1940).

served Judaism and the Jews well in the bitter centuries that followed his time.

Under the stresses of the first Christian century the rabbinical schools grew in both importance and number; by the year 135 every Jewish town maintained some kind of a school for the study of the law.

During the "great rebellion" Rabbi Jonathan, one of Hillel's disciples, founded a school at Jabneh. He taught patriotism to the law, not to the land—the best defender of Judaism, he said, was he who studied longest and taught best. He and the other great rabbis of the first and second centuries are called the Tannaim; they gave enduring form to the Mishnah. The council of Jamnia, which fixed the canon of the Jewish Bible, was led by Akiba (*ca.* 50–132). Pharisaic influence was responsible for the inclusion of the Song of Songs and the Book of Ecclesiastes in the canon. Akiba was also an early leader in the reaction against Christianity, a notable influence in the development of Judaism after the first century; in fact, the fixing of the canon of the Hebrew Scriptures was a primary aspect of this reaction. Later the reading of the Ten Commandments was eliminated from public recitations. Special prayers against heretics were introduced. The Septuagint and the allegorical method of interpreting sacred verses were repudiated. A highly literal Greek translation was made. Aramaic was barred from the synagogues. The missionary propaganda so widely spread after the Maccabean age was given up. Proselytes, it was said, were as troublesome to Israel as a tumor. And the tendency of the Jews to huddle together, especially on the Sabbath, was strengthened. Most of the outward characteristics of Judaism in Christian times are traceable to this reaction.[1]

Rabbi Mier, the greatest Jewish scholar of the second century, completed the work of codifying the Mishnah; its final statement, unwritten of course, was produced by Judah the Prince about 220. The contents were grouped under six headings: "Seeds," "Feasts," "Women," "Damages," "Sacred Things," and "Purifications." Its spirit, thoroughly legalistic, was expressed in the admonition, "Be equally conscientious in small as in great precepts, for ye know not their individual rewards."

2. *The Gemara and the Completion of the Talmud.* Once authoritatively rendered, the Mishnah became the basis of a secondary interpretation of the law; this took form in the Gemara, produced by scholars known as the Amoraim, who labored during

[1] See Louis Finkelstein, *Akiba: Scholar, saint and martyr* (1936).

the period from the early third to the sixth century.[1] At first the elaboration in this secondary manner went on in the rabbinical schools of Palestine, but slowly intellectual leadership passed to Babylonia. There labored Mar Samuel (*ca.* 165–257) and Abba Arika (fl. *ca.* 219–247), or Rab, who for eight centuries was the greatest Jewish authority; together they created the Babylonian Talmud. Mar Samuel introduced the innovation which declared the law of the country in which they lived binding on the Jews. Rab founded the school at Sura where the Babylonian Talmud was reduced to writing; this rendering was made partly because the oral tradition had become unwieldy and partly because Persian persecution was disturbing the congregations. The redaction was prepared under the leadership of Aschi (352–427), who, as head of the school at Sura, labored for thirty years, with a corps of rabbis, in editing and arranging the tractates of the Mishnah. The Palestinian oral tradition was also written down, but it never possessed the authority of the Babylonian compilation.

In consolidated form the religion of Judaism rested on a three-fold tradition: (1) the Torah, the divinely revealed law which had been given permanent form early in the fourth century B.C., (2) the Mishnah, the authoritative interpretation of the law, and (3) the Gemara, consisting mainly of disputes and contentions arising in specific cases. Together they formed the Talmud, which is to be understood, therefore, not as a single book but as a mass of literary materials of diverse content and form.

3. *The Essentials of Judaism in the Talmudic Rendering.* Under the political and social circumstances of Jewish life after the destruction of the Jewish state, its three chief institutions were the family, the synagogue, and the rabbinical school.

The Talmudic marriage laws were minute and strict. Every individual was in duty bound to assume the marital relation. Men were allowed to marry as many wives as they could support, but poverty limited most of them to one. The fidelity of the wife was taken for granted. Adulterers were punishable with death— a sentence the Jewish community could not enforce because it had

---

[1] On the Talmud see Meyer Waxman, *A History of Jewish Literature from the Close of the Bible to Our Own Day* (2 vols., 1938); H. L. Strack, *Introduction to the Talmud* (trans. from the 5th German edition, 1931); Dudley Wright, *The Talmud* (1932); A. Cohen, *Everyman's Talmud* (1934); M. L. Rodkinson, *The History of the Talmud, from the Time of Its Formation about 200 B.C. to the Present Time* (1903); M. L. Rodkinson, *New Edition of the Babylonian Talmud* (20 vols., *ca.* 1896–1903), reputed to be a poor English rendering. For selections see David Morantz, *Talmudic Tales* (*ca.* 1934); Moses Geldman, *Proverbs of the Sages: Collection of proverbs . . . from the Talmud and Midrashim* (1911).

no political power. Illegitimate children were considered outcasts. Under these and other regulations which governed family relations in every detail, the Jewish family became a closely knit unit, bound together by religious sentiment and mutual affection; it was, indeed, the very core of Judaism. Family descent remained an important form of social distinction among the Jews.

Just as the family bound together individuals, so the synagogue united the families in a community. It was the center of community life where the law was read, school was held, and charity administered. After the second century a liturgy was developed, standardized prayers were introduced, and hours of services were fixed. Inasmuch as the Jews did not think of the synagogue as a building, they used all sorts of structures as meeting places.

The rabbinical schools were the flowers of an educational system which had its roots in every synagogue. For every twenty-five children a teacher was appointed; thus literacy spread among the masses. The brightest scholars finally entered the rabbinical schools, where complete mastery of the Talmud was the goal of study. Scholars enjoyed high prestige, serving as the leaders of their communities but drawing little direct economic reward from their achievements. Most of them, it seems, lived by a craft or trade. Their rewards were immaterial:

A scholar always had precedence in the synagogue, in social gatherings, and even in court proceedings. Once having won great distinction, he was assured of immortality. For centuries to come, disciples would recite his words orally and finally they would be included under his name, in a sacred legal collection.[1]

The Talmud embodied the high intellectual tradition of Hebrew culture, and the men who studied it and read and interpreted it in the synagogues were a proud and haughty lot. They looked upon the common man and his objects as likely to be unclean, they deplored his laxity in paying tithes, they refused to summon him as witness in lawsuits or to appoint him guardian of orphans, and they disapproved of marriage between him and a member of their own families. Like other literate intellectuals, the Hebrew rabbis were aristocratic in outlook. And their intellectual methods were similar to the methods of the bearers of other high intellectual traditions, for in elaborating the Torah they argued by analogy, told fables, parables, and anecdotes, made puns, and sought

---

[1] Salo Wittmayer Baron, *A Social and Religious History of the Jews* (3 vols., 1937), Vol. I, p. 288. By permission of the Columbia University Press, New York.

allegorical meanings. Above all they regarded the law as perfect for all time, so that the glory of the law—its divine morality— became a worldly rigidity, and literate learning was devoted entirely to its perpetuation.

The doctrinal development in Talmudic Judaism was not rich. To the ancient beliefs in One God and the chosen people, the revealed moral and ritualistic law, the teachings of the Prophets about sin and the sufferings of the nation, and the belief in a Messiah, the rabbis added little but a clear view of life after death. On a universal day of judgment the dead would rise from their graves, and souls would unite with bodies no longer subject to infirmities; then the righteous would be rewarded with eternal life on a purified earth and the wicked would be punished in the everlasting fires of hell. After the disappearance of the Sadducees, who opposed the Messianic hope and the beliefs about life after death, the Pharisees made these doctrines dogma. The belief in the Messiah received less emphasis after the disasters of the second century A.D.

Besides the foregoing theological concepts the Talmud perpetuated the two main elements of ancient Judaism: (1) the ritualistic observances and (2) the moral law. The rabbinical regulations of rituals, particularly the observance of the Sabbath, the dietary regulations, the festivals, and the proper treatment of women and diseased persons were minute and prolix. The rabbinical interpretation of the moral law inculcated purity of personal life, family affection, mutual helpfulness in the community, and honesty in business. The economic outlook of the Talmudic teachers was purely rational; in other words, they approved of turning a penny any way that would make another penny. When political repression drove the Jews from agriculture, they took up urban economic pursuits, and when the Roman economic system declined they were left to carry on commerce, banking, and the slave trade—a calling which they monopolized during the early Middle Ages. The provision of the moral law which allowed them to charge interest to gentiles gave them freedom for business enterprise. They placed a high value on labor and disliked providing charity for those able to work. "Earn your wage" was their advice to the laborer.

The social attitudes of the rabbis were as harsh as those of their contemporaries.[1] Slaves, who after Nehemiah's time were non-

[1] On the social attitudes of the rabbis see Solomon Zucrow, *Women, Slaves, and the Ignorant in Rabbinic Literature* (1932).

Jews, were regarded as "mere asses," *i.e.*, beasts of burden. Although they were permitted a family life, masters could force them to exchange mates. All property acquired by a slave belonged to his owner, even money given to him by a benevolent person for the purchase of emancipation. If a slave was injured a master could collect damages to the extent of the work that might be lost in the present and in the future, but he was not required to feed a useless slave. The rabbis held that a master could refuse to feed a slave and still force him to labor, provided it was not a famine year, because the slave could beg food from kindly persons. The rabbis never expressed a kind sentiment toward the slave; in fact, they believed that one of the sins which brought poverty upon the well to do as a divine punishment was the sin of liberating slaves. The attitudes of the rabbis toward the "people of the land" were only a little less harsh than those toward slaves. Agriculture was not highly approved as a calling. The shepherd—the original Hebrew—was regarded as an uneducated and unworthy man. Such a man could not act as a witness in a lawsuit, could not serve as a trustee of charitable funds, and could not be appointed a guardian of orphans. Rabbis were not permitted to marry into the "people of the land," nor to eat with them. The knowledge of the curative properties of certain drugs was withheld from them, and in times of famine it was lawful to refuse to give them food. If among the "people of the land" there were some intelligent and well-mannered individuals who studied the Torah, the rabbis denied their ability to understand it. The effect of these attitudes was to set the rabbis in a privileged position quite like that which every priest class attempted to hold. Most of their harsh economic and social attitudes were merely doctrinal renderings of the class prejudices of urban cultures. Insofar, therefore, as the rabbis taught kindliness, charity, respect for labor, and the dignity of the individual, they limited the operation of such sentiments to Jews; for out-group individuals they preserved the traditional animosities and the practices of exploitation justified by them.

In final form Judaism was distinguished by a unity of observ-ances and a diversity of doctrinal speculations. Thus Jewish com-munity life everywhere followed the same pattern, while Jewish intellectual life, although confined to the study of the Torah and its elaborations, was free and active. But no important doctrinal divisions appeared among the Jews for several centuries after the formation of the Talmud, so complete was its authority. Judaism, more than any other religion, preserved not only the cultural tradition of a people but also a people. When the last disasters of the second century A.D. completed the dispersion of the Jewish nation, the nation lived only in Judaism; *i.e.*, Judaism received the in-group loyalties commonly organized in political forms. This result was the outcome of the early Hebrew identification of social experience with divine action.

THE SECULAR ASPECTS OF HEBREW CULTURE.

Scattered through the Bible and the Talmud, incidental to religious discussions, were bits of secular learning. Some of it survived from tribal times, a fair portion was Babylonian in origin, and a large part of it was borrowed from Greek and Hellenistic sources. The Hebrews neither produced nor possessed systematic scientific or philosophical works.[1]

The composite character of Hebrew secular learning is evident in mathematics. The decimal system of notation used for numbering the commandments and counting military forces and cattle probably survived from tribal times. The sexagesimal system, borrowed from the Babylonians, was used for measuring time, numbering sacred objects, and, until superseded in Hellenistic times, counting money. Thus the Hebrews spoke of the twelve months, the twelve tribes, the twelve gates of Jerusalem, the twelve precious jewels, and sixty shekels. The number 40 probably indicated an indefinitely large, not an exact, number. The Hebrews did not know abstract mathematics. One part of the Talmud deals with geometrical forms, such as the circle, the triangle, and the parallelogram.

In the Bible astronomical knowledge was cast mainly in Babylonian patterns. The cup-and-saucer view of the universe was accepted. God was believed to look down from heaven on men whom He viewed quite as men saw grasshoppers. By the late second century B.C. Hellenistic astronomical ideas became known to educated Hebrews but apparently they were not concerned with contradictions between these and the older Babylonian notions. The Talmud was permeated with astrological beliefs. The stars were described as armies fighting for orbits. The quality of Hebrew scientific thinking in astronomy is indicated by the fact

---

[1] On secular learning among the Jews see Alfred Bertholet, *A History of Hebrew Civilization* (1926), pp. 275–384; Salo Wittmayer Baron, *A Social and Religious History of the Jews* (3 vols., 1937), Vol. I, pp. 272–306; Charles J. Brim, *Medicine in the Bible* (1936); W. M. Feldman, *Rabbinical Mathematics and Astronomy* (1931); Jacob Snowman, *A Short History of Talmudic Medicine* (1935).

that the language contained no words for "world" or "universe"; the concepts "heaven" and "hell" were sufficient for the discussion of sky and earth phenomena.

Probably the most important Hebrew geographical idea was the belief that Palestine was the center of the earth; it was also believed that Palestinian air had a stimulating effect on the intellect. Arabia and Ethiopia were said to be connected, while the Nile, the Tigris, and the Euphrates were regarded as rising in the same place. The position of the lands about the Mediterranean Sea, even after the Dispersion, were only vaguely known.

Talmudic anatomical, physiological, and medical knowledge was simple.

The organs of the body, although clearly distinguished, were not understood as to function. The bones with muscles attached were numbered one hundred and one. The stomach brought sleep; the nose awakened and the liver generated anger. The eye, the most accurately observed organ, was regarded as a microcosm. Tears were classified as harmful and useful; those shed after an individual attained the age of forty were believed to be especially dangerous. God and both parents participated in conception. God gave life, the soul, facial expression, speech, vision, and hearing, the capacity for movement, and intelligence. The father contributed the bones, the tendons, the nails, and the brain. From the mother came the skin, the flesh, the blood, the hair, and the iris and pupil of the eye. The rabbis of Talmudic times were the advocates of prolonged nursing of infants.

The physician, who had a high reputation among the Jews, was commonly called "healer," a term also applied to God. The legal status of the physician was Babylonian in origin. Folk medicine permeated the Bible; in the Talmud it was mingled with Hellenistic lore. Very little of the scientific contents of Hellenistic medicine was known by the great rabbis. Rabbi Samuel, who wrote the medical precepts of the Talmud, claimed to know the cures for all ills except those that came from eating bitter dates on an empty stomach, from covering one's loins with a damp cloth, and from eating bread without walking four cubits afterwards. To his credit, he was opposed to many popular medical superstitions, although he had a high reputation as an astrologer. Diseases were believed to be caused mainly by violations of the dietary laws, which were regarded, of course, as sins, not as unhealthful acts. Compounded with this belief that disease was mainly a result of sin was the daimonic theory of disease, and exorcism, although not found in the Talmud, was long a prominent element in therapeutics. The Jews made no classification of diseases. Diseases of the mouth, colds in the head, and worms in the bowels received much attention. A fever was said to be a "fire from heaven." Rabbi Samuel had a specialized knowledge of eye diseases, said to have been acquired during a sojourn of eighteen months with flocks and shepherds. Epilepsy was believed to be hereditary; among its most likely causes were violations of the sex regulations. True leprosy—identified by the color of the lesions—was severely stigmatized; baldness was also regarded as deserving of social disapproval.

Therapeutics was as unscientific as other branches of medicine. Rabbi Akiba held the Hippocratic idea that every disease runs a course which could be offset by drugs administered at proper times. Vegetable drugs were believed to be the most efficacious remedies. The study of the law was recommended as a cure for headaches. Prayer was the common treatment for epidemics. The Hebrews objected to the taking of a census on the grounds that when large numbers of persons were gathered together epidemics were likely to occur. The pig, whose internal organs were like those of man, and the rat were believed to spread epidemics. Sanitary measures were taken to prevent disease. After meals, living rooms were fumigated. Clothes were not to be washed within a fixed distance of a well. A baker's oven was not to be kept under a house where fruit was stored. Threshing was not to be done inside a city. And tanyards were to be located on the east side of a city, at least fifty yards from the gate. An open wound or sore was not to be touched with the hands. Abscesses were opened, and cavities scraped. Water full of little reptiles was to be avoided. Vinegar and salt were used as mouth washes. Fractures were set with high skill. Because the extraction of teeth was condemned, an artificial tooth was commonly substituted for the one removed. The most dreaded injury was the bite of a mad dog. The desires of pregnant women were to be satisfied at all costs, because prenatal influences were regarded as having special significance for offspring.

After the Jews had fixed their religious and moral tradition they lost interest in social phenomena. They stopped writing history, and social and economic speculation was limited to matters arising in the application of the law. Their most important contribution to historiography was the teleological view of history, reinforced by a religious faith which made the view a basis of action. The Messianic idea was a corollary of the teleological interpretation of national history.

Recent archaeological discoveries indicate that the arts had a higher place in the life of the Jews of the Diaspora than has been commonly supposed. They made mosaics, rendered Biblical themes, including the female form, in murals, and developed an architectural pattern for the synagogues. The small place that art has had in Hebrew culture was due in part to religious beliefs and in part to life in foreign social environments.

THE GENERAL CHARACTERISTICS OF HEBREW CULTURE.

Viewed against the background of antecedent social and cultural developments, Hebrew or Jewish culture does not appear to be greatly different from the cultures of contemporary peoples. The basic assumptions of Hebrew thought were derived directly from primitive beliefs, and in spite of great refinements these presumptions were never abandoned. The monotheistic idea, developed largely as a result of an intense feeling of in-group solidarity, was after all a rendering of the concept "daimonic universe"; its identification with the concepts "righteousness" and "social justice" was the outcome, as in other cultures, of the consideration of social problems which the rise of cities caused. The law was formalized custom rather than a legal system given coherence by clearly formulated principles.

The weak elements in Hebrew culture were corollaries of the dominant ones. The concentration of attention upon the religious significance of phenomena obscured their natural aspects, which, if there was to be science, would have been its basis. Although the hatred of foregoing cults inspired the repudiation of idolatry and omenology, rationalism did not develop, for the Hebrews continued to believe in miracles and inspired visions. Their greatest art—poetry—reflected the emphasis on social experience in their thinking, for it expressed subtle psychological states with rare accuracy. This accuracy was due partly to the primitive tendency to emphasize striking details at the expense of abstract concepts and partly to the fact—again primitive—that their vocabulary was almost completely concrete. The lack of abstract terms in the Hebrew language undoubtedly contributed to the extremely important fact that the Prophets and later religious teachers kept the expression of religious ideas within the range of the understanding of the masses. In fine, the Hebrew low and high intellectual traditions never grew so far apart that either was not to be understood in terms of the other.

Certain by-products of Hebrew religious thought were extremely important; like its distinctive elements, these by-products had their origin chiefly in the fact that the Hebrews interpreted their social experience as aspects of the spiritual overworld. This orientation necessarily gave social experience through time, *i.e.*, history, special significance. Although the Hittites compiled the first historical chronicles, the Hebrews developed the first coherent view of the past, *i.e.*, an interpretation of history. This interpretation declared that through all past experience ran a purpose and that future events also would occur in accordance with the achievement of this purpose. For the Hebrews, of course, this end was the fulfillment of Yahweh's covenant with their nation; obviously, however, other peoples might conceive other final ends, and hence the teleological interpretation of history— once it was conceived—could have, as it has had, many renderings. In a similar manner the Hebrews invented a theory of politics, namely, that government is bound by a superior law. From this point of view authority, in whomsoever vested, is not free to act arbitrarily. For the Hebrews the limitations on authority were God's command; other peoples, of course, could devise other limitations. A third by-product of Hebrew religious thinking was the first system of popular education; this arose because of the belief that only through a knowledge of the religious law could an individual carry out the responsibility of observing God's commandments. Although this education taught individual moral responsibility, it was, as a matter of fact, the chief means of inculcating loyalty to the nation which survived only in religious observance. The Jews invented formal religious education as a mode of social control. These by-products, as well as the distinctive achievements, of Hebrew culture have had far-reaching influence in the development of the Western cultural tradition.

In conclusion, it may be observed, the evolution of the Hebrew cultural tradition ended as it began—in the sublimation of in-group feeling—for the belief in personal immortality, the distinctive addition to the tradition made in the Talmud, was conceived not so much as the mode of individual salvation as the means of the ultimate reunion of the nation. It was the religious concept necessary to restoration of the nation after the Diaspora.

CULTURAL DEVELOPMENT IN CENTRAL ASIA

Between the highland zone and the great northern forests stretched the plains of eastern Europe and central Asia; some places were well grassed, others sparsely, and in a few areas, which came to be especially prized, vegetation grew in both summer and winter. Across the grasslands—from the Hungarian plain in Europe to eastern Siberia—movement was easy. On the north the dense forests halted movement; to the south there were a few passages into the lands beyond the mountains—through the lower Danube valley into the Balkan peninsula and Asia Minor, through the passes of the Caucasus into the Armenian Highland, between the Kopet Dagh and Hindu Kush ranges into Iran and, by difficult passes, India, and by way of the Jungarian Gate to the Mongolian plain and the Huang valley.

Toward the end of the fifth millennium B.C. a peasant-village culture, known originally at Anau, appeared at the edge of the grasslands just east of the Caspian Sea; a millennium later other peasant-village cultures had arisen, in southwestern Russia the Tripolje culture and in north central China the Yang Shao culture. The similarities of their painted pottery permit a surmise that they were related; if this relation existed, it is possible to conjecture that peasant-village culture spread slowly between the grasslands and the forested foothills of the mountains, finding a home wherever water and soil were available. At any rate, throughout the known history of central Eurasia peasant villagers have clung precariously to scattered areas along its southern edge. The peasant was not an unknown sociocultural type in central Eurasia.[1]

On the grasslands, at least from the early third millennium B.C., pastoral or nomadic peoples found homes. Although cattle and sheep were important to them, horses were their distinctive possession. When they first became known in the ancient-oriental urban areas, they used the horse as the draft animal for carts, which they made their houses, and for chariots in which they went to battle. A little later, however, they began to ride the horse, and as horsemen they made their mark in history. Their culture has been well designated a "horse culture."

Because of the nature of the vast Eurasian plain the migration of the "horse nomads" over long distances was possible, so that the favorable areas were points of concentration. Such areas were found in the lower Volga valley, the Oxus valley, the Jaxartes valley, north and east of Lake Balkhash, and in Inner Mongolia bordering the Huang valley. The cultural development of central

---

[1] On the early Asiatic peasant-village culture and the environmental conditions which affected its spread see Raphael Pumpelly, editor, *Explorations in Turkestan Expedition of 1904. Prehistoric Civilizations of Anau Origin, Growth, and Influence of Environment* (2 vols., 1908).

CENTRAL ASIA

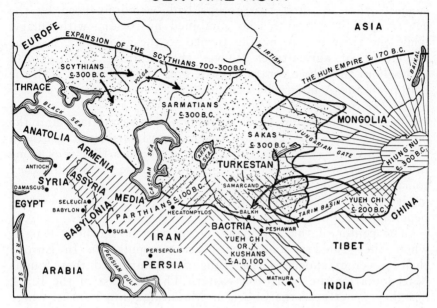

Asia was influenced, therefore, by constant interaction between these areas, as well as between them and the southern urban culture areas.[1]

THE INDO-EUROPEAN PEOPLES OF SOUTHEASTERN EUROPE AND CENTRAL ASIA: THE SCYTHIANS.

As previously mentioned, the place of origin of the Indo-European peoples is uncertain. But regardless of the exact location of their homeland, they appeared in history as a people of central Eurasia and until almost the close of the period surveyed in this book were dominant there.

At least three groups of Indo-European peoples emerged into recorded history—the Hittites and related peoples at the end of the third millennium B.C., the Celts, Achaians, Phrygians, Iranians, and Aryas about the middle of the second millennium B.C., and the Scythians, Sarmatians, Cimmerians, and Sakas and their neighbors in the eighth century B.C. Whereas the two earlier groups

[1] The best discussion of the horse nomads is William M. McGovern, *The Early Empires of Central Asia: A study of the Scythians and the Huns and the part they played in world history* (1939). See also M. I. Rostovtzeff, *Iranians & Greeks in South Russia* (1922); E. H. Parker, *A Thousand Years of the Tartars* (1924).

were peasant-pastoral peoples, the last were nomadic. This fact suggests that the first two groups had been influenced by the central Asiatic peasants who combined husbandry with tillage, while the third group, having turned to the grasslands, lost the knowledge of agriculture. It was their culture which spread throughout the whole central Asiatic area and interacted with the European and Asiatic urban cultures.

1. *The Scythians and Their Culture.* After the eighth century B.C. the Scythians and their neighbors, the Sarmatians and the Sakas, occupied the central Asiatic grasslands from southern Russia to Outer Mongolia. In Europe it appears that they came into contact with the Celts, while in Chinese Turkestan they touched an Indo-European people which held Kashgaria and lands toward the upper Huang valley; the Chinese knew these people as the Yueh Chi.

The center of the Scythians' power was in southern Russia, where they ruled a conquered peasant population. In Europe their power extended to the Hungarian plain, and they fought Macedonia for the control of eastern Thrace. East of the Black Sea they penetrated the Caucasus Mountains into Pontus, where they became a settled horse-raising people. Beyond the Caspian Sea they were a menace to the Persians, whom, like the Greeks, they had also encountered in the west.

The height of Scythian power coincided with the ascendancy of the Macedonians and Greeks, with whom they maintained close commercial relations. To the Greek merchants who brought them textiles they gave a protection under which, it seems, the merchants penetrated the lands east of the Caspian Sea; besides herds of horses and cattle, their wealth was derived from wheat grown by the conquered peasants and exported to Greece. In the third century B.C. the Sarmatians, having acquired a superior scale armor and a new type of sword, overthrew the Scythian empire; the remnants of the Scythians, like other defeated plains peoples both before and after them, seem to have taken refuge in the Crimea.

Scythian culture was an adaptation to the conditions of life on the grasslands.

The material aspect of the culture exhibited this fact in many ways. Horses, cattle, and sheep were the chief forms of wealth. The horse was primarily a military animal, although its flesh was eaten and mare's milk, especially when fermented, was used as a beverage. The main weapon was the bow, which was discharged from the back of a galloping horse with high accuracy. A short sword was employed for close fighting. The Scythian costume, adapted to horseback riding, consisted of trousers, boots, blouse, and cap. Originally these garments, except the boots, were made of leather, for the Scythians did not possess textiles. The boots were felt, of which their tents, or yurts, were also made. The Scythians lived in semipermanent tent towns, which were moved at the beginning and end of the winter season. Their domestic utensils were wooden, and their furniture consisted mainly of felt mats, carpets, and rugs. Metal, which was worked skillfully, was used only for weapons, for the fittings of saddles and bridles, which they greatly elaborated, and for jewelry. Since wood was scarce on the grasslands, they burned dung; they regarded fire as very precious.

As nomads the Scythians had a tribal organization, consisting of loosely knit units under chiefs who recognized the leadership but not the authority of a king; after creating an empire they were a warrior aristocracy ruling a conquered population. This development increased the power of the king, but his relation with the warriors remained feudal in character. Groups which moved away from the center of the empire were likely to become independent. Until they founded an empire the Scythians killed war captives, for they had no use for them as slaves; in the empire they possessed both slaves and serfs. Private property in herds, slaves, and consumption goods was recognized, but grazing lands were possessed in common. The boundaries of the grazing lands of the respective tribes were closely marked and guarded. The family was patriarchal and polygamous; and women were kept under severe restrictions. The aged and those regarded as incurably sick or injured were thrown to the dogs. Warriors gained prestige by collecting the scalps of the enemies they had slain.

The Scythian religion was polytheistic like the pre-Zoroastrian beliefs of the Iranians. Mithra and Anahita were the most important deities; Papoeus was a supreme father god. Sometime after contact with Asia Minor they borrowed the cult of the Mother Goddess, whom they knew as Tabiti; in general, however, they opposed the adoption of foreign religious beliefs. The chief intellectual figures were wizards who read omens and practiced magic, especially for treating disease. A special kind of magic was reserved for the treatment of the king's ailments. The metals were believed to have fallen from heaven. Gold was the symbol of the sun and the king. An artistic tradition, characterized by animal motifs and a polychrome style of surface decoration, was highly developed; the animals were commonly represented in combat or as slain by the hunter. The horse was the leading motif.[1]

Recent archaeological investigations indicate that this grassland culture carried eastward, long before the Hellenistic age, some Greek materials. The Scythians seem to have learned the making of textiles and the artistic working of the metals from Greek sources. Indeed, the transformation of tribal nomadism into the loosely knit warrior kingdom probably occurred in the course of the interaction between the Scythian tribes, the peasant villagers of southern Russia, and the Greek traders who began to come to southern Russia early in the eighth century B.C.

2. *The Indo-European Peoples in Turkestan after the Fall of the Scythian Empire.* After the fall of the Scythian empire before the Sarmatians, the center of Indo-European power shifted eastward. The Sakas pushed southward into the Jaxartes and Oxus valleys, where they founded a state; after Alexander's campaign it became, under independent Greek rule, the kingdom of Bactria and was noted for possessing a hundred cities. The height of its power was in the second century B.C. Late in this century, however, the Yueh Chi, driven from the Tarim Basin by the Huns, occupied the Oxus valley and created the Kushan empire, which shared with the Parthian kingdom the domination of central Asia and Iran until the third century. As previously noted, the cultures of both the Kushan and the Parthian empires had a Greek veneer, but their basic elements were Scythian and Iranian.[2]

THE RISE OF THE HUNS.

Chinese tradition from Shang times recorded the existence of non-Chinese people on the upland plains north of the Huang valley, but they were not horse nomads. Probably the first considerable impact of the horse culture of central Asia upon eastern Asia occurred about the time the Chou descended into the Huang valley and overthrew the Shang. The evidence now available indicates that the Tarim Basin, Outer Mongolia, and Inner Mongolia were inhabited at this time by a people now commonly known as the Turki; racially they have been identified as a highly specialized branch of the Alpine division of the white race. Ap-

---

[1] For a discussion of the Scythian religion see O. G. von Wesendonk, *Das Weltbild der Iranier* (1933).

[2] See W. W. Tarn, *The Greeks in Bactria and India* (1938); Neilson C. Debevoise, *A Political History of Parthia* (1938).

parently they occupied these lands before the rise of the Hiung-nu, or, as later known, the Huns. This Mongoloid people seems to have originated from a mixing of the Chinese with the Turki in Inner Mongolia. About the beginning of the sixth century B.C. they began to borrow the Scythian horse culture and, shortly afterwards, to create an empire.

1. *The First Hun Empire, Third and Second Centuries B.C.* During the period of the rise of Ch'in to the overlordship of China, the Huns created a center of power in Inner Mongolia; Shi Huang Ti, the first Ch'in emperor, built the Great Wall to hold them in check. Under Maodun, or Baghdur (*ca.* 209–174 B.C.), who took the title Heaven's Son Immense, they drove the Yueh Chi westward, conquered Kashgaria, and took possession of Outer Mongolia. Maodun improved the tactical efficiency of the horsemen by introducing the practice of shooting at a command and centralized his rule by establishing an elaborate feudal hierarchy. He was able to check the Han, who succeeded the Ch'in in China, but later under Wu Ti the Chinese broke the Hun control over the routes to the west and occupied Kashgaria.[1] Once the Chinese obtained the "supernatural horses" of central Asia they adopted cavalry as the chief military arm and, because their metalwork was superior, crowded the Huns out of the areas suitable for tillage.

After the second century B.C. the first Hun empire slowly declined, but the Huns absorbed as much of the Chinese urban culture as their poor land would support. Thus they mixed the Scythian horse culture with Chinese urban materials to create that power which, when the great empires weakened in the third century, swept like wildfire through central Asia and to the very centers of urban culture.

2. *The Huns as a World Power in the Fourth and Fifth Centuries A.D.* Throughout the second and third centuries the power of the Huns in Mongolia increased, and they spread westward as far as the Oxus. In the fourth century they entered on the career of conquest which shook every center of urban culture from China to western Europe.[2]

After the fall of the Han Dynasty the Huns were called into China as mercenary troops, and they remained to become conquerors. Shortly after the opening of the fourth century they established a kingdom in Shansi and a few years later conquered

[1] See p. 804.
[2] See W. M. McGovern, *The Early Empires of Central Asia: A study of the Scythians and the Huns and the part they played in world history* (1939).

the Huang valley, sacking the Chinese capitals, Changan and Loyang. Their inroads into southern China were not checked until near the end of the fourth century. Meanwhile their compatriots on the central Asiatic steppes pushed westward into southern Russia, where, on the Dniester River, they halted the eastward march of the Goths, a Teutonic people. After this defeat the Goths pushed into the Roman Empire, and the Huns followed them westward, settling on the Hungarian plain. Around this center they created a shadowy empire, and after 433, when Attila became king, they struck out in all directions. In 435 they subdued southern Russia; in 445 they attacked Constantinople; in 451 they penetrated Gaul, where they were turned back by a Teutonic-Roman army in the battle of Châlons.[1] From central Asia the Huns menaced Persia and India. In 425 they crossed the Oxus River. In 455 they invaded India and, a little later, destroyed the empire of the Gupta Dynasty. In 484 they broke the power of the Sassanian Dynasty in Iran. But the force of the Huns, except in China where they controlled the Huang valley, was finally spent. Shortly after Châlons they retired from the Hungarian plain to southern Russia. Early in the sixth century they were expelled from India, and a little later from Iran. Between 563 and 567 the Persians and the Turks drove them from the Oxus valley.

The extent of the Hun conquests is evidence of the cultural unity which, with the rise of the great empires, bound all centers of urban culture together.

THE SIGNIFICANCE OF CENTRAL ASIATIC CULTURAL DEVELOPMENTS.

There is little reason today to believe that these movements of the horse nomads over central Asia and into the peripheral areas of the urban cultures were due to periodical droughts; rather they were due to an interaction between the nomads and the urban peoples which contributed to the cultural advance of the nomads. The Scythians rose to power through contacts with the Greeks, the Parthians through contacts with the Hellenistic rulers of Iran, and the Huns through contacts with the Chinese. Because the lands of these peoples did not provide the economic base for an urban culture, they tended, as they borrowed industrial and military techniques from the neighboring urban culture areas, to become a greater and greater menace to them. But their activity was predatory: they plundered and then dispersed after the loot

[1] See p. 1091.

By the courtesy of the India Office. From Sir Aurel Stein, *Innermost Asia (4 vols., Clarenden Press, 1928)*

HORSES FROM CHINESE TURKESTAN

This is a drawing on paper from Khotan in Chinese Turkestan; it is dated in the sixth or seventh century. The nearest horse is roan, the next gray and brown, and the third sorrel. The life-like quality of the drawing testifies to the keen attention the peoples of the central Asiatic horse culture gave to their all-important animal.

had been consumed. This fact accounts for the relatively short life of the empires set up by these peoples of the plains and steppes. Few, indeed, were the nomadic conquerors who learned to rule a settled people. But the force of their conquests was great. They destroyed populations and broke up local institutions. They killed men and seized women, leaving a trail of half-breeds in their wake. For a time their violence paralyzed all resistance, and its ultimate result was to stamp even the ancient-oriental monarchy with their predatory characteristics. Government became harsher, and exploitation more cruel.[1]

Yet, the central Asiatic nomads made some contributions to civilization. Aside from the horse, which they domesticated, chief among them is the now prevalent male costume, especially trousers. This garment was their invention, and from them it was diffused into China, Iran, and Europe. The continental Celts were the first people in Europe to wear trousers; the garment spread from them to the Teutons, and from the Teutons to other European peoples. The nomadic costume was taken over by the Chinese, for both men and women, probably in the fifth century B.C. The nomadic artistic tradition also had wide effect, especially in jewelry design.

Finally, the nomadic peoples opened the first channel of communications between western and eastern Eurasia and served for centuries as the chief intermediaries between their respective cultures. Recent discoveries indicate that the northern route across central Asia was important before, during, and after the burst of traffic over the southern route through Bactria and the Tarim Basin in the period from the first century B.C. to the third century A.D.[2]

---

[1] *The Cambridge Medieval History*, Vol. 1, *The Christian Roman Empire and the Foundation of the Teutonic Kingdoms*, (1936), p. 359.

[2] G. F. Hudson, *Europe & China; a survey of their relations from the earliest times to* 1800 (1931), p. 37. See map facing p. 664.

Chapter XIII

THE CONSOLIDATION OF THE INDIAN
CULTURAL TRADITION

≪≪-≪≪-≫≫-≫≫

Over the thousand years from the middle of the last millennium
B.C. to the middle of the first millennium A.D., five among several
dynasties—the Mauryan, the Sunga, the Andhra, the Kushan,
and the Gupta—exercised imperial sway in India or in parts of
it, and under them Indian culture developed the main patterns
that even now shape Indian life. The chief factor in the consolidation of the Indian cultural tradition was the struggle of the Aryan
Brahmans to maintain their position against domestic rivals and
foreign foes. This struggle generally took form in the rivalry of
Brahmanism and Buddhism. The Sunga Dynasty promoted a
Brahmanical reaction, and the Andhra kings championed the
Brahmans. The Buddhists had the support of the Kushan invaders. During the first and second centuries A.D. Brahmanism
became identified with Indian in-group loyalty, while Buddhism
was more and more associated with foreign influences. Under the
Gupta Dynasty Brahmanism, especially in eastern and southern
India, achieved a golden age, while Buddhism, except in the north-
west, began to decline.[1]

THE EBB AND FLOW OF IMPERIALISM IN INDIA

The roots of Indian imperialism were in the rivalries of the
states which had appeared in the central Ganges valley in the

[1] On the development of Indian culture in the early Indian empires see H. G. Rawlin-
son, *India: A short cultural history* (1937); G. T. Garratt, editor, *The Legacy of India*
(1937); P. Masson-Oursel, *Ancient India and Indian Civilization* (1934); A. A. Macdonell,
India's Past: A survey of her literatures, religions, languages, and antiquities (1927); R. C.
Dutt, *A History of Civilization in Ancient India Based on Sanscrit Literature* (3 vols., 1889);
Sri Ramakrishna Centenary Committee, *The Cultural Heritage of India* (3 vols., 1936).
For material from non-Indian sources see J. W. McCrindle, *Ancient India as Described in
Classical Literature* (1887); S. Beal, *Buddhist Records of the Western World* (1865). Archae-
ological data are to be found in two works by John Marshall, *Guide to Taxila* (1921) and
Guide to Sanchi (1936).

sixth and fifth centuries B.C., but it flowered under the stimulus of foreign invasion. Darius, the great organizer of the Persian empire, held Gandhara in the upper Indus valley, and Alexander, the Macedonian conqueror, merely followed his footsteps to India. Under the influence of the former a few of the Indian princes seem to have reorganized their governments and their armies, and the latter's invasion roused them to active resistance.[1] Throughout this early period Iranian influence was undoubtedly a decisive factor at every step in the organization of an imperial regime.[2]

The Mauryan Dynasty (*ca.* 321–184 B.C.): the Golden Age of Buddhism.

The first of the several Aryan states in the central Ganges valley to rise to political prominence was Magadha, consisting, it is said, of eighty thousand villages. Its first great king was Bimbisara (*ca.* 540–490 B.C.), who checked the pacifistic influence of Buddhism by an arrangement with Buddha which hindered the entrance of village supervisors and soldiers into the sangha. He seems also to have paid great attention to the army. The imperial career of Magadha began with Chandragupta Maurya (*ca.* 321–297 B.C.), who, having seized the throne by force and introduced Persian military practices, drove the Greeks from the Indus valley and organized a state covering central India from Magadha to Gandhara. Under his grandson, Asoka (*ca.* 274–236 B.C.), the empire was extended westward toward Iran and southward into the Deccan.

But the misery and destructiveness of war led Asoka to abandon imperial projects in favor of peaceful achievements. He is commonly known as the imperial apostle of Buddhism; for a time at least he was a monk. He conceived that as a king he should instruct his subjects in the duty—*dhamma*—of right living;[3] to do this he introduced Buddhistic teachings into a series of edicts which, inscribed on pillars, survive today as the first written documents of Indian history.

---

[1] See p. 608.

[2] See D. B. Spooner, "The Zoroastrian Period of Indian History," *Journal of the Royal Asiatic Society*, 1915, Part II, pp. 405–455. For the political history of ancient India see E. J. Rapson, *Ancient India* (1914); V. A. Smith, *The Early History of India* (1924); K. P. Jayaswal, *History of India 150 A.D. to 350 A.D.* (1933); R. Basak, *The History of North-eastern India . . . (c. 320–760 A.D.)* (1934).

[3] The words *dharma* and *dhamma* signify "law," the former in Sanskrit and the latter in Pali, the language in which the Buddhist scriptures have survived. When speaking of Buddhism the correct word is, therefore, *dhamma*, and when speaking of Aryan orthodoxy

THE MAURYAN EMPIRE c̲250 B.C.

At the core of Asoka's instruction was the doctrine of harmlessness. He forbade the killing at any time of parrots, wild geese, bats, ants, tortoises, squirrels, porcupines, lizards, rhinoceroses, pigeons, and all quadrupeds neither useful nor edible. Fish were not to be caught or sold on fifty-six days of the year; on some days it was forbidden to brand horses. The slaughter of domestic animals was strictly limited. No animal was to be killed until it was six months old. This passion for the protection of life did not extend to human beings. Men were put to death for killing animals, even for eating meat. Asoka kindly allowed condemned men three

---

the correct word is *dharma*. It should be noted also that the Buddhist concept of the law embodies more of the idea "duty" than does the Aryan orthodox concept.

days to prepare for death. The duty of men to each other was summarized in the commandments to revere parents, to tell the truth, to be charitable, and to be tolerant. Superiors were required to treat inferiors with kindness. In addition to gifts to the needy, which were administered by special officials, the charitable Asoka planted shade trees along the roads, dug wells at regular intervals, established resthouses, and cultivated herbs useful as medicines. His care of travelers was merely an official support for the custom of making religious pilgrimages. There is no record indicating that he lightened the burden of the peasants upon whom Chandragupta had imposed a yearly tax of one-fourth of the produce of the soil.

The tolerance which Asoka taught was grounded in the conception that at the heart of all religions was a universal morality; as universal king, he was merely performing his proper royal duty in aiding all sects to realize what was, after all, their common purpose. Although he taught Buddhist doctrines, he never repudiated the caste system. As a matter of fact, he heaped favors upon Brahmans and Jains as well as Buddhists. His conceptions of empire and kingship were derived from Persian sources, but whereas the Persians allowed various subject peoples and sects to retain their own customs, he undertook to develop among his subjects the observation of a universal moral law. His benevolence was well expressed in the formula: "Law aims at the happiness of all creatures."[1]

The Theory and Practice of the Oriental Monarchy. In spite of the humanitarian tone of the Mauryan regime, it was actually a monarchy of the traditional oriental type, and it produced the fullest statement of the theory of that form of government to be found in any language. Its author is said to have been Chanakya, or Kautilya, the chief minister of Chandragupta; however this may be, for there is evidence that the work—the *Arthasastra*—was compiled at a considerably later time, it sums up the practices and precepts of the early Mauryan age.

Chanakya did not regard the king as a god; however, the king was divine in nature—the soul of the body politic—and performed his religious duty only by performing his secular task, which was to enforce order as it had evolved through the ages. Only by holding fast to the ancient customs could a king keep the affection of the people; therefore, only in righteousness, according to the established religion, was there political

---

[1] V. A. Smith, *Asoka, the Buddhist Emperor of India* (3d ed., rev., 1920); V. A. Smith, *The Edicts of Asoka, in English with an Introduction and a Commentary* (1909); J. M. McPhail, *Asoka* (1918); D. R. Bhandarkar, *Asoka* (1925); Francis J. Monahan, *The Early History of Bengal* (1925); Edmund Hardy, *Indiens Kultur in der blütezeit des Buddhismus; König Asoka* (1902).

security. The choice of a successor required the utmost skill, for the wives and concubines of the harem and their respective sons were always a source of faction. Great care was given to the education of the heir, for a dynasty was safe only so long as its members were well disciplined in the exercise of power. Chanakya constructed a schedule which regulated every detail of the king's daily life. Certainly this schedule was not adhered to in practice, for the king undoubtedly enjoyed a gross luxury. But his was also a life of fear. Chandragupta never slept two nights in succession in the same room; nor did he dare to nap during the day. He was surrounded by a bodyguard of foreign women, and his intimates, except for a few advisers, were the members of his harem. Megasthenes, a Greek ambassador at his court, well indicated its atmosphere by the comment that the murderess of a king became the wife of his successor.

The functions of government were four in number: (1) to expand the country by conquest, (2) to preserve what was gained, (3) to increase the wealth of the country, and (4) to enjoy it. This conception of government made warfare and diplomacy the leading activities of the state. Chanakya laid down definite rules for their conduct: "He who has the advantage should march"; "He who is growing strong should make war"; "He who is weak should make alliances against a strong neighbor"; "Evil conditions among the people are an opportunity to the enemy"; and "Treat a newly conquered people kindly and do not disturb their customs." Special care was given to the army. Its main divisions—elephants, cavalry, chariotry, and infantry—were equipped with the best possible weapons. These were to be obtained mainly from state shops. Chandragupta is said to have maintained an army of 9,000 elephants, 30,000 horse, and 600,000 infantry. In order to prevent revolts by the army, different nationalities were mixed together and sent to parts of the country where they were strangers. Diplomacy was carried on chiefly by matrimonial alliances; its objectives were to win allies and to sow discord among enemies and rivals. The height of success was "to bind the princes with the fetters of cleverness and play with them at one's pleasure." Treachery was the leading practice of statecraft.

The preservation and increase of the wealth of the country was the duty of boards which maintained a strict regulation over every aspect of economic life. Chanakya named departments for goldsmiths, warehouses, trade, forests, mines, weights and measures, tolls, textile manufacturing, pastures, cows, slaughterhouses, ships, passports, and agriculture. Highways and ships were provided for merchants. Craftsmen were subject to boards of conciliation and arbitration which seem to have guarded them against the abuse of employers. The workers were fined for delays in performing their tasks. Agriculture, the chief economic support of the state, necessarily received constant attention. The killing of milch cows, bulls, and calves was prohibited. A department of meteorology was established to forecast weather conditions. The clearing of lands and the

By the courtesy of SIR JOHN MARSHALL

PATALIPUTRA

Recent excavations have verified the Greek tradition that Pataliputra, the capital of the Mauryan empire, was surrounded by well-built wooden walls. Parts of them are to be seen in this photograph. The timbers were fastened together with irons.

construction of irrigation ditches were prime duties of the state. In order to promote production, the encouraging of migration, the founding of new villages, and the building of fortresses to protect the cultivators also were important and continuous tasks. Manufacturing, carried on largely in the king's shops, was another leading source of wealth. In the markets the king's merchandise was displayed in special booths. Prices were fixed in each market by inspectors.

In Chandragupta's time six commissions sat at Pataliputra, the capital of Magadha; besides guiding the paternalistic administration of the economy, they performed the king's duty of protecting the people against the eight visitations of god—fire, flood, plague, famine, rats and mice, beasts of prey, snakes, and daimons. Asoka seems to have increased greatly the duties of the inspectors who acted under these commissions.

Chanakya recognized the value of humanitarian measures to the king. He recommended that special care be given to aged persons, orphans, and pregnant women. Poor women, widows, crippled women, and reclaimed prostitutes were provided with jobs in state textile factories. Orphans were fed and clothed. The sale of spoiled meat in cities was prohibited, as was also dealing in liquor near forts and camps. Prostitution and gambling were minutely regulated. State endowments were established to maintain amusements for the people. Actors, dancers, mimics, jugglers, and scribes were supported at the king's expense. The medical profession was required to serve the sick and the needy at fixed costs. The state searched for and grew herbs useful as medicine. In time of famine the king prevented the well to do from hoarding grain, but no supplies were set aside regularly for such an emergency.

The king's revenues were derived from several sources, chief of which, of course, were the royal estates. From earliest times land revenue was the basis of Indian state finance. Forests, mines, factories, and markets also were exploited for the enrichment of the royal treasury. The state was, in fact, the leading economic enterpriser. Fees were charged to landowners and cultivators who drew water from royal irrigation ditches. One-sixth of the produce was taken from each cultivator. Cultivators were also subject to forced labor. Robbery was likewise considered a proper means of obtaining revenue. Chanakya advised that heretics, guilds of laborers, and rich widows could be robbed without arousing antagonism. He also noted that thieves could be incited to plunder merchants, and that after they had done so they could be executed as criminals and the plunder seized. He recommended, too, the setting up of false religious shrines in order to obtain funds. Royal accounts were kept by a large staff of clerks, divided into sections according to the various departments of the government. Embezzlement, of which forty kinds were recognized, was punishable with death. Of special importance in fixing the revenue was the census, organized in a permanent office under an inspector general. The villages were classified according to the amounts and kinds of revenue they paid; the census of cities was made by special officers. Much of the work of the spies charged with maintaining domestic order was carried on in connection with the census.

The chief support of social order was an impartial justice administered under a stern code. "Government," said Chanakya, "is the science of punishment." There were two levels of courts, village and royal, and besides the judges an army of inspectors, spies, informers, and *agents provocateurs* participated in bringing evildoers to their bars. These secret agents—nine classes of them—were the chief arm of the state in maintaining domestic peace. Spies adapted their methods to the four classes into which the people were believed to fall—the haughty, the greedy, the angry, and the timorous. Some operated under the cloak of religion. Others used torture. Still others incited disputes in order to learn who was hostile to the king. The criminal code of the Mauryan state, in line with Chanakya's views, was extremely cruel. There were fourteen kinds of common torture and eighteen kinds of superior torture. Adulterers were forced to embrace a red-hot image. Anyone who committed a crime against a member of the king's harem was cooked in a great copper kettle. Plotters against the king were compelled to sit on a red-hot iron throne. Most common criminals were executed by trampling or impalement, but some were subjected to such refined methods as the pouring of molten metal down the throat, skinning alive, and starvation. Mutilations and fines were imposed on criminals not sentenced to death. Drunkards were branded. Caste status was taken into consideration in ordering punishments.

It is incorrect to think of the Indian oriental monarchy as a state organized under law; rather it was a military regime extracting wealth from its subjects by terror. It produced no civil law distinguishable from the customs of the villages and the regulations of castes. The sentimental gentility of Asoka's Rock Edicts was the expression of religious feeling rather than the rendering of any conception of justice. Just as India never developed a conception of political liberty, so she never arrived at the idea of legal justice; government was not extricated from the maze of religious speculations which pervaded the Indian mind. In fact, Chanakya went into considerable detail about the use of magic in politics. He regarded it as a means of protecting the people from calamities, of keeping the armies from fatigue, and of making secret agents invisible. He advised that during a war the enemy be proclaimed a defiler of the gods and an associate of the evil spirits. To the mentality of his age such acts as the defilement of shrines and the association with evil spirits were the supreme atrocities.[1]

IMPERIAL DYNASTIES IN INDIA, 200 B.C.–A.D. 500.

After the death of Asoka the Mauryan empire slowly disintegrated. The spread of Buddhism undoubtedly weakened the princely group by drawing its members into the sangha, where, under the rules of celibacy, their lines died out. At the same time lax military organization hastened the collapse of the army; the last Mauryan emperor was slain at a review of the army by its commander, who became the first of the Sunga line (*ca.* 184–72 B.C.). The last of this dynasty was also destroyed by an assassin, a slave girl whose lover became king.

In early Mauryan times Aryas filtered into the Deccan, whose peoples took over from them the Vedic religion and the Aryan village structure. In the third century B.C. a dynasty known as the Andhra (225 B.C.–A.D. 225) arose in the delta of the Godavari and Kistna rivers; late in the first century B.C. an Andhra ruler conquered Magadha and won control of the lower Ganges valley.

---

[1] On the political ideas of Chanakya or Kautilya, see Beni Prasad, *Theory of Government in Ancient India* (1927); U. N. Ghosal, *A History of Hindu Political Theories* (1927). See also M. H. Gopal, *Mauryan Public Finance* (1935); N. N. Law, *Studies in Ancient Hindu Polity (based on the Arthasastra of Kautilya)* (1914).

THE GUPTA EMPIRE c. A. D. 400

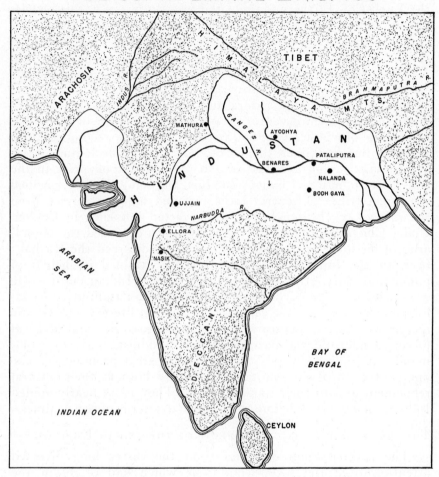

At its greatest extent the empire of the Andhras, included most of the Deccan and central India.

In northern India the Bactrian Greeks followed eastward the retreating Mauryan power, until Milinda or Menander (*ca.* 180–160 B.C.), the greatest of the Greek princes to rule in India, attacked Magadha itself. His power was confined, however, to the upper Indus valley. As indicated by the Indian work, *Milinda Pandha* or "The Conversations of Milinda,"[1] the Greeks adopted the culture of the land. They fell before the Scythians, who, in

[1] See p. 779.

turn, were overwhelmed by the people whom the Chinese called the Yueh Chi. In the middle of the first century B.C. this people, known as the Kushans, invaded northwestern India; under their greatest king, Kanishka II (*ca.* A.D. 120–162), they ruled an empire which included Bactria, Afghanistan, Gandhara, and Kashmir. Its capital was at Peshawar. The Kushan empire was the creation of the last Indo-European invaders of India.

On the ruins of the Andhra and Kushan empires, which alike broke up in the third century, rose a second empire of Magadha, the revival of whose power had begun in the early second century. Its new imperial line, the Gupta Dynasty, ruled from about 320 to 535. Samudragupta (*ca.* 330–375), who took pride in the title "exterminator of kings," subdued the Ganges valley, pacified the forest tribes of central India, exacted military service from the princes of the northwest, and exerted influence in Ceylon. Under Chandragupta II (*ca.* 375–413), who extended the boundaries of his dominion to the Arabian sea and forced the Kushans back to the Indus, the Gupta Dynasty attained its height of power and glory—the golden age of classical Indian culture. He was believed to be Vishnu's regent on earth. Pataliputra, Ayodhya, and Ujjain were the centers of a brilliant literary and artistic life, as well as the focuses of commercial prosperity and political power. Under Gupta patronage the Buddhist monastic community and university of Nalanda rose to great prominence. The fine gold coins of the Gupta kings testify both to their cultural refinement and to their imperial glory. They more nearly unified India than any rulers before the English overlords of recent times.

The Social and Economic Aspects of the Indian Empires.

The concentration of interest on the castes long diverted attention from the social conditions which had origin in the technological and economic aspects of early Indian culture; glimpses of these conditions are provided by meager references scattered through religious writings.[1]

[1] On the social and economic history of ancient India see, Pran Nath, *A Study in the Economic Condition of Ancient India* (*Asiatic Society Monographs*, Vol. 20, 1929); U. N. Ghoshal, *The Agrarian System in Ancient India* (1930); N. Banerjee, *Economic Life and Progress in Ancient India, Being the Outlines of an Economic History of Ancient India* (1925); Richard Fick, *The Social Organization in North-East India in Buddha's Time* (1920); E. H. Warmington, *Commerce between the Roman Empire and India* (1928); H. G. Rawlinson, *Intercourse between India and the Western World from the Earliest Times to the Fall of Rome* (1916); S. C. Britton, "Iron in Ancient India," *Nature*, Vol. 134 (1934), pp. 238–241.

1. *The Growth of Indian Commerce.* As previously noted, commercial contact between the Indus valley and Mesopotamia existed certainly in the third millennium B.C., and there is little reason to believe that it was ever completely broken off. When Alexander the Great arrived at Taxila it was a thriving commercial center frequented by a cosmopolitan group of traders from both east and west.

In Mauryan times India took a permanent economic place in the world of urban cultures and, in later times, broadened its influence. Routes through Bactria and Arachosia led to Persia and Transcaspia. A sea route connected the lower Indus and Narbudda valleys with Mesopotamia by way of the Persian Gulf and with Egypt by way of the Red Sea. Over these routes flowed the commerce that, until the opening of modern times, was the main channel of cultural intercourse between the East and the West. In Kushan times the routes through the Kabul River valley to Persia and through Kashmir and across the Tarim Basin to China were alive with traders and, perhaps, religious teachers; rivalry between the Kushans and the Parthians for the control of the trade with the West led the former to cultivate friendly relations with the Romans, who avoided the Parthians by using a route across southern Iran. At the same time mariners from Egypt developed a direct route by sea to the western coast of the Deccan and Ceylon. Broach, at the mouth of the Narbudda River, became the entrepôt of this trade. The Gupta age found Indian and Chinese merchants moving around the Malay Peninsula; perhaps the Chinese reached India, but the Indians hardly went farther than Java and Sumatra. Ujjain became the center of the internal trade flowing westward through Broach.

Because the religious law forbade Hindus to go overseas, India's external trade remained mostly in the hands of foreigners. The internal trade was both wholesale and retail. Merchants traveled in great caravans, sometimes comprising, it is said, as many as a thousand bullock carts. The retail trade was carried on by local shopkeepers, who dealt mainly in salt, spices, textiles, and rice. Every village had a trader or two. Robbers and petty thieves constantly preyed on them.

2. *The Indian Crafts.* Besides semitropical and tropical plant products—poisons, medicinal herbs, aphrodisiacs, and spices—India's exports were mainly fine goods and wares produced by her craftsmen. With simple tools they created fabrics, jewelry, and metalwares surpassing those of any other land in refinement

of workmanship and design. The source of their skills was undoubtedly the ancient village technical traditions; however, their perfection in many crafts was probably due to the introduction of iron tools, presumably a little after the opening of the first millennium B.C. Indian ironworkers performed feats impossible to Western workers until modern times. An example of their skill is the Iron Column of Delhi (A.D. 310), almost twenty-four feet high and weighing about six tons. It was built up by welding together thin disks of pure, rustless, malleable iron. Indian metallurgists were probably the first makers of steel. When money was introduced the Indian metalworkers did not borrow the Western method of striking coins.

Traders and craftsmen were organized in guilds, partly for purposes of royal regulation and partly for reasons of self-government. The guilds were cooperative associations which preserved the traditions of the crafts. In the main they centered about the temples and the markets. The merchants joined together more for protection on the highways than for control of trade. Except for the heavy tolls levied by the king or prince in whose domain the merchants gathered, trade was free.

3. *The Development of Money Economy in India.* Before Mauryan times the merchant guilds, towns, and a few private merchants cast crude coins; the Mauryan emperors made minting a royal monopoly, but they never developed a regular coinage. They commonly used Athenian or Persian pieces. The Kushans introduced a gold coinage based on the Roman model, and the Guptas followed their lead, issuing two kinds of gold coins. Only in areas of Greek influence did Indian coinage progress; outside those areas most of the coins were crude squares or strips of metal, usually copper or silver, marked with a punch. Except in the commercial centers, money never played an important role in Indian economic life. There, however, banking appeared and interest taking became common. The usual rate of interest was 15 per cent, although it sometimes went as high as 25 per cent. Among the concessions made by the Brahmans was the recognition that men who took usury did not lose their caste status.

4. *Indian Urban Life.* The Indian cities increased in size rather than multiplied in number, with the result that urban influences instead of penetrating more deeply into the life of the people remained concentrated at a relatively few points. Thus the cities produced a growth of luxury among the well-to-do classes rather than an awakening of social movements among the people.

The merchants, probably as often foreign as they were native in origin, never became sufficiently numerous or wealthy to challenge the princes or the Brahmans, who alike drew support from the peasant-village masses. For this reason the Indian empires never possessed the power or cohesion necessary for a long life.

Before the Indian cities were centers of trade they had been shrines or fortresses, and so they remained. They were fortified with walls, bastions, and gates. Tall polished pillars supported the gabled fronts of the houses of the well to do. Windows were covered with brightly painted lattice work. Semicircular stairways led from floor to floor; some buildings are said to have had seven stories. Paintings and draperies ornamented the walls of incense-filled rooms, usually furnished with upholstered beds and large, soft cushions; the floors were sometimes bare and highly polished, sometimes covered with rugs. On the roofs were terraces for gazing at the stars and the moon. The bazaars were centers of a ceaseless chaffer. There, along with false weights, counterfeit coins, and adulterants, were to be found the products of the seventy-two recognized crafts. The temples were quite as much amusement centers as places of worship. They were built in parks and surrounded by pools, flower beds, shelters against the sun, and sight-seeing stands, to which the people flocked when religious processions were held. These processions were enlivened by acrobats, dancing girls, pantomimists, jugglers, and singers. On less noisy occasions the temples and parks became the haunts of amorous couples. The princes went about always on parade, sometimes on elephants, at other times on horses; frequently they were carried in palanquins. Always they were protected by umbrellas and accompanied by standard bearers, musicians, and dancers; often they added the color of garlands of flowers to the hues and tints of their richly embroidered robes. Luxury was most resplendent at the baths, to which came rich and poor, men and women alike. Mauryan women went about freely; restrictions of their movements came with the rise of Hinduism. Both Brahmanical and Buddhistic rites emphasized cleanliness, a virtue encouraged by the pleasures of scented waters, oils, unguents, and massage. Through this life of display and luxury ran a strain of licentiousness.

5. *The Indian Aristocracy.* The Indian aristocracy was composed of princes, who, as landowners, lorded it over the peasant villagers and, as warriors, conspired against their kings. The politico-economic unit of Indian life was the great estate, consisting of many villages from which the princely or royal owner drew

income in kind. Every day the cultivators supplied their lords with fresh vegetables and fruits, and in the year they paid a share of their crop—sometimes an eighth, at other times a fifth, or a fourth, or a third, and on occasions a half. Royal officials received milk, grass, firewood, and vegetables wherever they went. In return for the land granted from the king, the princes were obligated to furnish troops, which were subject to the king's order. To guarantee the performance of duty the king held some member of the prince's family, usually the heir, as hostage. The princes also paid a lump sum each year as a tribute; Indian kings knew twenty-five kinds of tribute to levy on their vassals.

The kings and the princes never formed a consolidated ruling class, for they were usually at odds with one another. Federations of princely families constantly menaced royal power, and plots were endless. Sometimes even thieves and wild native tribes were brought into them. Political disorder was, therefore, a normal condition in Indian states.

When opposed to the peasant-village masses the aristocracy was, however, a united class, possessing a monopoly of political power and maintaining a social superiority which its members understood quite as the Western world in more recent centuries has understood the concept "gentleman." The arts and luxury—refinements in every form—were for their enjoyment. They were above labor; love, intrigue, and warfare were their proper occupations. The Indian aristocracy was probably smaller in proportion to the total population than the ruling class of any other urban culture.

6. *The Indian Peasant-village Masses.*　At the base of Indian culture were the tillers of the soil who lived in the self-governing villages. A few craftsmen, who served the village needs for manufactured wares, also lived there. Each village had a watchman, an accountant, a headman, and a special officer to look after watering places. The overlord was represented in the village by the headman, often his appointee, and a tax collector. Local affairs were supervised by a council of patriarchs, *i.e.*, the heads of the local castes. Each head of a family had rights in the land, which, however, was owned by the prince or king; when computing the yearly revenue, the village council dealt with the tax collector. The accountant kept the village land register, and the headman rendered justice in disputes between the villagers. These officials lived in fairly well built houses of seven or eight rooms. Ordinary villagers dwelt

in one- or two-room structures of sun-dried brick; the poorest villagers had only huts of branches and leaves. Every village had a shrine or a temple, a bazaar, and a special meeting place where gossip was the main business. Astrologers, bards, and wizards found ways of living in every village. Chanakya recommended that actors, jugglers, and buffoons be kept away from the villages in order to prevent disturbances. Two kinds of magic, the charming away of tigers and of hailstorms, were universally practiced. Sometimes the villages were fortified with a mud wall for protection against robbers; at times thieves who had bribed the officials terrorized the countryside.

Among the peasant villagers were different social levels; all were toilers, but their conditions varied. Many of the farmers were Aryan freeholders; some, however, were tenants and subtenants, who had little or no right in the land. Then there were landless laborers who worked for hire, many of whom had only a temporary right of residence in the village. In accordance with Chanakya's teachings, all tillers of the soil paid a share of their crop to the overlord and were liable to forced labor. There were two grades of workers—the *Sudras* and those having no caste status. The Sudras were fit only to work for the upper classes; they were compelled to wear clothes thrown away by the twice-born castes and were not allowed to accumulate money. Those outside the caste system were the dregs of society; under no circumstance could they acquire a right to land or practice an honorable profession. There were fifteen varieties of slaves. Some were born to servitude; others were captives of war or of raids, commonly made by robber bands for the purpose of catching men and women to be sold into slavery; and still others were freemen who had lost their liberty. If a freeman left home to become a monk and failed to do so, he became the king's slave.

The poverty of the Indian masses was never ameliorated, for, regardless of rulers, India remained a poor land. Crop failure from drought and flood was common. Technical advance was unbelievably slow. In agriculture it seems to have halted very early; in the crafts, however, there were advances throughout the imperial age. The metals were scarce. Depopulation by famine and pestilence was recurrent. Migration was continuous. A wandering existence was sanctioned by religion. Warfare and banditry took a constant toll of life and property. At best government was only an orderly exploitation of the masses. Thus in the villages were always the miseries of a life that became old and impoverished before it was young and prosperous.[1]

THE REORIENTATION OF INDIAN CULTURE IN THE IMPERIAL AGE

Along with the rivalry of Brahmanism and Buddhism played other factors which helped to give Indian culture its enduring form. The spread of literate learning among the princes compelled the Brahmans to modify the ancient Vedic religion so as to accommodate the princely ideal. The growth of the non-Aryan population —a result of the Aryan penetration of southern India—replaced old rituals and dogmas with even more primitive practices and beliefs. These two developments aroused the fear of the Brahmans that the caste system, which the Kushan emperors, inspired by Buddhism, repudiated, would break down completely. At the same time Greek cultural materials, notably coinage, military tactics, and artistic methods and motifs, and Persian craftsmanship and religion filtered eastward and southward from the Indus Valley. The product of these developments was Hinduism—a blend of Brahmanical philosophies, princely ideals, and primitive beliefs. Under it the Brahmans preserved their ancient social ascendancy at the expense of unity of religious beliefs.[2] They continued to be the spiritual advisers of the kings and princes and the guardians of the sacred law which was enforced in secular, as well as in caste, courts. In contrast to the Vedic religion the distinctive element in Hinduism was an emotionalism which permitted the common Indian to attain through worship the salvation Brahmans gained by ritualistic performances and mental discipline. The root of this emotionalism was, perhaps, the psychological reaction of the masses to the disturbance of their primitive way of life caused by the development of urban economic and political organization.

The Development of Literate Learning and Literature in India.

The original stimulus to learning in India was the debates between heretics—the Jains, the Buddhists, and others—and the

---

[1] On the relation of the poverty of the Indian people to the development of their religion and philosophy, see P. Masson-Oursel, *L'Inde antique et la civilisation indienne* (1933), pp. 134–135.

[2] D. R. Bhandarkar, *Some Aspects of Ancient Hindu Polity* (1929), pp. 30–31: "When the power and glory of the old Kshatriya families was supplanted . . . the only indigenous class in India who profited by this political upheaval was the Brahmans, who were chiefly instrumental in Hinduizing the alien tribes by converting them to brahmanism and above

orthodox Brahmans. In the Mauryan age the kings promoted such discussions, and men who excelled in them ranked with princes. But these disputations produced only an oral learning. Neither the heretics nor the orthodox believers seem to have rendered their traditions in writing until late in Mauryan times. Although, as suggested by Asoka's edicts, a wide knowledge of writing may have existed in ancient India, there is no evidence that his age knew written books. The earliest known Indian manuscript dates from about 350, when books were in common use all over northern India. But the dates of their origin and their first multiplication are not known. The oldest known books of northern India were written on birch bark; in the south they were written on specially treated leaves. Perhaps the fragile character of these writing materials accounts for the disappearance of India's earliest written works. Inasmuch, however, as Indian learning long remained primarily oral, this loss has probably not obscured the general outlines of Indian intellectual development.[1]

1. *The Rise of Universities in India.* The chief intellectual institution of ancient India was the university, a center where many scholars gathered to pursue various branches of learning. The roots of the university, like those of the Buddhist sangha, were undoubtedly in the shelter or "rain retreat" to which the Brahmans went during the monsoon, and its development was advanced by the growth of the sangha. In Buddha's time there were two centers of learning, Kasi and Taxila, where the Aryan religion and language were studied, but the earliest university may have been the product of his movement—Nalanda, founded, perhaps, about the opening of the fourth century B.C. It has been called the Oxford of Buddhist India. Other Buddhist universities arose at Taxila and Peshawar. Brahmanical universities, the greatest of which seems to have been at Kasi, appeared first just before the opening of the Christian era.[2]

The curriculum of the universities grew out of the specialization of various fields of learning. At its base was grammar, to which Panini (fl. *ca.* 350 B.C.) had given a scientific analysis; it was

---

all furnishing them with an epic-old pedigree and thus conferring social status on them. The power of the Brahmans gradually increased in this manner until they became supreme. And there was hardly any part of the social fabric or any branch of literature to which they did not give a shape which was consonant with their power and importance." Benares Hindu University.

[1] S. V. Venkateswara, *Indian Culture through the Ages*, Vol. I, *Education and the Propagation of Culture* (1928).

[2] See Hasmukh D. Sankalia, *The University of Nalanda* (1934).

By the courtesy of SIR JOHN MARSHALL.

NALANDA

Nalanda, located in Bihar, the original home of Buddhism, was long the intellectual center of the Buddhist world. Besides the monasteries, whose ruins are seen here, its chief structure was a great stupa. Recent excavation, which revealed that the stupa was enlarged on six different occasions, brought to light many evidences of the encroachment of Hinduism upon Buddhism.

regarded as the open door to all higher intellectual pursuits. His book, *Doctrine of Words*, explained the origin of words (from verbal roots) and the functions of suffixes. His successors of the second and first centuries B.C. refined his rules and conclusions. Medicine, the fine arts, logic, and philosophy were introduced into the curriculum as time went on; the Brahmanical universities studied politics and caste law as well as these subjects. Some universities specialized in one or two fields of learning. It became customary for students to nail topics, *i.e.*, theses, which they would defend, to the doors of the pavilions where public discussions were held. Indeed, these universities were the original centers of that type of learning known in Western intellectual development as scholasticism.

The earliest type of scholasticism was the Buddhist, and this is just what we should expect, considering that Buddhism was at once a very early religion, antedating Christianity by some five centuries, and that it manifested from the beginning a scientific attitude. In fact, pure Buddhism was the most scientific of all religions and Buddhist scholasticism developed rapidly and reached its climax, the Hindu climax, under Buddhaghosa in the first half of the fifth century. . . . [1]

Buddhaghosa (fl. *ca.* 425), the greatest representative of Buddhist scholasticism, is said to have written commentaries on the entire canonical literature of Buddhism. In connection with the development of scholasticism, it should be noted that the useful arts were not admitted to the university curriculum; only the fine arts, such as dancing, mimicry, antics, magical tricks, and the aesthetic furnishing of bedrooms, were thought worthy of study.

Most of the great emperors were patrons of the universities, and some of the scholars had political influence. Because both the scholars and the students at the universities formed cosmopolitan bodies, sectarian zeal was low and the patriotic bias weak. Foreign learning was appreciated. In this connection it may be pointed out that Greek learning did not promote in India either a literary development or an intellectual movement; its influence was exerted chiefly through a slow infiltration into the sciences and, perhaps, the philosophies.

2. *The Beginnings of Secular Literature in India.* As if to balance the elaboration of religious and philosophical studies among the Brahmans and Buddhist monks, new intellectual interests appeared among the princes and the people. The princes took to writing poetry and debating philosophical ideas, and the people called for household guides for ritualistic practices and caste law. These popular law books, compiled of course by Brahmans, circulated mainly in low-caste circles. At the same time writing came into use in the law courts, for public business, the registration of land and taxes, and the keeping of both public and private accounts. Chanakya's organization of administrative departments presumed the continuous keeping of full records and accounts.

The language of this spreading literate learning was Sanskrit, the tongue of Brahmanical oral learning. In the second Christian century Sanskrit became the official language of the more impor-

---

[1] George Sarton, *Introduction to the History of Science*, Vol. 1, *From Homer to Omar Khayyam* (1927), p. 26. Published for the Carnegie Institution of Washington by the Williams & Wilkins Company, Baltimore.

tant northern Indian states; in southern India native languages
were adopted as official.

The spread of literate learning gave India a secular as well as a
religious literature. The chief literary products of the Indian
imperial age were (1) the great epics, the *Mahabharata* and the
Ramayana, (2) the *Upanishads*, short religious poems for memorizing, (3) *sutras*, brief philosophical guides, in prose, for learning,
(4) *sastras*, didactic verses presenting philosophical and legal principles, (5) *dramas*, *i.e.*, plays of secular interest, (6) *animal tales*,
and (7) the *Puranas*, the scriptures of later Hinduism.[1] Under the
Guptas, scholars gathered the scattered materials of earlier
centuries in the enduring codifications of Indian learning. Beside
the epics, which were given a final editing about A.D. 200, the chief
works of this character were the *Arthasastra*, the political treatise
ascribed to Chanakya, the *Dharmasastra*, a compendium of the
laws of caste credited to Manu (fl. *ca.* A.D. 100), the *Panchatantra*, a
collection of animal tales, and the eighteen Puranas, accounts of
creations, the descent of the gods, and the genealogies of kings.
The earliest philosophical and scientific works also were made
in these times.

Since the religious literature will be dealt with in the discussions
of Hinduism and Buddhism, only the epics, the dramas, and the
animal tales will be noted here.

3. *The Indian Epics.*   The *Mahabharata*, a long poem of over
twenty thousand verses, described the struggles of kings and the
rise of a great empire under the direction of the mighty warrior-god
Krishna, who was noted more for trickery than for piety.[2] The
composition of the poem probably was begun in the course of the
eighth-century B.C. struggle between the two waves of Aryan
invaders in the upper Ganges valley; the great empire which it
reflected was probably the early Mauryan state. In the second
century B.C. the princely caste began to elaborate the poem, and
the Brahmans introduced into it didactic material explaining their

---

[1] For the history of Sanskrit literature see H. H. Gowen, *A History of Indian Literature
from Vedic Times to the Present Day* (1931); A. B. Keith, *A History of Sanskrit Literature*
(1928); Moriz Winternitz, *A History of Indian Literature* (1927); Ernest P. Horowitz, *A
Short History of Indian Literature* (1907); A. A. MacDonell, *A History of Sanskrit Literature* (1900).

[2] See R. C. Dutt, *The Ramayana and the Mahabharata Condensed into English Verse*
(1929); J. C. Oman, *The Great Indian Epics; The stories of the Ramayana and the Mahabharata* (1899); E. W. Hopkins, *The Great Epic of India* (1902); G. J. Held, *The Mahabharata:
An ethnological study* (1935).

philosophy, theology, and law. Thus by the second Christian century the poem was not only a narrative of warfare and political intrigue but also a vast compilation of religious teachings. The *Bhagavad-gita*, or "Divine Song," which states the ideal of the new Hinduism, is part of it.

The *Ramayana*, composed by Valmiki (fl. *ca.* 200 B.C.), was the first narrative poem in Sanskrit; it gave an account of the great hero, Rama, an incarnation of the god Vishnu, who brought to an end a conflict that disturbed all India. The events of the story seem to reflect the struggle between the Kshatriyas and the Brahmans during the period of Aryan penetration of southern India:

The Ramayana. The gods were troubled. Ravana, a daimon, had obtained power over them by performing the astounding ascetic feat of standing on his head amidst five fires for several thousand years. Escape from his tyranny could be made only with the aid of men and monkeys.

In this crisis Vishnu volunteered to come to the aid of the gods by being born into the royal family of the king of Ayodhya; thus when the king's three wives bore sons, Rama, the child of the first wife, was one-half Vishnu, Bharata, the child of the second wife, was one-fourth Vishnu, and twins, the offsprings of the third wife, were each one-eighth Vishnu. As a baby Rama put his big toe in his mouth, cried for the moon, and spoke brokenly. But he grew rapidly and, at the age of eleven, was initiated into the princely caste.

His adventures began at once. In a distant realm, to which he had made a dangerous journey, he won a beautiful bride, Sita, and obtained possession of the great bow of the god Siva. On the way home he encountered and killed a notorious enemy of the princes; in this fight he proved that he could bend the great bow of Vishnu. At his father's court he encountered intrigues. The mother of his half-brother Bharata brought the king to appoint him heir to the throne and order Rama into exile. But Bharata, more noble than his ambitious mother, refused to rule except as Rama's regent.

Upon going into exile Rama, accompanied by his bride, Sita, and one of his half-brothers, Lakshmana, went toward Ceylon where Ravana, the daimon, ruled. On the way he was met by the sister of Ravana, who promptly fell in love with him. When the daimoness, enraged by frustrated passion, attacked Sita, Rama cut off her nose and ears. War with Ravana followed immediately. Although defended by the king of the vultures, Sita was captured by the daimon; before dying the bird told Rama and Lakshmana that only with the aid of the monkeys could they destroy their enemy. But the throne of the kingdom of the monkeys was in the hands of a usurper, whom Rama had to overthrow before the rightful king would be free to join in the war against the daimon and his hosts. Once this noble work was completed, the monkeys, under the great general Hanuman, who took leaps sixty miles long, marched southward. He first attacked Ravana by means of a stratagem. Disguised as a cat he invaded the court, where he heard Ravana's plea for Sita's love and her haughty refusal, to which the daimon replied with a threat to devour her. At this point Hanuman was recognized by the daimonesses of the court; in the fight which followed, he killed many of them and then escaped northward, spreading destruction far and wide, by means of the torch he made by setting his tail on fire. In the north he recruited an army of monkeys and bears which he led to Ceylon, crossing the sea on a bridge built by Rama. Squirrels had filled the cracks between the timbers of the bridge by carrying dust in their tails. The new army of bears and monkeys met the daimonesses in battle outside the walls of Ravana's stronghold. At the outset of this battle Indrajit, son of Ravana, entangled Rama and Lakshmana in a noose of serpents from which they were rescued by Vishnu's bird, whose odor the snakes detested. But the heroes were finally slain by Ravana's brother. In order to restore them to life Hanuman dashed northward to obtain a sacred herb; when it could not be found, he carried The Himalaya south and with their odor brought the princes and the slain monkeys back to life. This feat turned the tide of battle against Ravana. He fled into his city, set it on fire, and with his son perished in a final bloody struggle.

With the rescued Sita, Rama returned northward, where he became maharaja not only over his native realm but also over the conquered dominions of his enemies. The gods again received the sacrifices the daimons had been stealing, and all was well again on earth and in heaven.

When translated into the vernaculars of India, the *Ramayana* became the favorite poem of the nation and Rama its leading hero. Statues of Hanuman were placed at the doors of the temples of Vishnu, and in the city of Ayodhya troops of sacred monkeys were kept at public expense. Scenes from the poem were used as motifs in the arts, particularly sculpture, and many of its legends became folk beliefs. Among the most charming of these legends is the account of the churning of the ocean to produce a beverage that gave immortality.

4. *The Indian Drama.* The drama developed in India as a part of the temple worship of the new Hindu gods, Vishnu, Siva, and Krishna. The first Indian treatise on the theater was written about the end of the first century B.C.; the earliest dramas survive from the close of the second Christian century. The plays had simple plots that always ended happily. Actors depended on

gestures and dancing for effects quite as much as on interpretation of character. No scenery was used on the stage.[1]

Among the early dramas the best-known is *Mrichchakhatika*, or "The Little Clay Cart," which tells how a Brahman, although a merchant, won a courtesan for a second wife. Everything came out all right in the end because, when a revolution put a herdsman on the throne, he lifted the courtesan out of her lowly caste by making her priestly husband the governor of a province. The moral of the play is:

> Fate plays with us like buckets at a well,
> Where one is filled and one an empty shell,
> Where one is rising, while another falls;
> And shows how life is change—now heaven, now hell.

Kalidasa (fl. *ca.* 400), the most famous poet of India, rendered ancient legends and popular tales in both dramas and lyrics. His *Sakuntala*, which has been played on the Western stage, deals with the love of a prince and a maiden, who, kept apart by parental objections and public interest, are finally united. A ring, which is lost and found, plays a great part in the plot. His *Ritusamhara*, or "Cycle of the Seasons," contains lovely pictures of nature, for example, the following description of Autumn:

> . . . a maiden fair
> In slenderness and grace,
> With nodding rice stems in her hair,
> And lilies in her face.

Some of Kalidasa's dramas and poems were translated into the languages of Tibet and Ceylon, where his renown became as high as it was in India.

5. *Indian Animal Tales.* The animal tale was probably a creation of preliterate men; its greatest literary development occurred in India. Apparently the earliest collection of animal tales was made late in the third century B.C. in Kashmir, a land where Greek influence may have been at work. The *Panchatantra*, the most widely known collection of animal tales in the world, was completed in the age of the Guptas; since then the tales have been reproduced in twenty-five different recensions in India and diffused through Persia, China, and Europe.[2] These tales form a "textbook

---

[1] See A. B. Keith, *The Sanskrit Drama* (1926); A. W. Ryder, *Kalidasa, Translations of the Shakuntala and Other Works* (1928); and Mary B. Harris, *Kalidasa, Poet of Nature* (1936).
[2] A. W. Ryder, *The Panchatantra, Translated from the Sanskrit* (*ca.* 1925).

of wise conduct"; in other words, they explain how to get along in the world as it is. They mark no saintly path, only the path of wit, fair dealing, and good judgment. Most of the characters are animals, like the friends, Lion Rusty and Bull Lively, who fall out, to their mutual loss. The social attitude of the tales reflects an aristocratic bias:

> The wind is friend to forest fire
> And causes it to flame the higher;
> The same wind blows a candle out.
> Who cares what poor folks are about?

Apparently the tales were used in both Buddhist and Brahmanical schools.

In the general qualities of ingenuity of plot, lively imagination, sound observation of nature and men, and dramatic arrangement of material, the literature of India compares favorably with the literature of any other country. In range of sentiment—from austere religious feeling on the one hand to unashamed eroticism on the other—it exceeds all ancient literatures except the Greek.

The Rise of Hinduism.

Those developments in Indian society which weakened the position of the Brahmans caused them to accept modifications of their beliefs that would hold new adherents. Since these adherents came almost exclusively from the native peoples that filtered into the lowest caste, the modifications generally tended to strengthen the primitive at the expense of the philosophical and the emotional at the expense of the ritualistic elements. The competition of Buddhism and Jainism favored the growth of asceticism. The combined effect of these tendencies was to make Hinduism a religion of composite beliefs and practices which, centering around the acceptance of the social leadership of the Brahmans, was quite unlike such dogmatic religions as Christianity and, later, Mohammedanism.[1]

In the growth of Hinduism three main phases are recognizable. (1) From the third century B.C. to the second century, as evidenced

---

[1] On Hinduism see J. N. Farquhar, *A Primer of Hinduism* (2d ed., rev., 1912); J. N. Farquhar, *An Outline of the Religious Literature of India* (1920); Charles N. E. Eliot, *Hinduism and Buddhism* (3 vols., 1921); and L. D. Barnett, *Hindu Gods and Heroes: Studies in the history of the religion of India* (1922). For discussions of Hindu customs see L. S. S. O'Malley, *Popular Hinduism, the Religion of the Masses* (1935), and Stanley Rice, *Hindu Customs and Their Origins* (1937).

in the *Mahabharata* and the *Ramayana*, native beliefs were mingled
with the teachings of the Vedas and the Upanishads; the chief
result of this mingling was the advance of the gods Vishnu and
Siva to positions of prominence alongside Brahma in the Hindu
pantheon. (2) During the second, third, and fourth centuries the
new sectarian beliefs were correlated with the chief philosophical
ideas of the Brahmans; the outcome of this correlation, best
expressed in the *Bhagavad-gita*, was an ideal, which in spite of the
almost infinite variety of belief and practice, gave a central point
of spiritual orientation to Hinduism. (3) In the fifth and sixth centuries the new beliefs were codified in the Puranas which explained
the mythological descent of some god or the mystical significance
of some doctrine. The Puranas, pieced together from earlier
materials, formed a Hindu sectarian literature. Together with the
epics they became the sacred work of popular Hinduism. The
Bhagavad-gita has been honored by Hindus as the New Testament
has been cherished by the Christians and the Koran by the
Mohammedans.

1. *The Theology of Hinduism.* The chief gods of the new
Hinduism were Brahma, Vishnu, and Siva. As previously noted,
Brahma was the sublimation of the Brahman caste as the universal
soul, the single principle of reality, pure spirit. As creator of the
universe all things flowed from Brahma and back to him; associated
with him was Sarasvati, the goddess of learning. Vishnu, known
in the Vedas as Rudra, a storm- and thunder-god, was identified
with Brahma as the "Absolute One"; actually he became a
personal god, whose *avatars, i.e.,* incarnations, took many forms—
animals, men, and gods. The great heroes of the epics, Krishna
and Rama, were avatars of Vishnu. Krishna, originally a dark-
skinned charioteer, became the Savior-God—the "blessed lord"
of Hinduism. Vishnu's consort was the goddess of wealth, Lakshmi.
Siva, who personified the abstract forces of nature, was known both
as "the destroyer" and as "the merciful." As the destroyer he
was depicted as a fierce and cruel dweller in graveyards; as the
merciful god of creative powers he was conceived as a garland-clad
dancing figure. He was also thought of as a sage, an ascetic, and a
musician. Associated with him was Parvati, the daughter of The
Himalaya, an Earth Mother; chief among her forms were Uma the
Gracious and Kali the Black—a terrible goddess of destruction—
with four arms, fanglike teeth, and red eyes. Siva and Parvati
represented the male and the female principles of procreation;
when they embraced the world shook.

The emergence of these gods as the principal Hindu deities did not weaken the belief in many other gods. In fact, the whole host of deities, spirits, and devils of the daimonic universe remained, and the dread of their influence was universal. Every local village had its own godling to which the natives turned when the great gods seemed far away, particularly on occasions when suffering was great. And everywhere the ancestral spirits were regarded with awe and reverence. Thus the mingling of Brahmanical and popular beliefs resulted in little more than the reshaping of the conceptions of the leading gods of the pantheon. In the first place they became personal gods, *i.e.*, easily approachable by men. This development transformed the Aryan nature religion into a theism. In the second place goddesses were associated with the deities, largely in accord with the Dravidian emphasis upon the female principle in nature. And in the third place the gods took many forms—for example, Vishnu was believed to have had ten important avatars. By means of this belief in incarnation the multitude of gods was blended together in a grand unity, conformable to the whole of nature; at the base of the hierarchy was the host of spiritual beings known to all primitive peoples, while at its summit was Brahma, the principle of pure spirituality. Hinduism compounded gross superstitions with a philosophical conception of the deity.

Under these gods man could win either an absolute or a relative immortality. By austerities and meditation he could achieve complete absorption in the absolute deity, Brahma; by devotion and strict adherence to the rules of his caste he could win a residence of thousands of years in heaven, after which he would be reborn into a fine family on earth. Complete release from the cycle of births and deaths was attained only by those who were merged with Brahma. Those who achieved relative immortality were born again into one or the other of the four ages through which the universe was believed to move. In the first, or golden, age, which after a dawn of four hundred years endured four thousand years, men lived happily under a single Veda; this age brought the development of castes. During the second age, which after a dawn of three hundred years lasted three thousand years, virtue declined one-fourth, numerous religious rites appeared, and asceticism became a means to the attainment of spiritual perfection. During the third age, which after a dawn of two hundred years endured two thousand years, virtue declined by one-half, passion became dominant, ceremonies were multiplied, increasing ignorance led to the appearance of four Vedas, and sin and disease beset men.

In the fourth age, which after a dawn of one hundred years lasted only a thousand years, virtue declined three-quarters, religion decayed, the Vedas were ignored, and sin became unbearable. At the end of this age—the Brahmans of the Gupta era interpreted their time as such a period—a universal destruction, first by fire and then by flood, occurred, and all things, gods as well as men, were absorbed in Brahma, who then fell into a great sleep of one thousand cycles of twelve thousand years each. At the end of this period Brahma would awake and recreate the universe, which would repeat the movement through the four ages. Such absorption in Brahma and re-creation by Brahma, it was contended, went on endlessly.

Hindu theology not only set before men gods who were near to them but also provided an explanation of every phase of existence in terms of the activity of universal reality—the absolute god, Brahma.

2. *The Religious Ideal of Hinduism.* Since Hinduism declared all men potential incarnations of the divine, it called upon them to realize the ideal of perfection, for man could be at peace only when he became like a god. In the *Bhagavad-gita* Krishna refuted the pacifist doctrines of Buddhism and preached the rightfulness of action so long as action fulfilled a duty.[1] For the warrior, he argued, fighting in a righteous war was a sacred obligation. But duty must be performed without desire for or hope of reward: "Thy concern must be with action, not with fruits. . . . He who forsakes desire and goes detached through life, with no thought of I or mine, attains to peace." Only complete renunciation of desire leads to the attainment of peace, but without unselfish love such renunciation was impossible. In practice, therefore, Hinduism became a way of life:

> Who fixed in faith on Me,
> Dotes upon none, scorns none; rejoices not,
> And grieves not, letting good or evil hap
> Light when it will, and when it will depart,
> That man I love! Who, unto friend and foe
> Keeping an equal heart, with equal mind
> Bears shame and glory; with an equal peace
> Takes heat and cold, pleasure and pain; abides
> Quit of desires, hears praise or calumny

[1] See Nicol Macnicol, editor, *Hindu Scriptures: Hymns from the Rigveda, Five Upanishads, the Bhagavadgita* (1938); John Davies, *The Bhagavadgita, or the Sacred Lay: A Sanskrit philosophical poem* (1892); and Edward J. Thomas, *The Song of the Lord: Bhagavadgita; Translated with introduction and notes* (1931).

> In passionless restraint, unmoved by each;
> Linked by no ties to earth, steadfast in Me,
> That man I love.

This way of life, however, by ennobling suffering and the performance of duties accepted the world as it is, so that the quest of perfection was a purely spiritual undertaking. "The body dies, only the soul lives on," said Krishna.

In calling upon men to keep their souls at peace—"still as a candle in a windless place"—Hinduism subverted action to the maintenance of a static social order and denied duty the enlightenment that altruism gives.

Like the Vedic religion, Hinduism set before men the goal of release from the cycle of birth and death, but it offered ways to achieve this goal that were open to all men rather than only to the members of the twice-born castes. In the *Bhagavad-gita* these ways are three: (1) *karma*, *i.e.*, the way of good actions, (2) *jnana*, *i.e.*, the way of knowledge, and (3) *bhakti*, *i.e.*, the way of devotion. The way of good actions consisted of performing the duties of one's caste. The way of knowledge was followed not in learning but in meditating upon the "Absolute One." The way of devotion, unknown to Vedic teaching, offered to the lowest caste an open road to the goal of release, for, by dedicating oneself to Krishna, abandoning all desire, and loving him without hope of reward, peace was attainable. Thus Hinduism, while preserving the essentials of the old Brahmanical religion, became a popular religion of salvation in which emotionalism was quite as effective as the performance of rituals and asceticism in attaining the soul's release. By linking emotionalism with the acceptance of the world as it is, Hinduism reduced further its power to promote the advancement of knowledge and social amelioration.

3. *Hindu Worship*. In the course of the mingling of Brahmanical and primitive beliefs, a temple worship in which the new gods received the devotion of their adherents emerged as a new form of religious expression. Temples to Vishnu and Siva appeared throughout India, and the use of cult symbols, such as idols, hymns, and liturgies developed. Thus members of one section of the Brahman caste became ministrants in these temples, where dancing, singing, and emotional excess combined with a lively faith and elaborate ritual to shape a devotion into which everyone could enter. The old Brahmanical rites survived mainly in the family. With the reinvigoration of primitive beliefs, pilgrimages to

shrines, especially sacred rivers whose waters were believed to give spiritual strength, became a universal form of religious expression. The rivalry with Jainism and Buddhism led to the formation of new monastic groups and the multiplication of ascetics or holy men, whose self-mortification was believed to lead to spiritual release. Hinduism gave India a rich and diversified worship, which in its highest form promoted true self-abnegation and in its lowest form fell into the grossest sensualism.

4. *The Social Outlook of Hinduism.* The unifying factor in the diversity of gods, ways of salvation, and forms of worship of Hinduism was a social outlook which had its chief expression in the concept "dharma." Theoretically dharma consisted of the supernaturally sanctioned duties and rights which individuals were bound to follow if they wished to achieve their soul's release from the cycle of births and deaths; actually it was a body of customs through which the Brahmans exercised social domination, and its institutional realization was the caste system. When the Brahmans won new adherents among the non-Aryan population, they were required not to change their beliefs but to adopt the social code of the Brahmans. Thus Hinduism has known neither religious conversion nor intolerance; it has known only social acceptance of custom and intolerance of its violation. But Hinduism recognized no single definition of rights and duties; each group possessed its own code and enforced its own obligations, and individuals by virtue of birth into a group were subject to its code.

According to Manu four fundamental rules permeated Indian social organization: (1) birth determined caste status; (2) marriage within the caste was compulsory; (3) occupation and caste status were correlative; and (4) the observation of caste status was compulsory.[1] Chief among the laws were the rules not to take a meal with a member of a lower caste, not to travel by sea, and not to neglect such traditional observances, for example, as the rituals of keeping the cow sacred. Each caste had its own enforcement agent, the *panchayat*, or committee; such bodies existed in every village and city. They imposed penances and, in extreme cases, excommunicated offenders against caste rules. By excommunication the culprit was excluded from associating and eating with his fellows and was deprived of all care when he fell sick or died. Since the excommunicated one received service from neither Brahmans nor barbers nor washerwomen, he became both spirit-

[1] See E. W. Hopkins, *The Ordinances of Manu* (1884); Kewal Motwani, *Manu: A study in Hindu social theory* (1934).

ually unclean and physically dirty. Since he could not marry his sons and daughters with Brahmanical sanction, he committed the sin that brought upon him all the torments of hell. In some instances an offender could perform acts of purification which would restore his caste status; chief among the acts was tasting a mixture of the five sacred products of the cow—milk, curds, ghi (butter clarified by melting), dung, and urine. Habitations were purified by washing the walls and covering the floor with a mixture of cow dung and water. Persons expelled from their caste and persons never granted a caste status formed the great body of "untouchables" which existed in India after the consolidation of Hinduism.

Secular law was much less complicated than the religious law. In addition to the princely governments and the guilds of craftsmen, organized chiefly around the temples, the chief secular institutions of Hindu society was the *joint family*. In this family, fundamentally patriarchal in structure, property was held collectively by all the males descending directly from the head down to the degree of great-grandson. After three generations of male descendants, daughters became inheritors. There is no Hindu word for "will" or "testament." Many diversities of practice complicated the relations of members of the joint family. The wife, who could not hold property, was enjoined to worship her husband as a god; she was subject to physical punishment. Polygamy was allowed, and child marriage was approved. The burning of widows on the pyres of their husbands was not known when the laws of Manu were drawn up. Property rights in land were regulated by intricate rules.

Buying and selling were carried on only in the open market; secret bargaining was regarded as fraudulent. Prices were fixed by public authority and wages by custom. A herdsman was entitled to one-tenth of the milk of the cows he tended. Bargains could be canceled by either party to them within ten days after their making. Moneylending was a recognized business, exorbitant interest charges were allowed, and creditors could recover from debtors by either force or fraud. The son and grandson were under the religious obligation of paying the debts of the father or grandfather, who endured torment in hell until the debts were paid.

Labor was regulated through guilds, to which the law gave strong support. Every caste was also a craft or a trade organization which trained young workers, enforced an ethical code, and offered social services to its members. The ethical standards and regulations of these guilds were regarded as parts of the dharma under which all life moved. Many of the craft guilds were organized around the temples, where skilled workers of all kinds found employment. The craftsmen's way to salvation was the skillful performance of appointed tasks.

Criminal law was also closely bound up with religious customs and practices. The five principal crimes—abuse, assault, theft, robbery, and illicit sexual relations—were also mortal sins. Cattle stealing was a common offense, as were also drunkenness and the practice of magic for the injury of persons. The three upper castes generally paid fines; the Sudras alone were subject to corporal punishment.

These distinctions in punishments indicate the class character of Hinduism. The social superiority of the Brahmans was declared in both doctrine and law. When sacred water was drunk by a Brahman it reached the heart, by a Kshatriya it reached the throat, by a Vaisya it remained in the mouth, and by a Sudra it touched only the lips. In court the Brahman swore by his own veracity, the Kshatriya by his chariot and arms, the Vaisya by his cattle, and the Sudra by his guilt of sins. A ten-year-old Brahman, it was declared, was as wise as a Kshatriya one hundred years old; also a single Brahman, when angry, could destroy an army of princes. If a Sudra sat on a bench with a Brahman, he was whipped and branded; if he reviled a Brahman, a red-hot spike was driven down his throat; if he pulled a Brahman's hair, his hand was cut off. But Brahmans were generally punished with nothing more severe than the shaving of the head; their torments were believed to occur in the next world. If a Brahman intrigued with a low-caste woman, his soul went to hell; if he disregarded the rites of his caste, his forefathers would fall into hell, and the world would be destroyed. All things belonged to the Brahmans, and all other mortals existed only through their benevolence.

The excessive claims of the Brahmans to superiority indicate that the upper-caste Hindu had no idea whatever of social progress, and the lower castes were helpless to improve their lot as long as they recognized the Brahmanical claims which were implicit in the caste system. If the Sudras should dominate a state, the Brahmans taught, the state would perish. If the Sudras became rich, the Brahmans suffered great pain. In effect, therefore, Hinduism reduced the lowest caste to a form of slavery; only the fact that the Brahmans did not regard the accumulation of wealth as a worthy objective saved the masses from the severe economic exploitation that usually accompanied compulsory labor.

THE DEVELOPMENT OF BUDDHISM.

After the Buddha's death five hundred of his followers gathered in a council which shaped an oral rendering of his teachings, and from it sprang ultimately the written scriptures of Buddhism. They have survived in Ceylon, to which Buddhism was carried in the Mauryan age, in a dialect known as Pali, which is native not to Ceylon but to Bihar in central India. They consist of three *Pitakas*, or Baskets: (1) the *Vinaya*, regulations of monastic life, (2) the *Sutta*, stories and sayings, and (3) the *Abhidhamma*, the philosophy. The *Jatakas*, or folk tales of Buddha, found in the second Basket, were elaborated by many authors during the early Mauryan age; they contain references to the popular life of the time. Just when these materials were reduced to writing is not known. In the fourth and third centuries B.C. dissension among the monks about their content was more or less continuous. The canonical works were determined by a council held under the patronage of Asoka. In final rendering they were known as the *Tripitaka*, or "Three Baskets."[1]

Although Buddhism was originally a rationalistic revolt from Brahmanical daimonism, it developed a mythology which was, in fact, a rendering of the traditional Aryan beliefs. Among the gods, Brahma and Indra alone retained individuality, becoming servants of the Buddha. Brahma was commonly described as the supreme ascetic. Mara, the Satan of Buddhism, tempted men with the pleasures of the senses, delaying both the preaching and the accepting of the law. He had three daughers—Thirst, Sexual Pleasure, and Carnal Desire—who distracted men. Four kings, each reigning over a point of the compass, ruled the world of spirits. The king of the north reigned over the Yakshas, the good and evil genii who symbolized the world as it is. The subjects of the king of the south were pot-bellied gnomes. The king of the east marshaled the celestial musicians. The king of the west ruled the Nagas, the snakes that lived in marvelous palaces at the bottom of lakes; they gave both good and bad luck. As masters of rain, they assured prosperity or brought famine; their enemies were giant birds

---

[1] For the writings of the Buddhists see Edward J. Thomas, *Tripitaka Buddhist Scriptures: A selection translated from the Pali* (1913); Edward J. Thomas, *Early Buddhist Scriptures: A selection, translated and edited* (1935); Mrs. Rhys Davids, *Dhammapada: Verses on Dhamma* (1931); Irwin Babbitt, *The Dhammapada, Translated from the Pali, with an Essay on Buddha and the Occident* (1936); Mrs. Rhys Davids, *Buddhist Birth Stories (Jataka Tales)* (rev. ed., 1925); E. B. Cowell, *The Jataka* (1907); H. T. Francis and Edward J. Thomas, *Jataka Tales, Selected and Edited, with Introduction and Notes* (1916).

By the courtesy of the Museum of Fine Arts, Boston

A YAKSI

The Yaksi, a good or evil female deity, symbolized the acceptance of life as it is. The figure is clothed in a muslin so fine that the cloth is visible only when folded. Only the Greeks and the Hindus, among the ancient urban people, made the female form a leading motif in their art. This rendering, which was probably a part of a gate of the Stupa of Sanchi, dates from the second or first century B.C.

known as garudas. Between the earth and the other world wandered the pretas, ghosts with mouths as small as a needle and bellies great-ly distended by the suffering of eternal hunger. In a variety of hells hosts of souls endured an infinite diversity of punishments. These beings and souls, it should be remembered, were alive and transmi-grating, *i.e.*, in each form approaching or falling away from nirvana.[1]

[1] On the mythology of Buddhism see J. Hackin and others, *Asiatic Mythology* (1932).

From differences of belief among the early Buddhist monks issued two enduring forms of Buddhism. The earlier perpetuated the beliefs and rules of the original sangha; it was known as *Hinayana,* or the "lesser vehicle," and survived in the "south-ern church," which, until a later diffusion, was strong only in Ceylon. The later form *Mahayana,* or the "greater vehicle," developed into the "northern church." It undoubtedly originated in central India, for its great scholars attended Nalanda, but it became clearly differentiated only in the Kushan empire, where Western beliefs—Iranian, Greek, and perhaps Christian—cer-tainly contributed to it. The spread of Buddhist monasticism into Bactria and along the land and the sea routes eastward and west-ward was an important element in the general interaction of Eastern and Western ideas after the rise of Mahayana Buddhism.[1]

1. *The Emergence of Mahayana Buddhism.* In the second century Kanishka II, the Kushan emperor, who had accepted Buddhism, assembled the monks of his realm in the fourth and last council, and, although it was Hinayana in outlook, from it sprang new doctrines, mainly mythological and metaphysical, and a new literature in Sanskrit.[2] The leading figure but certainly not the only one at the source of these developments was the poet and philosopher Asvaghosa (fl. *ca.* 150), whose learned but highly imaginative work, *Buddhacarita,* or "Life of Buddha," was for a long time the main statement of Mahayana doctrine. Asvaghosa, it should be noted, was a man whose wide learning also expressed itself in a bitter hostility to the caste system. Nagarjuna (fl. *ca.* 200) gave Mahayana doctrines a new philosophical orientation. From the principle that no part can be known separate from its whole, he developed the view that all being has unity and reality only in the primal Buddha. The practical effect of this doctrine was to declare existence known to man an illusion. These ideas were, of course, the Buddhist counterpart of the Brahmanical belief in the Absolute One.[3] The monk Asanga (fl. *ca.* 300–350), who intro-duced Yoga, made Mahayana a full-fledged religion of salvation, quite as emotional as the Krishna worship of Hinduism.[4]

---

[1] O. G. von Wesendonk, *Das Weltbild der Iranier* (1933), p. 254.

[2] See W. E. Soothill, *Saddharmapundarika: The Lotus of the Wonderful Law, or the Lotus Gospel* (1930); also G. K. Nariman, *Literary History of Sanskrit Buddhism* (1920).

[3] See p. 393.

[4] On the rise of Mahayana Buddhism see E. J. Thomas, *A History of Buddhist Thought* (1933); Kenneth J. Saunders, *Epochs in Buddhist History* (*ca.* 1924); Kenneth J. Saunders, *The Gospel for Asia: A study of three religious masterpieces, Gita, Lotus, and Fourth Gospel* (1928); D. T. Suzuki, "The Development of Mahayana Buddhism," *Monist,* Vol. 24

After the second century A.D., when Mahayana beliefs began to be rendered in dramatic dialogues, epic poems, stories, and treatises, Mahayana literature grew rapidly. The chief Mahayana doctrinal work was the *Saddharmapundarika* or "The Lotus of the Good Law," a statement of faith comparable with the Hindu *Bhagavad-gita* and the Christian Fourth Gospel. Addressed to the simple layman, it portrayed the "coming Buddha," Maitreya, who taught the way of salvation:

> Buddhas ye shall all become;
> Rejoice and be no longer uncertain
> I am the Father of you all.

The poem, somewhat longer than the New Testament, described the one way to salvation, the one eternal Lord, and the one living church. Maitreya was similar in many ways to the Iranian Mithra. The liturgy of Mahayana embodied, it seems, many Christian elements. And the philosophy of Nagarjuna was, like Plato's, a subjective idealism. But, since these foreign elements, whether great or small, were suffused with the mood of Hinduism—emotionalism and mysticism—Mahayana must be regarded as a true product of Indian cultural development.

2. *The Theology of Mahayana Buddhism.* The central Mahayana belief was in Buddha, the Savior-God, who, sitting alone on a mountain peak, gave reality to all things; through the endless variations of change, he endured, eternal and absolute. When the world became too evil, he descended to it in a new form, shedding light and mercy, as well as teaching the way to salvation. Thus from the original primal Buddha issued a series of Buddhas, each of whom played a significant role in the evolution of the universe and the moral growth of mankind. Buddha, like Vishnu, had a number of avatars.

The traditional arhat ideal was replaced by a new ideal, the *bodhisattva*. The bodhisattva, having achieved Buddhahood by a righteous life, postponed the enjoyment of immortal bliss in order to serve and teach men. Since the way to Buddahood was open to all men, this doctrine gave rise to many saviors, each with his heaven. The virtues of the bodhisattva were ten in number: liberality, morality, forebearance, rapt contemplation, transcendental wisdom, intuitive knowledge, moral strength, resolution,

(1915), pp. 565–582; D. T. Suzuki, *Outlines of Mahayana Buddhism* (1907); Th. Stcherbatsky, *The Conception of the Buddhist Nirvana* (1927); Paul Carus, *Amitabha: A story of Buddhist Theology* (1906).

skill in teaching, and compassion. Self-mastery was the cardinal individual virtue; compassion, or the love of others, was the supreme social virtue; and one without the other was meaningless. This doctrine broke down the traditional social division between the monastic orders and the laity. Under Mahayana Buddhism the teacher became more a priest than a monk.

There was a single road to salvation, but it had three gates: one for arhats, another for those who excelled in meditation, and still another for the altruistic and sociable. This belief led to the multiplication of rites and ceremonies. Chief among the influences dominant in Mahayana Buddhist devotion was the ascetic practice yoga, which the grammarian Patañjali (fl. *ca.* 140 B.C.) systematized from early Vedic practices; it claimed to make possible the realization of the absolute, *i.e.*, the attainment of salvation, by certain breathing exercises, which were conducive to mental concentration. Such concentration was believed to culminate in an ecstatic communion with God. Yoga, it must be remembered, was not peculiar to Mahayana; as a matter of fact it was quite as important in Hinduism as in revised Buddhism. It strengthened the theistic elements of both religions. Prayers and magic, especially the utterance of sacred words, were also believed to be useful in the quest of salvation. But the last thought at the moment of death was held actually to determine the fate of the soul. Nothing in Mahayana weakened the ancient belief in transmigration; in fact, for Mahayana thinkers it explained the great inequalities among men.

Chief among the some six thousand Buddhas who ultimately appeared was Amitabha, who reigned over the "western paradise"; he saved the faithful by admitting them to this "pure land." A goddess of mercy reigned with him. Among the innumerable bodhisattvas four were especially important. Avalokitesvara—wise, merciful, and kind—protected men from evil, distress, and thievery and granted children to women. Mañjusri personified thought and meditation. Maitreya lived innumerable lives as a human being. Kshitigarbha was a kindly keeper of the inmates of hell; sometimes he released them.

In developing a vivid conception of the afterlife, Mahayana made a noteworthy contribution to the traditional religions of eastern Asia. At death the soul went to a purgatory where it suffered many torments. The hells, where different kinds of sinners were punished, numbered sixteen. Buddhist imagination ran riot in peopling these abodes of pain and suffering. Among the wicked persons receiving severe punishments were those who hindered good causes, who burned incense without a sincere heart, who did not believe in rewards and punishments after death, who burned good books, who persisted in eating meat, who participated in religious festivals without fasting beforehand, who were stingy, who threw tiles and stones over their neighbors' walls, who sowed salt on the ground, who did not bury dead cats and snakes very deeply, who caused workers to dig frozen ground, who compelled neighbors to move their kitchen stoves, and who appropriated public property. Clearly the population of hell consisted mostly of antisocial peasant villagers.

Although each bodhisattva had his own heaven, the ultimate abode of the blessed was the "western paradise" of Amitabha. There seven fountains flowed with the waters of the right virtues. For six hours each morning and evening there was a rain of celestial flowers. Varicolored birds, singing continuously and harmoniously, flew about everywhere. Each morning the blessed offered the celestial flowers to the countless Buddhas who returned to their land at mealtimes. The continuous repetition of Amitabha's name was a sure way to reach this heaven.

3. *The Social Outlook of Mahayana Buddhism.* Mahayana teachers accepted the doctrine of the inequality of men and the distinctions of the caste systems; in fact, many Brahmans entered its ranks, and its monks were organized in four grades, duplicating the castes. But caste exclusiveness was weakened rather than strengthened by Mahayana. The *Milinda Pandha*, a second-century B.C. dramatic dialogue, which is sometimes said to be the greatest Indian prose work, advanced the argument that the Buddhist teacher is both a Brahman and a Kshatriya, *i.e.*, a kingly teacher. In line with this conception the Buddhists favored the princes and, under the Kushan emperors, attacked the Brahmans. The social outlook of Mahayana was, therefore, aristocratic not sacerdotal. For the masses it advocated simple devotion, humility, and the giving of gifts to the monks. For the monks it set the ideal of social service: "Servant of all, a sweeper for humility, friend of those who need a friend, food for the hungry, medicine of the sick." But to all men, indeed to all women too, it offered immortal bliss.

THE INDIAN ORTHODOX PHILOSOPHIES.

In the competition between Buddhism and Hinduism for the allegiance of the Indian masses, Buddhism became a religion of salvation and Hinduism drew out of the great well of Brahmanical speculations philosophies, which, while holding fast to the fundamental tenets of the Vedic religion, were quite as intellectualistic as Buddhism. Just as the Sanskrit literature of Mahayana was the rival of the orthodox sacred writings and epics, so the Brahmanical commentaries, especially on the Upanishads, were an offset to Buddhistic philosophical treatises. The scholasticism which, as previously noted, became the distinctive element of Indian literate learning was a product of these developments.[1]

In the Buddha's time sixty-two religious sects, orthodox and heretical, existed; as time went on, they decreased in number until Jainism and Buddhism remained the dominant heresies, and Hinduism, buttressed by six schools of philosophy, assimilated all orthodoxy. The victory of Hinduism, which after the sixth century slowly drove Buddhism from India, was due partly to its acceptance of popular customs and partly to the development of the philosophies that made possible the retention of the loyalty of scholars. It was the victory of a priesthood, whose members were strong in the villages, over the monks, who lost contact with the people; by means of the philosophies the priests and others sought, without disorganizing ordinary social life, the ends which the monks hoped to attain. A by-product of the formation of the philosophies was an increase in the numbers of fakirs, prophets, and recluses.

The development of the orthodox philosophies was the work of several centuries. Their beginnings were in the early period of clashes between the Vedic religion and the heresies. The original statements of their doctrines seem to have been made in the first and second Christian centuries. By the fifth century commentaries on these original statements were the normal products of orthodox scholars.

1. *Sankhya: a Matter-Spirit Dualism.*   Kapila (fl. *ca.* 580 B.C.), the lengendary founder of the philosophy known as Sankhya, taught that primordial matter—*prakriti*—was the complete basis of nature but through it ran a changeless spirit—*purusha*—which, in man, was the soul, or *atman*.[2] Man's proper quest was for the knowledge that would release the soul from the body. This knowledge was declared to be external to the knower. Nature was

---

[1] On the Indian philosophies see S. Radhakrishnan, *Indian Philosophy* (2 vols., 1927), Vol. 2, *The Six Systems;* Surendranath Dasgupta, *A History of Indian Philosophy* (2 vols., 1922); Mysore Hiriyanna, *Outlines of Indian Philosophy* (1932); and Otto Strauss, *Indische Philosophie* (1925).

[2] See p. 393.

knowable by enumeration; thus there were the five elements, the five senses, and the five organs. The mind, a subtle but material force, arrived at knowledge by perception, inference, and analogy. Since human suffering had origin in the failure to distinguish between matter and spirit, the knowledge that liberated enabled man to become conscious of the soul alone. Such knowledge, it was held, cut the bonds that enmeshed the soul in matter. In the quest for this knowledge man advanced or regressed according to his virtues and vices or, in other words, under the influence of his karma. The quest was pursued chiefly by speculation guided by twenty-five formal intellectual principles.

Sankhya was the basis of all subsequent orthodox philosophical speculation. Its literature took form in the early Christian centuries. The pursuit of release according to its teachings was open only to the twice-born castes.

2. *Yoga: a Discipline for the Will.* Whereas Sankhya was agnostic, Yoga was theistic. There was a supreme lord, eternal, perfect, and without karma. His name was the mystic syllable *OM*,[1] and in ancient days he had taught the primal sages the way of release. This way was meditation, which had for its functions, first, the overcoming of disease, doubt, and secular-mindedness and, second, the attainment of knowledge. Meditation was cultivated by concentration, benevolence, indifference to happiness and misery, and bodily exercises which suppressed the functions of the mind that attended to worldly affairs. These exercises consisted mainly of physical postures and a control of breathing, which withdrew the mind from sensual experience and fixed attention on spiritual being. Ascetic practices, which were regarded as disintegrating egotism, *i.e.*, the desire to live, also were helpful in achieving liberating knowledge. To abstain from worldly activity was believed to be a way of avoiding its future effects through karma. From a worldly life developed in these terms and pervaded by a devotion to the Lord, man ascended through seven stages to the possession of knowledge. Its possession gave occult powers, such as the capacity to see the past and future, to make oneself invisible, to converse with spirits, and to fly through the air or walk on water, as well as the liberation that wiped away the effects of all previous works.

As a philosophy Yoga agreed in the main with Sankhya, except for the emphasis on deity. But its method of attaining liberation was completely nonintellectual:

[1] See p. 390.

What we stand in need of is not subtleties of disquisition but control of will. We must subdue the inner turmoil of emotion and passion. The true philosopher is a physician of the soul, one who helps us save ourselves from the bondage of desire.[1]

The Yoga exercises long antedated philosophical speculation, and their practice was not confined to any religious sect or school.

3. *Nyaya: a Logical Method.*   Nyaya, sometimes known as the Aristotelianism of India, was primarily a system of logic. As such, of course, its object was to win the knowledge that gives liberation. It seems to have originated as a method of settling disputes regarding the meaning of texts. The proof of a statement rested on perception, inference, analogy, and verbal testimony; the formal reasoning was developed in a syllogistic pattern, for example:

1. The hill is fiery.
2. For it smokes.
3. Whatever smokes is fiery, as a kitchen.
4. The hill is smoking.
5. Therefore it is fiery.

By this method of reasoning fundamental knowledge was developed about the soul, the body, the senses, the mind, virtues and vices, transmigration, karma, and emancipation. The supreme soul, it was held, was a unity, and emancipation was achieved only in union with it.

Nyaya became a stock study among Indian scholars, promoting a precision of statement and an almost endless refinement of thought. It was even more intellectualistic than Sankhya. In this connection it should be noted that Buddhist thinkers were especially prominent in its development. They are credited with having first distinguished logic from general philosophy in India. Dignaga (fl. *ca.* 500) did some original work in developing the syllogism.[2]

4. *Vaiseshika: Atoms and Universal Harmony.*   The distinctive element in Vaiseshika was an explanation of physical nature and virtue in terms of the concept "atom." All objects consisted of aggregates of atoms brought together by force—not by the will of God. Disintegration was as much a normal aspect of nature as aggregation. Change was the rule of all being. And diversity was the fundamental fact of universal existence. The universe was understood in terms of seven concepts: "substance," "quality,"

---

[1] S. Radhakrishnan, *Indian Philosophy* (2 vols., 1927), Vol. 2, p. 364. By permission of George Allen & Unwin, Ltd., London.
[2] See Satisachandra Vidyabhusana, *History of the Medieval School of Logic* (1907).

"action," "community" or "genus," "particularity," "coherence," and "nonexistence." There were four atoms—earth, water, light, and air—from which all substances were formed. Aether, an undifferentiated entity, pervaded all existence. The simple objects, having particularity, were time, space, soul, and mind; they were not aggregates of atoms. The universe was regarded as a harmony of relations, and so long as man was unable to harmonize jarring elements, such as desires, impulses, and passion, he was unable to find the enlightenment that gave freedom. The object of the quest for knowledge was to gain this experience of harmony; its methods were the study of philosophy, reflection on what has been learned, and meditation on nature itself. In the quest, endurance of pain, benevolence, and selflessness were aids. The mind, it was held, could directly perceive knowledge; it was the organ by which the soul had contact with the senses.

5. *Mimamsa: a Philosophy of Revealed Truth.* Mimamsa, developed by two schools—both orthodox—was grounded in the doctrine that the Vedas contained revealed eternal truth. But this truth was difficult to know through words. Mimamsa considered, therefore, the problem of the relation of thought to words, that is, the problem summarized by the word "semantics." The concrete result was an elaboration of rules for interpreting texts and an emphasis on the singing of hymns in worship. Through an examination of the Vedas its followers hoped to teach men their duties, discover the order of their performance, define the purpose of their performance, and guarantee their efficacy. The Vedic sacrifices were, therefore, the chief mode of liberation, defined as the cessation of the union of the body and the soul. Considerable attention was given to the psychological status of waking, dreaming, and sleeping, as they were related to the atman.

The creation and cultivation of Mimamsa doctrine was almost exclusively the work of the Brahmans.

6. *Vedanta: Idealistic Monism.* The word *Vedanta* means "end of the Veda," and the philosophy was conceived as the culmination of the quest for saving knowledge, by whatever methods the quest was made. The basic treatise of the system is credited to Bardarayana, who may have lived about the end of the second century A.D. This treatise consists of five hundred and fifty-five verses of two or three words each, which, without interpretation, are hardly intelligible. Inasmuch as the philosophy taught that revealed truth is self-evident, this obscurity was not a difficulty. Metaphysical knowledge, it was held, could not be

attained by logical method or reflection. As a body of doctrine the Vedanta philosophy consisted almost exclusively of ideas drawn from the Upanishads; it was, in fact, an exegesis of the Upanishads.

The supreme spirit—Brahman—was a being capable of all knowledge and feeling: all else was illusion. He was the universal soul and the all-pervading breath. Although impassive, he was both cause and effect in the universe. The individual soul—atman—was a spark of the supreme being; by transmigration it passed from state to state until it attained release in the loss of individual identity with the "Universal One." The final state was "god-vision." Pious meditation was the chief method of attaining god-vision; the performance of rites was only a preliminary discipline. Women and low-caste men could gain salvation by the grace of Brahman.

The standpoint of the Vedanta philosophy was idealistic monism; behind the matter and spirit of the Sankhya philosophy was the Universal One—pure spirit. This doctrine had affinities with Buddhistic teachings—which, as a matter of fact, it superseded as the dominant philosophical system as Buddhism became more and more a religion. Just as Hinduism represented the victory of the Brahmans in the struggle for the allegiance of the masses, so Vedanta symbolized their triumph among learned men.

INDIAN SCIENCE.

Although Indian science had roots in Vedic lore, it became a recognizable body of thought only with the rise of urban culture. By that time some Babylonian and Iranian materials had reached India, and later, in the Mauryan and Kushan periods, Greek influence became important. The first, indeed the chief, Indian achievement of the mode of thinking that characterizes science was grammar; as previously noted, it became a complex but systematic body of learning in the fourth and third centuries B.C. By this time, it seems, mathematics, astronomy, and medicine were also separate fields of learning. The history of their development is obscure, for few scientific documents have survived, and their chronology is uncertain. Indian science, like law, never escaped the influence of religious speculation; in fact, grammar attained its high development largely because it was useful in religious studies.[1]

---

[1] On the general history of science in India see Abel Rey, *La Science orientale avant les Grecs* (1930), Livre V, "La Science hindoue"; Brajendranath Seal, *The Positive Sciences of the Ancient Hindus* (1915). Indian treatments of the history of science are prone to overstate the achievements of the ancient Aryas.

1. *Indian Mathematics.*   Among the early urban peoples only the Greeks excelled the Indians as mathematicians. Early in the second century B.C. Apastamba wrote a practical geometry for the guidance of masons in building altars; he dealt empirically with acute, obtuse, and right angles and stated the Pythagorean generalization, for which, however, he offered no proof. Indian geometry never progressed from rules to the systematic proof of rules. Under Greek influence some skill in trigonometry appeared.

The great Indian mathematical achievements were the inventions: (1) the numerals now known as Arabic, (2) place notation, and (3) *zero*. The numerals were known in Asoka's time; in the third century A.D. they took their now common forms. Originally, it seems, the Indians had signs for numerals up to and including 19. They also used words for the numerals. The earliest known numbers written in the place-value system date near the end of the sixth century. Apparently, however, place notation was invented in the first century B.C., and the concept "zero" was known to Indian mathematicians perhaps a century earlier. From the first Indian mathematicians treated zero as a number and used it as such in all kinds of arithmetical computations. The earliest sign for zero seems to have been a dot. The synthesis of these developments was achieved by Aryabhata (fl. *ca.* 475–500), whose work remained for a considerable time the high point of Indian mathematical learning. He was familiar with a system of place notation based on 10; the largest number he used had ten places, but the largest of which he spoke had eighteen. He used Greek methods for computing the volumes of pyramids and cones, gave the value of π as $3^{177}/_{1250}$, or 3.1416, stated the correct formula— πR^2—for finding the area of a circle, and handled quadratic equations.

From very early times the Indian mathematicians were competent arithmeticians, except in division, which they neglected; they were especially expert in handling fractions. The beginnings of their algebraic operations are lost. There can be no doubt that much of the mathematical learning which spread through the West from Arabic centers was originally received by them from Indian sources.[1]

[1] See B. Datta and A. N. Singh, *History of Hindu Mathematics: A source book*, Part I, "Numerical Notation and Arithmetic" (1935); W. E. Clarke, *The Aryabhatiya of Aryabhata* (1930); Louis C. Karpinski, "The Unity of Hindu Contribution to Mathematical Science," *Scientia*, June, 1928, pp. 382–388.

2. *Indian Astronomy, Physics, and Chemistry.* The chronological calculations necessary for the determination of the calendar
of Vedic sacrifices were at the base of Indian astronomy, but its
development, as far as it ever became scientific, was due largely
to Babylonian and Greek influences.[1] After Mauryan times a
considerable number of astronomical works were composed, but
the first important authors were Aryabhata, the mathematician,
and Varahamihira (*ca.* 505–587). Aryabhata calculated the positions of the planets in the Babylonian manner and developed a
theory of epicycles like that of Ptolemy. He understood the true
causes of lunar and solar eclipses. Astrological ideas were prominent
in his work. Varahamihira used many Greek terms in explaining
equinoxes, solstices, and the movements of heavenly bodies. The
moon, he said, revolves around the earth and the earth around
the sun.

The chief astronomical speculative doctrine of the Brahmans
was the theory of cycles of universal creation and destruction, more
religious than scientific in quality. According to this theory the
earth was a circular flat plain. At its center was the mountain
Meru, behind which the heavenly bodies were hidden when they
were not visible. India was shaped like a lotus petal. Seven concentric oceas surrounded the earth. In formulating this theory the
Brahmans developed the concepts "void," "unlimited space,"
"infinite time," and "atom." In comparison with the speculative
thinkers of other urban cultures, the Indian priests and philosophers
were unique in predicating the enormous duration of the many ages
of the universe.

The atomic theory of the Indian philosophers[2] seems to have
been derived from a Greek source. They conceived that the physical
universe was an aggregation of atoms suspended in space and time.
The earth was composed of four elements—air, earth, water, and
light; around the earth was the aether. The smallest visible object
was believed to be the mote seen in the sunlight; it was said to
consist of six atoms. As among the Greeks, these speculations had
no practical results. Useful chemical and physical knowledge was
almost completely bound up with the technical processes of tan-
ning, dyeing, bleaching, compounding cements, mixing pigments,
making soap and glass, and working metals, and was, of course, in
the hands of craftsmen, not priests and philosophers. The Indian

[1] Sukuman Ranjan Das, "Scope and Development of Indian Astronomy," *Osiris*,
Vol. 2 (1936), pp. 197–219.
[2] See p. 782.

dyers invented fast colors and discovered indigo, and, as previously noted, the Indian ironworkers may have produced the first steel.

3. *Indian Medicine.* Indian medicine, rooted in folk beliefs, never abandoned the daimonic theory of disease or gave up magic and incantations as treatments. Fever was said to be the "king of diseases." The itch was caused by the fever daimon's brother. A dog-daimon caused whooping cough.

Inasmuch as a considerable part of Indian medicine, including surgery, developed in northwestern India about the opening of the Christian era, it seems likely that it owed much to Greek influences. Although the oldest medical works quote earlier sources, nothing at all is known about the development of Indian medicine until this time. It is impossible to date the two earliest medical writers, Susruta and Charaka. Susruta, who described several operations, such as removing cataracts and closing hernias, listed over a hundred surgical instruments and a thousand medicinal herbs, most of which were poisons, antidotes to poisons, soporifics, and aphrodisiacs. The Indians were expert in extracting substances from plants; they also used skillfully many metallic derivatives. Susruta, who recognized the value of different kinds of symptoms in diagnosis, made cleanliness and close attention to diet important elements in the treatment of disease. Charaka noted the peculiarities of many diseases, including fever, leprosy, epilepsy, and tuberculosis; he seems also to have been aware that certain diseases are likely to become epidemic. His medical encyclopaedia, which is first met with in the second Christian century, was the leading guide of Indian medicine until recent times.

Later Indian physicians divided medicine into eight branches and enumerated sixteen fearful diseases. They developed a theory of diseases (in which were compounded, it seems, both Greek and Chinese ideas) based on a classification of breaths and a conception of the circulation of the breath through tubes, *i.e.* the nerves and the blood vessels. They called the nerve centers "lotuses." Anatomical students described five hundred muscles, three hundred and sixty bones, and two hundred joints. They counted the teeth, the nails, and the cartilages among the bones. They distinguished the chief internal organs. They recognized the heart as the center at which the arteries meet. They knew the difference between the white and gray matter of the brain. The atman or soul, was believed to enter the individual through the sutures in the skull. Among the physiological processes digestion and the sexual function were the best understood; the function of the gastric juice seems to have been known. Indian physicians were skillful in the use of emetics, purges, massage, and baths in treating diseases; they used cold applications for fevers.

A theory of functioning of the various organs of the body that was in harmony with Indian philosophical ideas is found in the Upanishads, especially the earlier ones. The influence of Yoga produced a belief in a system of arteries through which five vital airs circulated. The process of living consisted of an interaction between an inward fire of the body and the breath. The soul was believed to reside in the heart, where the mental functions were also said to be located. In deep sleep the soul wandered through the body.[1]

Man, the Indian physicians and philosophers believed, came from fire and returned to fire; he was to be understood only as part of the physical and moral universe. They recognized five physical types or races and three moral classes—those who yearn to be free, those who desire to become free gradually, and those who want offspring and cattle. They called health the greatest of gifts, and dreaded old age as a time of decay and pain. They counted the natural span as one hundred years.[2]

4. *Indian Geography.* The Indians had only a slight knowledge of geography. They were generally aware of the existence of China and the Western lands but had no accurate idea of the size or the distance of these lands from India. To the north, the Indians knew, were The Himalaya, the Kwen-Lun, the Tian Shan, and the Altai Mountains, and somewhere in these mountains was the sacred lake, Manasarowar. In spite of the common use of plant motifs in art and of plant substances the ancient Indians developed neither a botanical nor a zoological science. The beginnings of botanical geography were made in the discovery that certain kinds of plants grew only in certain kinds of climate.

The Art of Ancient India.

The diversity of social customs and religious beliefs which characterized Aryan culture had its correlative in the multiplicity of forms—most of them symbolical—of the arts. Buddhistic or

---

[1] See George W. Brown, *The Human Body in the Upanishads* (1921).

[2] On Indian medicine see D. Chowry Muthu, *The Antiquity of Hindu Medicine and Civilization* (1931); A. F. R. Hoernle, *Studies in the Medicine of Ancient India*, Part I, "Osteology or the Bones of the Human Body" (1907); F. S. Hammett, "The Anatomical Knowledge of the Ancient Hindus," *Annals of Medical History*, Vol. 1 (n.s., 1929), pp. 325–333; F. S. Hammett, "The Ideas of the Ancient Hindus concerning Man," *Isis*, Vol. 28 (1938), pp. 57–71.

Hindu, they were conceived as manifestations of the Universal One, as indeed was every natural form, and aesthetic feeling was never differentiated from religious feeling. Artists, like craftsmen, were almost exclusively members of the low castes; indeed, the practice of an art was so completely bound up with the practice of an occupation that the "artist" as understood by the modern Western world can hardly be said to have existed. Art was not so much the representation of nature as objective form, as it was an effort to understand nature as a divine force manifested in subjective moods, which, as evidenced by the Indian religions and philosophies, were regarded as the true approach to reality. No purely secular art has survived from ancient India; the priests completely monopolized its motifs.[1]

1. *Indian Architecture.* Apparently three streams of architectural achievement flowed together in pre-Mauryan times: (1) the brickwork of the early Indus valley cities, (2) the wooden construction of the natives of the Ganges valley and southern India, and (3) the timberwork of the invading Aryas. In Mauryan times, when the use of stone was begun, Persian designs and methods of construction were introduced, but the ancient wood forms survived. There were then three main architectural forms: (1) the palace, (2) the rock-hewn cave, and (3) the stupa. Asoka's palace at Pataliputra is said to have been a duplicate of the Persian royal residence. The rock-hewn temple was probably elaborated from the native cave shrine. In Buddhist hands it became the tour de force of Indian art. Its chief elements—cut from solid rock—were a hall with a high vaulted roof, a row of columns along each side of the hall, a narrow aisle between the columns and the outer wall, and cells cut into the walls. Sometimes the columns and cells also circled the back wall. Light was let in through a great horseshoe shaped window placed over the ornate portal that served as an entrance. At Ajanta—called the "cradle of Asiatic art"—there are thirty of these cave temples. Some of them were the dwellings of Buddhist monks; others were shrines. The oldest date from early second century B.C.; the last were hewn probably in the seventh century. The stupa—a shrine for relics—was a Buddhist elaboration of the ancient Aryan burial mound. Its

[1] On the art of ancient India see G. T. Garratt, *The Legacy of India* (1937); Ananda K. Coomaraswamy, *Asiatic Art* (1938); Vincent A. Smith, *A History of Fine Art in India* (2d ed., rev., 1930); E. B. Havell, *A Study of Indo-Aryan Civilization* (1915); E. B. Havell, *The Himalayas in Indian Art* (1924). For a pictorial record of Indian art see Kenneth de B. Codrington, *Ancient India from the Earliest Times to the Guptas* (1926); Odette Bruhl and Sylvain Lévi, *Indian Temples* (1937).

Indian Railways

THE STUPA OF SANCHI

The stupa, developed from a simple burial mound, became the symbolical monument of
Buddhism; it was usually built over a receptacle containing some relic of its founder or of
one of its saints. The structure was solid masonry and earth. The great Stupa at Sanchi,
which may have been begun by Asoka, is undoubtedly the oldest standing architectural
work in India.

chief elements were a mound, sometimes with several levels, a
rectangular shrine, and a pillar which frequently supported an um-
brella-like roof. Around the mound was a stone railing, often
with elaborately built gates. The great stupa at Sanchi, dating
from the second century B.C., is probably the oldest Indian construction now standing. Its mound is a solid stone dome; its railing

and gates are among the most notable of all ancient Indian works of art. After the rise of Mahayana Buddhism many stupas were built in northwestern India, but their classic home, as of the Indian arts generally, was in the central Ganges valley and the upper Deccan.

In post-Mauryan times two additional architectural forms developed: (1) the monastery and (2) the temple. The monasteries —Jain, Buddhist, and Brahmanic—were great brick structures of cells, kitchens, storerooms, and shrines, arranged around a central hall. Pavilions of timber construction usually dotted the grounds around the monasteries. Although some of the temples were rock-hewn like the cave shrines, most of them were built of brick or stone. The chief elements of the temple were a rectangular shrine and a tower, usually well proportioned and richly decorated with sculptures and reliefs. The finest early temples were Buddhist, notably at Bodh Gaya (second century); later they became the chief architectural expression of Hinduism. In the Gupta age temples arose in all parts of India; they are the evidence of the cultural unification which Hinduism achieved.[1]

2. *Indian Sculpture.* The oldest known Aryan stone monuments were the six pillars set up by Asoka to advertise his edicts. They were monolithic columns between forty and fifty feet high. They were round and polished, set on a circular base, and crowned with animal figures. These figures, which showed Assyrian influence, were as perfectly done as any animal figures in the world. A few human figures surviving the Mauryan age are heavy and stiff, lacking especially that feeling of subtle movement characteristic of later figures.[2]

In spite of the fact that Buddha laid down rules against the representation of the human figure, Indian sculpture found its first great exponents among his followers. The railing of the stupa at Sanchi was decorated with reliefs having the delicacy of carved ivory and showing considerable interest in social life. In these reliefs, as well as those of Mathura, Bharhut, Ajanta, and Amaravati, there is exhibited a mastery of the human form so complete as to render all Indian types, their movements, and their moods. These figures were, however, like the plant and animal motifs combined with them, symbolical. The scenes generally depicted incidents in the legendary life of Buddha. Buddha was symbolized by the footprint, the "wheel of the law," the bodhi tree—the

---

[1] See J. Fergusson, *The History of Indian and Eastern Architecture* (1910).
[2] See Stella Kramrisch, *Indian Sculpture* (1933).

British Museum   *General Museum, Lahore*

THE BUDDHA SYMBOL

The Buddha symbol was a product of the contact of Indian and Greek cultures. These figures, which date from the second or third centuries A.D., are in the style of Gandhara, the northwest province of ancient India. The first represents the Buddha in the conventional Yoga pose; the second, remarkable as a rendering of the state of complete emaciation, represents the Buddha as a penitent. A representation more native and less Greek in features developed at the same time at Mathura in the Jumna valley.

scene of his enlightenment—and the umbrella. The lion symbolized his first preaching. The elephant represented the dream of his mother. The lotus, which became the most popular Buddhist motif, symbolized the universe.

The most important art development of post-Mauryan times was the creation of Buddhist and Hindu cult images.[1] This development undoubtedly had its source in the anthropomorphic elements of the primitive cultures of southern India. But in the northwest Hellenistic influences contributed significantly to its advance. The transition from the symbolical representation of Buddha to the cult image is evident in the reliefs at Mathura, where Hellenistic influences penetrated under Kushan rule. This influence affected

[1] J. Ph. Vogel, *Buddhist Art* (1936); A. Foucher, *Beginnings of Buddhist Art* (1917); Ananda K. Coomaraswamy, *Indian Origin of the Buddhist Figure* (1928); and Ananda K. Coomaraswamy, *Elements of Buddhist Iconography* (1935).

Jain and Hindu, as well as Buddhistic, iconography. The first image of Buddha—set up early in the second century by Kanishka —was a product of Mahayana thought. The Buddha—seated on a lion throne—was a yoga, calm and holy but not without humor, as he meditated on universal being. The lack of a head covering and the short hair, curled to the right, symbolized the abandonment of worldly interests and desires. Although Greek influence was apparent in the shape and tilt of the head and in the manner of using drapery, the figure remained Indian in both physical form and mood. In the Gupta age the Buddha figure was developed in the patterns that subsequently spread throughout western Asia.

Hindu cult images arose as a result of the fusion of feeling and belief which produced the great epics. Figurines of the Vedic gods were produced in the second century B.C.; in the second Christian century the now well-known representations of Siva, Krishna, and Hanuman, the monkey-god, appeared. The common rendering of Siva showed him with four arms and three heads. With the development of temple architecture Hindu sculpture found in the great epics innumerable motifs which were rendered with infinite detail. The sensuous quality of Hindu figures is achieved not only by the forms given to the various limbs but also by the seeming bonelessness of the body.

Hindu sculptured figures always represented acts and personality traits of gods. Realism, when achieved, was conceived as identification of the artist with his subject; furthermore, it aided others to achieve this identification. In view of the erotic quality of many Hindu figures, it should be realized that the artists were interested in the physical basis and the emotional content of sexual passion mainly as a mode of religious expression and feeling. This dominance of religious motivation prevented the development of portrait sculpture.

3. *Indian Painting.* Although painting was a widely practiced art in ancient India, the antecedents of the wall paintings of the Ajanta caves are unknown. The earliest of these paintings date from the second century, the greatest from the Gupta age. The pictorial principles embodied in these paintings have origin in the fundamental outlook of Indian culture, for they are rendered not as if man were groping in a dark world, but as if the universe were forcing itself upon him. Thus, instead of having depth and leading the eye into a vista, they seem to press forward upon the senses and consciousness. There is no background, but a welling-up

at the edges of the pictures of diverse forms and movements. There is no depth of shadow, only light, out of which come recognizable forms. In the rendering of these forms the rhythm of life is exhibited in curves and waves. Reality is depicted in terms of plastic volume and harmonious movement.[1]

The motifs were derived from Buddhist legends and the classical Sanskrit literature. Under Mahayana influence the bodhisattva was rendered in every degree of compassion and every mode of understanding. In the Gupta age the avatars of Vishnu and scenes from the epics were popular. Herds of elephants and monkeys were favorite themes. About the same time a form of portraiture, showing lovers, appeared in court circles.

These paintings were rendered with a mastery of line and color not equaled certainly until the European Renaissance. The usual technique was to outline the figures with a fine red line and fill in the form with glowing colors. The peculiar effect of pressing in upon the beholder was achieved by painting so that the scene seems to be tilted forward at the top. The pictures were done on especially prepared plastered surfaces.

Examples of Indian painting have been found at a few places in India besides Ajanta, in Ceylon, and recently along the great inland road to China. The art was a strong influence upon the painting of all Far Eastern lands.[2] Its diffusion was closely bound up with the spread of Buddhism.

4. *Indian Music.* Indian music was rooted in religious feeling. The Vedic hymns were sung, and later Hindu ritual embodied instrumental music and the dance. Secular music was the product of the court and the village. The chief instruments were a simple guitar, an elementary violin, the flute, and a great variety of drums. The dance was a synthesis of rhythmic motions symbolizing the movements of the universe. Indian music, like that of the Greeks, was melody rather than harmony. When different instruments were played together, the musicians, producing different notes, converged upon an identical note and, thereby, created a cross rhythm. Many notes were "graced," *i.e.*, accented as

---

[1] Stella Kramrisch, *A Survey of Painting in the Deccan* (1937); for a reproduction of an early Ajanta painting, see article "Ajanta" in the *Encyclopaedia Britannica* (14th ed.). The most recent reproductions of the Ajanta paintings, in color photography, are found in G. Yazdani, *Ajanta: The colour and monochrome reproductions of the Ajanta frescoes based on photography* (1933).

[2] See Joseph Strzygowski *et al.*, *The Influence of Indian Art* (1925); also J. H. Lindsay, "Indian Influences in Chinese Sculpture," *Indian Art and Letters*, Vol. 10 (1936), pp. 125–133.

violin players "slide" a note. There were thirty-six traditional *ragas*, or themes, which, although they were regarded as possessing supernatural charm, the players were free to embroider. Skill was manifested chiefly in the rendering of moods, both natural and human. Singers, dancers, and musicians were low-caste. Brahmans would not play or dance in public, nor would they put an instrument to their lips.[1]

5. *The Indian Minor Arts.* The minor arts were in the hands of the village craftsmen. Their wood and ivory carvings were the most delicate ever produced. Their fabrics, especially cottons, were finer in texture and brighter in hue than those of any other land; they were also notable for colorful designs combining plant, bird, and animal motifs. The chief products of the metalworkers were hammered brass, fine enamels, and exquisite jewelry. Only the art of pottery making, choked by religious prohibitions on preparing and eating food, did not thrive in India. The high quality of Hindu craftsmanship gave Indian furniture, jewelry, and cloth a foremost place in the luxury trade that flowed westward to the Mediterranean lands.[2]

THE RELIGIOSITY OF INDIAN CULTURE

When the Aryas, under the leadership of the Brahmans, rallied against foreign conquerors and foreign cultural penetration, they found their chief support in native masses, whom the Brahmans admitted to the traditional social system. This amalgamation of the Aryas with the native peasantry was, it seems, the decisive factor in fixing the enduring characteristics of Indian culture.

Economically Indian culture remained on a peasant-village basis. Although commerce expanded, it never penetrated deeply into Indian economic life, nor did it give rise to a significant merchant class or a numerous urban working class. The craftsmen, organized in guilds, were commonly attached to temples where Brahmanical influence was supreme. The weakening of the military class, the princes, in the course of the constant wars with invaders, deprived Indian agriculture of that systematic organization which dominant military classes imposed on the peasants of Persia, the Hellenistic kingdoms, China, and the Roman Empire. The persisting belief in the sacredness of the cow—at first, perhaps, a device for increasing the supply of cattle in an economy passing

[1] See B. D. Krishnaji, *The Hindu Musical Scale and the Twenty-two Shrutees* (1910); H. A. Popley, *The Music of India* (1921).
[2] See Ananda K. Coomaraswamy, *The Arts and Crafts of India and Ceylon* (1913).

from hoe culture to husbandry or a way of protecting Aryan property from the native masses—is evidence of the failure of the Indian landholders to shift from the religious to the secular practices of economic exploitation.

The low efficiency of economic production led, of course, to the slow growth of the economic surplus and the further consequence that Indian culture was never fully organized on the urban level. In the first place this circumstance accounts for the fact that neither centralized government nor codified law attained full development. In the second place it accounts for the military weakness of the Indian states; they were weak in the face of invaders and weaker still as imperial forces. In the third place it explains the gross poverty of the people; their productivity was so low that the exploitation of labor by slavery was never developed on a scale similar to that of the Mediterranean lands or of China. In this connection it is fair to note again that the Brahmans did not regard the accumulation of wealth as a worthy objective. And lastly the circumstance meant that all those social and intellectual tendencies which had their source in competition for possession and control of the economic surplus remained weak, so that tradition, rooted in primitive beliefs and practices, survived in almost unimpaired strength.

On the social side the persistence of tradition was manifest in the triumph of the caste system over the forces that worked for its disintegration. This survival was probably due to the fact that social groups which might have become the successful rivals of the Brahmans never achieved economic strength.

On the intellectual side the survival of tradition was manifest in the reversion of both Brahmanical and Buddhist thought to forms more primitive than they had at the opening of the Mauryan age, when urban social forces were first powerful. As previously noted, this reversion was due to the assimilation of primitive beliefs and practices from the natives admitted to the Aryan social system. It was due also to the fact that social groups having tendencies toward secular-mindedness, namely, merchants and princes, remained weak. In this connection it is significant that all Indian thought, religious and philosophical alike, held fast to the ancient beliefs in the transmigration of the soul and the quest for release, and, furthermore, that they found release chiefly in subjective states of mind which, however attained, were believed to bring the mergence of the individual soul in universal being. Thus Indian thought, regardless of its diverse forms, retained a fundamental unity in which animism and metaphysical speculation were not only present but actually harmonious. Indian thinkers did not set between the low and the high intellectual tradition a system of logic which could give the latter a coherence not shared with the former; that Indian thought systems found their main literary expressions in scriptures (*i.e.*, sacred books), epic poems, and compilations of aphorisms, is evidence of this failure of speculative thought to rise to the level of logical systematization. Not one of the Puranas, Buddhist scriptures, or philosophical treatises set forth a closely and consistently argued doctrine.

Lastly, the survival of tradition was sealed in the identification of custom with Universal Being; from inorganic substance to the Universal One, everything was under the domination of dharma. As a part of nature, man, although he had a sense of order and beauty in nature, never felt impelled to master it. Nature was imperfect because universal law was disobeyed—living men suffered because of the sins of their ancestors—and ultimately, indeed, the universe would be destroyed because men violated the universal law.

The Hindu ideal was implicit in these correlative social and intellectual systems: the holy one is he who lives detached from the world, having compassion for suffering, remaining dutiful but desireless, and finding bliss in an inward unity with the Universal One. For the masses this ideal meant stagnation in misery, superstition, and sentimentality; for the twice-born castes it meant altruism without amelioration, refinement without gentleness, violence without vindictiveness, and thought without action.

After the Hindu reorientation Indian culture was more resistant to change than any other culture, not excepting the Egyptian, with which, indeed, it shared religiosity as a dominant quality.

Chapter XIV

THE CONSOLIDATION OF THE CHINESE CULTURAL TRADITION

≪≺-≪≺-≫≻-≫≻

The consolidation of the Chinese cultural tradition occurred in the course of economic, social, and political changes which transformed the Chinese cultural area from an array of feudatories into a centralized empire; the changes also promoted an·expansion of the cultural area. Underlying them was the increase of wealth due to the introduction of iron implements and tools, the traction plow, and large-scale irrigation. The political aspects of the transformation which culminated in the establishment of the centralized empire were (1) the rise of new social groups and, consequently, the reorganization of the feudal states, (2) a bitter struggle between the feudal states for supremacy, and (3) the rise of border peoples to political prominence and their intervention in the struggles of the feudal states. In the interaction of these developments Confucianism, which had originally declared the feudal regime to be the central political element in the Chinese cultural tradition, was reorientated so that, when the empire superseded the feudatories as the enduring political form, Confucianism was identified with it. The culmination of the transformation was the rise of the Confucian scholars to leadership in the empire.

THE RISE AND DECLINE OF THE CHINESE EMPIRE

Like other great empires, the Chinese empire began in the career of a conquering state, extended its power over a vast area, and finally collapsed from the weakening effects of both external and internal forces it had created.[1]

[1] For the general history of the ancient Chinese empire see Henri Maspero, *La Chine antique* (1927); K. S. Latourette, *The Chinese: Their history and culture* (2 vols., 1934); Marcel Granet, *Chinese Civilization* (1930); Friedrich Hirth, *The Ancient History to the End of the Chou Dynasty* (1911); and Richard Wilhelm, *A Short History of Chinese Civilization* (1929). A useful brief account is found in E. T. Williams, *A Short History of China* (1928). On the phases of Chinese history see H. T. Lei, " Periodization: Chinese History and

WARRING STATES AND IMPERIAL DYNASTIES.

Although the transition from feudal anarchy to the centralized empire was brought about abruptly in the third century B.C. the empire was not fully identified with Chinese culture until two centuries later.

1. *The Warring States* (403–221 B.C.). The final crisis of the Chou feudal regime began in the fifth century B.C., when seven powers, known as the "seven martial states," entered upon a bitter struggle for supremacy. Among these states, six—Han, Wei, Chao, Ch'u, Ch'i, and Yen—were in the Huang and Yangtze valleys; the seventh, Ch'in, was within the mountain barriers of Shensi. Of those in the river valley, Ch'i in the western part of the Shantung peninsula, Yen to the west of the Huang delta, and Ch'u in the central Yangtze valley were the most important. In 403 B.C. Han, Wei, and Chao dismembered a minor state known as Chin. But Ch'i, under the rule of an adventurer who organized the iron and salt industries as government monopolies, advanced most rapidly in power. Yen and Ch'u, like Ch'in, had large non-Chinese populations, and their rulers were adventurers, warriors, and scholars, who did not come from the old nobility. They conscripted armies, built great walls around their territories, and fought to the death to gain the coveted supremacy. For a time, however, Ch'i held off all rivals for ascendancy with a formidable light cavalry, armed with "magic swords" made of iron. After 312 B.C., when Ch'u was defeated by Ch'in, Ch'i and Ch'in faced each other and for a time divided the "world." The ruler of each country bore the title emperor—*ti*.[1]

2. *The Triumph of Ch'in.* The development of the power of Ch'in was begun under Duke Hsiao (361–338 B.C.), who supported Wei Yang (d. *ca.* 338 B.C.), commonly known as Shang Yang, in carrying out a program of political, economic, and military reorganization. Feudalism was abolished, private property in land was established, taxes were levied according to the area and not the product of the land, border regions were opened for settlement, a severe legal system was introduced, and compulsory military service was made universal, for able-bodied women as well as all but old men. In order to break up the traditional

---

World History," *The Chinese Social and Political Science Review*, Vol. 20 (1936–1937), pp. 461–491.
[1] See H. T. Lei, "The Rise of the Emperor System in Ancient China," *The Chinese Social and Political Science Review*, Vol. 20 (1936–1937), pp. 251 *ff*.

THE CHINESE EMPIRE c. 220 B.C.

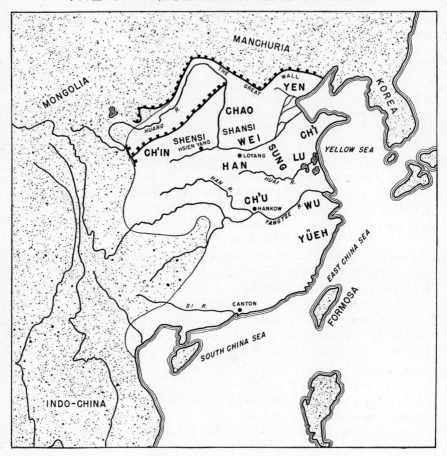

social system, the younger sons of nobles were compelled to farm, and a father and his sons were forbidden to live in the same house. As a result of these measures, Ch'in became a strong centralized monarchy, the peasants owned the land and paid a direct tax to the king, and wealth increased greatly, partly because of the new system of land tenure and partly because of the construction of great irrigation projects. Although Shang Yang favored agriculture over commerce, many merchants became rich and some of them rose to political prominence.[1]

[1] See J. L. L. Duyvendak, trans., *The Book of Lord Shang: A classic of the Chinese school of law* (1925).

As far as Ch'in was concerned, the traditional feudal regime was a thing of the past. Under the all-powerful king, a hierarchy of appointed officials ruled the people. The peasants, free of the obligation of working the land but owing taxes to the king, formed a base of wealth and military power. Merchants, adventurers, and scholars found opportunity to serve the state in many ways. And the hill people of the west, kinsmen of the king of Ch'in, furnished soldiers for a standing army that soon exceeded in numbers and excelled in equipment the armed force of any rival.

Ch'in, however, was not recognized by the other states as a part of China; it was feared but not admired. Throughout the fourth century B.C., as its power grew, the absorption of the culture of the Huang valley went on; the decisive step of introducing the ritual of the other states was taken in 326 B.C. In the third century B.C. Ch'in overcame all opposition. In 299 B.C. the king of Ch'u was dethroned. Six years later Han and Wei were defeated. In 260 B.C. Chao fell, and a large army which had been starved into submission was slaughtered. In 256 B.C. the Chou dynasty was destroyed. In 222 B.C. the last feudal prince was overthrown, and in the next year the remnant of Ch'i was conquered.

After 247 B.C. the leader of Ch'in was the man—Chêng—who is known to history as Shi Huang Ti—the first sovereign emperor of China; he took the title in 221 B.C. and reigned as emperor until 210 B.C. His chief minister, Li Ssǔ (280?–208 B.C.), an itinerant scholar, was largely responsible for the program that unified his conquests into a centralized monarchy. The theory of unification, drawn from the political philosophy of the Legalists, made power— *shih*—the chief end of all governmental action. Li Ssǔ gave this theory practical application in measures which kept alien scholars and soldiers in the service of Ch'in, made the ministers dependent on the king, set the people at productive labor, and reduced the danger of internal disorder.[1]

Shi Huàng Ti's rule is well symbolized by the unsheathed sword, which he held while sitting on the throne, for his policies cut through the ancient institutions as the blade of his sword had cut through his opponents. In order to destroy the old nobility, he transported thousands of families to Shensi, where they sank into peasantry. All arms not in the hands of his own soldiers were confiscated and melted down. In order to silence the scholars, especially the Confucianists, who idealized Chou, he ordered that

[1] See Derk Bodde, *China's First Unifier: A study of the Ch'in Dynasty as seen in the life of Li Ssǔ (280?–208 B.C.)* (1938).

the copies of the classical books of history and poetry and all works of philosophy should be burned. Works on divination, medicine, pharmacy, agriculture, arboriculture, astrology, and history, especially works treating the rise of Ch'in, were impounded in the imperial library, where only authorized persons could consult them. Education became a monopoly of the state. Over four hundred magicians who had duped the emperor in his quest for an elixir of life were buried alive. The attack on the scholars is understandable when it is realized that most of them came from the ranks of the lower nobility—a fertile source of intrigue and insurrection.

Such destructive acts were supported by constructive measures aimed to promote unification. The laws of Ch'in, as well as its systems of land tenure and taxation, were extended to all China. Weights and measures, the system of writing, and even the length of the axles of carts were standardized. And to facilitate the collection of tax grain and the movement of troops, a vast road system radiating from the capital, Hsien Yang, in Shensi, was built. By connecting existing structures, the Great Wall, extending from the sea to Kansu, was raised; over a million workers, it is said, died before this vast undertaking was completed. It was an effective defense against the raids of the Hiung-nu, known later as the Huns, who held the sparse grasslands of Mongolia.

3. *The Han Dynasty* (202 *B.C.–A.D.* 220). The death of Shi Huang Ti was followed by a conspiracy, which raised his second son to the throne, but at the court power passed to eunuchs and in the provinces to military officers. Both proved irresponsible, increasing the harsh taxes, the ruinous levies of forced labor, the cruel confiscations, and the tortures and mutilations of the first emperor. In 209 B.C. popular discontent, taking fire from a revolt in Ch'u led by a farmer-soldier, inspired a general insurrection. Representatives of the old ruling families and common adventurers, although momentarily held in check by the Ch'in, quickly acquired all power. In the east Hsiang Yü, a member of the ancient nobility, organized a confederacy of states and attempted to restore the feudal regime. In the west Liu Chi, known after his coronation as Liu Pang, held Ch'u and soon won control of Ch'in. In the duel between Hsiang Yü and Liu Chi the economic resources of Ch'u and Ch'in gave the latter military superiority and, after a brief struggle, he won the supreme power (202 B.C.).

As founder of the Han Dynasty, Liu Pang preserved some of the reforms of Shi Huang Ti but was careful to cloak them in a restored feudalism. Although recognized, the princes were completely without power, and the emperor, remembering how he had made war against his rival, Hsiang Yü, took care that no general should ever become firmly planted in a command. The people were no longer required to provide food for the army from their own stores and were even permitted to advise officials in the conduct of their offices. Measures of leniency, such as the granting of amnesty to political opponents and the liberation of slaves, were taken on occasions of imperial celebration. And the graves of the ancient kings were cared for so that their ghosts, remaining quiet, would not excite the people.[1] Underlying the success of Liu Pang was the national resentment aroused by the Ch'in's violent disturbance of tradition, and his successors were the heirs of the favor he won by seeming to return to the past. Actually, however, the Han Dynasty consolidated the reforms of the Ch'in and, as a result, led China into a new era. Under Wu Ti (140–87 B.C.) the Chinese empire experienced a golden age.

4. *The Expansion of the Chinese Empire under the Early Han Emperors.* The original center of Chinese culture was the lower Huang valley. By the opening of Chou times it had spread to the Wei and Feng valleys. In the eighth century B.C. the Han and central Yangtze valleys were drawn into its area. At the same time it was pushed northward and southward from the lower Huang valley. When Shi Huang Ti built the Great Wall, China was a consolidated state and an integrated culture area covering the lands between Tibet, the Mongolian plateau, the southern tributaries of the Yangtze River, and the sea. He colonized the area around modern Canton and sent expeditions into Korea.

Under the early Han emperors the imperialistic forces of urban culture promoted further expansion.[2] To the south, southwest, and north the expansion was mainly a colonizing movement which bound new peoples into the Chinese culture area. To the northwest and west it was both a commercial and a political movement. The original impetus to expand in these directions was provided by border troubles with the Hiung-nu, who were at war with the Yueh Chi, another neighboring people. Under Wu Ti a considered policy of western expansion was adopted; its immediate objective, besides the pacification of the border, was to acquire the spirited

[1] See H. H. Dubs, *The History of the Former Han Dynasty by Pan Ku* (1938).
[2] See G. E. Hudson, *Europe & China: A Survey of Their Relations from the Earliest Times to 1800* (1930); also Friedrich Hirth, "The Story of Chang K'ien, China's Pioneer in Western Asia," *The Journal of the American Oriental Society,* Vol. 37 (1917), pp. 89–136.

horses, known in China as the "supernatural horses," of the central Asiatic grasslands. Until this time China, it should be remembered, possessed mainly small Mongolian ponies.

In 138 B.C. Wu Ti sent Chang Ch'ien on a mission to the Yueh Chi, but he reached them in central Asia only after having been held captive by the Hiung-nu for ten years; in 126 B.C. he returned, bringing much geographical information, the first definite news of India and Bactria, the seeds of the grape and alfalfa, and "supernatural horses." The Chinese followed up his success with a military expedition which in 121 B.C. drove the Hiung-nu northward and established Chinese rule in the area around Lop Nor. Chang Ch'ien again went west in 115 B.C. Caravan trade between central Asia and China seems to have started in 106 B.C. In 104–100 B.C. a Chinese military expedition captured Ferghana on the Jaxartes River in a campaign designed to force the sale of the much desired "supernatural horses." The success in obtaining these animals led to the displacement of the chariotry by a heavy-armed cavalry in the Chinese army, and the contact with the central Asiatic lands established the trade in silk—"the most far reaching large-scale commerce of antiquity."

The Great Silk Road passed from China through the Tarim Basin to central Asia. This basin—a vast area of 350,000 square miles—lay between The Gobi and The Pamirs and the Kwen Lun and Tian Shan ranges. Its chief river, the Tarim, was over a thousand miles long; it rose from the melting snows of the western Kwen Lun mountains and sank finally into the marshes of the Lop Nor district at the western edge of China proper. Most of the Tarim Basin, except for small oases at the foot of the mountains, was desert. Two routes led westward through its marshes, dunes, and oases—one along the southern rim to Khotan and the other around the northern edge to Kashgar. Khotan was located in the largest oases of the basin; its prosperity rested on the agricultural exploitation of a loess soil which, when irrigated, yielded good crops. Khotan became the main point of contact with India. Kashgar was the terminus of the routes from Balkh, which was the central Asiatic place of exchange with lands farther to the west. The journey from Changan to Kashgar required seven months; probably few Chinese merchants went beyond this point. In order to protect the trade with these cities the Chinese established military garrisons along the routes beyond Tunhuang, the farthermost outpost of the empire on the west; these garrisons supported themselves by farming in the oases about the edges

THE CHINESE EMPIRE UNDER THE HAN DYNASTY

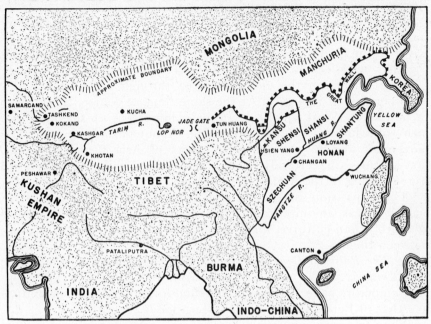

of the Tarim Basin.[1] Trade with the central Asiatic lands was promoted mainly by sending embassies to their rulers. These embassies commonly remained away from China for a period of ten years.

After Wu Ti's successes in the west, Chinese activity declined for a time, partly because the Hiung-nu disrupted intercourse by the northern route and partly because drifting sands in the Tarim Basin made the journey increasingly difficult. In the first century—74 to 94—renewed military activity under the great general Pan Ch'ao (32–102) brought the oases of Turkestan under Han rule. His army marched to the shores of the Caspian Sea and one of his messengers reached the Persian Gulf. Parthian tales of the terrible hardships to be encountered in western lands, rather than Parthian power, halted his advance, which, it seems, may have been aimed at opening direct communication with

[1] On the Tarim Basin see Sir M. A. Stein, *On Ancient-Central-Asian Tracks* (1933); Sir M. A. Stein, *Ancient Khotan: Detailed report of archaeological explorations in Chinese Turkestan* (3 vols., 1907); also R. C. F. Schomberg, "The Climatic Conditions of the Tarim Basin," *The Geographical Journal*, Vol. 75 (1930), pp. 311–323.

Rome or rather with the eastern Mediterranean lands ruled by Rome. They called these lands Ta Ch'in.

Under Wu Ti the Chinese also won a foothold in Korea and brought southern China—from the headwaters of the Mekong River to the Gulf of Tonkin—under Chinese rule. These advances, together with the occupation of the Tarim Basin, established Chinese culture in the enormous area through which it was to have permanent influence. At the same time, of course, those contacts with the West which were to be so important for the development of Chinese culture were made. About this time, too, the movement around the southern coasts of Asia began. By the first century A.D. certainly, Indian and Chinese sailors and traders were meeting in the Malay Archipelago.

The expansion of the Chinese empire under the early Han emperors was an important development for both Eastern and Western urban cultures, for it established the first direct contacts between them.

5. *The Political Organization of the Chinese Empire under the Han Dynasty.* The political innovations of the Ch'in and the Han emperors gave China a monarchial form of government quite like that of Persia, India, and Western lands.[1]

The emperor—an absolute despot—governed through an appointive bureaucratic hierarchy. At its head stood several boards, which actually, although charged with supervising military affairs, public works, justice, provincial administration, and newly settled areas, were concerned with ceremonials. Under Liu Pang a threefold division of territorial administration was devised: provinces, prefectures, and districts. Under Shi Huang Ti there were thirty-six provinces, under Wu Ti thirteen. Vice-governors, comparable to the Persian satraps, ruled the provinces. The truly active agents of the imperial authority were magistrates who resided in the districts. They supervised public works and famine relief, tried criminal cases, and performed certain religious ceremonies. Since the taxes were passed from the lowest official to the official next in rank above him until they reached the imperial treasury, there was a steady dissipation of funds in the course of transmission. This peculation was unofficial but not illegal. The magistrates dealt with the village headmen and elders, who were the real governors of the people. If the magistrates maintained order, government was good; if they permitted dis-

[1] K. Bloch, "Reflections on the Social Structure in China," *Social Research*, Vol. 4 (1937), pp. 490–508.

orders, which meant that others besides imperial officials preyed upon the peasant villagers, government was bad. Of course the people, according to Confucian theory, had the right of revolution, which, if conditions became too bad, they could exercise by supporting a conspirator against the emperor or an audacious bandit daring to aspire to be the Son of Heaven. Unfortunately only rare candidates were successful, and still rarer were those successful ones who gave serious thought to the welfare of the common people.

The Chinese never produced a theory of jurisprudence, except insofar as li^1 may be regarded as one, nor a complete legal system. Public law as opposed to rites appeared in the sixth century B.C. and was developed by the Legalists. But they were more interested in power than in justice, for they looked upon reward as well as punishment as a device to get the people to serve the state. Private law was never clearly differentiated from custom. Contracts rested on the good faith inculcated by Confucian ethical teachings. A distinction between personal debts and debts on land was recognized. Enslavement for debt was allowed. If a debtor sold his family into slavery and disposed of his land to satisfy a creditor, the creditor had no further claim on him. The criminal law was very harsh. The five punishments for criminals—beheading, cutting off the nose, chopping off the legs, castration, and burying alive—were believed to have been established by one of the early traditional emperors. It was also believed that the Shang Dynasty had introduced the practice of commuting the death penalty to transportation, as well as the rule that, in case extenuating circumstances existed when a man committed a crime or if there was any doubt as to his guilt, he should be shown leniency. Ch'in law was especially brutal; the Han emperors reverted to the milder tradition of the Shang. Liu Pang reduced the crimes punishable with death to three—murder, mayhem, and robbery. The codification of the laws began in the time of Confucius, when some of them were recorded on bamboo tablets. Legalist influence produced codes in several of the warring states. The Ch'in, although they made law the support of their rule, do not seem to have produced a general code. The Han developed a code of the private law in sixty sections which became the base of later dynastic compilations. Although the criminal law always provided for atrocious punishments, the need for revenue caused fines to be substituted for many of them; for this

¹ See p. 423.

reason the enforcement of the law was probably milder than its provisions.[1]

Besides the village elders and headmen, who had charge of such local affairs as the assessment and payment of taxes and the organization of relief in time of public calamity, the family and the guild governed the people.

Theoretically the family was a patriarchate, but actually the mother's influence was strong. The family, consisting of the father, the mother, the sons, the sons' wives and their children, and sometimes the father's brothers, was in reality a clan; its members, who lived about a common courtyard, were entirely subject to its rule. It administered all family property on a communistic basis. It decided which son should be educated and what occupations the other children should take up. It determined whom the sons should marry, and when; daughters passed, at marriage, into the families of their husbands. It was collectively liable for the crimes of its members. It was responsible for its sick, aged, and orphaned. Ancestor worship, which together with numerous animistic superstitions constituted the religion of the masses, bound the family into a tightly knit unit, and filial piety was the greatest of virtues.

The guild was the chief instrument of economic government. All those engaged in an occupation within a recognized area were members of that occupation's guild; as a matter of fact, the guilds were exclusively urban. Different kinds of merchants, craftsmen, and professional men had separate guilds, which fixed prices, hours, qualities of workmanship, and punishments for violations of the rules. Guild courts heard cases involving such violations. Like the peasant-village patriarchal families, these urban guilds checked the competitive struggle for riches and assured at least the maintenance of a common level of poverty.

Because the family controlled almost every act outside the economic sphere, which was under the guild, the imperial regime hardly touched the people, except when by royal edict some reform of the chief social and political institutions was proclaimed. After the triumph of Confucianism, which made tradition the norm of virtue and justice, such edicts became more and more rare. The real law of China was an unwritten common law applied in village courts, and every village had its own legal tradition.

Except as regards obedience to the supreme authority and the payment of uniform taxes, the people of China lived under the

[1] Jean Escarra, *Le Droit chinois, conception et évolution* (1936).

empire much as they had lived under the feudal regime. Local affairs were under their control, and prosperity was a gift of nature —which, indeed, the emperor claimed to have obtained from Heaven. His magic, as wrought in rituals, was the chief factor in maintaining the harmony between Heaven and men upon which prosperity depended.

6. *The Later Han Dynasty, A.D.* 25–220. After the great expansion under Wu Ti, social and economic development stimulated by the growth of commerce and industry produced new controversies over policies, and new social groups rose to political power. On the one hand the owners of large landed estates, the manufacturers of iron, and the boilers of salt were continually at odds with the philosophers and scholars, while on the other hand the peasants, sometimes under rebels and sometimes under religious leaders, sought over and over again to use the power of the state for social amelioration. Wang Mang (A.D. *ca.* 9–23), a descendant of a Han emperor through a concubine, seized the throne and undertook sweeping reforms favorable to the peasants.[1] Resistance by the scholars and property-owning classes finally raised to the throne a member of a southern family, who, known as Kuang Wu Ti (*ca.* 25–57), pacified the empire. He moved the capital from Changan, where the first Han emperors had established it, to Loyang; for this reason the dynasty he founded is known as the Eastern, or Later, Han. Under its leadership internal order was restored and Chinese culture was pushed southward across the Yangtze valley in the direction of the region known later as Annam.

In this extension, as well as in internal conditions and in contacts with the peoples to the north and west, were circumstances which ultimately caused the disorganization of the empire. The new areas, especially in the lower Yangtze valley, became centers of wealth production which could be made the basis of political and military attacks on the imperial regime. At the imperial court intrigues continually disturbed the government, and among the peasantry the burden of taxation produced distress. In the west and north, as trade expanded and new military techniques were borrowed, the non-Chinese peoples grew stronger and, consequently, became a menace. The combined effect of these developments was so to alter the balance of power in favor of border lands, that they could become centers of attack upon the heart of the empire.

[1] See p. 824.

By courtesy of the Museum of Fine Arts, Boston

KUANG WU TI

After Wang Mang failed to win the support of the people for reforms that were meant to ameliorate their lot, Kuang Wu Ti, the founder of the Later Han Dynasty (A.D. 25–220), restored order in the patterns of the Confucianist tradition and Legalist practice. This portrait is from a seventh century scroll.

The crisis which disrupted the Chinese empire began, however, within the court and among the peasantry of the Huang valley early in the second century and continued through several phases until the Later Han Dynasty was overthrown in 220. Toward the end of the second century, when female favorites rocked the court with rivalries, when the court eunuchs fought the philosophers, and when agitators proclaimed the Confucian doctrine that the people have a right to overthrow an unjust ruler, a great uprising broke out in the central provinces. Its partisans, known as the Yellow Turbans, were mainly members of a Taoist sect; the officials called them "rice thieves," a name which suggests the economic character of the insurrection which quickly swept over the whole empire. The leaders of the movement combined religious with economic motivation by promising immortal life to every follower who died on the field of battle.

The imperial forces, which suppressed the revolt, were mainly barbarian mercenaries from the north, and after the victory they quickly fell to fighting over the throne. Rival generals killed one another, and the court eunuchs plotted the destruction of the survivors. Finally in 220 a victorious commander purged the eunuchs and set aside the Han line.

7. *The Disorganization of the Chinese Empire after A.D.* 220. The successors of the Later Han Dynasty did not rule a united empire. In the Huang valley was one kingdom, around the mouth of the Yangtze river another, and in the middle Yangtze valley still another centering about Szechuan. These states were constantly at war with one another.

Shortly after the middle of the third century a dynasty which divided the empire into two kingdoms—an eastern and a western—won power, but it did not halt the process of disintegration, for no less than sixteen kingdoms, most of them ruled by short-lived barbarian dynasties appeared. Changan and Loyang were sacked by the Hiung-nu during wars that tossed up these kingdoms, and from time to time Nanking was the seat of a weak imperial rule. Early in the fifth century the empire was divided again, this time into a northern and a southern kingdom. The southern kingdom in the Yangtze valley was ruled by Chinese princes. In the Huang valley a dynasty of Tatar origin held dominion over a turbulent population of mixed Chinese and barbarian stocks.

In the Chinese empire, as in the Roman, intrigues, insurrections, civil wars, invasions, and the overthrow of dynasties were the external manifestations of fundamental changes. Behind political disorganization were shifts in the centers of wealth production, caused mainly by the construction of water-control projects and the dislocations of the basic peasant-village population. Each of these developments so affected the sources of power that political adventurers could contest with established rulers for the rule of the state. In the course of these contests the lower Yangtze valley became the center of Chinese culture, and the old culture area of the Huang valley became the home of the new mixed population. Among its members foreign cultural materials, mainly associated with Buddhism, were assimilated into almost every element of the traditional culture, and from them spread southward. The Chinese empire, like the Roman,[1] went down because imperial expansion set in motion a social and economic process which collapsed its foundations—the peasant-village population; in this process, however, new materials were organized in Chinese life, so that the people of China, like those of the Roman ruled Mediterranean lands, emerged with a reorientated cultural tradition.

ECONOMIC AND SOCIAL ASPECTS OF THE CHINESE EMPIRE.

From earliest times Chinese culture was rooted in villages. The developments that produced the empire multiplied and integrated the villages but did not change their fundamental character. Neither trade nor industry ever disturbed the fundamental localism of the rural economy, and political organization advanced only as modes of control applicable to many villages were developed.[2]

1. *The Development of Water Control in China.* The floods and droughts that afflicted the river valleys set for the Chinese the problem of controlling water, both as a means of protection to settled areas and as a way of increasing production. Simple methods of irrigation were in use very early, but systematic projects were undertaken only when the feudal regime began to break down. During the feudal struggles rival princes found the building of dikes and canals a method of increasing their economic resources and gaining popular support. In fact so important was this work that its performance came to be regarded as a duty of officials. From the eighth to the fifth century B.C. six irrigation projects were undertaken and completed, from the fifth to the middle of the third century B.C. eight more. The advance of Ch'in was hastened by the opening in 246 B.C. of a canal which carried the waters and silt of the Ching River over a large part of central Shensi. It was the king's control of this project that made possible the complete destruction of the feudal nobility and the introduction of private property in land, with the peasants paying taxes directly to the state.

---

[1] See pp. 934 *ff.*
[2] On the economic history of China see K. A. Wittfogel, *Wirtschaft und Gesellschaft Chinas* (1931); Chao Ting-Chi, *Key Economic Areas in Chinese History as Revealed in the Development of Public Work for Water Control* (1936); Mabel Ping-hua, *The Economic History of China* (1921); and Wan Kuoh-Ting, *An Agrarian History of China* (1933).

The triumph of the Han had origin in the seizure of these irrigated lands. Together with parts of Szechuan and Kansu, they were a "heavenly storehouse," which, although forming only one-third of the area of China, had, it is said, three-tenths of the population and three-fifths of the wealth. Fifty-six water-control projects are known to have been undertaken by the Han emperors. Wu Ti was very active in repairing and extending canals and dikes. The shift of power to the Later Han Dynasty was due, in part, to the development of systematic water control in the lower Huang, Han, and Hwai valleys. From the fall of the Han empire to the end of the sixth Christian century many water-control projects, mainly in the Yangtze valley and farther south, were completed. The extension of water control in these regions, as well as the neglect of canals and dikes in the northern provinces, was a factor in the disorganization of the empire during these centuries.

With the increased production which large-scale irrigation supported, the wealth of the prince who directed it grew in amount so rapidly that the local feudal rulers could not stand before him. Thus as water-control projects were developed the nobles were weakened and the struggle of the states became more intense. The creation of the empire reflected the economic supremacy of the Shensi area, and the shifts of power within the empire in later times had origin quite directly in the rise of various regions to economic leadership and their decline. Always this leadership rested on water control and agriculture, however much industry and commerce contributed to it. The shifts also reflected the results of the reclamation of old areas and the opening up of new regions which came with the extension of water controls.

2. *The Advance of Chinese Agriculture.* Although the spread of irrigation was the decisive factor in the expansion of the Chinese peasant-village economy, several other developments contributed to an elaboration of its techniques and crops. About the middle of the last millennium B.C. iron implements superseded the stone hoes and spades which had remained in use since early neolithic times. The Chinese peasantry, it seems, never passed through a bronze age. At the same time the traction plow and the ox, used exclusively for draft purposes, reached China. In the southern provinces the water buffalo was employed for plowing and hauling. The horse was never made a work animal. Another innovation of this period was the application of manure to the soil. These advances did not alter the traditional intensive character of Chinese tillage; it remained, at base, a hoe culture, and its typical

unit was the garden or small plot rather than the field. However, they did bring a considerable increase in the productivity of labor.

The original Chinese cereal was millet; when rice and wheat arrived from foreign lands is not known, but in the period of the rise of systems of water control they became common crops. Soy beans and buckwheat also were staples. After the penetration of central Asia in Han times many new plants were carried eastward. Tea was known in early Chou times but was not widely cultivated until the fourth century A.D. The expansion of the area of rice tillage was achieved by developing the technique of terracing hillsides. Where the hilltops were not cultivated they quickly became deeply eroded. The Chinese, who used human excrement as a fertilizer, never learned to rotate their crops. Their chief domestic animals were the pig and the sheep, and their common fowls the chicken and the goose. The cow was never kept for dairy purposes. The Chinese had an aversion to milk and its products which may have been an expression of their bitter hostility to the men of the "Devil's Country." After Han times few improvements were made in the methods of Chinese tillage.

3. *The Chinese Crafts.* The crafts of China, although developed in distinctive ways, were like those of Western lands.

Among the building crafts carpentry was most important, for wood was always preferred to brick and stone for building purposes. Pounded clay was, of course, a favorite material, used mainly for walls and military works. After bamboo, introduced from India, spread through the southern provinces, it was used in combination with wood. Painting and carving developed as adjuncts of the building crafts, as did also the manufacture and application of lacquers. Furniture making became an important craft in Han times, when, it seems, couches, armchairs, and small tables became popular.

The earliest Chinese pottery dates from about the opening of the third millennium B.C. The painted pottery of the middle of this millennium gave way ultimately to a fine ware made of white material but painted black. Recent archaeological finds indicate that colored glazes were in use in Shang times. However, a primitive buff ware remained common until the end of Chou times. Early in the Han era, perhaps as a result of contacts with the West, lead glaze, clay slips, and coloring with copper oxide came generally into use. Porcelain, the greatest Chinese ceramic achievement, was developed probably as the result of attempts to imitate glass. Glass has been discovered recently in the tombs of Han officials.

The great advance of Chinese ceramics in post-Han times was due, there is good reason to believe, to the diffusion of Western techniques.

The metal crafts in China were, it is almost certain, based on borrowed techniques. The Shang bronze products, almost perfect of their kind, have no antecedents in China except in pottery forms. The copper phase of the development of metallurgy was hardly known in China, and the transition to iron was relatively abrupt. It has been noted in a preceding paragraph that the tools of the peasants passed directly from the neolithic to the iron age. Since bronze was identified with the nobility, its chief uses were for weapons and ritual vessels, and these persisted long after iron was used for the implements of the field and the tools of the crafts. Iron displaced bronze for military uses during the period of the warring states. Passages in the *Chou-li*, a Han compilation, indicate that the Chinese, although excellent smiths, knew little about the metals and their alloys. Gold and silver were never plentiful. The finest known metal products of ancient China are the Shang bronze ritual vessels and the Han bronze or copper mirrors. By the second century B.C. iron was in general use for weapons, tools, utensils, and chariot fittings, but the great age of Chinese ironworking was, like the great age of ceramics, still in the future.

The major Chinese contribution to the world's textiles is silk. The date of its invention has not been determined, but there is reason to believe that it was known by the opening of the second millennium B.C. However, it remained a rare and expensive material until the economic expansion of the middle of the last millennium B.C. When the Han penetrated the central Asiatic lands it was treated as a commodity suitable to be possessed only by princes and its manufacture was a carefully protected monopoly. The sumptuary laws of the early empire indicate that its use was spreading from the aristocracy to the new merchants. The loom with which the Chinese wove silk was more efficient, it seems, than the Western loom. Recent discoveries of bits of Han silk show that it was made with many figured designs, some of which show Hellenistic influence. From the very earliest times the Chinese common people wore clothing made from a kind of grass cloth. The date of the arrival of cotton from India is not known; it was probably not later than the end of the Han era. The styles of Chinese garments were fixed about the end of the fifth century B.C., when a king of Chao borrowed certain kinds of garments, including trousers, and the practice of quilting cloth from the

From WILLIAM CHARLES WHITE, *Sometime Bishop of Honan, Tomb Tile Pictures of Ancient China* (1939).   *The University of Toronto Press*

THE SCYTHIAN COSTUME

The recently discovered tiles of Han graves in the valley of the Lo River afford an interesting record of many aspects of ancient Chinese life. This galloping horse and rider with a Scythian cap testify to central Asiatic influences in ancient Chinese culture.

northern nomads; these styles spread first in the armies and then among the common people. The aristocratic costume seems to have remained true to the Chou style.

The most original Chinese invention—paper—was made probably early in the second Christian century; it was soon produced in several varieties from different materials, such as tree bark, hemp, rags, and old fish nets. The archaeological exploration of the trade routes of the Tarim Basin has yielded bits of early Chinese paper, as well as pieces of silk. Probably the earliest known samples of Chinese paper date from the sixth or seventh century.[1]

4. *The Growth of Chinese Commerce and the Formation of a Money Economy.*   Trade did not play an important part in Chinese life until about the middle of the first millennium B.C., when the salt and iron of the seacoast states found a demand in the interior. Foreign trade became important only after the Han westward advance, which led to the growth of the silk trade with

[1] On Chinese technical achievements see Frederick Hung, "Early History of Tea in China," *The Chinese Social and Political Science Review*, Vol. 16 (1932–1933), pp. 260–268; Berthold Laufer, *The Beginnings of Porcelain in China* (1917); Berthold Laufer, *Paper and Printing in Ancient China* (1931); T. F. Carter, *The Invention of Printing in China* (1925).

the Mediterranean lands. Besides silk, rhubarb, jade, lacquer, and iron, the last probably not a product of China itself, passed westward. This trade was at its height in the first and second centuries. About this time, also, a sea-borne commerce grew up between China and India by way of the Strait of Malacca. Some goods also passed between China and the Mediterranean lands by this route. At the same time internal trade expanded considerably, mainly because transportation was improved by the building of roads and canals and by the development of navigation on the great rivers. The trade was mostly an exchange between the centers of craft industry in the lower valleys and raw material areas in the upper valleys and highlands.

The earliest medium of exchange in China was the sea shell, which, although known before, was first widely used in Shang times.[1] Early in Chou times, probably in the eighth century B.C., a metal medium of exchange consisting of pieces shaped like the knife, the bell, and the spade appeared. It was minted by various feudal dignitaries and had a fiat value. Money economy spread widely only in the fifth century B.C., with the growth of trade. In 335 B.C. the ancient shell currency was suppressed and the round metallic pieces—the ancestor of the traditional Chinese cash—were issued. In 221 B.C. the round coin with the square perforation—"round as the sky and square as the earth"—was cast, and barter was prohibited.

All Chinese coins, it should be noted, were cast, not struck. Inasmuch as the coins were given values higher than their intrinsic worth, there was constant confusion in their exchange, and counterfeiters found profit in imitating them. The Han emperors dealt with these evils in several ways. In 175 B.C. the right of private minting was withdrawn, without appreciable effect on counterfeiting. Wu Ti undertook to circumvent the counterfeiters by issuing a currency made from the skin of white stags kept only in royal parks; this is the first known experiment with a redeemable nonmetallic currency, so familiar now in paper money. But the experiment was a failure. Finally, in 113 B.C., after an issue of copper coins with red borders, all current coins were declared valueless and a new money having only the value of the copper it contained was issued. With the centralization of minting at Changan, the western Han capital, and the abandonment of coins having arbitrary values, the Chinese empire arrived at a metallic

[1] See Harry Glathe, "The Origin and Development of Chinese Money," *The China Journal*, Vol. 30 (1939), pp. 97–107, 210–218.

currency suited, because of the small value of its copper pieces, to the local traffic that formed the bulk of its commerce.

After the opening of the trade with the West large amounts of precious metal were imported, and gold became more plentiful. However, a gold coinage was not minted.

Elementary forms of banking and credit operations appeared in the course of the growth of trade and the development of money economy. Moneylending was mainly a local business. Some bankers found it highly profitable to speculate in coins. Under the Han, especially in the second century B.C., the state depended on loans from bankers for "cash" to cover extraordinary expenditures necessitated by wars and revolts. Money was borrowed to pay troops in the field, and, in some cases, action against rebels was delayed until the bankers decided upon the advisability of making loans. Private fortunes based on commerce and banking appeared for the first time in the fifth century B.C., when new fields of enterprise for private investment, such as iron mining, smithing, and salt boiling, began to develop.

5. *The Full Emergence of the Urban Social Structure in China.* The decline of feudalism and the rise of the empire were the political correlatives of the changes which gave China an urban social structure similar, at least in its main elements, to those of other urban cultures. The full emergence of this social structure occurred under the Earlier Han Dynasty. Of the great cities of this age very little remains; for example, at the site of Changan only a part of a wall of pounded earth has been found.[1]

Four new social groups appeared: (1) military leaders whose power was relative to the economic resources they could command, (2) merchants and capitalists engaged mainly in trade, iron mining, and salt boiling, (3) free peasants having a title to land and owing obligations in kind to the state, and (4) landless laborers who could be recruited for either warlike or peaceful enterprises.[2]

As a representative of the anti-Ch'in movement, Liu Pang outwardly harked back to the Chou order. Thus he encouraged agriculture at the expense of commerce and imposed harsh taxes on merchant-capitalists and artisans, whom he excluded from office. His policy toward the old nobility, which he pretended to restore, and the military leaders was shrewd and far-sighted. He reduced the nobles to helplessness by giving them fiefs surrounded by

[1] C. W. Bishop, "An Ancient Chinese Capital Earthworks at Chang-an," *Antiquity*, Vol. 12 (1938), p. 68.

[2] See Marcel Granet, *Chinese Civilization* (1930).

military districts; the generals commanding the districts he frequently displaced and often degraded and executed. Only members of the imperial clan retained positions as princes. By the time of Wu Ti, the old nobility had ceased to be important, and a court clique of princes, female favorites, and eunuchs monopolized the privileges of aristocracy.

The weakening of the old ruling orders opened the way for the advancement of the mercantile and industrial magnates, and the needs of the state gave them opportunity to enter its service. The alliance of the emperor and the merchant-capitalists had origin in the fact that the new standing army required constant supplies of iron weapons, grain, and horses. The Ch'in establishment of private property in land permitted the merchant-capitalists to buy estates. Under the early Han emperors, it was said, the peasants did not own enough land to plant a needle, and the new merchant-capitalists, having become urban-dwelling landlords, ruled the countryside with bands of hired retainers.

At the same time the dispossessed peasants supplied labor under compulsion for the industries of the capitalists, for state projects, and for transportation. Most of the slaves were children sold by the peasants in times of famine; some of them were prisoners of war. There was no organized slave trade. Forced labor, however, was a universal burden inflicted on the peasants. Except in periods of danger from foreign invasion, or after a military disaster, the slaves on state projects were not treated severely; the road to freedom was open to those who could purchase their release. The Chinese never developed an agricultural or industrial slavery comparable to that of the Romans.

During these developments the Han reaction to the Ch'in policies promoted a revival of the traditional scholar group. Liu Pang requested provincial rulers to send only educated men to the imperial court, and his successors broadened the policy by constantly favoring the Confucianists. In 191 B.C. the order against possessing the classical works was rescinded, and in the course of several succeeding decades many of these works were recovered from places where they had been hidden. By the time of Wu Ti an education in the classics was necessary to ennoblement; in this connection it should be noted that the policy of selling titles, which of course were purchased mainly by the new merchant-capitalists, promoted the formation of a new aristocracy. It was, however, much more an aristocracy of wealth and learning than of political power and privilege.

In a sense the empire was the creation of the military class, but its consolidation was the outcome of an alliance of the emperor and the merchant-capitalists and its perpetuation was the work of the scholars, who, although the Confucian tradition praised feudalism, found reason to approve of the centralization of authority. The welding of these elements in the enduring imperial organization was achieved in the course of a controversy over policies that raged under the early Han emperors.

The Controversy Over Social Policy under the Early Han Emperors: State Capitalism vs. Laissez Faire. The Chinese feudal regime fell because technological advances created new wealth, which, since it flowed from new kinds of agriculture, commerce, and industry, could not be acquired through the traditional methods employed by the princes. This wealth was the support of the new centralized empire, but because of its character it accumulated mainly in the hands of traders and manufacturers. The problem faced by the Han emperors may be stated in a question: How was this new wealth to be secured for the state? According to the advice of a tutor of an early Han prince, success depended on supplies: "Now, stores are the life of the Empire. If there is much grain and treasure in abundance what undertaking will not succeed?" Liu Pang dealt with the problem of the relation of the state to the new economy by traditional methods, favoring agriculture and issuing edicts against merchant-capitalists holding offices, wearing silks, and riding in carriages, *i.e.*, against their acting like princes. As time went on, however, their numbers increased, their wealth grew, their estates expanded, their luxury became notorious, and their economic power disturbed the social order. Their speculations in money, which affected prices, were especially disturbing. Moreover, they began to advance in the court hierarchy by purchasing titles. This practice had been initiated by the Ch'in, and in 124 B.C. the Han openly adopted it. The object of the emperors, of course, was to derive wealth from this new body of well to do.

In Wu Ti's reign circumstances greatly increased the need of the state for revenue. The wars with the Hiung-nu were expensive, the westward expansion was costly, and the court spent money extravagantly. In 122 B.C. a flood devastated the lower Huang valley, forcing the government to provide relief on a great scale. Almost a million persons migrated as a result of the catastrophe. The merchant-capitalists fattened on war contracts, the new trade, and the expenditures of the court, and the moneylenders found the needs of the people a golden opportunity for usury. At the same time they hid their wealth from the state, so that taxation was difficult, and were quite indifferent to the relief crisis caused by the flood. Faced with these problems Wu Ti turned from the advisers who had guided his policy to the Legalists for new methods of finance.

The reforms they proposed and, with the aid of the great merchant-capitalists, put into practice were fourfold. First, in order to prevent counterfeiting and halt speculation in coin, the new deerskin currency was issued. As previously noted, this device failed and was displaced by an issue of "cash" having only the value of the metal it contained. Second, heavy taxes were levied on business. All businessmen were required to report their investments as a basis for computing taxes. Manufacturing, moneylending, trading, transporting, and storage enterprises were taxed at high rates. The rates were lower for craftsmen than for business operators. Those who did not report were subject to confiscation of property and transportation to the frontier. Those who informed against violators received one-half of the confiscated property. And traders paid a tax double that of others if they drove a carriage, even if the carriage was used in their business. Third, the iron and salt industries were declared government monopolies, and their administration was placed in the hands of the three most important merchant-capitalists in the empire. The effect of this action was to give the great merchant-capitalists the status of public officials, to ruin the small manufacturers and traders, because all individuals were prohibited from dealing in the monopolized commodities, and to transform the workers in the industries into state slaves or serfs. Fourth and last, a new system of agricultural taxation was introduced. All taxes were paid in the produce most plentiful in a province. These products were stored in public granaries. When a famine occurred in a province, grain was brought to it from these stores. Prices for agricultural produce were set by the government. To this system of storing and distributing agricultural products the names "ever normal granary" and "balanced standard" were given. The first name implied that supplies throughout the empire were kept at a normal level, and the second indicated that prices were not allowed to fluctuate as the yields in various areas were high or low. The operation of the system depended on the roads which the Ch'in and Han emperors had built in order to move the taxes in kind from the rural districts to the urban centers. The cost of transportation was nevertheless high. Thus the government took over the operation of the iron and salt industries and went into the business of distributing the most essential commodities; the system was state capitalism, designed to increase the imperial revenue. These changes were accompanied by a relaxation of the sumptuary laws against the merchant-capitalists.

The reforms augmented the revenue, but their operation produced discontent. The salt, it was said, was bitter and the agricultural implements blunt. The laborers in the mines and monopolized industries felt themselves to be enslaved. The relaxation of the sumptuary legislation against merchant-capitalists was followed by a wave of luxurious spending, and the repeal of the law permitting the denunciation of a merchant-capitalist for failure to report investments caused an uproar. The occurrence of a drought raised the cry that the emperor had angered Heaven and the demand that the administrator of the monopolies be boiled alive. The Confucianist scholars, it should be noted, added greatly to the clamor. When the son of Wu Ti ascended the throne, he called upon the scholars and national worthies to report the distresses of the people. Sixty Confucian scholars answered the call, and between them and the officials a sharp debate took place.

The central issue was the rightfulness or wrongfulness of the state's engaging in mercantile and industrial pursuits for gain, in competition with private individuals. The Confucianists, expressing the traditional contempt for traders, said that the offices were filled with "jackasses." The officials, foreshadowing the recent claim that only those who have "met a payroll" are qualified to speak on economic matters, asked, "What do poor scholars know about the affairs of the state and the business of the officials?" More to the point than the mutual recriminations were the different points of view and the arguments elaborated in terms of them.

The Confucianists, arguing from the classical texts, held that the state had nobler ends to serve than the pursuit of profit; its proper function was to promote the education in virtue that meant national well-being and social order. This contention was supported by the charge that the policy of favoring the merchant was destructive:

"The great merchants accumulate money and get interest at the rate of one hundred per cent; and the smaller ones sell goods in the market. They control extraordinary profit, and speculate around the market day by day. Taking advantage of any immediate demand of the government, they double the price. Therefore, although their men do not cultivate and weed the land, nor their women raise silk worms and weave, yet save elegant raiments they wear not, save savory meat they eat not. They toil not like the farmers, yet they make a hundred, nay, a thousand, times as much profit. On account of their wealth they connect themselves with the princes and the marquises and their powers exceed those of the officials, and they control society by money."[1]

The effects of this disturbance of social order, the Confucianists argued, were far-reaching. Agriculture was deserted for trade. Improper wants were stimulated among the people. The small landlords lost their acres, and the peasants were deprived of their subsistence. Hatred was aroused, wantonness encouraged, and greed rewarded. Simplicity, thrift, and hardihood—the primordial virtues of the people—were lost. Inasmuch as the argument turned on the point of the state's need for revenue, the Confucianists asserted that these developments produced the appetites that necessitated excessive expenditures—in other words, that the need for revenue was engendered by the circumstances that accompanied the adoption of the new policies.

[1] Chun-Ming Chang, "The Genesis and Meaning of Huan K'uan's 'Discourse on Salt and Iron,' " *The Chinese Social and Political Science Review*, Vol. 18 (1934), p. 14. See also E. M. Gale, *Discourses on Salt and Iron: A debate on the state control of commerce and industry in ancient China, Chapters I–XIX. Translated from the Chinese of Huan K'uan with Introduction and Text* (1931).

The merchant-capitalists, Legalists, and officials defended their position ably. Trade, they held, was useful to the state. It balanced the products of one region against those of others, and caused the wealth of the world to circulate. The drawing of people to the cities increased rather than decreased wealth. Getting rich was not so much a matter of work as it was a matter of calculation; it increased rather than disorganized production. The monopolies, they held, were necessary because the salt and iron industries were so large and important that their conduct could not be safely left in the hands of private individuals. They pointed to the princes who had created armies by giving weapons to peasants, saying, "Iron implements and soldiers' weapons are important in the service of the Empire and should not be placed in the hands of the masses." The monopolies also kept down prices and held up quality, preventing the enrichment of the well to do at the expense of the poor. The need for revenue was occasioned not by extravagance but by the cost of defense of the empire against warlike neighbors, especially the Hiung-nu, who, greedy and lacking honor, understood only force as an instrument of persuasion. Practical considerations of state, not selfish desire, required a firm control of economic production and distribution.

In rebuttal the Confucianists made several points. To prevent revolts, they said, it was necessary to instruct the people in their virtues. To equip the farmer with good tools, it was desirable to have private traders who, seeking profit, would not only make strong and sharp implements but also adapt them to different soils and carry them to the farmers' doors. The way to increase wealth was to bring more land into cultivation. To the argument that revenue was required to conduct the war against the Hiung-nu they answered that the war was useless. The proper action was to inculcate in them a respect for honorable commitments and thus to achieve a lasting peace, not a temporary victory that would be followed by an even more expensive war. In effect, therefore, the Confucianists called for a return to agriculture as the source of national wealth, to the classics and custom as guides not only in domestic affairs but also in foreign relations, and, as a result, for their own restoration as the officials of the state. In fact, this debate should be understood partly as the outcome of the philosophical discussion of social policy that had begun with the early disorganization of feudalism and partly as an episode in the struggle for position and power between the scholars and the men of affairs who had created the empire. The emperor and his clique, interested mainly in revenues, forced the argument to turn about financial practices.

The debate did not lead to the immediate restoration of the Confucianists, and the reforms remained in effect for a century. But the difficulties of their administration increased. After the first successes in the west, the Hiung-nu again became troublesome. There were famines and revolts, especially in the mines, and insurrectionary movements spread among the peasants. Slavery increased, and the masters were cruel.

From these disorders emerged finally Wang Mang, who attempted to restore the traditional well-field system of Chou times. He forbade the buying and selling of land, abolished slavery, and extended cheap loans to the peasantry. Also he set up, in addition to the monopolies of iron and salt which he retained for their revenue, monopolies of wood, copper, and wine. To protect the peasants against the merchant-capitalists he fixed prices. In spite of the "socialist emperor's" attempt to disguise these measures as a return to the ancient ways, the scholars repudiated him and the propertied classes turned to banditry. The result was the transfer of the throne to Kuang Wu Ti and the restoration of offices and properties on the grounds of re-establishing "the ancient loyalty between servant and prince." This justification reflected the fact that after a century of controversy the Confucianist scholars and officials had drawn together.[1]

Under the Later Han, therefore, the bureaucracy represented the propertied classes in industry and commerce, as well as on the land, and possessed the learning the Confucianists so prized. "The master stroke of the Han Emperors was to enlist in the support of the centralized state the very school which had upheld feudalism to the last."

Practically, these developments meant the restoration of private property in land, the revival of landlordism, the abolition of the state monopolies, the dependence for revenue upon the land and the peasants— accounted for under a national census—and the re-establishment of a condition not greatly different from serfdom among the peasantry. This status was modified by the custom of the villages, which, however, were subjected to harsh laws that laid down severe punishments for those who failed to fulfill their obligations. In effect, therefore, although Confucian ideas were prominent in the theory of government, the practice, as far as the masses were concerned, came from the Legalists.[2]

6. *The Chinese Peasant-village Masses.* Under the Chinese empire the typical peasant, it has been said, was a "resigned and needy insect," whose ideal was bounded by the hope of a good harvest; it is a fair description.

When first sighted in the villages on the loess deposits of the Huang valley the typical Chinese was a hard-working and super-stition-bound, but nature-loving, tiller of the soil. Later, when he added the crafts to his employment, he neither left his hut nor lost his peasant character. He has been the constant factor in Chinese history, the norm of Chinese culture. In Chou times he lived as a serf on land belonging to his feudal overlord, giving up part of his crop as tax. Although the amount of the tax was changed from time to time, its basic principle was never altered: "Leave only

[1] See K. Bloch, "Reflections on the Social Structure in China," *Social Research*, Vol. 4 (1937), pp. 503–504.
[2] See C. P. Fitzgerald, *China: A short cultural history* (1938), p. 103.

enough in the hands of the peasants to maintain them until another crop grows." A change in the tax rate was actually little more than a revision of the estimated amount of food necessary for the subsistence of the peasant and his family. The Ch'in introduced large-scale forced labor and military conscription. In Han times the enforcement of these obligations was somewhat less rigorous.

After the Ch'in established private property in land, the peasants lost their security, but the village organization of life persisted. Wu Ti undertook to ameliorate the evils that came with money economy by altering the tax rate, on one occasion reducing it to one-thirtieth. In times of famine and flood he remitted all taxes in the stricken areas. Wang Mang's reforms failed mainly because the peasants were so inert that they could not come to his support when the aristocratic classes took arms against him. From pre-Confucian times came the lament of the Chinese masses:

> How free are the wild geese on their wings,
> And they find rest on the bushy yu trees!
> But we, ceaseless toilers in the king's service,
> Cannot even plant our millet and rice.
> What will our parents have to rely on?
> O thou distant and azure Heaven!
> When shall all this end?

From the same times came their boast:

> At dawn we rise,
> At eve we rest,
> Dig wells to drink,
> Till fields to eat;
> What is the might of the Ruler to us?

The Chinese peasantry never influenced political developments. Like the voice of God, which Confucius declared its opinion to be, its voice was never heard. Chinese revolutions were mainly struggles between factions. Ignorant of everything but his calling, bound to tradition by ancestor worship, and limited in outlook by the horizon of his native village, the Chinese peasant was almost as much a part of nature as the earth he tilled, the plants he tended, and the animals he kept. As a worker he was despised by the cultivated hierarchy, and he accepted his inferiority just as he accepted drought, flood, and plague. The vermin crawled over him; he crawled over the earth; both were tao—all was tao. As bearer of a moral tradition which united the performance of customary social obligations with lively sentiments, he needed no law to guide him. The restraints inculcated by the village, the

family, and the guild gave him a seeming dignity—actually a
passivity, which, except when goaded to action by famine or
terror, he never broke. Over him passed unheeded the stream of
history: "The famous empire called 'celestial' has been constantly
broken up—torn into fragments by attacks from the outside and
interior crises. Never has a country undergone so many revolutions,
civil wars, and wholesale massacres. Apart from certain brilliant
periods, which have been as rare as they were short, the whole
history is lamentable and painful. . . . "[1] "Injustice, cruelty, and
indifference to the welfare of the masses were accepted as the
natural state. But all this was equally true everywhere else in
the world. . . . It must be remembered that the humanitarian
ideal, the ideal of the welfare of the commonalty, may always
have been professed in the Occident, but not until the nineteenth
century was it seriously regarded as a practical aim and seriously
advocated as a social policy."[2]

Correctly viewed, the Chinese empire created by the Ch'in and
Han Dynasties consisted of a vast number of peasant villages
loosely knit together under an aristocracy whose members justified
their rule by a decorative learning made possible only by a continuous exploitation of the villagers. Thus the China of the next
two thousand years was born. "Even to-day the Chinese proudly
call themselves *Han Jên*, 'the men of Han.' "[3] When Western men
have judged this regime they have commonly criticized it for
conditions which, in their own regimes, they have disregarded
as unimportant or forgotten entirely.

THE INTELLECTUAL PATTERNS OF CHINESE CULTURE

Shi Huang Ti's attempt to obliterate the philosophies did not
destroy them; rather it created for later scholars the task of
restoring China's traditional learning. Han scholars devoted
themselves earnestly to this work, but, inasmuch as they seem to
have found room for their own ideas in the texts they edited, it
seems certain that much of the restored learning was adjusted to
new interests. Not the traditional learning itself, but the Han
version of it, became the enduring intellectual content of the
Chinese cultural tradition.

[1] A. F. Legendre, *Modern Chinese Civilization* (1929), p. 12. Jonathan Cape, Ltd.,
London.
[2] N. Peffer, *China: The collapse of a civilization* (1934), p. 14. The John Day Company,
New York.
[3] K. S. Latourette, *The Chinese: Their history and culture* (2 vols., 1934), Vol. 1, p. 145.
The Macmillan Company, New York.

CHINESE LITERATE LEARNING AND LITERATURE.

In the Chinese cultural tradition social prestige and the possession of literate learning were more closely united than in any other cultural tradition, at least in the sense that skill in literate learning, along with wealth and military capacity, was a prerequisite to obtaining political office. This circumstance greatly affected the development of Chinese literate learning, but Chinese literature was a product of forces not unlike those that influenced literary developments in other urban cultures.

1. *The Chinese Language and Writing Systems as Factors in the Development of Learning.* Certain peculiarities of the Chinese language and writing system contributed to the formalizing of literate learning, which became the distinctive element in the Chinese cultural tradition.

The relation between a language and the method of thinking that prevails among the people who speak it is very close. For the Chinese this relation was developed in a concrete view of life or, rather, in a view which approached the abstract always through the concrete. In terms of this view generalization and summarization were difficult, whereas the association of phenomena in picturesque combinations was easy. Inasmuch as intellectual conceptions are most easily stated in abstractions and emotions are most easily expressed in vivid images, the Chinese language favored the latter against the former. For this reason Chinese words commonly have a cluster of meanings, each of which carries a particular emotional accent; the effect of this aspect of the language has been to make thought diffuse, rather than precise; *i.e.*, it has taken form in an aggregate of related concepts closely attached to images rather than in concise predications developed in terms of closely reasoned concepts. The following example of a Chinese syllogism suggests this looseness of thought:

Subjects without depravity, then Heaven-below (*i.e.*, the empire) peaceful.

Heaven-below peaceful, then ruler awe-inspiring venerated.

Ruler awe-inspiring, then supervision holding-responsible definite.

Supervision holding-responsible definite, then that-which sought obtained.

That-which sought obtained, then State-home (*i.e.*, nation) prosperous.

State-home prosperous, then ruler(s) joy abundant.

Although brevity and vigor of expression were notable qualities of both Chinese poetry and prose at a very early date, the reason for their prevalence was also a cause of difficulty in shaping abstract ideas.[1]

The Chinese language, as finally developed by the scholars, is known as "Mandarin." Since it consists of about three hundred and forty monosyllabic vocables, each sound necessarily expresses several meanings. Words are built up by compounding vocables; several devices, such as prefixes and the doubling of syllables, are employed in this process. Meanings are distinguished also by the use of four tonal qualities. A fixed word order in sentences helps to differentiate the several meanings a monosyllable may convey. Parts of speech are not defined, nouns being known as "dead words" and verbs as "living words." Such linguistic practices, because they hinder the expression of fine distinctions of meaning and their integration in generalizations, have also been a handicap in the development of abstract thought.

Chinese writing is pictographic, for at the base of each character is a representation of a single object or idea. A full character, however, is a compound of an aural symbol and an ideograph and, as such, stands for a word or a concept. As previously noted, the original pictographs probably appeared in Shang times; if this is true the Chinese writing system is about as old as Western alphabetical writing. The development of the Chinese pictographs into their enduring forms was completed by Han times. In early Chou times the signs were elaborated in a style of writing known as the *Large Seal*, but an older style of writing persisted until at least the time of Confucius. Under the Ch'in, when Li Ssŭ standardized the writing system of the empire, a style known as the *Small Seal* was introduced; it was derived mainly from the *Great Seal*. At the same time an abbreviated form of the signs, known as the *Li* script, was widely used in everyday life. From it, under the Earlier Han Dynasty, sprang the modern Chinese writing system. The Li style was much less pictographic, *i.e.*, far more conventionalized, than any of its predecessors. In early Han times the number of signs was about four thousand; by the end of the second Christian century probably as many more had been added. Several men contributed to the consolidation of the writing system under the Later Han Dynasty. Hsui Hsin (fl. *ca.* 100) compiled the

[1] See Derk Bodde, *China's First Unifier: A study of the Ch'in dynasty as seen in the life of Li Ssŭ (280?–208 B.C.)* (1938), Chap. XI, "Types of Reasoning"; also Derk Bodde, "Types of Chinese Categorical Thinking," *Journal of the American Oriental Society*, Vol. 59 (1939), pp. 200–219.

first dictionary of the Chinese language, which, because it classified the symbols by the signs that determined meaning, drew the characters and the spoken words together, and Tsai Yang (fl. *ca.* 150) first formulated the rules of writing. Wang Hsi-chih (*ca.* 321–379) created the "model style" of writing, which with only slight modifications remained in use until very recent times.

The materials for writing in China were significant factors in the development of the characters. Originally the signs were scratched on bone or tortoise shell. But the brush, it seems now, came into use in Shang times, and writing with ink and brush on bamboo tablets developed in Chou times, at least by the age of Confucius, when books were common. The Han artists depicted the scholar carrying a bamboo book. When silk and, later, paper came into general use as writing materials, calligraphy became a fine art, and the brush stroke developed in writing was soon carried over into painting.

There was no break in the evolution of the Chinese writing system from Shang times onward—a fact which meant that intellectual development was also continuous from those times. The language of the characters, it should be remembered, became different from the popular speech, but whoever learned them, regardless of his dialect, entered into the possession of a body of thought shared by all Chinese learned men. The difficulty of mastering the thousands of characters required for complete familiarity with this body of thought limited the number of scholars able to advance knowledge; indeed, it has been held that the Chinese writing system was far more useful in preserving the unity of Chinese culture than in facilitating its intellectual enrichment.[1]

2. *The Triumph of the Confucian Scholars.* As previously noted, the outcome of the controversy over social policy under the early Han emperors gave the Confucian scholars a privileged position.

Favors heaped upon the Confucian scholars from the beginning of Han times contributed much to their advancement. After the order against possessing the classical books was rescinded, early in the second century B.C., the work of recovering the ancient texts was begun in earnest, at first by private scholars and later with imperial patronage. Wu Ti, who established a new imperial library in which hundreds of copies of the classical books, along with books

[1] See article "Chinese Language" in the *Encyclopaedia Britannica* (14th ed.): also Arnold Silcock, *Introduction to Chinese Art* (1935).

on mathematics, medicine, war, and agriculture, were collected, founded an academy for the study of the classics and instituted the practice of giving state examinations to those who studied them. Thus the basis of the future domination of Chinese intellectual life by the Confucianist scholars was laid; its chief element was the identification of scholarship with antiquarian researches. Sometime in the period of the Earlier Han Dynasty the *Chou-li*, or "The Rites of the Chou," which embodied the social ideal of the scholars, was composed; Wang Mang, who made much of the work, was accused of interpolating passages favorable to his reforms. However this may be, it is certain that the work of editing the classical texts was carried far in his reign. The greatest of the editors was Liu Hsin (d. *ca.* A.D. 22), who drew up a catalogue of the ancient works. Under Kuang Wu Ti, the founder of the Later Han Dynasty, schools for the study of the classics were established in many parts of the empire.

The different attitudes of the philosophies toward knowledge was probably the decisive factor in the survival of classical learning as the chief intellectual element in the Chinese cultural tradition. When the Moists denied the validity of tradition, they came shortly to a situation in which, lacking a body of scientific knowledge, they had nothing to replace it. The Taoists, because they regarded the pursuit of knowledge as a subjective effort, were not impelled to undertake systematic studies or develop organized statements of their findings. The Legalists desired only well-established laws, which, from their point of view, it was best not to discuss. The Confucianists, however, because they believed the true guide to knowledge to be the study of the past, necessarily cherished the ancient writings, produced commentaries upon them, and transmitted them from generation to generation. The result, it is easy to see, was the creation of a body of writings not only more bulky but also more coherent and authoritative than that possessed by their rivals. Thus the pursuit of literate learning and the study of Confucianism tended to become more and more united.

The most remarkable element in Chinese literate learning was the examination system by which scholars were selected for promotion through different grades of achievement. Although the antecedents of this system were deep in China's past, it was evolved slowly under the empire. The theory, if not the practice, of the system was outlined in a Confucianist work of the Han period known as *Ta Hsüeh*, or "The Great Learning." After passing from a village to a district and then to a provincial school, each step by successfully completing an examination, the scholars entered a college, where each year they devoted themselves to prescribed studies and every two years faced an examination:

In the first year it was seen whether they could read the texts intelligently and explain the meaning of each; in the third year, whether they were reverently attentive to their work and took pleasure in the community life; in the fifth year, how they broadened their studies and became intimate with their teachers; in the seventh year, how they could discuss what they had studied and what friends they selected. This was called the small completion. In the ninth year, when they knew the different classes of subjects and gained a comprehensive knowledge; were firmly established and would not fall back; this was called the great completion. After this their training was sufficient to transform the people and change the customs, so that those near at hand would pay allegiance to them with delight and those far away would think of them with great longing.[1]

Thus by successfully passing examinations—which, it is worth noting, could be repeated until they had been passed—the scholar moved upward in a hierarchy of learned men.

The passing of an examination did not automatically lead to appointment to political office; it did, however, give social prestige. Of course, many officials were appointed from the successful candidates, and unsuccessful ones commonly served in subordinate positions. The system bound the entire learned group to the throne; it was justified under the ancient rule: "Employ the able and promote the worthy." Popular education was neglected, and those who set out on a scholarly career required the support either of considerable wealth or of a family whose members were willing to make sacrifices in order to place one of their number in the bureaucracy. Theoretically the examination system established a democracy of the intellect; however, it tended to restrict admission to the ranks of officialdom mainly to those who could afford the cost of a lengthy education. In this connection it should be noted that, because promotion in the learned hierarchy and titles of nobility could be purchased and military achievement was commonly rewarded with office, the scholars shared imperial favor and political privilege with the well to do and the soldiers. Scholars, however, were always looked upon as the possessors of the most eminent virtues.[2]

[1] Quoted in Fung Yu-lan, *A History of Chinese Philosophy: The period of the philosophers* (1937), p. 363.

[2] K. S. Latourette, *The Chinese: Their history and culture* (2 vols., 1934), Vol. 2, p. 205.

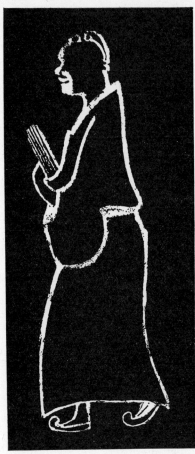

From WILLIAM CHARLES WHITE, *Sometime Bishop of Honan, Tomb Tile Pictures of Ancient China* (1939). *The University of Toronto Press*

THE ANCIENT CHINESE SCHOLAR

This ancient Chinese scholar is carrying a bamboo book. Every cultural tradition is transmitted partly by an intellectual type shaped by its peculiar body of literate learning. For this reason the Chinese, the Greek, and the Greco-Roman sophisticated literates were slightly less religious in outlook than their correlatives, the Indian Brahmans, the Buddhist monks, the Iranian Magi, the Hebrew rabbis, and the Christian priests.

In many respects the bearers of the Chinese classical learning were the most remarkable intellectual class ever developed. Their learning was traditional, largely moralistic, and supremely ritualistic. Their method of study was mainly the memorizing and the repeating of fixed comments. The emperor and, under him, the officials were priests of the state cult, and if learning was not specifically concerned with the overworld of spirits, it was at least the refined precipitate of ages when, so everyone believed, the spirits had instructed the ancestors. Supernatural sanction, age, and the authority of the sages combined to give validity to the learning of the Chinese literati. And they always conducted themselves as a superior and privileged class. As Mencius said, "Those who labour with their minds govern others; those who labour with their strength are governed by others. Those who are governed by others support them; those who govern others are supported by them." This was a forthright declaration of the almost universal relation of the governing and the governed. Thus the Confucianist scholars united learning and power in a regime which, although outwardly more orderly and elegant than the ancient-oriental monarchy, was no more concerned with social amelioration. They gave stability to Chinese culture because they merely perpetuated the codified mores of the ancient peasant villages; their teaching never went so far beyond the mental range of the "blue-coated masses" that the masses could not accept it. And the territorial bulk of China prevented military conquerors from displacing any considerable number of scholars in the bureaucratic hierarchy which, if the conquerors were to rule at all, they had to maintain.[1]

3. *Chinese Literature*. The main literary achievement of Han times was the recovery and editing of the literature of the Chou period.[2] The Han Confucianists came to regard thirteen works as canonical, *i.e.*, as authoritative guides to learning. First among them were the Five Classics: the *I Ching*, or "Book of Changes," the *Shu Ching*, or "Book of History," the *Shih Ching*, or "Book of Poetry," the *Li Chi*, or "Record of Rites," and the *Ch'un Ch'iu*, or "Spring and Autumn Annals." In the second group were the Four Books: the *Lün Yü*, or "Analects of Confucius," the *Ta Hsüeh*, or "Great Learning," the *Chung Yung*, or "Doctrine of the Mean," and the *Mêng Tzŭ Shu*, or "Book of Mencius." The works which completed the canon were the *Êrh Ya*, a dictionary, the *Hsiao Ching*, or "Classic of Filial Piety," the *I Li*, a collection of rites, and the *Chou-li*, or "Rites of the Chou," which set forth the ideal society. While the bulk of this literature undoubtedly originated in Chou times, some of it was composed at a later date. The exact dates of the composition or recovery of the several works is not known. The Five Classics were originally Chou works. The Four Books were probably Han renderings of earlier works; the "Great Learning" and the "Doctrine of the Mean" were taken from the "Record of Rites."

Among the commentators on the classics Tung Chung-shu (fl. *ca.* 100 B.C.), who directed the restoration of Confucianist studies under Wu Ti, was probably the greatest. The leading editors of the texts were Liu Hsiang, who flourished in the first century B.C., and his son, Liu Hsin, who, as previously mentioned, worked under Wang Mang. In pursuing a Confucianist education the pupil began with the Four Books. After the Han period various parts of this literature were from time to time given different degrees of emphasis.

[1] Paul F. Cressy, "The Influence of the Literary Examination System on the Development of Chinese Civilization," *American Journal of Sociology*, Vol. 35 (1929), pp. 250 *ff*.

[2] The treatments of Chinese literature in Western languages are quite inadequate. See article "Chinese Literature" in the *Encyclopaedia Britannica* (14th ed.); A. Wylie, *Notes on Chinese Literature* (1902); Herbert A. Giles, *A History of Chinese Literature* (1901); Shih Min, *An Anthology of Chinese Poetry from Chou and T'ang Dynasties* (1933); and Lim Boon Keng, *The Li Sao: An elegy on Encountering Sorrows by Ch'ü Yüan* (1929).

The Taoist and Confucianist belief that the way of Heaven is to be known from past experience necessarily turned attention to the study of history. Han times were notably conscious of the past, and among its scholars none is more worthy of note than Ssŭ-ma Ch'ien (*ca.* 135–85 B.C.), a court astrologer, who set the pattern of historical study and writing that was followed in the composition of the official histories of the twenty-four Chinese dynasties. It became a custom for each emperor to appoint an official historian. Ssŭ-ma Ch'ien's great work, the *Shih Chi*, or "Historical Memoirs," was an attempt at "a connected history of the whole Chinese world." It was written from ancient texts, contemporary records, and governmental documents and dealt not only with chronology and reigns but also with irrigation, divination, music, and rites. The author was skillful in composing biographies of famous men and geographical accounts of the many regions he had visited. He was the first scholar to point out certain fundamental differences between north and south China. The remarkable objectivity of the "Historical Memoirs" can be traced probably to Moist influences. Another historical work, composed by Pan Ku (fl. *ca.* A.D. 90), gave an account of the Earlier Han Dynasty; it contained considerable information about contemporary peoples.[1]

The poetry of the Chou period is known from the *Shih Ching*, or "Book of Poetry"; it contains songs and hymns in honor of ancestors, poems for ceremonial occasions, and bits of folk verse which show the people in all the activities of life. Some of these verses are biting satires on social conditions. The earliest Chinese poet whose name and work have survived is Ch'ü Yüan (*ca.* 338–288 B.C.); he lived in the period of warring states and his poem, the *Li Sao*, or "Encountering Sorrows," reflects its disorders. This work, Confucianist in outlook, has been almost as famous in China as the great epics in India and in the Western lands have been. The Chinese did not produce an epic poetry. The *Li Sao* embodies the reflections of the author on the problems of his age from which, in spite of an ascent to heaven, he is unable to escape. His sweetheart is wanton. The good man is scorned. The rake is admired. The masses are ignorant. Scheming courtiers trick the emperor. The times, indeed, are out of joint:

> The hawks do not unite and fly in flocks;
> From ancient times, such has been nature's way.
> How can the square just fit the circle right?
> With views opposed, who can unite in peace?

[1] See Charles S. Gardner, *Chinese Traditional Historiography* (1938).

And when he returns to his old home he finds only strangers who do not know him. The concern of the poet with his own moods sets a pattern of literary interest that endured for almost a thousand years, and his reintroduction into poetry of heavenly beings, whom Confucius had taught it was best to forget, contributed something to the development of Taoist fantasy.[1]

In fact, the mood of Chinese poetry throughout the Han Dynasty and even later times was Taoist; it was characterized by a deep sense of the artificialities of life, a love of nature, and a world-weariness. These qualities are exhibited in the following poem by Wang Ts'an (fl. *ca.* 177–217), one of a group known as the Seven Sages of the Bamboo Grove who found escape from ritual in humor, winebibbing, and devotion to nature.

> Grief is with me—my lonely life has crossed the dusk:
> bitterness—are not my parents long dead? As I order the
> silent house, my thoughts turn back, to linger over motes
> and dust as if they were jade. I look up, my eyes
> search far and wide—before, they search, and behind,
> over and over, finding no one. This then, is solitude—
> to stand alone unpropped, exposed; my heart is fixed
> on vanished things and shrinks, remembering time.

Many of the poems of the Han era were odes, brief but poignant in feeling and sharp in imagery:

> The wind of autumn rages, white clouds race,
> Trees and grasses wither, geese fly south apace.
> Yet orchids bloom and sweet chrysanthemum
> To call to mind my love; I cannot find relief.

As time went on the love of nature became more and more the dominant motif, in the other arts as well as in poetry. But the poets also had an eye for the human scene:

> Green grows the grass upon the bank,
> The willow-shoots are long and lank;
> A lady in a glistening gown
> Opens the casement and looks down.
> The roses on her cheeks blush bright,
> Her round arm is a dazzling white;
> A singing girl in early life,
> And now a careless roue's wife. . . .
> Ah, if he does not mind his own,
> He'll find some day the bird has flown.

[1] See Lim Boon Keng, *The Li Sao: An elegy on Encountering Sorrows by Ch'ü Yüan* (1929).

Shên Yo (fl. *ca.* 450) is credited with having first composed with tonal values, the style which reached its highest form in the golden age of Chinese poetry under the Tang Dynasty (618–907).

The Han historians did much to set the prose style of later periods; the Han poets, although less important in the general development of Chinese literature, foreshadowed the future of their art.

CHINESE PHILOSOPHY AND RELIGION.

The philosophical controversies of the late Chou period, it must be realized, did not disturb the fundamental religious beliefs of the Chinese people; the worship of Heaven, ancestors, and nature survived and, in the Han era, entered into a syncretism which blended them with the philosophies. This syncretism was nourished by the credulity of the scholars, the superstitions of the imperial family, and the pessimism of the people. The early Han emperors were greatly influenced by Taoism. The assimilation of border peoples into the empire added primitive materials to those surviving among the native masses. Wizards, magicians, and astrologers were prominent at court, where they shared with the eunuchs and harem favorites the control of policy and intellectual life. Wu Ti, who did so much to revive Confucianism, not only continued the old practices of divination by tortoise shells and bones but also became the high priest of a new cult. Emperor after emperor squandered large sums of money on projects for finding the philosopher's stone and for transmuting base metals into gold. The pessimistic mood which supported the resurgence of superstition was probably not unlike the so-termed "failure of nerve" which contributed to the rise of Christianity in Greco-Roman times; it was a reaction to the uprooting of the masses that came with the changed economic organization and imperial expansion.[1]

1. *The Reorientation of Confucianism.* During the advance of Ch'in to supremacy over the feudal states, the ancient conception of the Above or Supreme Ruler, known as Shang Ti or Heaven, was elaborated into a belief in the Five Heavenly Emperors, and in the Han era this anthropomorphic polytheism was introduced into the state cult. Behind all deities was, of course, the supreme power, Heaven. The chief state sacrifice was made by the emperor

---

[1] On the general development of Chinese religion and philosophy under the empire see E. Seetwood, *The Three Religions of China* (1923); E. T. C. Werner, *A History of the Religious Beliefs and Philosophical Opinions in China* (1927).

to these heavenly rulers, who, it was believed, had delegated earthly power to him. This sacrifice was performed on a mountain top in Shantung; if, when the emperor ascended the mountain, violent storms occurred, they were believed to show the anger of Heaven with the emperor. The destruction of the Ch'in state was explained on the grounds that its rulers had neglected the ancient rituals. Under Wu Ti the state ceremonials were given enduring form, and correctness in ritualistic procedure became a leading ideal of his successors. The Confucianist scholars took the lead in this elaboration of the imperial cult. At the same time local deities were bound into the state worship. The eight principal provincial gods were moved to the capital, and the gods of the soil and crops received imperial patronage. Ancestor worship became the universal popular cult.

The political theory of the Han state was orientated in religious terms. Commentators on the classics asserted that (1) the authority of the emperor was derived from Heaven, (2) the way—tao—of government was exhibited in the rule of the ancient emperors to whom it had been revealed by Heaven, and (3) the calamities which befell the people and the state were manifestations of Heaven's anger at an unworthy emperor. Tung Chung-shu, who, as previously noted, guided Wu Ti's adoption of Confucianism, expounded these beliefs in a commentary on the Spring and Autumn Annals:

The principle of government is to follow the action of Heaven by governing with uprightness, for the ruler must act as Heaven acts.

The *Tao* of Heaven summons the *Yin* and the *Yang*. *Yang* signifies virtue, while *Yin* signifies punishment or killing. To emphasize virtue is to aid growth. *Yang* is the source of life in the spring, while *Yin* destroys in the autumn. From this we can see that Heaven also emphasizes *Yang*. *Yang* is used to give life, and is assisted by *Yin*, for without *Yin*, *Yang* cannot be complete. The ruler merely carries out the intention of Heaven, and so he should endeavour to develop virtue and education, not depending upon punishment. To depend upon punishment would be like relying upon *Yin* to give growth during the course of the seasons. . . . A year is a unit and exhibits the greatness of all things. It must have a foundation in unity, in order that all may prosper, and therefore a ruler of men, like a year, must unify his heart, making it upright, for if his heart is rectified, the state will have unity and uprightness. Then officials will follow his examples, the people also, until the whole world will be upright and things far and near will possess unity. In such a land evil will hardly appear, *Yin* and *Yang* will be harmonized, wind and rain will come at the right seasons, while life will be peaceful, and the people settled in good order.

As Mencius said, "To follow Heaven is to be preserved; to act contrary to Heaven is to perish."

The Confucianist political doctrine was simply an up-to-date rendering of the theory by which the Chou had justified the overthrow of the Shang. Thus the Confucianist scholars recognized the right of the people to depose and murder the emperor who lost the favor of Heaven; lack of benevolence, famine, flood, and invasion were evidence of this loss. However, the scholars knew no form of government other than monarchy, so that revolution merely brought a change of ruler, never a new political organization. The welfare of the state depended on the character of the emperor, not upon its political institutions.[1]

Among the original elements of Confucianism the Han scholars emphasized three doctrines: (1) history reveals the will of Heaven; (2) ceremonials nourish culture and refinement; and (3) education is a corrective for man's selfishness. To these elements they added the belief in the Five Heavenly Emperors, the recognition of several new gods, many elaborate rituals, and, finally, the worship of Confucius as a god.[2] Sacrifices at the tomb of Confucius began early in the Han era. By A.D. 37 the worship had become official, and twenty years later it was made compulsory in the schools. Han Confucianism was a blend of ancestor and hero worship; its establishment as the state cult was the work of the scholars who, acknowledging the leadership of the sage, had won a dominant political position.

In order to protect this position the scholars advocated a prohibition of the teaching of rival doctrines. Tung Chung Shu said, "My meaning is that all that is not in the six sciences [propriety, marksmanship, music, chariot-driving, study of books, and arithmetic] and the canon of Confucius should be discouraged, and the teaching and spread of these doctrines hindered, in order that false and corrupted principles may be stopped." Thus the scholars combined intolerance with the monopoly of education as a defense of their power. In view of the fact that social and intellectual conditions favored the revival of superstitions, these defenses meant chiefly that the rationalistic elements—particularly Mo Ti's skepticism—were submerged by religious beliefs. Han scholars

---

[1] See Gilbert Reid, "Revolution as Taught by Confucianism," *International Journal of Ethics*, Vol. 33 (1922–1923), pp. 188–201.

[2] See J. K. Shryock, *The Origin and Development of the State Cult of Confucius* (ca. 1932).

formed, therefore, a kind of priest class, and in many respects the Han empire was a glorified priestly monarchy.

With such interests the Confucianist scholars had little energy for philosophical inquiry. But they did produce several generalizations about li. They emphasized the need of preserving class distinctions in order to maintain social order. They counseled great care in dealing with life and death. They found in the cultivation of music a way to create that harmony which obstructs the rise of social discontent. Above all they pointed to the past as revealing the norms of morality and justice. Ultimately, however, intellectual enterprise departed from them:

> Confucianism came to be an ossified system of pedantic erudition and dry ceremonial, with no inspiration for the people or even for the intellectuals.[1]

2. *The Elaboration of Taoism.* The resurgence of primitive beliefs and religious fervor, which gave added vigor to Taoism, produced a remarkable elaboration of belief in miracles, allegorical interpretations, and occult speculations. Notable among these innovations was the belief in, and quest for, an elixir of life, which won the support of Shi Huang Ti and many succeeding emperors. Shi Huang Ti's actions in several instances are to be understood only in terms of Taoist and related superstitions. In accordance with the theory that all existence consists of five elements—earth, wood, metal, fire, and water—the Taoists taught that five ages, each associated with one of these elements, succeeded each other in a fixed order, and since the Chou age had been under the rule of fire, the Ch'in period was dominated by water. Thus, under their influence, Shi Huang Ti made the imperial flags, standards, and costumes black, because this color was associated with water, and required that official hats be six inches high, the wheels of carts be six feet apart, and the horses attached to a carriage be six in number, because the number six, like the color black, was associated with water. The first emperor thought of himself as the True Man of Taoist belief—the man who enters water without becoming wet, who touches fire without being burned, who rides on clouds and vapors, and who exists as long as the universe endures. Many of the changes which were made in Confucianism after the founding of the empire were brought about by Taoist influence.

[1] H. T. Lei, "Periodization: Chinese History and World History," *The Chinese Social and Political Science Review*, Vol. 20 (1936–1937), p. 477.

Chief among the new elements that found a place by the side of the traditional doctrines of tao and wu wei was the belief in personal immortality. By attaining virtue in an etherealized body, the soul could rise from earth through the clouds of heaven. Breathing exercises, strict attention to diet, and the use of drugs, particularly cinnabar, were considered effective aids in achieving the proper degree of etherealization. Wizards, exorcists, and charm makers found in these beliefs opportunities for all kinds of magical practices, and the people took from them a hope for an immortal life in heaven. Thus Taoism became a salvation religion.

Because of its popular appeal, Taoism was always closer to the masses than Confucianism, with the result that demands for social amelioration occasionally became associated with it. In the first century B.C., it seems, a considerable body of Taoists called for the abolition of slavery and a redivision of the land according to the principles of the *Chou-li*. Indeed, it may be that Wang Mang, in spite of his close relations with the Confucianist scholars, received inspiration from these Taoist ideas. At any rate, after Wang Mang's failure many Taoists migrated to the hinterland province of Szechuan and set up a state on Taoist principles. The leader of the movement, Chang Tao-ling (fl. *ca.* 135), founded many semimonastic communities, which, after his death, were united under a priestly hierarchy, headed by a "celestial preceptor." The Taoist priests—great magicians that they were—cared for the health and morals of their subjects, built roads and bridges, cleared lands, and ruled mildly, appealing to the sense of shame rather than to the fear of physical punishment in order to obtain obedience. The subjects paid them five bushels of rice per head a year. The successors of Chang Tao-ling inspired the popular revolts, particularly the great rising of the Yellow Turbans, which had something to do with the overthrow of the Later Han Dynasty, and after its fall Taoist influence increased.

Much of this development of Taoism was undoubtedly stimulated by contact with Buddhism. Early in the fourth century Taoists argued that Buddha had been a convert of Lao Tzŭ, created books imitating the Buddhist scriptures, and organized temple worship with a regular priesthood. With these innovations innumerable native elements survived which clouded tao in supernaturalism. In fact, Taoism ceased to be a philosophy and became a religion, organized as a church.

3. *The Arrival of Buddhism in China.* Although Buddhism may have reached China in late Chou times, it became an impor-

tant factor in Chinese cultural development only after the Han expansion into central Asia. As early perhaps as 121 B.C. traders from Khotan carried Buddhist images into China and monks enjoying imperial patronage preached its doctrines. In the first century A.D. the emperor Ming (*ca.* 58–78) sent an embassy to India to obtain Sanskrit books. It seems likely that he promoted the diffusion of Mahayana Buddhism as a means of counteracting the socialistic Taoism which Wang Mang had espoused. The cult of Amitabha, known to the Chinese as Omito-Fo, spread rapidly after his reign. Hinayana Buddhism also reached China, but its influence was never great.

After the third century Buddhism won a firm hold on the Chinese mind. Treatises on monastic law filtered into China from central Asia, and the Buddhist scriptures became generally known. "The Lotus of the Good Law" was rendered in Chinese about the opening of the fourth century. Terms borrowed from Taoism were found to be most suitable for expressing Buddhist ideas. Kumarajiva (*ca.* 344–413) of the Mahayana school was the most active translator; he arrived in China in 383. As in other countries to which it spread, Buddhism absorbed native beliefs; chief among the Chinese accretions was ancestor worship, which the monks adapted to the service of their interest:

Nothing can help thy parents, except my monks. They only can work in their behalf. This must thou do. On the fifteenth day of the seventh month go offer a rich gift of food and drink, of garments, and other choice offerings to the Brethren. They are a field of merit, in which if thou sowest, thou shalt reap a rich harvest, and shalt help thy dead even to the seventh generation.

The sweep of Buddhism sent a stream of pilgrims to the "Buddha land," among whom Fa Hsien was the most famous. He spent the period 399–414 on an Indian journey, learning Sanskrit and collecting many manuscripts.[1]

Occasionally during these centuries Buddhism encountered both popular and official intolerance, but opposition failed to stop its spread. And finally it was fused with Chinese culture. This fusion was socially expressed in an order of Chinese monks. The first Chinese were ordained as monks about the end of the second century. Legal ordination was established early in the fourth

[1] On Buddhism in China see James H. Cousins, *The Cultural Unity of Asia* (1922); Lewis Hodous, *Buddhism and Buddhists in China* (1924); and Helmuth von Glasenapp, *Der Buddhismus in Indien und im Fernen Osten* (1936).

century. The first Buddhist emperor reigned about the opening of the fifth century. At this time, also, Buddhist architecture and art spread, Mahayana works were translated, and a native Buddhist literature appeared. The intellectual fusion is exemplified in a third century poem which blended the Chinese feeling for nature with the Indian religious aspiration that characterized the Mahayana cult:

> One long deep breath, a sigh from sleeping earth,
> As though in troubled dreams her spirit stirred,
> And all is still. No call of wakeful bird,
> No life of leaf on trembling wave of air,
> But soulful silence brooding everywhere;
> The stars are veiled, and from their heights are heard
> The noiseless sweep of spirit forces, stirred
> As at the moment of some wondrous birth;
> Before each household shrine the candle gleams;
> Then food is spread for guests that come unseen;
> And human faith in simple ways is fed.
> The air is filled with lucent, mystic beams;
> They come indeed, the loved and lost, I ween;
> And human hearts by lowly ways to God are led.

With the establishment of Mahayana Buddhism in China, the Far East came to possess a religion of personal salvation not unlike the cults that arose in India, Iran, and the Mediterranean Basin in the first five Christian centuries.

CHINESE SCIENCE.

The Chinese, like other early peoples who developed an urban culture, possessed a large body of factual knowledge which they used mainly in agriculture, the crafts, and the arts. The invention of paper and porcelain testifies to their capacity to use knowledge in new ways, and the construction of the Great Wall and many irrigation projects bears witness to their skill in engineering. In fact, the Chinese were as scientific in outlook as their Western contemporaries, but like these contemporaries they failed to develop a secular study of nature. It is unfortunate that most of the Chinese scientific literature has not yet been studied.[1]

1. *Chinese Mathematics.* Like every other element of Chinese culture, mathematics is said to have a very ancient origin, but the earliest evidences of its existence date only from the second century

[1] J. K. Shryock, *The Study of Human Abilities: The Jen wu chih of Li Shao* (1937), pp. 157–160.

B.C.[1] From this century survives a commentary on an ancient "sacred book on arithmetic" and a treatise, ascribed to Chang T'sang (d. *ca.* 150 B.C.), called *Chui-chang Suan-shu,* or "Arithmetical Rules in Nine Sections." This treatise contains evidence of a long evolution of mathematics, for it deals not only with arithmetical but also with geometrical and algebraic problems. The handling of fractions, the measurement of plain figures and solids, and the extraction of square and cube roots were fairly well understood. It is said that the discussion of equations having one or more unknown terms mentioned the concept "negative quantity." The relation summarized for the Western world in the Pythagorean theorem was stated in mathematical form. The value of π was given as 3.

The most elaborate ancient Chinese mathematical work, *Suan-ching,* or "Arithmetical Classic," was composed by Sun Tsŭ, who flourished about the beginning of the third century A.D. In this work the decimal system of numeration, without the zero, was used. The numerals were written: 1 | or —, 2 ‖ or =, 3 ‖‖ or ≡, 4 ‖‖‖ or ≣, 5 ‖‖‖‖ or ≣, 6 ⊤ or ⊥, 7 ⊤ or ⊥, 8 ⊤ or ⊥, 9 ⊤ or ⊥. Position seems to have been given value; thus 6,728 was written ⊥⊤=⊤. Large numbers were handled without difficulty, especially in addition, subtraction, and multiplication. Among the problems given in this work was the following:

There are three sisters, of whom the eldest comes home once in every five days, the middle in every four days, and the youngest in every three days. In how many days will all three meet together?

The answer—60 days—was correctly found. The last problem in the book lapsed into fortune telling. It was concerned with the determining of the sex of an unborn child.

A pregnant woman, who is 29 years of age, is expected to give birth to a child in the 9th month of the year. Which should be her child, a son or a daughter?

The method of solution was given as follows:

Take 49; add the month of her child-bearing; subtract her age. From what now remains, subtract heaven 1, subtract the earth 2, subtract the man 3, subtract the four seasons 4, subtract the five elements 5, subtract the six laws 6, subtract the seven stars 7, subtract the eight winds 8, subtract the nine provinces 9. If then the remainder be odd, the child shall be a son; and if even, a daughter.

[1] Yoshio Mikami, *Development of Mathematics in China and Japan* (1912).

The Hai-tao Suan-ching, or "Sea-island Arithmetical Classic," by Liu Hui (fl. *ca.* 200) explained methods of measuring magnitudes at a distance. It is said to contain material which suggests the existence of the mathematical procedures known later in the Western world as algebra.

The Chinese use of the abacus for arithmetical computation is first known to have occurred in the third century after Christ, although there is reason to believe that it was known much earlier.

2. *Chinese Astronomy, Physics, and Chemistry.* In astronomy, physics, and chemistry the Chinese developed theories but no systematic bodies of knowledge.

From earliest times Chinese priests and diviners observed sky phenomena in order to determine the "order of the seasons" so important to agriculture. In this connection it must be noted that in northern China, where a cyclonic climate prevails, a correct calendar was especially necessary if the planting of crops was to be made at the time that would make certain full use of the growing season. For this reason a dynasty was always associated with a calendar. When the calendar in use no longer coincided with the growing season, this was evidence of the loss of the favor of Heaven, and the favor was to be recovered only by a change of dynasty and the introduction of a new calendar.[1] For this reason every emperor kept, along with other diviners, a court astrologer, who studied the clouds and winds as well as the movements of the heavenly bodies. The career of an emperor was believed to be determined by the combination of clouds and winds at the time of his coronation. The fate of the people was believed to be revealed in the movements of the planet Jupiter. Astrologers distinguished five kinds of clouds and twelve kinds of winds. It is thought that Babylonian astrology became known in China as early as the sixth century B.C., although how the knowledge reached China is not clear.

Records of Chinese astronomical observations are known from Chou times on. The first eclipse was recorded in 775 B.C. A comet was noted in 613 B.C. A map of the stars was made in the third century B.C. Chang Heng (*ca.* 78–139), probably the greatest Chinese astronomer, knew 320 large stars and 11,520 small ones. He constructed a celestial hemisphere, corrected the calendar, and

[1] Wolfram Eberhard, "Contributions to the Astronomy of the Han Period III," *The Harvard Journal of Asiatic Studies*, Vol. I (1936), p. 201: "To change the calendar and to create a new calendar, for the Chinese, is to form a new dynasty." The "socialist emperor" Wang Mang, for example, introduced a new calendar.

fixed the value of π at the square root of 10. Liu Hung's (fl. *ca.* 190) observations were a landmark in fixing the length of the year and correcting the calendar.

During the period of the classical philosophers, speculation about the physical universe somewhat similar to that of the Greeks appeared. A theory of five elements—water, fire, wood, gold, and earth—became the classical conception of Chinese chemistry. A theory of creation affirmed that originally there were two factors, *chaos* and *force*. From them arose eight *substances*, which separated into *forms*. The *light* substances rose, making heaven; the *heavy* ones sank, becoming earth. Heaven was commonly thought of as a blue vault, the earth as an inverted yellow bowl. In the third century B.C. the original universe was said to be a gigantic monad, which had two modes, heaven and earth. All forms of existence developed through the transformation of yin and yang. Life, it was held, originated in water and developed through a series of forms into men. At death the human body was believed to dissolve into particles of the five elements. When superstition was at its height under the early Han these speculations were blended with Taoism, and the yin and yang theory triumphed over rival concepts of the fundamental process of nature. From tao, which originated in a great void, was generated a universal fluid. When this fluid was separated into particles, the bright, thin, and pure made heaven, and the coarse and turbulent ones formed the earth. The essence of earth was yin, and the essence of heaven was yang. Through the activities of yin and yang, the actions of which were said to be like those of flames in a furnace, the four seasons were produced. A dispersion of particles during the seasons spread the ten thousand living things over the earth. The stars were the children of the sun and moon. Universal existence was, therefore, a great equilibrium, within which there was constant but orderly change. Disorderly change brought catastrophe to men.[1]

3. *Chinese Medicine.* The earliest Chinese medical work, *Nei Ching*, "Internal Classic," or "Canon of Medicine," was compiled in late Chou times; it combined an anthropomorphic conception of the functions of several internal organs with a somewhat realistic view of the causes of disease. In the organization of the body the heart was the prince. The liver was the general. The gall bladder was a central office. The lungs were ministers.

[1] See Alfred A. Forke, *The World Conception of the Chinese: Their astronomical, cosmological, and physio-philosophical speculations* (1925); Masumi Chikashige, *Alchemy and Other Chemical Achievements of the Ancient Orient* (1936).

And the kidneys were skilled workers. These descriptions were ways of saying that these organs were the seats, respectively, of the vital spirit, strategy, courage, regulation, and skills. The blood was believed to flow with respiration. Some diseases were caused by external factors such as wind, cold, drought, and moisture; others were caused by internal factors such as joy, grief, anger, and fear. Hemorrhages were most likely to occur in spring, diarrheas in summer, ague fevers in the fall, and fits in the winter. The naturalistic approach to disease in the "Internal Classic" is evidence of the separation of the physicians from the priests and diviners in late Chou times.

Four ancient Chinese medical practioners and writers were remembered for their achievements. Pien Chao (fl. *ca.* 255 B.C.) gave narcotics to produce insensibility. He asserted that (1) if a man had led a dissipated life, (2) if he valued money more than health, (3) if he lacked proper food and clothing, (4) if he suffered from a fatal disease, (5) if he was so emaciated that he could not swallow a medicament, and (6) if he believed in sorcerers instead of doctors, a physician could not cure him. These conditions affecting the success of medical treatment suggest that Pien Chao's outlook was almost as realistic as that of his Mediterranean contemporaries. Ch'un Yu-i (fl. *ca.* 180 B.C.) wrote clinical descriptions of twenty-five ailments, but they do not compare in accuracy of observation with those of the Hippocratic school. Chang Chung-ching (fl. *ca.* 175), the "sage of medicine," is famous for a treatise on typhoid fever; his knowledge of this dread ailment was derived from experience with village epidemics. He advocated the use of cooling baths as a method of treatment. His work, motivated by zeal and high ethical principles, stimulated the study of diseases from the point of view of identifying their symptoms. He left to his successors 397 rules for treating disease and 113 prescriptions. Hua T'o (fl. *ca.* 190), the most famous surgeon of ancient China, was credited with having known anesthetics and performed many kinds of operations. He was an advocate of physical exercise as a therapeutic.

Along with these advances in medical knowledge went developments which harmonized anatomy, physiology, the theory of disease, and methods of treatment with the belief in yin and yang; in other words, the naturalistic elements of medicine were sacrificed to the desire for philosophical unity. Chief among the theories which had this effect was an eastern counterpart of the Western concepts "macrocosm" and "microcosm."

The universe with its dual forces is a macrocosm. Man is a microcosm, a little universe. Thus we read that as heaven is round and the earth square, so a man's head is round and the foot square. As heaven has its sun and moon, its order of stars, rain and wind, thunder and lightning, so man has two eyes, a set of teeth, joy and anger, voice and sound. The earth with its mountains and valleys; rocks and stones; trees and shrubs; weeds and grasses; has its parallel on the human body in the shoulders and armpits; nodes and tuberosities; tendons and muscles; hairs and down. The four limbs correspond with the four seasons; the twelve joints with the twelve months. . . . There is a brain reservoir, an air reservoir, a blood reservoir, and a water reservoir to agree with the four seasons. The pulse is of twelve kinds to agree with the twelve rivers.[1]

Yang was identified with the skin and the external organs; yin was associated with the interior parts of the body. Fevers were yang diseases; chills were yin diseases. The five elements were believed to form a harmonious mixture in the body, and each of the internal organs, of which there were five—the heart, the liver, the spleen, the lungs, and the kidneys—communicated with an external organ. Thus the heart communicated with the tongue; the liver with the eyes; the spleen with the mouth; the lungs with the nose; and the kidneys with the ears.

The effect of this conception of the body and its functioning was to make the Chinese develop internal medicine. The purpose of medical treatment was to restore the harmony of yang and yin that meant health, and every substance taken into the body was believed to affect them. As a means of diagnosis, a branch which the Chinese emphasized, there developed a great attention to the pulse. The places where the pulse was to be felt were believed to be different in each of the seasons of the year. The normal rate of the pulse was four beats to each respiration, and every variation of the pulse was believed to indicate a disharmony, *i.e.*, a disease. Besides the rather skillful use of mineral concoctions, the chief method of treatment was acupuncture, which consisted of puncturing the body at different points with a needle; it was believed that this brought about the escape of substances contributing to disharmony within the body. The blood, which circulated in twelve channels, flowed from the heart to the various parts of the body; in the kidneys it was purified. The points at which punctures were made numbered 367; they were located with reference to the twelve channels through which the blood flowed. The results of puncturing at these points depended upon the kind of needle used; long, short,

[1] K. C. Wong and Wu Lien-teh, *History of Chinese Medicine* (1932), p. 12.

cold, hot, coarse, fine, silver, gold, brass, copper, iron, and steel needles were employed in different diseases. Acupuncture, it may be believed, at least had the effect of a counterirritant. This method of treatment was never separated from magical practices designed to expel daimons. Taoist treatment, which involved elaborate relations with spirits and genii, undertook to make the mind a blank and the body motionless so that both natural and supernatural forces could work for a cure.[1]

Since many of the physicians of ancient China came from the northwestern provinces, where contacts with central Asia and India were most numerous, it seems that the medical advances of Han times may have been stimulated by foreign materials.[2]

4. *Chinese Geography.*   Until the expansion of early Han times the Chinese had a very limited knowledge of geography. When they penetrated central Asia by way of the Tarim Basin and Bactria, they first learned of India and the lands of southwestern Asia and the Mediterranean Basin. Although their armies reached the Caspian Sea and their couriers the Persian Gulf, they always exaggerated the distances between China and Rome. But there is reason to believe that the Chinese knew more about Rome than the Romans did about China. With the spread of Buddhism into China, intercourse between India and China became more or less constant. It flowed over three different routes: (1) by way of the Tarim Basin and Gandhara, (2) from the upper Yangtze valley through Burma, and (3) around the Malay Peninsula by sea. By the third century the knowledge of China was so complete that a map according to scale was drawn; it showed Greek influence. By the fifth century certainly the Chinese had a working knowledge of the area from the Caspian Sea and the Persian Gulf in the west to Java and the islands, now known as Japan, in the east—an area quite as large as that known by the Romans. This growth of knowledge of the world was largely the result of the going and coming of imperial embassies, religious pilgrims, and traders.

The earliest Chinese work on botany, written in the third century A.D., was a product of this growth of knowledge of the world; it contained descriptions of eighty species of herbs, bamboo, fruit trees, and forest plants.

5. *The Decline of the Secular Elements of Chinese Thought.*   The resurgence of traditionalism, superstition, and religious feeling in

[1] E. Y. Cowdray, "Taoist Ideas of Human Anatomy," *Annals of Medical History,* Vol. 3 (1921), pp. 301 *ff.*

[2] *The Harvard Journal of Asiatic Studies,* Vol. 1 (1936), p. 235.

Han times, which resulted in the reorientation of Confucianism, the elaboration of Taoism, and the acceptance of Buddhism, disintegrated the secular outlook and rational methodology which, although they were never clearly developed in the philosophies, might have produced a science if social and economic conditions had strengthened them. The philosophers turned to subjective interests.

> The Chinese philosphers . . . had no need of scientific certainty, because it was themselves they wished to know, so in the same way they had no need of the power of science, because it was themselves they wished to conquer. To them the content of wisdom is not intellectual knowledge and its function is not to increase external goods. To Taoism external goods seem to be something that can only bring confusion to man's mind. To Confucianism, while they are not so bad as Taoism supposes, they are by no means the essentials of human welfare. Then what is the use of science?[1]

The Moist logic was forgotten. The love of system imposed the yin and yang dynamics and the pentagonal pattern (five elements, five tastes, etc.) upon nature, and observation, except to verify these stereotypes, came to a dead stop. The Confucianists pursued a literary learning that had for its end product a cultivated elegance. The Taoists sought drugs to rejuvenate the body and postpone death and speculated on ways to make gold, float through the air, walk on fire and water, and command spirits. They discovered the magnetic needle but used it chiefly to find good locations for graves, and invented gunpowder but employed it—a use better than some others—only to scare away evil daimons. Since the Taoists came generally from the lower classes, they were carriers of the popular superstititions. Thus science became identified with the Chinese low intellectual tradition, while the Chinese high intellectual tradition developed mainly as a body of ritualistic and decorative learning. Only a sentimental attitude toward nature and an imaginative outlook upon the spiritual overworld relieved the traditionalism of Chinese mentality, and these qualities were expressed more in poetry than in religious or philosophical doctrines.

CHINESE ART.

Like Chinese writing and learning, Chinese art had a continuous development from very early times. Types of neolithic pottery

[1] Fung Yu-lan, "Why China Has No Science," *The International Journal of Ethics,* Vol. 32 (1922), p. 261.

Ewing Galloway

THE GREAT WALL OF CHINA

Every ancient Chinese city was surrounded by a wall built of clay. In the period of the Warring States the rival kings constructed walls around their territories. Shi Huang Ti, the first emperor, planned the Great Wall as a defense of the empire against invaders from the north and west. Little, if any, of his work exists in the present wall which, as is indicated by the brick and stone work, was erected long after his time.

persisted. And motifs first found on the Shang bronze ritual vessels—for example, the stylized "ogre mask," the dragon, the silkworm, and the cicada—became permanent elements of design and decoration. There is also evidence that the architectural achievements of the Shang had lasting significance.[1]

1. *Chinese Architecture.* Almost nothing is known about Chinese architecture and the allied decorative arts before the age of Ch'in, except that the most popular building materials were "rammed earth" and timber. Stone architecture appeared at this time, when city walls of rammed earth were crowned with crenelated towers and bastions. The Great Wall, the most famous of all Chinese structures, was originally a series of towers connected by earthen ramparts. Shi Huang Ti's Palace of Delight, probably the most elaborate building of ancient China, was made of stone and timber, set amidst artificial terraces and lakes. The best-known Han buildings are tombs consisting of timber structures within underground chambers, which, covered with rammed earth and rubble, were commonly crowned with earthen mounds. Temples and pavilions, set on terraces after the Shang manner, were typical Han buildings. They were constructed of wood and roofed with tile, both clay and wooden. The Chinese became experts in building light wooden walls that would support a heavy tile roof. The designing and erecting of city gates also called forth the best in Chinese architectural practice.

Under Buddhist influence the Chinese elaborated from the Indian stupa the peculiar towerlike building known as the pagoda. These structures were first built under the Later Han; the oldest one standing dates, it is said, from 523. It is characterized by solidity of construction and grace of line. The superimposed roofs of the pagoda were repetitions of the umbrella—a symbol of Buddha's sovereignty—which crowned the Buddhist stupa. The curved roof, which became common in Chinese construction, may also have been derived from India, although some authorities believe it originated as an imitation of the sag in poorly constructed early roofs. If this should be its origin, its persistence is further evidence of the Chinese attachment to tradition.

2. *Chinese Sculpturing, Painting, and Decorative Arts.* Although many figurines of animals and men have survived from Chou times, the earliest known sculptures were made under the Ch'in. Shi Huang Ti cast colossal images of the "great barbarians"

[1] See Arnold Silcock, *Introduction to Chinese Art and History* (1935); Osvald Sirén, *A History of Early Chinese Art* (1929); John C. Ferguson, *Chinese Painting* (1927).

By the courtesy of the Freer Gallery of Art, Washington, D. C.

A CHINESE PAINTING

This painting is part of a twelfth-century scroll which is regarded as having been made after a design of Ku K'ai-chih. It illustrates the technique of Chinese painting as developed from calligraphy. The motifs, especially the figures in the sky, indicate the supernaturalism which persisted in Chinese culture, mainly in the influence of Taoism.

from the metal of confiscated arms and set them up before one of the royal residences. The Han era produced reliefs and some figures in stone. The finest reliefs have been found in tombs, where, because they faced inward, they were meant, it seems, to serve the ghosts of the dead. In them and the remains of metalwork have been identified the influences that gave Han art its new elements. Greek and Bactrian influences gave a rounded shape and a clarity of line to the rendering of forms; together with Scythian influences they made animals distinctive motifs. The galloping horse, one of the most persistent of all Chinese motifs, attained prominence for the first time; other animals frequently rendered were the bear, the lion, and the buffalo. The working of gold, learned from Bactria, was united with Scythian motifs to create numerous decorative pieces, especially buckles, girdle clasps, necklaces, and ornaments for saddles and bridles. Along with the ornaments for saddles and bridles, Taoist motifs, such as heraldic beasts—notably the dragon—floral arrangements, and clouds, also attracted the interest of artists who, as in India and southwestern Asia, were probably craftsmen. The earliest Chinese sculptured figures date from the second century B.C.

Painting developed under the influence of calligraphy. Its chief technique was the ink line, executed with a brush; colors, usually subdued in tone, were laid on as washes. Probably as early as the time of Confucius temples were decorated with painted frescoes. Later these frescoes were rendered as reliefs. Many of the Han tombs were decorated with frescoes and mural paintings as well as with reliefs. The earliest Chinese painting, known, of course, only in reproduction, is dated about A.D. 100, when the technique of painting on silk was invented. The reproductions of four paintings by Ku K'ai-chih (fl. *ca.* 350–412) have also survived; among them "The Admonitions of an Imperial Instructress" is most famous. Ku K'ai-chih is credited with having written the first Chinese treatise on painting. From these examples it appears that the early Chinese painters handled figures of animals and birds, ceremonial groupings, and drapery with great delicacy. Landscapes, although done with simple strokes of the brush, were remarkable for atmosphere. Portraits of emperors and famous men were done with great precision of line. In the fifth century the imaginative artists who pictured the "fairy paradise" of the Taoist and the figures and scenes of Buddhist legends became prominent; one of these artists, it was said, rendered dragons so spirited that, when he gave them eyes, they burst from the paintings and spread terror and devastation among the people.

Both sculpturing and painting were closely related to the decorative arts, such as inlaying, lacquering, and enameling, which were carried on with great skill. The notable aspect of these arts was the use of designs covering all available surface; among the motifs commonly used in a variety of arrangements were the galloping horse, heraldic animals in procession or combat, the dragon, the phoenix, fairies, ordinary animals and fowls, flowers, trees, processions of various human figures, and clouds. The same motifs were used in making figured silk and, later, porcelain. The bronze or copper mirror, superstitiously regarded as the source of light, was a typical Taoist art object; commonly it was decorated with arabesques.

Not the least important aspect of the consolidation of the Chinese cultural tradition was the fixing of the motifs of the arts; in this phase of Chinese culture, as in many others, the influences which turned the Chinese mind to mythological speculation were dominant, with the result that eerie figures sitting on haze-shrouded mountain tops or floating on clouds, dragons, and heraldic animals came to be repeated over and over again. Taoist and Buddhist legends provided many subjects for artists.

3. *Music.* Music, which played a significant role not only in the religion but also in the recreation of the people, was probably the leading art of the ancient Chinese. It seems that they were a "singing people." The earliest poems, which were accompanied by music, were written for singing, and Confucius, who edited them, also selected music to be played with them. Just as he excluded from his collection poems of passion, so he suppressed seductive melodies. The music was composed in a five-toned scale, and all instruments—wind, string, and percussion—were adapted to its rendering. The Chinese did not develop either a musical theory or a musical education; both remained on an empirical and popular level. Hence, although scholars and emperors alike emphasized the place of music in education, Chinese music never possessed that quality which the Western world knows as harmony.[1]

THE STABILITY OF CHINESE CULTURE

The stability of Chinese culture was due to several factors. Natural barriers between the Chinese and other culture areas ensured that foreign cultural traits were introduced in a manner making certain their fusion with Chinese materials; thus they fertilized but did not change Chinese culture. The economic foundations of Chinese culture were so widely laid among the peasant-village population that neither commerce nor warfare was able to displace the essentially primitive psychology of the culture as a whole; the inertia of the Chinese peasant-village masses guaranteed the stability of the Chinese cultural tradition. Among the literate intellectuals tradition reigned supreme, because the writing system was both a preservative of ancient meanings and a hindrance to the development of new abstractions. Furthermore, since only the most brilliant minds could master its numerous characters, literacy never spread widely enough to enable new

[1] See John H. Lewis, *Foundation of the Chinese Musical Art* (1930).

social groups to carry out an orientation of traditional ideas in terms of their interest. Thus Chinese culture developed little under the impact of advancing special-interest groups. In Han times the struggle between the new industrial, financial, and landed plutocrats and the peasant-village masses took the form of an intellectual conflict between Confucianism and Taoism. By reorienting the Confucian social teachings in the traditional religious beliefs of the masses, the literati led the masses away from the socialistic doctrines of Taoism. The otherworldliness of Buddhism, which quickly absorbed the Taoist superstitions as well as the ancestor worship of Confucianism, completed the diversion of the peasant demand for social amelioration to a quest for heavenly bliss.

Thus arose a culture whose chief social elements, the peasant-village masses and a highly educated literati, possessed a common intellectual outlook. The differences between the two groups were more matters of refinements of taste and social usage than of belief and thought. For the peasant-village masses the violation of tradition was tabu; for the literate few the adherence to tradition was the supreme virtue. Thus literate learning sanctioned the virtue of the few in terms of the religious beliefs of the many. Under Heaven the emperor reigned supreme; under the emperor the literati ruled serenely; under the literati the peasant-village masses looked stolidly toward Heaven. Chinese culture embodied an almost complete union of superstition, intellectual refinement, and social acquiescence.

Chapter XV

THE ROMAN EMPIRE

≪≪‹≪‹-›››-››

In the Western world Rome built a dominion comparable to the great Eastern empires, and during the period of its formation and its rule the social forces having origin mainly in the Hellenistic age carried Western culture toward a consolidation similar to that which had occurred in the other urban culture areas. Rome was the heir not of Greece but of the Hellenistic kingdoms, and its conquest of the Mediterranean Basin gave impetus to the development of the cosmopolitan culture which was rooted in the mingling of Greek and Asiatic materials. The ultimate result— Christianity—was a consolidation of the chief cultural achievements of the peoples Rome united; when both Rome's empire and the conquered peoples disappeared, it remained to organize Western life for more than a thousand years.[1]

THE EXPANSION OF THE ROMAN REPUBLIC

The expansion of Rome in Italy and in the Mediterranean Basin was in no sense the result of a considered policy. But since the Romans always had an eye for a danger to be averted or an advantage to be gained, they easily followed the path to empire. It would be a mistake, though, to assert that they were more warlike than the peoples they conquered. They rose to power slowly, but as they rose they learned well its uses, so that they not only reaped its rewards but also compensated its victims. If the last three centuries B.C. were filled with wars and enslavements, the first and second centuries were an era of peace, not without

---

[1] On the general history of Rome see Max Cary, *A History of Rome down to the Reign of Constantine* (1935); M. I. Rostovtzeff, *A History of the Ancient World* (1927), Vol. 2, *Rome;* A. E. R. Boak, *A History of Rome to A.D.* 565 (1929). The classic study of Roman history is by Theodor Mommsen, originally published in German in the late nineteenth century; it is to be found in English as Theodor Mommsen, *The History of Rome* (4 vols., 1929–1931), trans. from the German by W. P. Dickson.

distresses but, on the whole, more orderly than the Mediterranean peoples had enjoyed before or have known since.[1]

THE SUPREMACY OF ROME IN ITALY.

After the founding of the republic, the relations of Rome with its neighbors—the Etruscans, the cities of Latium, and the hill peoples of central Italy—were continually disturbed, and its position uncertain. The Etruscan city Veii was a rival of Rome for the control of the Tiber crossing. The Latin cities were organized in a league to resist Roman encroachments. And the hill peoples threatened constantly to invade Roman lands as well as those of their Latin neighbors. Leadership in the conflict of the lowland and the west coast against the hill peoples was Rome's first step toward supremacy in Italy.

After 448 B.C., when the plebeian element began to play a more important role in the state, Rome's advance was rapid. Early in the fourth century B.C. Veii was destroyed and the hill peoples were checked. The capture of Rome by the Gauls in 390 B.C., although a setback, was followed by the erection of new walls and by other military measures which improved its position, so that by the middle of the fourth century B.C. it was overlord of the Latin cities, no longer feared the Etruscans, whom the Gallic inroads had weakened, and held enough lands to give its power a firm base.

These developments drew it into the situation to the south where the Samnites, a hill people, who had pushed along the Apennine ranges, were threatening the Greek coastal cities.[2] As early as 420 B.C. they captured Cumae, the first Greek city on the western Italian coast below Rome, and throughout the early fourth century B.C. they raided the rich agricultural plains of Campania. Shortly after the middle of this century Rome began a series of wars with the Samnites which, although they forced it to meet all of its enemies again, ended in its domination of the entire Italian peninsula. After the First Samnite War (343–341 B.C.), which expelled the Samnites from the coastal plain, the Latin cities rose against Rome. Rome beat them one by one, and fixed upon them a settlement which incorporated some of them in the Roman state, bound others to furnish troops, and left all

[1] On the history of the Roman Republic see H. L. Havell, *Republican Rome: Her conquests, manners, and institutions from the earliest times to the death of Caesar* (1914); Franz Altheim, *Epochen der römischen Geschichte*, Bd. 1, *Von den Anfängen bis zum Beginn der Weltherrschaft* (1934); W. E. Heitland, *The Roman Republic* (3 vols., 2d ed., 1923); André Piganiol, *La Conquête romaine* (1927).

[2] See J. W. Spaeth, *A Study of the Causes of Rome's Wars from 343 to 265 B.C.* (1926).

of them without freedom of action. After this victory Rome had no rival on the western coastal plain. In the Second Samnite War (326–304 B.C.) Rome suffered some severe defeats, but by making alliances and establishing strong military colonies it planted Roman power firmly across the north central part of the peninsula and confined the Samnites to the southern highlands. An ascendancy in the Etruscan cities was established when the aristocrats, faced with the revolts of their serfs, were forced to call for aid. Although the Third Samnite War (298–290 B.C.) saw an attempt to unite against Rome all of the Italian enemies, including the Etruscans and Gauls, the city emerged victorious, largely because it opposed a well-organized power to a loosely knit combination of foes. In 290 B.C., when the Samnites asked for peace, they were enmeshed in a network of alliances that gave central Italy an enduring peace.

The victory in central Italy turned Rome's attention both northward and southward. In the north the last Gallic raiders were destroyed, and the Etruscan cities were finally reduced. In the south, war with Tarentum, the most prosperous of the Greek cities, broke out.

When Pyrrhus, king of Epirus, across the Adriatic Sea, invaded Italy at the invitation of Tarentum, Rome's power was put to a severe test, for it faced not only the Greek cities and Pyrrhus but also the Samnites. Success came this time not as a result of a decisive battle but as the outcome of a slow attrition of the forces of its enemies. The defeat of Pyrrhus at Beneventum in 275 B.C. assured to Rome the supremacy of Italy or rather, as Pyrrhus said, a struggle for it with Carthage. In 272 B.C., when Tarentum accepted a Roman garrison, the supremacy was complete.

In the course of these wars Rome forged the instruments of its imperial rule. Beside the legions, which were organized as mobile units rather than as solid ranks, in the Greek manner, these instruments were: (1) military and civil colonies planted at strategic points; (2) roads, such as the Appian Way, which led from Rome across Campania, over which its troops could move quickly; and (3) the policy of "Divide and rule," which by keeping its enemies separated lessened their capacity to resist. This policy, worked out in alliances with different tribes and cities, gave some full Roman citizenship, others partial citizenship, and still others only rights of local government. All allies furnished military levies and allowed Rome to direct their foreign relations. The chief means of Romanization was the civil law, which was enforced by

Roman officials, *praefecti*, who resided in the colonies and among the allies.[1]

THE DUEL OF ROME AND CARTHAGE.

The unification of Italy, the necessary preliminary to the extension of Roman power beyond Italy, brought Rome face to face with Carthage. The immediate cause of the struggle between them, which began in 264 B.C., was rivalry in Sicily, especially in Messina, the port that controlled the strait between Sicily and Italy. When Rome succeeded in forcing the withdrawal of a Punic military force, Carthage declared war. In the First Punic War (264–241 B.C.) Rome built a war fleet and carried the struggle into Africa; at its close Carthage surrendered Sicily, the chief center of the fighting, and paid a large indemnity. After the war Carthage, under the able leadership of Hamilcar, recouped its loss of Sicily by conquering Spain as far as the Ebro River. Silver mines were the first objective of the campaign. Rome met this advance, when Carthage was engaged in suppressing a revolt in its army, by seizing Sardinia and Corsica and by forcing the payment of a second indemnity. Rome's munition manufacturers added to the difficulty of Carthage by supplying its enemies with weapons.

Troubles in Spain, as well as Carthaginian interference with the trade of Massilia, friendly to Rome, led to the outbreak of the Second Punic War (218–201 B.C.). This bitter struggle was waged in all parts of the western Mediterranean Basin. Hannibal (247–183 B.C.) harried Italy from end to end for fourteen years; in 216 B.C. he inflicted on Rome its greatest military disaster, the destruction of an army of about 85,000 men in the battle of Cannae. Publius Scipio (237–183 B.C.), known afterwards as Scipio Africanus, countered Hannibal by invading Spain and then Africa, thus forcing the withdrawal of Carthaginian arms from Italy. In 202 B.C. Scipio overthrew Hannibal in the battle of Zama by employing tactics similar to those used by Hannibal at Cannae.

In the First Punic War Rome won command of the sea; in the second it destroyed Carthaginian power on land. But it is fair to say that it learned the art of warfare, both by sea and by land, from its enemy. After Zama, defenseless Carthage surrendered Spain and the western Mediterranean islands, agreed to pay a huge indemnity, and gave up the rights to maintain an army and navy and to conduct an independent foreign policy. Rome, having

[1] See Hans Rudolf, *Stadt und Staat im römischen Italien* (1935).

WESTERN MEDITERRANEAN LANDS DURING THE SECOND PUNIC WAR

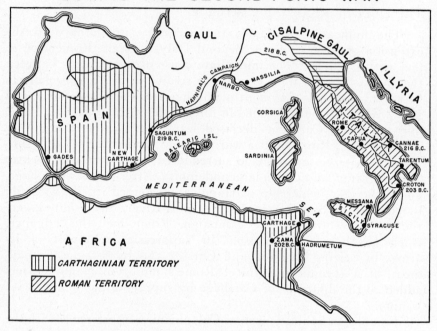

learned to profit from warfare during the duel with Carthage, emerged from the struggle a predatory power.[1]

THE ROMAN CONQUEST OF EASTERN MEDITERRANEAN LANDS.

Just as Rome's advance in Italy brought conflict with Carthage, so victories over Carthage led to eastward expansion.

In 215 B.C. Macedonia, stirred by the debacle of Cannae, entered the war on the side of Carthage and threatened to invade Italy, but Roman naval power in the Adriatic Sea and Roman diplomacy in Greece, where the cities were resisting a restoration of Macedonian overlordship, thwarted the design. Soon after

[1] See *The Cambridge Ancient History*, Vol. 7, *The Hellenistic Monarchies and the Rise of Rome* (1928), Chap. XXI, "Rome and Carthage: The First Punic War," Chap. XXIV, "The Carthaginians in Spain"; Vol. 8, *Rome and the Mediterranean, 218–133 B.C.* (1930), Chap. II, "Hannibal's Invasion," Chap. III, "The Roman Defensive," Chap. IV, "Scipio and Victory." Discussions of the wars between Rome and Carthage are also to be found in R. B. Smith, *Rome and Carthage* (1905); T. A. Dodge, *Hannibal* (2 vols., 1891); C. Torr, *Hannibal Crosses the Alps* (1924); B. H. Lidell Hart, *A Greater than Napoleon: Scipio Africanus* (1926).

Zama, Rome, at the request of Athens, intervened directly, liberated the Greek cities, and, in 196 B.C., forced Macedonia to abandon its fleet and pay tribute. Further advance in the East followed the intrigues of Hannibal, who, having been driven from Carthage by his enemies, aroused the Seleucid king of Syria to attack Rome in Macedonia; his scheme involved the raising of Macedonian, Greek, and Carthaginian arms against the all-conquering city. Rome halted the attack at Thermopylae and imposed on the Seleucids terms similar to those Macedonia had been compelled to accept (189 B.C.). Rome took no eastern territory but dictated the disposal of lands, giving Asia Minor to Pergamum, and Caria and Lycia to Rhodes, whose fleet had given aid against the Seleucids. A third war with Macedonia (171–168 B.C.) led to its partition into four self-governing republics. Rome's failure to take political responsibility in the new republics allowed dissatisfaction to grow, not only in them but also in Greece, Pergamum, Rhodes, and Carthage, each of which had grievances; the dissatisfaction finally flared up in the widespread but unorganized revolt—the Third Punic War (149–146 B.C.)—that ended with the destruction of Corinth and Carthage in 146 B.C. Then Rome took the inevitable step of annexing eastern territory, and Macedonia, like Carthage, became a Roman province. In 129 B.C. Pergamum, bequeathed in 133 B.C. to Rome by its king, also became a Roman province.[1]

At last Rome was mistress of the Mediterranean Basin. During the Second Punic War, Cisalpine Gaul had been brought into the Roman system of alliances. About the same time the king of Egypt became a ward of the Roman people. Under the provincial system of government, which Rome had first applied in Sardinia and Sicily, Spain, Africa, Macedonia, and Asia Minor received Roman governors, paid taxes to the Roman state, and gave up all arms. And there was no rival to resist advance over territories not yet conquered.

THE SOCIAL REVOLUTION UNDER THE LATE ROMAN REPUBLIC

The Roman Republic was mistress of the Mediterranean world. But who ruled Rome? Who had ruled Rome? Who would rule Rome?[2]

---

[1] See *The Cambridge Ancient History*, Vol. 8, *Rome and the Mediterranean, 218–133 B.C.* (1930), Chap. IX, "Rome and the Hellenistic States," Chap. XV, "The Fall of Carthage." See also M. Holleaux, *Rome, la Grèce, et les monarchies hellénistiques* (1921).

[2] On this phase of Roman history see T. R. Holmes, *The Roman Republic and the*

There was no single answer to these questions, for at different times different special-interest groups were dominant. In the fifth and fourth centuries B.C. the patricians ruled. In the third century B.C. the patricians and the plebeians, especially the small landowners, moved hesitantly along the path to imperial power. Toward the close of the third century B.C. a narrow senatorial oligarchy, partly patrician and partly plebeian, walked firmly in this path. The constitutional struggles which transformed Rome into a mature timocracy were bound up with the wars that gave supremacy in Italy. The wars that carried Rome's power throughout the Mediterranean Basin so disturbed the elements of this regime that domestic strife became continuous, especially after the middle of the second century B.C. Behind this strife lay the economic and social consequences of expansion, and within it the military force which expansion created became always more important. The republic was overthrown finally in a protracted struggle which brought into action not only the special-interest groups that expansion had created in Rome but also the Mediterranean peoples who had suffered at Rome's hands. The empire emerged at the end of the struggle, ruled by the victor in both the imperial and the domestic arena.

THE ECONOMIC CONSEQUENCES OF THE ROMAN CONQUEST OF THE MEDITERRANEAN BASIN.

Rome became a significant factor in Mediterranean commerce only as its dominion was extended.[1] Its industries, particularly the manufacture of weapons, throve as the market widened. The destruction of Carthage gave it the trade of northern Africa and the western Mediterranean coasts of Europe. As its armies moved east, Greek and Asiatic traders and craftsmen moved west, and its own merchants followed in the paths of the legions. By the end of the third century B.C. Roman traders were familiar figures in all parts of the Mediterranean Basin.

This sound economic growth was not, however, so significant for the future as developments traceable directly to the waging of successful wars. Agriculture underwent a profound change, a

Founder of the Empire (3 vols., 1923); F. B. Marsh, *A History of the Roman World from 146 to 30 B.C.* (1935); A. H. J. Greenidge, *A History of Rome from the Tribunate of Tiberius Gracchus to the End of the Jugurthine War, B.C.* 133–104 (1904); G. Bloch and J. Carcopino, *La République romaine de* 133 *à* 44 *avant J.C.* (2 vols., 1936); Guglielmo Ferrero, *The Greatness and the Decline of Rome* (5 vols., 1908).

[1] On the general economic history of the Roman Republic see Tenney Frank, *Economic History of Rome* (2 vols., 2d ed., 1927).

new kind of business enterprise developed, and political dominion gave rise to a kind of capitalism.

The agricultural change was the result, on the one hand, of the destruction of the small landowners in the incessant wars and, on the other hand, of the ruining of the market for domestic grain by the opening up of foreign sources of supply, particularly Sicily. The ruin of the Italian countryside dated from the first war with Carthage, which bore most heavily upon the small farmers. The campaigns of Hannibal destroyed domestic animals, tools, and farmsteads as well as men. Roman campaigns outside Italy took men away from the fields for such long periods that they lost the habits of rural life. Furthermore, after the introduction of the vine, the olive tree, and the fig tree, small farmers lacked the capital necessary for profitable production.

These circumstances combined to promote the growth of a system of cultivation based on the large estate—the *latifundium*—producing cattle, wine, oil, and figs. Near Rome and other growing cities a diversified production appeared. These developments were, of course, the economic foundation of the new patrician-plebeian nobility, whose members possessed the capital necessary to organize production. Their political power enabled them to hold the public lands, to which every war added; to them also went the bulk of the slaves who flowed into Italy after every victory. They used the mortgage and even harsher methods, such as driving cattle over the fields of small farmers, to crowd out their weaker competitors. The Licinian laws proved ineffective to check their aggressions. Poor men who received allotments as colonists frequently sold them and joined the streams of dispossessed men flowing to the cities, especially Rome. The economic revolution which swept the countryside added to the wealth of those already rich, deprived the poor of what little they possessed, and planted on the land a vast and cruelly exploited slave population. Hellenistic methods played a large part in the evolution of the new agrarian system.

The expansion of business enterprise which imperial aggrandizement nourished was fivefold; it embraced (1) the manufacture of munitions, (2) the building of roads, harbors, bridges, and temples, (3) the leasing of state-owned enterprises such as mines, fisheries, salt works, and timber regions, (4) the loaning of funds to the state and municipalities, and (5) the farming of provincial revenues. The capital for these enterprises was derived chiefly from the booty seized during the wars; like the public lands, it went mainly into the hands of those already well-to-do. Thus movable wealth became a factor in Roman life alongside the traditional landed property. To facilitate its manipulation companies, or syndicates, arose. The first were organized to supply the legions that Scipio led to Spain during the Second Punic War. Early in the second century B.C. syndicates were formed to farm customs, exploit mines and forests, and manage the Sicilian corn lands. Such companies had three grades of members: (1) the *socii*, an inside circle of promoters, (2) *participes*, an outside circle of subscribers, and (3) *partes*, ordinary investors in stocks and shares. Each syndicate had a manager, who remained in Rome, and staffs of agents, accountants, collectors, and couriers, most of whom worked in the provinces. As Rome's dominion grew, speculation increased and the gambling spirit rose, attaining its height in the century before the fall of the republic. The temple of Janus became the Wall Street of Rome.

Closely bound up with these agricultural and business developments was the exploitation that was organized by means of the provincial governments. As previously noted, early urban political and legal institutions functioned chiefly as the means of transferring the economic surplus from the working masses to some ruling class. The Roman system of provincial government served this traditional purpose, taking from conquered nations and giving to the Romans not only the accumulated economic surplus that could be seized but also the new surplus produced by labor. The simplest means of such transfer, besides the seizure of booty, was the levying of tribute and indemnity. The sale of captives as slaves not only realized great sums for the victors but also confiscated the labor force of conquered nations. When a provincial government was fully organized, a land tax, usually 10 per cent, custom duties, and collections in kind wrung other sums from the subject peoples. The seizure of mines, forests, quarries, and salt deposits, as well as land, gave the natural resources of conquered areas to the victors. The extension of the Roman system of lending money at usurious rates intensified the exploitation that, after the middle of the second century B.C., became universal in the provinces. As a matter of fact, the growth of business enterprise was incidental to the rise of political exploitation, for the political rulers, interested mainly in income, found it advantageous to allow speculators to take the risks of enterprise and make what profits they could: (1) by leasing estates, mines, forests, and fisheries for fixed annual rents and (2) by farming the taxes of the provinces for fixed payments to the state treasury. Thus political dominion and business grew together: "War gave birth to capitalism in Rome."[1]

THE SOCIAL CONSEQUENCES OF THE ROMAN CONQUEST OF THE MEDITERRANEAN WORLD.

This combination of political and economic factors created a new social structure of two main divisions: (1) the groups within the body of Roman citizens and (2) the groups within the conquered populations.

The Roman groups were: (1) the senatorial nobility, (2) the *equites* (equestrians or knights), and (3) the poor citizens.

The nobility of the late Roman Republic consisted of those families, about six hundred in number, whose members traced descent from magistrates. After the close of the struggle of the orders many rich plebeians became magistrates, and in time their descendants intermarried with the relatively small number of patrician families that survived. As time went on, however, fewer plebeians entered the nobility, and it became a new oligarchy. In this connection it should be noted that the plebeian offices were ultimately organized in the *cursus honorum*, and so they also came to give the rank of nobility. The nobility, as a whole, felt that its members alone were entitled to hold office, and the censors came generally to act on this principle in selecting senators. The senate, the seat of the oligarchy's power, made imperial policy and provincial government its chief concern. The oligarchy was united by common interests, on the one hand in the distribution of public lands and on the other hand in the holding of public offices which opened the public purse to the incumbents. Political power was a means to great wealth, and great wealth was a prerequisite for a political career. By the end of the Punic Wars a newly rich plebeian found it almost impossible to break into the senatorial circle.

By this time also there had formed within the oligarchy an inner circle or clique whose members came from the families descended from consuls; known as *nobiles*, they guarded jealously access to the senate and the consulate. Both patrician and plebeian families belonged to the group, and competition among them for preferment was keen. Family prestige, money, and marriageable

---

[1] J. F. Toutain, *The Economic Life of the Ancient World* (1930), p. 250. See also A. E. R. Boak, *A History of Rome to A.D. 565* (1929), p. 131: "Rome was now living largely from the exploitation of the provinces. The income derived from this source passed mainly into the hands of the office-holding aristocracy and, to a lesser degree, the business class. The lower classes profited little therefrom, and their conditions had deteriorated steadily as the empire had expanded." By permission of The Macmillan Company, New York.

daughters were valuable assets in conducting the intrigues by which position was won and kept. Most of the patrician families in the group remained there only by virtue of alliance with powerful plebeian families.

The equestrians, or knights, were the businessmen of Rome. Year by year, as new conquests were made, they became richer with the profits of government contracts, transport, leases of state-owned resources, and farmed taxes, which, in turn, they invested chiefly in Italian land. And through wealth they exerted political power. Among them the *publicani*, who followed the conquering armies, systematizing their exploitation, became especially active in politics. Many senators, either in partnership with them or in debt to them, found their interests best served by voting as the publicani wished. In the provinces the publicani put pressure on the governors; in Rome, when opponents attempted to punish them for extortion, they bribed officials and corrupted juries. Furthermore, since cases involving the penalty of a large fine were tried by the comitia tributa, the knights controlled the juries that heard not only the cases in which they were interested personally but also the trials of provincial administrators; for this reason the knights were able to use the judicial power to advance their interests in the provinces at the expense of the senatorial nobles. In the absence of a civil service the knights formed the administrative corps of the all-conquering republic. The greater part of the knights probably were without economic interests beyond Rome and Italy and sought security for property rather than new opportunity for vast accumulation; in this desire they were, of course, the opponents of any proposal affecting the existing distribution of wealth.

Together the senatorial nobles and the knights formed the property-owning class. Although they were united by a hatred of the Roman poor, family rivalries and conflicting economic and political interests within their ranks were the sources of most of the internal struggles that finally wrecked the republic.

The poor citizens were mostly small landholders who, having lost their property, had flocked to Rome. They lacked the capital to enter business and the skill to compete with the eastern craftsmen brought in as slaves. During the First Punic War the democratic party which had forced the patrician-plebeian nobility to make concessions to the small landholders held together, but the disasters of the Second Punic War destroyed both its members and its leaders. Its last important leader, the tribune C. Flaminius, who fought a desperate struggle with the senatorial oligarchy over a policy of colonization that would have given the public lands to the poorer citizens, perished in 217 B.C. Like the nobles and the knights, the poor citizens supported imperialism, for as legionnaires they shared somewhat in the booty and as colonists they sometimes received lands. But ultimately they profited most by selling their votes in the assemblies to the nobles and knights who had political ends to further.

The non-Roman groups in the new social structure were: (1) the allies, mostly Italians, (2) the provincials, and (3) the slaves. These groups, deprived of political power, were at the mercy of the rulers of the Roman state.

The Italian allies were practically in the position of the Spartan perioikoi. They fought Rome's wars but did not enjoy the advantages citizenship gave. Like the poor citizen landholders, they suffered greatly during the struggle with Carthage as well as from that universal scourge of the countryside, the usury of the capitalists. Two important groups can be identified among the Italians: the poor Italians, who joined the legions and made imperialism and civil war the means of economic and political advancement, and the well-to-do Italians, whose members increased steadily as Italy was transformed by the wealth seized in conquered lands. They opposed the Roman oligarchy which denied them political privileges and resisted the poor who attacked the rights of property. Although the mergence of these groups with the Roman citizenry was a slow process, it was a decisive factor in the social and political movements that overthrew the republic.

The composition of the Roman people was rapidly changing at this time because of the addition of large numbers of freedmen and allies to its ranks. The wars of the second century had depleted the old Roman stock, and families became small as the men were kept away for years in interest of the state. Many Romans sought relief from their economic distress by migration to the newly won provinces where opportunity was beckoning. Additions to the body politic were made from time to time, but usually grudgingly, since the old citizens were not inclined to share their privileges with others. Even after citizenship was bestowed, the new citizens were hampered with restrictions. As a result of these factors a proletariat came into being at Rome which was largely composed of the step-children of Italy. It was this downtrodden class which was chiefly responsible for the violent outbreaks of the late republic and the resulting anarchy.[1]

[1] From *Illinois Studies in the Social Sciences*, Vol. 23, (1935), No. 4, John W. Heaton, 'Mob Violence in the Late Roman Republic, 133–49 *B.C.*," p. 4.

The provincials, regardless of class status, were helpless before their conquerors. Upon them fell the burden of the irresponsible greed of the Roman nobles and knights. Each province, it was said, had to yield three fortunes to its governor—"one to pay his debts, one to bribe his judges, and one to recompense him for his arduous and disinterested labors." In 167 B.C., when the direct taxation of Romans was stopped, the bulk of state expenditure was levied on the provincials. But they suffered quite as much under the financial operations of the knights as they did under the political exploitation of the officials sent to govern them; usually, of course, the knights and officials were partners. They regarded the province as an estate from which to wring the last penny. Only by appeal to Rome could provincials obtain any redress, and there corruption denied them a fair hearing. The kings and wealthy families of despoiled lands often became the clients of the Roman commanders who had conquered them and found in the relation some protection. The commanders in turn made the formation of such bodies of clients the means of political advancement in Rome.

Roman exploitation fell heaviest upon the slaves, whose numbers increased rapidly during the period of expansion. Every battle, siege, and war ended with the enslavement of the conquered survivors. In Italy only the citizens of Tarentum escaped this fate. At the close of the First Samnite War 36,000 were sold into slavery. The destruction of Carthage sent 50,000 over the block. The advance in the east was marked at every stage by enslavements; Asia Minor was partly depopulated. In 101 B.C. Marius sent 100,000 Cimbri south to the slave pens of Italy; during the Gallic Wars, it is said, Caesar sent 400,000 captives across the Alps. The supply of slaves, it seemed, was unfailing.

The Roman slave system grew steadily more cruel after the Second Punic War. Like any domestic animal or other piece of movable property, the slave was a chattel. He had no rights, not even that of marriage. His children were slaves at birth. He was subject to severe discipline under the whip, but the master did not possess the right of life and death. Cato the Elder recommended that at the end of each day a recalcitrant slave be flogged. In case a master was murdered in his house, every one of his slaves became subject to the death penalty. No slave could make an accusation against his master. Worse than legal disabilities was the torture of labor. On occasions slaves actually were worked to death, and those too old or too sick to work were turned out to die. But Roman slave management generally followed the rule of profit. If

Hamilton M. Wright

THE ROMAN FORUM

The Forum was the center of the Roman world. In the foreground are remains of the rostrum on which Mark Antony made his famous funeral oration over Caesar's body. In the center is the arch of Septimius Severus to commemorate his victorious campaign against the Parthians. On the right, is the Phocas Column, 608 A.D., the last monument erected in the Forum.

kind treatment paid, it was given; if cruelty paid, it was un-hesitatingly employed. Expensive slaves, for example apothecaries, were carefully guarded. Free labor was sent to work on malarial lands so that the capital invested in slaves might not be endangered. The spirit of the Roman slave system was well described by Varro (*ca.* 116–27 B.C.), the greatest Roman writer on agriculture:

> Slaves should be neither cowed nor high-spirited. They ought to have men over them who know how to read and write and have some little education, who are dependable and older than the hands whom I have mentioned; for they will be more respectful to these than to men who are younger. Furthermore, it is especially important that the foremen be men who are experienced in farm operations; for the foremen must not only give orders but also take part in the work, so that his subordinates may follow his example, and also understand that there is good reason for his being over them—the fact that he is superior to them in knowledge. They are not to be allowed to control their men with whips rather than with words, if only you can achieve the same result. Avoid having too many slaves of the same nation, for this is a fertile source of domestic quarrels. The foremen are to be made zealous by rewards, and care must be taken that they have a bit of property of their own, and mates from among their fellow-slaves to bear them children; for by this means they are made more steady and more attached to the place. Thus, it is on account of such relationships that slave families of Epirus have the best reputations and bring the highest prices. The good will of the foremen should be won by treating them with some degree of consideration; and those of the hands who excel the others should also be consulted as to the work to be done. When this is done they are less inclined to think that they are looked down upon, and rather to think that they are held in some esteem by the master. They are made to take more interest in their work by being treated more liberally in respect either of food, or of more clothing, or of exemption from work, or of permission to graze some cattle of their own on the farm, or other things of this kind; so that, if some unusually heavy task is imposed, or punishment inflicted on them in some way, their loyalty and kindly feeling to the master may be restored by the consolation derived from such measures.[1]

Slaves manned almost every part of the Roman system of production. After the conquest of Greece and Asia Minor, artists, musicians, grammarians, teachers, engineers, physicians, architects, and philosophers were owned as slaves. Domestic slaves were employed in every branch of household labor. At the door of the house of a noble or a knight usually two slaves stood, chained like watchdogs. Most of the craft industries were carried on by slaves

[1] Marcus Terentius Varro, *On Agriculture*, Book I, XVII.

from the Hellenized East. Slaves who qualified as gladiators were greatly prized. Four classes of slaves were treated with gross inhumanity: contract slaves, agricultural slaves, mine slaves, and galley slaves. Many knights owned great numbers of slaves who were let out under contract to work on public or private projects. When not at work they were kept in stockade-like pens. The estate system of agriculture was based entirely on slave labor. Masses of slaves worked in the fields in chains; at night they were housed in a half-underground prison—the *ergastulum*. In fact, since most of the managers of estates—bailiffs—were slaves who profited as production increased, they had little regard for either the diet or the health of the creatures who worked under them. The mine slaves frequently lived, married, begot children, and died underground. The galley slave, driven to monotonous labor by the lash, became a figure symbolical of all the terror and misery of the slave system. Among the many varieties of Roman slaves, probably the herdsmen who were sent into the hills and mountains to care for cattle and sheep fared best. They lived entirely in the open, ate only the meat and milk they took from the herd, and enjoyed the companionship of the female slaves who shared their lot.

The progressive enslavement of the Mediterranean masses from the third to the first century B.C. was a profound social development of far-reaching consequences, for it carried on, in an intensified form, the process of uprooting which had begun in Hellenistic times.

THE SOCIAL STRUGGLE IN THE LATE ROMAN REPUBLIC.

In the second century B.C. the institutions of the Roman Republic were not greatly different from those of three hundred years earlier. But behind the institutions was the new social structure, embodying conflicts of interest and forms of power which made the institutions ineffective. Four factors were important in this situation: (1) the rivalry of consular nobles for power and glory, (2) a clash of interests between the senators and the knights, (3) the corruption of the poor citizens by the great wealth holders, and (4) the advent of the army as an independent political force.

The rivalries of the consular nobles caused them to take advantage of every opportunity they could find in the cupidity and discontent of other groups; for this reason their conflicts and intrigues were important not in themselves but in relation to the interests of other groups. The unprincipled, opportunistic, and violent actions of these high-born politicians were the chief cause not of the fall of the republic but of the bloody disasters that accompanied the struggles in which it was overthrown.

The clash between the senatorial oligarchy and the knights was chiefly a quarrel over the spoils of victory.[1] The senators not only fixed the conditions of exploitation of the provinces but also, regardless of their legal exclusion from trade, entered various enterprises as "silent partners." The knights objected not so much to this competition as to the political control of their own activities. In 184 B.C. when Cato the Elder, then censor, made some contracts that were unfavorable to the knights, they forced him to cancel them. In 169 B.C. when certain knights were excluded from negotiating for contracts, their colleagues were greatly angered, and two years later when the senate refused to lease the Macedonian mines their bitterness was increased. Open conflict between the two wealth-holding groups followed the assumption by the senate in 149 B.C. of judicial control over the provinces. In view of the fact that many of the knights had become politically ambitious this measure incited them to take whatever action was possible against the senatorial nobles.

The knights found in the assembly of tribes a means of retaliation. They increased their power there by creating freedmen who were registered in the urban tribes. The full struggle between the senators and the knights developed in the rural tribes, whose members, mostly dispossessed peasants, were willing to sell their votes. By the opening of the first century B.C. the corruption of this element of the electorate was complete. Bureaus were maintained for the purchase of votes. "Bread and show" were provided on a lavish scale. And gangs of poor citizens, freedmen, and clients were organized to influence elections. The nobles vied with the knights in bribing the electorate, so that Rome was at the call of the highest bidder. Such corruption made easy the advance of men who did not scruple, if occasion demanded, to add violence to bribery.

Such men appeared among both the nobles and the knights, but the instrument of violence par excellence, the army, was to be won only in the provinces. The development of the provincial command as a means of dominating the state was the inevitable result of imperial expansion. The necessity for continuing campaigns after

[1] Léon Homo, *Roman Political Institutions from City to State* (1929), p. 153: "The conflict dividing the two kinds of nobility doubtless took the form of a caste-rivalry, but what was much more serious, it was above all a question of material interests, or, to put it plainly, a matter of money. That rivalry was aggravated more and more every day by the increasingly intensive exploitation of the Mediterranean domain of Rome." By permission of Alfred A. Knopf, Inc., New York, and George Routledge & Sons, Ltd., London.

the expiration of the yearly term of a commander led to the extension of the term; at first such extensions were made for one year, but later they were made for two or three or five years. Thus the authority of the proconsul, as the provincial commander was called, acquired a permanency not possessed by the authority of any civil magistrate. Although commands were determined by the senate, authority to command, as well as extension of term, was given by the assembly of tribes. Originally the senate controlled the proconsuls by selecting the provinces to which they were sent, by fixing the size of armies, by appointing the officers of the legions, and by voting money; more important, perhaps, for the senate's control was the fact that ambitious men who desired advancement in the *cursus honorum* had to hold its favor. But successful commanders found in the prestige and wealth won by war the means of weakening these controls. By sending trusted lieutenants home to stand for the magistracies they were able to create their own political faction, often only after bribing a part of the citizenry, and contest directly for political power. At the same time, because of the increasing technical character of warfare, the senate was less able to remove a proconsul from his command. In other words, the senate, no longer able to send inexperienced nobles into the field, was forced to retain experienced and successful generals in their commands, and the generals, as a result, tended to become more and more prominent politically. Scipio Africanus, the conqueror of Spain and Carthage, was the first commander of an army outside of Italy to make military success the basis of political preferment. He claimed the right to dispose of his army as he saw fit, while the citizens, among whom were his veterans, wanted to make him consul and dictator for life. Cato the Elder fought a long battle, ultimately successful, against these threats to the constitution.

After the destruction of the small proprietors the dependence of the ordinary soldier on his commander became immeasurably greater, for only through the commander's success were booty, land, and advancement to be won. As a matter of fact, as soon as the assembly of tribes obtained the right of lawmaking, the imperial motive became stronger and more open; it was the assembly of tribes that voted to go to war with Carthage. The army began to have a political significance of its own: for the poor citizens it was *empire*, *i.e.*, the means of participating in prestige and plunder. The creation of six independent provincial commands raised up that many competitors for honors and power and deposited in the body politic voters who would support rival claimants. Because the resort to violence was a normal form of behavior both for the generals and for the veterans, the materials of civil strife accumulated as the armies marched from one victory to another.

But quite as important as a cause of civil war was the intervention of armies in the feud between the senatorial oligarchy and the knights, for it extended the struggle from the assembly and courts to the provinces. And the knights won, for through the power of the comitia tributa to bestow commands they deprived the senate of the control over military operations. In the last period of the republic such men as Marius, Pompey, Crassus, and Caesar received their commands from the assembly of tribes. When Pompey and Caesar won the right to appoint the officers of their legions, their armies became personal forces. At the same time the armies became professional and found it easy to identify their commander's authority, which was the best servant of their own interests, with the right to rule.

THE FALL OF THE ROMAN REPUBLIC

In the disorganized political conditions of late republican Rome, it is easy to confuse the activities of individual politicians with the dynamic factors that were driving the republic to its fall. The dynamic factors were the conflicting interests of the several groups of the new social structure, especially of the senatorial nobles, the knights, the poor citizens, the well-to-do Italians, and the legionnaires. Because the constitution of the republic did not give these groups power in the government according to their respective capacities to exert power, the struggle to change the organization of the government became more and more acute. The constitution was a sham, and change was necessary. But those Romans who were served by it were unwilling to surrender their advantage without a resort to violence, and those Romans and Italians who were not served by it were prepared to use violence to alter it. In the serving of these social groups the politicians found opportunity for the aggressions and shifts that gave office, and at their beck and call was an ever changing crowd of adventurers who offered their services—for buying votes, for rioting, and for murder —to the highest bidder. And the bidders were numerous. By promoting a social revolution, conquest generated the forces of a political revolution that ran through a little less than a century. Civil strife, foreign wars, national revolts, and slave insurrections contributed to the universal chaos.

THE FORMATION OF THE POPULAR PARTY: THE GRACCHI.

Tiberius Gracchus (163–133 B.C.), elected tribune in 133 B.C., was disturbed by the plight of the poor citizens who filled the ranks of the legions. "The private soldiers," he said, "fight and die to advance the wealth of the great, and they are called masters of the world, while they have not a foot of ground in their possession." His fear that Rome would lack soldiers in time of need was shared by a small group of consular nobles who were among his supporters. There was good reason for this fear, because in Sicily 250,000 rebellious slaves were spreading terror through the rich grain lands. (They were starved into submission in 132 B.C., and thousands were crucified.) Tiberius proposed that the lands held contrary to the Licinian laws should be restored to the state and divided among the poor citizens in unalienable twenty-acre homesteads. The knights, the plebeians, and the Italian allies—the last because he proposed to grant them citizenship—supported him. But the senatorial nobility induced another tribune to veto the scheme. When Tiberius appealed to the citizens against the oligarchy, they ousted the rival from the tribunate, thereby violating the constitution by an act of force. Tiberius then created an agricultural commission which set about making allotments. The senate, of course, hindered its action in every possible way. In order to be certain of carrying the work of redistributing the land, Tiberius took the step—of doubtfully legality—of standing for re-election to the tribunate. He gained additional popular support by advocating the sale of the legacy left to Rome by the king of Pergamum and the distribution of the proceeds to those who received homesteads, so that they could buy implements and livestock. As a protection against his aristocratic enemies, he went about with a bodyguard of three thousand poor citizens. The comitia tributa supported him, but the senatorial nobles, having spread the rumor that he aimed at absolute power, stirred up a riot in which he and three hundred followers were killed.

In these events began the internal political strife and class warfare that ended only with the establishment of the empire; the external conditions that contributed to the disorder were evident in the year after the death of Tiberius Gracchus, when mercenaries, slaves, and despoiled men throughout Asia Minor revolted against senatorial rule. They aimed to set up the revolutionary "sun city." Two years later the slaves of Delos rose against their masters.

Although the death of Tiberius Gracchus halted the work of the agricultural commission, the new agrarian law still stood, and in 123 B.C., when his brother Gaius Gracchus (153–121 B.C.), was elected tribune, reform was again the order of the day. To the soldiers Gaius Gracchus offered free clothing and shorter enlistments under a less stern discipline. To the poor citizens he gave doles, employment in public works, twenty-acre homesteads, and opportunity to migrate as colonists. To the knights he gave the control of juries that tried cases arising in the provinces, the right to organize companies (with silent partners) to farm the taxes of Asia Minor, the removal of the senators from the centuries of the knights, and the right of the assembly of tribes to assign military commands. To the Italian allies he wished to give citizenship. After his re-election the senate induced another tribune to outbid him for popular favor, and in the next year he was defeated in the assembly of tribes and driven to suicide.

THE SENATORIAL REACTION.

The return of the senatorial nobility to power brought an immediate reaction. The consuls, armed with dictatorial powers, dispersed and suppressed the poor citizens. Laws forbidding public meetings except at the call of a magistrate and limiting the right to speak at such meetings were passed. In 118 B.C. the allotting of land to poor citizens was stopped, and seven years later all public lands were declared, in effect, the private property of those who held them. These measures wiped out all that the Gracchi had accomplished for the poor citizens and the Italian allies. But several by-products of their activities remained. The tribunate had become an office to be held from term to term. The power of the assembly of tribes had been increased. And the knights, more powerful than ever, made it plain that they would punish any official who interfered with their business activities. If the Gracchi had aimed, as rumor had it, at absolute power, the tribunate had proved too weak an instrument for the purpose. And the non-Roman elements in Italy had become an important political factor.

THE REVIVAL OF THE POPULAR PARTY: MARIUS.

Repression at Rome was accompanied by disorder and corruption in the provinces. In Africa the rebel Jugurtha, who aspired to the throne of Numidia, bribed the nobles sent against him and, when called to Rome, frustrated an attempt to punish him by corrupting a tribune. He then returned to Africa, where, after destroying and enslaving a Roman army, he bribed Roman ambassadors to make a treaty satisfying his claim to the Numidian throne. One of the guilty bribe takers escaped the senate's anger by becoming a member of the commission to investigate the conduct of the ambassadors. Another army under the command of a consul was sent against Jugurtha; while its commander pursued the rebel, his chief lieutenant Marius (155–86 B.C.), who had risen from the ranks, returned to Rome and stood for the consulate. He was elected (107 B.C.) by the poor citizens and knights interested in exploiting Africa; his aim was to break the senatorial monopoly of patronage in the provinces. Many men from the Italian towns, who saw their interests served by this aim, were drawn into his faction. When the senate refused to give him the command in Africa, he appealed to the assembly of tribes, which bestowed it upon him. He used the tribunate to continue the agitation for reform and introduced certain innovations in military organization. The poor citizens were enrolled in the legions, the equipment of the individual legionnaire was standardized, and great stress was laid on swordsmanship. Because the poor citizens were interested in booty and lands, they began to pay attention to the prestige and soldierly capacity of the commander under whom they enlisted. The success of Marius against Jugurtha was due mainly to the skill of Cornelius Sulla (138–78 B.C.), a cavalry commander belonging to one of the most prominent noble families. With Marius, a party was formed which sought reforms that would give the poor citizens, the knights, and the Italians a large share of the spoils of conquest.

Meanwhile a new danger to Rome appeared in the north, where the Cimbri and Teutons were ready to attack. When Marius led his new legions against them and defeated them in two battles, he was immediately hailed in Rome as the savior of his country and, in the next year, 100 B.C., was elected consul for the sixth time.

The rise of Marius brought back to power the sympathizers with the poor citizens. Their leader, Saturninus, who, as tribune, in 103 B.C. had made a deal to give lands to Marius's veterans and in 101 B.C. had exposed the corruption of the senate's ambassadors sent to negotiate with Mithridates VI (*ca.* 120–64 B.C.), king of Pontus, proposed to give lands in southern Gaul to poor citizens and grant citizenship to the Italian allies. When the senatorial nobles attempted to defeat these measures by a resort to violence,

Marius beat them down. But, never a politician, Marius wavered between the parties, and his indecision gave the nobles an opportunity to have Saturninus murdered. At the close of his consulship Marius abandoned Rome to the nobles, going to the East on a diplomatic mission. However, with his advent the political forces decisive for the immediate future had clearly emerged—the military commander, the army, and the urban mob.

While these struggles filled Rome with clamor and bloodshed, the slaves again terrorized Sicily.

In the lull that followed the murder of Saturninus the quarrel between the nobles and the knights and the agitation of the Italian allies for citizenship continued. The demand of the Italians for the franchise was motivated by a fear that the agrarian reforms would again be imposed on them. In 91 B.C. M. Livius Drusus, a tribune, brought forward proposals designed to compromise the issues that disturbed the factions. He proposed: (1) to create three hundred new senators from the equestrian order, (2) to restore the control of juries to the nobles, (3) to grant citizenship to the allies, and (4) to supply cheaper grain and provide an easier opportunity for the poor citizens to migrate. His aim was essentially conservative. But unfortunately each group felt it was called upon to give more than it was to receive, and Drusus, like the other tribunes who advocated reforms, was murdered.

THE SOCIAL WAR, 91–88 B.C.

When the opponents of Drusus carried a law making it treason to advocate the extension of the franchise, the Italian allies revolted, and for three years, 91–88 B.C., the peninsula was in a turmoil. Eight peoples joined a holy alliance which aimed at nothing less than the destruction of Rome; the well-to-do Italians were the chief supporters of the alliance. Marius, who returned from the East, took the field against them, but probably from design, he failed to push the advantages he won, for among the allies were many members of his faction. Fear that the Etruscans might join the Italians induced the Roman nobles to make concessions. In 89 B.C. all Italians who laid down their arms within sixty days were granted citizenship. The Samnites, who refused all concessions, were finally beaten by Sulla.

At the close of the Social War, as this rising of the Italian allies is called, practically all Italians became Roman citizens. The well-to-do Italians, who had feared land reforms of the kind proposed by the Gracchi, were now in a position to advance in the Roman political system without calling upon the poor citizens for support. But their opposition to the senatorial monopoly of patronage was not abated.

The Triumph of the Senatorial Reaction: Sulla.

The admission of the Italians into the assembly of tribes immediately became an issue between the Roman factions. The popular party, led by Marius, desired to register the new citizens in all the tribes, but the senatorial party, supported by Sulla, who had been elected consul, opposed the proposal. The senatorial nobles wished to admit the Italians to a small number of tribes, so that their influence would be limited. When the tribune Sulpicius Rufus combined measures with the proposal of Marius that would have purged the senate of insolvent members, enrolled freedmen in the rural tribes, recalled exiles, and given the command in Asia Minor to Marius, Sulla marched his legions into Rome, and the senate outlawed Marius, who fled to Africa. Sulla, forced to choose between remaining in Rome and going to Asia, chose the proconsular command, leaving the senatorial nobles in control of the state.

In Pontus Mithridates VI raised a revolt that swept through Asia Minor and Greece; it was a combined national rising and popular insurrection. Mithridates offered the cancellation of half their debts to men who killed their creditors, and eighty thousand Romans and Italians are said to have perished as a result. Sulla met this greatest of all threats to Roman power in the East by invading Greece and Macedonia. Athens was starved into submission and sacked. Mithridates was defeated in Macedonia. Then the wealthy Greeks and Asiatics, fearing the success of the rebellious peasants and slaves, turned to Sulla, with whom in 84 B.C. they made a peace. Sulla, who had collected a large indemnity and much loot—without the consent of the senate—then marched his legions toward Rome, where the popular party had returned to power.

Led by Cinna, who as consul had revived the legislation of Sulpicius, canceled debts, and lavishly distributed corn to the poor citizens, the popular party undertook to undo the work of Sulla's intervention in 88 B.C. When his colleague attempted to prevent the new citizens from voting, Cinna, with the support of a few Marian sympathizers in the senate, among whom was young

Julius Caesar (*ca.* 100–44 B.C.), and the Italians, killed a number of nobles. Marius seized this opportunity to return from Africa and wreak vengeance on the nobles who had outlawed him. With a force of slaves and Numidian horsemen he seized the port of Ostia, where the grain ships lay, and starved Rome into submission. Once again powerful in Rome, he murdered as many of his enemies as he could catch, forced the senate to repeal the act of outlawry, and had himself elected consul for the seventh time. Cinna shared power with him, and together they forced the outlawry of Sulla.

In 83 B.C. Sulla landed in southern Italy and moved on Rome. The leaders of the popular party fled, and the Samnites, who supported them, were defeated at the gates of the city. Sulla's quick victory was largely due to the excellent work of two lieutenants, Pompey (*ca.* 106–48 B.C.) and Crassus (*ca.* 117–53 B.C.). Sulla celebrated a triumph, proscribed the leaders of the popular party, and reformed the constitution in favor of the senatorial nobles. The power of the tribunes was reduced. Consuls were declared ineligible for immediate re-election. The abolition of the censorship stopped the enrollment of new citizens. The number of quaestors and praetors chosen from the nobility was increased. The priestly colleges were closed to the poor citizens. The courts were put under the control of the senate. The knights were deprived of the privilege of farming the taxes of Asia Minor. The corn doles were abolished. About six hundred of Sulla's followers were introduced into the senate, and 100,000 of his veterans were settled on the lands of his enemies. A private police, created by admitting some eight thousand ruffians into Sulla's gens, terrorized the city.

Thus Sulla became dictator. Crassus laid the foundations of an enormous fortune by dealing in the confiscated properties of the adherents of Marius, a few of whom found refuge in Africa and Spain. Pompey obtained a command in Africa. And young Julius Caesar, who refused to divorce his wife, a daughter of Cinna, at Sulla's order, lost his property and his priesthood in the temple of Jupiter. His life was saved only by the pleas of aristocratic relatives and the vestal virgins.

Marius made massacre the instrument of party vindictiveness; Sulla made it the means of constitutional reform—perhaps as many as two thousand senators and knights were massacred. His constitutional changes favored the oligarchy. The tribunate became subservient to the senate. In Greece and Asia Minor the government of the towns was settled, and limitations were placed on the activities of the tax farmers. After two years as dictator,

Sulla retired in 79 B.C., and an aristocratic clique, known as the *Optimates*, *i.e.*, the "best," inherited his work.

THE DEATH STRUGGLE OF THE ROMAN REPUBLIC WITH ITS EXTERNAL AND INTERNAL ENEMIES: MITHRIDATES, SERTORIUS, AND SPARTACUS.

The death of Sulla was followed immediately by an attempt to overthrow the nobility. In 77 B.C. Lepidus, a consul of the popular party, re-established the corn dole and proposed to restore the power of the tribunate, reinstate dispossessed landowners, and recall exiles. The nobles defeated him before the gates of the city and destroyed his army after a retreat to northern Italy. But other dangers beset the oligarchy on every side. In Spain Sertorius, a lieutenant of Marius, built up an independent power; because of his success in organizing the wild Spanish tribes, Rome knew him by the dread appellation, "the new Hannibal." In the east Mithridates plotted a new war. On the Mediterranean Sea the thousand ships of the Cilician pirates reigned supreme. In 74 B.C. they burned a Roman fleet in the harbor at Ostia. In the next year all Italy was shaken by a slave revolt. Its able leader, Spartacus, organized an army of about 70,000 men—Thracians, Gauls, and Teutons—defeated a consul, forced Romans to fight as gladiators, and celebrated a triumph, dragging senators behind his chariot. He planned to set up the revolutionary "sun city" in southern Italy. Rivalry between the Gauls and other nationalities led to his downfall. Crassus defeated him in the field, and Pompey destroyed his army. Six thousand of his followers were crucified along the Appian Way. In 72 B.C. Sertorius, who had attempted to form an alliance with the slaves, the pirates, and Mithridates, was struck down by an assassin. Pompey resorted to this method to destroy an enemy whom neither he nor other commanders had been able to destroy in battle.

Meanwhile the senate's agents ravished the provinces. Lucullus, without the senate's consent, raided Pontus and held its entire population for ransom. He sent so many slaves to market that the price dropped to seventy-five cents a head. Verres devastated Sicily, robbing temples and private houses as well as extorting enormous sums from tax collectors. His rule, said Cicero, who persecuted him before the senate, was more ruinous than the Punic Wars or the slave revolts. Rome no longer knew either responsibility or security; she knew only Fortuna—Sulla's god—and violence.

THE RISE OF POMPEY.

The ambitions of Pompey and Crassus gave the popular party an opportunity to undo Sulla's work. Since under existing laws both Pompey and Crassus were ineligible to the consulate, their ambitions could be realized only by violating or by reforming the constitution. They did both. With the support of their legions, camped outside the gates of Rome, and the votes of the poor citizens and knights, they were elected consuls for the year 70 B.C. In return for its support the popular party obtained reforms. The old powers of the tribunate were restored. The senate was purged of Sulla's partisans. The knights recovered control of the juries and the privilege of farming the taxes in Asia Minor. But confiscated properties were not restored. Pompey retired from the consulate in 69 B.C., but his power was supreme among the poor citizens and the knights. In 66 B.C. a tribune proposed that he be given a command against the Cilician pirates, and the assembly of tribes granted it in spite of the opposition of the senatorial oligarchy. By this grant he held proconsular authority over the coasts of the Mediterranean Sea; no province was beyond his power. His military campaigns were brilliant successes on both sea and land; when he annexed Syria in 64 B.C. Rome became mistress of southwestern Asia and faced Parthia across Mesopotamia. As Pompey's power and prestige increased, he settled kings on thrones and attached them to himself as clients.

THE REVIVAL OF THE PARTY FEUD: CICERO AND CATILINE.

While Pompey restored Rome's power in the east, new politicians arose in Rome. Cicero (*ca.* 108–43 B.C.) who had first won political favor by prosecuting Verres, the despoiler of Sicily, became the champion of the senatorial oligarchy. He thought that a union of the nobility and the knights would save the republic from revolutionary democracy, which he believed was dangerous to the rights of property. Opposed to him were two young "patrician demagogues," the shrewd and ambitious Caesar and the headstrong Catiline (*ca.* 108–63 B.C.)

Caesar courted popular favor in order to gain power. As aedile he provided extravagant gladitorial shows, a form of entertainment established by Marius, whose portrait Caesar paraded with his ancestral images. He brought to trial men who had done murder for Sulla. He offered citizenship to the allies of Cisalpine Gaul. In 63 B.C., when he was chosen pontifex maximus in an election rife

CICERO

Cicero was a small-town lawyer who made learning and opportunism the means of advancement in the service of the Republican oligarchy. His enduring reputation flowed from the literary and intellectual expression he gave to that conservatism which masks reaction with refinement.

with corruption, he became head of the state religion. His capacity for intrigue was only exceeded by his political realism.

Catiline was the leader of the discontented—poor citizens, ruined nobles, despoiled knights, and Sulla's veterans—who wanted reform. His program called for the cancellation of debts and a redivision of the land. Twice frustrated by Cicero in campaigns for a consular post, he finally determined upon a resort to violence. His plan of action included the arming of the slaves in Italy and the people of Greece for war against the oligarchy. He had some support among the Roman and the Italian poor. Cicero, who was kept informed by the mistress of a member of the conspiracy, finally denounced Catiline before the senate and the citizens. Catiline fled to his army in Etruria, where he perished in battle with a consular force.[1]

In all probability Caesar and Crassus (whose enmity to Pompey had led him to seek an alliance with Caesar) were implicated in the plot; certain evidence suggests that Crassus was to be made dictator, with Caesar as his lieutenant. But both escaped the penalty of death which the senate imposed on several members of the conspiracy.

In the meantime Pompey with his veteran legions approached Rome. The people acclaimed him and bestowed upon him the unique title "warden of earth and sea." But the senatorial oligarchy feared him, and he hesitated to use force against the government. The Optimates, powerless to resist him openly, worked in the government and by private intrigues to frustrate his designs. Cato the Younger (*ca.* 95–46 B.C.), their leader, made constitutional principle serve so completely the interest of party that he became the great exemplar of conservative integrity. More astute politicians found Pompey's return the reason for making new arrangements.

The Struggle of the Military Commanders: Pompey and Caesar.

Among these politicians Caesar was the most active, and in 62 B.C., by supporting measures favorable to Pompey, he won a command in Spain, where the conqueror of Asia still retained control. In order to conduct a campaign Caesar borrowed a great sum from Crassus. The venture was fortunate, for in a year Caesar returned to Rome a successful general and a rich man. And there he found a situation to his liking. The vain Cicero had irritated Pompey, and the senate, under the influence of the Optimates— especially the younger Cato—refused to ratify Pompey's arrangement of the eastern provinces, although it had granted him a triumph. When the Optimates caused the senate to refuse Caesar a triumph, he turned to Pompey, and in 60 B.C., when Caesar was consul, they, together with Crassus, made what may be considered the greatest political deal in history. Technically the deal is known as the First Triumvirate. Pompey's acts in Asia were ratified,

[1] E. G. Hardy, *The Catilinarian Conspiracy* (1924).

and his veterans were provided with lands in Campania. The tax farmers of Asia Minor got their payments to the treasury reduced, a measure desired by Crassus and opposed by Cicero. And Caesar was made proconsul to Gaul, with powers equal to those of Pompey in the east. The money to buy the votes necessary to carry these measures in the assembly of tribes was furnished by Crassus and the Egyptian prince Ptolemy, who desired to be recognized as king of Egypt. When the other consul resisted these schemes at the bidding of the Optimates, Caesar called out the democratic gangs and forced him into virtual retirement. Pompey sealed the agreement by marrying Caesar's daughter Julia. The First Triumvirate was an alliance of money power in Rome and military power in the provinces against the senatorial oligarchy.

Caesar's command in Gaul gave him the opportunity to become the military rival of Pompey. He recruited legions among the Italians, who had been embittered by the Social War, and gave positions to the survivors of the faction of Marius. His successful campaigns soon won him prestige and, more important, great resources, partly from gold mines and partly from the sale of captives.

Meanwhile the factions in Rome were as active as ever. The Optimates hoped to play off Caesar against Pompey. Clodius, Caesar's agent, who had been elected tribune, harried Cicero out of Rome and advanced his own and Caesar's interests in spite of Pompey's opposition. Pompey seems to have contrived a famine, which had the desired effect of obtaining for him a special commission for five years to supply the city with grain. And Cicero, who had come back to Rome with Pompey's favor, proposed the repeal of the legislation of Caesar's consulship, a measure which would have destroyed the triumvirate.

In the face of this danger Caesar, Crassus, and Pompey renewed their alliance. Doles were given to the poor citizens. Caesar retained the command of Gaul for another five years. Pompey and Crassus, who had been consuls, became consuls again and, in the following year, were to take commands, the first in Spain and the second in Syria. In due time Crassus went to the East, where he fell in battle against the Parthians in 53 B.C. But Pompey, at the request of the senate, remained in Rome, ostensibly to put down popular riots but actually to act as head of the state. Clodius had been killed in these riots, but Caesar found other agents whom the people elected to the tribunate. The Optimates attempted to break up his army by intrigue and to call him to Rome, where he could be tried for breaking the constitution. In 50 B.C. he led a single legion into Cisalpine Gaul so that he could watch closely the moves of his enemies. When he demanded the right to become a candidate for the consulate although absent from Rome, Pompey joined the Optimates in ordering him to resign his command. If he refused they planned to make war on him. The tribunes, Quintus Cassius (d. 42 B.C.) and Marcus Antonius (*ca.* 83–30 B.C.), usually known as Mark Antony, vetoed the order and fled the city. Caesar now had to choose between giving himself up to his enemies or making war on the state.

His choice was quick and his action rapid. When he crossed the Rubicon (49 B.C.), disarmed the Italian militia raised against him, and seized certain cities, the magistrates and most of the senators hastily left Rome, and Pompey withdrew across the Adriatic. In three months Caesar was master of Italy and entered Rome without opposition. There he seized the treasury, the storehouses of the state, and the machinery of government, paying little or no attention to constitutional forms. He forced the granting of citizenship to Cisalpine Gauls and, in order to ensure the food supply of the city, undertook a campaign in Spain, where some of Pompey's legions were stationed. They were outmaneuvered and soon capitulated. Upon returning to Rome Caesar, who had been designated dictator, stood for the consulate and was duly elected. It was, therefore, as head of the state that he marched against Pompey. The battle of Pharsalus, fought in Thessaly in 48 B.C., destroyed a considerable number of Caesar's aristocratic enemies. Pompey fled to Egypt, where he was murdered as he landed. Caesar followed him—met and loved Cleopatra, queen of Egypt—and brought the east under his control. In 47 B.C. he pacified Asia Minor, and a year later Africa.

In July of the year 46 B.C. Caesar finally celebrated a triumph. On four successive days, to the delight of a frenzied people, a prince followed after his chariot. First the Gaul, Vercingetorix, who had been kept in prison six years, then the Egyptian, then the Pontic, bearing a tablet marked with the legend "Veni, vidi, vici," and lastly the African were exhibited to the populace. On the first day the conqueror wore a purple robe taken from a statue of Jupiter and a crimson sash; in the one hand he carried a laurel wreath, in the other an ivory scepter crowned with an eagle. Unfortunately, when he put his foot on the floor of his chariot, the axle broke, and the multitude marked the accident as a bad omen. To quiet the superstition he crawled on his knees up to the temple of Jupiter on the Capitoline hill. His bounty was unsurpassed. Each soldier received about two thousand dollars, and each citizen about a tenth as much, with an additional allowance of corn and oil, as outright gifts. The games exceeded all previous ones in lavishness. A mock naval engagement was fought in an artificial lake dug in the Campus Martius. Gladiators and wild beasts struggled in the arenas. A giraffe brought from Africa and a hundred elephants bearing torches marched in the processions. Wild songs and drunken soldiers filled the streets, the people ran from entertainment to entertainment, the town was in a tumult, and the cost was seventy-five million dollars. Caesar gave the show, but the entire Mediterranean world paid the bill.

THE ROMAN EMPIRE

No date can be given for the founding of the Roman Empire. Caesar acted always in some legal capacity, and his actions were, in fact, neither subversive nor revolutionary. They tended, however, to one significant end, namely, the aristocracy was no longer to govern and exploit the provinces in its own fashion. With Caesar a new group—a heterogeneous crowd of adventurers, mainly the heirs of the members of proscribed factions, bankers, talented young men on the make, knights (the "flower of Italy"), and soldiers—rose to power. And Caesar never forgot the army, an example his successors remembered. In these aspects of his rule was the basis of the new imperial regime.[1]

Caesar's Reorganization of the Roman State.

Caesar, the proconsul, won power over the Roman state when he was made dictator, and, as previously noted, in this capacity he held the election which made him consul in 48 B.C. After the defeat of Pompey he received additional grants of power. He was made tribune for life and authorized to stand for consul for a period of five years. He was given the right to declare war and make peace, assign provincial commands, and, as dictator, to reform the constitution. After the final defeat of the oligarchy he was given still other grants of power. He became censor with the power to name magistrates and to "reform morals"; at the same

[1] See *The Cambridge Ancient History*, Vol. 9, *The Roman Republic* 133–44 *B.C.* (1932), Chap. XVII, "Caesar's Dictatorship"; W. Warde Fowler, *Julius Caesar and the Foundation of the Roman Imperial System* (1904); Guglielmo Ferrero, *The Life of Caesar* (1933); G. G. Brandes, *Caesar* (1918); H. P. Judson, *Caesar's Army: A study of the military art of the Romans in the last days of the republic* (1888).

CAESAR

For Western men Caesar symbolizes great evil and great good—the evil which springs from the lust for power and the good which rises from the right use of power.

time the inviolability of the tribunate was extended to the provinces and the title "imperator" was made permanent. Also he was empowered to appoint a commission to make allotments of lands in Italy.

Caesar's honors were no fewer than his powers. The senate authorized him to wear the red boots of the ancient kings and the red robes of triumph at all times. It designated him "father of his country." He was also authorized to carry in his procession a statue of himself bearing the legend "To the unconquered god." His statue was set up in every temple, and with reluctance he refused the title "king."

But Caesar did not reform the constitution. No republican institutions were abolished, and no new institutions were created. His method of ruling was to concentrate in himself, as consul, tribune, censor, dictator, and pontifex maximus, every essential power and to replace the elected magistrates—quaestors, praetors, and aediles—with officials of his own choosing. Money—the gold of Gaul—and the control of patronage were the means of this distortion of the constitution. His chief reform was the reconstitution of the senate which, as a result of the addition of about three hundred new members, became a body of "moneyed mediocrities." It acted merely as a ratifying agency for his acts. Rearrangements of ranks and honors altered the nobility somewhat, as did also the admission of some Italians to the senate. Thus the government was given a little wider basis than the city. But there was no proscription, partly because Caesar did not desire it and partly because, on account of the slaughter of his enemies at Pharsalus, he did not need it. However, the property of opponents was confiscated and sold. Property was the cement of the new ruling group, as it had been of the senatorial oligarchy.

Caesar dealt soundly with the conquered lands. The policy of planting colonies was extended from Italy to the entire Mediterranean area. Sites favorable to commerce were occupied and developed. A strict control was maintained over provincial governors and commanders, who, of course, were his and not the senate's agents. For the irresponsible exploitation the oligarchy had countenanced he substituted ordered government; of course, this change did not mean the end of heavy taxes, merely their regularization.

There is little evidence that Caesar entertained grand schemes of political reorganization. Perhaps he did dream of a career of conquest in the East. And the tendency of his measures, regardless of the fact that he preserved republican forms, was the creation of an "absolute, hereditary monarchy of the Hellenistic type, the perfect pattern of which was furnished by the East."[1]

THE RISE OF OCTAVIANUS.

Opposition to Caesar came to a head in a conspiracy which, although led by members of the senatorial oligarchy, notably

---

[1] Léon Homo, *Roman Political Institutions from City to State* (1929), p. 191. Alfred A. Knopf, Inc. See also Pierre Jouquet, *Macedonian Imperialism and the Hellenization of the East* (1932), p. 304: " . . . the system placed in the hands of the masters of Egypt an instrument, so adaptable and so powerful that in many points the administration of the Ptolemies was taken as a model by the Roman Emperors." Alfred A. Knopf, Inc.

Gaius Cassius (d. 43 B.C.) and Marcus Brutus (d. 43 B.C.), had support among both knights and poor citizens. His assassination (44 B.C.) was the work of men who looked upon themselves as the liberators of Rome from a foreign system of government. But their act solved no problems. Its immediate effect was confusion; its ultimate effect was proscription, civil war, and a permanent military monarchy.

Antonius, who was a consul, succeeded Caesar as the dominant political figure, but he made no attempt to avenge the murder of his former commander. Its perpetrators celebrated their act in public banquet. Far away in Illyria another individual, the youthful Octavianus, the grandson of Caesar's sister and his heir by adoption, turned a sharp face toward Rome.[1] History has dealt gently with him; known by the title Augustus—"the revered"—he has seemed the exemplar of statesmanship. Actually, though, he won the empire by intrigue, propaganda, revolutionary violence, and warfare. From Caesar he inherited a name and a cause—revenge; by his realism and opportunism he completed a social revolution and reconstituted the state. By virtue of his origin—he was the son of a banker in a small Italian town—he was well qualified to represent those forces in Italy which were hostile to the Roman oligarchy.

Octavianus, who took care to keep in touch with Caesar's veterans, demanded his uncle's ready money from Antonius and called for the punishment of the assassins. While Antonius temporized, he spent his entire fortune on games for the poor citizens and raised a private army. In this rivalry the senatorial oligarchs, led by Cicero, believed they saw an opportunity to rid themselves of both men by setting them against each other. To further this scheme the senate made Octavianus a praetor with consular rank and gave his troops legal status. As a result Antonius was brought to bay. But the oligarchs misjudged Octavianus, who turned on Rome and forced his election as consul. He was not yet twenty years old. With the state treasure he gave his soldiers ten times a

---

[1] Recent political events have directed the interest of historians to a study of the crisis of the Roman Republic from which Octavianus emerged as imperator. Among the works which express this interest are Ronald Syme, *The Roman Revolution* (1939)—an incisive study of men and parties in the days of Pompey, Caesar, and Octavianus; Karl Hönn, *Augustus* (1938); B. M. Allen, *Augustus Caesar* (1937); Léon Homo, *Auguste 63 av. J.-C.—14 ap. J.-C.* (1935); Helmut Berve, *Kaiser Augustus* (ca. 1934).

Other works dealing with Augustus and his times are T. R. Holmes, *The Architect of the Roman Empire* (2 vols., 1931); V. Garthausen, *Augustus und seine Zeit* (3 vols., 1891–1904); René Francis, *Augustus: His life and work* (1914); E. S. Shuckburgh, *Augustus: The life and times of the founder of the Roman Empire* (1905).

year's pay. And with political status, he dealt with Antonius as an equal. In 43 B.C., together with Lepidus, another of Caesar's lieutenants, they formed the Second Triumvirate and divided the state. To pay the costs of their enterprise, they proscribed their enemies; about 130 senators, among them Cicero, and many more knights and citizens perished. The proscription had the characteristics of a class war, for the soldiers and the little magnates who could buy the confiscated estates—they were chiefly Italians—were ranged against the Roman nobles. By corruption the triumvirs controlled the magistrates and by intimidation they forced the senate to take an oath to maintain the acts of Caesar. Throughout these events Octavianus invited those to join him who had nothing to lose by war.

Once established in Rome, the triumvirs gave attention to their enemies in the provinces. They destroyed Cassius and Brutus and forced Sextus Pompeius, heir of the great Pompey, who was terrorizing the sea with a fleet manned by fugitive slaves, to relax a blockade of Rome. After the defeat of the liberators, Antonius went east, where he was captivated by the Egyptian queen, Cleopatra, and Octavianus returned to Italy, where he found a confused and dangerous situation. To make matters worse he settled 170,000 veterans on lands taken from Italian towns. But with aid from Gaul and the support of the soldiers he overcame the resistance of the propertied classes. In this circumstance the remnants of the oligarchy turned to Antonius, who found an excuse to approach Italy. But he was checked at Brundusium, where, after negotiations which terminated in his marriage with Octavia, the sister of Octavianus, he and Octavianus made a peace. And shortly they adjusted relations with Pompeius, who held Sicily.

As a result of these arrangements many partisans of the republic returned to Rome, and Octavianus, who courted their favor, became master of the west. In a war with Pompeius, a constant menace to Rome, Agrippa (*ca.* 63 B.C.–A.D. 12), the chief lieutenant of Octavianus, won control of the sea.[1] Following this victory, Octavianus banished Lepidus and seized Africa. Meanwhile Antonius, who was preparing for a campaign against the Parthians, fell again under the influence of Cleopatra, a turn of affairs which gave Octavianus an opportunity to assert that Antonius was trying to subvert the liberties of the Romans and to

[1] See M. Rheinhold, *Marcus Agrippa: A biography* (1933); F. W. Shipley, *Agrippa's Building Activities* (1933).

subjugate the West to the East. This propaganda was eagerly believed by those Romans and Italians who found that the policy of Antonius in settling the subject Eastern nations was limiting their profits. In 33 B.C. Octavianus was elected consul for the second time, and in the next year the people of Italy, in a plebiscite, took an oath of personal allegiance to him. At long last he was the leader of a patriotic movement against his only remaining rival, for his feud with Antonius was disguised as a war against Cleopatra. The outcome of the war was determined in the naval battle of Actium (31 B.C.), from which Octavianus emerged the victor. Immediately he moved against Egypt, where, after the suicides of Antonius and Cleopatra, he assumed the role of the pharaoh. With this success, he stood alone, the unchallenged master of the Mediterranean world.

IMPERATOR CAESAR AUGUSTUS, 31 B.C.–A.D. 14.

The political structure which Octavianus erected on Caesar's foundations endured for over three hundred years.

1. *The Principate.*   In 29 B.C. Octavianus returned to Rome, where a docile senate ratified his acts in the east and conferred on him the title *princeps civitatis*—"the first citizen of the state." From this title was derived the name of the imperial government— the *principate*. A year later he was elected consul for the sixth consecutive time, and Agrippa, the companion of his youth as well as his wars, was his colleague. Octavianus was thirty-five years old, and Agrippa a year older. At the end of this consulship— January, 27 B.C.—Octavianus announced his resignation of all powers, both in Rome and in the provinces, and the restoration of the republican constitution. But upon the senate's protest at this action, he accepted a special command in Gaul, Spain, and Syria. Egypt, of course, he continued to rule as a private possession. When the grateful senate bestowed upon him the designation "Augustus," he became Imperator Caesar Augustus. Further changes in the organization of his power occurred in 23 B.C., when he ceased to be consul. After this date he was proconsul, having command of all armies, and tribune, having the supervision of magistrates and the control of legislation. In theory the senate was still the central organ of the state, but actually the princeps, who presided over its sessions, held all effective power. It rested on force. Its popular basis was the oath of personal allegiance taken by the people of Italy in 32 B.C. Its legal forms were the proconsular command and the tribunate. A last conspiracy against

OCTAVIANUS

This worldly-wise young man, known to history as Augustus—the "revered"—built the heritage of Caesar's name into supreme power in the Roman state; the methods of his achievement have long been obscured by its splendor.

the triumphant "monarchic demagogue" was suppressed in 23 B.C. Eleven years later, when Lepidus, who, although banished, had been pontifex maximus, died, Octavianus took that office, becoming the head of the state religion.

2. *The Social Basis of the Principate.* The foregoing picture of the absolute power of the princeps obscures the social basis of the regime which he headed. The basis was a renovated oligarchy, revolutionary in origin but plutocratic in character. Its backbone consisted of knights, mainly men from the Italian cities, who rose in the army until they reached the senate. To them had gone the

spoils of victory in the civil wars; with victory and the consolidation of their position they profited from the revenues that flowed into Italy from the East and from the rise of land values in Italy. When Octavianus won Egypt he acquired not only the richest land in the Mediterranean Basin but also the last great hoard of wealth not yet seized and transported to Rome. Most of this wealth passed in due time into the possession of his supporters. The abolition of direct taxation in Italy released them from the burdens of the state. After 28 B.C., when the senate was purged or, in more delicate terms, purified, they—"hard faced men, enriched by war and revolution"—became, in fact, the state.

Clustered about this core of the new oligarchy were many of the adherents of Caesar, some old republicans who found it to their interest to adorn the state in order to share wealth and prestige with the knights, and even freedmen who had grown rich by dealing in the properties of the victims of the proscriptions. At the outer edge of the oligarchy were provincials who, having been rewarded for valor with citizenship, advanced themselves by the performance of military service.

In the republican plutocracy wealth and family connection were the means of advancement; in the new, merit was rewarded by easy promotion through the ranks of the army and in the magistracies. Final control over advancement was in the hands of the princeps, who admitted to the senatorial rank those he wished to reward and ennobled those whose services to him were greatest by designating them to the consulate. A monopoly of patronage was the means of control of the social composition of the new oligarchy.

In effect, therefore, Augustus, after having completed the destruction of the old patrician-plebeian nobility, reconstituted the aristocracy by assimilating its survivors into his party and by preserving its social privileges as distinctions for the men who had risen to wealth and power with him. In this fusion the class antagonisms which had destroyed the republic were abated. The new provincial policy, which gave the imperial provinces to the knights, while Greece, Asia Minor, and Africa were left to the senatorial nobility, also contributed to the appeasement. This social policy was carried out with great regard for old forms and usages.

3. *The Imperial Government.* Although Augustus declared he had restored the republic, actually his revision of the constitution shaped a supergovernment. To him belonged the executive

power.[1] To aid him in exercising it he created boards, or commissions, composed of senators and knights, who drew their authority exclusively from him. To aid in shaping policy he formed a kind of cabinet—*consilium principis*—whose members were drawn from the royal family, the senate, and the magistrates. As tribune, or through republican magistrates whose election he controlled, he initiated legislation. As supreme commander he functioned through the prefect of the Praetorian Guard, who served as a kind of chief of staff.

In the provinces under his control Augustus ruled through governors who were his legates and through procurators who were his financial agents. These officials, who were paid salaries, were held to a strict accountability. For the financial practices of the old provincial system he substituted a direct land tax levied according to an imperial census and collected by his own representatives. The farming of indirect taxes was continued, but extortioners were severely punished. Throughout the first century of the empire the trials of extortioners were frequent, and, as a result, the old publicani were destroyed. The stabilization of the financial policy in the imperial provinces eased their burdens; the senate followed a similar policy in the provinces it controlled with a similar result. The right of appeal from the decision of a provincial governor became the basis of a new imperial court. The heart of the imperial idea was the conception that the provinces were part of a single state.[2]

Except in the provinces under the control of the senate, the imperial government was the emperor's private establishment.

[1] On the political organization of the Roman Empire see *The Cambridge Ancient History*, Vol. 10, *The Augustan Empire 44 B.C.—A. D. 70* (1934); F. B. Marsh, *The Founding of the Roman Empire* (2d ed., 1927); A. D. Winspear and L. K. Gemerke, *Augustus and the Reconstruction of Roman Government and Society* (1935); M. Hammond, *The Augustan Principate in Theory and Practice during the Julio-Claudian Period* (1933); H. Mattingly, *The Imperial Civil Service of Rome* (1913); W. Schulz, *Das Wesen des römischen Kaisertums der ersten zwei Jahrhundert* (1916).

[2] On the provinces of the Roman Empire see V. Chapot, *The Roman World* (1928); T. Mommsen, *The Provinces of the Roman Empire from Caesar to Diocletian* (2 vols., 1909); W. T. Arnold, *The Roman System of Provincial Administration* (3d ed., 1914); M. I. Rostovtzeff, *Social and Economic History of the Roman Empire* (1926); E. S. Bouchier, *Syria as a Roman Province* (1917); E. S. Bouchier, *Spain under the Roman Empire* (1914); C. H. V. Sutherland, *The Romans in Spain: 217 B.C.–A.D. 117* (1939); J. G. Milne, *A History of Egypt under Roman Rule* (2d ed., 1925); Allan C. Johnson, *Roman Egypt to the Reign of Diocletian* (1936); Eugène Albertini, *L'Afrique romaine* (1937); Eugène Albertini and others, *L'Afrique du nord française dans l'histoire* (1937); F. Koepp, *Die Roemer in Deutschland* (2d ed., 1912); C. Jullian, *Histoire de la Gaule* (8 vols., 1908–1926); F. Haverfield, *The Romanization of Britain* (4th ed., 1923); R. C. Collingwood, *Roman Britain* (1923); G. Macdonald, *Roman Britain* (1931).

The senate had no voice in the selection of the boards, the provincial governors and procurators, the prefects, or the members of the cabinet. The staffs of these agents were recruited mainly, at first, from freedmen and, later, from knights. Together they formed a well-paid imperial bureaucracy. The emperor's control of the surviving republican institutions was largely indirect. It was exerted in several ways: (1) by supervision over the membership of the two privileged orders, (2) by the nomination of individuals to be elected magistrates, and (3) by the determination of the qualifications for the beginning of the *cursus honorum* and the control of promotion in it.

In the perpetuation of a regime, especially one established by a revolution, the decisive problem is the mode of transfer of power from the holder of supreme authority to a successor, for upon the ease of this transfer depends the orderly development of the regime. The succession was the weak point in the new government. Octavianus had won power by validating the inheritance from Caesar in revolution and civil war. Did he now have the power to designate his heir as his successor? Or did the senate or the people have the right to elect the emperor? Or did the army have the final choice? Augustus exercised the right to designate his successor, but after him these questions rose in forms that contributed to disorder.

4. *Imperial Policy.*   Having won power by violence, Augustus exercised it to restore order and security of life and property.

The protection of property was the chief element of economic policy. This protection was, of course, a primary need of men who had won property by revolution. Peace and the suppression of the abuses of senatorial government contributed to a return of prosperity which affected the provinces as well as Rome and Italy. The release of the hoard of the Ptolemies greatly relieved the shortage of capital which had been continuous throughout the civil wars. Great building operations in Rome and then in the Italian and provincial cities stimulated production in many lines, and the protection of transportation by land and sea facilitated the growth of orderly trade. No important changes in the relation of government and economic activity or in organization of enterprise were introduced by Augustus.

The effort to stabilize the social basis of the imperial regime was far stronger than the effort to ensure its economic support. In order to protect the oligarchy from internal decay legislation against the abuses which weakened the family under the late republic was enacted. Adultery was converted from a private offense to a public crime. The marriage of a senator with a freed-woman was prohibited. Rewards, mainly in the form of rapid promotions, were given to husbands who became fathers. The education of young aristocrats was reorganized. Apprenticeships for military service were introduced, and the ancient military exercises were revived. Oratory and law, not philosophy, were the proper subjects for study by a member of the senatorial class. Inasmuch as propaganda had played an important part in the success of Octavianus, he made it an effective support of his regime. The literature of the Augustan age may be read as the carefully prepared propaganda of a successful revolutionary;[1] its chief purpose was to cloak the victor in the sanctions of tradition. With imperial patronage Vergil and Horace, the poets, and Livy, the historian, contributed to the realization of this purpose. Ovid, who refused to serve the state, was disgraced, but when he turned from politics to love for motifs Latin literature was the gainer. Artists made the imperial portrait a universal presence, and the interpreters of signs found in past events omens that foretold every event in the emperor's life. Finally religion was made the servant of the new order. The civil wars, it was declared, had occurred because the ancient gods had been neglected. The *pietas*—religious faith and observance—and *virtus*—manly courage—of the ancient Roman peasant were proclaimed the primary virtues of a social group which, upon investigation, turns out to be composed mainly of small townsmen grown rich and powerful by revolution. Old temples were restored. The old priesthoods were reorganized. And an attempt, perhaps half-hearted, was made to suppress the Egyptian cults in Rome. This effort was probably connected with the propaganda which gave glory and nobility to Octavianus by picturing Cleopatra as the villainess of the imperial drama. Finally, the worship of the emperor, which was quite as much a form of patriotic expression as a mode of religious devotion, was established. It embodied the then universal belief that the welfare of the state was dependent on the good will of the national god in a form suitable to the new regime.

In taking these measures Augustus was careful to remember the poor citizens, whom, at the outset of his career, he had carefully wooed. To them he gave lavish games and cheap food. From Egypt came a secure supply of grain, and no senator was allowed to approach the corn ships when they were at anchor in the new

[1] See p. 960.

port of Ostia, near the mouth of the Tiber. Among the numerous architectural embellishments of the city which he constructed were the first of the great baths for which Rome became famous. Agrippa was especially active in restoring and building aqueducts and in improving sewers. When Augustus gave back the right to elect magistrates, the citizens knew well how to use it in the service of their benefactor.

Whereas Caesar had dreamed of conquering Parthia, Augustus recognized that the Roman world had boundaries at which dominion should stop. But he added more provinces to the empire than any other man—annexing Egypt, absorbing Numidia, conquering Rhaetia, Noricum, Pannonia, and Moesia, and pacifying Gaul and Spain. At the end of his reign, of the Mediterranean coasts only Mauretania was outside the Roman state. Of the territories added to the empire after his death, only Britain became a permanent part of the Roman world. The Rhine frontier was, of course, a second choice, necessitated by the victory of the Germans in the battle of Teutoberg Forest in A.D. 9; the boundary had been originally set at the Elbe River.

5. *The Roman Army: the Dominant Power in the Roman State.* Behind the work of Augustus—the new ruling class, the stabilized administration, the cloak of piety, and the well-drawn frontiers—stood the real force of the empire: the army. Octavianus had recruited, armed, and trained the legions that lifted him to supreme power, and only when he became the legal head of the state did they become the legal force of the state. Their oath of allegiance, like that of every other Roman army, was to their commander, not to the state. And the legionnaires looked to their commander, who was always generous, for rewards—pay, booty, land, and, finally, pensions. They were not disappointed; and in A.D. 6, when an inheritance tax was levied on property in Italy to provide money for pensions for veterans, Augustus transferred to the state the obligation which he had always been careful to perform.

For the defense of the empire Augustus maintained an army of about 300,000 men; for his own protection he kept a bodyguard of Germans. The Praetorian Guard was stationed at Rome. Eight legions were on the Rhine frontier, the same number on the Danube, and half as many on the Euphrates. Eight others were scattered through Africa and Spain. Associated with the legionnaires were provincial auxiliaries. They served as border patrols and, if war broke out, did most of the fighting. The legions were mainly an engineering and a supporting force. Most of the legions were settled in permanent camps which became centers of Romanization. Even in the time of Augustus, it should be noted, legions were raised in Spain and Asia Minor. But most of the legions were recruited in Italy. At the end of the term of enlistment, which was long, the legionnaires received lands; often they married and settled in the villages which grew up outside the camps. In the course of time this circumstance contributed greatly to a change in the composition of the legions, for the son commonly followed the father into the ranks. The national army quickly became a fiction.

Agrippa had organized Rome's first permanent navy in the war with Sextus Pompeius. After the establishment of the principate the main force policed the Mediterranean Sea, keeping down pirates, while squadrons plied the Rhone, the Danube, the Euphrates, and the Black Sea.

THE ROMAN PEACE.

The question as to who would rule Rome was now answered. The answer was: the commander of the armies that survived the war of classes which imperial expansion had generated. In fact, as well as in form, the Roman Empire was the culmination of the Roman Republic. In 13 B.C. the senate voted the erection of an altar of peace to commemorate the achievements of Augustus; it was quite as much a memorial to the long career of conquest that had reduced the peoples of the Mediterranean Basin to submission. The Roman peace was the peace of a conquered world.[1]

THE HEIGHT OF THE ROMAN EMPIRE

Tiberius (14–37), a stepson of Augustus, was associated with him in the government for a decade before he succeeded to the principate. But Tiberius had won power only after family intrigues in which Augustus had tried to make a young grandson his heir. Tiberius, an experienced general and administrator, continued the policies of Augustus, especially in the careful attention to the provinces, and their effects became increasingly evident in

---

[1] On the general history of the Roman Empire see H. S. Jones, *The Roman Empire* 29 *B.C.–A.D.* 476 (3d imp., 1916); Tenney Frank, *Roman Imperialism* (1914); M. P. Nilsson, *Imperial Rome* (1926); G. H. Stevenson, *The Roman Empire* (1930); Eugène Albertini, *L'Empire romain* (1929); Gustave Glotz, *Histoire generale*, Troisième partie, *Histoire romaine*, Tome 3, *Le Haut-empire par Léon Homo* (1933), and Tome 4, *L'Empire romain de l'avènement des Sévères au concile de Nicée* (1937); H. Dessau, *Geschichte der römischen Kaiserzeiten* (2 vols., 1924–1930); T. Mommsen, *The History of Rome* (4 vols., 1929–1931), trans. from the German by W. P. Dickson.

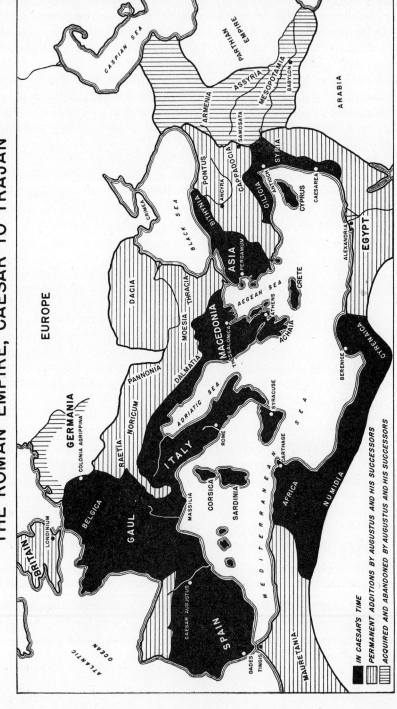

THE ROMAN EMPIRE, CAESAR TO TRAJAN

greater security of property, improved transportation and communication, and orderly administration of justice. The imperial power continually increased, the imperial bureaucracy, recruited largely from Greek and Hellenized oriental freedmen, became well organized, and great public works began to appear in all parts of the empire. Above all, the new conditions favored the growth of cities, which were everywhere the centers of imperial administration as well as the beneficiaries of its activities.[1]

The heirs of Augustus, known as the Julian-Claudian line, held the principate until the death of Nero (54–68), when the great weakness of the state was revealed in a struggle over the succession. From this struggle, in which the army of Spain, the Praetorian Guard, the army of the Rhine, and a coalition of the armies of the Danube and Euphrates participated, Vespasian (69–79) emerged victorious. His sons, Titus (79–81) and Domitian (81–96), succeeded him. In their hands the principate became less a personal possession and more a legal power of the incumbent. After the murder of Domitian, the senate, which had been neglected and insulted by these representatives of the army, made one of its members, Nerva (96–98) emperor. He and his successors, Trajan (96–117), Hadrian (117–138), Antoninus Pius (138–161), and Marcus Aurelius (161–180), are known as the Antonine emperors. The succession was hereditary, but actually the emperor appointed a successor by adopting him as a son.

Under the Antonines the Roman Empire attained a height of peace and prosperity.[2] Trajan overhauled the military system and encouraged the formation of workingmen's guilds under imperial license. Under Hadrian the imperial bureaucracy became so well organized that knights were given places without risk of corrupting the administration. Imperial finance was placed under a central

[1] On the Roman Empire under the successors of Augustus see *The Cambridge Ancient History*, Vol. 10, *The Augustan Empire* 44 B.C.–A.D. 70 (1934); Joseph Wells and R. H. Barrows, *A Short History of the Roman Empire to the Death of Marcus Aurelius* (1931); G. B. Baker, *Tiberius Caesar* (1928); F. M. Marsh, *The Reign of Tiberius* (1931); A. Momigliano, *Claudius: The emperor and his achievement* (1934); B. W. Henderson, *The Life and Principate of the Emperor Nero* (1903); B. W. Henderson, *Civil War and Rebellion A.D. 69–70* (1908); B. W. Henderson, *Five Roman Emperors (Vespasian to Trajan)* (1927); Christine Longford, *Vespasian and Some of His Contemporaries* (1928); S. Gsell, *Essai sur le règne de l'empereur Domitien* (1894); G. Boissier, *L'Opposition sous les Césars* (1900).

[2] On the Roman Empire under the Antonines see Joseph Wells and R. H. Barrows, *A Short History of the Roman Empire to the Death of Marcus Aurelius* (1931); *The Cambridge Ancient History*, Vol. 11, *The Imperial Peace A.D. 70–192* (1936); M. Pelisson, *Rome sous Trajan* (1886?); E. Gregorovius, *The Emperor Hadrian* (1898); B. W. Henderson, *The Life and Principate of the Emperor Hadrian* (1923); H. D. Sedgwick, *Marcus Aurelius: A biography* (1921).

control. The franchise was extended. The law was consolidated and more and more provincials obtained the advantage of imperial jurisdiction. The conquered people began to have some part in local government, other than that taken by the urban oligarchies.[1] Gambling in foodstuffs ceased, and other kinds of speculation became fewer. Under Nerva a last attempt at agrarian reform in Italy was made. A by-product of this effort, developed by his successors, especially Antoninus Pius, was the creation of endowments for the support of free children of both sexes. This action was motivated partly by a desire to give small farmers cheap credit, partly by the need to train children for citizenship, and partly by the failure of the citizens, particularly the ruling classes, to rear enough children to replace themselves. Although this action was taken against the background of the historic agrarian problem, its adoption pointed to the conditions that were carrying the empire toward an unsuspected crisis.[2]

Under Claudius (41–54) the policy of conquest had been revived, with the result that Britain had become a Roman province, and the early Antonines continued it. Trajan rose to prominence in campaigns against the Germans, and his reign brought the conquest of Dacia, where a king by the name of Decebalus (fl. 100–117), with the aid of Roman drill masters, had established a military regime. After the conquest Trajan placed an absolute embargo on the export of arms and forbade drill masters, on pain of death, to instruct the barbarians in military exercises. Trajan drove the Parthians from the Euphrates to the Tigris but died before he could undertake a campaign in Iran. Hadrian, who made the provinces the special field of imperial administrative care, established the fortified lines that protected the empire during the greater part of the third and the fourth century.

The Antonines, especially Antoninus Pius and Marcus Aurelius, the "philosopher emperor," suffused the imperial regime with a humanitarian spirit which, along with the growing cosmopolitanism, gave the Mediterranean peoples a sense of participation in a beneficence that Roman peace and order bestowed upon all alike. This feeling was well expressed by Aristides (117–189), a Greek rhetorician, in his "Panegyric on Rome":

Now the whole world keeps holiday and laying aside its ancient dress of steel has turned in freedom to adornment and all delights. The cities

[1] See p. 917.
[2] See Hazel G. Ramsay, "Government Relief during the Roman Empire," *Classical Journal*, Vol. 31 (1935–1936), pp. 479–488.

ANTONINUS PIUS

That good fortune which brought the Antonine emperors to power in the peaceful time between imperial conquest and imperial crisis, more than their understanding, gave them a reputation for wise government. Antoninus Pius remitted the taxes of cities and lightened the burdens of provinces. But mere relief did not abate the evils from which the distress arose, and the empire drifted steadily into an unsuspected crisis.

have abandoned their old quarrels, and are occupied by a single rivalry, each ambitious to be most pleasant and beautiful. Everywhere are playgrounds, fountains, arcades, temples, workshops, schools. To use a metaphor from medicine, the world sick from creation has recovered its health. Gifts never cease flowing from you. One cannot find one place more richly endowed than another, for your beneficence is equally shown to all. Cities are ablaze with brightness and beauty, and all the earth is adorned like a king's garden. . . . You have made into a reality the saying of Homer that the earth belongs to all, for you have meted out the whole world, bridled rivers with many a bridge, cut mountains into carriage roads, filled the deserts with outposts, and civilized all things with settled discipline and life.

The conqueror had won finally not only the allegiance but also the acclaim of his victims.

ECONOMIC ASPECTS OF THE ROMAN EMPIRE

The Roman Empire united under a single sovereign a territory comprising about 1,300,000 square miles and gave to it an internal peace lasting almost two centuries. This peace was more important for the economic and social development of the diverse peoples— equal to about one-fourth of the present population—who inhabited the territory than any technological or intellectual advance, and the results—widespread prosperity and social intercourse— were the chief elements in that beneficence which the panegyrist praised. This beneficence should not obscure, however, the central fact that the primary function of government was to transfer wealth from the producing population to the ruling classes. State policies were shaped to perform this function, and changes in policies should be understood as adjustments to new conditions affecting its performance. This relation between politics and economics should not be forgotten in the discussion of any political, economic, or social aspect of the Roman world.[1]

Economic Enterprise in Roman Times.

Economic enterprise under the Roman Empire was conducted in ways long known in the ancient Near East and the Mediterranean lands. In the early empire, when interest sank to the unprecedented rate of 4 per cent, private investment was at a height. The chief investment was in agriculture, although opportunities also existed in trade, manufacturing, mining, and shipping. The farming of the taxes of cities continued to be a lucrative business. But banking hardly existed. Small enterprise was especially active in local trade and the craft industries. State enterprise—imperial or urban—monopolized mining, large-scale building, and the trade in grain so necessary for the provisioning

---

[1] See *The Cambridge Ancient History*, Vol. 10, *The Augustan Empire* 44 B.C.–A.D. 70 (1934), Chap. XIII, "The Economic Unification of the Mediterranean Region: Industry, trade, and commerce." See also, on the general economic history of the Roman Empire, M. I. Rostovtzeff, *Social and Economic History of the Roman Empire* (1926); Tenney Frank, editor, *Economic Survey of Ancient Rome* (5 vols., 1933–1940); Fritz M. Heichelheim, *Wirtschaftsgeschichte des Altertums* . . . (2 vols., 1938).

of cities. Some of the state-owned mines were leased to private operators. The long-distance trade in luxury goods was mainly in the hands of rich Syrian and Jewish merchants, who took great risks in order to make greater profits. As time went on state enterprise and large-scale farming tended to crowd out all kinds of small enterprise, except in local trade and the craft industries. This development was caused mainly by an increasing cost of capital and a decreasing supply of labor.

A money economy spread through the entire Mediterranean Basin under the Roman Empire, but a uniform coinage never was achieved.[1] The senate, the emperor, and some cities, especially in the east, operated mints. The senate, which surrendered the minting of silver and gold coins to Augustus, continued to strike copper and bronze coins. The imperial coins were generally issued in connection with the military needs of the state. The gold *aureus* was coined by Augustus at the rate of 42 to the pound. The *denarius*, originally silver but later an alloy of silver and copper, was $\frac{1}{25}$th of the aureus. Four *sesterces*, also silver, equaled a denarius. Except for slight variations the values of these coins remained constant until the reign of Marcus Aurelius. But as economic conditions worsened, the emperors debased the coinage, until it became worthless. At the same time the trade with the East and the policy of buying off threats of invasion, especially in the north, drained the empire of precious metal. In this situation the government paid its debts in bad money, except obligations to the armies, and insisted that taxes be paid in gold. Financial chaos was universal in the third century. But it disturbed economic life far less than similar conditions do in the modern Western world, because, after all, a large part of all economic enterprise was conducted, as always, upon a barter basis.

AGRICULTURE IN ROMAN TIMES.

The Romans were always farmers; their deep interest in agriculture is well illustrated by the fact that they developed a greater body of factual and theoretical materials about it than about any other occupation. Many prominent Roman literate intellectuals, such as the elder Cato, Varro, and Vergil, wrote agricultural treatises. And the senate authorized the translation of the works of Mago (dates unknown), the Carthaginian authority on agriculture. Columella, the last important writer on agriculture,

[1] See H. Mattingly, *Roman Coins* (1928); Mattingly-Sydenham, *The Roman Imperial Coinage* (5 vols., 1923–1933); J. G. Milne, *Greek and Roman Coins* (1939).

From Greece & Rome, May 1937

ROMAN COINS

(For descriptive legend see opposite page)

flourished in the middle of the first century; like other Roman writers on farming, he drew heavily on Hellenistic sources.[1]

Roman farming was distinguished more by a management that systematized old practices than by improved methods. Above all the Roman farmer knew that the first step in the production of a good crop is a well-plowed field. But the ancient clumsy implements remained in common use, and fertilizers and crop rotation were not well understood. Although legumes were grown, the usual rotation was based on fallowing. Seed selection was not widely practiced. The leading field crops were barley, wheat, millet, and the chick pea. The olive, the fig, and the grape also became staple crops.

The Romans were excellent husbandmen, and stock raising was quite as important as tillage in every part of the empire. When the small farmers were dispossessed in the third and second centuries B.C., their lands went into the great estates largely given over to herds and flocks. Under the empire small farms were the rule in some areas, but slowly the large estate spread everywhere. The slave labor necessary to operate the estate was much less than that required for grain or vine growing. The barn was an original Roman contribution to rural architecture, and the field cart was a Roman invention. Forage crops were widely grown. Horses were used for warfare, transportation, and sport, but not for field work. They were bred chiefly in northern Africa, Spain, and Syria. Camel breeding centered in Syria.

[1] On Roman agriculture see W. D. Hooper and H. B. Ash, *Marcus Porcius Cato, On Agriculture; Marcus Terentius Varro, On Agriculture* (1934); Lloyd Storr-Best, *M. T. Varro, On Farming* (1912); F. Harrison, *Roman Farm Management* (2d ed., 1918); A. Geikie, *The Love of Nature among the Romans during the Later Decades of the Republic and the First Centuries of the Empire* (1912); W. E. Heitland, *Agricola: A study of agriculture and rustic life in the Greco-Roman world* (1921); Emile Savoy, *L'agriculture à travers les âges* (2 vols., 1935); Raymond Billiard, *L'agriculture dans l'antiquité d'après les Géorgiques de Virgile* (1928); Raymond Billiard, *La vigne dans l'antiquité* (1913).

ROMAN COINS

These coins are evidences of Roman history in imperial times. No. 1 is a sestertius of Vespasian, A.D. 71, commemorating the fall of Jerusalem; the reverse, pictured here, shows Judea mourning by a palm tree. No. 2 and 3 are seterces of Domitian, ca A.D. 87. No. 2, the reverse, shows a German man and woman amidst conquered arms. No. 3, also the reverse, portrays Domitian granting a pardon to a kneeling German. No. 4 is a sestertius of Trajan; it bears the dedication to the "best of emperors." No. 5, 6, 7, and 8 are sesterces of Hadrian. No. 5 and 6 show Britannia in forms known to modern British symbolism. No. 7 pictures Hadrian speaking to some standard bearers; no. 8 shows him about to raise the kneeling Gallia to her feet. No. 9 is a sestertius of Antoninus Pius; Britannia with standard, and spear is seated on a globe above waves. No. 10 is a gold medallion of Constantius I Chlorus, ca. A.D. 297, who held the command in Britain before he became emperor; the reverse shows him before the walls of Londinium (London), retaking the city from a rebel and restoring the "eternal light" of Rome.

The Romans developed a large-scale agriculture for profit; under the drive of this motive they brought the arable lands of the whole empire into cultivation and added continually to the tilled area by cutting back forests and draining swamps. Except in northern Africa, where aqueducts were numerous, irrigation was not highly developed. The increased yields generally obtained by Roman farmers were due largely to a wise adaptation of crops to soils.

For Western culture the most important work of Roman farmers was the completion of the transfer to Mediterranean lands of the agricultural complex that had developed in the Near East since neolithic times. The apple, the pear, and the plum, which the Greeks knew, became common in Italy, Spain, and northern Africa. The quince and a better grape also came west from Greece. The cherry from Pontus, the apricot (perhaps originally cultivated in China) from Persia, the peach from Armenia, and the fig from Syria were carried to Italy and then to the coastal lands of the western Mediterranean Sea. Vegetable growing as practiced in Egypt and around the Fertile Crescent was introduced to Italy, Spain, and Gaul. Among the garden plants that reached western Europe in this way were the radish, the onion, and the sugar beet. The melon was brought from Mesopotamia, the almond from Anatolia, and the pistachio nut from Syria. The date palm, originally at home along the shores of the Persian Gulf, and the lemon, originally from India, spread throughout the southern Mediterranean lands. Poultry keeping, originally Egyptian, bee-keeping, rabbit breeding, and fish breeding became important subsidiary rural industries. The chicken, the duck, and the cat probably came to western Europe in the first Christian century. The most important result of this diffusion of the Asiatic agricultural complex was the transplanting of the vine, the olive, and the fig to Italy and then to northern Africa, and the vine to southern Gaul, whence, along with the apple, the cherry, the peach, and the plum, it spread northward. In return for these gifts the Near East received mustard, rye and oats, and a few varieties of nuts.

The changes in the organization of agricultural enterprise were few in number but important in effect. The Roman law of property was introduced everywhere, with the result that the ancient free peasants generally lost their lands to the owners of great estates. Only in the neighborhood of the cities, which were ready markets for all kinds of foodstuffs, did the free peasants prosper. In time, however, the estate system, modified somewhat in order to accommodate survivals from the old village system of tenure and tillage, spread everywhere. Estate owners made good use of their capital but did not increase their investments to any extent. In the main the latifundium was not progressive in developing either new crops or new methods of tillage, and with its triumph agriculture settled into the patterns it was to keep for a thousand years.

Industry in Roman Times.

Roman industry, like Roman agriculture, made good use of old methods. This was especially true of mining, smelting, forging, and building—the industries in which the Romans were particularly efficient. There were some technological advances. The Hellenistic inventions, such as the crane and the water wheel, were widely used. The cylinder pump was developed. The processes of tempering iron and steel were improved, new alloys were introduced, and ways of making hollow pipe and wire were invented. In Syria the methods of dyeing and finishing cloth were considerably elaborated. The economic demand, which expanded as cities grew, provided the main stimulus for industrial development. The construction of temples, circuses, arenas, theaters, forums, aqueducts, and roads called for continuous supplies of sand, gravel, lime, brick, tile, and stone. Quarries and brickworks were found in all parts of the empire. Shipbuilding and the improvement of harbors also employed hosts of carpenters and masons. Timbering developed in every forested region. The pottery industry, which continued to decline artistically, produced chiefly crocks, tiles, and statuettes. The largest pottery works were in Gaul. The textile industry flourished. The manufacture of linen and woolens was carried on everywhere. Fine fabrics of silk, cotton, and gold and silver threads, as well as wool, were made in Egypt, Syria, and Asia Minor, still the leading centers of the luxury industries and trades. Egypt had almost a monopoly on the weaving of carpets. Greece made hats. Spain and northern Gaul produced coarse fabrics and common garments. Glassmaking, which originally centered in Egypt and Syria, was improved by the introduction of blowing, probably in Syria, about the opening of the Augustan age; after this improvement the industry spread widely, in both the eastern and the western parts of the empire. It was established in Italy about the time of Nero. By the third century the making of glass in the West attained an excellence not surpassed until the rise of the Venetian glass industry a thousand years later. Glass bottles and tableware were especially popular.[1] Furniture, rope, and leather goods, notably shoes and sandals, were made locally in all parts of the empire. The bulk of all industrial production was marketed among urban dwellers, for the peasant villagers supplied their own needs with homemade goods.

The early Roman Empire possessed a rich mining and metal-working industry. Every important province maintained forges and shops for making arms, and almost every village supported a smith, who not only mended but also made the chief implements of the farmer, the carpenter, the mason, and the woodsman. As iron-working everywhere became the leading metalworking indus-try, the use of bronze, except as an artistic material, declined. Cyprus, Lusitania, and Britain supplied copper. Etruria, Elba, Gaul, Styria, and Illyria furnished iron. The eastern sources of iron were still located mainly in Anatolia, Armenia, and Iran. Spain, the greatest mining region of the empire, produced iron, lead, silver, and gold. Sardinia supplied silver, and Sicily sulphur. Petroleum came from Anatolia. Gold was sought in all parts of the empire but mined profitably in only a few localities, particularly Spain and northeastern Italy. The emperors controlled all important gold deposits.[2]

COMMERCE IN ROMAN TIMES.

The expansion of commerce played an important part in the development of the Roman Empire. Roman traders entered Epirus and Greece shortly after the beginning of the third century B.C. In the next century they reached Africa, Spain, Ionia, and Egypt. The destruction of Carthage was caused largely by the desire of the great Roman landowners to exploit the lands upon which were grown the dried figs used everywhere as a common foodstuff. And Roman traders pointed the way that Caesar followed in Gaul. In the first century B.C. Roman traders penetrated Asia Minor, the Black Sea coasts, and the Fertile Crescent; in the first Christian century they reached Britain, the Danube valley, and equatorial Africa. A century later, it seems, they regularly went to southern India and, on a few occasions, even to China. After Augustus every important trading center had a cosmopolitan

[1] See E. B. Harden, "The Glass of the Greeks and Romans," *Greece & Rome*, Vol. 3 (1934), pp. 140–149; A. Kisa, *Das Glas im Altertum* (3 vols., 1934); Morin-Jean, *La Verrerie en Gaule sous l'empire romain* (1913).

[2] Oliver Davies, *Roman Mines in Europe* (1935); T. A. Rickard, "The Mining of the Romans in Spain," *The Journal of Roman Studies*, Vol. 18 (1928), pp. 129–143.

population, in which Jews, Syrians, and Greeks were most prominent. In fact, the business enterprises owned by Roman citizens were commonly managed by Syrians and Greeks.

The trade of the Roman Empire was threefold: (1) a traffic in locally produced commodities, (2) an exchange between the chief regions of the empire of their typical products, and (3) a commerce with areas beyond the frontiers. Each of these businesses was organized independently of the others. The retail trade was mainly in the hands of shopkeepers and peddlers. Great merchants, always few in numbers, dealt in the goods for which the well to do would pay a high price. The trade in commodities required for the support of urban populations was managed by either the municipal or the imperial government.

Most of the local trade around the towns, camps, and villages, was carried on as barter, although the peasants depended on selling some products for money so that they could pay their taxes. Inasmuch as the peasants bought almost no town-made goods, whatever money they received could be used in this manner. They depended on the village craftsmen for manufactured wares.

The interregional trade was the most important part of Roman commerce. It centered in a few cities such as Lyon and Massilia in Gaul, Thessalonica in Macedonia, Ephesus and Caesarea in Asia Minor, and Damascus and Palmyra in Syria. Almost every province of the empire contributed some article to the stream of foodstuffs that flowed toward the great cities. North Africa and Spain supplied dried figs and olive oil; Gaul, Dalmatia, Asia Minor, and Syria wine; Spain and Egypt salted meats; the Black Sea countries salted fish; the Danubian lands, Gaul, and Britain pork; and Egypt, northern Africa, Sicily, and the Black Sea countries grain.

The trade in manufactured goods was as extensive but not as great in quantity as the traffic in foodstuffs. Industrial specialization fostered a widespread trade in fine metalwork, the better grade of pottery, high quality textiles, perfumes, ointments, jewelry, and other luxury goods. In the great towns it was possible to buy any commodity produced in the empire in ordinary retail shops; peddlers carried articles in popular demand to outlying towns. The trade in manufactured goods hardly touched the villages.

The traffic in raw materials was of considerable importance. Illyria, northern Africa, Gaul, and Asia Minor supplied timber. Pitch and naval supplies were furnished by the Danubian provinces and Asia Minor. Hemp for ropemaking also came largely from Asia Minor. Hides and leather came from Britain, Gaul, the

Danubian provinces, and Asia Minor. Wool was produced almost everywhere.[1]

Rome's extensive foreign trade developed mainly after the founding of the empire. Germany exchanged amber, hides, and slaves for weapons and tools. The Scythian country supplied grain, hides, furs, and precious stones. Arabia furnished myrrh, spices, and precious stones. Over the Saharan routes and down the Nile equatorial Africa sent ivory, gold dust, slaves, and wild beasts. The trade between the Roman Empire and India and China was significant not only for economic life but also for social, intellectual, and artistic developments.

The trade with India, especially after the monsoon route from Egypt to India came to be generally used, about the middle of the first century A.D., centered in Alexandria. Vessels left Egypt in midsummer, took a month to reach Aden, and then, with the trade winds, another forty days to reach the Malabar Coast. The return voyage began in December. On the Malabar Coast and in Ceylon this western route connected with another route, known as the Golden Route, which went to China. But the Romans seldom went beyond Ceylon. The Chinese came around the Malay Peninsula to southern India more easily than the Romans reached Ceylon. The chief commodities in this trade were silks, cottons, spices, precious stones, fine metalwares, perfumes and cosmetics, slaves, and wild animals.

The overland trade with the Asiatic countries followed different routes at different times. Its western terminus was Antioch, which lost importance after the development of the sea route to India. Palmyra, in Syria, rose to prominence as a center from which the Romans gave police protection to the trade from Mesopotamian centers to this western terminus. When the Parthians, who levied a heavy toll on the silk trade, held northwestern Iran, the Romans turned southward, crossed southern Iran, and reached Kabul, where they were received in a friendly manner by the Kushans.[2] During the first and second Christian centuries the Kushans controlled the western ends of the overland route to China and the northwestern route to India. After the rise of the Sassanian Dynasty this trade swung back over the route that ran from

---

[1] See M. P. Charlesworth, *Trade Routes and Commerce of the Roman Empire* (1924); L. C. West, *Roman Gaul: The objects of trade* (1935); L. C. West, *Imperial Roman Spain: The objects of trade* (1929); L. C. West, *Roman Britain: The objects of trade* (1931); L. C. West, "Commercial Syria under the Roman Empire," *Transactions of the American Philosophical Association*, Vol. 55 (1924), pp. 154 ff.

[2] See p. 752.

Seluecia through Ecbatana, to Bactria. From China came the silk which, after the middle of the first century B.C., was increasingly fashionable among Roman aristocrats. Cleopatra made silk fashionable for women; in the reign of Augustus men took to wearing it. Much of the silk came west in the raw state; it was woven, along with other fibers, into various kinds of fabrics in Syria. The Chinese silk with allover designs never became popular in the West. The journey of a commodity from China to Syria required about a year, and silk, worth its weight in gold, was about the only article sufficiently valuable to pay the cost of transport. The iron which is supposed to have come west from China probably originated in Chinese Turkestan or central Asia.[1]

Rome, of course, was the center of the luxury trade which was the chief commerce of the times, but every city depended on it for many articles. In the East its leading entrepôts were Antioch, to which came Chinese goods, and Alexandria, to which came the products and wares of India. Among these products was pepper, for which each year the Romans paid a pretty penny. Ostia was the port of Rome's trade in grain and other foodstuffs; it was a prosaic town of warehouses, shops, and tenements. Puteoli, known as "little Delos" because it was center of the slave trade, received most of the Eastern goods that reached Rome. Rome and Italy paid western lands mainly with metalwares and fabrics, but for the eastern wares she had to send gold and more gold. The extent of Rome's commercial influence is clearly marked by the Roman coins which have been found over the entire area from Scandinavia to Ceylon.

TRANSPORTATION IN ROMAN TIMES.

Like agriculture, industry, and commerce, transportation reached a new height of development under Rome. But as in the other phases of economic activity, the achievement was largely the result of the systematic use of old means.[2] The great roads which

---

[1] On Rome's trade with Asiatic peoples see M. I. Rostovtzeff, *Caravan Cities* (1932); Wilfred H. Schoff, "Some Aspects of the Overland Oriental Trade at the Christian Era," *The Journal of the American Oriental Society*, Vol. 35 (1915), pp. 31–41; Wilfred H. Schoff, "The Eastern Iron Trade of the Roman Empire," *The Journal of the American Oriental Society*, Vol. 35 (1915), pp. 224–239; Wilfred H. Schoff, "Navigation to the Far East under the Roman Empire," *The Journal of the American Oriental Society*, Vol. 37 (1917), pp. 240–249; G. F. Hudson, *Europe and China* (1931).

[2] On Roman roads see J. W. Gregory, *The Story of the Road from the Beginning down to A. D. 1931* (1931); R. J. Forbes, *Notes on the History of Ancient Roads and Their Construction* (1934); A. M. Ramsay, "The Speed of the Roman Imperial Post," *The Journal of Roman Studies*, Vol. 15 (1925), pp. 60–74.

radiated from Rome, bringing the farthermost province within a six weeks' journey of the capital, were developed from the Hellenistic elaboration of the Persian system. The courier service which carried official dispatches followed closely the Persian pattern. Shipping and navigation remained much as they had been in Hellenistic times. Rome added to these means of transportation a police protection, which often broke down, regular posthouses and inns, and travel aids such as guides, guidebooks, and road signs. The mile post and the road sign were Roman inventions. Travel was easier, speedier, and safer under imperial Rome than at any time until the stagecoach era of the late eighteenth century. However, the Romans' road system was built to serve not an economic but a military purpose.

In the time of Trajan there were about forty-seven thousand miles of road throughout the empire. From Rome five great highways led northward, southward, and eastward to provinces beyond Italy. Twelve minor roads served Italy. Two roads crossed the Alps to Lyon, from which roads radiated to northern Gaul, Germany, and Britain. Each province had its own system of subsidiary highways. In Italy the main roads were fifteen to twenty feet wide; in the provinces they were little more than wide paths. Various types of construction were employed. The best method seems to have consisted of putting down a layer of flat rock, covering it with a layer of loose rubble and another of small stones, and topping them with a surface of paving stones. These upper stones were generally set on edge rather than on the side. No roads have ever surpassed the Roman roads in technical excellence. Average speed was about four miles an hour; high speed was eight miles an hour. Caesar once did eight hundred miles in ten days. Most travelers rode horses or asses; a few were carried in litters, and fewer still rode in light carriages. Many, of course, went on foot. The emperor and high provincial officials usually traveled with a large retinue and a full baggage train. The traveling public consisted mainly of officials, merchants, legionnaires, and professional men, such as physicians, astrologers, and rhetoricians.

The life of the roads was varied. The inns were smelly and noisy, their keepers dishonest, and their barmaids gay, to say the least. The hostlers were rough, the tollkeepers ill-mannered. And brigands lurked near by, ready to rob or kidnap.

Transportation by sea was largely a servant of trade. Regular routes led from Alexandria to Rhodes and Delos, whence passage could be taken directly for Italy, Gaul, Spain, or northern Africa. The crossing from Alexandria to Rhodes was made in four or five days. A direct passage from Alexandria to Puteoli, the great Italian port, could be made in nine days. The Egyptian grain fleet took fifty days to make the passage from Alexandria to Ostia. Inland waterways, especially the rivers, were widely used for transporting agricultural products to the towns. Among the very few canals built by the Romans was one across the Isthmus of Corinth. This transportation system served well the political centralization and economic interdependence upon which the empire rested and sustained the wide social intercourse which was characteristic of Rome's great age.

The Economic Significance of Rome in the Development of Western Culture.

Rome's contribution to the agricultural and industrial development of the Western world marked a chapter in its economic history. The most important of these contributions was the completing of the transfer of eastern agricultural products and methods to the Mediterranean Basin and western Europe; for a thousand years after the collapse of the Roman Empire the European countryside exhibited the patterns of Roman agriculture. These patterns were mingled with but did not entirely displace native peasant tillage. Only slightly less important than the Roman achievement in agriculture was the diffusion of eastern industrial techniques. By the middle of the second century Gaul was producing excellent pottery and fine woolen and linen fabrics. Glassmaking was brought to Italy, then to Gaul, and finally to the lower Rhine valley. By the opening of the third century the glassmakers of Cologne had won almost a monopoly of the industry in the West; by this time, also, Belgic Gaul, *i.e.*, the Low Countries, had begun the economic development which was to make it the center of western European trade and industry until the opening of modern times. With the spread of Roman ironworking techniques western Europe completed the transition from the bronze to the iron age. Among Roman methods of economic organization which endured, the estate system of farming and the principle of hereditary employment were foundations of the feudal economy of succeeding centuries. And in still later times, when modern capitalism began to develop, the Roman law of property and persons, especially concerning corporations, became increasingly important.

SOCIAL ASPECTS OF THE ROMAN EMPIRE

The Roman Empire was a "vast federation of self-governing towns and territories with a central government at Rome." In fact, the imperial administration was a superstructure resting on local municipal governments. Caesar and Augustus had been the leaders of the chief urban groups of their age—the knights and the poor citizens—and the empire, in its every significant aspect, was a realization of the interests of these groups. Wherever the power of the empire extended, cities grew and a mingling of peoples took place. The mingling of peoples—occurring mainly in the great cities—was the result, first, of agression and, second, of the wide social intercourse the conqueror's peace made possible. However, from another point of view, the Roman Empire, like the Persian, the Mauryan, and the Chinese empires, as well as the Hellenistic kingdoms, was a political organization superimposed on a "sea of villages" where native languages, customs, and beliefs persisted. The ruling classes of the empire drew their primary wealth from the land and the peasants; they obtained the service necessary for a life of ease and the production of the goods that made luxury possible from the urban working classes whose members came from many lands. If the ruling classes were differentiated from the peasant-village masses by power, wealth, luxury, and refinement, the urban workers were as sharply set off from them by a cosmopolitanism which increased rather than decreased as time went on.[1]

THE CITIES OF THE ROMAN EMPIRE.

"Rome," it was said, "may be fairly called the nation of the world"—an epitome of all cities, lands, and peoples, the beginning

[1] See Max Cary, *A History of Rome to the Reign of Constantine* (1935), Chap. XXXIX, "Roman Society from A.D. 70 to 180"; F. G. Moore, *The Roman's World* (1936), p. 58; *The Cambridge Ancient History* Vol. 12, *The Imperial Crisis and Recovery, A.D.* 193–324 (1939), p. 235; C. N. Cochrane, *Christianity and Classical Culture* (1940), p. 144.

On the social organization and social conditions in the great age of the Roman Empire see Ludwig Friedländer, *Roman Life and Manners under the Early Empire* (2d ed., n.d.); Jérôme Carcopino, *La Vie quotidienne à Rome à l'apogée de l'empire* (1939); H. W. Johnston, *The Private Life of the Romans* (rev. ed., 1932); Herman Bender, *Rom und Römischen Leben im Altertum* (1893); Hugo Blümner, *Die römische Privataltertumer* (1911); Helen McClees, *The Daily Life of the Greeks and Romans* (1933); A. M. J. Festugière, *Le Monde gréco-romain au temps de Nôtre Seigneur* (ca. 1935); Lillian M. Wilson, *The Clothing of the Ancient Romans* (1938); W. C. Firebaugh, *The Inns of Greece and Rome* (1923).

For discussions of social conditions at various times see H. A. Treble, *Everyday Life in Rome in the Time of Caesar and Cicero* (1930); Ch. Dezobry, *Rome au siècle d'Auguste et pendant une partie du regne de Tibère* (1835); W. A. Becker, *Gallus, oder römischen Scenen aus der Zeit Augusts* (1938); M. J. Rivenburg, *Fashionable Life in Rome as Portrayed by Seneca* (1939); W. R. Inge, *Society in Rome under the Caesars* (1888); Samuel Dill, *Roman Society from Nero to Marcus Aurelius* (1904); T. G. Tucker, *Life in the Roman World of Nero and St. Paul* (1916); M. R. Bell, *Roman Society from Commodus to Alexander Severus* (1937).

and the end of all things, a universal market! The philosopher Seneca (*ca.* 4 B.C.–A.D. 65), the tutor of the emperor Nero, probably described its inhabitants accurately:

Behold this multitude to which the habitations of a city scarce suffice: It is mainly composed of peoples not born at Rome. From country towns, from colonies, from the whole wide world, they flow hither as a river. Some are spurred by ambition, others came to fulfill public functions. Debauchees seek here a place where every vice may be indulged. Some among us have come to satisfy their taste for letters and the arts, others their cravings for spectacular shows. People flock hither in the wake of friends, to display their talents on a wider stage. Some are here to sell their beauty, others to sell their eloquence. In short, the human race forgathers here, in a city where virtues and vices alike are paid at higher rates than elsewhere in the world.

Only guesses exist about the size of the population of Rome at any time. Under Augustus, who added to the city's housing facilities by building several new residential areas, the population has been estimated as low as 650,000 and as high as 1,200,000. Inasmuch as the maximum population, reached under the Antonines, is placed between 1,200,000 and 1,600,000, it is likely that Rome housed probably slightly fewer than a million persons in the Augustan age.

After Rome, Alexandria was the second city of the empire, with Antioch a close third; they were respectively the London, the New York, and the Paris of the age. A new Carthage held second place to Rome in the western Mediterranean area. Corinth and Thessalonica were the principal Greek cities; Athens, after the sacking by Sulla, was repopulated by immigrants from all parts of the East. Ephesus and Pergamum were the chief cities of the Asiatic coast; the island of Rhodes was a main point of contact between the East and the West. In Spain, Gaul, and Britain new cities, situated on rivers and plains, took the place of the old Celtic hill towns. Gaul had many cities. The Eastern provinces were more densely populated than the Western; probably one-seventh of the total population of the empire lived in Egypt. Only the center of political and military power had moved westward; economically and culturally the Hellenized East dominated the empire.

1. *Imperial Urban Policy.* Under the republic Rome had no policy toward the cities that fell before its arms, except irresponsible exploitation; but under the empire a permanent policy was developed. As a matter of fact the development of this policy was a necessary support of the empire. If the crisis from which Rome

and its empire emerged is viewed as a whole, it is seen as having had two fundamental aspects, (1) a struggle among rival cities for supremacy and (2) a conflict between the urban classes for the control of the cities. Rome's victory ended the struggle for supremacy, and the policy adopted in dealing with conquered cities settled the conflict between the classes for almost two centuries, or until changes so altered the relation of the classes that a new conflict broke out. The chief element of this policy was Rome's support of the well to do of the cities, with a grant of a relatively free hand in local government, in return for their acceptance of domination.

The practical application of this policy involved the arrangement of the constitutions of the cities so that the well to do formed a tightly knit oligarchy. The councils or senates were made up of wealthy men who sat for life; in the cities where there were assemblies, mostly Greek, the council had the power to veto their acts. In time most of the assemblies disappeared, and the right to elect the magistrates passed to the councils. Inasmuch as the magistrates came to be required to make contributions to the maintenance of various urban activities and institutions, only the wealthiest men could aspire to municipal offices. In every city, therefore, political power came to be possessed by a rich and exclusive clique whose members divided among themselves the power and duty of governing. The people, it is fair to say, had no influence on urban government anywhere.

Rome recognized several kinds of urban status. (1) Some cities ratified an irrevocable treaty of mutual guarantees. (2) Other cities accepted a unilateral guarantee which could be modified by the senate. (3) A few cities were colonies, *i.e.*, extensions of Rome, and their citizens were Roman citizens. (4) Some provincial municipalities received a grant of Roman citizenship. When, in 212, citizenship was given to all provincials, the urban oligarchies were so well entrenched that the gift meant nothing politically. Since the Roman armies were normally settled in camps, the cities seldom received garrisons. Military control, although a fact, was kept at a distance. However, financial and judicial controls were continuous and effective. Most of the cities levied and collected their own taxes. Some paid a fixed sum to the imperial treasury. Others paid the receipts from certain specified taxes. Under Augustus most of the revenue received from the cities was derived from direct taxes on land and personal wealth. Rome did not permit the cities to lay new taxes or undertake what were regarded as excessive expenditures. As time went on Rome's judicial control broadened, mainly as a result of the extension of the right of appeal to the imperial courts.

Rome's power over the empire was exercised directly in the rights to make war and peace and to suppress factions in the cities. Every city was required to enforce the prohibition against political clubs that might become centers of political agitation. The security of the Roman ruling classes was buttressed by protecting the privileges of the urban oligarchs.

2. *The Functions of Urban Governments.* In noting the functions of urban governments it should be remembered that the community life of the cities, if not their political institutions, had developed in the pattern of the Greek polis. The cities were both a concentrated population living in a small area and a scattered population dwelling in rural districts contiguous with the urban area. Urban, not imperial, magistrates maintained law and order, a task they seem to have done badly rather than well. Few cities maintained either a police force or a night watch. Mounted constables, often drawn from the local landlords, rode the countryside, putting down banditry and catching runaway slaves; sometimes they were called into the cities to assist the police attached to the local courts in dealing with disorder. A well-filled jail, usually kept by public slaves, was almost a universal urban institution.

The services such as the providing of water—a most important function—the maintaining of fire protection, the keeping open of sewers and other drainage channels, the building of roads and bridges, and the removing of obstructions in the streets were generally carried on by boards which employed large numbers of public slaves. A close watch was kept over markets, so that trading was conducted fairly according to the city's laws regulating measures, weights, and coins. A first need of all cities was an adequate supply of foodstuffs. In times of dearth the town officials undertook to find supplies, to keep prices down, and to raise money to buy food for the poor. The inspection of millers and bakers was necessary at all times.

Health protection was afforded by a staff of doctors who, although allowed to take fees, treated many ailments at no cost to the patients. Doctors who worked with the magistrates were required to report the causes of all deaths that came to their attention. Similarly most cities maintained a number of teachers of grammar and rhetoric and a number of athletic trainers and assistants. However, of more importance than these services was the support of the local priesthoods, the conduct of public games, and the construction of public buildings, for these activities were the major forms of communal life.

3. *Urban Finance.*   The weak point of urban government was finance. Inasmuch as the Greeks and Romans paid little attention to the economic functions of cities, it is not surprising that this was the case. Few cities drew up budgets. Most of them farmed the collection of the local revenues. In addition to indirect taxes, the chief sources of income were profits from monopolies, rents from lands, and contributions by wealthy individuals who accepted election to the magistracies. During the early period of the empire the enormous wealth of these individuals made easy this kind of financing; in fact, wealthy persons had no opportunity for the use of their great wealth other than in expenditures which improved or decorated their city.[1]

The chief urban expenditures were for the wages of a small corps of clerks and constables, for the keep of a large number of public slaves, for the conduct of public games and festivals, and for the construction of public buildings. Among the special obligations which a city might be called upon to assume were the maintenance of ambassadors in Rome, the support of imperial officials traveling through the city, and a contribution for the support of the army. This contribution, known as the *annona*, was usually made in kind—wheat, barley, beans, meat, oil, wine, vinegar, hides, shafts for spears, and fabrics for uniforms. Under the early empire it was sometimes transported to Rome; in the third century, when military disorders broke out, the requisitioning of supplies became a great evil and contributed to the general economic disorganization.

THE SOCIAL CLASSES IN THE ROMAN EMPIRE.

Under the empire the social classes were more sharply defined than they had been under the republic, and the structure which they formed was more rigid. However, movement upward, at least from the unfree to the free status and from the knightly to the senatorial order, was easier than it had been. In determining class status inheritance was less important than merit proved by performance. But the possession of great wealth was, as always, the primary condition of admission to the privileged orders.

1. *The Roman Ruling Classes.*   As previously noted, in the Augustan arrangement of ranks both privileged orders survived.

[1] A. H. M. Jones, *The Greek City From Alexander to Justinian* (1940), p. 250.

But the relations between them were considerably different from what they had been under the republic.

The emperor controlled admission to the senatorial class, and elevation to it was primarily a mark of his favor. The old qualifications of opulence—an annual income of 1,000,000 sesterces[1]—and the holding of office in the *cursus honorum* were not changed. These offices, of course, were at the disposal of the emperor, who, by giving short tenures, promoted men rapidly. The senators continued to monopolize the highest magistracies, the governorships of the senatorial provinces, the memberships in the *consilium principis*, and the high military commands. The decimations of the patrician-plebeian nobility during the last decades of the republic destroyed many old families, but their places were taken by new ones. Caesar first admitted non-Romans to the senatorial order. Claudius introduced Gauls. Vespasian recruited Italians. In Hadrian's time only one patrician family survived. In the second century men from Greece and Asia Minor were admitted, and in the next century men from other parts of Asia. All senators were required to own land in Italy. From birth a senator's son ranked as a knight.

The knights formed a nonhereditary nobility whose members filled the jury lists, the civil offices of the emperor's staff, the provincial administrative positions, and the municipal posts. Chief among the offices held by them were the personal offices of the emperor, such as the provincial procuratorships, the governorship of Egypt, the prefectures of police, the fire brigade, the imperial posts, and the criminal courts, and the commands of the auxiliaries, fleets, and the Praetorian Guard. They held most of the offices in the army except the high commands and the lower posts filled by men promoted from the legions. The wealth required for the rank of knight was 400,000 sesterces. Admission to the order of knights was controlled by the emperor, but any man having the necessary financial qualification could apply. After admission, advancement to the senatorial rank was not only possible but easy if the favor of the emperor was gained.

The economic positions of the aristocratic orders were similar. The senators possessed heavy investments in slaves and lands, the chief forms of wealth. But many were also interested in manufacturing, mining, transportation, and moneylending. A few senators owned inns. As the holders of the offices in the *cursus honorum*, they received the great state salaries. Caesar barred senators

[1] Perhaps $50,000 today.

from trade and shipping; Hadrian prohibited them from farming taxes in their own names. The knights, besides holding slaves and lands, were the bankers, tax farmers, contractors, purveyors, and business enterprisers of the empire. Most of the imperial properties which were not managed by slaves or freedmen were leased to knights, many of whom were richer than senators.

The social positions of the two wealthy classes were slightly different. The senators maintained great dignity and made a show of munificence by spending money freely on games and shows and by bestowing gifts and legacies on friends and clients. Augustus ordered the senators to wear purple garments. They sat in the seats of honor at the theater and the games. The knights wore tunics bordered with a purple stripe and gold rings and occupied seats in the first row at the theater and the games. The children of both orders wore gold necklaces. Certain punishments, such as flogging, torture, condemnation to the mines, crucifixion, and being thrown to the animals, were not imposed on them. An insult to a senator or knight by a plebeian was severely punished. Senators were required to maintain a certain standard of living. In the first century 60,000 sesterces were hardly sufficient for the yearly rental of a senator's residence. Tiberius deprived a senator of his rank because he attempted to practice economy. It was considered undignified for senators to carry cooking utensils and articles of food. Both senators and knights gained social prestige by maintaining great numbers of clients to whom they paid regular fees. These hangers-on gathered at their patron's house every morning, followed after his litter when he moved through the streets, applauded his speeches in the senate or the forum, and took part in his plots, agitations, and election campaigns.

Beneath the senators and the knights were the provincial nobles—the *curial* class—who were established in a privileged position by the imperial urban policies. They were the members of the senates and councils of the cities. The distinction between them and ordinary citizens and plebeians was sharply marked. When money was distributed by a public-spirited magistrate they often received larger amounts than the common citizens. If one of them was accused of a crime, his case was heard not by a local but by an imperial court, and if he was convicted he could not be flogged or sent to the mines. Like the senators and knights, the curial nobles were required to possess a certain fortune—100,000 sesterces. In Trajan's time the rank became hereditary.

After Augustus the senatorial and equestrian orders were merely sections of a single ruling class, *i.e.*, an urban-dwelling plutocracy whose members held the political offices of the empire and possessed its wealth of slaves, lands, mines, and industries. The curial class was a source of new members for both orders. The destruction of the republican senatorial oligarchy opened the way for the advancement of new men, and the emperors kept the way open, so that the imperial nobility, although one body, continually received new blood and new talent. However, by the early second century the fluid conditions of the privileged classes had hardened, and social stratification was well advanced.

The luxurious life of the Roman ruling classes, which the Christians so harshly condemned, developed in the second and first centuries B.C. Except for the debaucheries of Nero and Caligula, excesses were probably greater in number under the late republic than under the empire. Lucullus dined on singing birds, peacock brains, and flamingo tongues. Caesar carried a mosaic floor from camp to camp while campaigning. Antony had a carriage drawn by lions. After Actium the aristocratic standard of living settled into a pattern. A building boom covered Italy with villas of stone and brick, decorated with imported colored marbles. The Roman residence aimed more at elegance than comfort. Such residences were frequently built on streams or at the seashore. Almost always they were surrounded with groves, gardens, and artificial lakes. The violet, the rose, and the lily were the common flowers used for outdoor planting. Furniture was well made and artistically designed; the chief pieces were couches, chairs, tables, and cupboards. Decorations of silver, gold, and bronze were popular. Walls were covered with imitations of Greek frescoes. Tableware was chiefly wrought silver, gold plate, and rock crystal. Meals were elaborate and banqueting became a vice. When the discomfort from overeating became too great, it was relieved by the taking of emetics. Foreign cooks and oriental dishes were immensely popular. The diet of the well to do commonly included oysters, fish, game, rabbit, kids, poultry, chestnuts, almonds, figs, dates, wines, puddings, and various sorts of breads. The chief vegetables were onions, leeks, lentils, peas, and asparagus. Spices were popular and plentiful. The aristocrat's clothing was simple and rich, rather than ornate; scarlet and purple were common colors. Jewelry—colored jewels inlaid in gold or silver, gold rings and necklaces, and silver buckles, belts, chains, and hilts—was mostly oriental in design. Diamonds were worn only in rings. Pearls were highly popular. Perfumes were used lavishly, especially by women. Bathing in asses' milk was a well-known beauty treatment. The chief amusements were gaming and eating. Drunkenness was common. But generally the aristocrats found their entertainment with the people at games, shows, and theatricals. Although a few rich men found pleasure in literary pursuits, the vast majority were content with gratification of the senses. The taste for art was the noblest trait of the aristocracy. Sexual excess was the most common vice. It is a mistake, however, to condemn the Romans for an extravagant and corrupting luxury beyond that of Western aristocratic groups of later times, whose members, as a matter of fact, derived their standards from the Roman source.

2. *The Roman Poor Citizens.* The poor citizens had fought with the knights in the final struggle against the republican oligarchs, and so under the empire they received their reward—the life of "bread and show." Under Augustus they numbered about 200,000; under Marcus Aurelius about 300,000. At least these were the numbers in each reign receiving free grain or bread. They were mainly an idle and petted class, accustomed to getting what they wanted by clamor. The politicians despised them but courted their favor. In the course of time every important city had a citizen mob similar to that of Rome and adopted similar measures to keep it quiet.

Originally the poor citizens were the farmers, driven from their lands by war and usury, but under the flattery of the politicians, who stooped to every device to win their favor at elections, they became men who would not work. Nor did they long continue to serve in the army after the empire was set up, for by the second century the military establishment was manned almost entirely by provincials. Many of the poor citizens were clients of the nobles, from whom they received, in addition to pitifully small sums of money, occasional gifts of oil and wine. Grain was furnished by the state, *i.e.*, the emperor, either free of charge or at a low price. The corn dole, established by the Gracchi, became a permanent feature of Roman life in the last decades of the republic. Only Sulla, the partisan of the senatorial oligarchy, undertook to abolish it; it was both a bribe to the electorate and a palliative for unemployment. The only alternative was a distribution of lands, which neither the senatorial nobles nor the knights were prepared to carry out.

The domestic life of the Roman poor citizens was bare and harsh. Their single garment was a toga, which served at night as a bed covering. They lived in the several-storied tenements—*insulae*—built in the valleys between Rome's hills.[1] They reached these warrenlike habitations by climbing stairs and ladders, sometimes as many as a hundred steps. The single room, used only for eating and sleeping, was furnished with bits of crockery, broken pieces of furniture, and a pile of straw. And sleep was hard to get. "It costs a fortune to get a sleep in the city" was a common complaint. Under such conditions family life was impossible, vice and crime thrived, illness was a usual condition. The streets of Rome were not safe day or night; cutthroats and pickpockets lurked everywhere. There were no police in the slums. Fires and falling walls added sudden hazards to these ever present dangers. Fights and domestic quarrels were continuous. Besides the state grain, which was made into a tough bread, the chief articles of diet, when they could be obtained, were onions, beans, turnips, a sour wine, a little cheese, salt meat, and bits of fresh meat from the heads of sheep, calves, and goats. Olive oil was a luxury obtained only as a gift from the well to do. Water, furnished by the state, was the single plentiful article at the disposal of the poor citizens—who were, in fact, a horde of paupers camped among the owners and rulers of the Roman state. Their power in the assemblies had been destroyed when the princeps took control of the magistracies.

The bread and bed of the poor citizens were hard; their shows were gaudy, bloody, and obscene. There were five main types of public entertainment: (1) chariot racing in the circus, (2) gladiatorial combats in the arena, (3) animal fights in the arena, (4) plays and dances in the theater, and (5) athletic contests in the gymnasium.

[1] George La Piana, "Foreign Groups in Rome during the First Centuries of the Empire," *Harvard Theological Review*, Vol. 20 (1927), pp. 209–210: "Endless blocks of 'insulae,' poor tenement houses, towering high on the narrow streets, were the result of the unavoidable overcrowding of the people in the central and cheaper districts. Greedy speculators were ready to grasp the opportunity; flimsy tenements of wood and plaster of rapid and cheap construction filled all the available space and returned large profits to the owners and to legions of middle-men who rented and subrented small apartments and rooms, fleecing the unfortunate tenants. Forced evictions, exposure, confiscation of furniture and household goods were common events, and not seldom riots and tumults of exasperated tenants kept the whole city in a turmoil. Not only were the rents high and the accommodations primitive; these tenements were also dangerous fire-traps. The population of Rome lived under the constant fear of ruin and fires. . . . The great monuments of the empire were built of solid bricks and stone covered with marble and could defy the centuries, but the tenement houses were of cheap material and wood, and often collapsed, unexpectedly burying under their ruins lodgers and passers-by."

Horse racing was the original public amusement in Rome. Both men and women attended the races. Betting was universal. The chariot race was seven laps around the course; usually there were four participants. Successful charioteers were public figures; unsuccessful drivers frequently died under the hoofs of the horses.

Gladiatorial combats were first held in Rome in 264 B.C.; as previously noted, they were first given officially by Marius as part of his program of recruiting the legions from the poor citizens. During Caesar's aedileship an extravagant standard was set for such exhibitions, which other politicians maintained. Augustus outdid Caesar as Caesar had surpassed Pompey in providing this kind of entertainment. Only Trajan, who gave shows lasting through four months, sent as many gladiators—ten thousand— into the arena as did the first emperor. The vast crowds at the exhibitions, sometimes as many as 200,000, served as popular assemblies, because the citizens informed the emperor of their wants by their clamor.

The fights were preceded by banquets, parades, and mock combats. Every sort of weapon was introduced into the contests, and various types of opponents were matched. A favorite contest was a fight between a Samnite armed with a square shield and a short sword and a Thracian bearing a round shield and a short sword. Sometimes women were matched with women; in A.D. 88 dwarfs fought women. And men were pitted against all kinds of wild animals. Occasionally full-fledged battles were staged. Claudius engaged 19,000 men in a mock sea fight. Often cavalry was sent against infantry. The frenzied crowds clamored for blood. To the coward, for whom they had only contempt, they shouted, "Whip him on, kill him, burn him, why does he fear the sword . . . why does he die so sullenly?" Mercy was shown to a fallen gladiator by raising the little finger of the left hand; the down-turned thumb meant death. At the close of a contest sand was shoveled over the bloodstains, the wounded were killed, and the corpses were hauled away in hearses.

Gladiators were recruited among criminals, slaves, and prisoners of war; some were volunteers. Toward the end of the first century both men and women of noble rank engaged in sanguinary combats. The lure of the arena was undoubtedly strong, and its reward great. Victors dressed in gold ornaments and ostrich plumes, women were at their feet, and money was showered upon them. Such men were generally of marvelous physique. Schools for training gladiators were set up in the first century B.C., and regular traders traversed the empire buying slaves who seemed qualified for the arena.

Animal fighting was an adjunct of the gladiatorial shows. Elephants, lions, tigers, crocodiles, rhinoceroses, hippopotamuses, leopards, panthers, bears, and almost every other dangerous beast within the ken of Romans appeared in the arena. Bulls were not popular. The first animal fights were given in 186 B.C. Professional animal hunters traveled in the frontier provinces seeking beasts. Animal training was a regular profession by the time of Augustus. Sometimes animals were pitted against each other. Sometimes they were sent against unarmed men and women. Occasionally they were set on men tied to stakes. Animal hunts by night were very popular.

What the theater lacked in violence it made up in obscenity, for the Roman theater never attained the intellectual level of its Greek prototype. The most popular show was a kind of Punch-and-Judy affair, with the dullard, the soothsayer, the glutton, and the booby as chief characters; its leading competitor was a low comedy of popular life. Dancing girls and noisy bands enlivened the performances.

Athletic contests, also introduced in 186 B.C., never excited the populace to the pitch to which they were aroused by the chariot races and the combats of the arena. Most of the competitors were Greeks.

Bathing was the universal pastime of the Romans; at the baths —*thermae*—men and women of every rank gathered to read, gossip, play ball games, and cast dice. Imperial Rome had eleven great thermae. Stealing the clothes of bathers was a common petty crime.

In the second century the life of the Roman proletarian, *i.e.*, the citizen who possessed no wealth except his children, was precarious but exciting. His typical day went off in about the following manner:

He leaves in the morning the little room which he rents by the day or the month in the top storey of some tall house in the Suburra, if he is not lodged gratuitously by some rich or generous patron. He then goes from palace to palace presenting his *sportula* [little basket], which is returned to him full of provisions and money. When it is time he takes his *tessera* [ticket] to the dispenser of public wheat. Some rich person with whom he is connected as a client invites him to one of those repasts by which all sad or joyful circumstances were celebrated, as the anniversary of a death or of a birth, or a funeral, a marriage, the ceremony of taking office, the dedication of a monument. When the hour of bathing comes he hastens to the free baths. He takes his afternoon nap under some marble portico, exposed to the gentle rays of the setting sun. Then he finishes the day at the theater, or the circus, or the Coliseum, where at the expense of some rich man some hundred gladiators kill each other for his amusement. When he returns at night to his little lodging, he may say to himself, more happy than Titus [emperor, 79–81]: "I have not lost my day"; and he can certainly add: "It has cost me nothing."[1]

The Roman proletariat, it should be remembered, was not a section of the working class.

It would be incorrect to conclude from the preceding paragraphs that only the poor citizens went to the shows and games; they were regular attendants, but the other divisions of the population also had appetites for displays of the race course and the arena. There is not a single protest in Latin literature against the continuance of gladiatorial combats.

3. *The Working Classes of the Roman Empire.* Only the members of the ruling orders were regarded as having a class status; the classless population was recognized as falling into two groups, the *honestiores*, who had yearly incomes of at least 5,000 sesterces, and the *humiliores*, who were without capital of any kind. These groups were differentiated from one another by the punishments to which they were subject. The heaviest punishments, such as crucifixion, running the gauntlet, being sent to the mines, and being thrown to the beasts, fell on the humiliores. The honestiores were punished by either exile or imprisonment. Except for the shopkeepers, almost all of both groups belonged to the working[2] classes.

The organization of enterprise as well as the prevailing technology fixed the conditions of life of the working classes. In industry the chief enterprises were owned by the emperor and big capitalists, who employed large numbers of slaves; the direction of these enterprises were often left to slaves or freedmen. In some industries the establishments, although they lacked mechanical power, had some of the characteristics of the modern factory. But many industries were carried on in small shops where slaves worked with free

[1] Paul Allard, *Les Esclaves chrétiens* (1900), pp. 40–41.
[2] On the working classes in the Roman Empire see Helen J. Loane, *Industry and Commerce of the City of Rome* (50 *B.C.*–200 *A.D.*) (1938); Helen M. Tanzer, *The Common People of Pompey: A study of Graffiti* (1939); E. H. Brewster, *Roman Craftsmen and Tradesmen of the Early Empire* (1917); J. P. Waltzing, *Les Corporations professionelles chez les Romains* (4 vols., 1895–1900); R. von Pöhlmann, *Geschichte der sozialen Frage und des Sozialismus in der antiken Welt* (2 vols., 1925).

laborers. In agriculture the latifundium was common everywhere. Since the senators and knights who owned the estates were almost universally absentee landlords, the management was left to bailiffs. The same system prevailed on the imperial lands, as well as on the temple lands in Asia Minor and Syria. Many of the imperial lands were leased to big tenants. On medium-sized holdings, which were numerous, slaves and free cultivators worked together, often under the owner's direction. Around every town small peasant proprietors were numerous. The working classes had, therefore, a fourfold division: (1) slaves, (2) freedmen, (3) free urban workers and (4) peasants.

The bulk of the slaves were owned by the emperor and the members of the ruling classes. The average Roman probably possessed no more than seven or eight.[1]

Toward the end of the first century the number of slaves began to decline and their condition to improve. The Roman peace cut off the supply, for war no longer sent hordes of captives to market. Enslavement for debt was also less frequent. Many new slaves were obtained through an extensive trade which found its sources of supply in Britain, Germany, Spain, Armenia, and Arabia. Kidnaping persons in order to sell them into slavery was frequent under these conditions. But the main source of new slaves was the breeding pens of Greece and the ancient-oriental lands; there *vernae*, as the young slaves were called, were the chief product of many estates. Productive females were released from hard labor. Although the worse features of the slave system were reformed by Augustus, it retained, as was inevitable, many harsh aspects. Slaves were still worked in chains in the fields, and were kept, when not at work, in chains and irons in barns. In the second century the sale of unsatisfactory slaves for gladiatorial combats was prohibited; about the same time the abandoned slave and the female slave prostituted by her master were declared free.

The need for increased income promoted a movement to free slaves. In fact, by the end of the first century the practice of manumission had become fashionable in aristocratic circles. Many slaves bought their freedom. Their economic advance was due to the widespread practice of placing properties in their hands for

[1] See article "Slavery" in the *Encyclopaedia Brittanica* (14th ed.); William Buckland, *The Roman Law of Slavery: The condition of the slave in private law from Augustus to Justinian* (1908); Eduard Meyer, *Die Sklaverei in Altertum* (1898); Henri A. Wallon, *Histoire de l'esclavage dans l'antiquité* (2d ed., 1898); A. M. Duff, *Freedmen in the Early Roman Empire* (1928).

management. Such a property, known as a *peculium*, belonged to the slave's master, but the slave treated it as his own and profited by its increase. Often he invested his own gains in the enterprise which he managed. Thus thrift and industry were stimulated and rewarded. Upon manumission the slave often received the entire peculium. Under these circumstances it is not surprising that freedmen, as manumitted slaves were called, became prominent in every phase of imperial economic life. Many of them rose to great wealth.

The slave population of the empire always remained large, and the line between the free and the unfree was a permanent element of the social structure. Nor did the fear of the slave rising die quickly. Mining was prohibited in Italy on account of this fear, and terror, as Tacitus said in the time of Nero, was the only safeguard of the ruling classes:

> Our ancestors always suspected the temper of their slaves, even when they were born on the same estates or in the same houses, and thus inherited from birth an affection for their masters. But now we have in our households nations with different customs than our own, with a foreign worship or none at all; it is only by terror that you can hold in such a motley crew.

About this time the senate, in spite of an aroused public opinion, voted according to the traditional practice, the sentence of death on all slaves in the house of a murdered prefect of police.

Perhaps the most remarkable social development of the early empire was the renaissance of the free urban working class. Every craft revived, and small shops and enterprisers employing a few slaves as well as free workers became numerous. Free men seem to have dominated such industries as baking, carpentry, smithing, brewing, and cloth working. In time they took over navigation and shipping. The free workers sprang from freedmen and immigrants; in the west a large number descended from free migrants of eastern origin. The increased prominence of free workers led to a revival of the guilds—*collegia*—which for political reasons had been abolished after the failure of Catiline's conspiracy. Augustus forbade them except when the senate authorized their organization. In the second century, after Trajan adopted a policy of licensing collegia, as many as one hundred crafts were organized in Rome, and similar movements occurred in other great cities. These organizations seem to have developed from the Assyrian model as eastern workers came west. Slaves, freedmen, and freemen, as well as enterprisers and workers joined them. Their functions, except for that of protecting members against financial exactions, were chiefly social. They served to provide fellowship, a common religious life, and burial. They never undertook to control wages or working conditions. Some of them dealt in foodstuffs in times of dearth. Members, admitted by vote, paid a small initiation fee and perhaps a small due. Every year a guild elected a master, and every five years the membership lists were checked. The collegia were the only working-class institutions of the Roman Empire.

Such improvements in the legal status of free urban workers did not bring an amelioration of their economic condition. They remained miserably poor, and any circumstance which disturbed the movement of food supplies to the cities quickly brought them to starvation. They were the first and greatest sufferers in time of famine. Their chief employments were the simple crafts and services, such as baking, pottery making, weaving, smithing, shoemaking, gardening, and keeping cheap inns. Many of them were muleteers, dock workers, and sailors. The chief cause of their poverty was the unequal distribution of wealth. The well to do, although possessing great wealth, were too few in number to provide a consumers' market for the wares the urban workers could produce, while the peasants, great in number, were too poor to buy them. Then, as now, urban and rural poverty were chained to urban riches.

The peasants were known as the *pagani, i.e.,* dwellers in the villages. In the period of conquest many of them had been reduced to slavery; in the period of peace many of them became *coloni, i.e.,* free workers with fixed obligations to the landowners. By the second century the coloni were probably more numerous than the agricultural slaves. They held lands as tenants and paid rents in kind. They marketed their own crops. They labored a certain number of days in their landlord's fields and worked for the state on roads and bridges. They also paid a poll tax. The Roman ruling classes, interested only in the peasants' productivity, made no effort to Romanize the pagani. In the few glimpses that the literary materials give of the peasant-village masses of the Roman empire, they are revealed as economically impoverished, socially inert, and completely superstitious—indeed, quite like the peasant-village masses in all times and places.

The working classes of the Roman Empire were at the mercy of their owners and rulers, indeed the victims of that parasitism which was the great internal weakness of all traditional urban cultures.[1] Whatever amelioration occurred in the first and second centuries was due, it may be believed, not to the humane sentiments of the Roman ruling classes but to their well-known eye for economic advantage. The advance of the working classes in these centuries is explained partly by the fact that a small portion of the wealth brought by peace, orderly government, stabilized finance, and the systematic exploitation of natural resources filtered down to them and partly by the discovery among the ruling classes that a material reward for enterprise and thrift was an aid to increased production. However, in fairness it must be recognized that the great age of the Roman Empire brought to urban working classes a freer opportunity for advancement, especially if they eschewed politics, than had ever existed before for any considerable body of common men or was to exist again until the opening of modern times. But for the peasant-village masses the Roman Empire was merely another incident which disturbed but did not change significantly the routine of their traditional way of life.

THE SOCIAL OUTLOOK OF THE ROMANS.

Above all the Romans held fast to tradition. In the bitter struggle that destroyed the republic the rival groups were alike in their appeal to the past. The people, looking back to the early order of farmers and soldiers, justified the overthrow of the senatorial oligarchies on the ground that they were usurpers. The defenders of the republic proclaimed the sanctity of private rights, especially the right of property, and called for an end to their invasion by irresponsible power. The victorious military demagogues claimed to be restoring the traditional order, purifying it by punishing corruption and immorality. And their work—the empire—was justified as the fulfillment of God's work in history.

---

[1] A. H. M. Jones, *The Greek City From Alexander to Justinian* (1940), p. 268: "Throughout the period under review the cities were, it would thus appear, economically parasitic on the country-side. Their incomes consisted in the main of the rents drawn by the urban aristocracy from the peasants, and the trade and industry which flourished in some of them catered largely for this class and were dependent on it for existence. The movement of urbanization was not, it is true, responsible to any large degree for the creation of the landlord class: only in the relatively few colonial foundations did the establishment of a city include the grant of estates to its members. But the growth of cities meant the concentration in towns of the larger proprietors and converted them into absentee landlords. This in itself was an unhealthy state of affairs. The wealth of the country-side—and it must be emphasized that the bulk of the wealth of the empire was derived from agriculture—was drained into the towns. The peasants were thus reduced to a very low standard of life, and this fact in turn impoverished the urban proletariat." By permission of the Oxford University Press, Oxford.

As conquerors the Romans saw themselves as the vindicators of liberty, the makers of order, the exponents of reason. But they ruled by right of their virtues—authoritative but not arbitrary, courageous but not arrogant, grave but not vain, just but not cruel. If this view of their virtues obscured their acquisitiveness, stubbornness, and duplicity, their success was an excuse for their blindness to their faults. It was altogether fitting that Octavianus, who rose to power by these faults, became the enduring symbol of the virtues. As a god he was the deification of the Roman tradition.

The Romans ruled as a conquering minority in an exploited world, and their attitudes toward other peoples reflected the relation between them. Foreign peoples lacked the wisdom and gravity necessary to exercise power with justice. A sense of humor was an evidence of corruptibility. Vulgarity was the mark of inferiority; inferiority was proof of vulgarity. Servility was the proper condition for the vulgar and the inferior, and the rightful lot of the servile was to labor. Slaves, said Varro, were "machines with voices." The term "machine" suggests the Roman's attitude toward the world he exploited: it existed to make him rich. That it was in any respect human made no difference. As conquerors the Romans despised labor and admired violence. "To be free," said Cicero, "it is necessary to be rich." And just as the Romans introduced every imaginable horror into the arena to satisfy their lust for violence, so did they stop at nothing to acquire wealth. Even under the empire the exploitation of the provinces went on unchecked. The contractors who built the aqueducts, roads, and public buildings used poor materials and charged excessive prices. Tenants bribed imperial inspectors, and inspectors bribed their superiors. The Romans could understand kindness to a rich man, for in return he might bestow a gift or leave a bequest. But as Cicero said, "What was the good of being kind to a poor man?" The poor were friendless. Moreover, all who befriended them were, so Cicero declared, traitors and fit to be murdered. The Romans reduced the laboring classes to inertia by violence, only to find that to satisfy the lust for wealth it was necessary to stimulate the workers with grants of freedon. Not even in their care for the poor citizen or in their new treatment of the slave were the Romans guided by any motive higher than the desire for gain.[1] They began

[1] Cyril Bailey, editor, *The Legacy of Rome* (1924), p. 481. "The average Roman was ever a keen grasping man, not given to neglect opportunities offered by fortune or the necessities of his neighbor." Oxford University Press, Oxford.

their career of conquest as farmers, the tillers of fields and the keepers of cattle; their empire was only an enlarged field and its population another kind of cattle. Their law recognized no sanctity of life and no rights of man; at its core was the right and sanctity of property, *i.e.*, their possessions, no matter how obtained.

THE TRANSFORMATION OF THE ROMAN EMPIRE INTO AN ORIENTAL MONARCHY

Absolutism was implicit in the Roman imperial structure from the beginning, but it became the overt fact only as the result of a crisis which threw the ruling classes and the masses of the empire again into turmoil. The central factor in this crisis seems to have been a disorganization of economic life which, because it did not permit the continuation of expenditure by the state, the municipalities, and the aristocracy at the rate of the early empire, brought a struggle among the various wealth-holding groups for shares of a decreasing wealth; as in the early crisis when the groups struggled for shares of imperial booty, the triumph belonged finally to the commander of the victorious army.

The Economic Decline of the Roman Empire.

The causes of the economic decline of the Roman Empire were exceedingly complex. Gone today are the simple explanations, such as increasing drought and a loss of soil fertility, which were offered not long ago. Although each occurred here and there, and both contributed a bit to a worsening situation, the decline itself seems to have been bound up with the nature of Roman imperialism.[1]

[1] The most easily available discussion of the third century crisis of the Roman Empire is *The Cambridge Ancient History*, Vol. 12, *The Imperial Crisis and Recovery, A.D.* 193–324 (1939). H. M. D. Parker, *A History of the Roman World from A.D.* 138 to 337 (1935), surveys the period of the crisis. The classic treatment of this phase of Roman history is Edward Gibbon, *The History of the Decline and Fall of the Roman Empire;* written in the late eighteenth century from the point of view of the rationalism of that time it explained the "decline and fall" as the result of the rise of Christianity. The work is available in an edition by J. B. Bury (1897–1906).

Recent writers have been inclined to view the "decline and fall" and the "rise of Christianity" as more or less parallel developments arising from underlying factors, but they have not agreed on the factors. Some have emphasized political disorder; others a scarcity of precious metal; others a decline of agricultural production; others the ravages of epidemics; and still others the effects of slavery. Discussion of one or another of these theories may be found in Otto Seeck, *Geschichte des Untergangs der antiken Welt* (6 vols., 1897–1920); N. A. Vavilev, *The Fall of the Ancient Roman Empire and the Disappearance of Ancient Culture and Law* (1921); Georges Sorel, *La Ruine du monde antique* (1925); G. Salvioli, *Le Capitalisme dans le monde antique* (1906); G. Mickwitz, *Geld und Wirtschaft in römischen Reich des Vierten Jahrhunderts n. Chr.* (1932); Hans Zinsser, *Rats, Lice, and History* (1935); Vladimir Simkhovitch, *Toward an Understanding of Jesus* (1923), the

Roman imperialism had three leading economic characteristics. (1) The Romans seized by violence the economic surpluses of the Mediterranean and ancient-oriental lands, including the labor forces that produced them.[1] (2) The Romans devised a system of

essay, "Hay and History." The most recent detailed examination of the crisis is M. I. Rostovtzeff, *Social and Economic History of the Roman Empire* (1926); M. I. Rostovtzeff, "The Decay of the Ancient World and its Economic Explanation," *Economic History Review*, Vol. 2 (1929–1930), pp. 197–214; also M. I. Rostovtzeff, "The Roman Empire," in Richard R. Ely, editor, *Urban Land Economics* (1922), p. 58: "Nothing explains why in the third century comes a social upheaval that almost destroys the Roman Empire. Scores of emperors proclaimed by the troops in a political hell for no reason. Why was it? I say it was the fight of the country population, which formed at that time the armies of the Roman Empire, against the city population. The fight of the country population against the city population. The fight of the peasants against the men of the city who exploited them and lived at their expense." If Rostovtzeff's view as stated in this quotation is interpreted in terms of the fundamental economic fact that the chief source of wealth was land, the crisis of the third century was a class struggle between the truly significant section of the working class and the urban-dwelling ruling class. Rostovtzeff's view is, however, not quite so crudely Marxian, for he finds that the deepest roots of the crisis were in a psychological change, expressed in a vulgarization of literature, art, religion, and philosophy, which engulfed the rationalism of the educated Romans in the superstition of the masses. The weakness of the Rostovtzeff theory of the crisis is that it neglects the ruling-class economic practices and outlook, which, because they entered into imperial policy, were decisive factors, first, in shaping the situation from which the crisis came and, second, in determining action by government after it came. The real point of the Rostovtzeff theory is that a movement by the masses against the ruling classes is certain to result in disaster; the theory is an excellent example of the fact that often erudite historical scholarship may be best understood as present politics.

It is worth noting, too, that contemporary journalistic comparisons between the economic and social crisis of the Roman Empire and economic and social circumstances in the contemporary world are commonly grounded in a misunderstanding of both situations. The situation in the contemporary world is fundamentally different from that of the Roman world in the most decisive respect, namely, as regards the tendency of the capacity to produce wealth. In the contemporary world the capacity to produce wealth has constantly advanced, even in the decade since 1929, while in the Roman world a combination of factors seems to have led over a period of time to a decreased capacity to produce. A decline of the population of the Mediterranean lands from about seventy to fifty millions accompanied by a growing impoverishment of the population would seem to leave no doubt as to the decreasing productivity. Although it may be pointed out that the present increased capacity to produce wealth is not being used, the fact is that it exists, so that current problems may be dealt with in ways fundamentally different from those possible in the Roman world.

[1] Guglielmo Ferrero, *Militarism* (1902), p. 124: "The chief results of the Roman conquests were not only to replace in circulation the wealth accumulated by the semi-barbaric Alpine, Gallic, Spanish, and Illyrian peoples, but also that of the civilized Asian states, which, since the days of Alexander had had time to re-accumulate and stagnate, using them for the advance of a new type of civilization. From the conquest of Carthage up to the time of Julius Caesar, Roman politics were directed by a crew of financiers whose sole object was to appropriate, by fair means or foul, the wealth lying dormant in the provinces." Ward, Lock & Co., Ltd., London. Also T. A. Rickard, *Man and Metals*, (2 vols., 1932), Vol. 1, p. 402: "The attitude of the Romans toward mines was that of military conquerors rather than of industrial exploiters; to them a mine was a prize of war, a place of treasure. Such ideas were due largely to the fact that in ancient times the metals were

taxation and finance which continuously transferred to them a large part of the new surplus as it was produced.[1] (3) And the Romans failed to make investments or develop enterprises that expanded production, or, in other words, they extracted wealth from an economy whose productive capacity they did not increase.[2] When viewed together, these aspects of Roman imperialism may be seen as a system of exploitation which, in time, was bound to yield decreasing returns.

An examination of economic developments under the empire indicates the ways in which this result followed from the conditions that brought the empire into being on a wave of prosperity.

When the direct spoliation of conquered peoples stopped, in the first century, the supply of capital was no longer replenished by the transport of confiscated wealth to Rome. This cessation was all the more a factor in decline because the wealth which had been carried to Rome was invested mainly in nonproductive works. The effect was, of course, a rising interest rate. In the Augustan age the price of money, as previously noted, was unprecedentedly low, but afterwards it steadily advanced.[3]

---

won mainly from superficial deposits; the yield represented a harvesting of the mineral crop, or outcrop, rather than the consequence of cultivation, or development. The Romans seized mines more frequently than they discovered or explored them; they availed themselves of the ores that others had uncovered; they reaped where they had not sown. Thus their mining was a depredation rather than an industry. . . . " The McGraw-Hill Book Co.

[1] J. B. Bury, *History of the Later Roman Empire from the Death of Theodosius I to the Death of Justinian (A.D. 395 to A.D. 565)* (2 vols., 1923), Vol. 1, p. 28: "The principle of this system was to transfer to the imperial treasury as much as possible of the wealth circulating in the Empire. Want of capital in the provinces was a necessary result; there were no means to repair the damages of time, fire, or earthquakes save by an application to the central authority, which entailed delay and uncertainty, especially in distant provinces. A decrease in the means of life was soon produced, and thereby a decrease in the population.

"The western suffered more than the eastern provinces, a fact which we must attribute primarily to a different economic condition, resulting from a different history. The distribution of property was less uneven in the East, and the social character of the people was different. For while the East was under the more genial and enlightened rule of Alexander's successors, the West was held by the cold hand of Rome." Macmillan & Company, Ltd., London.

[2] Tenney Frank, editor, *An Economic Survey of Ancient Rome*, Vol. 5, *Rome and Italy of the Empire* (1940), p. 295: "By the Augustan day the important men of the state had placed their investments in provincial real estate and mortgages, not industry or commerce, and the chief economic drive during the Empire was conditioned by this fact"; also p. 298: "Many of the owners were futile gentlemen farmers who drew their livelihood from old investments made elsewhere and sank their funds in rural show places, with studs, hunting lodges, and pleasure parks, not expecting to profit from them." By permission of Johns Hopkins Press, Baltimore.

[3] Paul Louis, *Ancient Rome at Work* (1927), p. 318: "Nothing proves better than the maintenance of exaggerated rates of interest the extent of the catastrophe which held the

A labor shortage developed for a similar reason. Under the later republic and early empire the Romans wasted labor recklessly, for the supply of slaves seemed endless.[1] But in the era of peace the supply of slaves decreased, in spite of the activities of slave breeders, traders, and kidnapers. At the root of the labor shortage, it has been suggested, were factors which lowered the fecundity of all classes. Indeed, the depopulation which followed the reign of Marcus Aurelius was probably as much a cause of economic decline as economic decline was its result.[2] The labor shortage was most acute in those industries, especially agriculture, which depended upon cheap labor and large-scale operations for making a profit. The effect was evident even in the first century, when some of the lands at the center of the empire went out of cultivation and soon lost population.[3] In an effort to maintain agricultural production, landowners began to grant favorable leases to small holders. But the desired result was only partially attained, because the small farmers, lacking both capital and labor, were unable to use the methods that yielded the greatest returns. As time went

---

Roman world in its grip: renewing itself incessantly, permanently exercising its fell influence, sapping energy, bleeding productivity and breaking the back of labor." By permission of Alfred A. Knopf, Inc., New York, and George Routledge & Sons, Ltd., London.

[1] Mary L. Gordon, "The Nationality of Slaves under the Roman Empire," *Journal of Roman Studies*, Vol. 14 (1924), pp. 102–103: "There can be little doubt that Rome in her wars of conquest made reckless use of the human material so acquired. . . . The nationality of the slave mattered little so long as his physical strength sufficed for the most exacting work. . . . If such labor killed him prematurely, the Roman master of Republican times might say with the concise brutality of Tacitus [*ca.* 55–120], *uile damnum:* there were plenty more." On the biological annihilation caused by slavery see Fritz M. Heichelheim, *Wirtschaftsgeschichte der Altertums* . . . (2 vols., 1938), Vol. I, p. 402.

[2] See Adolphe Landry, "Quelques aperçus concernant la dépopulation dans l'antiquité greco-romaine," *Revue Historique*, Vol. 177 (1936), p. 18.

[3] See Eugene Albertini, *L'Empire romain* (1929), p. 304. See M. I. Rostovtzeff, *A History of the Ancient World*, Vol. 2, *Rome* (1933), p. 296; also *The Cambridge Ancient History*, Vol. 12, *The Imperial Crisis and Recovery, A.D.* 193–324 (1939), p. 260: "The progressive change in agricultural production from the middle-sized specialized farm to the diffusely organized large-scale unit, the frequent nationalization of landed property, dating from the end of the first century, and the coming into being of the colonate, all testify to such a retrogression. The decline in the achievement in the industrial and technical spheres, and the gradual spread of the οικος-economy on the great estates, point in the same direction. The development of State-controlled commerce and the withdrawal of ships from service crippled free trade, and the intellectual and spiritual deficiency which became marked in cultural life as a whole during the second half of the second century affected the economic life of the community just as profoundly as it did other branches of human activity. Whole regions began to go out of cultivation, not only in Italy and Greece, but also in Spain under Marcus Aurelius. Wars, especially with the Marcomanni and Parthians, military conscription (as in Spain) and the great plague brought by the troops from the East in 165, accentuated the loss of land to cultivation." By permission of the Cambridge University Press.

on, therefore, agricultural production, especially in Italy, declined, and the centers of production moved to the provinces. This change was well advanced by the first quarter of the second century.

The shift of the centers of agricultural production to the provinces intensified a crisis in transportation which had origin in the shortage of labor, for it meant that more and more bulky goods had to be shipped in ever greater quantities longer and longer distances if the concentration of wealth supporting the empire and the ruling classes was to be maintained.[1]

At the same time the mines, especially the gold and silver mines, were worked out. This statement means that with existing tools and means of transport the limit of penetration of the earth was reached.[2] As in agriculture, this situation was immediately reflected in a change of organization of enterprise: large-scale operations with slave labor were replaced by small enterprises, often conducted by a single contractor and a few slaves. Roman methods in mining and metallurgy were not as efficient as those of the Hellenistic age.[3] The effect of the decline of mining was especially serious because it contributed to a failure of the supply of precious metal when trade and diplomacy called for an increase.[4]

The deterioration of technology which was so evident in mining was just as noticeable in agriculture.[5] In fact, the height of Roman agricultural skill was reached in the middle of the first century,

[1] See Sydney A. Reeve, "Ship Evolution and Social Evolution," *The Geographical Review*, Vol. 23 (1933), pp. 61–76, for a discussion of transportation as a factor in the expansion and decline of Rome. Probably by the third century the decreased labor supply (galley slaves) made necessary the use of smaller ships, just at the time when, without cheaper transportation, the products of the outlying provinces could not be brought to Rome.

[2] T. A. Rickard, "The Mining of the Romans in Spain," *Journal of Roman Studies*, Vol. 18 (1928), pp. 129–143. The author makes the point that "ancient mining was the merest grubbing in the ground."

[3] See M. I. Rostovtzeff, *A History of the Ancient World*, Vol. 2, *Rome* (1933), p. 297.

[4] See Oliver Davies, *Roman Mines in Europe* (1935), p. 2: "It is not until the third century that we hear complaints of the failure of Rome's mineral resources. . . . The archaeological evidence suggests that the western empire became bankrupt mainly owing to the failure of its mines, whereas the east survived because it reopened old workings, encouraged further prospecting, and appointed officers to supervise the mining districts." By permission of the Oxford University Press, New York.

[5] "So pressing had the labor problem become, and yet invention never came to the rescue. Farm implements remained what they had been for centuries. Plows were still too light to reduce seriously the labor of deep digging. Aside from olive presses and those for grapes we read of no machines in general use." Reprinted from Frank G. Moore, *The Roman's World* (1936), p. 74, by permission of Columbia University Press. On the relation of slavery, transport costs, and technological decline to the economic crisis see also *The Cambridge Ancient History*, Vol. 12, *The Imperial Crisis and Recovery, A.D.* 193–324 (1939), p. 253.

when Columella, noted previously as the last important writer on agriculture, flourished. The Roman attitude toward technological innovation is illustrated by the story of emperor Tiberius, who had an inventor of a shatterproof, or flexible, glass beheaded on the ground that the marketing of such a product would cause the collapse of all existing values in gold.[1]

If final and conclusive evidence of the economic decline of the Roman Empire is required, it is furnished by Egypt. For this land, to which nature gave an ever renewed soil, abundant water, and eternal sunlight, suffered a steady deterioration of prosperity under Roman management. As far as Egypt is concerned, the cause of economic decline is clearly a failure by the Roman ruling classes to maintain even the simplest conditions required for a prosperous agriculture.[2]

Economic stagnation became apparent throughout the empire as early as the second half of the first century, and from the end of that century one emperor after another made some adjustment to the situation. As noted previously, Nerva last attempted agricultural reform in Italy. Trajan revived the historic method of replenishing the supplies of both capital and labor by conquest; Dacia was seized mainly in order to obtain the product of its gold mines, and the campaign against Parthia was probably projected to obtain plunder. Hadrian turned from these projects to an improved internal administration, especially in the provinces, in

---

[1] C. N. Cochrane, *Christianity and Classical Culture* (1940), p. 143.

[2] J. G. Milne, "The Ruin of Egypt by Roman Mismanagement," *Journal of Roman Studies*, Vol. 17 (1927), pp. 11–12: "The intent of this survey has been to show that the prosperity of Egypt declined constantly under Roman rule from the time of the conquest till the central government lost its grip on the country; and, though the decline was more rapid at some periods than at others, there never was any sign of recovery or even a real check. The burden of supplying the tribute to Rome was first thrown on the upper and middle classes, then, as their resources were exhausted, it was passed on to the peasantry; the administrative changes of Severus were a fresh attempt to put the screw on the middle classes, those of Diocletian to do the like to the peasantry; but all through there was no departure from the general principle of policy, first laid down by Augustus, that Egypt was to be exploited solely for the benefit of the imperial treasury. It should be noted that the circumstances which contributed to the economic decay of the other provinces of the Empire did not affect Egypt. There was no question of the exhaustion of the soil; this is impossible in Egypt so long as the annual floods of the Nile continue, and though a 'bad Nile' may result in a poor crop, and bad Niles may occur in consecutive years, nature has always redressed the balance in due course. . . . Nor was there any permanent diminution of population; the numbers of the fellahin of Egypt respond almost as quickly as those of the lower animals to change in the food supply—there is a high birthrate—if there is sufficient food, the children live—if not, they die; and good government in Egypt, which means plenty of food, has always been accompanied by an increase in the agricultural population."

an effort to broaden the economic and social basis of the imperial structure. Unfortunately, the modes of state and urban expenditure and the habits of private consumption which had been formed under the early empire were not modified, and economy did not come to the aid of improved administration.[1] Under his successors, especially when the labor shortage became more acute as the result of a plague which swept through the cities in the reign of Marcus Aurelius, economic conditions grew steadily worse. And disaster was imminent when Commodus (180–192), extravagant and licentious heir of Marcus Aurelius, made the debasement of the coinage an expedient of imperial finance.

If the root of the economic decline of the Roman Empire is to be found anywhere, it must be found in the economic practices and outlook of the Roman ruling classes, who, because they had acquired wealth by noneconomic methods, could hardly be expected to know how to conserve it or increase it by economic means. They became *rentiers* in whom the desire for profit was choked by the desire for security.[2] They did not understand the function of investment in the production of wealth. They did not recognize the need for technological advance. They understood well how to wring the last penny out of a conquered people and how to adapt existing methods to continuous production. But they did not know how to create new wealth. The best evidence of their failure is the fact that the frontiers at which their armies halted, except in the East, were at the outer limits of the areas in which the native populations had built up sizable and, therefore, seizable surpluses. When confronted with the inevitable consequence of the failure to create new wealth, namely, the decline of production, they could do no more than attempt to hold their share of the decreasing production by resorting to violence and, along with this resort, by a tightening of controls over all kinds of labor—in fine, a progressive regimentation of economic life.

In a word, the decline of Rome may in the last analysis be attributed to the failure of vision on the part of the landed gentry: their willingness during the Republic to betray the free yeomanry for the sake of profitable

---

[1] A. T. Olmstead, "New Testament Times—and Now," *The Journal of the American Oriental Society*, Vol. 53 (1933), p. 322: "Too efficient administration had strangled local initiative and built up a powerful central bureaucracy. Government had exacted an increasing proportion of a declining national income, imposing buildings had frozen capital sorely needed for industry and trade, the resulting technical and artistic deterioration of their wares was becoming obvious. While encouraging urbanization, government had utterly ignored the farming population."

[2] M. I. Rostovtzeff, *A History of the Ancient World*, Vol. 2, *Rome* (1933), p. 294.

estates worked by slaves; and their readiness during the Empire to accept a totalitarian regime for the sake of the prospect of personal safety.[1]

THE CRISIS OF THE ROMAN EMPIRE IN THE THIRD CENTURY.

The emperors who took the foregoing measures were not aware of an approaching crisis. They were merely dealing with problems which disturbed the empire. But the tendencies of these problems are now clear: either they had origin in decreasing economic resources or they contributed to a further decrease of production; consequently, they intensified each other. The symptoms of crisis became more and more numerous under the late Antonines. Military costs mounted. Expenditures on the games and the dole increased. The cities overbuilt. Gold and silver mines went out of production. Additional lands became waste. Depopulation spread. Taxes became more difficult to collect and sometimes were remitted. Disorders were more and more frequent. And the frontiers became less secure. Internal and external dangers grew together.[2]

If at first, by new conquests, administrative changes, and new impositions upon the masses, the ruling classes sought to maintain the incomes they had been receiving, in time, when economic decline had proceeded further, they had either to accept lower incomes or to prey upon one another. In this circumstance the militarized section of the imperial ruling classes turned on the senators and the privileged urban groups. In other words, the knights, the bureaucrats, and the armies and their commanders attempted to hold their economic position at the expense of the two other wealth-holding groups. This attempt began with the advent of Septimius Severus (193–211), a commander of armies in Africa, Pannonia, and Illyria. He came to power after the failure of the senate to become a rallying point of resistance to the praetorian cohorts who put the emperorship to auction and sold it for 25,000 sesterces per man. He bluntly stated his policy: "Be of one mind, enrich the soldiers; trouble about nothing else." He put it into operation by levying heavy indemnities on towns

[1] Tenney Frank, editor, *An Economic Survey of Ancient Rome*, Vol. 5, *Rome and Italy of the Empire* (1940), p. 304. By permission of the Johns Hopkins Press, Baltimore.

[2] On the Roman Empire in the third century see H. M. D. Parker, *A History of the Roman World from A.D. 138 to 337* (1935); see also M. Platnauer, *The Life and Reign of the Emperor Septimius Severus* (1918); J. Hasebroeck, *Untersuchen zur Geschichte des Kaisers Septimius Severus* (1921); J. Stuart Hay, *The Amazing Emperor Heliogabalus* (1911); R. V. N. Hopkins, *Life of Alexander Severus* (1907); I. J. Manley, *Effects of the Germanic Invasions on Gaul, 234–284 A.D.* (1934).

that resisted him and by confiscating estates throughout the empire. He favored the knights who had military training. The senators were excluded from administrative posts, and deputy governors of equestrian rank were sent into the senatorial provinces. Many imperial officials now came from the eastern provinces.

Under Alexander Severus (222–235), who was influenced by his mother, a policy of rapprochement with the senate and re-trenchment of expenditures was followed, with good effects. Its objective was to win the support of the Roman poor citizens. Many new baths were built, the doles were well administered, and a scheme to improve the supply services of the cities was initiated. At the same time the collegia were brought under state supervision. A debasement of the coinage and economy at the court provided funds for these expenditures. When difficulties on the frontiers forced Severus to undertake a campaign, he encountered insubordination and was assassinated in a riot. This event was the signal for the struggle of the armies to control the principate. The senate resisted the military usurpations, and for a time it seemed that the ancient body might recover its once powerful position. But it could never command strength enough to check the provincial armies.

The crisis then shook the empire to its foundations.

Internal disorders everywhere broke out. Brigands—bankrupt farmers, ruined peasants, slave shepherds, and veteran legionnaires—pillaged far and wide in Gaul, Italy, Sicily, northern Africa, and Asia Minor. In 235 a robber band of six hundred men swept through Italy. "If masters treated slaves better," they said, "there would be fewer robbers." In 238 there was civil war in northern Africa. In 268 the Gallic peasants raided the cities. In the next year the slaves of Sicily rose in revolt. From 259 to 269 Gaul was ruled by a provincial emperor, and Spain and Britain recognized his authority.

The frontiers were broken. The Goths pushed down the Danube and, for a time, raided Asia Minor. The Alamanni, another Teutonic people, also crossed the Danube. In 251 the Goths defeated and killed emperor Decius. Then the Franks crossed the Rhine, raiding

---

THE WALLS OF ROME

Until the invasions and social disorders of the third century, Rome, outside the ancient walls of Servius Tullius, was an open city. Then the need for protection led to the building of the last and most enduring of the city's defenses—the walls of Aurelian (270–275).

Ewing Galloway

THE WALLS OF ROME

(For descriptive legend see opposite page)

as far as Spain in 257 and 275. Saxon pirates terrorized the English Channel. In 267 another Teutonic people penetrated Greece as far as ancient Sparta. Meanwhile the Berber people of northern Africa raided the frontiers, and the Sassanian kings, the new rulers of Iran, pushed into Mesopotamia. In 259 the emperor Valerian was captured and his army destroyed. From this time the Sassanian threat along the eastern frontier was never absent.

Insurrection and war necessarily accelerated economic decline. Bandits multiplied. Men fled from the towns. The labor shortage became more acute. Depopulation followed in the wake of pestilence. A reluctance to have children became widespread. In fact, the population, it is estimated, fell about one-third, from about seventy to about fifty millions.[1] Because the expenditures of the state were not reduced, the raising of revenue became more and more difficult. The burdens of the curial class were increased. Their fortunes became liable for deficiencies in the tax collections. The maintenance of imperial service became steadily more burdensome. At the same time the exclusion of the senators from the army gave the knights a monopoly of army commands and, as a result, the sole approach to supreme power, since the army now designated the emperor. Accompanying these changes were the multiplication of secret agents, changes in criminal procedure unfavorable to the old wealth-holding classes, the displacement of urban authorities by imperial officials, and the suppression of urban liberties. Like the soldiers the bureaucrats, *i.e.*, the personnel of the emperor's administrative staff, augmented both their power and their incomes at the expense of the old privileged groups.

These changes reacted on social organization in many ways. The peasants, goaded by increasing demands for labor and products, revolted against the landlords. But circumstances were not favorable to their success. Because the imperial bureaucrats, as they concentrated their attention more and more on obtaining revenue for the state, winked at new agrarian abuses, the landlords frequently were able to turn their estates into little principalities. In fact, the landlords, no longer able to collect their incomes in money, took up residence on their estates and lived by consuming the products of the field. Thus a natural economy slowly displaced the money economy in rural areas. By combining management of production with powers of government on their estates the landlords forced the peasants into a position of greater

[1] *The Cambridge Ancient History*, Vol. 12, *The Imperial Crisis and Recovery*, A.D. 193–324 (1939), pp. 267–268.

subservience and made themselves quite as much petty lords as property owners. At the same time suffering in the towns increased and life everywhere became harsher and cruder. The food supply became more and more insecure, and the plague—brought by soldiers returning from the campaigns against Persia—and earthquakes added to the distress. Although some of the free workers deserted their crafts and returned to the land, most of them, like many of the curials, remained in the decaying towns.

THE REORGANIZATION OF THE ROMAN EMPIRE: DIOCLETIAN.

As evidenced by the fact that between 235 and 285 only two of the twenty-six men who won the principate died a natural death, the emperors of the third century held precarious power. At one time there were thirty claimants to supreme power. But in spite of intrigue and assassination these emperors beat off invasion, suppressed rebellion, and moved slowly toward a reorganization of the state.

The principle of this reorganization was absolutism; its basis was a reconstructed army. The emperor, no longer regarded as a citizen, became the repository of abstract sovereignty. As such, he was above the law. At the same time, in line with the militarization of the state, he exchanged the costume of a senator for that of a general. The reconstruction of the army was accomplished in terms of the social and cultural changes that were affecting almost every phase of Greco-Roman life.[1] The heavier economic burdens imposed on the peasants necessitated the finding of a new source of man power for the army; for this reason provinces where men were most numerous, partly because new lands were recently exploited and partly because they received barbarians from beyond the frontiers, became the most important for military purposes. Foremost among these provinces were Illyria and Pannonia, from which, indeed, came the emperors that reorganized the state. The breakdown in transport weakened the influence of the legions of Syria, Gaul, and Africa in imperial politics. More important, however, than the changed geographical basis of military power was the introduction of new armor and tactics. The source of these innovations was the Sassanian heavy cavalry, which had demonstrated its superiority over the Roman infantry and auxiliaries. In the year 260 Gallienus (259–268) created a mounted army. Stationed at Milan, it could move quickly into

[1] André Alföldi, "La grand crise du monde romain au IIIe siècle," *L'Antiquité classique,* Vol. 7 (1938), pp. 1–18.

Italy, the Danube lands, or Gaul. Mobility and heavy armor made it superior to local forces organized in the traditional manner. After restoring imperial power in Gaul and Syria, Aurelian (270–275) carried further the military reorganization and projected the transformation of the principate into an absolute monarchy.

Diocletian (284–305), final victor in the struggle of the armies and their commanders, carried out this project. He ignored the senate and abandoned the old practice, still repeated as a matter of form, of electing the magistrates. The emperor was absolute, the sanctity of the state resided in his person, and his decrees—supplanting legislation—became sacred. To give the new regime prestige and splendor many practices of the Persian court were introduced. The emperor wore the diadem—symbol of eternity—purple robes, red boots, and a ring upon the big toe. All who came into his presence were required to prostrate themselves. Eunuchs ministered to his personal needs. Thus the principate became the *dominate*.

In order to supervise government more closely Diocletian associated with himself a second Augustus, Maximianus, and with each emperor a second official, almost a vice-emperor, who bore the title "Caesar." The two Augusti and the two Caesars shared a single power. Actually, however, Diocletian, as senior Augustus, had final authority, and order depended on his power to command his colleagues. The device of two Augusti each aided by a Caesar was meant to solve the problem of succession, for as each Caesar succeeded an Augustus he, in turn, selected a colleague. Diocletian also had in mind the practice—in fact he acted on it—of the Augusti resigning after holding office for twenty years. Beneath the "four sovereign gods" was a complete hierarchy of bureaucrats, consisting of the heads of four prefectures, twelve dioceses, and about one hundred provinces. The lower ranks of the hierarchy were made up of uniform grades of local officials. Each official was completely responsible to his immediate superior. This system of officials, whose members bore military titles, was known as a *militia*.

Financial reforms stabilized the economic support of the new regime. By means of a survey of the land, taxation was assessed on the basis of productivity, good land paying more than fair land and fair land more than poor land. Landowners were required to render accounts directly to the imperial treasury. Most of the taxes were paid in kind. The currency was restored, but the scarcity of metal prevented a widespread circulation of coin. An effort, which quickly failed, was made to increase production and prevent speculation by fixing prices. The collegia were strictly regulated. The coloni, now undoubtedly bound to the land on many estates, were closely supervised. Since all classes of citizens were hedged about with vexatious restrictions, the social structure assumed more and more the features of a caste system.

A unified army under the command of the emperor replaced the provincial legions, which, along with the auxiliaries, now disappeared. A new officer class, based on the independent landowners, superseded the old knights, who were confined to the lower ranks. The Praetorian Guard, long a disorderly element, was reduced in number. Heavily armed horsemen and archers, important elements in the Sassanian armies, became permanent parts of the new imperial force.

To protect this regime Diocletian initiated a fierce persecution of the Christians. The principle behind this action was undoubtedly the ancient belief that the stability and prosperity of the state were the gift of supernatural forces. If the state had decayed, was that not a sign that the ancient gods of Rome had deserted it? If the state was to be restored, was it not necessary to recover this support? Actually the emperor seems to have aimed to root the Christians out of the new classes holding property and power.

Diocletian's reforms merely brought into the open developments that had long been under way. Absolutism became a fact. Uniform administration was achieved. Law became the decree of a sacred sovereign. The civil establishment was approximated to a military hierarchy. The old national distinctions disappeared. Everything was Roman, but Roman had become oriental. "Thanks to the reforms of Diocletian, the Roman Empire emerged with renewed life from the crisis of the third century. From this date it became a vast *cosmopolis* of different races governed by the Asiatic despotism of four sovereign gods, subject to an innumerable bureaucracy depending on these sovereigns without distinction of nationality or social rank."[1] Thus the regime which had originated in the struggle of the Roman social classes for the possession of the wealth of the Mediterranean Basin was transformed into a regimented poverty. The regime was, of course, the ancient-oriental monarchy based on peasant-village masses having a very low capacity to produce wealth and ruled by allied military and

[1] Guglielmo Ferrero, *The Ruin of Ancient Civilization* (1921), p. 108. G. P. Putnam's Sons, New York.

priestly groups.[1] Diocletian's work was incomplete because he failed to solve the problem of the alliance of these ruling classes in terms of the religious changes that had accompanied the crisis; this failure was the opportunity of Constantine (306–337).

[1] See Fritz M. Heichelheim, *Wirtschaftsgeschichte des Altertums* . . . (2 vols., 1938), Vol. I, pp. 767–778.

Chapter XVI

THE ELABORATION OF THE WESTERN
CULTURAL TRADITION IN
ROMAN TIMES

〈〈〈·〈〈〈·〉〉〉·〉〉〉

By widening the area of social interaction the Roman conquest of the Mediterranean Basin and western Europe carried further the cultural tendencies of the Hellenistic age, particularly as they moved toward the creation of a cosmopolitan culture. Rome built a political regime suited to this culture, but the culture itself belonged to many peoples, among whom, of course, the Greeks were the most important. But local cultures did not disappear. Greco-Roman culture was peculiarly the possession of the thousand or more cities and towns which were the centers of Roman administration, and its social bearers were mainly the members of the aristocratic wealth-holding classes who resided there. In the second century, when Roman rule was at its height, there were three clearly marked culture areas within the empire: (1) the Greco-oriental, or Hellenized, East, (2) the Latin West—Italy, Africa, and Spain, and (3) the Gallic West—Gaul and Britain. And beneath the stratum of literate culture in both the East and the West persisted the ancient local cultures—mainly peasant-village in character—of the conquered peoples. In the fourth century, under the reorganized Roman Empire, the forces of cosmopolitanism reached their climax and found expression, as will be described subsequently, in the Christian reorientation of the Western cultural tradition. The Roman Empire was little more than the instrument that guided these forces to fruition.[1]

---

[1] The best short survey of Roman culture is Frank G. Moore, *The Roman's World* (1936). Albert Grenier, *The Roman Spirit in Religion, Thought, and Art* (1926), is a statement of the Roman outlook as expressed intellectually and artistically. Interesting commentaries on Roman culture are two works by Grant Showerman, *Eternal Rome: The city and its peoples from the earliest times* (2 vols., 1924) and *Rome and the Romans: A survey and interpretation* (1921). Cyril Bailey, editor, *The Legacy of Rome* (1924), is a discussion of

THE URBAN QUALITY OF GRECO-ROMAN CULTURE

The literary, intellectual, and artistic elements of Greco-Roman culture, as well as its political and economic organization, were identified with cities. "It would scarcely be an exaggeration to say that the history of Greco-Roman civilization is the history of cities."[1] Indeed, the great work of the Roman Empire, based as it was on the interests of urban groups, consisted of a stabilization and extension of urban life throughout the Mediterranean Basin. In the eastern Mediterranean area the work was mainly the matter of putting an end to the revolutionary movements that had threatened the Greek and Hellenistic cities. In Italy it was the organization of urban patterns among an ancient peasant population. In the western area it involved the founding of new cities among the peoples still at the tribal level of social organization. And Greco-Roman culture endured only so long as these cities retained their historic social structures; it disappeared when changes weakened the urban ruling classes, which were the carriers of its literary, intellectual, and artistic elements.

The great structures whose ruins give historic grandeur to a modern Rome that staggers with the memory of the past they represent suggest the fundamental patterns which, identified by buildings repeating their purpose if not their splendor in other cities, both large and small, in every part of the empire, were the characteristic elements of Greco-Roman culture. The Forum was the center of public life. About it were shops, markets, halls of justice—basilicas—and offices of the bureaucrats who really governed, and near by were the palaces of those who held power—the emperor and his associates. The Pantheon was originally the temple of local gods. Other temples, dedicated to the Divine Julius, Apollo, the Great Mother, and Fortuna, testified not only to the sources of imperial strength—genius, courage, fecundity,

---

Rome's contributions to Western culture; Cyril Bailey, editor, *The Mind of Rome* (1926), is a useful compilation of selections from Roman writers. W. G. Greene, *The Achievement of Rome* (1934), evaluates various elements of Roman culture. For a detailed topical treatment of Roman culture see Georg Grupp, *Kulturgeschichte der römischen Kaiserzeit* (2 vols., 1904).

The standard reference work for the history of classical culture is Pauly's *Real-Encyclo-pädie der classischen Altertums-Wissenschaft* (1894-1938, 19 vols. and several supplements).

[1] A. H. M. Jones, *The Greek City from Alexander to Justinian* (1940), p. 299. Oxford University Press.

THE PORTA OF OCTAVIA

Around this gate, which was built by Augustus in honor of his sister, Octavia, were clustered museums and libraries where poets and scholars gathered to study the works of their predecessors, both Greek and Roman. These institutions formed the intellectual center of Rome.

The Birmingham Art Gallery

THE PORTA OF OCTAVIA
(For descriptive legend see opposite page)

and luck—but also to the social amalgamation which had produced Greco-Roman culture. About the Portico of Octavia were grouped museums and libraries where artists, poets, and philosophers found the works of their illustrious predecessors. The first triumphal arches celebrated the victories of Roman commanders, but in time they were used for other commemorative and even decorative purposes. Among the many that graced imperial Rome those remaining are credited to the emperors Titus, Septimius Severus, and Constantine. Constantine's is decorated with sculptures from Trajan's arch. The Colosseum, the Amphitheatre, and the great baths recall the amusements which played such a part in the life of the populace. The walls, the aqueducts, the sewers, and the roads testify to the political and economic organization that supported urban life.[1]

Altogether these structures constitute an architectural rendering of the institutions, outlook, and values of Greco-Roman culture. They are even now beautiful and were in their day no doubt a fitting setting for a life of power, ease, and luxury. Indeed, they are the monuments of a culture which made an art of consumption but considered unworthy any effort to understand production. In this connection it is pertinent to emphasize that the tradition of rural life founded by the representatives of Greco-Roman culture was that of the gentleman landlord, not that of the working peasant. Its essential element was an amplification of the life of ease and luxury of the urban aristocrat with the pleasant aspects of life in the country. "If you read—read every ancient writer you like—you will find that life, really civilized life, was a city life."[2]

THE DEVELOPMENT OF LATIN LITERATE LEARNING UNDER GREEK INFLUENCE

Under Roman rule Greek literature, education, philosophy, and science were carried west, where, mainly in Latin renderings, they became the basis of the later intellectual development of western, if not central and eastern, Europe.

[1] On the monuments of Rome see A. W. Van Buren, *Ancient Rome as Revealed by Recent Discoveries* (1936); Léon Homo, *La Rome antique: Histoire-guide des monuments* (*ca.* 1921); Giuseppe Lugli, *The Classical Monuments of Rome* (*ca.* 1929); S. B. Platner, *A Topographical Dictionary of Rome* (1929); I. A. Richmond, *The City Wall of Imperial Rome* (1930).

On other Roman cities see R. C. Carrington, *Pompeii* (1936); C. G. Ellaby, *Pompeii and Herculaneum* (1930); Mattes della Corte, *Pompeii, the new Excavations* (1927); E. G. Barker, *Buried Herculaneum* (1908); Louis Barré, *Herculaneum et Pompéi: Recueil général des peintures, bronzes, mosaiques, etc.* (8 vols., 1870–1872).

[2] M. I. Rostovtzeff, "The Prehistoric Cities and the Cities of the Ancient Orient," in Richard T. Ely, editor, *Urban Land Economics* (1922), p. 19.

THE MOVEMENT OF GREEK LEARNING TO ROME AND ITALY.

The conquest of Magna Graecia was the decisive event in the development of Latin learning.[1] Following the fall of Tarentum in 272 B.C., Greek scholars, mainly as slaves, found their way to Rome, and there they became the instructors of the Romans in literature and other fields of learning. One, the most important of these early Greek teachers, Livius Andronicus (*ca.* 284–204 B.C.), translated the *Odyssey* and several Greek plays into a coarse Latin verse. Another of them turned a Greek history of Rome into Latin.

Latin literary activity along Greek lines began toward the close of the First Punic War. Naevius (*ca.* 264–194 B.C.) wrote an epic poem and experimented with comedy and tragedy. Ennius (*ca.* 239–169 B.C.), known as the "father of Latin literature," wrote an epic in Greek hexameters and composed Latin comedies and tragedies with Greek plots. Plautus (*ca.* 254–184 B.C.) was the first poet to use native materials for plots and characterizations; many of his comedies turn about the love of an aristocratic youth for a lowborn maiden. About 200 B.C. Latin prose reached a new level in a treatise on the law, which remained the core of Roman legal learning for almost two centuries.[2]

In the second century B.C. the Roman assimilation of Greek literary forms and intellectual materials went on rapidly. During the Second Punic War the Roman authorities sent a mission to Greece to consult the oracle of Delphi. When Rome intervened in Greece, ambassadors and hostages came to the city on the Tiber and after them quickly followed craftsmen, artists, traders, promoters, physicians, and quacks. Poor and needy Greeks taught the

---

[1] See page 522 for a discussion of the origin of Latin literate learning. On the early growth of Latin literature see *The Cambridge Ancient History*, Vol. 8, *Rome and the Mediterranean, 218–133 B.C.* (1930), Chap. XIII, "The Beginnings of Latin Literature," and Vol. 9, *The Roman Republic 133–44 B.C.* (1932), Chap. XVIII, "Literature in the Age of Cicero." See also R. S. Conway, *The Making of Latin* (1923); B. L. Ullman, *Ancient Writing and Its Influence* (1932); Tenney Frank, *Life and Literature in the Roman Republic* (1930); F. G. Kenyon, *Books and Readers in Ancient Greece and Rome* (1932); C. E. Boyd, *Public Libraries and Literary Culture in Ancient Rome* (1915); F. W. Hall, *A Companion to Classical Texts* (1913); F. F. Abbott, *The Common People of Ancient Rome: Studies of Roman life and literature* (1911); and Wilhelm Kroll, *Die Kultur der ciceronischen Zeit* (2 vols., 1933), especially Vol. 2.

[2] For the general history of Latin literature see John Edwin Sandys, *A History of Classical Scholarship* (3 vols., 3d ed., 1921) Vol. 1, Book III, *Latin Scholarship in the Roman Age;* J. Wight Duff, *A Literary History of Rome* (1936); H. J. Rose, *A Handbook of Latin Literature from the Earliest Times to the Death of St. Augustine* (1936); H. N. Fowler, *A History of Roman Literature* (1937); Wilhelm S. Teuffel, *History of Roman Literature* (2 vols., 1900); and Alfred Kappelmacher and Mauriz Schuster, *Die Literatur der Romer bis zur Karolingerzeit* (1934). See also J. A. Nairn, *Authors of Rome* (1924).

Romans every branch of learning, from rhetoric to tightrope walking. Each Roman political advance eastward was followed not only
by a further migration of Greeks and Hellenized orientals westward
but also by the introduction of more eastern slaves and the seizure
of additional Greek art objects. By 146 B.C. the gardens and temples
of Rome were filled with bronzes, marbles, and terra cottas
plundered from Greek cities. The effects of this increasing diffusion
of Greek cultural material was soon evident in almost every aspect
of Roman public and private life, particularly in trading and
aristocratic circles.

The Romans first came in contact with Greek science during
the siege of Syracuse, when a number of Archimedes' devices were
used against them; Scipio, in driving the Carthaginians from Spain,
made use of his knowledge of Greek science in naval warfare.
Ennius, who first wrote Latin in Greek hexameters, introduced
the philosophy of Skepticism. The first Latin philosophical work,
written a little before 100 B.C., dealt with Epicureanism. Stoicism
reached Rome in the second century B.C. and soon spread widely
in the growing literate group. At the center of this group was
Scipio Aemilianus (*ca.* 185–129 B.C.), the leading literary patron
of the age. Among the scholars in his circle the most notable was
Polybius (*ca.* 204–122 B.C.), who wrote in Greek a truly great
history of the Punic Wars.[1] The most significant Latin author was
Terence (*ca.* 190–159 B.C.), neither a Greek nor a Roman but
probably a Phoenician, who, brought to Rome from Carthage as
a slave, first gave Latin literature formality and polish; his works,
breathing the spirit of the new Greek comedy, provided intellectual
stimulus for the new literary circle.[2]

The growing enthusiasm for Greek culture aroused a reaction
which, headed by the elder Cato, brought the expulsion of the
philosophers in 161 B.C. Cato upheld the traditional virtues against
the newfangled foreign ideas and practices which, if adopted, he
feared would cost Rome its political dominion. As the author of
the first Latin history of Rome and a treatise on agriculture, he
was the founder of Latin prose as a medium of general intellectual
discourse.[3]

But the times were in favor of the new learning and manners,
so that by the opening of the first century B.C. the Roman nobility

---

[1] W. R. Paton, *Polybius, The Histories* (6 vols., 1922–1927).

[2] Gilbert Norwood, *Plautus and Terence* (1932); Paul Nixon, *Plautus* (5 vols., 1937);
and John Sargeaunt, *Terence* (2 vols., 1931).

[3] See R. E. Smith, "Cato Censorius," *Greece & Rome*, Vol. 9 (1940), pp. 150–165.

was almost entirely Greek in education and taste. Literary learning was greatly influenced by this development. Accius (*ca.* 170–90 B.C.) was the last and finest of the tragedians. Lucilius (*ca.* 180–103 B.C.) developed the most original form of Latin literature—satire; with him it ceased to be merely a mixture of this and that and became a witty, biting, even serious criticism of social, political, and intellectual affairs. After Stilo (*ca.* 154–74 B.C.) began to give lessons dealing with Latin literature, grammar, rhetoric, and etymology were quickly recognized as fields of learning quite as worthy of study as law, history, and philosophy. The Gracchi developed oratory, ultimately the most popular literary form, to a new height of appeal. By 100 B.C. almost every branch of learning could be studied in Latin.

The complete victory of eastern cultural materials in Rome followed the first century B.C. conquests of Asia Minor, Syria, and Egypt. Sulla's veterans introduced tastes for Hellenistic luxuries, such as scented waters, sharp wines, spiced foods, and soft, almost diaphanous, cloths. Heavy silver plate became a mark of social prestige. Pompey and Caesar imitated the Hellenistic kings. Roman authors and scholars aimed no higher than imitating Greek models. In fact, among educated aristocrats Greek became a second tongue, and they copied the Greek habit of letter writing. Roman deities were given Greek names and features. Roman mansions were designed and furnished in eastern style. The Roman dandy was an imitation of the Greek fop, and the Roman gentleman a model of Greek urbanity. Roman politicians even dared to believe that Rome was defending the Greek conception of liberty against the practice of Asiatic despotism. In fine, as Horace, one of the wisest Romans, said, the Greeks had conquered Rome.

ROMAN EDUCATION.

Roman education, rooted in religion and law, was from the earliest times traditional. At first, when its only method of teaching was repetition, its subject matter consisted mainly of old saws, ballads, rhythmical tales, and bits of history and law. Contact with the Greeks of southern Italy led to the addition of selections from the poets and orators. In the second century B.C., when rhetoric was introduced, declamation became the standard exercise of the classroom. Caesar and Octavianus delivered set funeral orations at the age of twelve; Cicero and Octavianus practiced oratory daily even after they became prominent public figures. When the victory of Octavianus put an end to the political struggles, the orators, along with other discordant elements, were quieted. Then rhetoric became the chief form of decorative learning for the aristocratic classes, and it soon developed in the schools of declamation, the ornateness of which made verbosity—"verbal honey-balls"—a mark of social, if not intellectual, achievement. Among the leaders in this development was Seneca the rhetorician, the father of Seneca the philosopher; he elaborated the style of speaking by introducing epigrams, antitheses, and picturesque digressions, and refined the form of address by formulating the modulations of the voice and the movements of the body, indicating even the proper times to step to the right and to the left.

The imperial schools, which served mostly the sons of the urban oligarchs, were of three grades: (1) the primary, taught by a *literator*, usually a slave or a freedman; (2) the secondary, taught by a *grammaticus;* and (3) the advanced, taught by a *rhetor*. In the primary school the boys learned to read and write. In the secondary school, which they entered at about the age of twelve, they studied literature—especially the poets, Vergil and Horace—and the related subjects, grammar and syntax. Prose authors, notably Cicero and, to some extent, Livy, were studied in the last year in the secondary school, when instruction in history, the traditional religion, and arithmetic were combined with literary studies. Students were promoted to the advanced school at the age of fifteen. There rhetoric, as a preparation for the practice of law and politics, was the all-embracing subject. The poets and orators were studied and imitated. Those who did not advance beyond the teaching of the *grammaticus* probably found their intellectual stimulation as adults mainly in pantomimes and gladiatorial shows.[1]

The emperors and the municipalities founded schools, especially for the study of rhetoric, and supported them with grants of money. Vespasian established various kinds of schools in the western provinces, and Antoninus Pius regulated the number of physicians and teachers the various-sized cities could maintain. The small city was allowed five physicians, three Sophists, and three grammarians, while the capital of a province was permitted ten physicians, five Sophists, and five grammarians. A notable aspect of this development of schools was the rise of centers of learning in Gaul—Massilia—and in Spain—Saragossa. And even faraway Britain had schools of its own. Northern Africa, of course, had received the elements of an eastern educational system in Cartha-

[1] See J. B. Poynton, "Roman Education," *Greece & Rome*, Vol. 4 (1934), pp. 1–12.

ginian times. The ordinary grammarian was overworked and underpaid, but a "prima donna," like Polemon (fl. *ca.* 120–150), for example, accumulated great wealth. He was the author of the earliest treatise on physiognomy. The public lecture was a favorite form of amusement among the sophisticated literates of the second century.

Cato the Younger and Cicero had great influence upon the development of Roman education. Its ideal was the creation of a country gentleman who, having a knowledge of literature and law, would be a good public servant. Because it aimed at moral as well as intellectual instruction, it emphasized literature, rhetoric, and philosophy and neglected science. Cicero was responsible for dropping mathematics, which played such an important part in Plato's system of instruction, from the curriculum of the Roman schools. Physical speculations were also denied a place in the course of study, which of course did not contain economics, statistics, sociology, or psychology because the subjects were nonexistent. Special schools were maintained by the state for the study of medicine. After the first century Greek methods in their worst forms of sophistry and the Asianic style of rhetoric were supreme in Roman education, and as time went on it became more and more traditional both in manner of instruction and in subject matter. The full effect of this type of education in literary style was evident in the literature of the third century, when such absurdities as picture poems (*i.e.*, lines and words arranged to form a picture of some object) and poems having as many lines as each verse had letters were popular. The blight of thought resulting from the popularity of the Asianic style of rhetoric was most completely evident in the fourth century practice of writing scientific treatises in florid verse.

Although a knowledge of reading was more widely diffused under the Roman Empire than at any other time before the nineteenth century, the Romans were a speaking, not a reading, people. Their distinctive contribution to education was that combination of literary knowledge and philosophical generalization, brightened by quaint observations from experience, which so long characterized the Western cultivated gentleman.[1]

[1] On Roman schools and education see A. S. Wilkins, *Roman Education* (1905); A. O. Gwynn, *Roman Education from Cicero to Quintilian* (1926); E. Jullien, *Les Professeurs de littérature dans l'ancienne Rome* (1886); H. O. Taylor, *Ancient Ideals: A study of intellectual and spiritual growth from early times to the establishment of Christianity* (2d ed., rev., 2 vols., 1913); F. P. Graves, *A History of Education before the Middle Ages* (1909).

LITERATURE IN ROMAN TIMES

Although the Romans produced a true literature, it is not unfair to hold that the typical product of Latin literate learning was a verbose composition designed to impress its audience by sound and gesture rather than by logic and depth of thought. Except in rare instances Roman intellectuals were shallow thinkers and second-rate imitators of bad Greek models. After the founding of the empire freedom of expression was greatly circumscribed, especially about all matters of current political interest. There is no clear evidence that a censorship of books existed in Rome.

THE GOLDEN AGE OF LATIN LITERATURE.

The last decades of the republic and the first decades of the empire were the golden age of Latin literature. The achievements of these times were based on the full mastery of Greek intellectual methods and the utilization of Greek literary devices.[1]

Each of the great figures of the last period of the republic gave some part of Greek learning a Latin rendering.

Varro (*ca.* 116–28 B.C.) was an encyclopaedist whose works covered many subjects—law, history, grammar, geography, botany, and agriculture, among others. Much of our knowledge of ancient Rome is based on his historical and archaeological writings. He had a fine feeling for nature and was one of the greatest authorities on farming—the traditional Roman occupation.

Cicero was the finest exemplar of the Roman assimilation of Greek culture. His intellectual outlook—thoroughly Greek—is well expressed in the apothegm "We who seek hypotheses are well prepared to refute them without prejudice and to be refuted without resentment." Besides the oration, of which he was the supreme master, his writings consisted mainly of letters and treatises on various phases of Greek learning. His *On the Nature of the Gods* and *On Duties* are among the best sources of our knowledge of Greek religious and ethical thought. His ethical principles, derived from Posidonius, were Stoic. The role of his works, which were studied both for their literary style and for their philosophical content, in the subsequent development of Western literate learning was so important that he is commonly recognized as second only to Aristotle among the contributors to the intellectual content of the Western cultural tradition. The grace of his literary style and

---

[1] For a summary discussion see *The Cambridge Ancient History*, Vol. 10, *The Augustan Empire*, 44 B.C.–A.D. 70 (1934), Chap. XVI, "The Literature of the Golden Age."

the urbanity of his thought entitle him to first place among Roman intellectuals.[1]

Lucretius (*ca.* 96–55 B.C.) was an apostle of Epicureanism. His poem *On the Nature of Things*, written to free men from superstition, was an exposition of the philosophy of atomism and its ethical and aesthetic implications:

> Look where the sun
> Through some dark corner pours his brightest beams,
> A thousand little bodies you will see
> Mix in the rays, and there forever fight
> Arrayed in mimic troops, no pause they give
> But meet and part again, nor ever cease.
>
> *   *   *   *   *
>
> For rising Beings still the old pursue,
> And take their place, old die, and frame the new:
> But nothing sinks to Hell, and sulphurous flames,
> The Seeds remain to make the future frames:
> All which shall yield to Fate as well as thou,
> And Things fell heretofore e'en just as now,
> And still decaying things shall new produce;
> For Life's not given to possess, but use.

The poem, probably the greatest philosophical scientific treatise in verse in any language, expressed a faith in the pursuit of knowledge as a means of release from distress as well as the conviction that nature does not know the distinctions men make among themselves:

> Fevers do not sooner quit your body if you toss on embroidered sheets than if you lie on a plebeian blanket.[2]

Catullus (*ca.* 84–54 B.C.) imitated Alexandrian verse, writing passionately of love, friendship, and patriotism. No one has dealt more successfully than he with the pleasures and pains of passing

[1] J. C. Rolfe, *Cicero and His Influence* (1925); G. C. Richards, *Cicero: A study* (1935); Herbert Eulenberg, *Cicero: Der Rechtsanwalt, Redner, Denker und Staatsmann sein Leben und Wesen* (1932); and Wilhelm Kroll, *Die Kultur der ciceronischen Zeit* (2 vols., 1933). Of Cicero's several works see H. Rackham, *Cicero, De Natura Deorum* (1933); C. W. Keyes, *Cicero, De Republica, De Legibus* (1928); W. Glynn Williams, *Cicero, The Letters to His Friends* (1927); E. O. Winstedt, *Cicero, Letters to Atticus* (1928); L. H. Greenwood, *Cicero, The Verrine Orations* (2 vols., 1928); E. S. Shuckburgh, *Cicero, Two Essays on Old Age and Friendship* (1927).

[2] A. P. Sinker, *Introduction to Lucretius* (1937); E. E. Sikes, *Lucretius, Poet and Philosopher* (1936); R. C. Trevelyan, *Lucretius, De Rerum Natura* (1937); John Masson, *Lucretius, Epicurean and Poet* (2 vols., 1907–1909); and G. D. Hadzsits, *Lucretius and His Influence* (1935).

hours. With Caesar Roman prose attained a clarity and flexibility reminiscent of the best narrative work of Xenophon. The *Commentaries on the Gallic War*, written about 51 B.C., was a political pamphlet designed to advance its author's interests in Rome. Sallust (*ca.* 86–34 B.C.) was more under the influence of Greek rhetoric than Caesar. His histories of Catiline's conspiracy and Caesar's war against Pompey were strongly biased against the senatorial oligarchy.

The writers of the early empire were both more nationalistic and more complacent than their republican predecessors. As propagandists of the new regime they asserted that the Romans, the equals of any other people in the world, had performed for these people the supreme task, namely, the achievement of unity. Augustus was not the conqueror but the defender of humanity.

Vergil (*ca.* 70–19 B.C.) is known as the poet laureate of the Augustan age. His *Georgics* embodied an understanding love of nature, a vibrant patriotism, and a deep religious feeling. The *Aeneid*—the Roman counterpart of the Homeric poems—idealized Augustus and the empire. Vergil believed that an all-wise Providence guided the destinies of Rome, giving through its dominion law, order, and peace to a harassed world:

> God's temple is the earth, the sea, the air,
> The sky, the pure in heart. Why seek we further?
> All thou dost see, all thou dost feel is love.[1]

Horace (*ca.* 65–8 B.C.) revealed the Romans at their best. His *Odes*, following Greek models, depicted the Roman aristocrat who, having won the overlordship of the world, gave up violence and arrogance for urbanity, moderation, refinement, and contentment. His *Satires*, which often described the seamy side of life, have never been excelled for honest realism and understanding of human weaknesses. Among the many tales found in the satires is the tale of the country mouse lured to a life of luxury by a city cousin.[2]

Ovid (*ca.* 43 B.C.–A.D. 18) described the aristocrat at ease, seeking amusement. His poems expressed the idle passion, the yearning for excitement, and the sense of worth of mere personal

[1] Tenney Frank, *Vergil* (1922); T. R. Glover, *Vergil* (1924); J. W. Mackail, *Vergil's Works: The Aeneid, Eclogues, and Georgics* (1934); H. Rushton Fairclough, *Vergil* (2 vols., 1937).
[2] J. F. D'Alton, *Horace and His Age* (1917); T. R. Glover, *Horace: A return to his allegiance* (1932); C. E. Bennett, *Horace, The Odes and Epodes* (1934); H. Rushton Fairclough, *Horace, Satires, Epistles, and Ars Poetica* (1936).

From EUGÈNE ALBERTINI, GEORGES MARCAIS, *and* GEORGES YVER, *L'Afrique du Nord
française dans l'histoire* (1937)

VIRGIL WRITING THE ANEID

No portrait statue of Virgil is known. This mosaic was found at Hadrumetum, near
Carthage, in northern Africa. Mosaics were very popular in Roman imperial times.

desires that characterize carefree wealth holders. The *Art of Love* is an epitome of romantic techniques and experiences.[1]

Livy (*ca.* 59 B.C.–A.D. 17) declared the Roman's satisfaction with his work. In the excellently written history bearing the title *Books from the Foundation of the City*, he narrated how Rome won and deserved to win world dominion, not failing in the run of the narrative to strip truth in order to adorn a tale or to applaud an ancient virtue in order to condemn a current vice. Like all patriots who idealize the past, he viewed the present with alarm:

> Our vices have attained to such a height
> of enormity that we can neither endure
> the burden of them nor the sharpness
> necessary to correct them.

Even a golden age, it seems, must have its pessimist.[2]

As a group the Augustan writers expressed the moods which accompanied national success.

The Decline of Latin Literature.

With the writers of the late first and the second Christian century, who emphasized style at the expense of intellectual content, a decline began in Latin literature, and the period is known as the "silver age."[3] Seneca (*ca.* 4 B.C.–A.D. 65), chiefly noted as a philosopher, rendered Greek tragedies in the rhetorical style of the declamation halls; his characters talked in quips and epigrams. Petronius (d. *ca.* A.D. 66) strung together tales, anecdotes, and witty conversations in a novel without a plot. Persius (*ca.* A.D. 34–62) rendered Stoic philosophy in poetic satires.[4] Quintilian (*ca.* A.D. 35–95) attempted to halt the literary decay with a textbook on oratory, in which was argued the obvious proposition that an author should have a real knowledge of his subject as well as a graceful style of expression; the work is the most exhaustive

[1] C. W. Bain, *The Poems of Ovid* (1902); F. A. Wright, *The Mirror of Venus: Love poems and stories from Ovid's Amores* . . . (1925); B. P. Moore, *Ovid's Ars Amatoria with the Art of Love, Verse Translation* (1935); J. H. Mozley, *The Art of Love, and Other Poems* (1929); F. J. Miller, *Ovid, Metamorphoses* (2 vols., 1936).

[2] On Roman historiography see J. T. Shotwell, *The History of History* (rev. ed., 1939). See also A. S. Peskett, *Caesar, The Civil Wars* (1914); B. O. Foster, *Livy* (8 vols., 1919–1936); A. Murphy, *Tacitus, Historical Works* (1915), and J. C. Rolfe, *Suetonius, Lives of the Twelve Caesars* (2 vols., 1935).

[3] See *The Cambridge Ancient History*, Vol. 11, *The Imperial Peace A.D.* 70–192, (1936), Chap. XVIII, "Latin Literature of the Silver Age"; W. C. Sumner, *The Silver Age of Latin Literature* (1920); H. E. Butler, *Post-Augustan Poetry* (1902).

[4] Michael Heseltine, *Petronius* (1930); W. Adlington, *Apuleius, The Golden Ass, Being the Metamorphoses of Lucius Apuleius* (1935).

treatment of the education of an orator ever written.[1] Tacitus
(*ca.* 55–120), Rome's greatest historian, was a master of Latin
prose; in the *Annals* he wrote a somewhat distorted account of the
events of the first century. Rome suffered disasters, he said, because
the gods were enraged at the city. His most interesting work,
Germania, is the earliest surviving account of the barbarians of
central Europe. Suetonius (*ca.* 70–130) compiled a mass of interesting material—*Lives of the Twelve Caesars*—which is today the
source of much of our knowledge of the early emperors; too frequently, it seems, Suetonius preferred the striking anecdote to
the historical fact.

The most original writers of the "silver age" were the satirists
Martial (*ca.* 40–104) and Juvenal (*ca.* 60–140).[2] Martial was the
master of the epigram—

> Cinna is said to libel me: who heeds?
> He does not write, whose poems no man reads

—and Juvenal of clear and vivid description. Both deplored the
artificiality of the poets, but their main concern was with the corruption of society. Juvenal had an eye for the misery of the poor
that lurked behind the ostentation of the rich:

> The feverish poor, by every sound distressed,
> Curse the slow hours, and die for want to rest:
> Sleep visits not their couch, it costs too dear;
> And hence disease makes such wild havoc here.

He originated many expressions which have become well known,
for example, "bread and circuses" and "a healthy mind in a
healthy body." To the pessimism of their contemporaries Martial
and Juvenal added an outspoken bitterness. In this connection it
is worth noting that as time went on the emperors, while they continued to patronize literature, became hostile to writings having
political implications. Oratory, as an art, died out completely.

In the "silver age" self-satisfaction, as well as excellence of
style, departed from Latin letters.

The development of Greek literature continued throughout
Roman times. In the Augustan age a revival of interest in Attic
authors gave it a new vigor, and under Hadrian a veritable renaissance of almost every thing Greek occurred. Among this emperor's

[1] A. O. Gwynn, *Roman Education from Cicero to Quintilian* (1926); H. E. Butler, *The Institutio Oratoria of Quintilian* (1933).

[2] Walter C. A. Ker, *Martial, Epigrams* (2 vols., 1930); G. G. Ramsay, *Juvenal and Persius* (1930); and Lewis Evans, *The Satires of Juvenal* (1931).

notable acts was the founding of the Athenaeum, known later as the University of Athens, as a center for the study of poetry and philosophy. Marcus Aurelius, who endowed four chairs of philosophy in the Athenaeum, one each for the teaching of the Platonic, the Aristotelian, the Stoic, and the Epicurean doctrines, aimed to make Athens the intellectual center of the empire.[1] The best-known representative of the revival of Greek literature is Plutarch (*ca.* 46–120). His *Parallel Lives* of Greek and Roman worthies has been more widely read than any other Greek book, excepting only the New Testament. Lucian (fl. *ca.* 150–180) is known as the wittiest author of Roman times. His *Auction of Philosophers* is an amusing evaluation of the leading schools of Greek philosophy. The auctioneer expounded the merits of the philosophers and knocked them down to the highest bidders. Pythagoras went for ten minas. Socrates was sold on credit for two talents. And Aristippus found no takers. In the second-century Greek literary renaissance, the chief figures were Sophists and rhetoricians who lectured to aristocratic audiences and tutored aristocratic pupils. Polemon, who traveled in his own yacht, received as much as twenty thousand dollars for one lecture. The style of these verbalists is well illustrated by Pollux (fl. *ca.* 170), who compiled a list of unusual words that would give color to any discourse.[2]

ART, SCIENCE, AND PHILOSOPHY IN ROMAN TIMES

The lack of creative ability apparent in Latin literature was also evident in Roman art, science, and philosophy. In these fields work was carried on mainly by Greeks and Hellenized orientals, whose significance lies chiefly in the fact that they elaborated materials mainly Greek and Hellenistic in origin. Although Greek science and philosophy, as well as literature, continued to develop throughout Roman times, they, too, lost vitality and, as a result, slowly hardened into rigid patterns. At best the Romans were merely patrons of the arts and sciences.

ART IN ROMAN TIMES.

Under the influence of motifs diffused from Rome, the arts became uniform throughout the empire.[3] However, these motifs

---

[1] See John W. H. Walden, *The Universities of Ancient Greece* (1909).

[2] F. A. Wright, *A History of Later Greek Literature from the Death of Alexander in 323 B.C. to the Death of Justinian in 565 A.D.* (1932); A. H. Clough, *Plutarch's Lives* (1914), and many other editions; and A. M. Harmon, *Lucian* (8 vols., 1927).

[3] On Roman art see *The Cambridge Ancient History*, Vol. 9, *The Roman Republic 133–44 B.C.* (1932), Chap. XX, "The Art of the Roman Republic"; Vol. 10, *The Augustan Empire,*

From Eugène Albertini, *L'Afrique romaine* (1937)

TIMGAD

These ruins of a Roman city in northern Africa exhibit the general pattern of urban development that spread throughout the Mediterranean Basin under Roman rule. In the center, right, are the forum and a triumphal arch; in the center, below, is a theater. Among the ruins is a building that was a public library.

were not Roman but blends of Etruscan, Greek, and oriental materials. The chief object of art in Rome was to give splendor and grandeur to the city; in fact, Roman art is best understood as a form of urban decoration, and its greatest surviving forms are almost exclusively the ruins of cities. Since the Romans, as evidenced by the material interests of their political and intellectual leaders, possessed little feeling, it is not surprising that few Roman artists are known by name.

    1. *Roman Architecture.* As the medium best suited to express the right to rule, architecture received original treatment at

44 *B.C.–A.D.* 70 (1934), Chap. XVIII, "The Art of the Augustan Age"; Vol. 11, *The Imperial Peace, A.D.* 70–192 (1936), Chap. XX, "Art from Nero to the Antonines"; E. Strong, *Art in Ancient Rome* (2 vols., 1928); Albert Grenier, *The Roman Spirit in Religion, Thought, and Art* (1926); Pierre Gusman, *Rome . . . Pastels* (3 vols., 1934–1935), especially Vol. 1 on ancient Rome; F. Wickoff, *Roman Art* (1900); Grant Showerman, *Monuments and Men of Ancient Rome* (1935); Arnold W. Lawrence, *Later Greek Sculpture and Its Influence on East and West* (1927); J. M. C. Toynbee, *The Hadrianic School: A chapter in the history of Greek art* (1934).

Roman hands. Roman buildings were *grand*, not only in size but also in decoration. To the Greek lintel and post the Romans added the Etruscan arch, which, since it could be made strong enough to carry great weight, permitted the construction of very large buildings; a further aid in such construction was the presence near Rome of a volcanic material which, when mixed with lime, made an almost indestructible cement. Roofs of large buildings were always supported by cross walls, usually perforated by arches. The use of the dome, because it was built only on a circular, never on a square, base, was limited. A characteristic feature of Roman construction was the use of false columns and arches to give ornate effects. Painted or colored stucco was a favorite wall covering. Wall surfaces and columns were usually brilliantly polished. Other forms of decoration were colonnades, balustrades, niches, frescoes, friezes, and mosaics.

The main Roman construction was the forum, *i.e.*, the public square, with various kinds of buildings grouped around it—temples, amphitheaters, circuses, colosseums, baths, and the basilica, or market place. Each of these buildings was constructed in a more or less uniform style. The villa—the country residence of the aristocrat—aimed more at the provision of comfort than at the expression of aesthetic tastes. What the villas lacked in design was made up for by the use of pictures, statuary, fine furniture, pillows, rugs, and awnings; great attention was given to the landscaping of grounds around these country places.[1]

No less typical of Roman architecture than the buildings noted in the preceding paragraph were the utilitarian structures of the ports, the highways, and the frontiers. The remains of these structures—aqueducts, causeways, roads, and walls—which today dot Europe from Britain to Iraq, testify to the power that once made stone and mortar the embodiment not only of grandeur but also of peace and comfort.

Until the time of Augustus, who boasted that he found Rome brick and left it marble, Roman construction was chiefly of brick, cement, and wood. Under the empire marble was the common material for urban buildings. Construction was at its height in the provinces under Trajan and Hadrian. Diocletian and Constantine were among the greatest builders of the empire, but their structures were distinguished chiefly by massiveness.

[1] Tenney Frank, *Roman Buildings of the Republic* (1924); W. J. Anderson and R. P. Spiers, *Architecture of Ancient Rome* (rev. ed., 1927); and G. T. Rivoira, *Roman Architecture under the Roman Empire* (1925).

2. *Roman Statuary.* Among the decorations of every Roman public building were sculptured figures of imperial and local magnates. Rome learned the art from Greece but gave it realism and portrayed men and women as individuals, not as types. Roman portrait statuary was at its best in the first century. At this time also, the Hellenistic use of sculpture in relief was adapted to the depicting of events of imperial history. The most notable work of this kind records the invasion of Dacia and other episodes on Trajan's column. Roman relief was characterized by deep cutting and rounded forms. Great attention was paid to the accurate rendering of national features and details of costume and to the expression of psychological moods. The artists had a fine sense of the relations between figures forming a group. Notable among the achievements of Roman art, especially in the second century, were the equestrian statue, ornamental pieces such as the triumphal arch, and the memorial column. They completed the pattern of urban grandeur which still survives in degenerate ugliness not only in Europe but also in the Americas.

3. *Roman Minor Arts.* Painting, which was never an important art among the Romans, declined rapidly after the first century, when mosaics became fashionable. The mosaics were frequently mere imitations of Hellenistic paintings. Pictures seem to have played a prominent part in public life. Some, depicting battles and conquered lands, were carried in triumphal processions. Others, showing the victims of tyranny, were circulated in political campaigns. Still others were posted in courts to illustrate criminal charges. Beggars carried pictures of shipwrecks, earthquakes, and conflagrations from which they had had narrow escapes. Portraits of emperors and municipal patrons were common in private houses. Lovers kept pictures of one another. And authors put their portraits at the head of their works. The wall paintings recovered from Pompeii, Herculaneum, and other sites show clearly the dependence of the artists on Hellenistic subjects and techniques, for most of the murals appear to be copies of Greek or Hellenistic pictures.

Gem cutting, goldsmithing, and wood carving were carried on with high skill. The engraved medallion was an artistic innovation of Roman times. Carriages and furniture were skillfully designed and well built. Pottery, except in Gaul, where native influence kept originality alive, became standardized. Fine textiles were produced chiefly in Syria and Egypt. These arts and crafts, generally carried on as mechanical professions in connection with industry, were almost entirely in the hands of eastern workmen.

Naples Museum. By the courtesy of Lesch

HERCULES AND TELEPHOS

This fresco from Herculaneum, which was buried with Pompeii by the eruption of Vesuvius in 79 A.D., is a fine example of the Roman use of Greek painting for interior decoration.

Telephos—in the picture he is nursed by the deer—was the son of Hercules and the Arcadian princess, Auge. When a plague fell upon Arcadia, Auge and her son were condemned to death. Hercules rescued Telephos, and he, after growing to manhood, found his mother in Mysia. The seated figure is Arcadia. Hercules stands between the eagle and the lion. The legend was the subject of a lost drama by Euripides.

4. *Roman Music.* Not the least interesting aspect of the development of the arts in Rome was the introduction of music into theatrical shows and public spectacles. The invention of the pantomime about 22 B.C. led to the creation of theatrical orchestras, and a little later oriental music arrived from Alexandria. With it came the Babylonian bagpipe, stringed instruments, and kettledrums and Alexandrian singers. At the games the musical accompaniments were noisy. Citharas as big as wagons were hauled about the amphitheaters, and trumpeters and cymbalists by the hundred tooted and clashed. Female singers became the fashion for private parties. Music in the modern sense of the word did not exist in Rome; what passed for music was either sensuous melody or cacophonous rhythm.

SCIENCE IN ROMAN TIMES.

The Romans applied science but did not study it.[1] Except for an expedition in Nero's time to search for the source of the Nile, they made no explorations, and they founded no scientific schools. Their greatest writers on nature did not have a scientific outlook. Varro made excursions into every field of science but contributed to none. Lucretius expounded an evolutionary scheme of natural development; its basis was the philosophical theory of atomism rather than observed facts. Seneca described nature in order to teach morality, confusing religion and philosophy with science.

Pliny the Elder (*ca.* 23–79), who compiled the greatest Latin scientific work, was almost devoid of critical faculty, quoting authors indiscriminately and accepting myth as readily as fact. To his credit, however, it should be noted that occasionally he doubted a very tall tale. His work, *Natural History* (in thirty-seven books), although projected as a systematic view of nature, is important mainly as a statement of the kind of information which passed for science among educated Romans and as one of the few sources from which Western men drew their scientific ideas and knowledge for about fifteen hundred years. Judging from its contents, Pliny missed his time and calling, for he was undoubtedly the master of those kinds of information which, lacking relevance to the understanding of any natural phenomena, find their best use in radio quiz programs.[2]

[1] Lynn Thorndike, *A History of Magic and Experimental Science* (2 vols., 1923); J. Clarke, *Physical Science in the Time of Nero* (1910); and John Masson, *The Atomic Theory of Lucretius* (1884).

[2] W. N. Wethered, *The Mind of the Ancient World: A consideration of Pliny's Natural*

The Roman feeling for nature was essentially agricultural, *i.e.*, utilitarian and sentimental. The murder of Archimedes by a Roman soldier at the siege of Syracuse symbolized well the fate of Greek science at the hands of the Romans. When they made popular superstition the support of political power, they struck a death blow at science and destroyed at the point of germination all the economic and social benefits that might have resulted from its progress.[1]

1. *Mathematics in Roman Times.* The weakness of the Romans in abstract thought was particularly evident in mathematics, which in their hands never rose above the level of arithmetic and surveying. Their notation system was originally Etruscan.[2] About the opening of the Christian era they adopted a system of finger computation, which lasted into the Middle Ages. They handled large numbers on the abacus. Only the most expert reckoners could multiply and divide large numbers. They applied simple geometrical principles in land surveys and accurate measurements of distance, as well as in architecture and city planning.

Abstract mathematics remained the possession of the Greeks throughout Roman times. Ptolemy the great geographer and astronomer, laid the foundation of spherical trigonometry in a study of chords. He gave π the value 3.1416. Pappus (fl. *ca.* 300) wrote a history of mathematics and a treatise on trigonometry and optics. He attempted to deal with the problems of the inclined plane, the center of gravity, and the lifting of weights by means of cogwheels. Diophantus (fl. *ca.* 325) produced the first known treatise on algebra, using symbols, equations, and analytical methods, and solving equations having one unknown. He did not recognize the negative number.

2. *Geography and Astronomy in Roman Times.* Although Roman traders visited the Baltic Sea, penetrated equatorial Africa, and even reached southern China, the Romans developed no interest in geography and allied fields of learning. To add excitement to the circus they searched the known world for wild animals, and to cure their ills they brought plants alleged to have medicinal value from far and near. But they learned little about zoology and botany. In the course of building their road system they

History (1937); John Bostock and H. T. Riley, *Pliny's Natural History* (6 vols., 1855–1857); H. Rackman, *Pliny's Natural History* (1938); Wilhelm Kroll, *Die Kosmologie des Plinius* (1930).

[1] See Benjamin Farrington, *Science and Politics in the Ancient World* (1939), pp. 231–232.

[2] D. E. Smith, *History of Mathematics* (2 vols., 1925).

acquired a good knowledge of distances and, in some areas, a fair acquaintance with topography. They did not, however, work out either the geography of their frontiers or a detailed survey of their dominion. The few official maps were based on distances between points and did not approximate the shape of the regions represented. Only one purely Latin geographical treatise is known, and its author, Pomponius Mela (fl. *ca.* 43), was a Spaniard. His work, although a fair summary of geographical knowledge, contained little that was new in fact and nothing new in theory. It stated clearly the prevailing conception of five zones—two frigid areas around the poles, two temperate regions, and one great torrid band around the center of the earth. Mela held that the southern temperate region, as well as the northern, was inhabited. He was the first author to mention the Baltic Sea.

The leading geographers of Roman times wrote in Greek. Strabo (*ca.* 63 B.C.–A.D. 21) gathered together mathematical, physical, political, and historical materials in the most comprehensive geographical treatise produced by Greek culture. He recognized that erosion by water creates alluvial deposits and explained the movements of the earth's surface as due to earthquakes. Volcanoes, he believed, were caused by winds pent up within the earth. Pausanias (fl. *ca.* 117–150) wrote a guidebook for travelers, more important as a guide to the art and architecture of Greece than as a contribution to geography. Ptolemy (fl. *ca.* 150–170), the greatest natural scientist of the imperial age, flourished at Alexandria. His chief work, known now as the *Almagest*, from the title of the Arabic translation, is a complete summation of ancient-oriental and Mediterranean mathematical and astronomical learning; it fixed the ideas of the Western world in these fields until the opening of modern times.

The earth, Ptolemy said, was a fixed sphere having a circumference of about eighteen thousand miles. His notions of the continents and the seas are illustrated on the accompanying map. The main seas, rivers, and mountains of western and southern Europe, northern Africa, and western Asia are correctly located, and their relations to one another are well understood. Ptolemy's knowledge of the Ganges valley and equatorial Africa was not excelled until the eighteenth century. He seems to have been better informed about China—"the land from which silk comes"—than about northern Europe. Probably Ptolemy's greatest achievement as a geographer was the location of more than five thousand places by latitude and longitude, with the lines of the Fortunate Islands and

THE UNIVERSE ACCORDING TO PTOLEMY

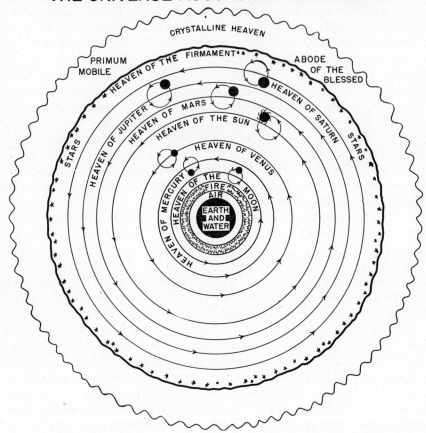

of the equator, which he located too far north, as bases. He made the first technical use of parallels and meridians.[1]

Around the earth, which was stationary at the center of the universe, moved the sun, moon, and planets. Ptolemy was not certain of their distances from the earth. Outside them were the firmament and the fixed stars, of which he catalogued 1028. Beyond the firmament was the crystalline heaven, made of fiery aether, where the *primum mobile*—the first mover—dwelled, and the blessed found an everlasting abode. In developing the theory

---

[1] On Ptolemy and his work see C. H. F. Peters, *Ptolemy's Catalogue of the Stars . . . : A revision of the Almagest* (1915); E. L. Stevenson, *Geography of Claudius Ptolemaeus* (1932); K. F. Koehlers, *Texte und Karten des Ptolemäus* (1932); and André Berthelot, *L'Asie ancienne centrale et sud-orientale d'après Ptolémée* (1930).

THE WORLD ACCORDING TO PTOLEMY

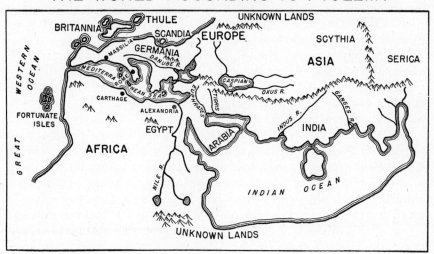

of epicycles and the geocentric theory of the universe according to the data at hand, Ptolemy fixed the chief astronomical concepts of late Roman and Christian times. The abandonment of the idea that the earth moves gave support to the popular notion of the universe and made difficult further astronomical speculation. Ptolemy's views, it should be noted, ran counter to the heliocentric theory held by many Hellenistic scientists.

The chief Roman application of astronomical learning was in a reform of the calendar. Upon the advice of Sosigenes (fl. *ca.* 46 B.C.), an Alexandrian astronomer, Caesar abandoned the traditional year of 354⅓ days and adopted a solar year of 365 days. By distributing the ten days added to the traditional year among the months, the dates of the Roman religious festivals were left as they had been under the old calendar. Every four years a day was added to the year in order to keep the year in harmony with solar time. The new calendar was instituted January 1, 45 B.C., New Year's Day being the day upon which the consuls for the year took office. This reform followed the calendar devised by Eudoxus and adopted in Egypt about 238 B.C.

About the time Caesar reformed the calendar the seven-day week began to spread about the Mediterranean basin. The background of its diffusion was not the Babylonian precedent but the growing influence of astrological beliefs among the masses. According to these beliefs, as previously noted, all life was under the influence of the seven planetary deities, each of which had a special day. Originally the Romans worked seven days and went to market on the eighth day, and the Greeks broke the month into three ten-day periods. By the beginning of the third century the observance of the planetary week was universal; its adoption by the Christians was due to the Hebrew beliefs about the creation. But the Hebrew beliefs, it should be emphasized, had little to do with the original adoption.[1]

3. *Medicine in the Roman Empire.* The Romans produced no important figure in medicine, anatomy, or physiology. Following Etruscan precedents, they paid close attention to the location and orientation of towns for water supply and drainage. Under the empire public physicians were appointed in the towns—five in small towns, ten in large towns, and as many as necessary in the cities. These physicians received salaries from the state and served the poor without cost. In the army there was a medical officer, usually a surgeon, with every cohort and a hospital with every camp. These military surgeons were trained in special schools. Because they were subordinate to the combat officers, their efforts to treat the wounded were frequently frustrated. The Roman hospital system, which became the basis of the religious foundations of Christian times, had a double origin. The first infirmaries seem to have been places to which sick and therefore useless slaves were sent to die; under the empire these institutions, combined with the military hospitals located at strategic points, became public hospitals. The organization of these institutions was Rome's greatest contribution to medical practice.

Greek medical learning reached Rome late in the third century B.C. but did not enter into Roman education until the late period of the republic.[2] The only significant Latin medical treatise was written by Celsus (fl. *ca.* A.D. 14). According to his medical theory, which was based on the philosophy of Democritus, disease was caused by disturbance of the atoms. He drew distinctions between internal and external ailments and described facial operations which today are classed as plastic surgery. His contemporary Scribonius (fl. *ca.* A.D. 25–50) compiled a collection of 271 pre-

---

[1] See F. H. Colson, *The Week* (1926).
[2] T. C. Allbutt, *Greek Medicine in Rome* (1921); Charles Singer, *A Short History of Medicine* (1928); E. H. Garrison, *Notes on the History of Military Medicine* (1922); W. G. Spencer, *Celsus, De Medicina* (3 vols., 1935); and J. S. Milne, *Surgical Instruments in Greek and Roman Times* (1907).

scriptions in which were used 242 drugs from plants, 36 from minerals, and 27 from animals. The work contains the earliest known description of the preparation of opium. Veterinary medicine, to which writers on agriculture such as Cato the Elder and Varro paid great attention, was a leading field of practice. In fact, the outlook of the Roman veterinarian, as evidenced in the well-organized treatise of Flavius Renatus (*ca.* 383–450), was probably more scientific than the outlook of all but the best physicians.

The state of the medical profession was low throughout the period of the empire. Midwives were often better educated than the ordinary physicians, many of whom, it seems, could barely read. The usual medical education consisted of listening to lectures by prominent physicians over a six months' period. No examinations were given at the end of the course, and no standards were imposed on practitioners. The chief requirement for practice was a collection of recipes, particularly for salves, which were in high favor, and commonly the highest priced was believed to be the most efficacious. Specialists existed for almost every ailment, fevers and eye and ear disorders in particular, and surgeons had great repute. Popular medicine was little more than a fusion of the universal folk medicine and Babylonian and Egyptian priestly lore.

The spirit of investigation which permeated Greek medicine in the Hellenistic age was displaced in Roman times by a doctrinaire approach which tended to formalize both diagnosis and therapeutics. This tendency produced a number of medical schools, or sects, each of which held fast to a theory of disease and a scheme of treatment.

The Dogmatics adhered to the Hippocratic tradition but diluted it with practices derived from almost every source of medical learning. Consequently treatment degenerated into a hodgepodge of prescriptions and physical manipulations.

The Empirics denied the usefulness of any theory of disease, relying on observation of the patient for both diagnosis and treatment. The autopsy, they said, was the basis of the medical art. Marinos (fl. *ca.* A.D. 50), who wrote a comprehensive treatise on anatomy in twenty books, was probably a member of this school.

The Methodics, founded by Asclepiades (fl. *ca.* 100 B.C.), was the most popular medical school of the imperial age. Its members explained disease in terms of the Epicurean metaphysics as the result of the constriction or relaxation of the pores among the atoms forming the body. Diseases characterized by congestion, disorders of elimination, and a rapid pulse—designated "acute"— were due to constriction. Diseases characterized by loss of energy, excessive elimination, and a slow pulse—designated "chronic"— were caused by relaxation. Although this theory was dangerously superficial, it had the good result of substituting simple treatments for such barbarous practices as burying patients under feather beds or exposing them to blazing fires in order to stimulate sweating. It led also to a decline in the use of harsh drugs and emetics. There was, said Asclepiades, no specific cure for any disease. The Methodic treatment of every disease began with a three-day diet, and thereafter food was given only every other day. Great attention was paid to the kind of bed, the light in the room, and the quality of air, for each of these physical conditions was regarded as affecting the atomic pores. Bleeding, massaging, and the applying of external remedies, such as mustard plasters, were common practices. The chief weakness of the Methodic theory of medicine was the refusal to recognize that each disease has a natural course. Soranus of Ephesus (fl. *ca.* 100–120), the recognized leader of the Methodic sect in Trajan's Rome, was the greatest specialist in women's diseases of Greco-Roman times. An exposition of the Methodic theory and practices of medicine survives in a work, written in bad Latin, by Caelius Aurelianus, who flourished in the fifth century after Christ.

The Pneumatic school, as the name implies, founded its theory on the metaphysics of Stoicism: disease was due to disorders of the *pneuma*, the igneous spirit of the universe, which in man resided in the arteries. The school, founded by Athenaos of Cilicia (fl. *ca.* 70–60 B.C.), was for a long time the leading rival of the Methodic sect.

The Eclectic school, which drew upon all sources of medical learning for its practices, produced the greatest physicians of Roman times. Aretaeos (fl. *ca.* 130–190) wrote a remarkable work on acute and chronic diseases, which embodied both Methodic and Pneumatic principles. He gave the first description of diabetes and made the first known reference to diphtheria of the pharynx and larynx. He also drew a clear distinction between cerebral and spinal paralysis. His treatment was based on dietetic regulation and the use of purgatives. Rufus of Ephesus (fl. *ca.* 100–125) made the first attempt to base pathology on anatomy and physiology. His anatomical researches included studies of the pig and the monkey. He wrote a treatise on the heart which gave clear descriptions of the pulse under different bodily circumstances. He improved the anatomical description of the eye and was the first to record that the liver has five lobes. He urged that water suspected of being dangerous to health be boiled before using. His reputation as a surgeon almost equaled his reputation as a physician. Dioscorides of Cilicia (fl. *ca.* A.D. 50) is commonly known as the "father of pharmacy." His great work on drugs, which gives a systematic account of remedies taken from the vegetable, animal, and mineral kingdoms, was the authoritative work on pharmacy for fifteen centuries. Besides containing accurate descriptions of many plants, it gives directions for the preparation of many simple chemical substances. Chemistry, it should be noted. was almost entirely a branch of pharmacy.

The greatest physician of Roman times was Galen of Pergamum (fl. *ca.* 130–200), whose voluminous works stand alongside those of Ptolemy as the enduring monuments of Greek science. He began his career as a gladiatorial physician in his native city. Subsequently he studied at Alexandria, where he saw a human skeleton and inspected the bodies of bears, pigs, sheep, oxen, dogs, and apes. After migrating to Rome, he won great popularity among both the poor and the rich. He treated as many as three thousand free patients a year; from rich patients, who came to him from all parts of the empire, he received very high fees. Because he was educated in rhetoric as well as in science, his works were marked by a literary style superior to that of the average scientific book of the time.[1]

Galen restored the Hippocratic tradition to the central position in medical science by reinterpreting its main elements in terms of the new knowledge and speculations of his age. His chief contributions were to anatomy and physiology. He discovered and described the cranial nerves and experimented with the spinal cord. He gave a valid explanation of the respiratory system. He knew that the heart is a motor and that the arteries contain blood. He described the muscles and bones with considerable accuracy. Much of this anatomical knowledge may have been derived from Marinos. Galen's physiological theory reveals his debt to the philosophers as well as his knowledge of anatomy:

[1] There is not a complete translation of Galen's works in a modern language. See A. J. Brock, *Greek Medicine, Being Extracts Illustrative of Medical Writers from Hippocrates to Galen* (1929); Emmanuel Chauvet, *La Philosophie des médecins grecs* (1886); and Joseph Walsh, "Galen's Writings and the Influences Inspiring Them," *Annals of Medical History,* Vol. 7 (n.s., 1935), pp. 428–437; Alfred E. Cohn, "The Development of the Harveian Circulation," *Annals of Medical History,* Vol. 1 (n.s., 1929), pp. 16–36.

From CHARLES SINGER, *The Evolution of
Anatomy* (1925). *Alfred A. Knopf, Inc.*

GALEN

This picture, a restored drawing from a late classical manuscript, is the sole representation
of the greatest physician of Greco-Roman culture. Like most of the other important
scientific and philosophical thinkers of Greco-Roman times, he came from the Hellenized
East. He wrote in Greek. His theory of personality types completed the development of an
integrated view of nature initiated by the Ionian nature philosophers.

The basic principle of life in the Galenic physiology was a *spirit* or *pneuma* drawn from the general World-spirit in the act of breathing. It entered the body through the windpipe or *trachea* and so passed to the lungs and thence, through the *arteria venalis*—which we now call the 'pulmonary vein'—to the left ventricle of the heart, where it encountered the blood. But what was the origin of the blood? To this question his answer was ingenious, and the errors that it involved remained till the time of Harvey.

Galen believed that food-substance from the intestines was carried as 'chyle' by the portal vein to the liver. There it was converted into blood and endowed with a particular pneuma, the *Natural Spirit*, which bestowed the power of growth and nutrition. Part of this lower-grade blood was carried from the liver to the right ventricle, where it gave off impurities by way of the *vena arterialis*, our 'pulmonary artery,' to the lungs, whence they were exhaled in the breath. The venous blood, thus continuously purified, ebbed to and fro in the veins for purposes of ordinary nutrition. A very small part of this venous blood passed through invisible pores in the muscular septum to the left ventricle. There it mixed with air drawn in from the lung by way of the *arteria venalis*, our 'pulmonary vein.' From this mixture was produced a higher-grade blood, the arterial blood, instinct with the principle of life and charged with a second kind of pneuma, the *Vital Spirit*. Blood containing this second kind of pneuma ebbed to and fro in the arteries endowing the various organs with function. Such as reached the brain became there charged with the noblest essence of all, the third pneuma, the *Animal Spirit* or breath of the soul. The *Animal Spirit* was carried from the brain by the nerves—believed to be hollow—and through them initiated the higher functions of the organism, including motion and sensation.[1]

This theory was the first coherent view of the life process set forth in terms of interaction between the external environment and the human organism, conceived as a structure of interdependent organs; it ranks among the major achievements of Greek scientific thought.

The theory, it should be noted, did not supplant the humoral theory of disease, which, as a matter of fact, Galen preserved and elaborated. Disturbances in the pneuma, which were evidenced in disease, were due to a disharmony arising among the four humors. Such disharmonies resulted from both external and internal causes. Among the external factors were air, food and drink, rest and exertion, sleep and waking, and mental states. Among the internal causes were the excess, insufficiency, and disintegration of any

---

[1] Charles Singer, *A Short History of Medicine* (1928), pp. 56–58. By permission of the Oxford University Press, New York.

one or all of the humors. These internal causes could be recognized only by symptoms, especially those relating to the pulse, the urine, and the respiration. Galen also believed that changes in the size and shape of organic parts caused disease.

Unlike the Methodics, whom he criticized severely, Galen believed that diseases have specific causes and based his entire method upon attacking these causes. For this reason diagnosis was all-important to him, and he paid attention not only to the condition of the organs involved but also to the age, sex, strength, and habits of the patient. In treatment he relied upon two Hippocratic principles: (1) Each disease passes through a number of stages. (2) The prescriptions of the physician should work with the curative powers of nature. He also followed the Hippocratic theory that a diseased condition of the body should be combated with its opposite, *i.e.*, when a disease is due to an overabundance of the cold humor, the proper procedure is to restore humoral harmony by a heating treatment. Although Galen used dietetic regulation and drugs, his treatment usually rested on bloodletting; he worked out carefully the amounts of blood to be let under various conditions. In order to increase his knowledge of drugs, which he used adeptly but sparingly, he traveled to various countries in search of new medicinal substances.

The systematic exposition which Galen gave to his theories, as well as his skill in applying them, combined with the literary merits of his work to establish him as the greatest Western medical authority until the opening of modern times.

Although the scientific elements in Greek medicine were notable, it should be remembered that the outlook on nature which led the Greeks to abandon the daimonic theory of disease and treatment did not culminate in a completely naturalistic conception of disease and its treatment. The popularity of the cult of Asklepios indicates the persistence of a religious view of sickness. Holy thoughts, it was believed, had therapeutic value. Dreams had medical significance. And miraculous cures were possible. After the first century, when the naturalistic basis of medicine, namely the dissection of human bodies, disappeared, these supernatural notions about disease and its cure spread more and more widely among both physicians and their patients.[1]

[1] See Ludwig Edelstein, "Greek Medicine in Its Relation to Religion and Magic," *Bulletin of the Institute of Medical History*, Vol. 5 (1937), pp. 201–246; Ludwig Edelstein, "The Development of Greek Anatomy," *Bulletin of the Institute of Medical History* Vol. 3 (1935), pp. 235–240.

4. *Psychology in Roman Times.* Although the Hellenistic advances in anatomical knowledge contributed to the development of psychology, it remained a facet of philosophy, having its center of interest in doctrines of the soul.[1] The Stoics taught that the soul, or pneuma, was a substance—a bit of the universal fire. Although it pervaded the whole body, its seat was the heart and the throat was its gateway. Its functions were the activating of the five senses and of speaking, procreating, and reasoning. The content of the individual mind was built up partly by contact with the world of objects and partly by social intercourse. That body of ideas possessed by all men was grounded in "common sense." Virtue was the result of the unimpeded activity of reason; vice had origin in the impulses, which reason might permit to guide behavior. Because impulse could not dominate conduct without the acquiescence of reason, the individual was morally responsible. This conception of man did not admit the existence of a spiritual world outside the physical universe. The Epicureans viewed the soul as a substance—the *anima*—composed of the subtle fiery atoms. Its seat was the heart. Sensations were caused by affluxes from objects. Thought arose through the impact of fiery atoms upon one another. Unlike the Stoics, who believed that the human soul was immortal because it was a bit of the world soul, the Epicureans denied the immortality of the soul. Like their metaphysics, their psychology was materialistic.

Among the writers on psychological topics in Roman times three are worthy of note: Artemidoros (fl. *ca.* 150), Galen, and Alexander of Aphrodisias (fl. *ca.* 200).

Artemidoros of Ephesus, who should, perhaps, be seen standing with Ptolemy and Galen as a codifier of Greek scientific learning, wrote a systematic treatise on dreams. By collecting accounts of dreams and classifying the principles of their interpretation, he undertook to prove the ancient, even primitive, proposition that dreams are messages foretelling the future. His rules of interpretation were based on nothing more substantial than coincidences, analogies, obvious vanities, puns, and caprice:

It may make the greatest difference whether the same dream comes to a rich man or a poor man, to a man or a woman, to a married woman or a virgin, to a king or a subject. . . . For instance, for a priest of Isis to dream of a shaven head is a good omen; to any other person it is ominous of evil. To dream that you have the head of a lion or elephant

[1] G. S. Brett, *A History of Psychology, Ancient and Patristic* (1912); A. J. Brock, *Galen, On the Natural Faculties* (1928).

is a prediction of a rise above your natural estate; but to dream that you have the horns of an ox portends violent death. To dream of shoe making and carpentry foretells happy marriage and friendship, but the vision of a tanner's yard, for its connection with foul odours and death, may foreshadow disgrace and disaster.[1]

That such a work could be compiled in the spirit of science and by the ordinary method of collecting information from any and all sources indicates the fundamental lack of a critical outlook which pervaded learning in Roman times. Educated men everywhere accepted the view of dreams which Artemidoros attempted to systematize.

From Galen's physiology developed one of the most influential psychological theories ever put forth, namely, the humoral theory of temperaments. It was grounded in the belief that the condition of the bodily humors determines the character of an individual. By combining the qualities warm and cold and dry and moist with the four humors—the blood, the phlegm, the black bile, and the yellow bile—Galen defined thirteen types of temperament. Later authors drew from these thirteen the four classic types which still serve to classify individuals: sanguine, phlegmatic, choleric, and melancholic. If an individual possessed a peculiar disposition, it was due to an idiosyncrasy, *i.e.*, a special combination of the humors. Galen conceived that the humors worked themselves into the temperament through the brain, the seat of the intellect, the liver, the source of desire, and the heart, the center of vitality. He recognized the distinction between motor and sensory nerves; reason, he said, derived its materials from the senses. This theory of temperaments, which was opposed to the Stoic doctrine that all men are fundamentally alike, had the merit of explaining character in terms of natural processes rather than on metaphysical or daimonic grounds.

In Galen's doctrine of the temperaments was completed the development of a coherent theory of nature which had begun with the Ionian nature philosophers and to which Empedocles, Hippocrates, and Aristotle had made significant contributions. The concepts "elements," "qualities," "humors," and "temperaments" were components of a synthesis in terms of which the physical universe, natural objects and conditions, bodily health and disease, and personalities were understood as related phe-

---

[1] Adapted from Artemidoros, *The Interpretation of Dreams* (Rendered into English by Robert Wood, 1644).

THE GREEK SCIENTIFIC SYNTHESIS

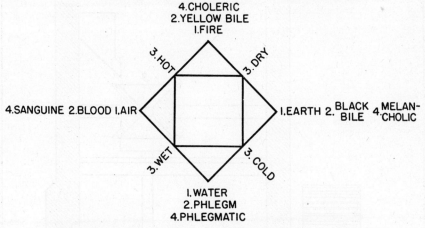

1. The Elements – Empedocles   *3. The Qualities – Aristotle*
2. The Humors – Hippocrates   *4. The Temperaments – Galen*

nomena. Thus was ended the nature philosopher's quest for unity in diversity.[1]

Alexander of Aphrodisias, who taught for a time at Athens (198–211), wrote a commentary on Aristotle's psychology, which was important for the growing synthesis of philosophical and religious thought. His original contribution was the making of a distinction between the *material* and the *active* soul. The material soul, which gave form to the body, had the capacity for but not the power of thinking rationally. The active soul, introduced into the body from without, aroused the material soul to action. As an emanation from the Divine Source, it was immaterial and immortal and possessed a rational power apart from the capacity for thinking of the material soul. This conception, it can be easily understood, aided greatly the growth of those theories of revelation, emanation, and intuition essential to the development of idealistic philosophy and mystical religion.

5. *Roman Engineering and Technology.*   Remains of buildings, aqueducts, and roads testify to the practical skill of Roman architects and engineers.[2] But their scientific knowledge was

[1] See Adolf Meyer, "The Tradition of Ancient Biology and Medicine in the Vitalistic Period of Modern Biology and Medicine," *Bulletin of the Institute of Medical History,* Vol. 5 (1937), pp. 800–821.
[2] Albert Neuberger, *The Technical Arts and Sciences of the Ancients* (1930); Frank

THE TRANSMISSION OF POWER BY VITRUVIUS

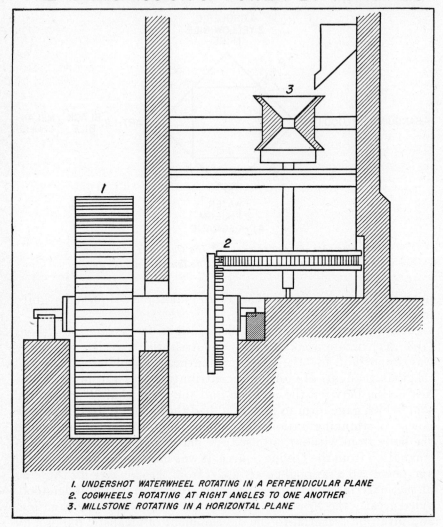

1. UNDERSHOT WATERWHEEL ROTATING IN A PERPENDICULAR PLANE
2. COGWHEELS ROTATING AT RIGHT ANGLES TO ONE ANOTHER
3. MILLSTONE ROTATING IN A HORIZONTAL PLANE

unbelievably elementary. Vitruvius (fl. *ca.* A.D. 1), author of the greatest Latin work on architecture, possessed little understanding of the abstract principles of construction. But he had a concrete

Granger, *Vitruvius, On Architecture* (2 vols., 1931); Charles E. Bennett, *Frontinus, The Stratagems and Aqueducts of Rome* (1925); Esther Boise Van Deman, *The Building of the Roman Aqueducts* (1934); Thomas Ashby, *The Aqueducts of Ancient Rome* (1935); A. P. Usher, *A History of Mechanical Inventions* (1929); Alexander P. Gest, *Engineering* (1930).

knowledge of the construction of such machines as windmills, wheels for measuring distance, windlasses, cranes, mills, mortars, and devices for raising water. His book contains the earliest discussion of architectural acoustics. Frontinus (*ca.* 40–103), superintendent of the water supply of Rome, wrote the oldest known treatise on engineering. It is chiefly a description of aqueducts and sewers. He knew that the speed of the outflow of water depends on the height of water above the outlet. The distinctive Roman achievements in the building arts, besides those already noted in the paragraphs on architecture, were in the heating and lighting of houses.

Many minor technological advances were made in Roman times. The common tools, such as the saw, the ax, the drill, and the plow were improved. The waterwheel was widely used to produce power; its gear was the only notable solution in classical times of the problem of transmitting mechanical power. Improvements in glassmaking brought glass into common use. Soap, originally invented it seems by the Gauls, became widely known as a medicine and a hair tonic. Under the early empire candles and lamps with adjustable wicks replaced torches for lighting houses; lanterns with glass panes came into use about the opening of the fifth century. Street lighting was first introduced in Antioch. In metalworking the chief Roman advance was the manufacture of wire and hollow pipe; in textile production, it was an improved method of dyeing; in pottery making, it was the production of cheap wares by a process of pressing out the forms. Although the contrivances of Archimedes and other Hellenistic inventors were known to the Romans, little use was made of them except in hoisting gear for unloading ships and raising building materials and in military machines, such as catapults, slings, and battering rams. These machines were expertly built. As previously explained, Rome's lasting contribution to the development of technology was the diffusion of eastern agricultural and industrial methods into western and central Europe.

The contrast between Roman engineering skills and technical knowledge is explained by the fact that the skills were embedded in the low intellectual tradition and transmitted in the industries, while scientific principles were at first only speculations divorced from the practical arts. The Romans shared the Greek disdain for the crafts and labor. Cicero—perhaps the most enlightened of the Romans—praised Socrates for pointing out that physical phenomena are too complex for human understanding, and Seneca, whom the Christians admired, said that inventors had their gaze bent on the ground.

Philosophy in Roman Times.

The few Roman speculative thinkers merely elaborated in Latin the ideas of Greek and Hellenized oriental philosophers, who, as in other fields of learning, displayed what little originality of thought there was.[1]

1. *Epicureanism.* Epicureanism—the first philosophy to reach Rome—won and held adherents chiefly among the well to do who cared little for political life. Although Lucretius, its greatest spokesman in Latin, developed a theory of social progress, in the main its followers, intent on finding contentment through refined intercourse with intimate friends, withdrew into brotherhoods and refrained from any participation in public action that might have promoted social amelioration. Roman Epicureans were quietists with little inclination to jeopardize their peace of mind by meddling in the affairs of others. Their brotherhoods had many of the characterististics of the religious associations which had spread widely among the lower classes in the cities during Hellenistic times.

The forthright materialism of Epicureanism nurtured what little skepticism opposed the rising religious mood, and its metaphysics—atomism—won a permanent place in scientific thought.

2. *Neo-Pythagoreanism.* The rising religious feeling was a strong factor in the revival of Pythagoreanism. This revival, carried to Rome through the influence of Posidonius on Cicero and pseudoliterary and philosophical figures of the early imperial age, was at its height in the first century. Ultimately it spread among both the aristocracy and the mixed peoples of the towns and agricultural estates. Its chief agents were missionaries, who went about continually among small groups of adherents.

Neo-Pythagoreanism, as the revival is called, was an assimilation of certain oriental beliefs into Greek speculations. According to its teaching the universe was divided into matter and spirit. All life was a unity, ever turning through the cycle of birth and death. Both God and man were eternal. Between them was a hierarchy of spiritual beings—evil daimons and kindly genii. The daimons, who governed the world, tormented men; the genii revealed knowledge to men. The human soul, having fallen from a state of purity, lived

[1] On the Roman adaptation of Greek philosophical ideas see J. E. King, trans., *Cicero, Tusculan Disputations* (1927).

amidst the evil that pervaded life on earth, but this existence was only a preparation for a future life beyond the grave. Preparation for eternal life was both sacramental and intellectual. Thus Neo-Pythagoreans, although they clung to the belief that a knowledge of numbers was a guide to spiritual perfection, frequently joined the mystery cults. They also practiced asceticism and self-examination in order to promote spiritual growth, which they believed expressed itself outwardly in a just dealing with other men. Beliefs in wonder working, omenology, miracles, and other forms of superstition clustered about these doctrines.

In Neo-Pythagoreanism emotion masked reason, and faith was confused with knowledge.

3. *Stoicism.* Stoicism, which, as previously noted, made its first appearance in Rome in the literary circle of Scipio Aemilianus, ultimately pervaded the aristocracy and became a significant influence in the development of policy and law.[1] The Gracchi were inspired by its social ideal. In the last century B.C. the group of nobles around the younger Cato, who wished to reform but not to overthrow the republic, were guided by its precepts; after the establishment of the empire the representatives of this group, known as the "old nobles," were persecuted. But official opposition to Stoicism was short-lived. By the end of the first Christian century it had become not only the philosophy but also the religion of educated Romans, and under its influence they made an earnest attempt to reconstruct the state.

The emperor Marcus Aurelius, whose *Meditations* is the best-known Stoic work, was the leading exponent of this phase of Stoicism; its prophets were Seneca and Epictetus (fl. *ca.* 100), a Greek slave, who became a teacher in Rome.[2] Both Seneca and Epictetus modified Greek Stoicism along the lines of intellectual change of their times. "The soul's entire struggle," said Seneca, "is with the flesh that oppresses it." After the confused struggle of earthly life, the soul lived a pure existence in a state of eternal peace. A moralizing tendency, which later made Seneca attractive to Christians, dominated his teaching. He disapproved of using marble as a building material, denounced the practice of warming houses with furnaces, and argued that taking baths was a violation

[1] E. V. Arnold, *Roman Stoicism* (1911); Frank Holland, *Seneca* (1920; John W. Basore, *Seneca, Moral Essays* (3 vols., 1928–1932); Henry D. Sedgwick, *Marcus Aurelius* (1921); C. R. Haines, *Marcus Aurelius Antoninus, Emperor of Rome—together with His Speeches and Sayings* (1930); C. H. S. Davis, *Roman Stoicism and Some of Its Disciples* (1903).

[2] W. A. Oldfather, *Epictetus, The Discourses as Reported by Arrian, The Manual, and Fragments* (2 vols., 1928).

of nature. To use feather pillows, he contended, was shameful, and to shield the head from the sun was silly. He condemned both art and technology as wrongful manipulations of nature. Such teachings were extreme conclusions drawn from the Stoic doctrine that man should live in harmony with nature. Epictetus left no writings, but his pupils collected his teachings in the *Enchiridion*, *i.e.*, handbook, which had a wide influence not only in Roman but also in Christian circles, particularly in early monastic communities. Its aphoristic declarations delineated the Stoic ideal—the sage who, unencumbered by personal relations and worldly interests, dedicated his life to the service of the all-wise deity.

Three ideas dominated Roman Stoicism: (1) an all-wise Providence guided the universe; (2) the universe operated under natural laws; and (3) man, knowing these natural laws, could act under providential guidance. Zeus or Jupiter or any other name was merely a designation for the all-wise Providence. Lesser deities, whose existence was not denied, were concerned with helping men. Both necessity and blind chance, besides Providence, operated in the world: the one, man could not resist, the other he need not obey. Man possessed a conscience, *i.e.*, a natural capacity to know virtue, and by means of his free will he could choose right forms of behavior. Earthly life was a preparation for the separation, at death, of the human soul from its earthly envelope. In this preparation the soul, ruled by reason, sought to act in accord with the righteous moral law, which the all-wise Providence had planted in the universe.

The Stoic saw human life as part of the universal process. The universe was a perfect sphere with the earth at the center and the heavenly bodies arranged in concentric spheres about it. The universal fire—the pneuma—energized all things; on earth it was active in warm air. As previously noted, the human pneuma was identified with the breath. At death the human soul rose to a purgatory near the moon, where it was cleansed of impurities remaining from earthly existence; each stage of its refinement was marked by ascent to a higher region, until at last it merged with the universal pneuma. Divine Providence, it should be noted, resided in the sun. The identification of deities with heavenly bodies led the Stoics to a strong belief in astrology.

Although the Stoics recognized that perfection is unattainable in earthly existence, they believed in making a serious effort to approach the ideal as nearly as possible. Knowing the confused state of the world, they were pessimistic; aspiring to perfection, they were dutiful and intrepid. Self-discipline, manifested in soberness, wisdom, courage, and justice, was the noblest goal men could attain. Virtue was the supreme good.

For individuals these concepts defined a way of life. The pursuit of wealth was ignoble. But economic independence was necessary if a man was to be free and honorable. The best professions were the law, the magistracy, teaching, and farming. Country life, because it preserved physical vigor, was to be preferred to city life. Celibacy was more virtuous than the married state. If a man married, he was obligated to rear a large family. Kindness to children and inferiors, especially slaves, was praiseworthy. Close friends, well chosen, were one of the few permissible pleasures of earthly life. An even temper was to be maintained under all circumstances. A well-grown beard was a thing to be proud of. But no parade was to be made of virtuous attainments. Marcus Aurelius, in a single reference to Christians, deplored the unseemly joy of martyrs at the prospect of the release of their souls by death. Even this joy the Stoics accepted calmly. Purity of thought and speech was promoted by meditation, prayer, and song. Each night the Stoic examined his conduct of the preceding day.

For society these concepts shaped a world "concord," characterized by peace and justice. The social form of this world at peace was a cosmopolis in which all human beings found their native land. Its government was a republic. Its rulers were sages, *i.e.*, men of wisdom who followed the all-wise Providence in ways that were justified to ordinary men by common sense. The state possessed neither coined money nor law courts nor temples. Justice reigned in every man's conformity to the natural law. Women were possessed in common, and children belonged to the state. Education, which was universal, taught men to love concord, not nations, and to follow the natural law, not selfish interests. So taught, men understood that they could attain individual well-being only by serving the common welfare. This ideal world order was attainable only as men learned to live in harmony with nature.

In Stoicism the Roman aristocrats found a philosophy which embodied the traditional ideals of their class, and of it they made a religion. Like other men they created a god in their own image: He ruled justly over a pacified mankind, and men aspired to rule their behavior as He ruled mankind, in the hope that ultimately they would share in His perfection. The Roman conquerors made the naked sword the symbol of peace and justice; the Stoics made military virtues the attributes of Deity. Western men have been a long time discovering the contradiction in the juxtaposition.

4. *Neoplatonism.* Although religious elements became increasingly important in Epicureanism, Neo-Pythagoreanism, and Stoicism, they preserved the outlook of philosophy, namely, that the universe is understandable through reason and the rational mind can shape a right way of life; ultimately, however, the philosophical outlook was abandoned in favor of the view that the highest knowledge is closed to human reason. Neoplatonism, the final product of Greek speculation, embodied this shift in outlook.[1]

The founder of Neoplatonism, Ammonius Saccas (fl. *ca.* 240), was an Alexandrian dock worker, and its greatest exponent, Plotinus (*ca.* 205–270), although he lived most of his life in Rome, was Egyptian born and trained.[2] These facts indicate that the system was originally a product of the interaction of Greek and oriental beliefs; in final form, however, it was a blend of Platonic and Aristotelian ideas with the rising religious mood. Ammonius Saccas left no written works, and Plotinus never looked at his words once they were set down. Thus the *Enneads*, his chief work, has no logical arrangement. This lack reflects the religious mood that dominated his thinking, a mood also expressed in his practice of magic—even for the discovery of petty criminals—and in his claim that in four separate trances he had experienced spiritual unity with supreme reality.

The followers of Plotinus, who were the defenders of the traditional culture against the Christians during the last two centuries of the empire, were imbued with this mood. With Porphyry (*ca.* 233–304) credulity became a virtue and religious disbelief a sin. In keeping with the metaphysical ideas of Plotinus, he arranged the

---

[1] On Plotinus and Neoplatonism see W. R. Inge, *Plotinus* (1929); W. R. Inge, *The Philosophy of Plotinus* (1929); C. H. Turnbull, *The Essence of Plotinus* (1934); A. H. Armstrong, *The Architecture of the Intelligible Universe in the Philosophy of Plotinus* (1940); K. S. Guthrie, *Plotinus, Complete Works, in Chronological Order* (*ca.* 1918); Stephen Mackenna, *Plotinus, On the One and the Good* (1930); Stephen Mackenna, *Plotinus, The Divine Mind* (1924); Stephen Mackenna, *Plotinus, Psychic and Physical Treatises* (1921); Stephen Mackenna, *Plotinus, The Ethical Treatises* (1917); E. R. Dodds, *Proclus, The Elements of Theology* (1933); and E. R. Dodds, *Select Passages Illustrating Neoplatonism* (1923).

On the place of Neoplatonism in intellectual development see especially Arthur Drews, *Plotin und der Untergang der antiken Weltanschauung* (1907).

[2] Eduard Zeller, *Outlines of the History of Greek Philosophy* (14th ed., 1931), p. 290: "Alexandria, where the Greek and oriental worlds met and mingled, had been the birthplace of the Hellenistic-Jewish philosophy (Philo), neo-Pythagoreanism and the revival of Scepticism. It was on this soil, too, that neo-Platonism came to life. . . . The idea of a graduated scale of existence that pervades its system was borrowed from Posidonius." By permission of Harcourt, Brace & Company, Inc., New York.

gods and evil daimons in a clear-cut hierarchy. The gods, he said, were satisfied with prayers, but the evil spirits hungered for the smoke of burnt blood. His *Introduction to the Categories of Aristotle* was the chief vehicle of the transmission of a knowledge of logic to the Christians and the Moslems. Iamblichus (*ca.* 280–330) projected a Neoplatonic church with a priestly system on the Egyptian pattern. Magic had a prominent place in his works. With Proclus (*ca.* 410–485), the last important Neoplatonist, the religious mood was completely dominant. Assailed by daimons and tortured by a sense of sin, he cried out against the evil of earthly life. For philosophical and literary learning he had little use; he prized oriental oracular compilations and the works of Plato, particularly the *Timaeus*. This dialogue, it will be remembered, gave a vivid description of the world in which the soul lived after death. In the rendering of Proclus, Neoplatonic doctrines became a logical system.

The central doctrine of this system was the existence of the *One*—absolute spiritual reality—from which by emanation all other forms of being were created. From the One, who knows without the need of actively knowing, proceeded the Nous, or divine mind. As the principle of becoming, it contained the spiritual forms the good, the true, and the beautiful—which shape the objective world. The emanation of the Nous left the One unchanged. From the Nous proceeded the World Soul, which gave life and motion to the realm of objects. Its emanation left the Nous unchanged. From it emanated the soul of man—his rational mind—and the lesser souls of animals and plants. The human soul had a real existence apart from the body. Its functions were to perceive through the senses, to remember, and to imagine. Since the senses were turned toward matter, the antithesis of the One, they could give man only error. In memory the soul, acting without sensory data, recalled its experience of spiritual reality. In imagination the soul transcended all experience, either immediate or remembered, and achieved a knowledge of the divine mind. In rare trancelike moments the imagination became conscious of the One. According to these doctrines man could have true knowledge only if he turned away from the sensory experience of the world and studied introspectively his own consciousness. Man was a "bridge-being," intermediate between the two worlds, the one of spirit and the other of sense.

Plotinus did not describe a dualistic universe of spirit and matter; for him all reality was spirit. Matter, as the antithesis of the One, possessed no qualities and no powers; it was the principle of nonbeing. Evil existed for men because their souls were enmeshed in a material foreign to them. Salvation was an escape from this alien material into the order of pure spiritual forms and unification with the One. This escape was to be made by leading a rational, as contrasted with a sensual, life, but identification with the One was possible only in the imagination. Most men, however, failed to achieve this supreme ecstasy; for them there was only the bliss of the heaven of the Nous—the order of pure spiritual forms—where perfected souls found happiness in a full knowledge of each other's perfection as well as in a clear experience of the divine mind. Such perfected souls kept on yearning for a full knowlédge of spiritual reality; only the One did not yearn, and only by unification with the One did souls cease to yearn. The One alone was completely real.

Of special note in this system was the threefold order of spiritual being—the *One*, the *Nous*, and the *World Soul*—sometimes called the Neoplatonic Trinity. The qualities of the human soul were derivatives from this concept of reality, and the mode and the goal of its salvation were developed in terms of the concept. In the doctrine of emanation the Neoplatonists found an explanation of the universe which, while accounting for the existence of matter and evil, made reality completely spiritual.

The feeling that pervaded Neoplatonism was expressed by Plotinus in many eloquent passages, none perhaps more eloquent than the one in which the Nous asserted the unity of all existence and its dependence upon the One:

I am made by a God: from that God I came perfect above all forms of life, adequate to my function, self-sufficing, lacking nothing: for I am the container of all, that is, of every plant and every animal, of all the kinds of created things and many Gods and nations of Spirit-Beings and lofty souls and men happy in their goodness.

And do not think that, while earth is ornate with all its growths and with living things of every race, and while the very sea has answered to the power of Soul, do not think that the great air and the ether and the far-spread heavens remain void of it: there it is that all good Souls dwell, infusing life into the stars and into that orderly eternal circuit of the heavens which in its conscious movement ever about the one Centre, seeking nothing beyond, is a faithful copy of the divine Mind. And all that is within me strives towards the Good; and each, to the measure of its faculty, attains. For from that Good all the heavens depend, with all my own Soul and the Gods that dwell in my every part, and all that lives and grows, and even all in me that you may judge inanimate.

The goal of striving for the human soul is no less eloquently set forth:

Suppose the soul to have attained: the highest has come to her, or rather has revealed its presence; she has turned away from all about her and made herself apt, beautiful to the utmost, brought into likeness with the divine—by those preparings and adornings which come unbidden to those growing ready for the vision—she has seen that presence suddenly manifesting within her, for there is nothing between: here is no longer a duality but a two in one; for, so long as the presence holds, all distinction fades: it is as lover and beloved here, in a copy of that union, long to blend; the soul has now no further awareness of being in a body and will give herself no foreign name, not man, not being, not all; any observation of such things falls away; the soul has neither time nor taste for them; This she sought and This she found and on This she looks and not upon herself; and who she is that looks she has not leisure to know. Once There she will barter for This nothing the universe holds; not though one would make over the heavens entire to her; than This there is nothing higher, nothing of more good; above This there is no passing; all the rest however lofty lies on the downgoing path: she is of perfect judgment and knows that This was her quest, that nothing higher is.[1]

The loftiness of Neoplatonic conceptions cannot be denied, nor can the fact that their makers abandoned the rational pursuit of secular knowledge for an intuitional quest of a knowledge of spiritual reality. They preserved the doctrine of the rational organization of reality but allowed man to know it only by suprarational experience. God, the *Good*, and the universe were the "fatherland." Men turned to them "with the unspeakable bliss of the man who, after long journeying, returns at last home," and knew them in a state of ecstasy—"of which the union of earthly lovers is but the reflection." "God," said Plotinus, "is neither to be expressed in speech nor in written discourse": He was knowable in a state of bliss, conceivable only as a blend of the two most powerful emotions, patriotism and passion, which have ever subverted logic to longing.

RELIGION IN ROMAN TIMES

The shift of outlook in philosophy was evidence that the religious currents which had run through the Hellenistic age ran still stronger in Roman times. More and more clearly were religious questions asked. What is the Deity's relation to the world and to

[1] See Stephen Mackenna, *Plotinus, Psychic and Physical Treatises* (1921). P. L. Warner, publisher to the Medici Society, Ltd., London.

man? How can a man save his soul? Why is there evil in the world? How can man know God? The traditional gods were true gods, but what were their roles in a universe over which, so educated men under the influence of philosophy and oriental religions everywhere came to believe, a single, all-powerful God ruled? To these questions were given answers almost as numerous as the sects and faiths; the answers, however, had certain striking agreements.[1]

THE PERSISTENCE OF TRADITIONAL RELIGIOUS BELIEFS.

Chief among these agreements was the universally accepted belief that earthly well-being, especially as realized in the political and social order, is divinely established and maintained. The fall of the Roman Republic, it was argued, had been caused by a neglect of the gods, and the success of the empire was due to the recovery of their favor. Augustus had won this favor by restoring the traditional worship. The cult of emperor worship which he introduced was an importation from the Hellenistic monarchies; actually it was the public worship of the domestic gods of the imperial family. For the Roman ruling class this worship was an expression of faith in the power which had brought imperial dominion; for the lower classes and conquered nations it was a testimony of loyalty to a power which they were no longer able to resist. The state cult was little more than a ritualistic expression of patriotism. Private Roman worship was, as it always had been, mainly a matter of keeping sacred the family gods and of observing the traditional agricultural festivals. Like Rome, whose chief gods were Jupiter and Mars, every city had its own deities. The temples of the gods were kept by priestly colleges whose members generally inherited their positions; Roman law recognized their sacred function by releasing them from civil duties. The Romans did not produce a consolidated priest class, but the priests of local cults, as well as of the national religion, were present in their religious life.

It is probably quite impossible for a modern student to comprehend the superstition that pervaded the mentality of educated as well as illiterate men in Roman times. Under the influence of the Greek tendency to systematize learning, many forms of superstition were cast in pseudoscientific patterns. The previously noted

[1] Franz Altheim, *A History of Roman Religion* (1938); W. Warde Fowler, *The Religious Experience of the Roman People* (1911); Cyril Bailey, *Phases of the Religion of Ancient Rome* (1932); J. B. Carter, *The Religious Life of Ancient Rome* (1911); E. R. Bevan, *Later Greek Religion* (1927).

Photograph by Burton Holmes. From Ewing Galloway, N. Y.

THE PANTHEON, ROME

This building, which has served a religious purpose for almost 2,000 years, originally housed the gods of the Roman Empire. It was begun in 27 B.C. by Agrippa and rebuilt by Hadrian. Its most remarkable architectural feature is the dome 144 feet in circumference. The pillars probably survive from Agrippa's building.

work of Artemidoros[1] on the interpretation of dreams is an example of this development. Astrology was similarly treated. The chief source of its literary growth among the Romans was a Greek poem by Aratus of Soli (fl. *ca.* 275 B.C.), which Cicero translated into Latin and upon which he wrote a commentary. Firmicus Maternus (fl. *ca.* 335), who wrote the greatest Latin work on astrology, described it as a "godly art" to be practiced only by pure priests. The systematization of astrological lore involved the correlation of beliefs about colors, metals, jewels, plants, and animals with ideas about the influence of the seven planets over human lives. Ptolemy produced a correlation of astrological and physiological concepts, connecting the influence of Saturn with the right ear, the bladder, the spleen, the phlegm, and the bones, the influence of Jupiter

[1] See p. 981.

with the sense of touch, the lungs, and the arteries, the influence of Mars with the left ear, the kidneys, the veins, and the male generative organs, the influence of the sun with the eyes, the brain, the heart, and the nerves, the influence of Venus with the smells exciting love, the liver, and the flesh, the influence of Mercury with the tongue and the gall, and the influence of the moon with taste, the stomach, and the female generative organs. He also attempted to correlate the influence of the heavenly bodies with the peculiarities of lands and the characters of their peoples. In fact, Ptolemy, the greatest representative of Greek scientific learning in Roman times, actually produced a synthesis of astrological, physiological, and geographic lore that ranked for centuries as scientific knowledge. Proclus identified the heavenly spheres with spheres of the human mind.

The medical art was heavily encrusted with superstition. From Alexandria issued a literature which, purporting to set forth the wisdom of the ancient Egyptians, described astrological cures of diseases. Dioscorides treated systematically the miraculous curative powers of gems and other rare substances. Sapphires, he said, would cure snake bites. Aristides, the Greek rhetorician whose "Panegyric on Rome" was quoted in the preceding chapter, taught that health is a matter of the harmony of the body with the heavenly spheres; he made incantation and the excitation of visionary experience normal medical practices. The wearing of amulets and charms, as well as the repetition of spells, as protection against disease and accidents were universal customs. Caesar, if he had an accident upon entering his carriage, was wont to repeat a spell three times before starting on his journey. The temples of the healing gods, served by priests, physicians, and nurses, were almost as numerous as those of Jupiter and Mars. Temples to the daimons of disease were not unknown, and exorcism was a favorite method of treating ailments among the illiterate city and country folk. After the second century, when epidemic disease again and again swept through the empire, superstition completely swamped what little science there was in the medical art.

Old and new superstitions were blended in many ways. The most notable example of this development was "judicial astrology," by means of which the emperors sought political guidance. In the second century, when Stoicism became dominant and the oriental worship of the sun well known, the casting of horoscopes was the form of fortunetelling cultivated by the educated aristocrats. Then it was proclaimed that a knowledge of letters and arms was far inferior to a knowledge of stellar portents. The old forms of political divination were not abandoned or suppressed. The state augurs still observed entrails, and the high command of an army in the field ordered the beginning of battle only when the behavior of sacred chickens, carried with the army, indicated that the time was favorable. In the last century B.C., when the eastern Mediterranean states fell before the Roman advance, the ancient oracles lost favor, but toward the end of the first Christian century, when Greek and oriental influences were a rising flood in the West, they revived and new oracles appeared. In the third century these oracles were patronized by individuals desiring a prophecy of the future rather than by politicians seeking guidance. The quacks— miracle mongers, diviners, and fortunetellers—forming the fringe of every learned class whose thought was orientated to the daimonic universe, thrived everywhere. The belief in visions was, of course, only another variety of thought orientated to the daimonic universe—which, as the foregoing paragraphs suggest, pervaded every form of learning and thought.

No less important than the pervasiveness of superstition in Greco-Roman times was its use as a means of political control of the population. When Augustus restored the traditional cult his motive was undoubtedly that which Polybius, two centuries earlier, had found praiseworthy:

> But the quality in which the Roman commonwealth is most distinctly superior is in my opinion the nature of their religious convictions. I believe that it is the very thing which among other people is an object of reproach, I mean superstition, which maintains the cohesion of the Roman state. These matters are clothed in such pomp and introduced to such an extent into their public and private life that nothing could exceed it, a fact which will surprise many. It is a course which perhaps would have been unnecessary had it been possible to form a state of wise men, but as every multitude is fickle, full of lawless desires, unreasoned passion, and violent anger, they must be held in by invisible terrors and such like pageantry. For this reason I think, not that the ancients acted rashly or at haphazard in introducing among the people notions concerning the gods and beliefs in the terrors of hell, but that the moderns are most rash in banishing such beliefs.[1]

This conception of the social function of religion was, of course, a reason for suppressing a movement if it led the masses away from the state cult and also, if the masses turned to a new faith, a reason for making it the state religion. Along with the principle of

[1] Polybius, *Histories*, Book VI, 56.

authoritarian government, this conception of the social function of religion survived in the Christian orientation of Western culture.

THE SPREAD OF THE MYSTERY RELIGIONS.

Besides the rise of Christianity, treated in the next two chapters, the chief religious development of Roman times was the spread of Greek and oriental mystery cults.[1]

The Anatolian cult of Cybele, the Great Mother, reached Rome as early as 204 B.C., and its first temple was built thirteen years later. Augustus gave it official recognition. Claudius inaugurated its spring festival. Its priests, usually eunuchs, maintained regular temple services. Aristocratic adherents sought immortality through austerity and asceticism. Members of the lower classes were attracted by the intense emotionalism expressed in the sacrifice of Attis, beloved of Cybele.

The Egyptian cult of Isis and Serapis entered south Italy in 200 B.C. but was not established at Rome until almost a century later. When Cleopatra came to Rome, Caesar gave it official toleration. Under Caligula an elaborate public ritual was established. Under Domitian, when the cult was at the height of its popularity, the images of its gods were placed on Roman coins. The cult found adherents among all classes.

Mithraism, an offshoot of Zoroastrianism, first reached Rome during Pompey's campaigns in Asia Minor and Syria. It was spread originally by soldiers and slaves, and its chief centers were always in the communities that grew up about the provincial camps of the legionnaires. In the second century it won a wide following in mercantile and official circles. In the third century imperial favor added greatly to its popularity. Partly because its centers were mainly provincial and partly because its outlook was military and aristocratic, the cult never won many adherents among the urban poor.

Originally Mithra, god of the dead, was a second-rank deity in the Zoroastrian pantheon, but in Hellenistic times, when

---

[1] On religious developments in Greco-Roman times see Clifford H. Moore, *The Religious Thought of the Greeks from Homer to the Triumph of Christianity* (1916); Carl Clemen, *Religionsgeschichte Europas*, Vol. I, *Bis zum Untergang der nachchristlichen Religionen* (1926); Samuel Angus, *The Mystery Religions and Christianity* (1925); Samuel Angus, *The Religious Quests of the Graeco-Roman World* (1929); M. I. Rostovtzeff, *Mystic Italy* (1927); Francis Legge, *Forerunners and Rivals of Christianity* (2 vols., 1915); Harold R. Willoughby, *Pagan Regeneration: A study of mystery initiations in the Graeco-Roman world* (1929); E. Bevan, *Sibyls and Seers* (1928); Walter Scott, *Hermetica: The ancient Greek and Latin writings which contain religious or philosophic teachings ascribed to Hermes Trismegistus* (4 vols., 1924).

Babylonian and Greek influences were brought together, especially in eastern Asia Minor, he was identified with the sun and rose to the dignity and power of a Savior-God. As god of light he was the protector of mankind and the mediator between men and the celestial deity. In accordance with the Zoroastrian doctrine that the life of man is a struggle between good and evil, Mithra led his followers in war against the daimonic hosts of Ahriman. To the Zoroastrian virtues of loyalty, honesty, and fortitude Mithraism added the ascetic virtue of celibacy and the social virtue of universal brotherhood. Like other salvation cults, Mithraism did not recognize nationalistic differences. At the end of life virtuous men attained immortality, but the wicked were condemned to eternal punishment.

The cult was organized in small circles, each with its own priests, whose duty it was to keep burning the everlasting fire. Women, who were not admitted to membership in these circles, were attached to the cult by associating the mother goddesses, Cybele and Isis, with Mithra. Members passed through seven grades before reaching the highest circle. In the third grade they became "soldiers" of Mithra and enjoyed communion with him in a sacred meal; in the seventh grade they became "fathers" of the church. The chief ceremony of the cult was the *taurobolium*, which involved the slaughter of a bull and the baptism of the communicant in its blood. In this ceremony, symbolizing the wars between Mithra and Ahriman, moral strength was given to the communicant just as Mithra gave fertility to the earth. Growing plants and heads of ripe wheat, as well as the sun and the bull, were common symbols of the cult.

Mithraism joined Zoroastrian ethics with those beliefs, mostly derived from the ancient fertility cults, which had produced the other mystery religions. Two elements of Mithraism have survived in Western culture: (1) the naming of the days after planets and (2) the celebration of December 25 as the birthday of the Savior God; almost nothing remains of its literature and monuments.[1]

GNOSTICISM.

Gnosticism was not a religion nor yet a philosophy; rather it was a confused mingling of religious, astrological, and philosophical

---

[1] See O. G. von Wesendonk, "Asia Minor and the Introduction of Kybele, Mā, and Mithra into Rome," *Journal of the Royal Asiatic Society*, 1932, pp. 23–31; A. D. Nock, "The Genius of Mithraism," *Journal of Roman Studies*, Vol. 27 (1937), pp. 109–113.

ideas.[1] Over thirty Gnostic systems are known. They began to appear in the second century B.C. and reached a high point of popularity in the second Christian century. They were the products of the syncretic tendencies of the revolutionary age that brought the fall of the Roman Republic. They developed mainly in the eastern Mediterranean area where Greek mystery religions and philosophy encountered Babylonian astrology and Egyptian mythology. Their creators were mostly men of some learning who claimed divine inspiration. Their adherents were drawn chiefly from the uprooted but not enslaved urban classes. Each sect had its own priests and admitted members only by a secret initiation. Whatever unity Gnosticism possessed was intellectual rather than social.

The common denominator of the Gnostic systems consisted of two beliefs: (1) Salvation can be won only by a special knowledge that makes possible an approach to supreme spiritual reality. (2) Matter, as opposed to spirit, is fundamentally evil. Closely associated with these beliefs were the ideas that the physical universe is a calamity, the body is a prison for the soul, and earthly life is sinful. Escape of the soul from entanglement in the material world was, therefore, the goal of earthly existence.

The Gnostic teachers elaborated endless variations on these themes. Long before the Neoplatonists gave the doctrine of emanation a philosophical rendering, they used it to explain the creation of both the physical world and the hierarchy of spiritual beings that stood between men and supreme spiritual reality. According to Valentinus (fl. *ca.* 135–160), the most prominent Gnostic teacher, there emanated from the unknown god—pure spirituality—pairs of ideal beings, such as Depth and Silence, Mind and Truth, Reason and Life, and Man and State. Altogether there were thirty pairs of these beings, forming the *pleroma*, an ideal order of spiritual beings. From Sophia, or Wisdom, the supreme female principle, who because of a fit of passion was cast out of the pleroma, was born Achamoth, who, in turn, created the material world. The angels who helped build the world also created man, but one of another order of spiritual beings, the *aeons*, unknown to the angels, planted in man the seeds of spirituality

[1] On Gnosticism see Hans Jonas, *Gnosis und spätantiker Geist*, Teil I, "Die Mythologische Gnosis" (1934); Richard Reitzenstein, *Die hellenistischen Mysterienreligionen nach ihren Grundgedanken und Wirkungen* (1920); Eugène de Faye, *Gnostiques et Gnosticisme* (1913); Luigi Salvatorelli, "From Locke to Reitzenstein: The Historical Investigation of the Origins of Christianity," *Harvard Theological Review*, Vol. 22 (1929), pp. 263–367.

so that he sought salvation. Because of this origin men, it was believed, were of three types: (1) the *pneumatic*, or those capable of receiving divine inspiration, (2) the *psychic*, or those who may understand a revelation received by a pneumatic person, and (3) the *hylic*, or those who, because they were incapable of understanding revelation, were doomed. The redemption of man was accomplished through the marriage of a heavenly Savior with the fallen Sophia. In the system of Basilides (fl. *ca.* 130), the Supreme Being created seven aeons, of whom two, Dynamics and Sophia, *i.e.*, Power and Wisdom, procreated superior angels. These angels built a heaven and in turn produced another order of angels; this process continued until there had been created 365 orders of angels. The lowest order of angels made the world and men. By the intervention of the Supreme Being men were given souls, and finally because the lowest angels, among whom the god of the Jews was the worst, ruled men badly, the Supreme Being sent the prince of the aeons to save men. Offshoots of these systems, as well as others, throve throughout the Roman world in the late second and the early third century.

In the quest for salvation man performed sacred rituals, practiced magic, sought spiritual knowledge, and followed an ascetic morality. Among the rituals baptism and ceremonies of confirmation, the bridal chamber, and breaking bread and sharing salt were prominent. Incantation, particularly the utterance of the seven vowels, which were believed to symbolize pure spirituality before its imprisonment in gross matter (represented by the consonants), was widely practiced. Knowledge was believed to be a "gift of the spirit," not to be won by unaided reason. Ascetic living was a way of rising above the sinfulness of worldly existence. Moral purification was not a means of winning salvation but the goal to be reached when salvation was won. The Gnostics denied the resurrection of the body because they believed that matter was completely evil and life after death was purely spiritual.

The intellectual methods of the Gnostic teachers were as diverse as their doctrines. They had dreams, visions, and visitations of the spirit. They found allegorical meanings in every word and event. They argued logically about propositions for which no basis in observed fact existed. They compiled sacred works and ascribed to them divine authorship and authority. They produced treatises as formless as the systems of thought they embodied. Above all, although they taught that salvation is possible only through knowledge, their knowing was an introspective process in which mythology and mysticism were blended in faith, and the knowledge thus obtained was useful chiefly as an instrument of warfare against the daimons who cut off human access to spiritual reality. The superhuman Savior, who was to save men, was to be a teacher of this knowledge.

Among the Gnostic sects only one—the Mandaeans, or Sabaeans —survived the breakup of the Roman Empire. This sect, pre-Christian in origin, had its center in Mesopotamia and the fringes of the Arabian desert. Its literature consisted of the *Geriza*, or Treasure, a sacred work, and the *Kolasta*, a collection of hymns and liturgies. Its mythology was a blend of Persian, Babylonian, and Indian teachings. The supreme god was a Light King against whom a female monster of chaos made war. Between men and the Light King was a complex hierarchy of aeons, angels, and daimons. The savior, Hibil Siva, was an incarnation of the Light King. Persian influence was evident in the moral doctrine that man must make the best of an evil world. Celibacy and asceticism were repudiated. The Sabaean holiday was Sunday and the chief ceremony baptism. The Christian savior was declared to be a devil. The sect was governed by a rigid priestly hierarchy.

From one point of view Gnosticism seems to have been merely a confusion of beliefs and intellectual methods; from another point of view it appears to have been a new effort to solve the problem of man's place in the universe. Actually Gnosticism was both of these things: it was the opening phase of intellectual and emotional development in the Mediterranean Basin which ultimately subverted the critical rationalism of Greek culture to the mysticism that found enduring expression in Christianity. The formlessness of Gnosticism was due to the fact that in the early period of the rising religious feeling there existed no principle to direct the selection and organization of beliefs and doctrines from the current mixture of Babylonian, Egyptian, Persian, Indian, Hebrew, and Greek ideas.

THE DIRECTION OF RELIGIOUS CHANGE.

An indication of what this principle of selection was to be is revealed by the direction in which religious developments were moving in Roman times. The primary movement was the displacement of the Greek confidence in man's intellectual and moral energy by the feeling that spiritually man was weak and helpless. Man was doomed to defeat in his quest for moral purity and immortality unless aided by a power greater than himself. How could man win spiritual aid? That was the burning question of the times.

The answer that was to be given to this question was implicit in the area of agreement among the philosophical and religious systems of late Roman times.[1] In brief this area of agreement included beliefs such as the following:

1. There is a single Supreme Being—Father.
2. Between the Supreme Being and men stands a host of lesser spiritual beings, of whom some aid men and others attempt to destroy them.
3. These spiritual beings constantly intervene in human affairs; in other words, miracles occur.
4. Worldly existence is wicked, sensual experience is evil, and contact with matter corrupts the soul.
5. Formal rituals and perhaps also magic and wonder working are necessary aids to man's striving for spirituality.
6. The knowledge helpful in man's quest for salvation is suprasensual and suprarational.
7. This knowledge is available to men either in direct revelations from the Supreme Being or in the utterances of inspired teachers or in the inner experience that men may have of spiritual reality.
8. Men can be saved only by a Savior God who acts with the knowledge and power of the Supreme Being; this Savior God teaches men the way of salvation.
9. The individual is spiritually reborn when he comes into the possession of that knowledge of spiritual reality which assures the salvation of the soul.
10. After death the individual human soul lives on in a spiritual world where moral perfection is achieved and sinfulness is punished.

Generally the philosophers and religious teachers of Hellenistic and Roman times wove some combination of these beliefs into a conception of cosmic struggle in which man's worldly life was only an episode. In this struggle there were two powers: (1) a supreme being, spiritually and morally perfect and (2) a monarch of evil. Both powers were surrounded by lesser spiritual beings— aeons and angels around the Supreme Being and daimons around the monarch of evil. These powers and their hosts waged eternal warfare for the control of the universe and the possession of men's souls. Men necessarily took part in this warfare, but as men they were helpless before the daimons. Only with the aid of a Savior God could they obtain the necessary spiritual strength to fend off the

---

[1] See E. R. Bevan, *Later Greek Religion* (1928), Introduction, pp. xxx–xxxi.

daimonic assaults. The climax of this warfare was a conflict in which victory came to the forces of righteousness and destruction or endless punishment to the forces of evil. In this final conflict, according to some teachers, the physical universe was to be purified; according to others, it was to be destroyed.

Not all of the foregoing ideas were found in every philosophy and religion of Roman times, nor were the ones embodied in the various philosophies and religions developed in the same manner. Furthermore, it must be remembered that each philosophy and religion embodied ideas other than these. But underneath the differences and contradictions among the philosophical and religious systems was this area of comparatively clear agreement, and as time went on beliefs contrary to these basic ideas tended to disappear. Above all the basic conviction that man, alone, is spiritually helpless grew stronger.

ROMAN LAW

The single intellectual development which the Romans initiated and significantly contributed to was the formation of a body of law which became as time went on an instrument to realize a justice based not on custom but on reason. The necessity of ruling the divers peoples of the conquered lands was the chief incentive to the substitution of principles for customs, and acquaintance with the laws of other peoples, as well as with Greek philosophy, guided the substitution. In the end, however, the systematization of the law was almost as much the work of non-Romans as it was of Romans. In fact when Roman law is viewed as a cultural growth and not as a creation of the Roman state, it appears as a product of the mingling of peoples and the assimilation of local cultures that influenced every other aspect of cultural change in Roman times.[1]

The Courts and the Law under the Roman Republic.

The advance of the plebeians to political power led to the establishment in 366 B.C. of a special court for the trial of cases between citizens and plebians. The magistrate of the court was known as the *praetor urbanus*, *i.e.*, the judge of the city. Each year this

[1] See *The Cambridge Ancient History*, Vol. 9, *The Roman Republic* 133–44 B.C. (1932), Chap. XXI, "The Development of the Law under the Republic"; Vol. II, *The Imperial Peace A.D. 70–192* (1936), Chap. XXI, "Classical Roman Law." See also H. F. Jolowicz, *Historical Introduction to the Study of Roman Law* (1932); C. P. Sherman, *Roman Law in the Modern World* (3 vols., 2d ed., 1924); W. W. Buckland, *A Textbook of the Roman Law from Augustus to Justinian* (2d ed., 1932).

official was elected from the ranks of the patricians. When he entered upon his office, he issued an edict setting forth the law he would follow during his term. Generally a praetor reissued the edict of his predecessor, but from time to time new rules were announced. Thus a secular official came to possess the power to modify the law by setting precedents and inventing legal fictions. Enactments by the centuries and the tribes also modified the law. About the beginning of the last quarter of the fourth century B.C. the right of a creditor to enslave a debtor was altered, and somewhat later the right to collect damages for injuries to property was redefined. When the plebeians were admitted to the priestly offices at the opening of the third century B.C. constant reforms in procedure were introduced, and finally in the middle of that century the first plebeian Pontifex Maximus released all legal "secrets." The creation of the praetorian court was the decisive step in the development of the *jus civile*, because it permitted the reinterpretation of old laws in accordance with changing conditions. The overthrow of the legal monopoly of the priests by the plebeians opened the way for the complete secularization of the law, for the judge, not the priest, became the guardian of justice.

Shortly after the middle of the third century B.C. a court was set up to try cases between citizens and foreigners. Its magistrate was known as the *praetor peregrinus*, *i.e.*, the judge of foreigners, and he, like the praetor urbanus, issued an annual edict. This departure led quickly to the recognition that among foreign peoples there were many legal systems but a few almost universal legal principles. The Romans did not regard these principles as foreign law; rather they looked upon them as common to all peoples, including themselves, and applicable in all circumstances. To this body of law they gave the name *jus gentium*. Cicero, from whom comes the first mention of the jus gentium, defined it as the law which natural reason has established among all nations. The jus gentium was, therefore, not opposed to the jus civile; it was, as a matter of fact, treated as a part of it. In applying the jus gentium the praetors invoked the traditional Roman concept "aequitas," *i.e.*, equity, and undertook to render justice according to reasoned principles. In the concepts "jus gentium" and "aequitas" were laid the foundations of abstract as opposed to customary law. The expansion of Roman rule led inevitably to the growth of the influence of the edicts of the praetor peregrinus, and appeals from the provinces kept his court constantly in touch with changing conditions throughout the Mediterranean world. These circumstances made his precedents the chief means of transforming the law of the city into a legal system universal in scope and application:

> What changed Roman law from a local rigid formal law into a world-wide rational formless jurisprudence? The answer is: the growth of foreign trade and commerce, the legal problems of which were solved by the praetor's applications of the rules of the law of nations (*jus gentium*).[1]

In 150 B.C. the praetor was given the power to alter both customary and statutory law in the light of right and reason.

Under the late republic the law began to be systematized. Procedure in cases at private law was formalized. A case was opened by a litigant presenting a claim to the praetor, who, if he found that the facts warranted a suit, called upon the defendant to reply. In this reply the defendant might deny the facts, set up a defense in law, or enter a counterclaim. After having heard both the plaintiff and the defendant, the praetor prepared a written statement of the issue. Sometimes as many as three or four declarations and replies were required of the parties to a suit before trial was held. Finally the case was referred to a *judex*, usually a senator, or a number of arbiters. In the trial witnesses were heard, documents examined, and arguments made. Praetors had the power to force parties to a suit to produce witnesses and documents in court. The criminal law was given enduring form under Sulla. He instituted special criminal courts, defined the various crimes, and fixed the penalties for each. In case capital punishment was ordered by the court, the defendant could appeal to the assembly of tribes. In such cases the large number of jurors gave opportunity for bribery, and corruption was common. Not the least important development during this period was the shift of the law from a personal to a territorial basis as a result of the Social War. This development, which meant that the law belonged not to the citizens of Rome but to the land of Italy, was the forerunner of the future unification of the empire under a single body of law.

[1] C. P. Sherman, *Roman Law in the Modern World*, (3 vols., 2d ed., 1924), Vol. 1, p. 37. Baker, Vorhis & Co., New York. Note also the comment on the impact of economic change on Roman law in P. Louis, *Ancient Rome at Work* (1927), p. 121. "The operations of lending and of selling, in particular, were freed from the formalities by which they had been previously impeded. The system of leasing became more and more current and as early as the third century, when Italians came in large numbers to reside in the capital, they took their houses on lease. . . . The economic revolution, favoured by the continued conquests, had abolished all the outworn conceptions which were based on the exclusive predominance of agriculture, upon the *gens* system and upon the divine right of ownership." By permission of Alfred A. Knopf, Inc., New York, and George Routledge & Sons, Ltd., London.

The Rise of Roman Legal Scholarship and Its Achievements.

Under the early republic every patrician was obligated to have a knowledge of legal tradition, and after the drawing up of the Twelve Tables patrician boys memorized the civil law in the same manner as they learned the other traditions of their class. Thus, as previously noted, the study of the law was from the first a branch of literate education. The chief early factor in the growth of legal scholarship was, however, the admission of plebeians to the senate and the magistracies, for in these positions they needed a knowledge of law and procedure. At the center of this growth were the praetorian courts, around which formed a steadily augmented body of students of the legal tradition, known as *prudentes*. The praetors, of course, were chosen from the ruling class, and their councils were filled with men of social position as well as of legal learning. The prudentes were, in fact, a specialized body of the ruling class; they kept alive the ancient legal tradition and adapted it to changing times, chiefly by creating new procedural precedents and by reinterpreting the provisions of the Twelve Tables. Roman law and the Roman legal profession were correlative developments.

About the opening of the second century B.C., when Sextus Aelius Paetus wrote the first legal treatise, the study of the law began to be influenced by Greek intellectual methods and philosophical outlook. The prudentes began to combine rhetoric, logic, and an ethical viewpoint with their legal learning. The results were a rapid literary elaboration of the law and the displacement of the traditional by an abstract conception of the law. With the elder Scaevola (d. 82 B.C.), who as author of eighteen books on the civil law is known as the "father of Roman jurisprudence," these influences were worked into a statement of legal principles. These principles, rendered as legal maxims or definitions, were comparable to the axioms in mathematics and the predications of metaphysics, for their validity was presumed to rest on the nature of things as understood by human reason. How this outlook transformed the traditional conception of the law is well indicated in the following quotation from Cicero, Scaevola's greatest pupil: "There is a true law, a right reason comfortable to justice, diffused through all hearts, unchangeable, eternal, which by its commands summons to duty, by its prohibitions deters from evil. Attempts to amend this law are imperious, to modify it wrong, to repeal it impossible." In the first century B.C. the prudentes trained in this outlook became the guardians of the law. In responses to questions asked by judges they had direct control over the determination of legal issues and the making of legal decisions. Thus the common opinion of the prudentes became the final legal resort.

The position of influence and distinction which the legal profession occupied in the great period of the empire rested on the official recognition given to the prudentes by Augustus and continued by his successors until Diocletian. This recognition consisted of the licensing of certain legal scholars, known as *jurisconsults*, to issue to judges statements of the law which, under imperial order, they were bound to accept. The jurisconsults also contributed to the formulation of imperial legislation. It is important to realize that the centralization of power in the hands of the emperor did not make him the source of the law; the law remained, as it had been under the republic, a thing apart from the mere exercise of sovereign power. As a matter of fact Augustus and his successors raised the legal learning elaborated by the prudentes to the status of imperial law.

Occupying a position only slightly less important than the jurisconsults was the main body of prudentes. They acted as counselors and teachers, giving advice to clients and training students. From the last period of the republic to the reign of Hadrian there were two great schools of the law; they were modeled on the Greek schools of philosophy. The Sabinian school, named for Sabinus (d. *ca.* A.D. 30), the first lawyer licensed to give responses, seems to have emphasized the philosophical view of the law. The rival Proculian school named for Proculus (fl. *ca.* A.D. 50) held fast to traditional views and methods. These schools were maintained by jurisconsults and prudentes, and students paid fees to attend them. Textbooks prepared for use in these schools exercised a powerful influence on the development of the law. In Hadrian's time most of the leading lawyers were members of the *consilium imperium*.

Ordinary lawyers, known as *advocates*, who argued causes in the courts, seem to have been in the main a greedy and venal lot. To make themselves appear important, they often carried about with them big bundles of documents, hired claquers to greet them when they entered a courtroom, and wore rich jewelry and gaudy clothing. Although the taking of fees was regulated, lawyers frequently grew rich on bequests from wealthy patrons. The Roman lawyers were generally in the service of the owners of property, who were, of course, mainly aristocrats. The poor man in Rome, it should be realized, went without legal aid and was at the mercy of the magistrate.

Under the empire the influences which had begun to shape the law in the third century B.C. carried it to maturity. The centralizing tendency led in Hadrian's reign to the substitution of a perpetual edict for the yearly edicts of the praetorian courts. This edict, formulated by the jurisconsult Salvius Julianus (d. *ca.* 169) and ratified by the senate in 131, became the permanent basis of imperial law. The universalizing tendency resulted in the extension of the law to the empire when in 212 Caracalla granted citizenship to all freedmen. The ethical tendencies had manifold results. At their base was the concept *jus naturale, i.e.,* the natural law, which, although derived from Stoic philosophy, was developed largely from the jus gentium—the law which Cicero had described as flowing from the hearts of all men. In order to attain the unity of the law, the legal scholars presumed that the jus naturale had been the original source of the customary law of ancient Rome, and in order to preserve the unity of the law they set themselves the task of defining its principles and applying them to all situations. Their work ranks as the greatest intellectual achievement of Roman culture.

Among the many contributors to Roman jurisprudence a few great names stand out. The elder Scaevola, previously noted, introduced the principle that the intention of the parties determines the validity of a contract. Gaius (d. *ca.* 180), probably a Syrian Greek, first compared Roman law with the laws of other nations on specific points. His great work, the *Institutes*, became the model for legal textbooks. Among the principles he developed were: (1) "A man's house is his castle." (2) "Want of skill is equivalent to negligence." (3) "A creditor who permits a thing pledged to be sold loses his security." His contemporary, Salvius Julianus, who drew up the perpetual praetorian edict, wrote a digest of the law in ninety books. Under his leadership the Sabinian school absorbed its rival. The flexibility of his thought is illustrated by the following opinions: (1) "Whenever a phrase has two meanings, that is to be accepted which is most fitted to the accomplished fact in the question." (2) "He ceases to be a debtor who has a just defense not inconsistent with natural equity." Papinian (d. 212), a Syrian, rose to criminal jurisdiction just below that of the emperor. His many legal works were noted for clarity of expression and profundity of thought; among them was a treatise on the law in Greek. From his pen came declarations such as: (1) "No one may change his purpose to the violation of another's right." (2) "A rule of public policy cannot be changed by a private contract."

(3) "The law draws an inference of fraud not from the event alone but from the intention." The Greek, Scaevola (d. *ca.* 193), was a voluminous author. He declared: (1) "It is theft when anyone knowingly has received money not owed him," and (2) "What a majority of a local government [*i.e.*, the government of a city] does is regarded as done by all." Paulus (*d. ca.* 222), who identified the law with all that is equitable and good, developed the principles: (1) "Ignorance of the law does not excuse; ignorance of the fact does," (2) "Whatever was originally void cannot be cured by a lapse of time," and (3) "No one is a wrongdoer except him who does what the law does not permit." Ulpian (d. *ca.* 228), the most quoted Roman jurist, was noted for lucid expression. The quality is well illustrated in the following propositions: (1) "The partner of my partner is not my partner." (2) "No one by his own wrong-doing can make his condition better." (3) "The judgment of a court is accepted as the truth." "The precepts of the law," he said, "were to live uprightly, not to hurt a neighbor, and to render to everyone his own." The last important Roman jurist was Modestinus (d. *ca.* 244). His statement of the function of the law was complete and unequivocal: "to command, forbid, allow, punish."

The foregoing examples of the thought of the great jurisconsults indicates clearly the abstract character of Roman jurisprudence. Although the philosophical outlook derived by the jurisconsults from Greek learning contributed most to the evolution of the law as an abstract system, the common practice of learned men of plagiarizing the works of their predecessors and contemporaries was an important aid in blending the work of individual jurisconsults into a single body of learning. The fact that the law was not codified preserved its flexibility. Its practical realism was due to the close contact of the prudentes with the work of government. They were not mere legal scholars; from the first they were immediately associated with the officials of the republic, and under the empire many of them had active political careers. Several of them perished in the disorders that engulfed the empire after the reign of Marcus Aurelius. Only after the emperor became absolute in Diocletian's time, did the Roman lawyers degenerate into compilers and commentators and the Roman law become ripe for codification.

The Roman Civil Law.

Although Roman public, religious, and criminal law had lasting influence, only the civil law, as elaborated by the jurisconsults, became a fundamental element in the Western cultural tradition; as Gaius said, it dealt with *persons*, *things*, and *actions*.

The Roman law of personality drew a distinction between a *man* and a *person*, with the result that a man might actually be several persons. For example, the Roman might be a magistrate, a head of a family, a soldier, a partner in a business, and an agent, and in each capacity special rights and obligations constituted him a person. Furthermore, individuals organized for a common purpose and having a common treasury were regarded as a person; this is the legal conception which survives today in the corporation. Such corporate persons, known to Romans as *universitates*, were common in municipal, religious, industrial, and commercial affairs. Because slaves had no rights, they were not regarded as persons. Foreigners became persons when granted rights under Roman law. Besides the rights to bear arms and to vote in the assemblies, the chief rights of the citizen were to head a family and to possess a patrimony, *i.e.*, to own part of the soil of Italy. The loss of citizenship deprived a man of these rights. Originally boys became persons only when admitted to citizenship by formal initiation. Natural facts recognized by the law of personality were the differences of sex, infancy and majority, and sanity and insanity.

Roman family law began as a branch of the law of things, for the power of the father—*paterfamilias*—over the members of the family was that of an owner over his chattels. The father was the priest of the family cult, the sole judge of right and wrong within the family group, and the owner of all property held or acquired by family members. He held the power of life and death over family members and could expose children at birth to die or sell them later into slavery. Sons acquired no rights of property so long as the father lived, and if he gave consent to their marriage their wives and children were under his power. The father gave daughters in marriage as he saw fit. No member of the family could take legal action against him. At the death of the father his sons became heads of their families; the eldest son had no special rights over younger sons.

The autocratic patriciate slowly declined, until, by the first century, it was little more than a shadow of its original form. In the Twelve Tables a form of marriage was allowed which permitted the wife to retain title to her property. Under the late republic the father's power to punish was little more than the right to chastise. By means of the *peculium*, property passed into the hands of sons, and the son became capable of binding the father in a contract. Property acquired by a son during military service belonged to him and could be disposed of by will. In the early empire women were freed from many legal disabilities under which the traditional family law had placed them. If unmarried, they became free at the death of their father. The form of marriage which allowed them to hold property was almost universal. And they, as well as their husbands, could dissolve a marriage by the withdrawal of consent. Divorce was remarkably free under the empire.

Marriage was originally a religious ritual and a contractual arrangement. Both the fathers of the parties to a marriage and the parties themselves were required to give their consent. Boys could give consent at the age of fourteen, girls at the age of twelve. After the betrothal the bride's dowry was given to the husband; the marriage was complete when the husband took the bride to his home. Marriage was legal within all degrees of relation beyond those of parent and offspring and of brother and sister. Marriage between a freeman or a freewoman and a slave was prohibited. As previously noted, the members of the families of senators were not allowed to marry within the ranks of freedmen. A married man was not allowed to keep concubines. Children born out of wedlock were commonly legitimized. By adoption a father could take into the family children not born of his marriage. Only minors could be adopted, and a difference of eighteen years between the father and the child was required. The relation established by adoption could not be broken once it was entered into. The practice of adoption was common among the aristocracy, chiefly as a means of obtaining an heir and of keeping a family line alive. Augustus, it will be remembered, was a nephew of Caesar and his heir by adoption. Adopted children had the same rights and obligations as blood children. By different forms of guardianship the education of orphaned children and the care of their property were legally provided for.

The Roman law of things, which was grounded in custom, recognized several classes of property, such as sacred property, *i.e.*, the lands, temples, and utensils which belonged to the gods; common property, *i.e.*, the air, the sea, and running water; public property, *i.e.*, walls, gates, streets, aqueducts, and roads; and private property, *i.e.*, things that could be owned by individuals. All things were divided into two classes, corporeal and incorporeal. Chief among corporeal things were lands, buildings, livestock, slaves, implements, and furnishings. Among incorporeal things were the rural and urban servitudes. The rural servitudes were the right to an eight-foot roadway for heavy traffic, the right to a footpath or a bridle road, the right to drive cattle to water across another's land, the right to take water in an artificial channel across another's land, and the right to draw water from another's well. The urban servitudes were the right to seat timbers in a neighbor's wall, the right to discharge rain water in gutters, and the right to allow water from a roof to drip on another's land. The urban dweller was required to build his wall strong enough to bear the weight of his neighbor's construction. The law defined three modes of private ownership: (1) the full right of use and abuse, (2) the right of usufruct, *i.e.*, the right to use but not to change, and (3) the right to use for a limited time under the compulsion of necessity. Originally the absolute right to use and abuse private property applied to all corporeal things, but in the course of time it was modified as regards slaves and lands. As early as the Twelve Tables the existence of a public interest in private things was recognized.

A large part of the law of things dealt with ways of acquiring ownership. Under the jus civile ownership was acquired in three ways: (1) by formal sale in the presence of five witnesses, (2) by transfer under the order of a magistrate, and (3) by use—one year for movables and two years for immovables. Less formal ways of obtaining title to things were recognized under the jus gentium: (1) by taking possession, as in the case of game and abandoned or lost articles; (2) by accession, as when a thing is joined to the property of another so that the two cannot be separated without destroying them (under this rule buildings became part of the land); (3) by using raw material belonging to another (a craftsman had ownership of his product if the raw material could not be restored to its original form); (4) by the right of treasure trove (if a man found treasure on his own land it belonged to him, but if he found it on another's land half of it went to the owner of the land); and (5) by delivery with the intention of giving ownership. This last method was sufficient for the acquisition of all things except Italian land, slaves, beasts of burden, and certain rural servitudes which could change hands only under the jus civile. If transferred under the jus gentium, title to these things was normally established by the right of use of the jus civile. By developing a special form of ownership for things sold under the jus gentium, the praetors replaced the formal process of transfer of the jus civile with a flexibility which, while protecting the rights of both the seller and the purchaser, permitted transactions of all kinds to be made easily. Ownership and possession were not regarded as identical. If a person claimed ownership of property in the possession of another, he was required to prove his claim, and the praetor protected the possessor until he did so.

With the development of flexibility in the law of transfer of property, came the elaboration of legal means of possessing and using it. Chief among these means were the leasehold and the loan secured by mortgage. Leases for a period, in perpetuity, and at will developed. Originally a leaseholder had no rights against an owner except those stipulated in a contract, and he could not assign the leased property to a third party. In time, however, he obtained the right of assignment. The loan secured by mortgage was a special form of credit transaction. The mortgage was dead property given by a debtor to a creditor as security for a loan. The debtor retained possession as a tenant at will, but ownership was transferred to the creditor by formal conveyance. The right of the debtor to recover ownership when the loan was repaid was provided for in a collateral agreement. If the creditor sold the property to a third party, which he had a right to do, the debtor could bring an action to protect his rights. If the debtor failed to repay the loan, his rights were completely extinguished by the sale of the property under the order of the court. Interest was the compensation due a creditor when a debtor failed to repay a loan. A sharp distinction was drawn between the principal of a loan and this compensation. Originally, although a creditor could enslave a debtor who failed to pay the principal, he had only a civil remedy for the failure to pay interest. For a time the praetors allowed creditors to avoid this limitation by permitting them to sue for interest as if it were money that had been lent.

The making of profit on lent money, known as usury, developed from this practice of allowing a creditor to collect compensation when a debtor defaulted. As the traditional agrarian economy gave way before the development of commerce, opportunities for lending money at a profit multiplied, and moneylending became a lucrative business. It was first subjected to legal regulation in the Twelve Tables. The rate of interest was fixed at 12 per cent, and those who collected more were punished twice as severely as thieves. From the fourth century B.C. to the end of the republic there is ample evidence to support the view that the struggle of debtors and moneylenders was a significant factor in politics. In 347 B.C. the legal rate of interest was fixed at 5, and five years later the right to collect interest was abolished. Since this law applied only to citizens, it was evaded by making loans in the names of aliens. Apparently the praetors winked at the practice for a long time, for it was not suppressed until the opening of the second century B.C. As Roman power grew, the profits of money-lending increased because in the provinces the moneylenders could charge as much as the traffic would bear. In some cases they collected about 50 per cent per year. In the time of the Gracchi open hostility between creditors and debtors appeared, and in the Social War violence broke out between them. Sulla eased the situation by fixing the interest rate at 1 per cent per month. In the middle of the first century B.C. this rate, which amounted to 12 per cent, was extended to the provinces. Caesar laid the foundation of the imperial law of debt by legislating further restrictions on usury. A schedule of graduated rates for different social classes—8 per cent for merchants, 6 per cent for persons not in business, and 4 per cent for distinguished persons and agriculturalists—was introduced. More important, however, than these limitations was the law of bankruptcy, which revolutionized the ancient law of debt by allowing a debtor to cede his estate to his creditors and begin anew with liability for obligations proceeding from the earlier periods only if they could be paid without financially ruining him. This reform, it should be noted, was designed more to protect the creditor against fraud than to ease the debtor's burden. All modern systems of bankruptcy stem from this legislation. In the course of these developments the ancient right of the creditor to enslave the debtor disappeared and a system of exemptions which withdrew certain chattels from seizure took its place. The extent of the exemption was left to the discretion of the magistrate. Normally a debtor was allowed to keep only the goods necessary for the sustenance of himself and his family—his plow, his cow, and his harness. Under the empire moneylending as a business declined, and the greatest evils of usury ceased. But the lower classes remained the prey of petty creditors. Imprisonment of the debtor and holding the debtor for ransom were common, as was the old custom of seizing the corpse of a defaulting debtor as a means of enforcing payment from his heirs. The general tendency of imperial legislation was to lessen the rights of the creditor over the debtor.

The jurisconsults treated interest as a penalty due the creditor from the debtor because (1) during the time the property lent was in the hands of the debtor the creditor was not able to deal with it for profit and (2) the debtor was responsible for losses that might be suffered by the creditor on account of his not having possession and use of his property. These doctrines, it should be noted, support the creditor's right to collect interest but not his right to charge usury. The importance of this distinction rests in the fact that when interest is regarded as a penalty the fixing of the rate by public authority is justified, but when it is regarded as a means of making a profit its rate, at least in the eyes of creditors, should be determined only by the demand of debtors for loans. Roman lawyers did not develop the view that the price of investment capital should be set by supply and demand.

The most distinctive element of the civil law was the law of contract. Like other elements of the civil law it was originally formal, but in time, largely as the result of the diversification of economic activity, it developed a high degree of flexibility. A contract was a legal form that made enforceable the promises of individuals, particularly those entered into by bargaining. A contractual relation was regarded as involving three distinct acts: (1) the offer, (2) the acceptance, and (3) the delivery or the performance. Offer and acceptance together constituted the agreement that was enforceable; delivery or performance was the act which the parties to the agreement could be legally compelled to perform. There were four types of contracts: (1) literal—originally an entry in a creditor's account book, (2) verbal—a formal declaration by both parties using the words "I promise," (3) real—an obligation entered into by one party only when the other party transferred to him actual things, as in the case of loans, deposits, and pledges, and (4) consensual—agreement to sell, to hire, to act as partners, or to act as an agent. Under the empire the idea of enforcing promises, particularly business bargains, grew, and the forms of agreement became more and more elastic. Various methods of extinguishing a contractual obligation, besides delivery and performance, were recognized. Among these methods were (1) a tender of payment, (2) a lapse of time, (3) the loss of a thing necessary to performance, (4) a mutual exchange of new intentions, (5) a merger of creditor and debtor interest, and (6) a plea at the bar. Every individual was responsible for his frauds, including the seller, who was responsible for the undisclosed faults of the articles he sold. The Roman law of contract standardized transactions involving property rights and the performance of labor by making the intentions of individuals in their private relations legally binding.

Originally the law of succession provided that property passed from the father to his sons. If there were no sons, it passed to his brothers, and if there were no brothers to his gens. Gentile succession disappeared under the late republic. At the same time the wife, if married by the legal form which permitted her to hold title to property, became the heir when her husband had neither sons nor brothers. Her brothers were her heirs. Under the empire a wife who had borne three children was given the right to succeed to the property of her husband, and her children became her heirs. These changes ran parallel to the modification in the power of the patriarch. Testate succession, *i.e.*, by will, was known in the early republic. Apparently early wills were made by verbal declaration in the assembly of centuries or before the army when battle was about to begin. The legal form consisted of (1) the transfer of the property to a trustee by formal conveyance and (2) the issuance of instructions to him for its distribution. In time the instructions, which had always been binding on the trustee, became a true will. Such wills, revocable during the life of the testator, were legal only when made over the signature of seven witnesses and the testator. The testator was completely free to choose his heir; furthermore, he was free to leave legacies which were a burden to the heir. Because the heir could succeed to the obligations as well as to the rights of the testator, he might be forced to pay out as a debtor more than he received as owner and creditor. The form of the will changed very little under the empire.

As previously noted, a lawsuit was brought by an appeal of a plaintiff to a magistrate, such as the praetor, but was decided by a private judge, the judex. The first part of the procedure was to determine an issue; the second part was to render a decision. Under the early republic the first part of the procedure was so formal that a mistake by a plaintiff in uttering fixed sets of words would lose his suit. After the middle of the second century B.C. this rigid procedure was superseded by the formula system. In this system the issue was arrived at by the merging of the plaintiff's charge and the defendant's answer in a statement, usually in a form which provided the alternative of condemnation or release of the defendant. By refusing to issue instructions to a judex, the praetor could force both parties to a suit to accept the formulation of an issue he saw fit to approve. Under the law of legal action all suits were settled by a kind of arbitration over which magistrates and judges acted as supervisors. Not until the rise of the absolute monarchy did the judges, using administrative powers, begin to impose justice; this modification of judicial practice, it is important to note, developed first in the provinces.

The Characteristics of the Roman Legal System.

The development of Roman law was continuous from the ancient tribes to the oriental monarchy—a period of about fifteen hundred years. Although the Twelve Tables and many legislative enactments contributed to this development, the enduring force was an unwritten legal tradition, originally preserved by priests but ultimately perpetuated and elaborated by lawyers. The process of legal growth was twofold: (1) modification of the tradition to meet changing circumstances and (2) perpetuation of the fundamental rule of the law through new circumstances. The concrete forms of this twofold process were (1) the judicial precedent and (2) the legal principle. Although each gave stability to the law, each also contributed to its flexibility, for as new circumstances appeared, the application of a principle involved the creation of new precedent. Thus the Roman legal system became systematic and abstract and, under the influence of Greek philosophy, rational, *i.e.*, the law was conceived as grounded in a fundamental order of justice which was worked out in practice by reason. In essence, therefore, the law grew by interpretation and comment. The role of the judge and the legal scholar was not only to render justice in specific cases but also to refine constantly the practical justice that stemmed from universal justice. Notable, in this connection, were the procedures which gave parties to litigation full opportunity to develop the issue according to their divergent interests, for by such procedure justice was rendered without arbitrary action. There was truth in the jurisconsult's assertion that the law is "the art of the good and the fair."

The distinctive achievement of Roman legal development was the most complete elaboration of the right of private property found in any legal system before modern times. By liberating individual intention from governmental control, this part of the civil law contributed to the free disposal of property and led to competition rather than regimentation in economic relations. This freedom, it is important to note, was largely restricted to property owners, because laborers, either as slaves or as coloni or as freemen organized in collegia, remained subject to legal compulsion. Furthermore, this freedom was not amplified by civil liberties, and so the individual, except in the restricted area of property rights, was at the mercy of the state. The conception of civil liberty as understood in recent modern times was unknown to Roman lawyers; on the other hand they developed the conception that crime can be committed against the state as well as against the individual. They invented the crime of *lèse-majesté*. In spite of these limitations, the Roman civil law embodied a notable contribution to a *free* as contrasted with an *authoritarian* society.

But Roman law, even in the hands of the jurisconsults, was a class law. The concept "persona" was a device permitting the legal recognition of degrees of social status. Slaves, it will be remembered, were not regarded as persons. Liberty was the attribute of a class status, for it meant primarily an immunity from burdens imposed on certain sections of the population. When the ancient distinctions between the citizen and the foreigner disappeared in the course of the second century, a new distinction arose between the citizen and the soldier favorable to the latter. In the criminal law class distinctions were sharp. Even at the height of the empire the "more honorable" classes, consisting of senators, knights, veterans, soldiers, and officials, were not subject to the punishments of crucifixion, exposure in the arena, penal servitude, scourging, and torture imposed on the "more humble" classes. For the "more honorable" classes the chief punishments were exile, confiscation of property, and infamy, *i.e.*, the refusal of appointment to public office. The procedure in cases against slaves was atrocious, and crucifixion was the usual death penalty. Under the early empire freedmen convicted of serious crimes were beheaded with the ax; under the late empire they were beheaded with the sword. Before he was beheaded, the criminal was tied to a stake and flogged. Capital punishment was symbolized from very early times by a bundle of rods from which projected an ax; from the designation for this bundle of rods and ax—*fascis*—is derived the modern term "Fascism." The Romans perpetuated the belief that the best method of suppressing crime is to make its punishment horrible. By assimilating a class outlook and the traditional attitude toward crime into the philosophical view of the law, the Romans gave social conservatism a new rigidity, and because their law was so significant as an intellectual achievement this rigidity, as far as the future was concerned, was the supreme attribute of the law.

THE FINAL DECAY OF GRECO-ROMAN LEARNING

The decay of Greek and Latin learning which began in the second century continued throughout the late period of the Roman

Empire. Originality disappeared from every field of literature and science. Copying, compiling, and abbreviating the works of earlier authors became the chief forms of literary enterprise. And, except in rare instances, the worst elements of the Asianic style of rhetorical expression were selected for imitation and perpetuation.[1]

THE FINAL FORMS OF LEARNING IN GRECO-ROMAN CULTURE.

Typical representatives of the foregoing tendencies were Aulus Gellius (*ca.* 130–180) and Diogenes Laertius (fl. *ca.* 250?). Gellius compiled a "warehouse of facts" having neither literary form nor intellectual coherence. The work of Diogenes Laertius, *The Lives and Opinions of Eminent Philosophers*, is the only surviving example of the many histories of speculative thought written in classical times. It is a dry-as-dust compilation from numerous sources, each considered as worthy of quotation as the other. The subject, it is worth noting, was treated under three main headings—physics, ethics, and logic. The author did not claim to have studied the subjects about which he wrote. The successors of these men produced mainly commentaries on the poets of the Augustan age, grammars and treatises on words, and poems characterized by shallowness of thought, fantastic vocabularies, and artificial forms. Many of the poems were didactic treatises on morals, philosophy, geography, hunting, and fishing. Among the *grammatici* of the period, three are noteworthy. Aelius Donatus (fl. *ca.* 330) wrote two Latin grammars that long served as textbooks in medieval schools. Servius (fl. *ca.* 375), the most learned man of his time, composed a commentary upon Vergil; in it was preserved the only complete edition of a classical author produced before the fall of the Roman Empire. Priscian (fl. *ca.* 500) wrote a systematic exposition of the Latin language. Like Servius, whose grammatical study was concerned mainly with meters and metrical endings, Priscian paid great attention to the sounds of words, their formation, and their inflexion. These authors exhibit clearly the subversion of thought to form which the Asianic style of rhetorical expression had nurtured.

The decay of learning in the special fields was as complete as in literature. The common philosophical work of the time was a compilation of moral maxims, often in short couplets, for school-

[1] On the decay of Greco-Roman learning see Percival R. Cole, *Later Roman Education in Ausonius, Capella, and the Theodosian Code* (1909); Charles Singer, *From Magic to Science: Essay on the scientific twilight* (1928); Thomas Whittaker, *Macrobius, or Philosophy, Science, and Letters in the Year* 400 (1923); T. O. Wedel, *The Medieval Attitude toward Astrology* (1920); and G. Lombroso-Ferrero, "Le Mécanisme dans l'antiquité," *La Revue du mois,* Vol. 21, pp. 459 *ff.*

boys to chant. The pattern of this type of work was set at the end of the third century. The typical historical works were abbreviations of earlier histories, especially Livy's, and anecdotal biographies. Science degenerated into fable rendered in bad verse. Solinus (fl. *ca.* 250) wrote an epitome of geography, famous for accounts of fabulous men and beasts. Sammonicus (fl. *ca.* 250) wrote a medical poem extolling the efficacy of many charms. Cassius Felix (fl. *ca.* 440), who compiled the last Latin medical work, repeated the worst instead of the best of his predecessors. Macrobius (fl. *ca.* 395–423) deserves special comment. His *Saturnalia*—a dialogue with no attempt at dramatic effects—combined a medley of comments on various literary, antiquarian, religious, physiological, and social topics with a Neoplatonic outlook. The work is interesting today mainly because it contains quotations from many authors. The comments on Vergil had great influence in Christian times.

The last representatives of Greek and Latin learning stood at the threshold of Christian culture. They wrote in the manner of their predecessors but thought in the mode of their Christian contemporaries and successors. In giving up the traditional learning they helped found Christian learning.

Martianus Capella (fl. *ca.* 400) wrote the last Latin treatise on education—*The Nuptials of Mercury and Philosophy*, an allegory in nine books. Behind the folderol of mythology, which narrated the wedding of Mercury to Miss Philosophy (after having been refused by Wisdom, Divination, and Soul) and her elevation to a place among the gods, was an exposition of a system of learning that was to survive from that day to our own. This system, derived from early Latin authors, was based on the "seven liberal arts"— grammar, rhetoric, and dialectic, which medieval scholars knew as the *trivium*, and arithmetic, music, geometry, and astronomy, which medieval scholars knew as the *quadrivium*. The discussion of each subject was merely an outline of a work by an earlier author, such as Varro, Pliny, or Solinus. Significant of the times and the mode of its thought was the dropping from the list of the liberal arts of the two applied sciences, architecture and medicine. Cicero had said that they did not contribute to the making of an honest man. Although a mixture of prose and verse, the work was dry and verbose—suitable, indeed, to be the favorite textbook of an age that subverted secular learning to the service of theology.

Among other works Boethius (*ca.* 475–525), of whom it has been asked, "Was he Christian or pagan?" wrote *Consolations of Philosophy*, the last treatise on pagan philosophy. Like the work of Martianus Capella on education, the book was an allegory. It narrated how a "majestic woman"—philosophy—led the author to a knowledge of God. The argument, colored by the Christian as well as the Neoplatonic outlook, contrasted the unreality of earthly greatness with the reality of the things of the mind. In the field of scholarship Boethius undertook to harmonize the teachings of Plato and Aristotle. He also studied the works of Cicero. He wrote a geometry, leaving out the proofs of the theorems, and treatises on arithmetic and music that served as textbooks in medieval schools. His philosophical works, which included a commentary on Porphyry's *Introduction to the Categories of Aristotle* and a tract on the Christian Trinity, also exerted considerable influence in Christian schools. He added the terms "specific" and "quality" to the vocabulary of philosophers.

Cassiodorus (*ca.* 480–575), whose work *Manual of Divine and Secular Learning* set the pattern of monastic education, marks the transition from Greek and Latin to Christian learning. "Constant and intent meditation," he said, "is the mother of understanding"; the liberal arts, he held, were secondary to theology. He contributed the terms "rational" and "irrational" to the philosophical vocabulary. These terms, like those contributed by Boethius, suggest the subjectivity that had come to pervade all learning.

THE FAILURE OF CLASSICAL CULTURE.

Why did classical culture decay? The answer to this question is, at least, two-sided: (1) some weaknesses brought its development to an end, and (2) changing social conditions nurtured a new culture to displace it. Here it is necessary to call attention only to the weaknesses, for the conditions producing a new culture are dealt with in the discussion of Christianity.

The weaknesses of classical culture had origin in the Greek mode of thinking, of which both Hellenistic and Latin literature, philosophy, and science were expressions.

When Greek, Hellenistic, and Latin learning is viewed as a whole, it is seen to have been a vast body of speculations, opinions, and guesses—some brilliant and some absurd. But behind it, diverse as were its forms, was a constant effort to know *unchanging reality*—the "elements," the "truth," the "moral law," the "absolute." This effort, it should be realized, promoted the formulations of systems of thought which explained the universe, defined the moral law, and sought first principles. But it did not promote a continuous expansion of factual information about man and his world. The Greeks and their successors never dealt with the finite world. They developed no means of accurately measuring quantities of matter, produced no mathematical calculus for describing matter in motion, and initiated no systematic investigation of natural phenomena. In fact, they never understood that the doing of these things was a part of intellectual activity. Logic, the only intellectual instrument they shaped besides allegory, is an instrument suitable for testing the coherence of predications but not useful in assembling and evaluating factual information. The mode of thinking which failed in these respects was consistent in that it nurtured the attitude that labor is degrading, the conviction that arithmetic is an egalitarian science, the idea that mechanics is a low and vile art, and the dogma that contact with matter is spiritually corrupting. The social science of the Greeks and Romans also failed to achieve any analysis of economic or political phenomena that was useful in formulating policies; in fact, the Greek thinkers considered such effort unworthy, and the Romans were less attentive to such phenomena than the Greeks. The great product of the classical mind in the field of social thought was Roman law, *i.e.*, a body of social controls which enforced policies that were not justified by the economic conditions prevailing in the empire. This statement means that the policies failed to serve the interests they were meant to serve. The triumph of rhetoric in literary expression and education was merely another form of the failure to deal with concrete experience.

The intellectual effort which directed men's minds toward unchanging reality left them helpless in a social order that changed in spite of them. Men, for whom the word "invention" meant only the discovery of verbal conceits in literature, were hardly the ones to find solutions for their problems in either technological or institutional innovations. Classical learning attempted to teach men how to act, not how to produce or construct, and when successful in this effort it produced closed minds, which, if change occurred, were necessarily blind.[1]

The manner of the disintegration of classical culture was bound up with its social and economic organization. Of primary significance in this respect was the almost complete restriction of classical learning to the urban ruling classes. The urban workers and the peasant villagers, it seems certain, possessed little of literary,

[1] See C. N. Cochrane, *Christianity and Classical Culture* (1940), p. 151.

philosophical, and legal learning.[1] This fact became decisive when economic decline began to weaken the ruling orders, for, as the spreading impoverishment steadily reduced the social classes whose members because of their education were the carriers of classical culture, the culture was engulfed by materials carried by the submerged classes. But this economic decline, as previously explained, was primarily due to the social and intellectual outlook of the ruling classes. When the carriers of classical culture, pursuing policies which supported their privileged position, were brought face to face with a situation arising from these policies, their understanding of economics, politics, and society was entirely inadequate; because this inadequacy left them helpless in a situation which was destroying them, they perished. Thus a social transformation produced by the economic consequences of the social and intellectual outlook of classical culture finally disintegrated classical culture.[2]

Insofar as classical learning stemmed from the Homeric poems, it perpetuated the primitive view that human life is under the control of uncanny powers that lurk everywhere. Indeed, the philosophers merely gave this primitive belief an abstract and universal form in the concepts "chance," "fate," and "fortune." The prosperity of the state, therefore, was due to the favor of the deities of the state cult, and disbelief in them was properly subject to punishment. Plato argued in favor of this form of intolerance, and ultimately the Romans acted in its terms. Public policy was developed only under favorable signs that were sought in oracles, dreams, and the movements of the stars. Among the Stoics this quest was understood as an aspect of the life of reason. As conditions worsened, first for the lower classes and then for the ruling classes, men on all intellectual levels turned to religions for a solu-

[1] A. H. M. Jones, *The Greek City* (1940), p. 287.

[2] C. N. Cochrane, *Christianity and Classical Culture* (1940), p. 157: "The debâcle, however, was not merely economic or social or political, or rather it was all of these because it was something more. For what here confronts us is, in the last analysis, a moral and intellectual failure, a failure of the Graeco-Roman mind. From this standpoint, we are not concerned to enter into a dispute as to the relative theories proposed, but may freely admit that they all have a place within the complex tissue of material fact. If, however, the Romans themselves proved unable to come to grips with that fact, the reason must surely be supposed to be in some radical defect of their thinking. In this defect we may find the ultimate explanation of the nemesis which was operating to bring about the decline and fall of ancient civilization." By permission of the Oxford University Press. The central difficulties of the classical mind—the failure to understand the nature of science and technology and the refusal to recognize work as a worthy activity—are dealt with respectively in Benjamin Farrington, *Science and Politics in the Ancient World* (1939), and Adriano Tilgher, *Work: What it has meant to men through the ages* (1930).

tion of their problems. And this revival of religious interests brought a reaffirmation of primitive beliefs of all kinds. Thus from Galen's works were drawn ideas that fitted in with the practices of folk medicine: to cure epilepsy, tie a bit of peony to the wrist; to stop a cough, wear the tongue of an eagle as an amulet; and to extract a tooth from the upper jaw, surround it with worms from top leaves of a cabbage. Such superstitions were only the popular form of the primitive mode of thinking which received its philosophical expression in the rationalized subjectivism of Neoplatonism. At best, Greek, Hellenistic, and Latin learning, except for a few rare insights which were soon lost, was as much an elaboration of primitive concepts as it was a departure from them. Its best elements, literary excellence and ethical interest, were not safeguards against the obscurantism which the philosophers developed in philosophic idealism and the masses retained in fervid superstitions.

The noblest ideals of classical culture—humanity and liberty— were meaningless except in terms of society; this relation the classical mind never understood, and in this failure was the fundamental cause of the disintegration of classical culture.

Chapter XVII

THE SOCIAL EVOLUTION OF CHRISTIANITY

≪-≪≪-≫≫-≫≫

The transformation of the Roman Empire into an oriental monarchy, the diffusion of Greek learning and its elaboration in Latin forms, and the spread of Eastern cultural materials, as noted in the two previous chapters, were merely phases of a process which began in Hellenistic times and continued throughout the centuries of Rome's imperial rule. "Historians do not now recognize that there was anything like 'decay' of civilization during these periods. What happened was a slow and gradual change, a shifting of values in the consciousness of men."[1] Rightly understood, Christianity is recognized as the embodiment of this shift of values.[2]

[1] M. I. Rostovtzeff, "The Decay of the Ancient World and Its Economic Explanations," *Economic History Review*, Vol. 2 (1929–1930), p. 198.

[2] For introductory accounts of the rise of Christianity see *The Cambridge Ancient History*, Vol. 11, *The Imperial Peace, A.D.* 70–192 (1936), Chap. 7, "The Rise of Christianity"; George Foote Moore, *History of Religions* (2 vols., 1929), Vol. 2; and Salomon Reinach, *Orpheus: A history of religions* (1930).

Satisfactory texts dealing with early Christian history are Edwin R. Goodenough, *The Church in the Roman Empire* (1931); Duncan Armytage, *Christianity in the Roman World: Its rise and progress to the fall of the Western Empire* (1927); Philip Hughes, *A History of the Church: An introductory study* (1935), *nihil obstat;* H. K. Rowe, *History of the Christian People* (1931); W. M. Walker, *A History of the Christian Church* (1918); H. Packenham-Walsh, *Lights and Shades of Christendom to A.D.* 1000 (1936); *The History of Christianity in the Light of Modern Knowledge: A collective work* (1929); and J. W. C. Wand, *A History of the Early Church to A.D.* 500 (1936).

More detailed accounts are L. M. O. Duchesne, *Early History of the Christian Church, from Its Foundation to the End of the Fifth Century* (from the 4th French ed., 3 vols., 1909–1924); Jules Lebreton and Jacques Zeiller, *Histoire de l'Église depuis les origines jusqu'à nos jours*, Vol. 1, *L'Église primitive* (1934); Vol. 2, *De la fin du 2e siècle à la paix constantinienne* (1935); Hans Lietzmann, *Geschichte der alten Kirche* (2 vols., 1932); B. J. Kidd, *A History of the Church to A.D.* 461 (3 vols., 1922); Johann P. Kirsch, *Kirchengeschichte, die Kirche in der antiken griechisch-römischen Kultur Welt* (1930); Julius Wellhausen and others, *Geschichte der christlichen Religion* (1919); H. M. Gwatkin, *Early Church History to A.D.* 313 (2 vols., 1909).

Paul Wendland, *Die hellenistisch-römische Kultur in ihren Beziehungen zu Judentum und Christentum* (1912), is an account of cultural development in Roman times from the point of view of religious development of Christianity and Judaism.

Useful reference works of different types are Henry Wace and William C. Piercy, *A Dictionary of Christian Biography and Literature* (1911)—the standard English work of its

GENERAL SOCIAL AND CULTURAL FORCES THAT SHAPED CHRISTIANITY

This shift of values was caused by the fundamental social transformation in Mediterranean life which was most clearly evident in the displacement of the old local communities, that had nurtured more or less independent cultural traditions, by the cosmopolitan society in which emperors, philosophers, soldiers, merchants, free craftsmen, and slaves mingled. This cosmopolitanism, in turn, was increased by (1) the constant flow of Asiatics, Greeks, and Africans westward and (2) the growth of cities in all parts of the Mediterranean Basin. These cities were, of course, the chief centers of cosmopolitanism, and its chief bearers were the large populations of freedmen that appeared as slavery declined. Some of these freedmen, it is true, became wealthy and powerful, but most of them remained the masters of professions, craftsmen, traders, and common laborers. In the course of time they were detached from the local cultural traditions in which they or their ancestors were nurtured and became embedded in the mingled cultural materials which they, by their presence in the cities, brought together. If, as it has been said, the freedmen and their descendants ruined Rome,[1] they were in turn the makers of Christianity, for it developed chiefly among them.

As the traditional local attachments disintegrated, emotions shaped in the events that created the cosmopolitan urban masses

kind; W. A. Smith, *Dictionary of Christian Biography, Literature, Sects, and Doctrines* (4 vols., 1877–1887); Otto Bardenhewer, *Patrologie* (1901)—a systematic discussion of Christian literature; Arthur S. Peake, *A Commentary of the Bible* (1936); W. E. Barnes, *A Companion to Biblical Studies* (rev. ed., 1916); James Hastings, ed., *Encyclopaedia of Religion and Ethics* (2d ed., 12 vols., 1925); Shailer Mathews and G. B. Smith, *A Dictionary of Religion and Ethics* (1923); Marcel Villers, ed., *Dictionnaire de spiritualité ascetique et mystique, doctrine et histoire* (Vol. 1, 1937); L. Elliott-Binns, *A Handbook of Church History from the Apostolic Era to the Dawn of the Reformation* (1937); Walter Lowrie, *Christian Art and Archeology, Being a Handbook to the Monuments of the Early Church* (1906).

For recent archaeological materials bearing on the Hebrew background and early development of Christianity see Sir Charles Marston, *The Bible Comes Alive* (1937); R. A. S. Macalister, *A Century of Excavation in Palestine* (1925). On New Testament times see C. M. Cobern, *The New Archaeological Discoveries and Their Bearing upon the New Testament and upon the Life and Times of the Primitive Church* (1929); S. L. Caiger, *Archaeology and the New Testament* (1939).

For bibliographical guidance see S. J. Case, J. T. McNeill, and W. W. Sweet, *A Bibliographical Guide to the History of Christianity* (1931); Gustav Krüger, "A Decade of Research in Early Christian Literature (1921–1930)," *Harvard Theological Review*, Vol. 26 (1933), pp. 173–321.

[1] A. M. Duff, *Freedmen in the Early Roman Empire* (1928), p. 207: "It seems, then, that the freedmen and their descendants ruined Rome." By permission of the Clarendon Press, Oxford.

became dominant, first among the urban masses and second among their rulers and the carriers of the high intellectual tradition. In the Hellenistic age the growing insecurity of life generated a pessimism which the career of all-conquering Rome intensified. War, enslavement, drudgery, and the disruption of old forms of life everywhere brought men face to face with a fearful present and a hopeless future. The brilliance of the early imperial age masked the widespread gloom, but the more thoughtful spokesmen of the Roman ruling class, like Seneca, felt it. In the second century the pessimistic mood was strengthened by an apathy among the ruling classes, and during the next century the severe measures taken by the imperial regime to hold its position in the face of economic decline added discontent to apathy and pessimism. The leading element in the new feeling for life has been aptly described as a "failure of nerve."

The new quality . . . is hard to describe. It is a rise of asceticism, of mysticism, in a sense, of pessimism; a loss of self-confidence, of hope in this life and of faith in normal human effort, a despair of patient inquiry, a cry for infallible revelation; an indifference to the welfare of the state, a conversion of the soul to God. It is an atmosphere in which the aim of the good man is not so much to live justly, to help the society to which he belongs and enjoy the esteem of his fellow creatures; but rather by means of a burning faith, by contempt for the world and its standards, by ecstasy, suffering, and martyrdom, to be granted pardon for his unspeakable unworthiness, his immeasurable sins. There is an intensifying of certain spiritual emotions; an increase of sensitivity, a failure of nerve.[1]

The sources of this feeling were deep in the experience of the uprooted masses. The class struggles and imperialistic wars were accompanied by a terror which only most recent events have prepared modern Western men to understand. The forcible removal of thousands from their native communities stripped them of traditional cultural materials and left them primitive in outlook, for most of them had been the carriers of the low intellectual traditions of their local cultures; thus they were prepared to accept any reorientation of daimonistic beliefs that offered release from their suffering. Evidences of these developments are found early in the Hellenistic age. The distinction between the Greek and the barbarian, as well as the prejudice of the free toward the unfree, disappeared in the great urban centers. A longing for peace spread

---

[1] Reprinted from Gilbert Murray, *Five Stages of Greek Religion* (1925), p. 155: by permission of the Columbia University Press, New York.

through the masses, who turned more and more toward a refuge in the hereafter. When finally all hope of worldy escape from terror and exploitation died with the failure of the great slave revolts, the masses turned toward renderings of daimonistic beliefs that offered an otherworldly refuge with a rising enthusiasm. The earthly "sun city" became a "heavenly city." Because social interaction bound the great Mediterranean cities more and more into a single psychological environment, the mood and the outlook of the urban masses became everywhere a pervasive influence in emotional and intellectual life. United with pessimism—the "failure of nerve"— this mood and this outlook, more than any other influences, produced the shift in values that was finally expressed in Christianity.

If the reaction of the masses to their uprooting led to their denationalization and their repudiation of the values of the ruling classes, the conditions under which they sought a better life emphasized to them certain other values.

He [the slave] lost the great gifts of nationality, its inheritances and inspirations, its vigorous creativeness, its unique individual quality; but he also escaped the limitations of race and tradition, and found it easy to become a citizen of the world. He had one great advantage over the free man—the habit of hard work, and, through the hope of emancipation, a constant incentive to work diligently and well. Work was the saving salt which kept the slave class from utter corruption, and gave it a certain unacknowledged dignity of its own. Moreover, the innumerable sepulchral inscriptions, on which freedmen and their sons record the loss of parent, wife or child (*pater carissimus, coniunx incomparabilis, filius culcissimus*), suggest that home ties must have had a peculiar preciousness to one who had emerged from the forlorn degradation of slavery. The slave had no *patria*, but emancipation gave him not only a city but a home; as a freedman, he could contract a legal marriage, his children were citizens, and he could found a Romanized and respectable family. How eagerly this privilege was accepted, how much affection and hope surrounded the children so born, and how tragic was their loss, is revealed in the abbreviated and laconic grief of the ancient grave-stones. . . . And if the home and its affections—that ancient foundation of Roman greatness—renewed its sacredness in the servile population, it was this same despised and degraded class which first received and transmitted the religion of αγαπη [brotherly love]. The earliest Christians were for the most part of humble and probably servile descent. It is as the first recipients of the new religion that the slaves and freedmen of the early empire have a claim to the highest historical importance. To Christianity they brought their traditional cosmopolitanism, their discipline for work and suffering, and that family affection which still smells sweet and blossoms in their dust; while from Christianity they received at once an inspiration greater than that of race, and a spiritual emancipation as daring as it was triumphant: "Art thou called, being a slave? *Care not for it.*"[1]

In cultural development both the positive and the negative emotional reactions to a condition of life are important. For Christianity the source of its complex of values was the reaction in both these aspects to the conditions of mass life that the last two centuries before Christ made universal among Mediterranean people. The consolidation of the Roman imperial regime provided the opportunity for this reaction to find a coherent organization.

The influence of this new element in Mediterranean mentality was evident in intellectual developments long before it received consistent expression in Christianity. The emergence of Hellenistic ethical speculations was an indication that the old local cultures no longer provided guides for right living. Pessimism and religious feeling united in the yearning for the "right way of life" which pervaded these speculations, and their antipatriotic biases, expressed in the idea of universal brotherhood, reflected the growing cosmopolitanism. As previously noted, Stoicism, Epicureanism, and Cynicism belong quite as much to the religious as to the philosophical history of the period. In the last century B.C. the pessimism of the Stoics gave rise to a cult of suicide. The Epicureans, of course, withdrew as much as possible from worldly pursuits, while the Cynics denied their worth. With Posidonius (*ca.* 135–51 B.C.) religious and philosophical speculations were compounded in an almost meaningless mixture, dominated by pious sentiments and orientated toward an unearthly reality. The tendencies attained their full expression in the Neo-Pythagoreanism and the Neoplatonism that were the final forms of Greco-Roman philosophy. The Christians, it is pertinent to note, recognized that the Neoplatonists had a true conception of God.

The obverse of this transformation of philosophy was the disintegration of the secular outlook that characterized Greek thought.[2] After Hellenistic times science and scientific technology,

---

[1] Mary L. Gordon, "The Nationality of Slaves under the Early Roman Empire," *Journal of Roman Studies*, Vol. 14 (1929), pp. 110–111.

[2] M. I. Rostovtzeff, *Mystic Italy* (1927), pp. 16–22: "Materialism gradually vanished; new-stoicism, new-pythagoreanism, orphism, hermetism, gnosticism, astrology, and the oriental religions gained daily in strength and influence. And above all gradually developed the new Christian faith, which knew how to find access to human souls, and how to amalgamate the lofty teachings of Christ with the mysticism toward which the minds of all men tended. . . . Little by little the dominant note in the spiritual life of all mankind all

which never entered into the daily life of any significant body of workers, less and less attracted the attention of the carriers of the high intellectual tradition. Even Pliny (*ca.* 23–79) held that only theoretical studies were worth while. At the same time both literature and art lost the realism which had made them mirrors of nature and wordly life.

As the secular elements in thought sank into the background or disappeared entirely, religious and mystical elements moved forward. The rise of the Gnostic schools was the first widespread manifestation of this tendency. Lucian (*ca.* 125–190), the last representative of the skepticism that had overthrown the Olympian gods, laughed in vain at the new superstitions. The spread of the mystery cults was possible only because men no longer believed in the power of rational inquiry to determine morality or win immortality. The ideas and attitudes which expressed the new outlook were noted in the discussion of the direction of religious change in the preceding chapter. Here it is necessary only to recall that the goal of life was salvation in an other world beyond the power of human minds to conceive or of human efforts to achieve. Only a supernatural strength, having its source in God, could assure men of the attainment of this goal. To this spiritual force, which was conceived as radiating from God as rays radiate from the sun, men—from the Hellenistic age on—gave many names: "the Word," "Savior," "Spirit," "Creator," "Lord," "Divine Law," "Natural Law," "Power of God," "Reason," and "Wisdom." And it came to men—"from a higher world"—as a "gift of the spirit," as an "illumination," or as a "radiant vision."

These intellectual trends made (1) syncretism (*i.e.*, the growing together of the religious elements of the local Mediterranean cultural traditions) and (2) religious speculation the foremost cultural activities of Roman times. Syncretism on a wide scale

---

over the Roman empire became religious and mystic. When the blessed period of peace and prosperity created by Augustus and by his successors came to an end in the bloody crash of ancient civilization, inaugurated by the terrible social and political revolution of the third century, the scientific and materialistic conception of life vanished forever. Religion and mysticism triumphed over all. Men cared little for life on earth, and concentrated their minds on their internal, spiritual life, in preparation for the real life which begins—after death.

"This is one of the most important and the least studied processes in the history of mankind. Its causes and its evolution are little known. Its result was the triumph of the Christian faith, and of the religious conception of life which our modern self-confidence and our materialism try in vain to overthrow." By permission of Henry Holt & Co., New York.

got under way in the last century of the Roman Republic.[1] About the same time religious feeling began to supplant reason as the guide of philosophy; thus in Roman hands Stoicism became always more religious in outlook. After the social crisis of the third century the traditional learning became stagnant, and religion, attracting every faculty of mind and heart, alone seemed to possess a capacity of growth.

With the cosmopolitanism and religious outlook of the age were united materials from the local cultures, particularly those of the eastern Mediterranean lands; in fact, these materials, largely mythological in character, steadily supplanted the secular materials of Greek origin, so that Mediterranean life was progressively orientalized.[2] Just as the empire finally became an oriental monarchy, so every other phase of Mediterranean life changed in quality. In this process intellectual leadership passed from the Greeks to Hellenized orientals in almost every field of learning; this development was correlative with the advancement of the freedmen in urban and imperial affairs. The religious syncretism of the age was merely one aspect of the assimilation of the local cultures into a general Mediterranean culture to which these social developments contributed.

Although Christianity possessed original elements, its external form and internal structure conformed to the pattern set in this general assimilation: it was cosmopolitan, otherworldly, and oriental.[3]

[1] J. W. C. Wand, *The Development of Sacramentalism* (1928), pp. 80–81: "Let us add to this a reminder that we are dealing with the most syncretic age in all history. Not far away, at Alexandria, Philo, a Jewish contemporary of Jesus, was busy combining Judaism, Platonism, Pythagoreanism, and Stoicism into one great system in which hard facts never fail to enshrine religious truths. Essenism had already shown its interesting 'example of elasticity within the pale of Judaism.' Before long the Fourth Gospel, the most definitely sacramental document in the Bible, will be written by an Aramaic-speaking Jew steeped in Hellenistic thought, while S. James, the most Judaistic of the Christian letter-writers, will borrow a phrase 'the wheel of generation' from the Orphic cult. And all around are Greek cities with their flourishing mystery cults." By permission of Methuen & Co., Ltd., London.
[2] F. J. E. Raby, *A History of Secular Latin Poetry in the Middle Ages* (2 vols., 1934), p. 1: "It is now generally recognized that if a conception is required to make intelligible the change from the ancient to the medieval world, it can be found in the progressive orientalization of that Graeco-Roman culture which is the basis of our modern western civilization." By permission of the Oxford University Press, New York.
[3] On the social and cultural developments of the last two pre-Christian centuries considered as the background of the beginnings of Christianity see Albert Dufourcq, *La Révolution religieuse* (1927); T. R. Glover, *The World of the New Testament* (1931); W. Fairweather, *The Background of the Epistles* (1935); Carl Clemen, *Primitive Christianity and its Non-Jewish Sources* (1912); Edward Bevan, *Hellenism and Christianity* (1921); G. H. C. MacGregor et al., *Jew and Greek, Tutors unto Christ: The Jewish and Hellenistic Background*

THE ORIGIN OF CHRISTIANITY

The adherents of Christianity have always believed that their faith has a divine foundation, first in revelations to the Hebrews and second in the mission of their Savior, Christ, the Son of God. The validity of these beliefs is not subject to verification by historical research, for obviously the acts of Deity cannot be studied by means of man-made documents. The historian, therefore, is limited to a discussion of the human aspects of the origin of Christianity.

THE MINISTRY OF JESUS (*ca.* 4 B.C.–A.D. 29).

Christianity sprang from an obscure religious movement among the Hebrews of the early period of the Roman domination of Palestine. The economic, social, and cultural conditions of this period have been discussed in an earlier section dealing with the consolidation of Hebrew culture.[1] At the outset the movement, it may be believed, was an attempt to orientate the Hebrew tradition in terms of these conditions. But its leader, Jesus, exercised such a remarkable personal influence over his followers that after his execution they remembered him as a divine being who had lived and suffered as a man. Thus, though the movement he inspired failed, Jesus lived on—the heart of a new religion of salvation.[2]

of the New Testament (1936); Bertram L. Woolf, *The Background and Beginning of Gospel Story* (1937); Thomas Walker, *Hebrew Religion between the Testaments* (1937); Joseph Thomas, *Le Mouvement Baptiste en Palestine et Syrie* (150 *av. J.C.*—300 *ap. J.C.*) (1935); Moriz Friedländer, *Die Religiösen Bewegungen innerhalb Judentums im Zeitalter Jesu* (1905); Martin Dibelius, *Die urchristliche Ueberlieferung von Johannes dem Täufer* (1911).

[1] See pp. 697, 706.

[2] No biography of Jesus was written until the nineteenth century. The first critical study of the subject was by the German author David Friedrich Strauss; his work *The Life of Jesus* is available in an English translation (1866) of the fourth German edition. *The Life of Jesus* by Ernest Renan, available in several editions, is one of the famous books of the nineteenth century; it is more a literary than a scholarly work.

The problem of untangling the career of Jesus from the snarl of religious tradition and myth has attracted the attention of many scholars. Useful works dealing with the problem are Friedrich Loofs, *What Is the Truth About Jesus?* (1913); F. C. Burkitt, *The Earliest Sources for the Life of Jesus* (new ed., 1922); Albert Schweitzer, *The Quest of the Historical Jesus* (2d ed., 1911); and Alfred Loisy, *Histoire et mythe à propos de Jésus-Christ* (1938). Shirley J. Case, *The Historicity of Jesus: A criticism of the contention that Jesus never lived* (*ca.* 1912), answers the arguments of those who have contended that Jesus is a myth. These contentions are forcibly stated in Georg Brandes, *Jesus, a Myth* (1926). E. J. Goodspeed, *Strange New Gospels* (*ca.* 1921), examines recently discovered materials purported to contain new facts about the life of Jesus. See also P. Alfaric, *Pour comprendre la vie de Jésus; examen critique l'évangile selon Marc* (1929), and J. F. Bethune-Baker, *Early Traditions about Jesus* (1930).

The life of Jesus has been treated by recent scholars from different points of view. Studies from the point of view of contemporary critical historiography are Joseph War-

1. *The Beginning of the Ministry of Jesus.* Jesus was born into a large and poor family of Nazareth in Galilee, a part of Palestine somewhat removed from the currents that were engulfing the country in foreign influences. It was, however, a center of intense patriotism and religious feeling. In A.D. 6, when Jesus was not more than ten years old, its herdsmen, fishermen, and craftsmen rose in revolt against Rome; at the same time the teachings of the Essenes spread among them.[1] Both movements intensified the hope for a Messiah. Jesus, it is safe to conjecture, was a sensitive boy upon whom these events and influences had a profound effect. The tradition of his boyhood discussion of the Jewish law with the Pharisees suggests his early reflection upon religious problems. Except for the customary family instruction in the traditional Jewish learning, Jesus had no formal education. He spoke Aramaic, probably was unable to write, and certainly had no acquaintance with the philosophies of the age. His was a personal message shaped in the Jewish tradition and vitalized by a profound emotional reaction to the sufferings of his poor and illiterate countrymen.

Jesus began his ministry under the influence of John the Baptist, an ascetic, who was probably identified with the Essenes; chief among his teachings were the need for repentance, the quest for spiritual cleanliness, and the coming of a "mightier one" who would set men in the path of righteousness. He denied the traditional belief that mere birth as a Jew was enough to win salvation. In the troubled atmosphere of the times every leader who won popularity became suspect in the eyes of the authorities, and so John, after a short imprisonment, was executed at the command of King Herod.

Jesus, who accepted the arrest of his teacher as a "sign" of the coming of the "mightier one," then began to preach. His simple tales—"parables"—and cures—"miracles"—won him a quick popularity among the superstitious folk of Galilee. Resent-

---

schauer, *The Historical Life of Christ* (1927); Maurice Goguel, *The Life of Jesus* (1933); and Charles Guignebert, *Jesus* (1933). Interesting treatments from the Roman Catholic point of view are Léonce de Grandmaison, S. J., *Jesus Christ: His person—His message, His credentials* (3 vols., 1934), *nihil obstat;* Joseph Pickl, *Messiaskönig Jesus in der Auffassung seiner Zeitgenossen* (1935), *nihil obstat;* and Jules Lebreton, *The Life and Teachings of Jesus Christ Our Lord* (2 vols., 1935), *nihil obstat.* Arthur C. Headlam, *The Life and Teaching of Jesus the Christ* (1936), is a scholarly Protestant study. Joseph Klausner, *Jesus of Nazareth: His life, times, and teachings* (1927), is a closely documented study by a famous Jewish scholar.

[1] See p. 721.

ment at the murder of John strengthened his following, particularly around the fishing village of Capernaum, where he found the men who became the "disciples" and began the missionary activity that placed him at the head of a growing religious movement. Always he spoke a personal message, appealing like the prophets of old to moral feeling and conscience rather than to law and doctrine.

The new teacher was soon confronted with difficulties. Herod suspected his motives. Townsmen generally refused his mission. When he repudiated the Jewish law, the Pharisees denounced him as a "false prophet" and a "sorcerer," and tradition demanded that anyone so accused be put to death. The enthusiasm of the countryfolk for him only increased the animosity of his detractors.

Attempts to escape from his enthusiastic followers, as well as from his enemies, took him into the hill country across the Sea of Galilee, then toward the seacoast, later into the Jordan valley, and finally again to Galilee. When his mother and brothers attempted to bring him back to Nazareth, he refused to come; in Nazareth, it is worth noting, Jesus performed no "miracles," for the people did not have faith in him. During these wanderings he consorted with sinners, publicans, and foreigners, as well as with the countryfolk; at all times, it seems safe to say, he sought for rest and meditation away from the crowd rather than escape from disputations and persecutions.

2. *The Culmination of the Ministry of Jesus.* Sometime in the course of these wanderings the disciples, especially Peter, recognized Jesus as the Messiah, and he accepted the recognition. In this turn of events lay the tragic future, for the Messiah must be the "king of the Jews" and claim in Jerusalem his "kingdom." Thus Jesus and his disciples were impelled, like all pious Jews, to visit Jerusalem at the Passover, when the escape of the nation from Egypt was celebrated. But they went not merely to celebrate; theirs was a mightier mission—the revelation to the nation of the Messiah and the proclamation of the "Kingdom of God."

Because Jerusalem at the time of the Passover was filled with men of every Jewish opinion and belief, the coming of Jesus with a following of Galilean villagers merely increased the commotion in an already excited city. His entry, planned to fulfill an old prophecy, attracted attention, and his mission necessarily took him to the Temple, the center of Jewish religious life. There, having revealed himself publicly as the Messiah, he denounced the political and economic corruption of the Jews and called upon them to repent, *i.e.*, to return to ways of righteous living, so that the Kingdom of God might come. Apparently Jesus believed that his call to the people was alone sufficient to bring about this great event.

Jesus entered Jerusalem five days before the Passover; daily he went to the Temple, but at night he and his followers, fearing that enemies might attack them, retired outside the walls of the city. As the days passed the commotion and the danger inside the city increased. The priests of the Temple and the scribes were outraged at Jesus' claim to be the Messiah. The people, excited by the claim, looked to him to overthrow the Romans, but he disappointed them, saying, "Give unto Caesar the things that are Caesar's and unto God the things that are God's." When Jesus refused to play the role of a rebel leader he lost the popular support that might have saved him from his priestly enemies. The Sanhedrin, controlled by the Sadducees, decided to arrest him, but, since Jewish law forbade arrests during the celebration of the Passover, they could not immediately seize him. The dangers of this situation, it seems, were clear to Jesus at all times.

Since, according to Jewish custom, the Passover could be celebrated only within the walls of Jerusalem, Jesus and his disciples made quiet preparations for the feast at a secret meeting place. Thus was held the "Last Supper." Afterwards Jesus and a little band of followers quickly left the city, for the fear of death had come upon him. Apparently at this time Jesus advised his followers to resist if enemies followed them; however, when the police of the Sanhedrin appeared, guided by Judas, one of the disciples who had become convinced that Jesus was only another "false prophet," they fled, leaving their leader to his fate. Judas, it is fair to note, seems to have been the only "educated man" among the disciples.

Immediately upon arrest Jesus was led before the high priest of the Temple, who, when Jesus persisted in the claim that he was the Messiah, declared him "to be worthy of death." Since the Jews could not execute a man for false prophecy—a political offense in the eyes of the Romans—the high priest hastened to turn the prisoner over to the Roman authorities. When Pilate, the Roman procurator, who knew of no overt act of rebellion committed by the prisoner, wished only to scourge him, the priests and the people excited by them clamored for his execution. And Pilate, caring nothing for the life of any Jew, found no reason to deny them. The Sadducean priests were moved to demand death for the prisoner lest he, stirring up the people to a rebellion against them, loose again the Roman terror upon their city.

In crucifixion Jesus suffered the death that Rome meted out to slaves, rebels, and the lowest criminals; his last cry, "My God, my God, why has thou forsaken me?" it may be believed, expressed the bitterness and terror of the thousands—Gentile as well as Jew—who had suffered like fates.

THE TEACHINGS OF JESUS.

A clear statement of the teachings of Jesus has not survived. Scholars recognize in the first three books of the New Testament certain passages which come, it seems, from a lost source called *The Sayings of Jesus.*[1]

1. *The Ethics of Brotherly Love.* The surviving sayings, although forming no connected body of doctrine, either theological or ethical, are pervaded by a mood which leaves no doubt as to the outlook of their author. To a world dominated by force and calloused to cruelty and suffering he brought the message of brotherly love which, functioning most easily in the daily life of poor men, had both source and culmination in God's mercy.

The classic expression of this mood is found in the passages from the Sermon on the Mount known as the Beatitudes:

"Blessed are you who are poor, for the Kingdom of God is yours!

"Blessed are you who are hungry now, for you will be satisfied!

"Blessed are you who weep now, for you will laugh!

"Blessed are you when people hate you and exclude you and denounce you and spurn the name you bear as evil, on account of the Son of Man. Be glad when that happens, and leap for joy, for you will be richly rewarded in heaven, for that is the way their forefathers treated the prophets.

"But alas for you who are rich, for you have had your comfort!

---

[1] Special studies of the teachings of Jesus are: B. W. Robinson, *The Sayings of Jesus: Their background and interpretation* (1930); Thomas Walker, *The Teaching of Jesus: Studies in its form and content* (1931); E. DeWitt Burton, *A Source Book for the Study of the Teaching of Jesus in Its Historical Relationship* (2d ed., 1924); Thomas Walker, *The Teaching of Jesus and the Jewish Teaching of His Age* (1923); Stanley Brown-Sherman and Harold A. Pritchard, *What Did Christ Think?* (1935); E. F. Scott, *The Ethical Teachings of Jesus* (1924).

"Alas for you who have plenty to eat now, for you will be hungry!

"Alas for you who laugh now, for you will mourn and weep!

"Alas for you when everyone speaks well of you, for that is the way their forefathers treated the false prophets!

"But I tell you who hear me, love your enemies, treat those who hate you well, bless those who curse you, pray for those who abuse you. To the man that strikes you on the cheek, offer the other also, and from the man who takes away your coat, do not keep back your shirt either. Give to everyone that asks of you, and if anyone takes away what is yours, do not demand it back. And treat men just as you wish them to treat you. If you love only those who love you, what merit is there in that? For even godless people love those who love them. And if you help only those who help you, what merit is there in that? Even godless people act in that way. And if you lend only to people from whom you expect to get something, what merit is there in that. Even godless people lend to godless people, meaning to get it back again in full. But love your enemies, and help them and lend to them, never despairing, and you will be richly rewarded, and you will be sons of the Most High, for he is kind even to the ungrateful and the wicked. You must be merciful, just as your Father is. Do not judge others, and they will not judge you. Do not condemn them, and they will not condemn you. Excuse others and they will excuse you. Give, and they will give to you; good measure, pressed down, shaken together, and running over, they will pour into your lap. For the measure you use with others they in turn will use with you."[1]

Difficult as it may be to comprehend and apply, the fundamental teaching of the Galilean carpenter is "Love thy neighbor as thyself." Only by sublimating self-interest in altruism can men become worthy of living with God. The vitality of Christianity resides in this making of the achievement of the social good the complement of the knowing of eternal reality. Between these two ideal aims men can, it seems, struggle endlessly: for the true followers of Jesus the realization of either aim leads to the achievement of the other. That is their "cross" and their hope: their

[1] *The Bible, An American Translation, The New Testament*, pp. 106–107, Luke 6: 20–38. By permission of the University of Chicago Press, Chicago.

cross because the certainty of spiritual perfection is impossible in the presence of social evil, and their hope because self-sacrifice in social service does have its own rewards.

Jesus, however, brought a religious rather than a social message to his age. For him these teachings were incidental to the immediate coming of the Kingdom of God.[1] So keen was the expectancy of this event among his disciples that they quarreled with one another about the positions they would hold after its occurrence. When Jesus called upon men to repent, he merely asked them to live as if the Kingdom of God were at hand. They were to give up worldly aims, foregoing riches, power, and fame. They were to forget their families, becoming "eunuchs for the sake of heaven," distribute their property, and avoid intellectual disputation. Jesus did not commend asceticism or excoriate luxury; men, he held, must work in order to live, but living "for the sake of heaven" necessitated only the simple satisfaction of a few wants. In the Kingdom of God men would live in "holy idleness." By virtue of their deprivations and sufferings the poor were naturally more self-sacrificing, meek, and lovingly kind than the well to do. This doctrine broadened the conception that the achievement of the social good is the way to eternal life, for, by identifying suffering with moral achievement it made common men the "chosen people." But the coming of the Kingdom of God did not involve a social revolution, only a purification of heart which was possible for both the poor and the well to do. God, the Merciful Father, closed his kingdom against no man, however sinful, who sought forgiveness. The tragedy and the glory of Jesus lay in the teaching "The Kingdom of Heaven is at hand": to the patriotic Jews of his time the kingdom, as he proclaimed it, was incomprehensible; to the Christians of later ages its nearness became the unshaken rock of faith.

2. *A Religion of Altruistic Behavior.* Less than any other great religious teacher Jesus emphasized the forms of worship. Although he observed the Jewish rituals, he considered them of little importance in comparison with the moral law. He seems to have misunderstood completely the relation of the ritualistic laws to the survival of the Jews as a nation, for he made no mention in his teaching of the commandments enforcing their fulfillment.

[1] See Alfred Loisy, *Les Origines du Nouveau Testament* (1936), p. 41. Jesus shared the popular belief in the Kingdom of God with John the Baptist and the Zealots. Jesus and John the Baptist believed that its coming would be according to God's will but had faith that His willing its coming was imminent. For the Zealots the belief had revolutionary significance; it inspired their rebellions from the last century B.C. to the final defeat of Bar Kocheba in the second century A.D. Librairie Émile Nourry, Paris.

Little can be found in his career or teachings that justifies the existence of a priesthood. Since righteousness was a way of life possible for the pure in heart, there was no need for formalism in worship. Since each man could know God, there was no need for priestly mediation. To his disciples he taught a daily prayer and with them he held a commemorative meal. For him the essence of the religious life was good works by men, who in serving one another sought only to serve God.

3. *The Relation of God and Man: the Concept "Suffering Messiah."* Although from the beginning of his mission Jesus was keenly aware of his closeness to God, he came slowly to a belief in himself as the Messiah. This belief had its source in the universal hope of the Jews of his age. But only as a wonder worker did Jesus conform to the ideal of this hope. Clearly he was no king to restore a sorely distressed nation. For him, however, the suffering not of the nation but of individuals became the manifestation of divinity; in his agony, he felt, God suffered in order that men might be saved for an eternal life. This departure from the Jewish tradition cost his life but saved his mission for the subsequent centuries.

The conception of the "suffering Messiah" reigns supreme among the beliefs about the relation of God and man. In it is personalized the doctrine of the achievement of the social good as the way to eternal life. In it suffering mankind, untaught yet right-hearted, poor yet unembittered, eager yet blind, becomes the measure of spiritual reality. The genius of the conception is almost proof of its divine revelation.

As a matter of fact, however, the concept was the evolutionary outcome of Jewish religious thinking. From the beginning of its development this thinking had interpreted social conditions in terms of divine intention; also, each succeeding disaster to the nation had brought a reorientation of previous thinking. Thus the national tradition had been orientated first about the Davidic kingdom, then about the Messianic monarchy, and then about the priestly state, and each orientation had failed to bring the nation to righteousness and salvation. When Jesus attacked the Pharisees and repudiated the law, he was merely abandoning another orientation which, in face of Roman conquest, had failed. Because of his origin and background he necessarily orientated the national tradition around the needs and in terms of the sentiments and understanding of common folk. His ethical teachings were a projection into universality of the morality of poor and helpless men who face together a common danger. His conception of God—

fatherly, kindly, and near at hand—was the expression of the longing for divine support that men who lack intellectual subtlety possess. His personalization of divine purpose in the suffering Messiah sublimated this longing. His Kingdom of Heaven was an inversion of the social order which everywhere had crucified common men. With Jesus the sentiments and ethics carried in the Jewish, as well as other, low intellectual traditions became the attributes of Deity: God was cast in the image of the suffering masses at the base of the original urban cultures. Only the Jewish tendency to interpret social phenomena in terms of God's purpose could have culminated in this conception.

THE EARLIEST CHRISTIANS.

When the police of the Sanhedrin seized Jesus, the disciples fled and his followers scattered. The followers who returned to Galilee soon forgot their teacher, but those who remained in Jerusalem never lost faith in him. They found a leader in Peter, who, alone among those close to Jesus, had not fled from the city. From his experiences after the burial of Jesus and from the lingering hope among the remnant of the followers that Jesus would yet triumph over his enemies sprang the belief that He, the Messiah, had risen from the grave and ascended into heaven, whence shortly He would descend, coming through the clouds in a burst of light and glory.

Under Peter's leadership this handful of the faithful—probably a few more than a hundred in number—lived in a state of preparation for the "Second Coming." Their dominant emotion was an enthusiastic hope. To their belief and hope they added baptism—a ceremonial initiation by which they entered into fellowship with the "saved ones"—and an evening meal—a ceremonial repast in which they shared in some manner a communion with their "Savior." Except for these peculiarities of belief and practice the earliest Christians were Jews even in their own thought. In fact, they claimed to be the only truly orthodox Jews. Thus they retained without modification the Jewish Scripture, the ritualistic law, the ethical teachings of the rabbis, and the traditional conception of God. For the later development of Christianity this retention of Jewish religious literature and theology was profoundly significant because it provided that link with the past which justified the Christians' claim that theirs was the only true religion. The interpretation of scriptural prophecies so that they seemed to explain and justify the mission of Jesus also greatly

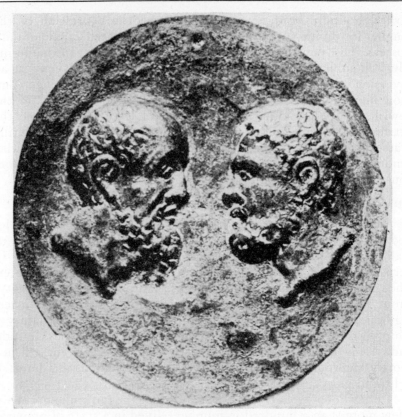

From F. X. ZIMMERMAN, *Die Kirchen Roms* (1935), *R. Piper & Co., Munich*

ST. PAUL AND ST. PETER

These portraits on a bronze medallion of the second century are typical of the representations of early Christian leaders that were painted on walls, carved on jewels, or made in
glass and mosaic. Peter has close curly hair, a short beard, and a full and strong face;
Paul, slightly bald, has a thin face and a long pointed beard. Christian tradition seems to
have preserved these characteristic traits from Apostolic times.

strengthened the new sect. The orthodox Jews, however, were
intolerant, and the little congregation grew slowly.

The social practices of the first Christians are largely to be
understood in terms of their ardent belief in the immediate Second
Coming. They worked little, shared their property, and abandoned
customary worldly interests and ranks, including those of the
family. There is nothing in primitive Christianity that justifies
the application of the word "communistic" if any modern meaning

is to be conveyed by the term.[1] The Christians lived for the divine event which would inaugurate the Kingdom of Heaven on earth. But the social aspects of this Kingdom were secondary to its religious elements. The poor, of course, were its chosen citizenry. But the Kingdom itself was only the prelude to an eternal life of spiritual bliss in heaven.[2]

In their hope of an immediate spiritual salvation for distressed common humanity, the primitive Christians prepared a gospel, *i.e.,* "good news," for the people of the Roman Empire.

THE DIFFUSION OF CHRISTIANITY IN THE MEDITERRANEAN LANDS

When the gospel began to spread among the Mediterranean peoples, it entered into the process which was changing their local cultures into an oriental cosmopolitanism. Primitive Christianity, of course, became a factor in this process and at the same time was influenced by it, so that ultimately the content and organization, as well as the triumph, of Christianity were its products. The evolution of Christianity followed the phases of Roman imperial development and decline.[3]

THE TRANSMISSION OF CHRISTIANITY TO THE GENTILES: PAUL OF TARSUS.

Among the Jews of the Diaspora the passionate in-group loyalty that characterized Jewish life in Palestine diminished, for they associated daily with Gentiles, took on their customs, and absorbed their learning. A third-generation Jew in one of the great eastern Mediterranean cities was commonly quite like

[1] See Johannes Weiss, *The History of Primitive Christianity* (2 vols., 1937), Vol. 1, p. 72. In the sharing of goods practiced by the earliest Christians there was no turning over of capital goods to the community.

[2] On the early Christians, their activities, and their communities see P. G. S. Hopgood, *The Religious Experience of the Primitive Church: The period prior to the influence of Paul* (1936); J. W. C. Wand, *First Century Christianity* (1937); Jules Lebreton, *La Vie chrétienne au premier siècle de l'église* (1927); Pierre Batiffol, *L'église naissante et le catholicisme* (7th ed., 1919). See especially H. J. Cadbury, "Between Jesus and the Gospels," *Harvard Theological Review*, Vol. 16 (1923), pp. 81–92.

[3] The most satisfactory account of the origin and development of early Christianity is Johannes Weiss, *The History of Primitive Christianity* (2 vols., 1937). Other useful discussions of this phase of the development of Christianity are Shirley J. Case, *The Evolution of the Early Christian Church in the Light of Modern Criticism* (1914); Otto Pfleiderer, *Christian Origins* (1906); MacKinley Helm, *After Pentecost: A history of Christian ideas and institutions from Peter and Paul to Ignatius of Antioch* (1936); A. C. McGiffert, *A History of Christianity in the Apostolic Age* (1897); Kirsopp Lake, *Apostolic Fathers* (2 vols., 1919); Alfred Loisy, *La naissance du christianisme* (1933).

the Greeks and the Hellenized orientals who made up the body of the population.

In the absorption of Greek learning, the Jews of the Diaspora became familiar with the idea of the Savior-God of the mystery religions and the philosophical conception of God's universal rule over man and nature. Both ideas were more generalized than the Jewish beliefs in Yahweh as the God of a chosen people and of the Messiah as a national savior. On the other hand, in the belief that the life of the soul is true reality, Greek philosophy and religion were more personal than Judaism.

To Jews with this changed outlook the claim that Jesus was the long-awaited Messiah had a truer ring than to the priest-ruled inhabitants of Jerusalem. As early as the day of Pentecost—fifty days after the second day of the Passover—some three thousand visitors to Jerusalem, tradition says, were converted by Peter. Although the number of converts is undoubtedly exaggerated, their enthusiasm cannot be doubted, for soon they were expelled from the city and one of their leaders, Stephen, was stoned to death for having spoken against "the Temple and the Law." Stephen's assertion that the heart is the true seat of holiness was a doctrine which permitted the Gentiles, who knew not the law, to become believers in the Messiah, who, as Stephen also asserted, had been repudiated by the adherents of the law only because they made formal obedience to it a substitute for righteous living. These early converts planted the faith of the Apostles in the great Hellenistic cities of Syria, Phoenicia, and Asia Minor, and from them it spread among the Gentiles.

How soon Gentiles began to stand by the side of Jews in Christian congregations is not known. Since, however, the whole Christian community was very soon disturbed by a contention over the question "Is the Jewish law to be applied to gentile converts?" it must have been shortly after the stoning of Stephen. The Apostles, including Peter, long resisted the admission of non-observers of the law to the Christian community, and apparently the congregation at Jerusalem never gave in on the point. Finally, about 49, at a conference of the representatives of the two parties to the contention, Paul of Tarsus (d. *ca.* A.D. 67) won Peter over to the view of the Hellenistic Jewish converts. Following this decision, Paul, who had been active in Syria and Cilicia, entered upon the career which won for him the title "Apostle to the Gentiles," and Peter, it seems, left Jerusalem—probably to go to

Rome. The original Christian congregation at Jerusalem soon sank into insignificance.

Great as was Paul's work in winning release for Christians from the bondage of the Jewish law, greater still was his transformation of the simple faith of the Apostles into a religion acceptable to the gentile, *i.e.*, Hellenized-oriental, mentality. Paul claimed a direct revelation from the Messiah, and the Apostles accepted his claim; this revelation, interpreted not only in terms of the Hebrew tradition but also in the light of Greek philosophical and religious beliefs, was an insight into the meaning of the career of Jesus. The result was a religion of salvation not unlike the mystery religions in form, but orientated about a new conception of the Savior-God.[1]

As a Jew Paul could make no compromise with polytheism. God was *one*, eternal and all-powerful, the creator and the ruler of the universe; from the beginning God had offered moral guidance to men and planned their salvation. Jesus was the "Son of God"— the "celestial man," who, sent from heaven, expiated Adam's sin by suffering a human death. Between God and man, Jesus Christ, *i.e.*, the Savior, was the sole mediator. Through "Him crucified" not only man but also the whole universe was reconciled with God; by *grace*, *i.e.*, by choice, God had sent Him as a sacrifice in order to redeem sinful man. This interpretation of the career of Jesus as a divine sacrifice was Paul's great doctrinal contribution to Christianity. Man could win redemption by faith in Christ; yet the faith was God's gift, and through it man entered into a spiritual union with Christ. To have faith was "to put on Christ as a sacred garment," triumphing over death and winning eternal life in heaven. From Paul's point of view Jesus superseded Moses as the

---

[1] On Paul's career and contributions to the development of Christianity see especially Johannes Weiss, *The History of Primitive Christianity* (2 vols. 1937), Vol. 2, pp. 180–445. Among the biographical studies of Paul the following are noteworthy: W. M. Ramsay, *St. Paul the Traveller and the Roman Citizen* (1895); Gustav Adolf Deissmann, *St. Paul: A study in social and religious history* (1912); B. W. Robinson, *The Life of Paul* (1918); T. R. Glover, *Paul of Tarsus* (1925); Lawrence O. Lineberger, *The Man from Tarsus: His world, personality and religious genius* (1933); F. A. Spencer, *Beyond Damascus: A biography of Paul the Tarsean* (1934); and Charles A. A. Scott, *Saint Paul: The man and the teacher* (1936). For discussions of Paul's teachings and their significance see Albert Schweitzer, *Paul and His Interpreters: A critical study* (1912); Albert Schweitzer, *The Mysticism of Paul the Apostle* (1931); H. A. A. Kennedy, *St. Paul and the Mystery Religions* (1912); W. Morgan, *The Religion and Theology of St. Paul* (1917); Fernand Prat, *The Theology of St. Paul* (from the 11th French ed., 2 vols., 1927); Charles A. A. Scott, *Christianity according to St. Paul* (1927); Robert W. Norwood, *The Heresy of Antioch: An interpretation* (1925); M. E. Andrews, *The Ethical Teaching of Paul: A study in origin* (1934); and Kirsopp Lake, *Paul: His heritage and legacy* (1934).

revealer of God's will with man; thus faith in Christ replaced the observance of the Jewish law as the mode of redemption. Like the Apostles, Paul believed the Second Coming was near at hand.

Man, said Paul, possessed an "in-dwelling spirit"—in later terms, a conscience; as a spark of divinity it made possible man's knowing Christ. In moments of highest knowledge of Christ man experienced ecstasy and had visions of heaven; in the ordinary state of faith he "knew" the *good*. Thus conscience guided the believer in Christ in the way of righteousness; its essential task was to bring man to put off the evils of the flesh—to release the spirit from the imprisoning body. This conception led, on the one hand, to an ascetic morality, especially as regards sexual expression, and, on the other hand, to an altruism pervaded by brotherly love. "Love" was the key word of Paul's moral teaching. God through love had sent His Son to redeem man, Christ through love had endured death in order to serve God and man, and men through love of God, Christ, and one another could become worthy of eternal life. After death the body was resurrected, but man lived a spiritual not a fleshly life.

Paul conceived of altruism only in its spiritual significance. "The ideal of social service was wholly lacking. Not the amelioration of society, not the service of the world, but one's own salvation was the supreme end of life, and if charity and kindness and generosity were recognized as Christian virtues, they were commonly practiced more for one's own sake than for the sake of others."[1] In calling upon men to abandon the world Paul condemned them to live under existing social institutions.

Although he gave Christianity no social program, Paul did create a new worship. Through baptism, which removed the stain of Adam's sin, man became spiritually purified—a state necessary for receiving the grace requisite to faith. In the "breaking of the bread" man entered into communion with the Savior and shared in His sacrifice and its reward. Through repeated performance of this ceremony the faithful were united in the sacred body of Christ. Paul, like other men of his time, could not conceive of a religion without rites almost magical in character and significance.

Paul's faith was unbending. God was the ruler of the universe. At its heart was Christ, the Son of God, who had lived and died as a man as a divine sacrifice in order that mankind might be saved

[1] A. C. McGiffert, *Christianity as History and Faith* (1934), p. 27. Charles Scribner's Sons, New York.

from spiritual destruction. His figure, radiant with heavenly light, was the Redeemer, near to every man who gave himself willingly and completely to the spiritual life. All those who believed in Christ constituted His church; He was its head and it was His body. Spiritual reality was knowable to man only through the divine grace which made possible a life of moral purity.

For Paul this faith was Jewish and orthodox; for his gentile auditors in the great Mediterranean cities it was chiefly an appealing combination of the familiar ideas of the mystery cults. Its new elements, which personalized the saving God as a "historic God-man," merely strengthened its appeal among men who feared both life and death. The psychology of religious ecstasy which Paul exemplified was more understandable to ordinary Gentiles than the reason extolled by the philosophers, and warmth of feeling in personal relations was a surprising moral tonic among men who experienced cruelty as a normal fact of life. In the "suffering Messiah," who died in order that all men might live eternally, pain became the stimulus of hope—and the greater the pain the greater the hope: this the gentile mind was fully prepared to understand.

In view of Paul's work as apostle to the Gentiles and his transformation of the religion of Jesus into the cult of the Christ, it is not incorrect to call him the true founder of the Christianity that was to enter so deeply into Western culture. The term "Christians" originated, it seems, in Antioch as an appellation for those Hellenized orientals who were among the first to accept the Christ.

THE CONVERSION OF THE MEDITERRANEAN PEOPLES.

The early Christians felt it their duty to carry the gospel to all men. At the outset of their missionary activities they were merely one variety among the many devotees of cults and philosophies who swarmed in the cities of the Roman Empire. The promise they brought of eternal life gained them a hearing and won them converts, who, participating in their earnestness, intensified the zeal to evangelize mankind. The opposition they encountered and the suffering they endured reminded them always of the career and fate of their Savior; to emulate Him by suffering for His church was the certain way to win immortality. These convictions made Christianity the world's greatest missionary religion.[1]

[1] An interesting recent account of the spread of Christianity is K. S. Latourette, *A History of the Expansion of Christianity* (3 vols., 1937–1939); Vol. 1, *The First Five Centuries*, deals with the period surveyed here. The classic study of the diffusion of Christianity about the Mediterranean Basin is Adolf von Harnack, *The Mission and Expansion of Christianity in the First Three Centuries* (2 vols., 2d ed., 1908). See also Johannes Weiss, *The History*

1. *Early Missions and Conversions.* Tradition asserts that the Twelve Apostles undertook missions far beyond Palestine; Peter, it is said, went to Rome, Thomas to India, and John to Asia Minor. Actually little or nothing is known about these activities; in fact, all the Apostles, except possibly John, disappeared leaving only the vaguest traditions of their work and fate. The earliest teachers of Christianity were Hellenized Jews, who wandered from city to city, first in Syria, Phoenicia, and Asia Minor, and then about the Mediterranean coasts. They traveled, it seems, after the manner of the Greek philosophical teachers and the Jewish rabbis, who relied upon the communities they visited for support.

Paul, the Apostle to the Gentiles, traveled in this way, at least until he went to Greece. His missionary career falls into three periods: (1) from his conversion (*ca.* A.D. 35) to the conference at Jerusalem (*ca.* A.D. 49), which decided that gentile Christians were not bound by the Jewish law; (2) from about A.D. 50 to 56, when he was active in Greece; and (3) from A.D. 56 to 64, when after returning to Jerusalem, he was sent as a prisoner to Rome. During the first period Paul, with the active support of Barnabas, a member of the congregation at Jerusalem, and others, made Antioch a center of missionary enterprise into Galatia and Cyprus. The converts were organized in churches under the leadership of elders, probably on the model of the Jewish synagogues. From Ephesus, which became the center of evangelization of Asia Minor, Paul went to Macedonia and Greece. A mixed congregation of Jews and Gentiles was founded at Philippi, and gentile congregations at Thessalonica, Corinth, and Athens. Corinth soon became a center from which Christian influence radiated. When Paul returned from Greece to Jerusalem, he was met by the open hostility of the Judaizing Christians, who, it seems, had him arrested as an inciter of rioting and imprisoned. By right of Roman citizenship Paul appealed to Rome; he was conveyed there as a prisoner about A.D. 58. The Roman congregation, whose foundation, although credited to Peter, is quite obscure, welcomed him, but the authorities retained him in custody. Tradition holds two views of his death: either he perished in a persecution under Nero or he died on a mission to Spain or England.

of *Primitive Christianity* (2 vols., 1937), Vol. 2, pp. 657–703, for the period A.D. 30–130; Gerhard Uhlhorn, *The Conflict of Christianity with Heathenism* (1879); Walther Classen, *Eintritt des Christentums in die Welt: Der Sieg des Christentums auf dem Hintergrunde der Untergehenden antiken Kultur* (1930).

On the phenomenon of conversion see A. D. Nock, *Conversion: The old and new in religion from Alexander the Great to Augustine of Hippo* (1933).

CENTERS OF CHRISTIANITY c. A.D. 100

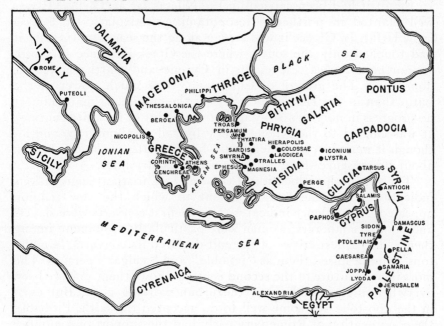

The apostolic period of the spread of Christianity closed with the destruction of Jerusalem in 70. Then the Judaizing congregation at Jerusalem was dispersed, and the life of the new church passed entirely to the mixed Jewish and Gentile groups of the great maritime cities. Nothing is known about the planting of Christianity in several of these cities, such as Alexandria and Carthage; probably it was the work of Hellenized Jews, who drew their inspiration from congregations founded by the Apostles. Paul's influence was far-reaching, as is testified to by his letters and also by the well organized life which characterized congregations wherever they appeared. It was Pauline Christianity that everywhere won acceptance.

During the great age of the Roman Empire Christianity spread gradually rather than rapidly. By the end of the third decade of the second century it had become quite at home in the gentile environment; by the close of the century the many local congregations were keenly aware of the greater Christian community of which they were the units. Most of these congregations were still in the eastern part of the Empire. In Asia Minor, the area with the oldest continuous Christian history, the faith had spread from the towns to the countryside, especially in Bithynia, Pontus, and Phrygia. In Egypt it had been carried up the Nile as far as Thebes. It was well planted in northern Mesopotamia, particularly at Edessa (now Urfa). In Greece it was strong along the seacoast. In Italy it had touched only the south, where the Greek influence survived. In northern Africa, especially in Cyrene and Carthage, it was flourishing. The growth of Christianity was much slower in the Latin than in the Hellenistic parts of the empire. It made almost no progress in northern Italy until the opening of the third century. It was carried to the Rhone valley by sailors about 170, and although it must have reached Spain by this date, nothing is known about its presence there until almost a century later.

The geographical location of these early Christian congregations indicates clearly the social element to which the new religion appealed. All evidence indicates that the first converts were slaves[1] and poor free laborers; women were particularly prominent among them. The earliest critics of the cult declared its converts "simpletons" and despised them as "ignoble" and "vulgar" persons. The mortuary furniture of the second century shows them to have been overwhelmingly members of the urban working class. But even in the apostolic age some well to do accepted the faith. Probably the congregation at Rome very early had the support of a number of influential persons. By the end of the second century the Christians not only recognized themselves as a "new people" but also boasted that they had entered every Roman place but the temples. The boast was hardly true, for, except in central Asia Minor and parts of Egypt, they had made almost no converts among the peasants.

The psychological conformity between Christianity and those who were won to it is probably too infrequently considered in explaining its spread:

When I try to realize it [Christianity] as a sort of semi-secret society for mutual help with a mystical religious basis, resting first on the pro-

[1] R. H. Barrow, *Slavery in the Roman Empire* (1929), p. 163: "Christianity, however, was notoriously spread by slaves; it is alike the reproach of its persecutors, and the glory of its apologists. In the *Octavius* of Minucius Felix, Caecilius the pagan taunts Christianity with having collected the dregs of the people, mere ignorant men and women, paupers; but the charge of poverty is caught up by Octavius: 'This is not a reproach but a glory; can he be poor who is rich in God?' Indeed the early churches contributed to a fund from which grants may have been made to ransom slaves who were Christians. The proper names mentioned in the Pauline epistles would by themselves be sufficient evidence, and the roll of martyrs contained the names of the slave-girls Blandina and Felicitas, 'who were celebrated in the festivals of the Church with honours denied to the most powerful and noblest born of mankind.'" By permission of Methuen & Co., Ltd., London.

letariats of Antioch and the great commercial and manufacturing towns of the Levant, then spreading by instinctive sympathy to similar classes in Rome and the West, and rising in influence, like certain other mystical cults, by the special appeal it made to women, the various historical puzzles begin to fall into place. . . . it explains its humanity, its intense feeling of brotherhood within its own bounds, its incessant care for the poor, and also its own comparative indifference to the virtues which are specially incumbent on a governing class, such as statesmanship, moderation, truthfulness, active courage, learning, culture, and public spirit.[1]

Christianity, which contained enough Oriental mysticism to appeal to the vast herd of Easterners in the West, and enough Hellenic sanity to captivate the rationalistic Westerner, found, even if one reckons only with social forces, the most congenial soil for growth in the conglomeration of Europeans, Asiatics, and Africans that filled the western Roman Empire in the second century.[2]

Christianity originated among the most despised people of the Roman Empire and spread among its most despised classes; and the fundamental Christian teaching, besides the doctrine that suffering is ennobling, was the prospect of immediate escape from earthly suffering. Not until toward the end of the second century did the belief in the imminency of the Second Coming begin to give way; as it gave way the Christians became more intent upon the earthly struggle with sin—a struggle which they understood as a conflict between daimons and Christ. Perhaps no aspect of early Christianity is more startling to contemporary Christians than this naive interpretation of the daimonic universe:

We say . . . that certain spiritual substances exist. Nor is the name unusual. The philosophers know of demons and Socrates himself waited on a demon's bidding. . . . All the poets know of them, and even the ignorant rabble make constant use of them for cursing. . . . The business of demons is the destruction of man. Thus from the beginning of things did spiritual wickedness aspire to man's ruin. Therefore while they inflict on men's bodies diseases and cruel accidents, they also inflict on the soul sudden and strange aberrations of violent madness. Their subtleness and fineness of texture give them access to both parts of man. Spiritual agencies have great power, and being imperceptible both to the eye and to the other senses they reveal themselves rather in their effects than in their actions; for example, when fruit or crops are by some unseen atmospheric blight nipped in the bud, killed in the seed, and damaged when ripe; or when the air polluted in some mysterious manner exhales

[1] Reprinted from Gilbert Murray, *Five Stages of Greek Religion* (1925), p. 233. By permission of the Columbia University Press, New York.

[2] Tenney Frank, "Race Mixture in the Roman Empire," *American Historical Review*, Vol. 21 (1916), p. 708.

pestilential vapours. By the same obscure method of contagion the breathing of demons and of angels upon us works corruption of the mind and brings attacks of raving madness, and disgraceful paroxysms of folly, and cruel lusts attended by perversities of various kinds. The most signal of these is that error which recommends the pagan gods to the enthralled and deluded minds of men.[1]

Thus Tertullian (*ca.* 150–230), the leading early expounder of Christianity in the Latin language, testified to the universal conviction. In the light of this conviction it is not remarkable that Christian missionary activity was everywhere accompanied by wonder working and the exorcism of evil spirits.

To demonstrate that the central doctrines of early Christianity were little more than a religious statement of the dominant emotions of the Roman urban masses needs little argument, and similarly it is not difficult to understand the orientation of these beliefs in the daimonic universe. Relevant to the first point is the fact that Christianity spread most rapidly among those social groups whose members had revolted against tyranny and exploitation during the second and first centuries B.C. It is more than a coincidence that Christian Messianism found ready acceptance among the same classes who had responded to the Greek ideal of a perfect worldly society.[2] The shift from a secular to an other-worldly ideal was probably inevitable because these classes, bearing the low intellectual tradition, were fundamentally primitive in outlook. Their belief in daimons was but one aspect of their primitive mentality. In a very fundamental sense the rise of Christianity was due to the displacement of the philosophical outlook which had originated in the Greek *polis* by an outlook more primitive in content because it was based on the experiences of the illiterate masses of the great Mediterranean cities. The ease of communication which the Roman empire brought was the social circumstance necessary for the unification of these masses under a single expression of their common experiences; at the same time

---

[1] F. A. Wright, *Fathers of the Church* (1928), pp. 36–37. By permission of G. Routledge & Sons, Ltd., London; note also H. B. Workman, *Persecution in the Early Church* (ca. 1906), p. 129: "In their belief in demons and other supernatural agencies the Christians were not before their age, save in their grasp of the supremacy of one benign Father of good. Behind every idol statue, however beautiful, they discerned the grinning face of a fiend. The devil and his angels were terrible realities, whose evil machinations were only thwarted by the ceaseless vigilance of the attendant spirits of good." C. H. Kelly, London.

[2] See Samuel Dickey, "Some Economic and Social Conditions of Asia Minor Affecting the Expansion of Christianity," pp. 399 *ff.*, in Shirley J. Case, editor, *Studies in Early Christianity* (1928).

the spread of literacy among a significant section of the masses provided the intellectual medium for the fixing of this expression in an enduring form.

Implicit in the conformity between the social experience of the Roman urban masses and religious doctrine was the ethical repudiation of the values accepted by their rulers and exploiters. This was the truly revolutionary element in Christianity. By their mutual helpfulness—every congregation was a kind of benefit association[1]—stern sexual morality, and loving care of the sick and the poor, the Christians exemplified their faith that self-sacrifice is the way to serve God. The spirit, if not the content, of this behavior, because it declared that the Christians serve no earthly city, was subversive.

2. *The Roman Persecution of the Christians.* The Roman attitude toward foreign religions was normally tolerant.[2] Under the late republic the orgiastic rites of the worshipers of the Great Mother and Isis aroused the sporadic opposition of the authorities, and in the first century of the empire Claudius suppressed the bloody sacrifices of the Druids. On the whole, however, the Romans acted on the ancient principle that the gods of all peoples are true deities, asking only that other peoples recognize Roman gods. After the conquest of the Mediterranean world and the inauguration of emperor worship, this recognition had a political significance, and failure to give it was a form of treason. In this connection it is well to emphasize that the Romans, like all other peoples, believed that the stability of the state and the welfare of society flowed from the continuing favor of their gods. From the Roman point of view any movement which might displease their gods was likely to bring public misfortune. From the first the Romans distrusted

[1] Alfred Loisy, *La Naissance du Christianisme* (1933), p. 168: "Although the Christian movement was not, in strictness, a kind of socialism coloured with religion, nevertheless it had at first and for a long time afterwards, and indeed has never wholly lost, the character of a popular association which offered a promising asylum to the disinherited classes of contemporary society, the slaves of the pagan world and the proletariat both Jewish and pagan . . . a vast mutual aid society where the unfortunate could find moral support and material help. Christianity, in short, had more to offer its adepts than an unrealisable hope doomed to indefinite disappointment; it brought healing to the grand miseries and led on to the institutions of equalitarian society." Emile Nourry, Editor, Paris.

[2] On the persecutions of the Christians see H. B. Workman, *Persecution in the Early Church* (1906); E. G. Hardy, *Christianity and the Roman Government: A study in imperial administration* (1925); Paul Allard, *Le Christianisme et l'empire romain, de Néron à Théodose* (1898); J. Zeller, *L'Empire romain et l'église* (1928); Gerhard Uhlhorn, *The Conflict of Christianity with Heathenism* (1879).

For a statement of the Roman attitude see Hugh Last, "The Study of the Persecutions," *Journal of Roman Studies*, Vol. 27 (1937), pp. 80–92.

the Christians, and peace between them was never more than a temporary cessation of a conflict which for the Christians was part of the realization of the plan of salvation. The persecution of the Christians can best be understood in the light of these attitudes, together with certain other factors that contributed to the hostility of the Roman state. Originally the Christians were confused with the Jews, that perverse and obstinate nation whose rebellious spirit was unbroken even by the destruction of their temple city.[1] Once this mistaken view was corrected, qualities peculiarly Christian were discovered to be obnoxious and, in some respect, treasonable. Furthermore, when the Christians first came to the notice of the Roman authorities, they were organized in congregations which were quite like the secret societies Caesar had forbidden, and their members were drawn from the classes which the rulers of the state feared might revolt.

The behavior and attitudes of the Christians in no way abated the antagonism these circumstances excited. Even when offering a surface loyalty, they maintained an inner revolt, not only against the Roman state but also against the entire social order, which they held in contempt as the work of daimons. They objected to holding public office. They refused to perform military service. They loathed warfare. They condemned the performance of the ritual of the state cult as idolatry and refused to burn even a pinch of incense on the altar to the emperor. Their hatred of idols won for them the designation "atheists." They condemned the popular amusements as gross barbarities and immoralities. They looked upon marriage and the begetting of children as regrettable concessions to the flesh. In their congregations they violated the social code by placing masters and slaves on the same level. Their condemnation of the wearing of jewelry and fine raiment interfered with trade and industry. One of the earliest outbreaks against them was stirred up by the silversmiths of Ephesus. Popular credulity charged them with immoral rites and ritualistic murder. Their practice of meeting secretly and at night gave inferential

[1] E. G. Hardy, *Christianity and the Roman Government: A study in imperial administration* (1925), p. 35: "We cannot judge the ordinary Christian of Corinth or Antioch, or Ephesus, or Rome from the leaders and teachers of the sect. The Christians of the Eastern provinces shared the characteristics of the Oriental population; they were not less fanatical or less ignorant, or less excitable, or less credulous. In the eyes of their fellow citizens there was nothing about them to justify what seemed the extravagant claims they made on behalf of their religion. They were fanatical, exclusive, and intolerant, and for a religion which, so to speak, to Gentile eyes, had nothing to show for itself, no stately temples, no famous shrines, no imposing priesthood, no impressive ceremonial." By permission of the Oxford University Press, Oxford.

validity to such wholly false accusations. Their uncompromising position in the face of criticism and persecution intensified the popular and official hatred. It became their claim that they were not bound to obey an unjust law and their boast that they had withdrawn from society. Finally, the divine event toward which they looked with fervid hope necessarily involved the overthrow of the state. Thus, in their own peculiar way, the early Christians were "revolutionaries."[1]

To maintain the faith which supported these attitudes, the Christians accepted martyrdom; to defend the state and society against their subversive influence the Romans became persecutors.

In the first century the outbursts against the Christians were sporadic and mainly inspired by local feeling. There is little evidence to support the view that Nero wreaked vengeance on the Christians for the burning of Rome and still less to warrant the assertion that he outlawed the Christian religion. In the second century Trajan and Hadrian tempered the growing popular antagonism by refusing to sanction any systematic hunting down of Christians and by imposing severe penalties upon their anonymous and false accusers. But Trajan also made the refusal to pay homage to the emperor a criminal offense punishable with death. Except for the obstinate refusal to participate in the customary demonstrations of loyalty, the Christians, although regarded as excessively superstitious, were not looked upon by official Rome with high disfavor. They were orderly, industrious, and peace-loving and not unwilling to pray to their God for the welfare of the state. Popular antagonism was the cause of persecutions until the reign of Marcus Aurelius, when imperial policy finally turned against the Christians.

This change was due chiefly to the factors that were carrying the empire toward the economic and social crisis of the third century; those emperors, it is interesting to note, who sought to stay these forces became the chief persecutors. The theory of their policy was simple: namely, the growth of atheism and disloyalty to the state caused the traditional gods to withhold the favor that made for stability and prosperity. In 248 when the Christians refused to take any part in the celebration of the thousandth

[1] E. G. Hardy, *Christianity and the Roman Government: A study in imperial administration* (1925), p. 35: "To a great extent it was the tendency to level distinctions of property or differences of social life, the hopes it held out of a shortly coming Saviour, and the idea of a future beyond the grave, in which compensation would be made for the inequalities of the present which drew the lower classes to Christianity." By permission of the Oxford University Press, Oxford.

anniversary of the founding of Rome, popular antagonism fell upon them, and in the succeeding year Decius, in order to restore the ancient *pietas et gravitas*, issued an edict requiring every person in every town to appear before a magistrate to offer sacrifice to the gods or to give evidence that he had done so. For two years after this edict many Christians were killed or banished to the mines and their property confiscated.

At this time the Christians probably numbered one-tenth of the population and were to be found in all but the outlying parts of the empire. The evil days that came to the state brought them many new converts, especially among the soldiers and the young intellectuals and in the higher ranks of society. Many young Stoics now entered their congregations. Valerian (253–260) undertook to check this development by laws which threatened senators and knights with loss of their properties and offices and, if they persisted in the forbidden faith, with execution by beheading. He sent members of the imperial household who became Christians to work as slaves at agriculture. But, even in the face of these severe measures, the Christians became bolder in their criticisms of the social order. They explained that the evils afflicting the state were the results of idolatry and polytheism. The avarice, luxury, immorality, and warfare of the times were proof that the state was possessed by daimons and ruled by the Devil. Their own sufferings were, they believed, God's punishment for living worldly lives. Thus the issue between the Roman rulers and the Christians became sharper and clearer, and the growing congregations and multiplying public meeting places of the Christians everywhere intensified it. It was not at all remarkable, therefore, that Diocletian, who reformed the state, should also have undertaken to root out the religion which, from his point of view, was partly responsible for the universal disorder. In 303 he purged the army of Christians and in the next year ordered the destruction of churches, the burning of sacred books, the removal of all Christians from public office, and the prohibition of the freeing of Christian slaves. Christians were also deprived of the right to appear in court. The primary aim of these harsh measures was to break up the congregations by destroying their leaders. Everywhere priests and bishops were arrested and punished by execution or imprisonment. In some places so many Christians were sent to the mines that they were able to organize congregations. The obstinacy of the Christians and their violent behavior in the courts increased the severity of their punishments.[1]

[1] See A. J. Mason, *The Persecution of Diocletian: A historical essay* (1876).

The occasion of this persecution—the only general attempt by the Roman authorities to suppress Christianity—reveals the essential difference of belief which was at the root of the conflict between the state and the Christian congregations. While observing entrails, *i.e.*, taking the official auspices, Diocletian saw a Christian attendant make the sign of the cross; this act, because it was irritating to the official gods of the state, the emperor believed made difficult the taking of auspices. This incident has meaning only in terms of the belief of both pagans and Christians, namely, that the welfare of the state depended on the favor of supernatural powers. In the face of the political troubles of the times, this belief strengthened the desire for religious unity. The question, however, was becoming: "Under what god will the state prosper?" The old pagan gods Jupiter and Hercules were commonly regarded as having lost the power to support the state.[1]

3. *The Christian Martyrs.*   The difference of belief about the Deity under whom the state would prosper was an evidence only of a far more fundamental clash between the Christians and the people among whom they appeared. From their Jewish background the Christians inherited a feeling of exclusiveness, and as time went on, especially in the face of persecution, this feeling took form in a recognition of their apartness: to themselves the Christians were a "new people," as has been noted; to the Romans and the Hellenized orientals they were a "third race."[2] At its base this

[1] Shirley J. Case, *Experience with the Supernatural in Early Christian Times* (1929), p. 214: " . . . Any emperor who sought seriously to stay the forces of disintegration that were already so clearly manifest in the Roman world felt it to be a serious obligation on his part to restore the rites of religion as a corrective, and, in the last analysis, the only sure corrective for the evils of the day. The more numerous Christians became, the greater was the menace to the state from their refusal to revere those supernatural sources of help which were assumed to be the only adequate guarantors of safety for the state.

"In their effort to alleviate the distress of the times, the more capable rulers sought not only to restore the worship of the traditional deities, but to supplement their apparently waning powers by the introduction of new gods who could be combined with the deities of tradition. Inevitably they turned to the East for these new increments of supernatural power. In the second and third Christian centuries, gods from the Orient were serving far more conspicuously the needs of the Roman government than were the native deities of Italy. In the reforms of Diocletian, for example, which were the most thorough-going that had been instituted since the time of Augustus, it was really the invincible sun-god of Syria to whom the Romans attached themselves in the hope of insuring restoration and permanence to their tottering Empire." By permission of D. Appleton-Century Company, New York.

[2] Adolf von Harnack, *The Mission and Expansion of Christianity in the First Three Centuries* (2 vols., 2d ed., 1908), Vol. 1, p. 277: "Plainly, then, Greeks and Jews and Christians were distinguished throughout upon the ground of religion, although the explicit formula of 'the third race' occurs only in the West. After the middle of the third century, both empire and emperor learnt to recognize and dread the third race of worshippers as a 'nation,' as well as a race. . . . The inner energy of the new religion comes out in its self-

recognition involved a repudiation by the Christians of the traditional in-group feelings of the Mediterranean peoples; naturally, therefore, these peoples turned against them the traditional antipathy toward out-groups. The persecutions were actually a clash of groups animated by the most primitive emotions that stir men. The Christians, of course, true to their beliefs, orientated their new in-group loyalty in theological doctrine: "Each organized gathering of believers seemed to itself to be visible realization of that Holy City of which the greatest Hebrew poets had sung and which the divinest seers had seen. Between the City of God, and the diseased and decaying society which surrounded it, there was perpetual and sharp antithesis."[1] Thus Cyprian (*ca.* 200–258), bishop of Carthage, praised martyrdom: "Let no one think of death, but of immortality, not of temporal punishment, but of eternal joy. . . . " This reorientation of emotions, because it touched the simplest feelings of the masses, was the most disturbing factor introduced by Christianity into the Roman world; it was, of course, the fundamental force which shifted loyalties from the old to the new culture that was taking shape.

In the clash of Christians with the Roman state it was inevitable, therefore, that they should have their heroes—those who died willingly and gloriously for the cause; such heroes are known as *martyrs*, *i.e.*, "witnesses" to the faith. By the opening of the second century this heroic service was willingly performed by Christian leaders, notably Ignatius (*ca.* 70–125), bishop of Antioch, and Polycarp (*ca.* 69–155), bishop of Smyrna. In the third century there was almost a fanatical desire for martyrdom. Christians deliberately neglected their public duties, insulted magistrates, and broke the statues of the gods. The mood of the times is well illustrated in the behavior of a Roman legion sent to Gaul and ordered to participate in a persecution. When its Christian members refused to obey their officers, they were twice decimated by command of the emperor, but still they refused to attack their fellow Christians. The leader of the Christian legionnaires declared that they were ready to obey the emperor in all things consistent with duty to God, but duty to God was above loyalty to the emperor.

chosen title of 'the New People' or 'the Third Race' just as plainly as in the testimony extorted from its opponents, that in Christianity a new *genus* of religion had actually emerged side by side with the religions of the nations and of Judaism." By permission of G. P. Putnam's Sons, New York.

[1] Edwin Hatch, *The Organization of the Early Christian Churches* (8th imp.. 1918) p. 69. By permission of Longmans, Green & Company, London.

The martyr, although often unstable emotionally, was not moved merely by his own impulses; on the contrary, he was a product of an inculcated faith in the worth of the sacrifice he made.[1] Explicit teachings held up the imitation of Christ's suffering as the highest worldly goal; to the questions which the official of the state asked, individuals were taught to answer, "I am a Christian." For suffering one hour of worldly torture, it was believed, the martyr would gain an eternity of immortal bliss. The image of the martyr, crowned and sitting among the angels, was presented over and over again to the congregations. Furthermore, the martyr, it was known, always won the high social approval of fellow Christians. Each congregation venerated its own heroes, and families and towns felt themselves honored if a member or a resident suffered martyrdom. Thus when persecution came, many Christians stood forth willingly to accept cruel punishment and death. To the Roman authorities such persons were evidence of the futility of violent measures. To the Christians they were a vindication of faith and exemplars to similar conduct. The blood of the martyrs, it was boasted, was the "seed of the church."

THE LEGALIZATION OF CHRISTIANITY.

The transformation of Christianity from a persecuted into a legal religion occurred in the course of the struggle for supreme power that followed the abdication of Diocletian in 305. Galerius (305–311), who succeeded Diocletian, kept up the persecution until 311, when, beset with political misfortune and a fatal disease, he sought supernatural aid by issuing an edict of toleration. The motive of the act was clearly stated, "In return for our indulgence the Christians are to pray to their God for our health, for the state, and for themselves, that the commonwealth may enjoy perfect prosperity, and that they be enabled to live at home in security." After his death Maxentius (306–312) reverted to the policy of persecution. But he faced as a rival for supreme power the son of a western emperor whose policy throughout the persecution had been relatively mild; this rival, Constantine (306–337), was told by Christian advisers that he would gain supernatural support if he granted them toleration, and he finally accepted this assurance and sent his troops into battle with Maxentius—the battle of Milvian Bridge (312)—with standards and shields bearing Christian devices. In gratitude for victory Constantine issued the famous Edict of Milan (313). He also set up in Rome a statue of

[1] D. W. Riddle, *The Martyrs: A study in social control* (1931).

himself holding the cross, which he described as the "salvation-bringing badge." By the terms of the Edict of Milan the Christians gained not only liberty of worship (which was extended, in fact, to the adherents of all faiths) but also the removal of all legal disabilities, the restitution of property, and the restoration of status in the imperial regime. The edict specifically mentioned the Christians in terms which leave little doubt as to the attitude that inspired its promulgator:

. . . We have thought that it was necessary above all to regulate all that concerns the worship due the Deity, in order to give both to Christians and to all free power to follow the religion of their choice. May, therefore, the Deity, in his celestial habitation show his satisfaction and his favours both to us and to the peoples who live under our authority.

Although Constantine's motives were undoubtedly superstitious,[1] he was enough of a politician to realize that the great Christian congregations were a political factor no ruler could longer afford to ignore.

THE SOCIAL CONSOLIDATION OF CHRISTIANITY

When Constantine issued his edict of toleration, Christianity had been planted in every part of the empire and even outside its borders. It was already the official religion of Edessa and Armenia. From Edessa it spread into Persia, and toward the end of the fourth century it penetrated Arabia and Abyssinia. In the west it was well rooted in Gaul and Spain, and at least a few congregations had appeared in Britain and along the borders of Germany. All northern Africa, including Mauretania in the far west, had felt its impact. But its main centers, in spite of the prominence of Rome (which, it should never be forgotten, always faced east), were in Greece, Asia Minor, and Egypt. In these lands not quite half of the population, it seems, had embraced the new faith; in the other parts of the empire certainly a far smaller proportion of the population had been converted. Constantine's pro-Christian policy accelerated the conversion of the middle and upper classes, but the peasants were everywhere slow to abandon the traditional beliefs.

---

[1] Ferdinand Lot, *The End of the Ancient World and the Beginning of the Middle Ages* (1931), p. 32; see also L. M. O. Duchesne, *Early History of the Christian Church* . . . (3 vols., 1909–1924), Vol. 2, p. 28.

On Constantine see J. B. Firth, *Constantine the Great: The reorganization of the empire and the triumph of the church* (1905); A. Piganol, *L'Empereur Constantine* (1932); Ernst Gerland, *Konstantine der Grosse in Geschichte und Sage* (1936); V. Burch, *Myth & Constantine the Great* (1927); C. B. Coleman, *Constantine the Great and Christianity* (1914); [Eusebius] *The Life of the Blessed Emperor Constantine* (Eng. trans., 1845).

Probably about one-twentieth of the population of the empire was Christian in 313.

THE CHRISTIAN ROMAN EMPIRE.

Under Constantine's pro-Christian policy the state became a full-fledged oriental monarchy, and it endured as such until its disruption in the late fifth century. During this phase of its career the Roman state is known as the Christian Roman Empire.[1]

1. *Constantine's Completion of Diocletian's Work.* In the main Constantine followed Diocletian's political and fiscal policies. The power of the emperor, however, was not divided, although the division of the empire into four parts was retained. Each part was governed by a prefect, who had full civil and financial but no military authority. The departments of the central administration, which were concentrated around the emperor, were declared to be sacred. The emperor, having dropped the titles and symbols of Mithraism, adopted Christian designations and emblems. Ultimately he bore the title "equal to the Apostles" and was represented as wearing the nimbus of a saint; he was addressed as "your eternity." But the oriental etiquette of the court remained unchanged. A new official known as the quaestor, who served as the emperors' mouthpiece, edited and issued edicts and laws. He was the administrative head of the government. The senate, deprived of its functions, survived chiefly as a social body; its members were deprived of financial immunity and the privilege of trial by their peers. The magistrates became courtiers dependent on favor rather than election for their positions. The whole body of administrative officials, whose numbers multiplied greatly, formed a hierarchy of four grades. The highest rank, which surrounded the emperor, was showered with wealth and titles; the lowest rank was burdened with the many duties of provincial posts. In spite of the absolute power of the emperor, the administration became more and more decentralized, for the provincial officials found many opportunities to avoid responsibility. This development was

[1] On the Christian Roman Empire see *The Cambridge Medieval History*, Vol. 1, *The Christian Roman Empire and the Foundation of the Teutonic Kingdoms* (1936), Chap. I, "Constantine and His City," Chap. II, "The Reorganization of the Empire," and Chap. IV, "The Triumph of Christianity"; H. St. L. B. Moss, *The Birth of the Middle Ages* (1935); Ferdinand Lot, *The End of the Ancient World and the Beginning of the Middle Ages* (1931); J. B. Bury, *History of the Later Roman Empire from the Death of Theodosius I to the Death of Justinian (A.D. 395 to A.D. 565)* (2 vols., 1923); Ernst Stein, *Geschichte des spätrömischen Reiches*, Vol. 1, *Von römischen zum byzantinischen Staate, 284–476 n. Chr.* (1928); John B. Firth, *Constantine the Great: The reorganization of the empire and the triumph of the church* (1923); and Pierre Batiffol, *La Paix Constantinienne et le catholicisme* (3d ed., 1914).

quite in line with the others that were giving the state oriental characteristics.

At the court conspiracy and intrigue reigned, with female favorites and eunuchs often enjoying power. Sometimes a strong man, acting in a military or a political capacity, became the real ruler. Spies lurked everywhere. Persons were arrested and imprisoned or executed on weak charges or no charges at all. Constantine, who had won power only after vanquishing five opponents, attempted to fix the succession in his line by destroying all possible rivals to his sons. But the policy failed, for soon the emperorship was to be had by any man who could win it. Hosts of barbers, grooms, cooks, and eunuchs ministered to the needs of the elaborate life of the court clique.

The revenues were derived almost exclusively from land and indirect taxes. The land was surveyed and its obligations fixed according to the size and productivity of estates. New taxes were levied on senatorial estates and the profits of trade. But mainly the lesser landlords and merchants bore the financial burden of the state, for the new aristocracy was relieved of taxation and the urban workers were no longer required to pay the head tax. The peasants paid their dues to the landlords. The members of the urban middle class, who were responsible for raising the taxes of the cities, were denied all means of escape from their burdens. The political hierarchy, as well as the luxurious court, was expensive to maintain; together with the costs of building enterprises and military levies, they sapped further the declining economic strength of the state. Almost all of the economic surplus, except that part which now began to flow to the Christian priests, was concentrated in the hands of the new aristocracy.

The army also underwent a further evolution. In 312, when the Praetorian Guard was abolished, a palace guard on the Persian model was created. Almost all of the old legions disappeared, their places taken by new legions posted as garrisons in the cities. The frontier was protected only by a screen of peasant soldiers. In each province a military official, known as a count, was in complete control of the army, for civil and military functions were now entirely separated. The counts, however, reported from time to time to the emperor about political affairs. In this way new great provincial commands began to arise. Constantine first introduced Germans into the upper ranks of the military establishment. In line with these developments in organization went further changes in tactics and arms. Since the legions were no longer capable of complicated movements, the mailed cavalry became the chief mobile force. The barbarian sword, the long pike, and the Parthian bow replaced the old Roman weapons, and standards bearing Christian and even barbarian devices were introduced. Military supplies were obtained almost entirely by levies of produce on the area in which an army was stationed. Finally, it should be noted, the soldiers in the ranks sank into a servile class while the officers, drawn from the aristocracy, tended to surround themselves with retainers.

The transfer of the capital of the empire to the new city Constantinople, which was founded in 330 on the ancient site of Byzantium, strengthened the Greek and oriental at the expense of the Roman elements of the state. The new capital, of course, was from the beginning a Christian city. Although pagan temples were demolished in order to obtain statuary for the city's decoration, no temples were erected within its confines; the city was officially dedicated to the Blessed Virgin. The building of Constantinople was undoubtedly motivated by the emperor's desire to make Christianity the official religion of the state.

Constantine remained the traditional head of the pagan religion, the Pontifex Maximus, but neglected to perform the duties of the office. He forbade the erection of new statues—idols—of the gods and prohibited the official performance of rites to them. Divination in private houses was made a criminal offense. In contrast to this hostile treatment of the traditional cults was the continuous granting of privileges to Christians. He made observation of Sunday obligatory in the cities, especially by craftsmen and judges. He restored the ecclesiastical properties confiscated during the persecutions, built new churches, identified holy spots, recovered relics, and granted alms to poor congregations. He suspended the laws against childlessness in favor of Christian priests and exempted them from political obligations and compulsory labor. At the same time he undertook to play an active role in Christian affairs, presiding over church councils and attempting to compel obedience to their decisions by force. In this role, however, he was inconsistent, for at different times he favored different ecclesiastical parties. Furthermore, he allowed the provincial rulers to choose their religious policies.

The results of Constantine's pro-Christian policy were far-reaching: (1) It opened the way for the conversion of the politically significant section of the population, *i.e.*, the aristocracy. (2) It brought to the state the support of the best-organized elements

By the courtesy of the Metropolitan Museum of Art

CONSTANTINE

With Constantine's recognition of Christianity as a legal religion, the Church entered into that uncertain alliance with political power which produced an enduring confusion of the things that are Caesar's with the things that are Christ's.

among the people, *i.e.*, the large urban congregations. (3) It placed the power of the state at the service of Christianity in converting the remainder of the pagan population, especially the peasants. (4) It made religious contentions significant political issues. (5) It led to modifications of the law. The first three of these effects, which worked themselves out in the suppression of paganism, the conversion of the greatest part of the population, and the establishment of *orthodox* Christianity as the official religion of the state are noted in this chapter. The rise of religious controversy as an aspect of politics and the changes in the law will be touched upon in the discussions of the development of theological doctrines and the relation of the church and the state.[1]

From the battle of Milvian Bridge, when he became a Christian, until baptism on his deathbed, Constantine believed himself to be guided by the Christians' God, and in this belief he was constantly encouraged by Christian advisers. They kept a record of the dreams and visions by which he received heavenly advice. Constantine, who became a Christian in order to win the support of the Christians' God, acted, of course, on the traditional belief that the well-being of the state depended on supernatural favor. If the advancement of Christian interests is considered, the action was a success; if the welfare of the population of the empire is kept in view, the policy was a failure, for economic and social distress was not ameliorated. Finally, it is fair to note, the pro-Christian policy failed politically, for it did not restore the unity of the empire; nor did it unify the Christians.

2. *The Suppression of Paganism.* Although the successors of Constantine quarreled among themselves, they continued to support Christianity. Death threats were made against those who violated the prohibition of the performance of the pagan sacrifices. Temple properties were confiscated and given to the churches. The statue of Victory, symbol of imperial dominion, was removed from the senate house. At the same time the doctrinal struggles of the Christians became more embittered, and those declared heretics were driven into exile. But the traditional cults survived, particularly in the west. Nicomedia, Diocletian's capital, was the chief center of pagan education. There the emperor Julian (*ca.* 361–363), who made the last attempt to restore the traditional cults, was trained in rhetoric and Neoplatonism.[2]

Julian aimed at nothing less than a reconstruction of the pagan cults along lines that would have given them an organization similar to that of the Christian churches. A new priesthood, whose members lived according to ascetic principles, was to devote its energies to social and intellectual, as well as pious, works; its leaders were to be somewhat like the Christian bishops. The chief expression of religious feeling was to be through good works; the

---

[1] See pp. 1124, 1133.

[2] See Victor Schultze, *Geschichte des Untergangs des griechisch-römischen Heidentums* (1887); J. Geffcken, *Der Ausgang des griechisch-römischen Heidentums* (1920); P. de Labriolle, *La Réaction païenne* (1934); G. E. A. Grindle, *The Destruction of Paganism in the Roman Empire* (1893); Gerhard Uhlhorn, *The Conflict of Christianity with Heathenism* (1879).

maintenance of orphanages, hospitals, and asylums was every-where encouraged. Measures designed to weaken the Christian churches were taken. The clergy were deprived of state aid and ordered to return to customary occupations. The giving of alms to the Christian poor was stopped. Christians were compelled to join in the rebuilding of temples, and garrisons were withdrawn from towns refusing to rebuild them. Julian's death in battle with the Persians after a reign of two years put an end to this single constructive effort to revitalize paganism.[1]

After Julian's death Constantine's legislation was revived, and Christians regained their favored position in the state. But the quarrels of the orthodox and heretical Christians continued unabated. In the east an attempt was made to stamp out the orthodox beliefs. In the west the orthodox party continually gained strength. In 382 the emperor Gratian (*ca.* 375–383), under the advice of the greatest Christian leader of the time, Ambrose (*ca.* 340–397), bishop of Milan, deprived the pagan priests of the last of their exemptions and privileges, confiscated much temple property, and prohibited legacies to the temples. These measures broke up the ancient priestly aristocracies. Theodosius I (*ca.* 379–395), who, like Constantine, succeeded in uniting the empire, ordered the closing of all pagan temples, forbade the maintenance of household shrines, and declared the making of public or private sacrifices treason. With these measures, which provoked an insurrection, the institutional organization of paganism came to an end. Theodosius also issued the first laws for the suppression of heresy. Heretics were deprived of their churches, denied the right to make wills and inherit property, disqualified from holding civil offices, and forbidden to assemble. Thus orthodox Christianity became the only religion recognized by the state. It is worth noting that the last emperor to rule over a united Roman Empire was also the first emperor to recognize orthodox Christianity as the single legal religion and that, like his predecessors, whether pagan or Christian, he sought religious unification in order to win supernatural favor for the secular state.

3. *The Social Basis of Triumphant Christianity.* The development of Christianity was bound up at every step of the way to its ultimate triumph with the depressed urban masses. For them it became a gentile religion. Through them it found a permanent place in Mediterranean life. From them it spread to the other parts of the social structure.

---

[1] On Julian the Apostate see J. Bidez, *La Vie de l'Empereur Julien* (1930).

We have often emphasized in the foregoing pages the significance which the great cities of the Mediterranean Basin had for ancient Christianity: Jerusalem, Antioch in Syria, Ephesus and Smyrna, Thessalonica, Corinth, to say nothing of Alexandria, whose outlines are now visible in the dawn, and finally Rome—all these have come into our view. From the great cities as central points the new faith expanded along the roads of every-day commerce, first to the smaller cities, and then into the country districts. We can only very occasionally observe Christianity, in the period which we have considered, among the rural people of such provinces as Bithynia-Pontus or Phrygia. This development which reached out from the large city was, moreover, decisively operative on behalf of an enduring unity. The small churches of the minor cities found unity and support in the churches of the greater cities. From the latter they had received their Christianity, there their members found a friendly reception if they came to the capital on their own business or for the church: it was not in vain that hospitality occupied such a conspicuous place in the circle of early Christian virtues. The great city churches were, furthermore, often of great antiquity; most of those enumerated above were of apostolic foundation, and their church tradition was superior to that of those which were later organized. Ephesus had the undisputed position of leadership among the churches in the province of Asia, as had Antioch in Syria and Corinth in Achaia. . . . By means of the active communication and intercourse, which we can clearly observe, there was possible a very widespread and uniform development of Christianity in the Roman empire among the widely dispersed churches, despite the weak position which Christianity had in the world at the time.[1]

Just as the spread of Christianity among the urban masses was partly a result of their worsening conditions of life, so it penetrated other social groups also as their positions were altered by social and economic changes. As the urban aristocracy was destroyed by economic decline, the bearers of the Greco-Roman high intellectual tradition tended to become fewer, and those who remained commonly turned from the traditional cults to some combination of philosophical ideas as a guide for living. Those who were politically minded found new opportunities for exercising power by entering the Christian congregations, where their social prestige gained a quick recognition for them. Julian is an example of the first development, Ambrose, the great bishop of Milan, of the second. Indeed, the final victory of Christianity was assured when the church became an avenue leading to political power. Constantine's supreme service to Christianity was the opening of this avenue.

[1] Johannes Weiss, *The History of Primitive Christianity* (2 vols., 1937), Vol. 2, pp. 864–865. By permission of Wilson-Erickson, Inc., Elmira, N. Y.

The legislation that gave the congregations the right to receive bequests suggests the manner in which they acquired property and grew in economic strength; this growth was undoubtedly a factor contributing to the shift of political influence from urban magistrates and provincial officials to ecclesiastical dignitaries. When the conversion of the urban masses was completed, during the struggle to suppress paganism, the peasants were left as the carriers of the traditional culture; since they had never acquired possession of its intellectual and artistic elements, they preserved mainly its vulgar content, and Christians, like Roman aristocrats, regarded them as rustics; thus paganism (as previously noted, this designation for the traditional religion was derived from the word *paganus*, which meant "dweller in the fields") was identified with vulgarity and doltishness, while Christianity was identified with social refinement and intellectual enlightenement. This shift of social approvals assured the triumph of Christianity.

THE FORMATION OF THE CHRISTIAN PRIEST CLASS.

Throughout the long period of Christianity's diffusion over the Mediterranean lands every development which furthered its advancement contributed not only to the growth of its congregations but also to the power and prestige of its leaders; at first these leaders were mere teachers, but ultimately they became officials—performing special duties, living according to established rules, and possessing special privileges. The formation of a priest class as the bearer of the Western cultural tradition was the most important social result of the rise of Christianity.[1]

1. *The Origin of the Christian Priesthood.* The first Christian leaders, the Apostles, were the successors of Jesus, from whom, it was believed, they had received divine appointment and inspiration. The founders of the first congregations were wandering teachers who bore the message of Jesus from the Apostles; they were believed to have received the "gifts of the Spirit," like Peter, who "spoke in tongues," or Paul, who had a vision while in a trance. The greatest sin a Christian could commit was to reject

[1] On the rise of the Christian priesthood see *The Cambridge Medieval History*, Vol. 1, *The Christian Roman Empire and the Foundation of the Teutonic Kingdoms* (1936) Chap. VI, "The Organization of the Church"; James Heron, *The Evolution of Latin Christianity* (1919); Robert Rainy, *The Ancient Catholic Church from the Accession of Trajan to the Fourth General Council (A.D. 98–451)* (1902); B. H. Streeter, *The Primitive Church Studied with Special Reference to the Origin of the Christian Ministry* (1929); Adolf von Harnack, *The Constitution and Laws of the Church in the First Two Centuries* (1910); Edwin Hatch, *The Organization of the Early Christian Churches* (8th imp., 1918).

or criticize their utterances. At the outset, therefore, the Christian leaders were the heirs of the Hebrew tradition of inspired prophecy. But once an apostle or teacher left a congregation he had founded, the congregation was dependent on local leadership. Usually it may be assumed that, like Paul, the original teachers appointed these leaders; at any rate, it is certain that they were regarded as having received the "gifts of the Spirit."

The elements of the Christian priesthood appeared in the course of the differentiation of these local leaders into grades of ecclesiastical functionaries and dignitaries. The original differentiation separated the elders, or presbyters, from the congregation. During the performance of the sacrament of the Lord's Supper[1] these leaders sat around a table while the members of the congregation stood. A second differentiation marked off the deacons from the elders; while the elders sat at the table, the deacons circulated among the members of the congregation. From the first the deacons were also employed in carrying on charitable work. The elders also gave instruction in the Christian way of life and administered the discipline necessary to maintain that way of life. By the year 70, when the first generation of Christian teachers had disappeared, the responsibility for the life of the Christian congregations passed entirely to local leaders. Since Paul regarded Jesus as the successor of Moses, whose teachings had been guarded and transmitted by the Hebrew priests, it was only natural that the Christians should regard these leaders as a divinely ordained body; at the same time, it should be noted, they were also believed to possess "the gifts of the Spirit."

Until after the beginning of the second century, it seems, the growing congregations of Asia Minor, Macedonia, Greece, and Italy were governed by a *college*, *i.e.*, a body of presbyters, whose members were aided by deacons. At Rome the number of deacons was fixed at seven, the number of subleaders first appointed by the Apostles at Jerusalem. To these leaders fell the duties of keeping pure the story of Jesus, of guarding morals, of administering the sacraments of baptism and the communion, and of supervising charitable work. They were chosen, it seems, with the consent of the congregations.

2. *The Growth of the Episcopate.* The full transformation of the Christian leaders into a priesthood was bound up with the rise of the bishops as the chief functionaries and dignitaries of the congregation. The term "bishop," it is worth noting, is derived

[1] See p. 1152.

from a Greek word meaning overseer. Originally the bishops were, apparently, merely the presidents of the colleges of presbyters, but in the second century several developments transformed them into the spiritual monarchs of the congregations and united in them the "gifts of the Spirit." One of the earliest known Roman bishops, Clement (fl. *ca.* 96), regarded the presbyters as the successors of the Apostles and looked upon their leader, *i.e.*, Peter, as the chief repository of the faith. At Antioch Ignatius set forth a clear doctrine of the elevated position of bishops: "We ought to look upon the bishop as we would upon the Lord himself." This view of the bishop as a spiritual monarch spread through Asia Minor and Greece and, about 150, united with the Roman doctrine of the apostolic succession. In the union of these two conceptions of the position of bishops the ideological basis of the supremacy of the episcopate over the other sections of the priesthood was established. In line with this development grew the conviction that those teachers who continued to speak with the "gifts of the Spirit" were dangerous to the traditional beliefs of Christians; as a result, the bishop began to exercise an authority over doctrines.[1] The outcome of these several developments was to concentrate in the hands of the bishops the functions of religious mediation between Christians and their God. They performed the sacred rituals, interpreted and explained the sacred works, and acted as judges of the moral life of the faithful. As the leaders of the Christian priest class, the bishops assumed the role of God's agents in the worldly lives of men.

To the Apostles themselves, in person, appeal is no longer possible; but their representatives and successors are to be found in every Church. The bishops, or the presbyters (for Irenaeus uses either word for the heads of the governing bodies of the Churches) were appointed at first and taught by them; and they in turn, generation by generation, in unbroken succession, have handed on to their successors the same tradition.[2]

Several factors contributed to the rise of the bishops to this supreme position. (1) As the growth of the congregations increased the administrative work, it became centralized under the leadership of the presbyters. Thus the bishops became charged with the

---

[1] On the factors that contributed to the early differentiation of the priesthood from the laity see S. B. Eaton, *The Apostolic Tradition of Hippolytus* (1934). The force of tradition in this differentiation is clearly revealed in this work.

[2] J. F. Bethune-Baker, *An Introduction to the Early History of Christian Doctrine* (6th ed., 1938), p. 56. By permission of Methuen & Co., Ltd., London.

duties of the performance of the Eucharist, the admission of converts through the sacrament of baptism, the administration of discipline to penitents, the supervision of the care of the sick, the poor, the orphaned, and the widowed, the ordination of priests, and the installation of new bishops. In obtaining the power to ordain priests and install bishops, the bishops gained control of the personnel of the sacred hierarchy. (2) The growth of the congregations in large cities led to the attachment to them of small congregations in small near-by towns and villages, with the result that the local presbyters and priests looked to the leader of the large congregation for guidance and support. In this way the local congregations became units—*parishes*—in larger bodies of Christians—*dioceses*—over which bishops ruled. Thus was created the rudiments of an ecclesiastical administrative structure. By the middle of the second century the bishops of the great Mediterranean cities—Antioch, Alexandria, Ephesus, Carthage, and Rome—were heads of such structures. (3) The need for church unity led to the development of a general episcopal jurisdiction over the congregations. This was probably the most important factor in the rise of the bishops.

The instrument of this general jurisdiction was an assembly of bishops, which acted in the name of the whole body of Christians. An assembly of the bishops of a province was a *synod;* an assembly to which all bishops were called was an *ecumenical council, i.e.,* a council representing the whole inhabited world. Such assemblies were first held early in the third century. The precedent for holding councils at regular intervals was set by the council of Carthage (*ca.* 251), summoned by Cyprian to deal with an issue that had arisen as a result of persecution. The issue was: "Ought Christians who abandoned their faith during a persecution to be received back into the church?" From the point of view of ecclesiastical organization, the question raised was whether the church, *i.e.,* the bishops, had the right to forgive all sins, including apostasy. If the bishops did not have this power, there was a limitation on their spiritual leadership. Those who denied that the bishops had the power to forgive the sin of apostasy were known as Novatians, after their leader, Novatian (fl. *ca.* 250). The council of Carthage upheld the broad view of the power of bishops. A similar dispute arose as a consequence of Diocletian's effort to destroy the church. After the persecution many Christians, including some bishops, who had surrendered their sacred vessels and scriptures, sought readmission to the church. They were known as *traditores, i.e.,* traitors. Opponents of their readmission raised a significant question as to the powers of a bishop who had been a traditor. Could he administer the sacraments or ordain a priest? From the point of view of ecclesiastical organization the question raised was whether an impure bishop could function spiritually. To have answered this question in the negative would have resulted in a disruption of the ecclesiastical organization, for then individual Christians could always have had doubts as to the efficacy of the sacraments. Those who denied the power of an impure bishop to function spiritually came to be known as Donatists, from the name of one of their leaders, Donatus (fl. *ca.* 316). The council of Arles (314) condemned the Donatist position, but its supporters long remained a disturbing element.[1]

The strife about and within Christianity during the second and third centuries produced a rounded faith to which orthodox believers adhered.[2] Besides the New Testament, a clearly formulated creed, and an established ritual, this faith included two fundamental ideas: (1) the church is universal, *i.e.*, there is no salvation except within it; (2) the bishops, as the successors of the Apostles, are the spiritual heads of the church, and anyone who disagrees with his bishop is not within the church. These ideas completed the ideological justification of the supremacy of the episcopate, *i.e.*, of the bishops, who, considered as a unit, ruled all Christians, as the single repository of the "saving truth." In this form Christianity is known as the Old Catholic Church.

3. *The Structure and Privileges of the Christian Priest Class.* During the third century the bishops everywhere increased their power, so that the other members of the priesthood and the ordinary Christians became almost completely subject to them. Closely associated with the bishops were the presbyters and deacons; together they formed an exclusive spiritual order. Above all, presbyters as well as bishops administered the sacraments. The deacons assisted the bishops in administrative, charitable, and disciplinary work. More and more the severe morality of the early Christians was confined to this upper order of priests. Although the bishops and presbyters did not yet forego marriage or withdraw from ordinary occupations, a celibate life devoted to study and meditation was becoming increasingly the priestly ideal. The lower rank of the priesthood was made up of a host of lesser functionaries—subdeacons, readers, exorcists, door-

[1] See p. 1202.
[2] See p. 1104.

keepers, gravediggers, notaries, and advocates, who did not withdraw from the ordinary pursuits of life. Thus subdeacons and the readers assisted in the performance of the rituals of worship and the teaching of morals. The readership was a preparative for the presbyterate. The exorcists, who originally had been bearers of the "gifts of the Spirit," were particularly important in the preparation of converts for baptism.[1] The lesser priests were chiefly engaged in carrying out the multiple administrative duties of the bishop's office. As a matter of fact, the bishop's administration took on the characteristics of a second urban government, so wide was its operation when the congregation became large and property began to accumulate. The bishop's office was supported mainly by contributions of the congregations, and the members of its staff were paid regular stipends. In return for "material gifts" the congregations received "spiritual gifts" from the priestly hierarchy. Although the congregations participated in the selection of the bishops, the possession of divine appointment and the "gifts of the Spirit" came only through installation in office by other bishops. As a whole, therefore, the episcopate was clearly set off from the other orders of Christians—the presbyters and deacons, the lesser priests, and the body of the faithful.

Constantine's recognition of Christianity won for him the support of this well-organized minority; for the bishops—its leaders—the recognition gave that association with authority which whetted the appetite for still more authority and led to the transformation which made the bishops as much secular rulers as they were spiritual leaders. The Greek and oriental mystery religions, it should be remembered, did not produce closely knit priesthoods, and the ultimate triumph of Christianity was largely the result of the consistent pressing of its priesthood's interest in every phase of social and intellectual life. After Constantine the power of the state was at the service of the bishops whenever they thought this interest was endangered.

---

[1] L. M. O. Duchesne, *Early History of the Christian Church* . . . (3 vols., 1909–1924), Vol. 3, p. 16: "People's minds at that time were greatly concerned in regard to evil spirits, their powers and the necessity of delivering from them not only the souls of men but their bodies and nature itself, whether animate or inorganic. Everything over which the name of Jesus Christ had not been vigorously invoked was deemed to be subject to the action of the evil spirit and capable of transmitting it. It was for this reason that exorcisms were multiplied over the candidates for baptism, and that it was insisted that they should descend in complete nudity into the sacred font without the smallest object, whether ornament, amulet, or binding for the hair, which could afford a lodgment for the enemy." John Murray, London.

No surprise, therefore, need be caused by the fact that soon the Christian priesthood became a privileged class. Constantine laid the basis of this status by extending to the Christian priests the traditional privileges of the pagan priests, *i.e.*, freedom from the financial and military burdens of the state. But more important was his grant to the bishops of the rights to hold courts and to receive bequests.[1] He permitted litigants to resort to either an ecclesiastical or an imperial court and recognized the bishops' verdicts as equally valid as those of secular judges. Thus was founded the civil power of Christian ecclesiastical authorities. As the result of the right to receive bequests, the bishops began to acquire property and to play an important part in economic life— managing estates, making loans, and collecting usury. Shortly the priests so successfully preached the merit of bequeathing property to the church that the emperors felt the need of limiting its right to acquire property. Lands which passed under the control of the bishops almost never returned to secular hands. Furthermore, the accumulation of property in the hands of the bishops diverted their attention from spiritual matters. As early as 306 the Council of Elvira prohibited bishops from directing commercial enterprises. They could, however, hire others to do so. The council of Nicaea (325) ordered all priests taking usury to be expelled from the sacred order. In this connection it is pertinent to note that Constantine's attempt to restrict the number of priests and to select them exclusively from the poor failed; as time went on, the bishops, especially, were recruited from the older aristocratic and great wealth-holding classes of the empire, so that the Christian priesthood was more and more assimilated into the traditional privileged classes. Under Gratian the first step in freeing the Christian clergy from the secular courts was taken in the promulgation of a law establishing the jurisdiction of the bishops' courts over all cases involving priests except those arising out of criminal charges. The privileges of the Christian priests were finally given explicit legal definition in the code of Theodosius II (*ca.* 408–450). They were

---

[1] Edwin Hatch, *The Organization of the Early Christian Churches* (8th imp., 1918), pp. 154–155: " . . . the clergy became not only independent, but in some cases wealthy. In an age of social decay and struggling poverty they had not only enough but to spare. They could afford to lend: and they lent. . . . The effect of the recognition of Christianity by the State was thus not only to create a class civilly distinct from the rest of the community, but also to give that class social independence. In other words, the Christian clergy, in addition to their original prestige as office-bearers, had the privileges of a favoured class, and the power of a moneyed class." By permission of Longmans, Green & Company, London.

freed of all secular duties and personal taxes. They could be tried only in bishops' courts. And they were given an intellectual monopoly by the declaration that heresy was a punishable offense against the state.

By the opening of the fifth century the Christian priest class not only had won supreme power over the Christian congregations but also had acquired those political, economic, and intellectual privileges which were to make it for a thousand years always an important and sometimes a dominant element in Western society.

4. *The Supremacy of the Roman Papacy.* As the Christian priest class advanced in power there took place among the bishops a struggle for primacy. This conflict had its roots in the conflict of the several cultures that contributed to Christianity, in the doctrinal controversies that disturbed the congregations from the second to the fifth century, and in the political circumstances which finally disintegrated the Roman Empire. Although no single bishop ever won complete dominance, the bishop of Rome asserted a universal supremacy and made it good in the western part of the empire.[1]

Theoretically, in the Old Catholic Church all the bishops were equal. But due to the fact that the original Christian congregations were in the most prominent cities of the empire, certain bishops possessed special prestige and were regarded with special reverence. In the early second century the bishop of Antioch was looked up to throughout the east; by the end of the second century the bishop of Rome held an equal status. In the third century the bishops of Carthage and Alexandria became prominent. After the founding of Constantinople, its bishop, who enjoyed imperial favor, became a rival of these early leaders of the congregations. These bishops in the prominent cities bore the title *patriarch;* beneath them, in only slightly less important cities, were the *metropolitans.* The ordinary bishop ruled a diocese; the metropolitan a province, and the patriarch a patriarchate. Although the first ecumenical council, convoked by Constantine at Nicaea in 325, recognized this system of church government, it was never completely worked out. Quarrels between the various bishops

---

[1] On the rise of the papacy see W. E. Beet, *The Early Roman Episcopate to A.D.* 384 (1913); A. K. Fortescue, *The Early Papacy to the Synod of Chalcedon* (1920); M. I. M. Bell, *A Short History of the Papacy* (1921); Pierre Batiffol, *Le Siège apostolique* (359–451) (1924); E. Caspar, *Geschichte des Papsttums von den Anfängen bis zur Höhe der Weltherrschaft*, Band I, *Römische Kirche und Imperium Romanum* (2 vols., 1930–1934); James T. Shotwell and Louise R. Loomis, *The See of Peter* (1927)—a collection of documents; S. H. Scott, *The Eastern Churches and the Papacy* (1928).

were continuous. The violence of these quarrels throughout the fifth century, especially in the east, sometimes even endangered the safety of the state.

The advance of the bishop of Rome to supremacy was slow but steady. At the root of his claim to primacy among the bishops was (1) the prestige of the congregation in the ancient capital of the empire and (2) the tradition that both Peter and Paul had come to Rome and had died there. Clement, the first known bishop of Rome (unless Peter is regarded as the first bishop of Rome) seems to have made no claim to a universal jurisdiction. A century later, however, Victor (fl. *ca.* 190–198), attempted to exercise such a jurisdiction by excommunicating certain eastern bishops who refused to accept his decision in a controversy over the date of Easter. Callistus I (fl. *ca.* 217–222), who reminded other bishops of the fact that he sat in the chair of Peter, asserted his authority in morals by absolving sins not absolved by any other bishop. His third-century successors constantly intervened in the ecclesiastical affairs of Spain, Africa, Gaul, Greece, and Asia Minor. The feeling of the other bishops toward this aggrandizement of Roman authority was expressed by Cyprian, who, while he vigorously declared that the unity of the church rested in the episcopate, just as vigorously denied the supremacy of the Roman bishop. The first ecumenical council, although it asked the Roman patriarch to issue its decisions, recognized the patriarch of Alexandria as having authority over Egypt and Libya equal to that he had over Italy. At this time the Roman bishop was regarded as having greater prestige but not greater legal or moral power than the other patriarchs.

After the seat of the empire was transferred to Constantinople and the church became closely allied with the state, conditions for the growth of Roman ecclesiastical power became more and more favorable. Those ecclesiastical officials who from time to time resisted imperial domination usually found a leader in the Roman bishop. Consistent orthodoxy also won him support, while heretical controversy weakened both the prestige and the power of his eastern rivals. At the council of Sardika (modern Sofia), in 343, a group of bishops passed a rule allowing any deposed bishop, regardless of his own metropolitan or patriarch, to appeal his case to the Roman bishop, whose decision was to be taken as final. This rule, which embodied the principle that the Roman bishop was supreme over the priestly hierarchy, was never accepted in the east.

The political decline of Rome during the fourth and fifth centuries gave the Roman bishops the opportunity to grasp powers that slipped away from the emperors. Pope Damasus (366–384), who won his election in a contest which cost the lives of 137 persons, assumed the social position the emperors had held. He kept a carriage, set an elegant table, built an ornate church, drained the hill where his residence stood—now known as the Vatican—patronized the arts, collected the relics of the martyrs, and made the tombs of the early Christians in the catacombs a spectacle for pilgrims. He was so adept at obtaining legacies that he became known as the "matrons' ear tickler." In 378 the emperor Gratian ordered all western bishops to consider themselves subject to his rule. Pope Siricius (fl. *ca.* 384–399) issued the first decree, founding that body of ecclesiastical law now known as the decretals; he claimed that the Apostle Peter was acting through him. Under Pope Innocent I (402–417) appeals came to Rome from all quarters regarding every branch of faith and discipline, and he dealt with them on the principle "Rome has spoken, the matter is closed."

Under Pope Leo I (440–461) Roman primacy became a fact.[1] Its doctrinal basis was found in the verse (Matt. 16: 18) "Thou art Peter, and upon this Rock I will build my Church," which was interpreted as meaning that Jesus had chosen Peter to be the worldly head of His church. This theory, which had been argued since the second century, was formally proclaimed by Leo I: "Whatever Christ gave to the other Apostles, He gave only through Peter; the firmness which was given to Peter by Christ was conferred upon the other apostles by St. Peter; Peter is the prince of Apostles, and rules personally those whom Christ rules supremely." The doctrine of the apostolic succession, of course, made the Roman bishop, according to universally accepted tradition, the direct successor of Peter. These theological claims were amplified by the declaration that anyone who separated himself from the rule of the Roman bishop had no share in the divine mystery of the church, in other words, that anyone who refused to accept the rule of the Roman bishop was damned. Quite as important as these ecclesiastical assertions was the legal recognition which Leo I won for the Roman claim. He prevailed upon Valentinian III (425–454) to decree that Rome was the chief seat of ecclesiastical power and to order that henceforth the decrees of the Roman bishop would have the force of law for the entire church. A further strengthening of the Roman claim was

[1] See Charles Gore, *Leo the Great* (1912).

From F. X. ZIMMERMAN, *Die Kirchen Roms* (1935). *R. Piper & Co., Munich*

A CHURCH IN THE ROMAN CATACOMBS

(For descriptive legend see opposite page)

won in 451, when the council of Chalcedon sanctioned Leo I's doctrinal position; however, it is pertinent to note that the council also recognized the bishop of Constantinople as coordinate with the bishop of Rome as a head of the church. Probably more important than these verbal arguments for the Roman position were Leo I's interventions in the ecclesiastical affairs of Illyria, Gaul, Spain, and Africa, where he acted as the sovereign he claimed to be. His temporal activities clinched the claim to supremacy, at least as far as the west was concerned. In 451 he induced the Huns to withdraw from Rome, and four years later he saved part of the city from the Vandals. At the same time he took over the civil authority, replacing the ancient Roman municipal administration with an ecclesiastical regime.

When Rome lost the emperor, she gained the pope. This designation, originally applied to all bishops, means father. Under Leo I it became the title of an ecclesiastical monarch whose power was declared to be universal. In the Latin west this conception was embodied in orthodox Christian doctrine; in the Greek and Semitic east and Egyptian Africa it was accepted, if at all, only in the moral sense, for the rules of the local patriarchs endured until political disasters destroyed them. The Christian priest class was, therefore, never united under a single head.

5. *The Rise of Monasticism.* By the evolution of the "sacred hierarchy" of Christian priests the "gifts of the Spirit" were given an institutional form; at the same time the quest for moral perfection at the heart of the Christian way of life developed an institutional form—monasticism.[1] At the root of monasticism was the belief that spiritual achievement involves the renunciation of worldly needs, desires, and ambitions; intertwined with this belief was the conviction that nothing, including life, is so precious that

---

[1] See *The Cambridge Medieval History, Vol.* I, *The Christian Roman Empire and the Foundation of the Teutonic Kingdoms* (1936), Chap. XVIII, "Monasticism"; E. C. Butler, *Benedictine Monachism* (1924); H. B. Workman, *The Evolution of the Monastic Ideal from the Earliest Times down to the Coming of the Friars* (1913); James O. Hannay, *Spirit and Origin of Christian Monasticism* (1903); Comte de Montalembert, *The Monks of the West from St. Benedict to St. Bernard* (6 vols., 1879); Dom John Chapman, *Saint Benedict and the Sixth Century* (1929).

A CHURCH IN THE ROMAN CATACOMBS

Few Christian chapels were built in the catacombs. Christian painting, not Christian architecture, sprang from the darkness of the subterranean chambers, where the early Christians, believing ardently in a heavenly life beyond the grave, associated with death without fear or horror of it.

it should not be sacrificed for the sake of Christ. The martyrs, of course, had made the supreme sacrifice.

The cradle of Christian monasticism was the depression of the Wadi Natrun, or "Valley of Soda," about a day's camel journey west of the Nile Delta.[1] There, as early as the middle of the second century B.C. an attempt was made to organize a brotherhood of hermits. A little more than a century later a hermit, known as Ammon, drew together a number of disciples who formed a community which soon attracted pilgrims, both male and female, from all parts of the Christian world. Each hermit quarried the rock from which he built a two-room cell roofed with rushes. With interruptions for prayer, meditation, and mortifying the flesh, the work required about a year. Most of the hermits made a scanty living by weaving mats or linen which merchants took to the market in Alexandria. Some of them worked as bakers to supply others. Anthony (*ca.* 251–350), a pupil of Ammon, set the original pattern of Christian monastic life. For twenty years he lived a solitary existence in the desert, fighting constantly the daimons which sought, by every form of trickery, to lure him into sin. His emulators chose to live in the desert not so much to escape from the wickedness of ordinary communities as to defy the innumerable daimons which according to traditional beliefs dwelt there. The accounts of the lives of early monks record fierce encounters with these foes of Christ. By the end of the fourth century as many as five thousand hermits lived in the Wadi Natrun.

At Tabennesi, six hundred miles up the Nile, Pachomius (*ca.* 292–346) formulated the first rule for a community of monks. They lived in individual huts, worked at various occupations, and studied the New Testament, learning much of it by heart. Because they believed that eating is an unbecoming act, they covered their heads with their hoods when at meals. Pachomius forbade washing except during sickness. The austerities of these early monks seem to modern men almost incredible.

In the fourth century a combination of factors promoted the rapid growth of monasticism; chief among them were (1) the cessation of the persecutions, which closed the way to martyrdom, (2) the economic decline, which everywhere made life harder, (3) the political disorders, which disrupted the traditional forms of secure life, and (4) the intellectual developments which made escape from worldly sin into an otherworldly bliss the chief hope of man.

[1] E. H. Sawyer, "The First Monasteries," *Antiquity*, Vol. 4 (1930), pp. 316–326.

From Egypt monasticism spread to Palestine, Asia Minor, and Arabia and then westward.

Basil (*ca.* 330–379), bishop of Caesarea in Asia Minor, first adapted monasticism to the organized life of the church. Under the rule which he formulated the daily life of the monks was closely regulated; among the objectives of the rule was the eradication of the extravagant austerities of illiterate ascetics. After the *novitiate*, a probationary period of systematic training, the monks became members of a community subject to the rule of a bishop. They devoted their lives to study, meditation, charitable work, and the exemplification of austerity in a routinized observation of the sacraments. The rule of Basil was generally adopted in the monasteries of the eastern parts of the empire.

The sources of western monasticism were partly indigenous and partly eastern. An early growth of nunneries was promoted by the feeling that widows ought not to remarry and that virgins possessed a peculiar moral purity which ought to be protected by a secluded life. By the opening of the fourth century such women frequently dwelt together, cut their hair short, wore voluminous black gowns and devoted their lives to the care of the poor and the sick. The original monks in Rome were known as "Egyptians." But pilgrims returning from Jerusalem were more important in the establishment of western monasticism than migrants from Egypt. The first monastic communities were founded in Gaul by Martin (*ca.* 316–397), bishop of Tours, and by Cassian (*ca.* 360–435), a migrant from Egypt. But the rule which gave enduring form to western monastic life was developed by Benedict (480–543), who established a monastery at Monte Cassino, about a hundred miles south of Rome. As a test of perseverance the candidate for admission to a Benedictine monastery was refused admittance for five days; if at the end of this waiting period he persisted in his determination to enter the monastery, he was received as a guest and given the status of a novice. As a novice he lived under the watchful eye of a veteran monk. After two months the entire rule of the monastery was read to him, and twice again in the year it was repeated to him; if, then, he continued in his desire to become a monk, he was granted *stability*, *i.e.*, membership in the house. Many monks were recruited from the boys entrusted to the care of the houses; they were educated under elaborate rules.

Members of the Benedictine houses took vows of poverty, chastity, and obedience and lived a communal existence—eating, working, and praying together. They slept in a common dormitory.

Gossip and idle conversation were suppressed. Each hour of the day had its allotted duties. Religious services were held several times during both day and night. About four hours in each day were devoted to worship and about seven to manual labor and study. Field work, charitable enterprise, especially among the poor, and study were the chief communal activities. No monk was allowed to undertake any special austerity without the permission of the head of his house. The clothing and the diet of the monks, although simple, were adequate. At each meal there were two dishes—one cooked, the other uncooked. No flesh of quadrupeds was eaten. In Lent food was served only once a day; during other times of the year there were many special fasts. The head of a monastic community—the abbot—punished violations of the rule by prescribing various penances or imposing physical chastisements, such as floggings. Punishments were carried out in public. Since the vows, once taken, were never to be violated, the monastic life, although in a milder form, became a profession in the west just as it had in the east. Originally there was no intention to organize the Benedictine monks in an order; each house was an independent community.

During the period of the final suppression of paganism and fierce controversies over heresies, the monks were generally a powerful force making for the victory of orthodoxy. Their activity had many aspects hardly in keeping with either the humility of the early Christians or the spirit of their own vows:

So long as the monks remained in the deserts and concerned themselves only with the progress of their individual perfection, it was still possible to manage with them. But they were soon to be seen everywhere and in large numbers, attracting attention by eccentricities of dress and by an asceticism which was often exaggerated or stamped with ostentation, mingling with the populace and with its religious life, espousing its quarrels and arousing its passions, even and especially when these were excited against the authorities. From time to time they rendered services as the active agents in strong measures or even in disturbances. They assisted in demolishing the temples, in chastising heretics, in making life a burden to officials whose conduct gave ground for complaint. At ordinary times bishops and prefects would gladly have been rid of such restless folk. The institution of monasteries which spread rapidly throughout the Greek Orient and even in the West, from the end of the 4th century onwards, afforded a means of stemming the torrent to some extent. But all the monks were not in the monasteries; there were many of them wandering about fields and the towns. Besides, the facility with which monastic institutions could be set up led to the establishment of some which were devoid of a serious purpose. The outskirts of the towns became covered with hermitages, veritable dens, which gave shelter to two or three monks, sometimes only to one: in these they lived the life of savages, emaciated, unclean, and in rags. Even in the best regulated monasteries the doors possessed no very effective fastenings; exit as well as entrance was allowed with the greatest ease. For one recluse who remained for forty years without crossing the threshold of his cell, there were hundreds of restless monks who passed from one monastery to another, roaming about through the different provinces of the Empire, and making their appearance in turn at Antioch, at Constantinople, on the highways of Pamphylia or in the deserts of Mesopotamia.[1]

The importance of the development of monasticism in the consolidation of Christianity can hardly be overemphasized. Under the rules of community living irregular austerities were replaced by devotional exercises and charitable work, and renunciation was manifested chiefly in celibacy, poverty, obedience, and meditation. Thus individuals whose thoughts and fervor were likely to lead them into heresy were brought into a way of life acceptable to the ecclesiastical hierarchs. In a sense, therefore, just as the episcopate compromised the desire for worldly power with Christian ideals, so monasticism blended individual moral striving with the conformity necessary for the maintenance of orthodoxy.

As a result of the growth of monasticism the Christian priest class came to have two sections: (1) the sacred hierarchy, whose spiritual gifts came through the apostolic succession and (2) the monastic orders, whose merit was won by renunciation of the world and by special spiritual exercises. Together they formed an ecclesiastical aristocracy raised above common Christians.

6. *The Definition of the Christian Laity.* As previously noted, the distinction between the priests and the ordinary Christian believers was recognized as early as the end of the first century. By the fourth century it had entered to a very marked degree into the customs and administration of the church. By the sixth century it was established in differences of costume, ways of life, and social function; then the priest class alone counted in the government of the church, except when, in the election of bishops, popular feeling was allowed expression. The respective positions of the two levels of Christian social organization were clearly described in the *Constitutions of the Holy Apostles*, a work whose title suggests an

[1] L. M. O. Duchesne, *Early History of the Christian Church* . . . , Vol. 3, pp. 22–23. John Murray, London.

origin in oldest Christian tradition but which was, at least as far as composition, a fourth or fifth century compilation. On the one hand stood the bishops:

A bishop must be no accepter of persons; neither revering nor flattering a rich man contrary to what is right, nor overlooking nor domineering over a poor man. . . . For your bishops are to be guides and watchmen to the people, as you yourselves have Christ for your guide and watchman. . . . Upon this account, therefore, O bishop, endeavour to be pure in thy actions, and to adorn thy place and dignity, which is that one sustaining the character of God among men, as being set over all men, over priests, kings, rulers, fathers, children, teachers, and in general over all those who are subject to thee: and so sit in the Church when thou speakest, as having authority to judge offenders. . . . Let the bishop esteem such food and raiment as suits necessity and decency. . . . Distribute to all those in want with righteousness, and yourselves use the things which belong to the Lord, but do not abuse them; eating of them all up by yourself: communicate with those in want, and thereby show yourselves unblameable before God.

And on the other hand were the people:

The bishop, he is the minister of the word, the keeper of knowledge, the mediator between God and you in the several parts of your divine worship. He is the teacher of piety, and, next after God, he is your father, who has begotten you again to the adoption of sons by water and Spirit. He is your ruler and potentate; he is, next after God, your earthly God, who has a right to be honoured by you. . . . Wherefore, you ought to love your bishop as your father, and fear him as your king, and honour him as your lord, bringing to him your fruits and the works of your hands, for a blessing upon you, giving to him your first fruits, and your tithes, and your oblations, and your gifts, as to the priest of God; the first fruits of your wheat, and wine, and oil, and autumnal fruits, and wool, and all things which the Lord gives thee. . . . When thou instruct the people, O bishop, command and exhort them to come constantly to church morning and evening every day, and by no means to forsake it on any account, but to assemble together continually; neither to diminish the church by withdrawing themselves, and causing the body of Christ to be without members. For it is not only spoken concerning priests, but let every one of the laity hearken to it as concerning himself, considering that it is said by the Lord, "He that is not with me is against me, and he that gathereth not with me scattereth abroad. . . . " Let the young persons of the church endeavor to minister diligently to all necessaries; mind your business with all becoming seriousness, so that you may always have sufficient to support yourselves and those that are needy, and not burden the Church of God. . . . Labour therefore con-

THE CHRISTIAN WORLD c. A. D. 325

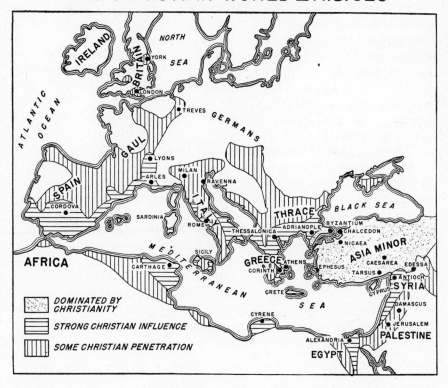

DOMINATED BY CHRISTIANITY

STRONG CHRISTIAN INFLUENCE

SOME CHRISTIAN PENETRATION

tinually; for the blot of the slothful is not to be healed. But "if anyone does not work, let not such a one eat" among you. For the Lord our God hates the slothful. For no one of those who are dedicated to God ought to be idle.[1]

A primary result of the evolution of the distinction between the priesthood, headed by the bishops, and the laity was to reduce ordinary Christians to a passive role in the congregations. They lost the right to preach, which all early Christians had been free to exercise. They were excluded from the dais where priests performed the Christian mystery—the Lord's Supper; in some parts of the east they were actually excluded from the chamber in which this ritual was performed. Generally they participated in worship only by uttering short prayers under the leadership of priests.

[1] A. Roberts and J. Donaldson, *The Ante-Nicene Fathers: Translations of the writings of the Fathers down to A.D. 325* (10 vols., 1899), Vol. 7, *Constitutions of the Holy Apostles*, *passim*. Charles Scribner's Sons, New York.

Their chief religious duties were: (1) to attend the rituals weekly, (2) to accept the teachings of the priests in all matters pertaining to doctrine and morals, and (3) to make gifts to the priests. If a layman faithfully performed these obligations, his spiritual welfare was secure. Among the ascetic rules of life, the layman was expected to obey only the prohibition against second marriages. Otherwise he was free to follow what was called the "lower morality"; this was generally, of course, simply the customs of his local community. The chief social obligation of laymen was to follow the ordinary pursuits of life.

The word "laity" means the people, considered as a vulgar and ignorant lot. Its use to describe the multitude of Christian believers as contrasted with their priestly leaders indicates the inferior moral, intellectual, and spiritual position they came to hold. Their religious obligations bound them to follow and support materially the priest class; their social obligation left them in the traditional ways of life. For them conversion to Christianity meant little more than the reorientation of their emotions and the acceptance of new symbols of their loyalties. If their hope for immortal life became stronger, their conception of life beyond the grave was no less superstitious than it had been in the past. The triumph of Christianity did not alter in any significant manner the traditional routines of the lives of common men.

THE DISINTEGRATION OF THE ROMAN EMPIRE

Since Christianity's aim was to win for its devotees an eternal life beyond the grave, it did not halt the operation of the forces which were transforming earthly society; in fact, as a product of these forces, it could hardly have changed their course. Thus the factors of decline which had emerged in the crisis of the third century finally worked the dissolution of the Roman state.[1]

THE TRANSFORMATION OF THE SOCIAL STRUCTURE OF MEDITERRANEAN LIFE.

Although the reforms of Diocletian and Constantine were partially successful, economic decay went on steadily. In the middle of the fourth century most of the parts of the empire were still in contact with one another, but the interruption of trade and the

---

[1] L. M. O. Duchesne, *Early History of the Christian Church* . . . (3 vols., 1909–1924), Vol. 3, p. 3; see also *The Cambridge Medieval History, Vol.* 1, *The Christian Roman Empire and the Foundation of the Teutonic Kingdoms* (1936), Chap. XIX, "Social and Economic Conditions in the Roman Empire in the Fourth Century."

increasing difficulties of transport during the next century reduced the old Mediterranean economy to a shell. At the same time both mining and manufacturing declined further. The chief effects of these tendencies, along with the increasing scarcity of coin, was to force a reorganization of production and distribution. Production was more and more limited to agriculture, and distribution was carried on by means of transfers of goods under political regulations. The cultivators tilled not only their own plots of land but also the domains of the landowners; thus the Roman system of agrarian management was replaced almost everywhere by the cruder methods of the peasant village, and the landowners, who generally came to reside on their estates, were almost completely dependent on the products of the soil.

In line with these economic changes went alterations in the social structure. The mode of this transformation was the interaction between declining production and the growing burden of taxation. Declining production meant decreasing wealth. Heavier taxation meant the transfer of an ever greater portion of the decreasing wealth from its producers and traditional possessors to that group which succeeded in retaining political power; this group had its base in the reorganized army and consisted of the members of the political hierarchy, particularly those who enjoyed imperial favor.

The evidence of the social transformation was everywhere apparent in the decline of the provincial cities, many of which by the fifth century were merely walled fortresses. The great cities alone retained the Roman ways of urban life. The most significant aspect of social change was the slow disintegration of the traditional urban-dwelling ruling class. This disintegration took several forms. (1) In order to escape the heavy burden of taxation imposed on them, some of its members fled to their country estates where, in time, they became members of a new powerful class. For the same reason others entered the Christian priesthood. Constantine sought to close this way of escape by commanding that priests be recruited exclusively from the poor; the rich, he held, were obligated to support the state. Many others, it seems, became impoverished and fell into the lower orders of society. (2) In the reorganization of the army members of senatorial families were excluded from the officer rank. (3) When the closing of the temples destroyed the pagan priestly colleges the last stronghold of the class disappeared. The emergence of a culture fully orientated in terms of Christianity was, of course, the inevitable result of this destruction of the chief carrier of Greco-Roman culture. Other destructive aspects of the transformation were: the recurrence of peasant revolts, the revival of piracy, and the passing of commerce almost entirely into the hands of eastern merchants.

Since every social transformation merely replaces an old with a new order, which in time comes to be recognized by those who live under it as the embodiment of right and justice, the creative developments under the Christian Roman Empire were those that gave rise to new social classes. The first of these developments has been outlined in the discussion of the formation of the Christian priest class, whose dominant members, the bishops, it should be remembered, took over many secular powers and duties. Two related developments combined with the emergence of the Christian priest class to give shape to the new social structure: (1) the growth of a new landed aristocracy and (2) the redefinition of the status of the masses.

The new landed aristocracy had its source in the flight of urban proprietors to their country estates, where, by means of the traditional Roman relation between patron and client, they brought the peasants, small free landowners, impoverished urban landlords, and traders seeking to escape taxation under their control. To the economically weak they offered lands and protection; from them they exacted labor and dues. The growth of the power of this new class was evident in several ways: (1) the refusal to pay taxes to the imperial treasury, (2) the maintenance of private military forces, (3) the assumption of judicial powers, especially over the tillers of the soil, (4) the establishment of private prisons, at first chiefly for debtors, (5) the intervention in litigation between other persons, and (6) the enforced alteration of private contracts to their own benefit. With these powers the great landlord became, in fact, the "true monarch of the countryside." To combat the growth of local jurisdictions the emperors attempted to prohibit patronage, but mere political authority was powerless to check a development which had its roots in economic decline. In this connection it is worth noting also that country life became fashionable and that the typical urban dwellers, bankers and lawyers, fell under a growing disapproval.[1]

The redefinition of the status of the masses was closely bound up with every aspect of economic decline and social change. As a matter of fact the masses remained as they had ever been—merely

---

[1] On the concentration of classical learning in the hands of the small class of rural aristocrats see C. E. Stevens, *Sidonius Apollinaris and His Age* (1933), pp. 79–83.

illiterate workers; the redefinition consisted only of an alteration in the social controls which forced them to work for their superiors. As previously noted, the need to maintain production caused the third century emperors to bind certain workers to their employment not only for life but also from generation to generation. In the fourth century this control was extended throughout the economic system. The state clerks and servants were militarized and freed from arbitrary dismissal but bound to prolonged service. The collegia, or guilds, of craftsmen were placed under public control, and their membership made hereditary. Workers particularly necessary to the state, such as minters, armorers, veterinary surgeons, sailors, and miners, were subject to special regulations. Weavers who spoiled fabric, scribes who placed wrong names on tax lists, and creditors who seized the oxen and implements of a debtor were liable to the death penalty. Even trade became a hereditary calling.

The peasants, now generally known as *coloni*, were bound to the soil, obliged to marry within the community on their landlord's estate, and subject to compulsory labor on his domain. Each colonus worked small plots for himself. To the landlord the colonus paid a small money rent as well as a part—probably a tenth—of his crops. The landlord could not increase these payments. The colonus had no public duties, but the landlord, who owed men to the imperial army just as he owed cattle and horses, might send him away as a conscript soldier. A landlord could not, however, sell a colonus from his estate, nor could he evict him for nonpayment of taxes. If a colonus ran away, he was subject to recapture, return, and physical punishment. Under this system of labor control, the powers of jurisdiction which the landlords had usurped from the imperial government placed the peasants directly under a local rule. When the Christian priest class came into the possession of lands it did nothing to alter this system of control, so that as imperial authority disintegrated, the agrarian masses passed entirely under the power of local magnates, both secular and ecclesiastical.

The combined effect of these social changes was to create a new social pyramid. At the summit was the imperial clique—factional, extravagant, and fanatical. At the base were the inert coloni. Between these two orders were the regimented craftsmen, transport workers, state servants, and the lower grades of the official hierarchy. Although the new landed aristocracy and the Christian priest class were integrated with this hierarchy, their positions were defined not by political forces but by the economic and intellectual trends of the age. This fact meant that when the imperial regime fell apart, their members, rising to political power by virtue of their economic and intellectual position, became the heirs to its authority.

THE STORM ON THE ROMAN FRONTIERS.

During the fourth century the external enemies of Rome everywhere became stronger, and emperor after emperor was forced to campaign against them. In these wars successful generals were frequently raised to the purple by their armies. This external warfare constantly nourished internal strife.

The Persians, dreaming of reclaiming the ancient dominion of Cyrus, seized Mesopotamia and Armenia. Both the Romans and the Persians called the wild Arab horsemen to their aid in conflicts of these areas, and they spread devastation far and wide. The Berbers, a desert people of northern Africa, ravaged the decaying countryside; farther west the partially Romanized Mauretanians threatened the coastal lands. Along the northern frontiers inroads were recurrent. At first the invaders, like the Celtic Picts and Scots and the Teutonic Franks and Alamanni, were driven back. After 375, when the Huns—the fierce horsemen from central Asia, who once had given Rome a respite by attacking the Persians—struck the Teutonic Visigoths in the Dniester valley, the pressure became too great to withstand. In 376 the Visigoths were permitted to cross the Danube River and settle in Pannonia; there they were given the status of *foederati, i.e.,* they held land under their own king, who was bound to render military service at the call of the Roman emperor. Unfortunately friction developed, and in 378 they defeated the emperor Valens at Adrianople. This battle, which opened the way for the general migration of the Teutons throughout the Western Empire, was decided by the mailed cavalry that was to dominate warfare for the next thousand years. The legions which the mailed horsemen defeated were not, however, the legions of old, for many of the officers as well as most of the rank and file were from the new peoples. The very power which had built the Roman state was no longer Roman.

Under Theodosius I, son of a Roman captain, who as emperor of the Eastern Roman Empire made orthodox Christianity the single legal religion of the state, peace and unity were restored, but only for a short time.

The Collapse of the Roman State.

During the fifth century the internal malady which was destroying the vitals of the Roman state entered its final phase, for everywhere poverty, disorder, and factional strife, both political and ecclesiastical, became more intense.

A fundamental change in political and military leadership occurred. The imperial armies were mostly non-Roman forces in the service of the emperors; and often their commanders, also non-Romans, were the real rulers of the state. At the death of Theodosius I his two young sons were left under the protection of the Vandal Stilicho (d. 408), the greatest commander of his age. Alaric (*ca.* 395–410), who led the Visigoths into Italy in 409, held the Roman command in Illyria. Aëtius (*ca.* 396–454), known as the "last of the Romans," was probably born a Teuton. With a combined force of Goths and Romans he won the last important military victory of the Western Roman Empire in 451 when he turned back the Huns. The exact place of the victory, which is usually called the battle of Châlons, is unknown; it was somewhere near Troyes in east central Gaul. Ricimer (d. 472), son of a prince of the Suevi and a princess of the Visigoths, held the Roman command in the west from 456 to his death in 472; during that time he made and unmade nine puppet emperors. Odoacer (d. 493), a member of an obscure tribe, commanded the mercenaries of Romulus Augustulus, a boy emperor, who had been set up by a rebel against the legitimate ruler of the west; when the rebel refused to grant lands to the mercenaries, Odoacer killed him, deposed the emperor, and seized power as king of Italy—the first barbarian to rule as king over the land of the Caesars.

In the eastern part of the empire a similar course of events moved toward a not greatly different climax. The Huns, although they had imposed upon the emperor the disgrace of paying tribute, invaded his dominions in 441, 443, and 447. When the defeat at Châlons broke their power in the east as well as in the west, Teutons replaced them as the dominant force in imperial politics. In 457 Aspar, an Alan, raised Leo (457–474), known as "the Thracian," to the throne; he was the first emperor crowned by a Christian ecclesiastical official. His son-in-law and successor, Zeno (474–491), was half barbarian. These rulers, unlike their western contemporaries, preserved the imperial name and dignity, but actually they were no more Roman than the kings who displaced the western emperors. Furthermore, the state which they and their successors ruled until 1453—the Eastern Roman Empire—was Greco-Oriental rather than Roman in culture.

Under Justinian (527–565), the greatest of these successors, that order which was to characterize the Middle Ages became clearly visible. The supreme ruler was God's vice-regent. Ecclesiastical officials sat in the supreme council of the state. Political issues were framed in theological terms. Monks swarmed everywhere. Every crisis brought multitudes into the churches to pray. And the theory that well-being was the fruit of priestly mediation with the Supreme Being was written into the law:

> If these pure hands and sanctified souls pray for the Empire, the army will be strengthened, the prosperity of the State will be increased, agriculture and commerce will flourish, under the assured benevolence of God.[1]

The settlement throughout the provinces of the Teutonic tribes as foederati had contributed to a change in the basic population which the invasions carried further. After 450 the Visigoths, Ostrogoths, Gepids, Alamanni, Suevi, and Burgundians occupied lands from Macedonia to Spain; farther north the Angles, Jutes, Saxons, and Franks merely conquered lands. But settlement or conquest, it seems, disturbed chiefly the landlords; the peasants remained largely unaffected by the change of masters. Few of them, however, had ever been Romans.

In the course of these developments the Roman state disintegrated. The year 476, which witnessed the deposing of the last emperor of the west, was not regarded as having brought a major catastrophe to the empire. In fact, political disorganization seems to have meant little, for religious unity had become the ideal, and to the Teutons it meant as much as, if not more than, imperial unity. An empire, an age, and a culture came to an end largely unnoticed by those who witnessed its passing. Present-day commentators upon their passing too frequently fail to recognize that the Rome that fell was not the Rome that rose. Between them had occurred a fundamental social and cultural transformation of Mediterranean life.

[1] From H. St. L. B. Moss, *The Birth of the Middle Ages* (1935), p. 93. By permission of the Oxford University Press.

Chapter XVIII

THE CHRISTIAN ORIENTATION OF THE
WESTERN CULTURAL TRADITION

《《-《《-》》-》》

In the shift of values that marked the transition from Greco-Roman to Christian culture the central factor was the emergence of a new attitude toward life. In psychological terms this attitude was a reaction to the harshness and cruelty of earthly life, sublimated in a faith that an otherworldly life was beautiful and joyous. This reaction involved the acceptance of the evil of earthly life as a factor in the cultivation of the moral purity necessary for attainment to otherworldly bliss. An elation accompanied this faith because it was predicated in the belief that man lived in accordance with a supernatural plan, participated in a sublime moral struggle, and might have the aid of divine power in the quest for otherworldly bliss. The faith and the elation together suppressed the pursuit of sensual pleasures; only inner satisfactions that came with moral striving were fit elements of earthly happiness. This suppression fixed attention upon subjective experience—the inner man, not the outer world—and emphasized in it those data supporting the new attitude toward life. This selection established a psychological unity between the attitude and the experience of individuals, and this unity gave stability to the attitude in terms of which Western culture was reorientated.

THE RISE OF CATHOLIC CHRISTIANITY

The gospel was the core of this reorientation. At its center was the faith "Jesus is Lord." At its circumference was the burning hope of the Second Coming, when the Lord would establish the Kingdom of God on earth. Between this faith and this hope was the way of life in which worldly satisfactions and interests were sacrificed in order to achieve the moral purity necessary for the winning of immortality. The rule of this way of life was "Love thy neighbor as thyself." These components were organized in a tradi-

1093

tion that flowed from the words and acts of Jesus. In this form Christianity was almost purely an expression of the new attitude toward life that had its source in the sufferings of common humanity.

Jesus wrote nothing. But he spoke with an authority that gave his utterances a unique value to the Apostles and their converts. Against the background of the Hebrew sacred writings they recognized his words as a further revelation and made them an oral tradition to which they held fast. Because they believed that other men might speak with the "gifts of the Spirit," this oral tradition long remained the authoritative rendering of Christian teachings. Early Christianity was, in fact, a nonliterary spiritual movement, hostile to the literate learning of both the Jewish and the gentile populations through which it spread. However, just as the growth of the congregations promoted the differentiation of the priest class and the laymen, so did it bring the transformation of the *oral* into a *written* tradition. Besides a body of literate learning, the outcome of this development was a canon of writings, a creed, and a liturgy. But it was part of the orthodoxy thus established that the church, as organized in the epicopate, was custodian of the living tradition descending from the Apostles, so that ultimate authority rested with the church and not with written texts.[1]

THE ORIGINAL FORM OF CHRISTIAN BELIEFS AND PRACTICES.

Although the early Christian congregations agreed about the fundamentals of their faith, they varied greatly in its expression in word and worship. Diversity, not uniformity, characterized early Christianity.

1. *The Earliest Christian Literature; Aramaic Writings.* When and by whom the first Christian writings were composed is not known. Present-day students believe that they have identified parts of two Aramaic works in the Gospels of Mark, Matthew, and Luke. The first, fragments of which are scattered through these Gospels, is known as *The Sayings of Jesus.*[2] The second, designated *A Book of Testimonies*, consists of passages from the Hebrew sacred writings purporting to prove that Jesus was the Messiah. It was, therefore, an appeal to the Jews and an argument for Christians. In addition to these works, a third—*The Teachings*

---

[1] On the beginnings of the Christian tradition see Gustav Adolf Deissmann, *The New Testament in the Light of Modern Research* (1929); Vincent Taylor, *The Formation of the Gospel Tradition* (1933); and Martin Dibelius, *From Tradition to Gospel* (1934).

[2] See p. 1037.

of the Lord by the Twelve Apostles, which besides presenting an "idyllic picture of primitive, guileless Christianity" was a guide to worship and church organization—survived, as parts were incorporated in later writings. Some early hymns and prayers also survived in this way. The literary forms of these works—the products of the spread of Christianity through Palestine and Syria, where Aramaic was spoken—were derived from Hebrew models.

The circumstances under which these writings arose fixed in early Christianity the Jewish attitude toward literate learning. The first Christians were Jewish converts who, having been expelled from the synagogues, set up circles of believers modeled on the synagogue. Such teachers and believers naturally felt the need of a sacred book and looked upon knowledge as a revelation which, although they were free to comment on it, they were obligated to preserve. Thus Christianity received an outlook upon learning which directed intellectual effort in the interpretation and preservation of old knowledge, not in the winning of new knowledge. This was, of course, the outlook which had long prevailed among the priests of the various local cultures of the Mediterranean world. The priests of Egypt preserved their ancient traditions in sacred works. The priests of Rome consulted the Sibylline Books when any crisis occurred in the affairs of the state. These books, written in Greek verse, were regarded as too sacred for any but priestly eyes; they were never published. And the Persian Magi, even after the Zoroastrian writings were dispersed, reshaped them in the Zend-Avesta. In creating a sacred tradition in written form the Christians were following old and almost universal precedents.

In this connection it should also be noted that early Christian liturgy was merely a continuation of the practices of the Jewish synagogue. The congregation was a brotherhood whose members read the Hebrew sacred books, chanted, and prayed in the manner of the worshipers in the synagogues. The shift of the day of worship from the traditional Sabbath to Sunday was due not to a rejection of the Jewish practice but to a desire to have a special day for Christian worship. By introducing into this Jewish heritage an emphasis upon certain practices the Christians gave worship a new content. Chief among these practices were: (1) the sacrament of baptism, by which new members were admitted to the brotherhood; (2) the sacrament of the Lord's Supper, or the "sacred meal" in which the members of the brotherhood entered into communion with Christ, the Lord; and (3) the "speaking with tongues" by which the Holy Spirit made truth known to the Christian faithful. This speaking usually followed the ritualistic services. Inasmuch as these practices were somewhat similar to the practices of the Greek mystery cults, early Christianity was not only an assimilation of the Jewish Messianic idea into the Greek belief in a Savior-God but also a blending of Jewish and Greek religious practices.

2. *The Beginnings of Greek Christian Writings.* Paul began the literary expression of Christianity among the Gentiles by writing letters to the congregations he founded. These letters gave advice and moral guidance but did not purport to be authoritative statements of doctrine. Doctrine was defined in the oral tradition; Paul was merely commenting on it. Neither he nor the recipients of the letters had any notion that in time the letters would become parts of a sacred book. The oldest letters, written about 50–51, are known as First and Second Thessalonians. Paul's other letters were written between this date and the year 56. Apparently they were the earliest elements in a popular literature that grew up in the Greek Christian congregations, especially after the original Jewish congregation was dispersed by the destruction of Jerusalem in the year 70.

About this date, perhaps a year or two earlier, a Greek work was produced at Rome which set forth the first complete account of the career of Jesus; it is now known as the Gospel of Mark.[1] Mark, who had been, it seems, a companion of Peter, wrote a simple book, suffused with a popular supernaturalism, that pictured Jesus mainly as a wonder worker and a forgiver of sins. This picture reflected the conception of Jesus that had existed among those simple countryfolk who became his first followers. During the first century, when the Christian congregations consisted almost entirely of slaves and poor urban workers, the book was popular; in the second century, after Greek learning began to

---

[1] On the origin of the New Testament writings see, in addition to the three works noted above, Barnard Weiss, *The Synoptists* (1904); Allan Menzies, *The Earliest Gospel* (1901); W. Sanday and others, *Criticism of the New Testament* (1902); A. Loisy, *The Gospel and the Church* (1903); Adolf von Harnack, *The Origin of the New Testament* (1904); F. C. Burkitt, *The Gospel History and Its Transmission* (1907); B. S. Easton, *The Gospels before the Gospels* (1928); B. H. Streeter, *The Four Gospels: A study of origins* (4th imp. rev., 1930); Vincent Taylor, *The Gospels: A short introduction* (1930); George A. Barton, *The Apostolic Age and the New Testament* (1935); and Martin Dibelius, *A Fresh Approach to the New Testament and Early Christian Literature* (1936). For a treatment of the Gospels from the literary, as well as the religious, point of view see J. Moffat, *Introduction to the Literature of the New Testament* (1918); E. F. Scott, *The Literature of the New Testament* (1932); R. H. Lightfoot, *History and Interpretation of the Gospels* (1935). Discussions of the literature of early Christianity in its historical setting are to be found in G. W. Wade, *New Testament History* (1922); H. M. Battenhouse, *New Testament History* (1922).

influence Christianity, it passed into disrepute. Its language was the *Koinē*, or colloquial Greek, with a sprinkling of Hebrew expressions; its style was Hebrew.

Between the years 70 and 90 other centers of Christian belief produced works that were to enter into the Christian literate tradition. Like Mark, their authors seem to have been men who had known the Apostles or had had a deep religious experience under the influence of their teachings. It is well to note also that these writings were probably inspired by the feeling that some record of the memories of the men who had known Jesus or the Apostles was highly desirable.

Shortly after the year 70, probably at Antioch, an account of the career of Jesus was written for Greek-speaking Jewish Christians; this work is now known as the Gospel of Matthew, or First Gospel. Besides almost all of Mark's book and a considerable portion of *The Sayings of Jesus,* it contained stories of the virgin birth and infancy of Jesus, a genealogy tracing descent in the Davidic line, and an account of the betrayal, trial, and resurrection. Written for Jewish converts, the book included numerous quotations from the Hebrew Prophets and emphasized the belief that Jesus was the Messiah. It was a manual of faith for both teachers and believers.

Perhaps a decade later a third account of the career of Jesus was composed by Luke, Paul's physician. Certain attitudes expressed in the book suggest that Luke may have been a Roman freedman. The account of the career of Jesus followed the main outlines of Mark and Matthew, but Luke added materials (probably taken from sources not used by his forerunners) dealing with cures, parables, sermons, and incidents. To the account of the career of Jesus he added a history of missionary activity, particularly that of Paul. This work, now known as the Acts of the Apostles, inspired the collection of Paul's letters, probably at Ephesus, about the year 90. The letters became popular immediately. Luke's writing had a Greek literary flavor; and the collection of Paul's letters was modeled on collections of letters made and circulated by philosophers.

If Mark recorded the tradition of the early followers of Jesus, Matthew and Luke developed it for the two groups of converts the Apostles had won. Matthew adapted it to the outlook of the Hellenized Jews, and Luke shaped it to the needs of ordinary Greeks.

Three other Christian works of the period 70–90 deserve notice. The Epistle of Barnabas (70–79) argued that the spiritual teachings of Jesus had superseded ceremonial Judaism. The Epistle to the Hebrews (80–90), an eloquent rendering of the same theme, was the first Christian work to embody Greek methods of argument and literary expression. The Book of the Revelation, or the Apocalypse (*ca.* 95–106), was a different kind of work. Its author, an unknown representative of early Christianity in Asia Minor, drew together several early visions of the Last Judgment of the Christians under their Savior and God. The work—the source of Christian eschatological beliefs, *i.e.*, the doctrine of "last things"— was a Christian rendering of a theme that had been popular among the Hebrews for three centuries or more. Its author seems to have been inspired by a burning faith in the immediate Second Coming.

3. *The Merging of Jewish and Greek Elements in Christianity.* Running through these writings of the late first century can be detected a conflict of Jewish and Greek elements in Christianity. After the destruction of Jerusalem the Jewish Christians were probably strengthened for a time by refugees, but in the face of the growing numbers of the gentile Christians they were unable to do more than preserve the original Jewish elements in Christianity. Since the elaboration of these elements was to be almost completely the work of gentile Christians, Greek influences soon became dominant in the Christian tradition. In this connection the significance of Ephesus as the first literary center of Greek Christianity should be noted.

Old Catholic Christianity.

The clash of Jewish and Greek elements in Christianity was merely a forerunner of the controversies that raged within and about it during its entire development. In the second century the Christians were forced to meet Gnostic arguments, heretical innovations, and philosophical contentions, as well as political harassment, and, as a result, were compelled to deal with the problem of *orthodox*, *i.e.*, right, as opposed to *heretical*, *i.e.*, self-chosen, doctrines. They found the solution of this problem in the Old Catholic Church and the modes of organization, faith, and ritual to which it held fast.[1]

1. *The Impact of Gnosticism on Christianity.* Gnosticism was already widespread when Christianity began to make itself felt

---

[1] On the history of Christian doctrines and institutions in the second and third centuries see MacKinley Helm, *After Pentecost: A history of Christian ideas and institutions from Peter and Paul to Ignatius of Antioch* (1936); James Heron, *The Evolution of Latin Christianity* (1919); W. Fairweather, *Jesus and the Greeks, or Early Christianity in the Tideway of*

in the Greek world; the immediate result of their contact seems to have been a reinterpretation of the career of Jesus. Although there is much speculation and not a great deal of factual knowledge about the origin of the Gospel of John, or the Fourth Gospel, scholars now generally recognize that the work was a product of the contact, perhaps in Ephesus.[1] Its unknown author was probably a Hellenized Jew, Christian born but Greek educated, at least in the philosophies. He was familiar with the Gospels of Mark and Luke, but he did not imitate them. His purpose was to present an interpretation of the career of which they gave a record. In making this interpretation he seems to have followed Philo, the Hellenized Jewish philosopher of Alexandria, for he identified Christ, the Savior, with the Logos as the instrumentality of God's action in the universe and among men. This identification was in harmony with the Gnostic doctrine of mediation. Also in harmony with Gnostic teachings was the author's identification of the Logos with light and life. In Christ, he held, light and life had become incarnate. Evidences of this incarnation he found in certain gospel events. By curing a paralytic Jesus gave "life." By multiplying the loaves and fishes Jesus gave the "bread of life." By raising Lazarus from the grave Jesus gave "eternal life." Thus by means of allegories the career of Jesus was harmonized with a widespread philosophical conception of divine action among men. Paul transformed Jesus, the Jewish Messiah, into a personal Savior like those of the mystery religions; John raised this Savior to the position of the highest mediator between God and men as conceived by the Hellenistic philosophers of the first and second centuries.

To counteract the danger of losing the person of Jesus as the historical basis of Christianity—a danger clearly evident in John's philosophical interpretation of his career—a combination of the Gospels of Mark, Matthew, Luke, and John was made at Ephesus about the year 125; during the next quarter century this "fourfold

---

Hellenism (1924); G. E. Edmundson, *The Church in Rome in the First Century* (1913); W. M. Ramsay, *The Church in the Roman Empire Before* 170 *A.D.* (1893); Ernst Barnikol, *Die Entstehung der Kirche im zweiten Jahrhundert und die Zeit Marcions* (1933); Friedrich Heiler, *Urkirche und Ostkirche* (1937), especially Part I, on the Old Catholic Church.

[1] For different views of the intellectual sources of the Fourth Gospel see C. H. Dodd, "The Background of the Fourth Gospel," *Bulletin of the John Rylands Library* (Manchester), Vol. 19 (1935), pp. 329–343; C. F. Burney, *The Aramaic Origin of the Fourth Gospel* (1922). Dodd discovers its source in the thought of the time but argues that the author accepted this thought not as doctrine but as a foundation upon which to build his own doctrine.

For a general discussion of the relation of Gnosticism to the rise of Christianity see L. G. Rylands, *The Beginnings of Gnostic Christianity* (1940), and Arthur Drews, *Die Entstehung des Christentums aus dem Gnostizismus* (1924).

A FRAGMENT OF ST. JOHN'S GOSPEL

This is a remnant of the oldest known manuscript of the New Testament; it dates about 140. Accumulating evidence supports the view that a true version of the Gospels was transmitted in the great manuscripts that survived from the fourth and fifth centuries.

document" completely displaced the individual Gospels that had been read in the various congregations; its combination of historical and philosophical material was particularly useful in combating the Gnostic heresies then threatening to engulf apostolic Christianity.

The character of these heresies was evident in the teachings of Valentinus (d. 160), the greatest Gnostic teacher of the second century.[1] The Hebrew sacred book, he said, was a false revelation and its god, Yahweh, was not the Supreme Being. The man Jesus, he contended, was a phantom and his sufferings on the cross were only a semblance of pain. In support of these assertions Valentinus argued that pure spirit, *i.e.*, the Logos, could not have contact with matter, which is evil. This doctrine that Christ had not led a natural life, known as the heresy of Docetism, persisted for centuries after Gnosticism had disappeared. Valentinus also had

[1] F. C. Burkitt, *Church and Gnosis* (1932), pp. 8–9: "Christian doctrine in the second century was still in the process of formulation. The great gnostic thinkers were Heretics, not in the sense that they left the high road, but in the sense that the track along which they went was not the direction along which the highway was afterwards constructed."

doubts about the efficacy of the Christian sacraments and the truth of the Christian claim that the body, as well as the soul, is resurrected.

2. *The Heresy of Marcion.* Closely related to the Gnostic heresies was the reformation of Christianity which Marcion (fl. *ca.* 144) attempted. Marcion, originally a rich shipowner of Sinope in Asia Minor, came to Rome, where, after entering the Christian congregation, he founded a sect that spread throughout Italy, northern Africa, Syria, and Asia Minor. For a century or more it threatened to supplant traditional Christianity. The orthodox Roman congregation expelled him in the year 144. His teachings, like those of the Gnostics, rested on a repudiation of the Judaistic base of Christianity. In *The Antitheses,* his chief work, many contradictions between the Hebrew sacred writings and Christian beliefs were pointed out. The ancient God of the Hebrews, he argued, was a wrathful Demiurge who created the universe and man out of matter and set over them a strict law. Man's failure to obey this law brought a curse upon him. Finally, in order to redeem man, a higher and kindlier God, who had remained unknown to men, sent His "only begotten Son" as a Savior. This Son, in the likeness of the man Jesus, preached in Palestine, but the Jews, hoping for a military Messiah, failed to recognize Him, and their ancient God caused the Savior to be crucified. By this act the ancient God sealed His own doom, opened the way for the release of the souls of all dead men to a spiritual life, and gave occasion for the preaching of the true salvation to living men. Paul, appointed by the Savior, rescued the true teachings from the Judaistic Apostles, and Marcion, likewise appointed by the Savior, was rescuing Paul's teachings from the same corrupting influences. He called upon men to win salvation by "faith" and looked forward to the redemption of mankind in the coming of "another" Savior. Unique among his doctrines was the belief that the God of love had remained unknown to men until revealed by Jesus. His morals were ascetic, and their purity won him many adherents.

Marcion's significance in the development of Christianity lay, however, not in any theological or moral teaching but in the clear formulation of the idea that Christianity should have its own sacred book. This was the necessary result of his rejection of the Hebrew sacred writings. He created the original New Testament from Paul's letters and the Gospel of Luke, expurgating from them passages which did not harmonize with his conception of Paul's teachings. Marcion, therefore, set in motion a process of selecting inspired works from the various Jewish and Christian writings; the outcome of this process was the formation of the Christian Bible with its two divisions, the Old and New Testaments.

3. *The Heresy of Montanus.* Montanus (fl. *ca.* 150–180), like Marcion, came from Asia Minor; originally he seems to have been a native of Phrygia and a devotee of Cybele, the Great Mother. When Christianity spread among the Phrygian peasants, they did not give up their ancient cults but introduced bits of them into their new faith. Notably they preserved the belief in communication, by individuals in trances, with the overworld of spirits. Montanus combined this belief with the Christian practice of speaking with the "gifts of the Spirit" in the doctrine that revelation is continuous, and from this doctrine he argued that the Christian priesthood should consist only of "inspired" prophets. Also contrary to ordinary Christian belief, he held that women, as well as men, could receive the "gifts of the Spirit." Thus he opposed to the official leaders of the congregation a priesthood of prophets and prophetesses into which any Christian, if he or she received the "gifts of the Spirit," might enter. The danger of such a doctrine to traditional Christianity was very great, for it meant that new individuals receiving new revelations might produce an endless variety of teachings in which tradition would be lost.

Actually, however, Montanism was more significant as a moral than as a theological movement. Its leaders, who taught a severely ascetic morality, denounced ordinary Christians for enjoying their food too much and proclaimed an immediate "visible" coming of the "New Jerusalem." The "metropolis of the Savior" was identified with a Phrygian village, Pepuza. There prophets and prophetesses gathered, and also a multitude of followers, who gave up their property and abandoned their lands, to await the opening of the "millennium," *i.e.*, the period during which Christ would govern the earth in person. To support the priesthood of prophets and prophetesses, who, it should be remembered, received revelations while in a state of trance, the Montanists introduced the practices of collecting fixed dues from individual members and of paying stipends to their leaders. They had no bishops but established an "overseer" of the prophets and prophetesses and recognized the leadership of presbyters in the congregations.

In two fundamental respects Montanism was an attempt to return to primitive Christianity: (1) it sought to revive the early purity of morals; (2) it asserted the authority of the oral tradition, as interpreted and elaborated by prophets and prophetesses, against the authority of the hardening tradition. The first was a protest against the nominal Christianity that was growing up among those born and reared in the faith; the second was a revolt against the growing power of the priestly hierarchy, particularly the bishops. The last elaboration of the Christian oral tradition, Montanism opposed individual moral purity to an institutionalized faith as the means of winning salvation. Like Marcionism, it was long a source of heretical teachings.

4. *The Apologists for Christianity.*   In the face of these movements, as well as the persecutions, traditional Christianity found many defenders. The apologists, as these defenders are now called, were chiefly preachers, who, like the sophistic philosophers, discoursed in public.[1] Early apologists, such as Clement, bishop of Rome, Ignatius, bishop of Antioch, and Polycarp, bishop of Smyrna, wrote relatively simple defenses of Christian faith and morals. Among the later apologists, some—Melito (d. *ca.* 177), bishop of Sardis, and Apollinaris (fl. *ca.* 170), bishop of Hierapolis— wrote appeals to the Roman emperors, while others produced elaborate treatises on doctrines and morals. Hermas (fl. *ca.* 110– 140), an obscure Roman author, wrote a book of visions, known as *The Shepherd*, which defended the Christian mode of redemption and the hope of the ultimate realization of the Kingdom of God. The work was a mild reply to the Gnostics. Justin Martyr (fl. *ca.* 150), wrote a more complete defense of Christianity. Although Justin knew the four Gospels, he made little use of them; his chief authorities were the Hebrew sacred writings, which are quoted over seven hundred times in his surviving works. To the Jews Justin pleaded that Jesus had fulfilled the ancient prophecies. To the Romans he protested that the Christians were not atheists. These arguments were elaborated by his successors. The one God, they replied to the Gnostics, is the "creator." To the Marcionists and Montanists they affirmed the validity of the gospel tradition. They denounced the pagans, including the Mithraists, as completely superstitious. And to the Romans they proclaimed the respectability and orderliness of the Christians. Although generally suspicious of Greek philosophy, they held that Christianity was not contrary to philosophical truth and accepted the identification of Jesus with the Logos as the divine instrument of revela-

[1] Philip Carrington, *Christian Apologetics of the Second Century in Their Relation to Modern Thought* (1921).

tion. The knowledge that saved was a knowledge not of divine mysteries but of God's will, character, and unity. This knowledge was possessed only by faith. They understood salvation as a freedom from the attacks of daimons. In the claim that Christianity was in accord with philosophical truth, the apologist opened the way for the amalgamation of the two bodies of thought.

5. *The Emergence of Catholic Christianity.* The crisis which the Gnostic, Marcionist, and Montanist heresies caused in the development of Christianity had far-reaching effects.[1] Gnosticism shook all traditional religions and, consequently, opened the way for the spread of new beliefs. As a positive force acting on Christianity, it stimulated theological speculation, particularly about the role of the Christian Savior in the universal process of creation and salvation, and strengthened ascetic tendencies. Marcionism gave birth to the idea of a distinct Christian Scripture, and Montanism forced an examination of the entire documentary record of Christian teachings. Above all, these movements, because they raised the fundamental question of the unity of all Christians under one faith and one discipline, compelled the Christians to formulate the true teachings. By its adherents this body of teachings was designated *Catholic,* or universal, *Christianity;* it was the faith of the Old Catholic Church.

A glimpse of the worship of Catholic Christians is provided in the following quotation from the *Apology* of Justin:

Then after the president has given thanks and all the people responded, the deacons as we call them allow everyone of those present to partake of the bread and wine and water for which thanks have been given; and for those absent they take away a portion.

And this food is called by us Eucharist, and it is not lawful for any man to partake of it but he who believes our teaching to be true, and has been washed with the washing which is for the forgiveness of sins and unto a new birth, and is so living as Christ commanded. For not as common bread and common drink do we receive these; but like as Jesus Christ our Saviour being made flesh and blood for our salvation, so also were we taught that the food for which thanks are given by the word of prayer that comes from him—food by which blood and flesh by conversion are nourished, is both flesh and blood of that Jesus who was made

[1] On early Christian doctrines see Jules Lebreton, *La Sainte Euchariste d'après le Nouveau Testament et la tradition patristique* (n. d.), *nihil obstat;* A. Lemonnyer, *The Theology of the New Testament* (1929); C. C. Richardson, *The Christianity of Ignatius of Antioch* (1935); Edwin R. Goodenough, *The Theology of Justin Martyr* (1923); Orazio Marrucchi, *The Evidences of the Catacombs for the Doctrines and Organization of the Primitive Church* (1929); Eduard Meyer, *Ursprung und Anfänge des Christentums* (3 vols., 1924); Albert Dufourcq, *Le Christianisme primitif: s. Paul, s. Jean, s. Irénée* (1929).

flesh. For the Apostles in the memoirs which they composed, which are called Gospels, thus delivered that command was given them—that Jesus took bread and gave thanks and said, This do in remembrance of me, this is my body; and that He likewise took the cup, and after He had given thanks said, This is my blood, and gave of it only to them. Which the evil demons imitated, commanding it to be done also in the mysteries of Mithras; for that bread and a cup of water are set forth with certain formulae in the ceremonial of initiation, you either know or can learn.

But we afterwards henceforth continually put each other in mind of these things, and those of us who are wealthy help all that are in want, and we always remain together. And for all things that we eat we bless the Maker of all through His Son Jesus Christ, and through the Holy Spirit. And on the so-called day of the Sun there is a meeting of all of us who live in cities or the country, and the memoirs of the Apostles or the writings of the prophets are read, as long as time allows. Then when the reader has ceased, the president gives by word of mouth his admonition and exhortation to follow these excellent things. Afterwards we all rise at once and offer prayers; and as I said, when we have ceased to pray, bread is brought and wine and water, and the president likewise offers up prayers and thanksgivings to the best of his power, and the people responds with its Amen. Then follows the distribution to each and the partaking of that for which thanks were given; and to them that are absent a portion is sent by the hand of the deacons. Of those that are well to do and willing, every one gives what he will according to his own purpose, and the collection is deposited with the president, and he it is that succours orphans and widows, and those that are in want through sickness or any other cause, and those that are in bonds, and the strangers that are sojourning, and in short he has the care of all that are in need.[1]

This statement is significant evidence of the central position the sacrament of the Lord's Supper had come to hold in orthodox Christian worship. Since in this sacrament Christians shared in the atonement for sins which they believed Christ had made by dying on the cross, its performance was logically the heart of Christian worship and the chief function of the church. Adherence to the doctrine of atonement and the performance of the sacrament which gave the believer Christ's spiritual support in gaining salvation constituted the Catholic reply to Gnostic and Montanist teachings about gaining salvation through mystical knowledge, or with the assistance of angels, or by means of ascetic morality.

Among the many men who contributed to the shaping of Catholic Christianity two stand out—Irenaeus (*ca.* 130–200) and Tertullian (*ca.* 155–225).

[1] H. M. Gwatkin, *Selections from Early Christian Writers Illustrative of Church History to the Time of Constantine* (1902), pp. 53–55, The Macmillan Company, Ltd., London.

Irenaeus, bishop of Lyon, was recognized as the greatest Christian of his time. He was educated in Asia Minor under the influence of the views that prevailed at Ephesus. His best-known work, *Against the Heresies*, was a vigorous defense of the accepted Christian tradition. As the Logos, he said, the Savior was not the *reason* but the *voice* of God, and the voice of God, he argued, was to be heard only through the traditional church:

The Church which has been planted throughout the world to the ends of the earth has received its faith from the apostles and their disciples. It is a faith in one God the Almighty Father who made the heavens, the earth, the sea, and all that is in them. In one Jesus Christ the Son of God, incarnate for our salvation. And in the Holy Spirit who by the prophets proclaimed His providence. It is a faith of the coming of our beloved Lord Jesus Christ, of His birth from the Virgin, of His suffering, of His resurrection from the dead, of His ascension in the flesh into heaven, of His coming from heaven in the glory of the Father to gather all things under His headship. It is a faith that all flesh of the human race shall rise again, so that every knee, whether on earth or in heaven or under the earth shall be bent before Christ Jesus our Lord, our God, our Saviour, and our King, and every tongue shall confess Him. And that He shall do just judgment on all. That He shall send the fallen and apostate angels, and the impious, unjust, and blasphemers from among men into everlasting fire; while on those who are upright and just, who have kept His commandments, who have preserved His love, whether from the first or after penance, He will bestow life, undying life, and will surround them with eternal glory. The Church has accepted his doctrine and guards this faith as we have proclaimed it. Though she is spread throughout the whole world she keeps this faith as though she dwelt in one place; she believes these things as though she had but one mind and one heart; she proclaims these things and teaches them as consistently as if she had but one mouth. There are indeed different languages in the world but there is only one and the same meaning of the traditional teaching.[1]

Irenaeus united with this clarity of doctrine a conception of the unity of all congregations in one church and an assertion of the supremacy of the bishops in its affairs. He is sometimes spoken of as the founder of the Old Catholic Church.

Tertullian was a Carthaginian, trained in Roman law, who, although he never rose above the rank of presbyter, exercised a strong influence over the western congregations.[2] His writings—

---

[1] Quoted in Edward Eyre, editor, *European Civilization: Its origin and development*, Vol. 2, *Rome and Christendom* (1935), p. 532. By permission of the Oxford University Press.

[2] Benjamin B. Warfield, *Studies in Tertullian and Augustine* (1930); T. R. Glover, *Tertullian, Apology, De Spectaculis* (1931).

the first important Christian works in Latin—reveal a fiery temper and a logical mind. Under the stress of the persecutions of the last decade of the second century he castigated Roman officials, scourged heretics, and upbraided Christians who fled from a martyr's death. To the theological question of the relation of the Father, the Son, and the Holy Spirit he gave the answer "One substance, three persons" and declared, "The Father is God, and the Son is God, and the Holy Spirit is God, and each is God." This is the doctrine of the Trinity, which, although always regarded as true doctrine by the adherents of tradition, became the declared teaching of the church only after bitter controversy. It is important to understand that Tertullian, as a lawyer, found in the Roman legal concept "persona"[1] the intellectual basis of the Trinity. To the Gnostic Docetism he opposed the belief that the human and the divine are permanently united in Christ. He drew the distinction between *venial* sins, *i.e.*, those the bishops can absolve, and *mortal* sins, *i.e.*, those for which there is no forgiveness. The deadly sins were idolatry, murder, and unchastity. Unfortunately his moral fervor led him to become a Montanist, and after the year 202 he denounced traditional Christians as fiercely as he had once defended them. Engrossed in saucepans and kitchens, they were, he protested, *animal*—the Montanists alone were *spiritual*. In spite of this lapse from the teachings finally triumphant in the church, Tertullian is commonly known as the "father of orthodoxy."

The chief support of the growing Catholic orthodoxy, besides the episcopate, was the *new* Scripture which, set alongside the Hebrew sacred writings, fixed the pattern of the Christian Bible as the *Old* and *New* Testaments. From the first the Christians had used the Hebrew sacred books in the Greek translation known as the Septuagint; this translation, the work of the Hellenized Jews of Alexandria, contained works not recognized by the Palestinian Jews as divinely inspired. Apparently the Christians were ignorant of this fact until late in the third century. The term "New Testament" was first used about the year 192. The "Muratorian Fragment," so designated after its discoverer, Muratori (1672–1750), which was written about this time, probably indicates the writings which the Roman congregation had long regarded as inspired.

[Gospel of Matthew] Missing but assumed to have been pres-
[Gospel of Mark   ]   ent once.
Gospel of Luke

[1] See p. 1011.

Gospel of John
The Acts of All the Apostles
Corinthians (I, II)
Ephesians
Philippians
Colossians
Galatians
Thessalonians (I, II)
Romans
Philemon
Titus
Timothy (I, II)
(Laodiceans and Alexandrians are spurious)
Jude
John (I, II)
Wisdom of Solomon
Revelation of John
Revelation of Peter (which some reject)
(The *Shepherd* of Hermas may be read but not publicly in
church)[1]

This fragment is the earliest known record of New Testament works arranged in order. As it indicates, there was not yet agreement as to the works that were regarded as inspired. But the basic principle of selection, namely, that only works of apostolic origin are inspired, was clearly understood. Irenaeus and Tertullian accepted the works of this list as canonical. By the year 200, therefore, Catholic Christianity was well on the way to becoming a religion of a book whose interpretation was the prerogative of a priest class. The *book* and the *priest class* were merely the correlative aspects of the hardening Christian tradition.

The supreme product of this hardening process was a *creed, i.e.,* a formal statement of the faith to be adhered to by all Christians. During the first and the early second century the various congregations used a "form of sound words" in the instruction of converts and baptismal confessions. But the form varied from congregation to congregation. Under the influence of the Logos doctrine, the early Christian formula "Jesus is Lord" expanded into the declaration "I believe in God, Jesus Christ, and the Holy Spirit." The

[1] See E. J. Goodspeed, *The Formation of the New Testament* (1927), p. 189. Lines *one* and *two* of the list are missing in the Muratorian Fragment, but it is assumed that they enumerate the Gospels of Matthew and Mark. By permission of the University of Chicago Press, Chicago.

Gnostic, Marcionist, and Montanist heresies caused a further elaboration of the statement of the faith. The product of this elaboration, rendered in Greek toward the close of the second century, embodied the tradition to which Irenaeus and Tertullian had held fast as orthodox; it seems to have been the creation of the Roman congregation.

> I believe in God the Father Almighty.
> And in Jesus Christ, his only son, our Lord;
> Who was born by the Holy Ghost of the Virgin Mary;
> Was crucified under Pontius Pilate and was buried;
> The third day he rose from the dead;
> He ascended into heaven, and sitteth on the right hand of the Father;
> From thence he shall come to judge the quick and the dead.
> And in the Holy Ghost;
> The Holy Church;
> The forgiveness of sins;
> The resurrection of the body (flesh).

When in the fifth century this statement of the faith became known as the Apostles' Creed, its authority was recognized as having basis in tradition rather than in the action of an assembly of ecclesiastical officials. Additions of the seventh and eighth centuries gave it the form familiar to later times.[1]

Between those who adhered to Christianity as expressed in these forms and those who did not, the Catholic Christians made an absolute distinction: the eternally *saved* and the eternally *damned*. And to opponents, whatever their beliefs, the Catholic Christians proclaimed their possession of the absolute truth; in this truth alone, they argued, could men become righteous and

---

[1] See Philip Schaff, *The Creeds of Christendom* (3 vols., 1905), Vol. 1, p. 21, The Apostle's Creed:
> I believe in God the Father Almighty,
> Maker of heaven and earth.
> And in Jesus Christ, his only son, our Lord;
> Who was conceived by the Holy Ghost, born of the Virgin Mary,
> Suffered under Pontius Pilate was crucified [dead] and buried;
> He descended into Hell (Hades).
> The third day he rose from the dead;
> He ascended into heaven; and sitteth on the right hand of God the Father Almighty.
> From thence he shall come to judge the quick and the dead.
> And I believe in the Holy Ghost;
> The Holy Catholic Church;
> The communion of saints;
> The forgiveness of sins;
> The resurrection of the body (flesh).
> And life everlasting.

gain salvation. Furthermore, they proclaimed that only because of their faith did the just and merciful God hold back from utterly destroying the earth and men. This dogmatism was the intellectual correlative of the in-group feeling that distinguished the Christians as the "third race."

Just as Ephesus was the center of the shaping of early Christianity by Greek influences, so Rome was the focus of the influences that produced Catholic Christianity. This role was the result partly of the prestige of the Roman congregation and partly of the strong attachment of the congregation to the apostolic tradition.

Because Old Catholic Christianity was mainly Greek in language, it should be distinguished from the later Latin rendering of Christianity known as Roman Catholic Christianity.

THE CONSOLIDATION OF ORTHODOX CHRISTIANITY

In Old Catholic Christianity the adherents to the apostolic tradition triumphed over interpreters who would have sacrificed some of its essential elements. But new circumstances soon brought new threats to the unity of the faith. So long as most Christians were drawn from the lower classes, tradition sufficed to define beliefs, but when members of the educated classes were converted in increasing numbers the problem of amalgamating Christian beliefs with Greek and Roman learning, particularly philosophy and logic, appeared. In the fourth and fifth centuries the most brilliant minds of the Mediterranean world struggled with this problem, and many disputes arose among them.[1] When the church, organized under the episcopate, came to be regarded as the divinely appointed depository of "the 'saving truth,'" the problem of orthodox as opposed to heretical doctrine became acute. Although the bishops rested their authority on their positions as the successors of the Apostles, they often disagreed as to the meaning of tradition, and, as a result, their assemblies were not only frequently disorderly but also sometimes contradictory in decisions. When Constantine established Christianity as the official cult of the state, he made theological and ecclesiastical policies matters of imperial concern. Unfortunately the emperors at different times found their interests served by different policies, so

---

[1] On the development of Christian theology see J. K. Mozley, *The Beginnings of Christian Theology* (1931); J. F. Bethune-Baker, *An Introduction to the Early History of Christian Doctrine* (6th ed., 1938)—the best survey of the subject in English; Charles Guignebert, *L'Evolution des Dogmes* (1910); Friedrich Loofs, *Leitfaden zur Dogmengeschichte* (1906); E. M. Pickman, *The Mind of Latin Christendom* 373–496 (1937), an excellent study of the intellectual history of the period covered.

that their intervention contributed no little to controversy. Because the great prelates of Rome, Jerusalem, Alexandria, Antioch, Ephesus, and Constantinople were rivals for power in the ecclesiastical hierarchy, they made doctrinal disputes the occasions for the advancement of their interest. A final factor working for discord was the monks, whose fanaticism often turned argument into violent conflict. Out of the crisis these circumstances brought to Christianity in the fourth and fifth centuries came finally an orthodoxy which, although never universally accepted, was the main form in which the apostolic tradition survived.

THE ELABORATION OF CHRISTIAN LEARNING.

Early Christian learning was little more than a statement and a defense of Christian beliefs, but after educated persons were converted, it was elaborated in the pattern of Greek and Roman learning. The languages of this elaboration were Latin and Syriac, as well as Greek; to the men who carried it out is commonly given the name *patres ecclesiae* or Church Fathers, and their works are called patristic writings. They did not pretend to add anything to the received tradition; they sought only to preserve and affirm it. Actually, however, they performed the stupendous labor of syncretizing the high intellectual tradition of Greek and Roman culture with the apostolic tradition so that the two became the intellectual content of the Western cultural tradition. This achievement gives the Church Fathers a position of enduring significance in the history of Western culture.

1. *The Rise of Christian Schools.* The centers of the elaboration of Christian literate learning were schools similar to those in which rhetoric and philosophy were taught.[1] The first of these was founded at Antioch; the most famous was at Alexandria. Other schools appeared at Edessa, Athens, Carthage, and Rome. In them Christian scholars adapted logic and rhetoric to theological disputation and filtered Christian beliefs through philosophy into systematic theology. The Antiochene and Alexandrine schools differed sharply in outlook. The former followed the literal meaning of the Scriptures and used historical and geographical data in interpreting them. The latter developed the allegorical method of

[1] On early Christian literate learning and education see Geraldine Hodgson, *Primitive Christian Education* (1906); Charles A. Briggs, *History of the Study of Theology* (1916); Augusta Theodosia Drane, *Christian Schools and Scholars, or Sketches of Education from the Christian Era to the Council of Trent* (new ed., 1924); P. J. Marique, *History of Christian Education* (3 vols., 1934); and E. C. Moore, *The Story of Instruction: The Church, the Renaissance, and the Reformation* (1938).

interpreting the sacred word, even to the point of finding hidden meanings in misspellings; by this method scriptural support was found for doctrines somewhat more mystical than those taught in the Antiochene school. This difference in outlook had far-reaching effects upon the development of theology. The distinctive element in Christian scholarship was exegetics, *i.e.*, the science of scriptural exposition, which grew out of the need, shared by all Christians, for an understanding of the inspired writings.

2. *The Greek Church Fathers.* The first important Christian scholars were products of the school at Alexandria, which, it is important to note, received from the pagan intellectual environment of the city the Platonic philosophical outlook and the syncretizing tendency represented by Philo, the Hebrew philosopher, and Valentinus, the Gnostic teacher. At the beginning of the school's development there was a close connection between it and the forces that produced Neoplatonism. At this time, too, so scholarly opinion is more and more inclined to believe, there was in the Alexandria environment considerable knowledge of Indian thought. Plotinus, the Neoplatonist, and Basilides, the Gnostic, it is said had gone east, if not to India, perhaps to Mesopotamia or Iran for study. Clement, noted in the next paragraph as the chief early representative of Christian philosophical speculation, seems to have possessed a knowledge of Buddhism. Although it is not now possible to identify clearly any body of Indian doctrines in the ancient Near East, it is a fair assumption that many of them had spread westward along the trade routes.[1]

Clement (*ca.* 150–216), second head of the Christian school at Alexandria, marked an epoch in the development of Christian learning by bridging the gap between pagan scholarship and Christian beliefs.[2] After him the minds of educated pagans and Christians were open to one another. Plato's *Timaeus*, according to Clement, outlined a Christian view of God and Plato occupied in the gentile world a position similar to that of the Prophets among the Hebrews. In his greatest book—*Pedagogus*, or The Instructor—Clement argued that knowledge rested on faith and only a simple faith was necessary to know God. The Logos was the divine instrument for the education of the human race in this faith. Only by self-conquest through mortification of the flesh and contempt of the world, which released men from corrupting passion, could the spiritual purity enabling men to contemplate God be

[1] See C. G. Rawlinson, *India: A short cultural history* (1937), p. 98.
[2] Charles Bigg, *Christian Platonists of Alexandria* (1913).

achieved. The goal of faith, which Clement, like the Gnostics, understood as a form of knowledge, was an effortless living with God. Clement recognized himself as a "Christian Gnostic." His significance in the development of the Christian intellectual ideal resided in his fusion of the Christian ideal of spiritual life and the Greek ideal of meditative rationalism.

Some years after a persecution drove Clement from Alexandria, Origen (*ca.* 185–254) reopened the school and made it the most influential center of Christian learning. Besides the pagan subjects of logic, rhetoric, geometry, astronomy, and the philosophies (except Epicureanism, which the Christians regarded as materialistic and atheistic), its curriculum included Hebrew and other oriental languages. A staff of copyists issued books after the manner of a modern press; Origen's many works, it is said, were dictated to shorthand writers and reproduced for publication. Among these works three deserve notice: (1) the *Hexapla*, the first work of Christian exegesis, (2) *Eight Books against Celsus*, the most effective Christian apology, and (3) *The Principles of Things*, the earliest systematic statement of Christian theology. The *Hexapla* presented in parallel columns the six leading texts of the Hebrew Scriptures:

1. The Hebrew text in Hebrew letters.
2. The Hebrew text in Greek letters.
3. The Greek translation of Aquila (*ca.* 128).
4. The Greek translation of Symmachos (*ca.* 180).
5. The Greek translation of "the Seventy" of Alexandria (*ca.* 280 B.C.). [Septuagint]
6. The Greek translation of Theodotion (*ca.* 170).

Origen also produced a text of the New Testament writings.

But more important for the development of theology than these texts was the theory of interpretation which he set forth; it asserted that each word and verse of Scripture had three meanings—(1) a literal, (2) a moral, and (3) an allegorical—and only in the allegorical meaning was to be found the revealed truth. In the *Eight Books against Celsus* Origen answered the anti-Christian views of a cultured pagan with arguments as sophistical and speculative as those of the critic; this work clearly indicates the debt which Christian learning was to owe to both the method of thinking and the trend of speculation dominant in pagan philosophy. In *The Principles of Things*, which Origen developed by arguments from pagan philosophy as well as from the Hebrew and the Christian

Scriptures, a Christian philosophy of universal order was outlined; the work is important not only as the first exposition of Christian theology but also as the first product of the mergence of Christianity with the high intellectual tradition of Greek and Roman culture.

Origen, who attended the lectures of Ammonius Saccas, the founder of Neoplatonism, owed much to this philosophy. He discussed the universe as a hierarchy of spiritual beings—God at the apex, the Devil and the fallen angels at the base. This hierarchy, however, had been created not by emanation, as the Neoplatonists held, but by generation, a process of creation rather than a mere flowing outward and downward of being from the central source. God—eternal, omnipotent, and righteous—was the principle of absolute causality, and creating was His constant work. Out of benevolence and mercy He had created the universe and man. He was knowable in nature, *i.e.*, the rationally ordered universe, and in Christ, who, generated from the essence of God, was the full revelation of His mercy and wisdom. The Logos was the instrument of creation and the mediator between God and all created beings. As the first of all created beings, the Logos was divine—as radiance is to light, so was He to God. As incarnated in Christ, the Logos was the express image of God, and His life and death as a human being was the sacrificial offering which set at work the forces of redemption making possible salvation not only for men but also for evil angels and even the Devil. The Holy Spirit, created by the Logos, was the instrumentality of revelation; possessed of a direct knowledge of God, the Holy Spirit refreshed and sanctified human souls. Although Origen argued against the heresy of Manichaeism, which declared God a single person, he did not arrive at a clear-cut conception of the Trinity. Of the Logos, he said, "There was a time when He was not"; and he associated the Holy Spirit with God only in a vague way. The Logos created a multitude of immaterial intelligences which differed only as they loved Christ. Those loving Christ most were angels; those whose love proved defective were daimons. Man, who possessed a rational soul in a body of flesh, stood between the angels and the daimons. In the body the soul was exposed to the corrupting influence of matter, and the material universe was the theater of the struggle of human souls for redemption. Differences of fortune, suffering, sorrow, and death were a form of justice imposed on men by a merciful God who had opened the way for the saving of all souls. Through Christ God had revealed this way, and men were free to choose to follow it. If they chose to live sinfully, they were damned; if they chose to live righteously, at death they entered upon a period of purification that ended in the attainment of a state of holiness and bliss. The goal of salvation was a life of purity with the Christ-Logos.

Origen rejected the elements of the Christian tradition which involved belief in materialistic phenomena such as the physical suffering of the Logos on the cross, the thousand-year reign of Christ on earth, the resurrection of the body, and the physical torture of souls in hell. The doctrines that even the Devil might win salvation and that souls having once won salvation might again fall into sin were also contrary to the accepted tradition. His conceptions of the Logos and the Holy Spirit, although falling short of the Trinitarian position, contributed much to its final clarification.

Athanasius (*ca.* 298–373), somewhat less a scholar than an ecclesiastical official, was the greatest of the Greek Church Fathers. Early in life he was taken into the household of the bishop of Alexandria, and in the year 328, at the early age of thirty, he was elevated to the see. He was well educated in the philosophies and the New Testament writings. Although he is best known for his defense of the Trinitarian doctrine against the heresy of Arius,[1] his work actually covered the whole life of the church. He opposed the interference of the state in ecclesiastical affairs. He was the first bishop to promote monasticism, and his *Life of St. Anthony* exercised a lasting influence on its development. His Easter Letter of the year 367 concerning the books of the New Testament was a milestone in the evolution of the canon of the inspired writings. His greatest service to the development of theology was to fix not only the doctrine of the Trinity but also the terminology of its orthodox rendering. The philosophical basis of his theory of the Trinity was the Aristotelian doctrine of essences which permitted the postulation of "one substance" behind the "three persons." Most of his books have been lost.

Among the scholars of the Antiochene school three are notable. Diodorus (*ca.* 330–394) developed the rational interpretation of the Scriptures for which the school was famous. John Chrysostom (*ca.* 347–407)—the "golden mouth"—was the greatest preacher of his time.[2] His sermons, ardent appeals for the simple and medi-

[1] See p. 1125.
[2] A. Puech, *Saint Jean Chrysostome et les moeurs de son temps* (1891); John Evelyn, *The Golden Book of St. John Chrysostom concerning the Education of Children* (1656); W. R.

tative life, exercised wide influence among unlettered as well as educated Christians. As bishop of Antioch and Constantinople he exemplified the Christian way of life in a disorderly and contentious age. Theodore of Mopsuestia (*ca.* 350–428) was probably the greatest theologian of the Antiochene school. The variety of his interests and the diversity of his writings won for him the title—indicative of universal learning—"polyhistor." His theological teachings, although regarded as orthodox, gave rise to the controversies over the relation of Mary to the Christ and the relation of the human and the divine natures in Christ.

Basil, the formulator of the rules of eastern monasticism, was representative of the moral outlook that prevailed in Asia Minor; associated with him were the two Gregorys, the bishop of Nyssa (d. *ca.* 395) and the bishop of Nazianzen (d. *ca.* 390).[1] The three men are sometimes known as the Cappadocian Fathers. Cyril (*ca.* 315–386), bishop of Jerusalem, produced the first formal statement of orthodox Christian theology in a work called *Catechetical Lectures*. He explained the sacraments, the relation of the body and soul, the miraculous power of the relics of the saints, the efficacy of exorcism and "crossing," and the proof of the resurrection. In this proof he made use of the Egyptian myth of the phoenix, the fabulous bird which after living five hundred years was consumed in fire, and rose restored to youthfulness from its own ashes. Although not representative of any school, Cyril's work exhibited that combination of dogmatism and mysticism which everywhere pervaded Christian learning.

3. *The Syrian Church Fathers.* Syriac, a Semitic tongue, became the written language of Syria, east of Aleppo, and Mesopotamia in the second century, and a Syriac literary tradition persisted in these lands from that time until the fourteenth century. The Syriac alphabet was derived from the old Hebrew and Phoenician writing systems. Syriac learning was from the outset a blend of elements—Gnostic, Christian, and Greek. A Syriac version of the Gospels, which combined the four books in a single narrative, was produced in the second century. In the third century Bardesanes (*ca.* 154–222), sometimes known as the "last of the Gnostics," won the city of Edessa for Christianity, and its school became the foremost eastern center of the faith. His teachings seem

Stephens, *St. John Chrysostom* (1871); and F. H. Chase, *Chrysostom: A study in Biblical interpretation* (1887).

[1] W. K. L. Clarke, *Saint Basil the Great* (1913); W. K. L. Clarke, *The Ascetic Works of St. Basil* (1925).

to have combined Persian dualism and Chaldean mythology with Christian beliefs; his hymns were the earliest form of Syriac poetry. Aphraates (fl. *ca.* 330–350), the "Persian sage," was the first expounder of orthodox Christian doctrines in Syriac. Ephraem (d. *ca.* 378), an unbending advocate of orthodoxy, was a prolific author of hymns and homilies. His commentaries covered the entire Bible. He alone among the Syrian Church Fathers won a reputation among the Greeks. Under Rabbulas, bishop of Edessa from 411 to 435, a firm supporter of orthodoxy, a new version of the New Testament was introduced and heretical teachings were suppressed.

The rendering of the Bible into Syriac was only a part of the work of translation which gave Syriac learning its fundamental materials. The chief translator of Greek works was Sergios of Resaina (d. *ca.* 536), a priest and physician, who wrote treatises on Aristotle, Plutarch, Galen, and Porphyry. Among Syriac secular writings a romance based on the life of Julian the Apostate, a history of the outbreak of the Roman-Persian war in the sixth century, and a treatise on logic deserve mention. The bulk of Syriac learning was, of course, theological and ecclesiastical.

4. *The Latin Church Fathers.* Christianity spread very early among the Latin-speaking folk of northern Africa, and there Latin Christian learning had its origin. The oldest known Latin work on Christianity was an apology composed by the converted Roman lawyer Minucius Felix about the year 190. The practical and severely moral outlook of Latin Christianity was first developed by Tertullian and Cyprian, both Africans, and the school of Carthage perpetuated their achievement.[1] Lactantius (*ca.* 260–340), who lost a Roman professorship when he became a Christian, is known as the "Christian Cicero." His great work—*Divine Institutes*—set forth Christian doctrine in a form similar to a jurisconsult's treatise on the civil law. Arnobius (*ca.* 280–305) was also a converted rhetorician. His works, which show little knowledge of the New Testament and none of the Hebrew Scriptures, argued that the disasters befalling the Roman state could not rightly be blamed on the Christians. These writers, like the western church as a whole, were less interested in philosophical speculations than in practical considerations of the supremacy of the faith and ecclesiastical organization.

[1] E. W. Benson, *Cyprian: His life, his times, and his works* (1897); also J. A. Donaldson, *Church Life and Thought in North Africa A.D.* 200 (1909); Dom H. Leclerq, *L'Afrique chrétienne* (1904); G. A. Poole, *The Life and Times of Saint Cyprian* (1840).

During the fourth century the scholarly treatment of Christian beliefs in Latin spread throughout the west. Gaul, especially, became a center of orthodoxy. Hilary of Poitiers (*ca.* 305–368) wrote the first formal treatise in Latin on the orthodox doctrine of the Trinity. Cassian, originally from Scythia but trained in Palestine and Egypt, settled at Marseille, where, after founding a convent, he expounded in Latin the rules of monastic living. Salvian (*ca.* 400–490), also of Marseille, advocated an ascetic morality on the grounds that only by withdrawal from the world can men escape from the daimons that seek to trap them. Each of these men was adept in the pagan arts of persuasion.

Ambrose, the great bishop of Milan, was the first important Roman Christian writer.[1] The son of a high official, he was trained for the law and prepared for an administrative career, but in the course of a dispute between the orthodox and the Arian parties he was elected bishop. He was only a catechumen at the time. As bishop he brought to the church not only ability as an orator and an organizer but also the outlook and training of a Roman official. The dominant element in this outlook, the conviction that "whatever is, is right," made him an ardent supporter not only of orthodoxy in theology but also of ecclesiastical supremacy over secular rulers. More than any other ecclesiastic he was responsible for the formulation of the theory of the relation of the church and state which became the accepted Roman position.

Ambrose's literary works show the influence of the theological speculation of the Christian scholars of Alexandria and of the moral outlook of the Cappadocian Fathers. His introduction into the west of the allegorical method of interpreting the Scriptures opened the way for the development of the mystical element in the traditional faith to which the Roman church so stanchly adhered; his emphasis on sin, divine grace, and faith pointed the direction Latin Christianity was to take in the development of its systematic theology.

Jerome (*ca.* 340–420), the greatest scholar of Latin Christianity, was born of a wealthy but orthodox Christian family.[2] In addition to a typical Roman education in grammar, rhetoric, and philosophy, he received training in Greek, Hebrew, and exegetics. His knowledge of eastern Christianity was derived from an early acquaint-

---

[1] On St. Ambrose see F. H. Dudden, *The Life and Times of St. Ambrose* (2 vols., 1935); P. de Labriolle, *The Life and Times of St. Ambrose* (1928); Richard Wirt, *Der heilige Ambrosius und seine Zeit* (1924).

[2] E. L. Cutts, *Jerome* (1878); C. Martin, *Jerome* (1888).

THE CHURCH OF THE HOLY NATIVITY, BETHLEHEM

In 330 Constantine built a basilica over the traditional birthplace of Jesus. The Chapel of the Nativity is beneath the Choir of the present building; opposite the Chapel is the Manger where, it is said, Jesus was born. From the Chapel access is had to the cell where Jerome made the Vulgate translation of the Scriptures

ance with the works of Origen and from travel in Egypt and Palestine. The greater part of his work was done in Rome, where he served as secretary to Damasus; the last decades of his life were spent in a monastery at Bethlehem.

Jerome's great contribution to Latin Christianity was a translation of the Bible, known as the Vulgate, which became, after much contention, the accepted rendering of the Scriptures in the Roman church. The New Testament was based on second and third century Latin versions of the Gospels; the Old Testament was based on Origen's Hebrew text. Jerome, more than any other western Christian scholar, was inclined to use geographical and historical data in interpreting the Scriptures. He also wrote letters, sermons, chronicles, biographies, and polemical works. His *Lives of the Monks* was modeled on the *Lives of the Caesars* by Suetonius. His interest in manuscripts and books contributed to the shaping of monastic education. His interest in the early history of Christianity made him the founder of Christian antiquarian study. Like his great contemporaries he was an ardent advocate of an ascetic morality.

Augustine (*ca.* 354–430), although a learned man, was less a scholar than a great intellect. Born of Roman parents in a small town in northern Africa, he received the education of a well-to-do Roman youth and set out on a career as a rhetorician. As evidenced by the fact that at the age of twenty he was the father of a son, whose mother was his concubine, the young Augustine followed the Roman moral code of the time. In Carthage, however, where he completed his education, he fell under the influence of Manichaeans and for nine years held their doctrines. Finally disgust at the lack of learning of their leaders drove him back to Greek Skepticism. The turning point in his life came when he accepted a professorship at Milan, the see of Ambrose. There under the influence of his mother, a lifelong Christian, and the teachings of the great bishop, he was converted to Christianity. Moral scruples then forced him to abandon his concubine and become betrothed to a girl too young to marry. After returning to Africa his devotion to the church won him quick recognition, and in the year 395 he was consecrated bishop of Hippo. His career as bishop was notable for the introduction of monasticism into northern Africa, kindly ministration to the poor, and close attention to the economic interests of the church.[1]

Augustine's literary work marked an epoch not only in the development of Latin Christianity but also in the evolution of Christian culture. Besides numerous books called forth by theological controversy in which he was constantly engaged, he wrote the definitive theological treatise, *On the Trinity*, the first autobiography, *Confessions* (a profound exposition of his psychological growth), and *The City of God*, generally recognized as the greatest Christian book after the Bible. This work, inspired by the sack of Rome by the Visigoths in the year 410, was an answer to the old charge that the Christians were destroying the Roman state:

[1] For St. Augustine's writings see Marcus Dods, *The Works of Aurelius Augustine.* . . . *A new translation* (15 vols., 1872–1934)—Vol. 1 and 2 contain *The City of God*, Vol. 14, *The Confessions;* William Watts, *Augustine's Confessions* (2 vols., 1912); J. G. Pilkington, *The Confessions of St. Augustine* (1927); G. Gibbs and W. Montgomery, *The Confessions of St. Augustine* (1889).

On St. Augustine's life and work see H. H. Lesaar, *Saint Augustine* (1931); Hugh Pope, *Saint Augustine of Hippo* (1937); E. L. Cutts, *St. Augustine* (1914); William Cunningham, *S. Austin and His Place in the History of Christian Thought* (1886); Pierre Batiffol, *Le*

The City of God. In the infinite ages before time began God was supreme and unchanging, and since time began with His creation of angels and man He has also been supreme and unchanging. As rational beings possessing free wills, angels were not bound to love God, and accordingly some chose to love self. Not by nature but by will did evil exist: "The bad will is the cause of bad actions." The angels who loved self were cast into the chains of darkness; the good angels were bright with the light that came from loving God. The first human parents lived shamelessly in Paradise until the serpent, chosen for the work by the Devil, the leader of the fallen angels, deceived Eve, who, in turn, deceived Adam by bringing him to eat the fruit of the forbidden tree of the knowledge of good and evil. Because of this disobedience the first parents were doomed to beget children in shame, to labor for their sustenance, and to suffer death, and their sin was transmitted to their offspring. But God in His mercy gave some angels and men the grace that made them love him. Since the beginning of time, therefore, angels and men had been divided into two kingdoms—those who love God forming the Holy City and those who love self forming the city of the Devil.

The careers of these two cities run through all time. Already five ages had passed and the sixth was passing. In the first age the sons and daughters of Adam multiplied. Cain built the first earthly city and murdered his brother Abel, a sojourner on earth, for he was a citizen of the City of God. Finally, because men found women too fair, God sent the deluge to destroy them. From this calamity Noah and his sons were saved. The Ark was the symbol of the Church which in time would be the instrument of salvation of all those who love God. In the second age the sons of Noah begat the nations, among which only the Hebrews were the citizens of the City of God. When pride led men to raise the tower of Babel, God struck down their vanity by confusing their tongues. In the third age the only true worship of God survived in the line of Abraham, to whom God promised (1) the land of Canaan as a dwelling place and (2) a blessing for all nations through him. In the Kingdom of Saul was foreshadowed the holy kingdom that was to remain through all eternity. The third, fourth, and fifth ages extended from David to the birth of Christ. In the division of the Kingdom of Solomon was foreshadowed the ultimate separation of the carnal and the spiritual. After the Prophets the Hebrew nation grew more sinful. With the birth of Christ the Word was made flesh, the Holy City became visible as the Church, and the Devil and his hosts of demons raged more violently than ever against those who loved God, but their raging did no harm.

Throughout these ages the City of the Devil had experienced the rise and fall of empires, each of which was the embodiment of human pride and vanity. Before Rome was Assyria, and before Assyria was Babylon.

Catholicisme de Saint Augustine (2 vols., 1920); James Morgan, *The Psychological Teachings of St. Augustine* (1932); H. I. Marrou, *Saint Augustin et la fin de la culture antique* (1938).

Rome was founded when Assyria fell, and like Cain, the founder of the first earthly city, its founder Romulus murdered his brother. Rome, having sought glory, had received its reward. Its success, however, was due to the one true God, not to its false gods, its grandeur to self love, and its licentiousness to the demons which gave moral instruction to its citizens. Its "most insane pomp of human glory" made a mockery of justice.

"Only let it [the Roman state] remain undefeated; they say, only let it flourish and abound in resources; let it be glorious by its victories, or still better secure in peace; and what matters it to us. This is our concern, that every man be able to increase his wealth, so as to supply his daily prodigalities, and so that the powerful may subject the weak for their own purposes. Let the poor court the rich for a living, that under their protection they may enjoy a sluggish tranquillity; and let the rich abuse the poor as their dependents, to minister to their pride. Let the people applaud not those who protect their interests, but those who provide them with pleasure. . . . Let the laws take cognizance rather of the injury done to another man's property, than of that done to one's own person. . . . Let there be a plentiful supply of prostitutes for every one who wishes to use them, but especially for those who are too poor to keep one for their private use. Let there be erected houses of the largest and most ornate description: in these let there be provided the most sumptuous banquets, where every one who pleases, may, by day or night, play, drink, vomit, and dissipate. Let there be everywhere heard the rustling of dancers, the loud, immodest laughter of the theatre; let a succession of the most cruel and the most voluptuous pleasures maintain a perpetual excitement. If such a happiness is distasteful to any, let him be branded a public enemy; or if any attempt to modify or put an end to it, let him be silenced, banished, put an end to."

Worse than the profligacy of the Romans was their refusal to learn the lesson calamities should have taught them.

For Christians, however, calamities, even so great a one as the plundering of mighty Rome, had no meaning because they were but sojourners on earth.

In the seventh age, the beginning of which no man would know, Christ would come to judge the living and the dead. With the Devil chained, Christ and the saints, *i.e.*, those who loved God, would dwell on a new earth for a thousand years. Then the Devil, loosed from bondage, would wage final war against the Holy City. At the close of this war, of three years and six months, the dead would be resurrected in the flesh, the damned would be cast into eternal fire, and the saints, knowing no longer death but remembering their earthly pains, would enter into the kingdom that has no end.

From the seventh age, which would correspond to the day of rest that followed the six days the Lord labored at creation, the eighth age—the "eternal Sabbath"—would proceed. Incorruptible in body, having no capacity to find delight in sin, and possessing no will to love self, the saints would see God. The women among them, more fair than ever, would excite men and angels only to the love of God. All would "rest and see, see and love, and love and praise"; theirs would be "the peace of blessedness and the blessedness of peace."

The significance of the work of Augustine was twofold. First, he gave final theological formulation to the doctrines of divine control over the destiny of men and of the divine mission of the church as the instrument of salvation. Incidentally he set forth many theological views, which although not all accepted by the church, fixed the pattern of Western religious thought for a thousand years and established Latin as the literary language of western Christianity. Second, he embodied in literary forms the psychological mood which lay at the base of the transformation of Greco-Roman into Christian culture. In other words, he achieved, especially in *The City of God*, the complete reorientation of values that was at the heart of this change. His education and experience had prepared him for this achievement. In northern Africa the Semitic and Greek renderings of Christianity flowed together with the Latin. Training as a rhetorician gave him the knowledge of Greco-Roman culture necessary for the work of evaluating it in Christian terms, and experience as a Manichaean emphasized the moral as contrasted with the intellectual approach to this evaluation. In Milan, it is important to note, the study of Cicero, which reinforced his conviction that there can be moral certainty, and the reading of Neoplatonic works, which argued the reality of the spiritual as opposed to the unreality of the material, prepared him for his conversion. The subjectivity which pervaded the mentality of his age became for him a poignant introspection in which human feeling was sublimated in striving for a knowledge of the divine.

It was Augustine's function in the evolution of Christian culture to reduce faith to regimen and lift hope to intellectuality. Thus history became the epic of the saints, and the physical universe the divine poem. With God all things had their beginning; through God all things moved; and in God all things had appointed ends. If there was knowledge, it was God's gift. If there was beauty, it was God's creation. If there was justice, it was God's love. If there was salvation, it was God's grace. No human thing mattered, except as it glorified God, and the church was the eternal embodiment of all that glorified God. It is a fair inference that for Augustine, man, God, and the church were the *actual* Trinity, and of the three the church was the greatest, for only through it did man and

God live as one. By reordering the past, Augustine gave order to the future; his achievement was the tour de force of Christian learning.

THE GREAT THEOLOGICAL CONTROVERSIES.

As late as the year 325, it is said, there were ninety Christian sects. Diversification, it seems, had been the main tendency of Christian development. As is evident, however, in the elaboration of Christian learning, the local cultures of the Mediterranean Basin were being drawn together in a universal organization of the Christian way of life; the great theological controversies of the fourth and fifth centuries were a further development of this universalism. Besides the intellectual issues, which in the main reflected the special outlooks of the local cultures, two factors contributed greatly to these controversies: (1) the imperial policy, which sought to promote religious unity, and (2) the rivalry of the great ecclesiastical centers, especially Alexandria, Constantinople, and Rome, for supremacy in a unified Christianity. Both of these factors tended to make the controversies political struggles in which intrigue, slander, and violence played normal roles. In the main the controversies turned on three points: (1) the unity of God, (2) the freedom of the human will, and (3) the nature of Christ. Bound in with the doctrinal issues were questions of discipline and ritual. Each party to the controversies, it should be realized, insisted upon its adherence to tradition, and no position was so extreme that it could not be defended as apostolic. Thus, although *apostolic* and *orthodox* Christianity were held to be identical, the latter was actually an intellectual version of the former, so encrusted with philosophical subtleties that faith could stand without reason but reason could not stand without faith.[1]

1. *The Arian Controversy.* The Arian controversy had its intellectual roots in the opposing views of the schools of Antioch and Alexandria. The Antiochene scholars, following Lucian (fl. *ca.* 300), who founded the theological system of the school, in asserting the unity of God, denied the divinity of Christ. This position was

[1] On the theological controversies of the fourth and fifth centuries see *The Cambridge Medieval History*, Vol. 1, *The Christian Roman Empire and the Foundation of the Teutonic Kingdoms* (1936), Chap. V, "Arianism," Chap. XVII, "Religious Disunion in the Fifth Century." See also W. Bright, *The Age of the Church Fathers* (2 vols., 1903); F. E. Humphrey, *Politics and Religion in the Days of St. Augustine (395–430)* (1912); Carl J. von Hefele, *History of the Councils of the Church from original documents* (5 vols., 1883–1896); Adolf von Harnack, *History of Dogma* (7 vols., 1894–1899); William Du Bose, *The Ecumenical Councils* (1906).

well stated by Arius (fl. *ca.* 310–336), a pupil of Lucian, who had the audacity to preach his master's doctrine in Alexandria:

God is One, Eternal, and Unbegotten, and all other beings are His creatures. The Logos, therefore, is a creature, and, in fact, is the first of all creation. . . . Jesus Christ is the first of created beings, above the angels, the agent through whom the universe was made. The title "Son of God" may be granted to him on account of his work in creation, but He does not share in the divinity of God, and has no true likeness to it. Since He was Himself created, He is not eternal, and therefore cannot be called God.

As previously noted, Athanasius rose to the defense of the traditional doctrine that, as Christ, God had become man. His support came mainly from the monks swarming in the Egyptian metropolis. Arius, who won a small body of followers by brilliant preaching, was soon driven from the city, but his partisans made life miserable for the bishop. Songs, set to popular tunes of the day, played a part in the Arian propaganda.[1]

Except for the fact that Constantine had made Christianity the state cult this controversy might have burned out as a mere sectarian squabble. But because the Arian doctrine reduced Christ to manhood it endangered the position of the church as a divine institution. Consideration of the church's newly won power necessitated that action be taken to settle the dispute. The emperor, desiring unity of faith for political reasons, initiated this action by calling the first ecumenical council at Nicaea in 325. Among the more than three hundred bishops who assembled, there were three parties: (1) a small group favoring Arius, (2) a somewhat larger group favoring Athanasius, and (3) the majority, which, although willing to condemn Arius, was not inclined to accept the Athanasian formulation of the orthodox belief. The doctrinal issue was clear: "Is God *one* or *three* persons?" The advocates of the Unitarian view opposed logical argument to scriptural citations; the supporters of the Trinitarian doctrine decried the intellectual subtleties of their opponents. Christ, they said, came not to teach men brittle arguments but to give them a simple faith and a good way of life. For two months the parties wrangled, sometimes with little dignity and less piety. The partisans of Arius produced a statement of faith, which their opponents

[1] See *The Cambridge Medieval History*, Vol. I, *The Christian Roman Empire and the Foundation of the Teutonic Kingdoms*, (1936), Chap. V, "Arianism"; H. M. Gwatkin, *Studies in Arianism* (2d ed., 1900).

promptly tore to pieces. Finally all but five of the bishops agreed to a decision upholding the doctrine of the Trinity.

We believe in one God, the Father Almighty, Maker of all things visible and invisible.

And in one Lord Jesus Christ, the Son of God, begotten of the Father [the only-begotten; that is, of the essence of the Father, God of God], Light of Light, very God of very God, begotten, not made, being of one substance with the Father; by whom all things were made [both in heaven and on earth]; who for us men, and for our salvation, came down and was incarnate and was made man; he suffered, and the third day he rose again, ascended into heaven; from thence he shall come to judge the quick and the dead.

And in the Holy Ghost.

[But those who say: "There was a time when he was not"; and "He was not before he was made"; and "He was made out of nothing," or "He is of another substance" or "essence," or "The son of God is created" or "changeable," or "alterable"—they are condemned by the holy catholic and apostolic church.]

The philosophical difficulty presented by the belief in the unity of the godhead and also in three persons was solved by the concept "of one substance." Each of the three persons of the Trinity was considered a *hypostasis, i.e.*, an essential principle of this substance. As previously noted, the mode of thinking which defined the godhead as three persons was derived from the Roman law of personality. To the creed the council added a condemnation of those who taught that there was a time when Christ was not, that He is of a substance other than God, and that He is subject to change. It banished Arius, and Constantine decreed death for anyone who kept his books.

The knotty problem of church government was also considered by the council. Its own authority resided partly in the fact that the emperor, having called the council and presided over it, gave official approval to its acts and partly in the theory that the opinion of the bishops was binding on all Christians. These bases, it is clear, are contradictory, for the former placed the state over the church and the latter implied the independence of the church. A third conception of church government existed in the claim of the bishop of Rome that he was sovereign in matters of faith and ecclesiastical policy. At Nicaea a clear decision on these conflicting theories was not made. The emperor was recognized as having a significant interest and voice in ecclesiastical affairs, and the bishop of Rome was accorded the "primacy of honor" among all the bishops as a

By the courtesy of Antiquity, Vol. 12 (1938)

THE WALLS OF NICAEA

Today a timeless mournful silence broods over the ruined city where Constantine and the bishops made the Trinitarian doctrine the dogma of the Christian church. The oldest parts of the walls were built in late Roman times; some of the arches in the gateways date from the first Christian century.

moral leader. In canons five and six a system of church government was sketched. In each province a bishop was recognized as leader of the church, but his decisions were subject to review by a provincial synod. The bishops of Rome, Alexandria, and Antioch were charged with preserving the ancient customs of their sees. Rome's authority was limited to Italy, Alexandria's to Egypt, and Antioch's to Asia. Actually, of course, the ecumenical council was presumed to have supreme authority over these bishops, as well as all others.

The firm acts of Nicaea did not end the Arian controversy. Constantine wavered in support of the Trinitarian doctrine—so much so, in fact, that when he was baptized on his deathbed he accepted its rival—and Constantius (337–361) his son and successor, openly favored the Unitarian position. In 343 a council at Sardica left the issue as clouded as ever, for, after violently disagreeing, each party withdrew and excommunicated the other. The partisans of Athanasius also passed a resolution allowing a deposed bishop to appeal his case to Rome. From the first Rome had supported Athanasius, and this resolution, which Rome ever afterwards remembered as a conciliar recognition of its ecclesiastical supremacy, bound it more firmly than ever to the cause of orthodoxy. Needless to say the eastern churches never accepted this resolution. In 353 a fierce attack forced Athanasius into exile in the west, and four years later another council adopted a creed declaring the Son unlike the Father. Constantius supported these councils by driving the orthodox bishops, including the pope, from their sees. The effort of Julian to restore paganism did not abate these contentions.

Under Valens (364–378) the Arians continued to hold the upper hand, but with the ascent of Theodosius I the orthodox party recovered imperial favor. The second ecumenical council, which Theodosius I called at Constantinople in 381, formulated the creed which, in Latin form, is used even now in the Roman Catholic Church.

> We believe in one God, the Father Almighty, maker of heaven and earth, and of all things visible and invisible.
>
> And in one Lord Jesus Christ, the only begotten Son of God, begotten of the Father before all Worlds (aeons), Light of Light, very God of very God, begotten, not made, being of one substance with the Father, by whom all things were made; who for us men, and for our salvation, came down from heaven, and was incarnate by the Holy Spirit of the Virgin Mary, and was made man; he was crucified for us under Pontius Pilate, and suffered, and was buried, and the third day he rose again according to the Scriptures, and ascended into heaven, and sitteth on the right hand of the Father, from thence he shall come again, with glory, to judge both the quick and the dead; whose kingdom shall have no end.
>
> And in the Holy Spirit, the Lord and Giver of life, who proceedeth from the Father, who with the Father and the Son together is worshiped and glorified, who spake by the prophets; in one holy catholic and apostolic Church; we acknowledge one baptism for the remission of sins; we look for the resurrection of the dead, and the life of the world to come. Amen.

This statement of the faith, commonly known in the west as the Nicene Creed, followed closely the baptismal confession of the church of Jerusalem.

On the issues of ecclesiastical government the council of Constantinople took an aggressive position. The east was recognized as divided into five patriarchates, and the bishop of Constantinople was accorded a position of honor second only to that of the bishop of Rome. This recognition was incidental to Constantinople's claim to primacy over the other eastern patriarchates. A strict injunction against bishops interfering in affairs outside their jurisdiction was issued.

The victory of the Trinitarian party at Constantinople did not destroy the Arian menace because Arius and many followers, having found refuge among the Teutons, had converted them, so that when they entered the empire they came not as heathens but as heretics. In one way or another the Arian heresy threatened for almost two centuries to disrupt the church.

2. *The Nestorian Controversy.* The declaration of the unity of the godhead raised in a new form the old question of the nature of Christ. If He were God become man, what was the relation of His divine to His human nature? If He were man become God, what was the relation of His human to His divine nature? Tradition held fast to the belief that He was one person with two natures. Tertullian had first formulated this belief as a theological doctrine. But other theologians had difficulty with the doctrine, and during the Arian controversy the problem became acute. Apollinaris, bishop of Laodicea (fl. *ca.* 370), denied that Christ was of the same substance as man. If Christ had a human soul, he argued, He was capable of moral change, hence his sinlessness was questionable. At the incarnation, he held, the Logos displaced the human mind so that Christ had but one nature, the divine. Athanasius held a modified form of this belief, and Cyril (*ca.* 376–444), also a bishop of Alexandria, gave it explicit theological formulation. The Logos, he said, formed one nature with the body by replacing the rational human soul. This doctrine, it should be noted, was a development of the teachings of the Alexandrian school which made Christianity a mystical religion of redemption.

Cyril's advocacy of the doctrine of one nature was bound up with a struggle to maintain the prestige of the see of Alexandria against the see of Constantinople, which, through the elevation of John Chrysostom and, later, John Nestorius, was in the hands of representatives of the Antiochene school.[1] Nestorius (d. *ca.* 451), following the teachings of Theodore of Mopsuestia, taught that Christ had a true human nature and a free human will and, as a result, His was the supreme example of divine life for men. The tendency of this teaching was to emphasize ethical as contrasted with sacramental and mystical religion. In arguing this view Nestorius protested against the orthodox practice of speaking of Mary as the "Mother of God." "Let no one call Mary the Mother of God," he said, "for Mary was a human being; and that God should be born of a human being is impossible." He also protested against speaking of God as if He were two or three months old. Cyril, whose episcopacy was blackened by the mob murder of Hypatia, a famous teacher of Neoplatonism (she was cut to pieces with oyster shells), fierce attacks on the Alexandrian Jews, and the confiscation of the property of the rich who aroused his ire, interfered against Nestorius when certain monks in Constantinople objected to these teachings. Cyril convoked a council at Alexandria which declared Nestorius a heretic and appealed to Rome for support. Because Rome was in conflict with the representatives of the Antiochene school over the doctrine of original sin, Pope Celestine (422–432) ordered Nestorius to retract and authorized Cyril to enforce the order.

At this point the emperor Theodosius II called the third ecumenical council to deal with the dispute. It met at Ephesus in 431. Cyril sent a rabble of monks "to slay the dragon in hell" and, in an unauthorized meeting, deposed Nestorius. The other eastern bishops replied by deposing Cyril. The Roman delegates, who arrived after these events, supported Cyril. Finally the emperor intervened and demanded the deposition of the bishop of Rome, as well as of the bishops of Constantinople and Alexandria. The council in the end affirmed orthodox teachings and deposed Nestorius. In its aftermath many followers of Nestorius, grievously persecuted by orthodox Christians, fled into Mesopotamia and Persia. The victory of Cyril failed, however, to bring peace to the harrassed church, for shortly it became evident that his doctrine was also heretical.

3. *The Pelagian Controversy.* Rome gave support to Alexandria in the Nestorian controversy, partly to weaken Constantinople and partly to resist the Syrian and Palestinian bishops, who had sided against Augustine and the western church in a con-

---

[1] Friedrich Loofs, *Nestorius and His Place in History* (1914); J. F. Bethune-Baker, *Nestorius and His Teaching* (1908).

troversy over the moral freedom of man. Pelagius (*ca.* 360–420), a representative of Christianity as developed among the Celts of Ireland and Britain, came to Rome about the year 400. In line with the general tendency of western theological speculation, he was concerned with problems of sin and salvation. His teachings, summarized in the declaration "If I ought, I can," affirmed man's power to live without sin. In arguing this position he came into conflict with Augustine's doctrines of the depravity of the human race, of the predestination by God of those to be saved, and of the gift of God's grace, which alone gave men the power to overcome sin. His argument ran as follows: (1) Adam was created mortal and would have died whether he sinned or not. (2) His sin hurt only himself, not the whole human race. (3) Children are born innocent. (4) The observance of the law, quite as much as belief in the gospel, leads to heaven. (5) Before Christ there were men who lived without sin. He admitted that men, once having sinned by their own free will, could be restored to holiness only by the gift of grace. Before these teachings attracted much attention, even in the west, Pelagius went to Palestine.

In 411, when Celestinus, a pupil of Pelagius, applied to the bishop of Carthage for ordination, Augustine succeeded in having a synod called to consider his beliefs, and they were declared heretical. Augustine followed up this victory by denouncing Pelagius, but an eastern synod, to which a bishop of Jerusalem summoned him, refused to condemn him. In 418 a council at Carthage affirmed Augustine's teachings, and the pope ordered the western bishops to repudiate Pelagius. The disappearance of the teachings of Pelagius, however, was due more to the dispersal of his adherents by the Vandals when they ravaged northern Africa (*ca.* 429) than to ecclesiastical suppression. They endured for a long time in Gaul, and in the east they were merged with those other beliefs that emphasized the ethical aspects of the Christian life.

4. *The Monophysitic Controversy.* The Council of Ephesus (431) condemned those who taught that Christ was man but not God. Among those who opposed this doctrine were many who held that Christ was God but never actually man. Cyril, bishop of Alexandria, who had fought Nestorius so bitterly, was the greatest of the advocates of this doctrine of one nature; apparently he thought the Council of Ephesus had declared the doctrine orthodox. Consequently there developed quickly a new controversy between the adherents of Cyril's doctrine (called Monophysites, from the Greek term meaning "one nature") and the adherents

of the traditional view of Christ's nature. The leading advocate of Cyril's doctrine was Eutyches (*ca.* 380–456), abbot of Constantinople, who went so far as to assert that Christ's body was not like the body of man. He found support in the emperor, Theodosius II, and in Dioscorus (d. 454), bishop of Alexandria. Leo I, intent on asserting the primacy of Rome, came to the defense of the orthodox position with a letter stating the traditional doctrine of two natures and arguing that the determination of doctrine was beyond the authority of a council. Dioscorus replied by obtaining from a council held at Ephesus in 449 both the deposition of Pope Leo and his condemnation as a heretic. Leo refused to recognize the authority of this council, which became known in the annals of the Roman church as the "robber" or "bandit" synod. Constantinople's jealousy of Alexandria led to the calling of the fourth ecumenical council at Chalcedon in 451 to settle the dispute. In matters of faith Rome was dominant, but in matters of ecclesiastical policy Constantinople had its way. Dioscorus was deposed, and Nestorianism, as well as Eutychianism, was condemned. A Greek version of Leo I's statement of the doctrine of two natures was declared the faith of the church:

> We, then, following the Holy Fathers, all with one consent, teach men to confess one and the same Son, our Lord Jesus Christ, the same perfect in Godhead and also perfect in manhood; truly God and truly man, or a reasonable [rational] soul and body; cosubstantial [coessential] with the Father according to the Godhead, and cosubstantial with us according to the Manhood; in all things like unto us, without sin; begotten before all ages of the Father according to the Godhead, and in these latter days, for us and our Salvation, born of the Virgin Mary, the Mother of God, according to the Manhood; one and the Same Christ, Son, Lord, Only-begotten, to be acknowledged in the two natures, inconfusedly, unchangeably, indivisibly, inseparably; the distinction of natures being by no means taken away by the union, but rather the property of each nature being preserved, and concurring in one Person and one subtance, not parted or divided into two persons, but one and the same Son, and only begotten, God the Word, the Lord Jesus Christ; as the prophets from the beginning [have declared] concerning him, and the Lord Jesus Christ himself has taught us, and the creed of the Holy Fathers has handed down to us.

Two significant decisions on church government were made at Chalcedon. First, monks were brought under the authority of the bishops in whose sees they resided. Second, in the famous twentieth canon Constantinople was declared the equal of Rome. Leo rejected this canon on the ground that it was contrary to the decision of Nicaea because it infringed upon the rights of Antioch and Alexandria. Antioch and Alexandria, however, were so aroused by the condemnation of Nestorius and Eutyches that they separated from both Constantinople and Rome. The breach which resulted was never healed, and the rivalry of Constantinople and Rome was not abated by the fact that they agreed on theological points.

CHRISTIAN CULTURE ABOUT A.D. 500

After Christianity became the state cult it developed under the influence both of the social and cultural factors in Mediterranean life and of the political forces of the empire. The theological controversies reflected these influences, and the conversions which brought the last of the Mediterranean peoples into the church were their result. Political influence was particularly significant because it led to the modification of religious feeling by considerations of ecclesiastical interests. It hastened the spread of Christianity from its original urban centers into the rural areas of the empire, but a fear of peasant revolts prevented the political and ecclesiastical authorities from suppressing paganism in rural areas until after the year 400. It led to an easy acceptance of local cultural materials in the Christian way of life, because the organization of the population under priestly rule was more important than the adoption of the Christian moral code. And it promoted, above all, a syncretism which gave the Christian way of life common characteristics, besides those arising in religious beliefs, throughout its entire area. This syncretism was the climax of that orientalization of Mediterranean life which had progressed along many lines since Hellenistic times. In the fifth century, therefore, Christianity was spread from Persia to Ireland and gave to the peoples of the many lands of this vast area a unity they had never before possessed. This unity was chiefly evident in the creeds and other symbols of the faith; clustered about these basic elements were materials from many sources, but they were so organized that they had meaning in terms of the faith. The boastful praise Tacitus gave Augustus had been prophetic:

For all nations you have made a fatherland.

THE NATIONAL CHRISTIAN CHURCHES.

In spite of the Christian claim that the faith and the church were universal, Christianity never achieved a single ecclesiastical organization; it existed, even in this period of widest unity, as several churches which reflected not only the fundamental cultural differences but also the national rivalries between the converted peoples.[1]

1. *The Roman Catholic Church.* The church at Rome, by virtue of its stanch defense of the apostolic tradition and the prestige of the ancient imperial city, was everywhere accorded "primacy of honor" among the churches. However, this position was not recognized, in spite of Leo I's exertions, as carrying with it a lordship over the other churches. Actually the power of the pope was restricted to Italy and the near-by islands. The churches of Gaul and Spain were self-governing, and the African church, until broken by the Vandal invasion, was a powerful factor in western Christianity. The invasion of the Teutonic tribes, already converted to Arian Christianity, confronted the Roman church with a struggle for survival, the outcome of which was not certain until 496, when the Franks accepted orthodox Christianity. Celtic heathenism was widespread in Gaul long after that date. The literature and liturgy of the Roman church were, of course, Latin, thanks to the great African and Italian Church Fathers. The organization of its priesthood was centralized after the manner of the Roman administrative system. Its political power was inherited from Roman municipal and imperial authorities when they disappeared during the barbarian invasions, and its religious ascendency was asserted in the doctrine that outside its jurisdiction no man could win salvation. Although claiming a universal lordship over Christians, the Roman church in the fifth and sixth centuries was little more than an Italian church. Its claims were significant for the future only if they could be made good.

2. *The Celtic Church.* Besides the Arian churches established by the Goths, Vandals, and Lombards in the Western Roman Empire, a Celtic church developed in Britain and Ireland. Pelagius, whose controversy with Augustine has been sketched, was a representative of the British church, which became well organized in the fourth century. The origin and history of Christianity in Ireland are obscure. Probably the Gaels first came into contact

[1] On the churches separated from Rome see Friedrich Heiler, *Die katholische Kirche des Ostens und Westens*, Band I, *Urkirche und Ostkirche* (1937); W. F. Adeney, *The Greek and Eastern Churches* (1908); L. M. O. Duchesne, *The Churches Separated from Rome* (1907); L. M. O. Duchesne, *L'Eglise au vi⁰ siècle* (1925); Walter F. Adeney, *The Greek and Eastern Churches* (1908); B. J. Kidd, *The Churches of Eastern Christendom to the Present Time* (1927); A. K. Fortescue, *The Lesser Eastern Churches* (1913); F. C. Burkitt, *Early Eastern Christianity* (1904).

with Christianity during the raids into Gaul. Missionaries dispatched by order of the pope at Rome appeared among them early in the fifth century. Patrick (*ca.* 389–461), noted as the first bishop in Ireland, carried on a struggle with the Celtic priests, *i.e.*, the Druids, through missions to various parts of the island. His work as an organizer gave permanent form to the Celtic church. It was tribal and monastic; the tribal chiefs commonly became abbots, and the tribal wars continued as conflicts between the monasteries. The bishops had little or no control over the monks, among whom, in spite of their warlike character, a high level of devotion, ascetic practice, and learning prevailed. Differences between the Celtic and Roman churches as to the date of Easter, the form of the tonsure, the position during prayer (prostration rather than kneeling), the method of baptism, and the subjects of monastic education indicate that the Celtic church received elements from other than Latin sources. During the barbarian invasions, which seem to have destroyed the British Christians, the Celtic church developed independently, preserving a body of learning and a missionary zeal which were highly significant later in the spread of Christianity through northern and central Europe.

3. *The Greek Catholic Church.* The Greek church shared with Rome the inheritance of the apostolic tradition, for at its base were the areas, outside of Syria, which first became Christian. But its organization was the work of Constantine and his successors, who united the church and state. As a result of this union the emperors presided over synods and councils, disposed of church offices, and issued edicts on theological doctrines. The role of imperial policy in the great controversies has been noted. In 381 Theodosius I made the patriarch of Constantinople the minister of state for religion and raised his see to a position second to that of Rome. The subservience of the patriarch to the emperor was galling, and constant disagreements arose between them. At times the patriarch would excommunicate the emperor, and the emperor would seek a way to depose the patriarch. The resistance of the patriarch to state interference usually had the support of Rome and Alexandria. The monks of Constantinople sometimes supported one side and sometimes the other, depending on the theological issues at stake. Frequently there were no significant differences between the religious and the political parties in Constantinople. The patriarchate of Constantinople was established as a result of action by the Council of Chalcedon, which raised the bishop of Constantinople to equality with the Roman pope. Besides Constantinople, the

patriarchate included Thrace, Asia Minor, and Pontus. Constantinople was the heir of the jurisdiction of Ephesus and Antioch.
Beside the rivalry of Constantinople and Rome for ecclesiastical
supremacy, the differences between Greek and Latin Christianity
were unimportant. The liturgy and literature of the Greek church
were, of course, Greek. Variations in vestments, the use of images,
and the ecclesiastical calendar distinguished its worship from that
of the Latin church. Except in the heat of controversy neither
church questioned the orthodoxy of the other.

The Greek Catholic Church occupied the most advanced parts
of the Christian culture area. After the fourth century the leading
cities of the Mediterranean Basin—Constantinople, Antioch,
Damascus, and Alexandria—were in the east where, as economic
decline occured, the centers of wealth production, both agricultural
and industrial, became relatively more important than those of the
west. Eastern Mediterranean life was Greek and Asiatic rather
than Roman. The government was the traditional oriental monarchy, now pervaded with ecclesiasticism as the result of the rise
of the Christian priest class. The economy was almost completely
regimented in the manner of Ptolemaic Egypt. Learning was the
mature product of that syncretism of Greek and oriental materials
which had begun in Alexander's time. The language was Greek,
although Syriac, Persian, and Arabic words were in common use.
And manners and tastes were Asiatic. They were evident especially
in an ornate luxury among the small aristocratic groups and in an
art which, having lost the Greek sense of form, relied upon an
elaborate decoration of surfaces to achieve its effects. The urban
population, the carriers of the culture, was mainly a mixture of
peoples who, from time to time, had been dispersed. The Jewish
Diaspora is remembered because the Jews survived in spite of it,
but the Greeks and, later, the Syrians were also dispersed, and from
them, along with the native elements among whom they settled,
was blended the population of the Byzantine cities.

4. *The Egyptian or Coptic Church.* The separation of the
Egyptian church from Constantinople and Rome occurred as a
result of the Monophysitic controversy. The roots of the break,
however, were far deeper than doctrinal differences. Christianity
was originally restricted to the Greek community of Alexandria,
but early in the fourth century, when the Scriptures were translated into Coptic, the language of the masses, the peasants were
converted. Antagonism between the ruling class and the peasants
found expression in the growth of monasteries, which provided a

refuge from greedy landlords. After Chalcedon, when the Eastern Roman emperor attempted to enforce the orthodox creed, a national movement led by the monks swept the country, and about 550 a national church was established. Officially Egyptian Christianity was Monophysitic, but many of its beliefs and practices were derived from the ancient cults. In fact, Egyptian Christianity, instead of being an elaboration of the doctrines of the great Alexandrian bishops, Athanasius and Cyril, was in many ways a reversion to the old popular religion of the peasant-village masses. The power of the monks was greater in Egypt than in any other Christian country. Only a monk could be elected patriarch.

5. *The Ethiopian Church.* Christianity was carried to Abyssinia first by shipwrecked sailors and slaves. The first missionaries went to the country from Constantinople, but the monks of upper Egypt converted the people. Apparently this conversion was accomplished, as among the Teutons, by winning the favor of royal personages. Athanasius ordained the first bishop of Ethiopia, but during the conflict in the fifth century the Ethiopian church broke away from the Egyptian church. Its Scriptures, translated into the Amharic language about the year 500, were based on Syrian texts, and its creed followed that adopted at Chalcedon.

6. *The Syrian Church.* The fate of the great Syrian church of Antioch was decided by the Nestorian controversy, which drove part of its adherents into Persia and attached the remainder to Constantinople. Rabbulas, the great bishop of Edessa, was chiefly responsible for the victory of Greek Christianity. After Chalcedon a Monophysitic movement spread through the areas adjacent to the Arabian Desert; its leader, Jacobus (fl. *ca.* 550), succeeded in establishing a loosely organized church which preserved Syriac learning.

7. *The Armenian Church.* Christianity penetrated Armenia from Antioch and Edessa in the third century. At the end of the century Gregory the Illuminator (fl. *ca.* 257–332) converted the king, destroyed the ancient temples, and broke the opposition of the military caste to the new faith. He was a member of the royal family, and for over a century the headship of the new faith remained in his line. The ordination of the sons of many of the priests of the traditional religion of the country transformed Christianity into the state religion and gave rise to a national church, headed by an official known as the catholicos. Under Nerses (fl. *ca.* 365) and Sahak (*ca.* 387–439), monasteries, schools, and charitable institutions were established, an Armenian alphabet

was invented, the Scriptures and many Greek and Syriac works were translated, and a well-disciplined clergy was organized. During the conflict between the Eastern Roman Empire and Persia in the early fourth century, the Armenian state was destroyed, but the Armenian church, in spite of fierce persecution, survived. Until the Council of Chalcedon it remained orthodox, but opposition both to Constantinople and to Nisibis, which adhered to the doctrines of Nestorius, finally drove it to adopt the Monophysitic creed. Final separation from Greek Christianity occurred in 491. The council of Tiben in 535 gave enduring organization to the Armenian church.

8. *The Persian Church.* Christianity spread among the working classes of the Mesopotamian cities in the third century, and by the opening of the fourth century Edessa had become one of the most active missionary centers. The Sassanian kings of Persia placed no obstacles in the way of the new faith until war broke out with the Romans in 337. Then the sympathy of the Christians for the Romans, the fanaticism of their bishops, and the hostility of the Mazdaean priests brought on a bitter persecution (*ca.* 339). In 344 death was decreed for all Christians, and as many as sixteen thousand, it is said, suffered martyrdom. A double poll tax was levied upon survivors. After the condemnation of Nestorius the Persians found in the theological strife a reason to relax their hostility toward those holding views condemned by Constantinople. As a result the partisans of Nestorius flocked to Edessa and Seleucia-Ctesiphon. Originally Persian Christianity had been orthodox, but this movement brought about its reorganization as an independent church. In 424 the Nestorians separated from the western churches, set up an independent patriarch, and adopted their own creed and canons. Their liturgy and literature were Syriac. Like the Monophysitic churches, they did not use pictures and images. Infant baptism was not practiced, and marriage was not considered a sacrament. An educational system which used Syriac translations of Greek materials was founded.

By 435 the Nestorian church had spread its influence throughout Persia, to Turkestan, to the Malabar coast of India, and to Ceylon; at that time it had five metropolitans and forty bishops. Barsuma (fl. *ca.* 450), who fled from Edessa when Rabbulas enforced the decisions of the Council of Ephesus, developed at Nisibis a flourishing center of Syriac Christian learning; under his influence Greek learning, as well as Christianity, was adapted to Persian culture. After 489, when the Syriac school at Edessa was closed, Nisibis became the chief intellectual center of Mesopotamia; to it flocked students from all parts of Syria, Asia Minor, and Armenia, and from it flowed a stream of scholars who made a portion of Greek learning familiar not only to the Persians but also to the Arabs.

At its height the Nestorian church of Persia was comparable to the Greek church at Constantinople and the Latin church at Rome. Moreover, its service in transmitting Greek culture to the Persians and Arabs was quite as important as the Greek church's dissemination of Greek culture among the Slavs and the Roman church's preservation of Latin learning among the Teutons. It was, of course, the channel through which Christianity originally penetrated central and eastern Asia.

THE ASSIMILATION OF THE LOCAL MEDITERRANEAN CULTURES INTO CHRISTIAN CULTURE.

In the fusion of Christianity with the local cultures of the Mediterranean Basin, largely through the national churches, many old cultural materials were lost and new circumstances of further development appeared; the result was the emergence of the general cultural situation which was to prevail as long as Christianity was dominant throughout the area over which it had spread.[1]

1. *The Persistence of the Cultural Traditions of the Peoples Converted to Christianity.* Wherever the local culture survived it underwent modifications. In Egypt the ancient tradition which had endured through Hellenistic and Roman times finally disintegrated. Horapollon, an Egyptian antiquarian of the fourth century, knew only fantastic meanings for the hieroglyphs; he wrote in Coptic, the Egyptian vernacular. As previously noted, Syriac learning was an amalgamation of Greek and Semitic materials; it spread through Palestine, Syria, and Mesopotamia. Except for a hardened tradition carried by the dispersed and persecuted Jews, Semitic culture was for a time submerged in Christianity. The center of Greek culture, which, although nominally at Athens, was actually at Alexandria, passed to the new imperial city, Constantinople; there the surviving elements of Greek culture were shaped into the Byzantine forms which persisted during the Middle Ages. With this development Greek culture ceased to be a recognizable influence almost everywhere outside of the Balkan Peninsula and Asia Minor. In the west, Latin materials, assimilated into Christian forms, became the basis of medieval European

[1] See E. L. Woodward, *Christianity and Nationalism in the Later Roman Empire* (1916).

POLITICAL DIVISIONS IN THE CHRISTIAN CULTURE AREA c. A. D. 500

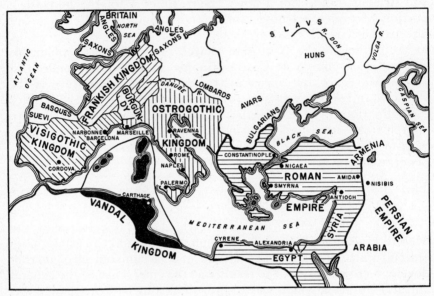

culture. In the lands penetrated by the Teutonic peoples, pagan cultural materials, except those assimilated into Christian forms, generally disappeared. Where the Celtic peoples remained dominant, *i.e.*, in Ireland and Britain, a mixture of Greek, Latin, and Christian materials preserved literate learning at a somewhat higher level than existed in the lands settled by the Teutonic invaders. Just as the foundation of western European culture during the Middle Ages was laid in this interaction between Teutonic and Celtic cultures and Latin Christianity, so was the groundwork of medieval cultural developments in eastern Europe and southwestern Asia established in the contacts of the Slavic peoples with Greek Christianity and of the Arabic peoples with Egyptian and Syrian Christianity. Within the Christian culture area there was unity superimposed upon the fundamental cultural traditions of its several peoples; at the borders of the Christian culture area there were contacts with peoples emerging from nomadic and peasant-village cultures into urban culture. Cultural developments in Europe, Africa, and southwestern Asia in the Middle Ages were greatly influenced by both these circumstances.

These changes were accompanied by the rise of new culture centers. In the Semitic East, Antioch declined and Jerusalem recovered, but more important were Edessa and Amida, where Syriac learning flourished, and Nisibis, where Persian culture absorbed Greek materials. In Egypt, Alexandria retained leadership, but the inland influences which later were to make Cairo the chief culture center of the Nile valley were already at work. In the Hellenized East, Constantinople quickly surpassed all the other centers; in Asia Minor, however, there were several important cities—Nicaea, Ancyra, Laodicea, and Caesarea among others. In Africa drifting sands and invading peoples reduced the old culture centers, and no new ones rose to replace them. In Italy, Rome shared with Milan and Ravenna, where Greek influence survived under imperial patronage, the cultural leadership of western Christianity. In Gaul, Christian culture centered at Marseille, Treves, and Bordeaux and in Spain at Lerida. Celtic Christianity took form at Bangor and Armagh in northern Ireland and Lismore in the south; from these centers it spread to Wales and Scotland. The rise of these new centers (often named after the original ones) reflected, in the shift from coastal to inland cities, the decay of commerce and the dependence upon agriculture which characterized the early Middle Ages.

2. *The Submergence of Pagan Cultural Materials.* From the first the Christians felt themselves at war with pagan culture; Christian writers commonly described it as the work of the Devil. This hostility was directed especially against the ways of living of the Roman ruling classes—their luxury, sensuality, and immorality—but it extended also to the literature, education, philosophy, and arts which were the main elements of their decorative learning. In the same way the amusements and arts which bound the masses to their aristocratic rulers were condemned. Thus the suppression of the pagan cults was accompanied by the disappearance of many other elements of pagan culture. The last prophecy of the oracle of Delphi was pronounced in the reign of Julian. The last Olympian games were held in 393. Three years later the Eleusinian mysteries were celebrated for the last time. Gladiatorial combats disappeared from the Colosseum in 404. Early in the sixth century the curtain came down on other Roman public amusements—the last animal hunt was held in 523, the last theatrical exhibition in 533, and the last race in the Circus in 549. Meanwhile in 529 the schools of Athens were closed, and the remnant of the philosophers and

rhetoricians fled to Persia. With their departure the last carriers of an organized body of pagan learning disappeared.

3. *The Assimilation of the Fundamental Elements of Local Mediterranean Cultures into Christian Culture.* Significant elements of every local culture superseded by the Christian culture found fundamental positions in it. From Sumer came the conception of the physical universe, which set the earth between heaven and hell. From Babylonia came the sense of sin that prostrated man before God. From Egypt came elements of the social outlook that made Christianity an ethical religion. From Palestine came the belief in one God, and the faith that His purpose is the redemption of mankind. From this source also came the belief that this purpose was to be achieved through the Messiah. From Persia came the vision of the hereafter, the array of spiritual hosts, and the conception of the cataclysmic denouement of the drama of redemption. Persian conceptions clarified the belief, strong in Judaism but also found in Egyptian and Greek culture, that earthly life is a moral struggle. From Greece came, above all, the conception of the Messiah as a personal Savior-God. Although the role of this Savior-God in the drama of redemption was developed in terms of the Gnostic doctrine of mediation, the manner of mediation was worked out in accordance with the Greek philosophical conception of the Logos. From Rome came the union of universalism and authority, having form in law, which set up orthodoxy as the necessary mold into which all of these materials should be cast. When the Christian argued that the Roman Empire had prepared the way for Christianity, he was simply declaring that Christian culture was the heir to the universal dominion Rome had exercised. By this assimilation of pagan materials Christianity was transformed from a religious into a cultural organization of life.

4. *The Role of the Priest Class in Christian Culture.* As the distinctive social product of Christianity, the priest class necessarily played the role of chief carrier of its organization of life. In the political struggles and the theological controversies of the fourth and fifth centuries, the interests of this new privileged order generally triumphed. In the main those theological doctrines which endangered the sacramental priesthood, like the Montanist doctrine of an inspired priesthood and the Donatist doctrine of a morally pure priesthood, were declared heretical, and those forms of worship which could be carried on only with priestly functioning became orthodox. That kind of learning which nurtured and

perpetuated the beliefs upon which rested the acceptance of priestly leadership by the masses was fixed in education. To make these statements does not mean that Christian culture was created by the new priest class; it means that Christian culture embodied fundamental psychological elements which could be organized socially only in functions performed by priests. These psychological elements were, of course, the reactions of the masses to repression and exploitation, which moved them to seek release in an other-worldly state combining justice and joy.

Chapter XIX

THE PATTERNS OF CHRISTIAN CULTURE

≪≪≫≫≫

When the shift of values begun in Hellenistic times was completed, earthly affairs went on much as they had always gone on, but they concerned western men less—their eyes were turned toward the New Jerusalem, to which bishops, priests, and monks, under Christ, promised to lead them. At the heart of Christian culture was the fear of hell and the hope of heaven—the sense of human guilt and the love of God; its patterns turned every aspect of life about this center. In the sense that Christianity embodied this center of orientation, it was a *new* culture; in the sense that the materials of its patterns were drawn overwhelmingly from antecedent cultures, it was a *reorientation* of elements of those cultures. In superseding them, its patterns became the enduring elements of the Western cultural tradition.[1]

THE CHRISTIAN RELIGIOUS SYSTEM

The distinctly new patterns of Christian culture formed a religious system having, besides the ecclesiastical structure previously outlined,[2] four main elements: (1) a canon of sacred writings, (2) a systematic body of beliefs, *i.e.*, a theology, (3) a fixed order of public worship, *i.e.*, a liturgy, and (4) a moral doctrine. The sociocultural type organized by these patterns was the spiritually perfect man, *i.e.*, the *saint*, found among men only through God's grace, but universal among those who won heaven through the church.

---

[1] There is no summary discussion of Christian culture at the time it became organized in the Western cultural tradition. Two very useful discussions of the process of this organization are E. M. Pickman, *The Mind of Latin Christendom* (1937), and C. N. Cochrane, *Christianity and Classical Culture: A study of thought and action from Augustus to Augustine* (1940). For discussions of the numerous aspects of Christian culture articles in *The Catholic Encyclopaedia*, Schaff-Herzog's *Encyclopaedia of Religious Knowledge*, and F. W. Hastings, editor, *Encyclopaedia of Religion and Ethics*, should be consulted. Bibliographies on the main aspects of Christian culture are given with the topics of this chapter.

[2] See pp. 1026, 1032.

CANONS OF CHRISTIAN SCRIPTURES.

Uncertainty about the content of both the New and the Old Testament continued through the third and fourth centuries.

1. *The Old Testament Canon.* Christian scholars of the third century became aware of the differences between the Hebrew Bible and the Septuagint, but habitual usage was not to be set aside by scholarship. Largely as a result of the influence of Athanasius and Augustine, the Greek version of the Hebrew sacred writings was adopted by the Greek and Roman churches. Jerome, it should be noted, favored the Hebrew canon. The Roman church recognized the canon of Alexandria at the council of Carthage in 397. The Syriac version followed the Hebrew canon. Chief among the works included in the Greek and Latin versions but excluded from the Hebrew canon were accounts of Hebrew history from the fall of the priestly state to the birth of Christ, notably the books known as First and Second Esdras and First and Second Maccabees.[1]

2. *The New Testament Canon.* Diocletian's attempt to destroy the Christian sacred books, as well as theological controversies, aroused concern as to which New Testament works were to be considered inspired.[2] Differences of opinion between the Antiochene and Alexandrian schools added to the concern. Doubts centered chiefly about the so-called Catholic Epistles—Hebrews, Second and Third John, Second Peter, James, and Jude—and the Book of Revelation. The Epistles were questioned because of their unknown authorship, Revelation because of its content. As was the case with the Old Testament, the influence of Athanasius and Augustine determined the New Testament canon of the Greek and Latin churches. Athanasius' Easter Letter of 367 was the decisive factor for the inclusion of the doubtful works. Under the influence of Augustine the councils of Hippo (393) and Carthage (397) adopted the Alexandrine canon. In 414 Pope Gelasius ratified the decisions of these councils. Jerome's version in the Latin vulgate fixed the canon of the Roman Catholic Church. The Syriac version, known as the Peshitta, excluded four of the Epistles and the Book of Revelation. The Ethiopic version, by contrast, included several works, notably the *Epistle of Clement* and the *Apocalypse of*

---

[1] W. L. Northridge, *The Old Testament To-day: A short Introduction* (1937).

[2] Theodor von Zahns, *Geschichte des neutestamentlichen Kanons* (2 vols., 1888–1892); B. F. Wescott, *A General Survey of the History of the Canon of the New Testament* (1881); D. S. Muzzey, *The Rise of the New Testament* (1900).

Peter, not accepted by the Latin, Greek, and Syrian churches. The *Apocalypse of Peter* and *The Shepherd of Hermas* were accepted as proper works for reading in the Greek and Latin churches until the fixing of the canon in the fourth century. The Armenian and Egyptian versions also differed somewhat from the Latin and Greek canon. Ulfilas (*c.* 311–383), the translator of the Bible into Gothic, did not include the Book of Revelation.

3. *The Apochryphal Christian Writings.* To the works finally excluded from the Old and New Testaments is given the name *Apochrypha.* Originally this word meant hidden or secret, but in the Nicene age, as applied to Biblical writings, it came to mean spurious or heretical.[1] The apochryphal New Testament writings, which survive mainly as fragments, consist of the same kinds of works as were accepted as inspired, namely, gospels, acts, epistles, and apocalypses. About fifty apochryphal gospels are known. Among them the Gospel of Thomas and the Gospel of Mary, both Gnostic in tone, had a wide appeal. Apochryphal acts were collected by the Manichaeans in support of their ascetic morality; those recording the works of Peter, Paul, John, and Barnabas were the most popular. The *Epistle of Clement to the Corinthians* was included, as previously noted, in the Ethiopic New Testament; it compares not unfavorably with the canonical books. The *Apocalypse of Peter* gave an horrendous account of the punishments of Hell. Mothers who abandoned their children were devoured by snakes springing from the milk that flowed from their breasts. Adulteresses were hanged by the hair over a lake of flaming mire. Adulterers were hanged by the feet with their heads in the mire. Worms swarmed over murderers so thickly that they knew only darkness, while the souls of the murdered looked on and cried, "O God, righteous is thy judgment." The entrails of persecutors were devoured by worms that rested not. The rich, clad in rags, turned and twisted on hot gravel sharper than swords. Usurers stood up to their knees in a lake of pus and blood. *The Shepherd of Hermas* described the efforts of a crude but pious herdsman to lead a Christian life in spite of the false prophets and evil daimons ever ready to lead him astray. He found salvation in the exercise of the virtues of faith, love of neighbor, truth, chastity, patience, mercy, and self-restraint. Both of these books suggest the popular, as contrasted with the ecclesiastical, Christian outlook, for their emphasis was on the ethical and daimonistic

---

[1] M. R. James, *The Apocryphal New Testament, Being the Apocryphal Gospels, Acts, Epistles, and Apocalypses* (1926).

rather than the sacramental elements of the faith. They ceased to be read in the churches when popular influence was displaced by hierarchical control.

CHRISTIAN DOGMATIC THEOLOGY.

To revealed truth, conceived as the body of authoritative teachings, is given the name dogmatic theology.[1] The word "dogma" means, basically, the tenets of a philosophical system, and the word "theology" refers to theories of the nature, activities, and purposes of the Deity. Dogmatic theology, therefore, is the systematic exposition of the Christian theories of God as taught by the organized church; it should not be confused with beliefs which an individual Christian may hold as his own. Reference to the creeds adopted by the councils of Nicaea, Constantinople, and Chalcedon will serve to review the general dogmas of the orthodox Greek and Roman churches.[2] Here a brief statement of these dogmas from two points of view is pertinent: (1) as they embody formal doctrines and (2) as they imply broad views of God, man, and the universe.

At the end of the age of theological controversies dogmas such as the following formed the core of the orthodox creeds:

1. *The Trinity:* God is one substance and three persons, the Father, the Son, and the Holy Spirit.

2. *The Fall:* God created man perfect, but Adam's sin of disobedience doomed the whole human race to the loss of fellowship with God.

3. *The Incarnation:* To achieve the purpose of restoring the fellowship of man with God, God became man as Christ.

4. *The Virgin Birth:* God as Christ was miraculously born of the Virgin Mary.

5. *The Dual Nature of Christ:* Christ was at once God and completely man.

6. *The Atonement:* God as Christ suffered and died as man as a sacrifice to redeem the whole human race.

7. *The Resurrection:* God as Christ rose from the grave as a promise of immortality to those who believe in Him.

8. *The Divine Foundation of the Church:* God as Christ founded the Church as the only mode of restoring man to fellowship with God.

---

[1] See W. R. Matthew, *et al., Dogma: Its history and thought* (1929); Lüdwig Ruhland, *Foundations of Morality* (2 vols., 1936); J. Tixeront, *Histoire des dogmes* (3 vols., 1906–1912); Philip Schaff, *The Creeds of Christendom* (3 vols., 1905); and Joseph Turmel, *Histoire des dogmes* (6 vols., 1931–1936).

[2] See p. 1132.

9. *Grace:* God gives to man, through His love, the spiritual assistance necessary for him to escape from sin.

10. *The Second Coming:* God as Christ will return to the earth, the dead will rise from the grave, the just will be saved, and the wicked will be damned eternally.

Clustered about these basic dogmas were other teachings, no less authoritative, which completed the Christian system of theology. The system may be considered under four main heads: (1) God, (2) the universe of created beings, (3) the plan of redemption, and (4) eschatology, or "last things."

1. *The Christian Conception of God.* The Christian conception of the Deity declared God to be a purely spiritual being—immense, unchangeable, omnipresent, omniscient, almighty, uncreated, and immortal. As a personal being He was infinitely perfect—holy, just, merciful, truthful, and faithful to promises. Possessed of supreme intelligence and free will, He was independent of all other beings. As the creator He made all things and fixed the purpose of all things; by His action alone were all things preserved. Although one in substance, God was three persons—the Father, the Son, and the Holy Spirit. As the Father, He created the world, marked the distinctions between good and evil, and set the rewards for merit and sin. The Father was distinguished by works that displayed omnipotence. As Christ He re-established the fellowship between man and Himself, which Adam's sin had broken, and inaugurated the plan of redemption. The Son was distinguished by works of wisdom. As the Holy Spirit He performed works of mercy and love; above all He acted as a teacher of the truth. Thus He bestowed saving grace upon men and gave them manifestations of the divine spirit, known as *charismata*. In the apostolic age these manifestations were nine in number: (1) the gift of speaking with wisdom, *i.e.*, from love of God, (2) the gift of speaking with knowledge, *i.e.*, with the certainty necessary to avoid sin, (3) faith, (4) the gift of healing, (5) the gift of performing miracles, (6) the gift of prophecy, (7) the gift of discerning spirits, (8) the gift of tongues, and (9) the gift of interpreting speeches. The orthodox churches regarded the dogma of the Trinity as embodying a mystery which could be understood neither by reason nor through revelation; because of man's imperfection it had to be accepted by faith. God was knowable, Christians believed, in nature, in the innermost heart (*i.e.*, by introspection), and by revelation. Revelation gave the most complete and certain knowledge because it gave supernatural knowledge. In this connection it should be noted

that Christians always held that God acted among men in ways inexplicable in terms of nature.

2. *The Christian View of the Universe of Created Beings.* The universe and all beings were created by God from nothing and in time. Before the universe was created, time was not; when the universe ended, time would cease. There were three orders of created beings: (1) plants and animals, (2) men, and (3) angels.

Plants and animals possessed only physical life; they were incapable of attaining immortality.

Man, his body created from slime and his soul generated from spirit, had both a physical and a spiritual life. As originally created, man was the image of God, *i.e.*, he possessed reason, intelligence, freedom of will, and freedom from passion and was immortal, both in body and in soul. The whole human race descended from Adam and Eve, the first parents. Adam's disobedience brought death to the body and sin to the soul. Man possessed three attributes significant for the attaining of immortality: (1) freedom of the will, (2) the impulse to sin, and (3) the capacity for faith. By virtue of his free will, man could choose to do good or evil. Under Augustine's influence it came to be held that the corruption flowing from Adam's sin was so complete that man alone was unable to do good. By the capacity for faith man surrendered his reason to God. As an act of understanding, faith involved an act of will, so that in assenting to the authority of God, by accepting His revelation, man placed himself in a state worthy of receiving grace. Thus faith was the primary condition necessary for attaining salvation. All earthly life of man was merely a preparation for the eternal life beyond the grave.

The third order of created beings were angels, who like men were originally destined for supernatural happiness. One among them, Lucifer, became proud and seduced others to commit his sin; for this they fell under God's wrath and were cast into hell. God permitted them to leave this terrible abode in order to tempt men, of whom they were the natural enemies. A man possessed by a devil was believed to have lost his reason and surrendered his will to Satan. Jesus, it was believed, had cast our devils, and the exorcist was long a recognized member of the priesthood. Under the distressing conditions of the third and fourth centuries the belief in daimons was greatly elaborated. Justin Martyr held that they were the offspring of the fallen angels and the heathen gods. Tertullian saw their action in every destructive occurrence, natural and moral alike:

. . . It is in their effects that they are frequently observed as when, for example, some mysterious poison in the breeze blights the blossoms of the fruit trees and the grain, or nips them in the bud, or destroys the ripened fruit, the poisoned atmosphere exhaling, as it were, some noxious breath. With like obscurity, the breath of demons and angels stirs up many a corruption in the soul by furious passions, vile excesses, or cruel excesses accompanied by varied errors. . . . Every spirit is winged, angel and demon alike. Hence in an instant they are everywhere. The world is just one place to them.[1]

The good angels were believed to aid God in the work of salvation, praying for human souls and exhorting men to do good. Clement of Alexandria and Origen developed the doctrine of angels as the guardians of men and nations. The good angels formed a hierarchy of three choirs: (1) angels, archangels, and princedoms, (2) powers, virtues, and dominations, and (3) thrones, seraphim, and cherubim. The last choir surrounded the throne of God; the first associated with men. The Christian belief in angels and devils was only a rendering of the primitive belief in good and evil daimonic powers.

3. *The Christian Plan of Redemption.*   After Adam's sin, God, out of His mercy, promised to restore men to divine fellowship. Originally this promise was made to all men. The central fact in the Christian process of redemption was the atonement. In suffering a sacrificial death, Christ gave full satisfaction for Adam's crime and opened the way to spiritual bliss which original sin had closed. In order that all men might recover fellowship with God, Christ established the church. Through its rites, known as sacraments, which were merely outward symbols of the transmission of God's grace to men, men shared in the spiritual merit Christ's atonement had won. Among the sacraments, two were most important: (1) baptism and (2) the Lord's Supper. Baptism destroyed original sin and regenerated the capacity for a spiritual life. The Lord's Supper, or communion with Christ, supplied the spiritual nutriment necessary for supernatural life. From the foregoing statements it is clear that the Christian process of redemption was entirely supernatural in character; for this reason the church was regarded as a supernatural institution, outside of which no salvation was to be won. It would exist during all time.

Besides having faith and receiving willingly the guidance of the Holy Spirit, the individual could contribute to the achievement

---

[1] Quoted in Adolf von Harnack, *The Mission and Expansion of Christianity in the First Three Centuries* (2 vols., 1908), Vol. 1, p. 138. By permission of G. P. Putnam's Sons, New York.

of his salvation by performing good works; they were understood to be the product of obedience to God's commandments and of the exercise of the virtues of faith, hope, and charity. They preserved and increased God's freely given grace but were not efficacious without it. Those receiving the saving grace became the adopted children of God.

4. *The Christian Eschatological System.* "Last things" necessarily received great emphasis in the apostolic church; however, when it became evident that the Second Coming was indefinitely postponed, the church prepared for a long career on earth and the next world lost some of the vivid reality it had had for the early Christians. At the same time, however, owing to pagan influences, notions of heaven and hell became clearer, and so Christians of the age of theological controversies were completely certain of the rewards or punishments that awaited them in the hereafter. At the Second Coming, which, it was believed, would be accompanied by heavenly signs and earthly disasters, Christ would judge the living and the dead. All would be resurrected in the flesh, and reward and punishment would be enjoyed or suffered in the flesh. The belief that Christ would reign on earth with the saints for a thousand years was not universally accepted. The damned would find eternal punishment in hell. Since this word meant hole, or cavern, it was believed, at least popularly, that hell was beneath the earth. There the fallen angels and lost human souls would burn in eternal fire. Consciousness of their loss and folly was even more painful to lost souls than physical suffering. Children who had died before baptism and men who died before the birth of Christ were confined to limbo. Souls that had died in venial sin were cleansed in purgatory. The doctrine that God could liberate any soul from hell at any time was not accepted. Souls that achieved spiritual perfection during earthly life went straight to heaven. Since, however, men generally died in sin, most souls dwelt for a time in purgatory. One of the chief works of the church was to secure their release and admission to heaven. Heaven was a "glorious abode" somewhere in the skies; pagan imagery gave it the aspects of the Elysian fields. There the saved would live free from sin, enjoy the supreme bliss of the beatific vision, *i.e.*, the contemplation of God, face to face, and act strictly under the inspiration of the pure love of God. Those souls that had won the veneration of men on earth would know a greater bliss than those that had failed to do so.

After the Last Judgment the universe, it was believed, would be destroyed, the damned would suffer forever without alleviation, and the saved would dwell in a state of immortal blessedness and glory.

CHRISTIAN LITURGY AND WORSHIP.

The forms of the public worship of the Christian congregations sprang from the practices of the Jewish synagogues.[1] At first selections from the Hebrew sacred writings, hymns—especially psalms—prayers, and preaching were combined differently by each congregation. The Apostles made no arrangement of rites. With the rise of the bishops, formal arrangements took shape, probably as early as the opening of the second century; they assumed elaborate forms under pagan influences in the fourth and fifth centuries. All worship was believed to be communion of man with God. Private devotion was also formalized, although not to the same degree as public worship, under the influence of the bishops.

1. *The Christian Sacraments.* At the heart of Christian worship were the sacraments, particularly the Lord's Supper, known in the east as the Eucharist and in the west as the Mass. Christians believed that it had been instituted by Christ when, in breaking bread at the last meal with the Apostles, He had said, "This is my body." Paul was inclined to regard the rite as a memorial; John, author of the Fourth Gospel, defined the rite as communion with Christ and established the belief that in partaking of the bread and wine the believer was eating the "flesh and blood" of Christ. When the belief that participation in this rite was necessary for salvation became established is not exactly known, but by the second century it was everywhere the foundation of orthodox worship. Numerous superstitions were attached to the rite at various times. In the early phase of its development the bread and wine were looked upon as luck charms. Under Gnostic influence the rite was regarded as a form of magic; orthodox opinion repudiated this view in favor of a conception that emphasized its moral significance. Bodies receiving the bread and wine were believed to be no longer perishable from the corrupting force of sin. Wine superseded water in the performance of the rite at the end of the fourth century; unleavened bread, similar to the bread of the Jewish Passover meal, was used from the first. Great care was taken by the priests to prevent the spilling of a crumb of bread or a drop of water or wine. In the third century certain churches arranged the bread in the form of a man, "so that one communicant should eat Christ's ear, another His eyes, a third

[1] L. M. O. Duchesne, *Christian Worship: Its origin and evolution* (1903).

His finger, and so on according to their social rank."[1] Cyril of Jerusalem first stated the philosophical doctrine that the bread and wine were changed into the flesh and blood of Christ. This belief, like the dogma of the Trinity, rested on Aristotle's doctrine of substances. Historically the Lord's Supper was the Christian counterpart of the sacred meal of the Greek and oriental mystery religions and Judaism; its ritualistic significance was similar to the chief rite of Mithraism.

Originally baptism seems to have been a Jewish ceremonial used in the initiation of gentile proselytes into Judaism. Christians believed that Christ had instituted it. Paul took it for granted. During the conversions it was extremely important, and a period of severe preparation was necessary before it was given. In the east it was believed that the rite made possible for the individual the beginning of a spiritual life; in the west it was held that the rite enabled the individual to turn from a life of sin to a life of moral striving. In either case it was regarded as making possible man's "union with Christ." As a result of the Pelagian controversy the baptism of infants became customary. Augustine's doctrine of original sin gave final theological justification to the rite. Natural water only was used in the performance of the rite; the words "with the Holy Spirit" were uttered by the priest just after the individual was touched by the water.

Other sacraments, probably as many as thirty, were observed by the early Christians. Some were based on Jewish worship; others sprang from New Testament sources. Of the latter kind was the practice of speaking with the "gift of tongues" which had a place in the worship of the early congregations; as previously noted, it disappeared as a result of rising priestly influence in the second century. The practice of the "laying on of hands" became the special sacrament of the priests, for by means of it their supernatural function was preserved and transmitted. The practice of anointing with oil, or unction, was originally a healing rite. Penance developed into a sacrament as a means of enforcing moral control upon the members of the congregations; it became more and more important as the power of the priesthood increased. The sacrament of marriage arose from Paul's teachings. These sacraments, along with baptism and the Lord's Supper, were practiced in different forms in the several churches during the age of the theological controversies; no clear sacramental system took form in that age.

[1] Arthur Weigall, *The Paganism in Our Christianity* (1928), p. 147.

The word "sacrament" was derived from a word signifying the pledge given by a participant in a lawsuit; in theology the sacrament was regarded as a physical symbol of supernatural action. The sacraments were God's way of dealing with imperfect man, and the church was their custodian. In Tertullian's view the sacraments were the entire church. Augustine considered them the only channels by which the supernatural grace necessary for salvation came to men; in fact, he always spoke of "sacramental grace." Contention over the efficacy of the sacraments and their ministration long disturbed the congregations. As previously noted, the Donatists held that an impure priest could not perform the sacraments; the orthodox church required only that the priest be duly ordained and the form of the rite strictly followed. Augustine expressed the orthodox view emphatically: "Between an Apostle and a drunken man there is a great difference; but between the baptism of Christ which an Apostle and that which a drunken man gives there is no difference." For the laity participation in the sacraments meant the winning of eternal life; for the priesthood they were the means of control of the spiritual life of the congregations; and for the church—if a distinction is to be drawn between it and the priests and the congregations—they were the instruments by which its supernatural function was performed. As the visible form of the invisible society of saints, the church, indeed, was a sacramental institution—the supreme mode of God's action among men: His pledge of redemption.

2. *Christian Worship.* Special orders of acts were developed for worship performed at different times. On Sunday, the chief day of worship, elaborate ceremonies, featured by hymns, processions, and prayers, particularly for the dead, were performed. The use of lights, incense, singing, various gestures (such as genuflection and prostration), and vestments were taken over mainly from the Greek and Egyptian mysteries.[1] From the same source came holy water, oil, candles, and beads. By the fourth century Sunday morning worship was begun by the singing of the Gloria in Excelsis Deo ("Glory be to God on high"), and evening worship was closed with the doxology. The wording varied according to the several theological dogmas of the nature of God and Christ. Wednesday and Friday were kept as fast days. The sacrament of the Lord's Supper was generally celebrated on these days. In the African church the sacrament was for a long time celebrated every day. Ordinary believers said prayers in the morning at cock's crow

[1] See article "Paganism" in *The Catholic Encyclopaedia.*

—*matins*—and in the evening at candlelight—*vespers*. In the churches the priests said prayers six times a day. At first ordinary believers participated actively in worship, saying "amen" and shouting "alleluia" and "hosanna." However, as priestly control developed, popular participation in worship was restricted to such simple acts as saying a few prayers, for example, "Lord have mercy on us" and "Peace be with you," singing the doxology, and receiving the sacraments.

The elaboration of vestments necessary for liturgical functioning was only an aspect of the several developments which contributed to the clear differentiation of the priesthood and the laity. In the fourth century differences in garb for the holders of the various church offices appeared. Great impetus was given to this development by Constantine's political recognition of the church. Before Constantine vestments generally followed the secular forms of dress of the early Greek Christians; after him oriental influence became dominant.

The outcome of these diverse movements was a worship consisting of elaborate rituals performed by an ornately vested priesthood, before which, indeed, it was fitting that the laity—the vulgar multitude—should stand penitent, humble, and awed.

3. *The Christian Religious Calendar.* By the fourth century a cycle of regularly recurring religious festivals followed the year around. The Christian religious calendar, although determined by the leading events in the life of Christ, was derived from the traditional religious calendars. The Greek church followed closely the Jewish calendar; the Latin church, the pagan. The climax of the religious year was the Easter festival commemorating Christ's work on earth. Holy Week began with Palm Sunday, commemorating Christ's entrance into Jerusalem, and ended with the close of Easter Sunday, commemorating the Resurrection. On Thursday of Holy Week, known as Maundy Thursday, was celebrated the establishment of the sacrament of the Lord's Supper. The Crucifixion and the Ascension were also observed during the week. Contention about the date of Easter, arising out of differences between Jewish and Greek practices, long agitated the church; the council of Nicaea decided in favor of the Greek practice. After Holy Week, rejoicing continued for a period of seven weeks, known as Eastertide. Lent was originally a forty-hour period of fasting and watching kept in the church of Rome; the council of Nicaea lengthened the period to forty days and extended it to the whole church.

The historical antecedents of the Easter festival were the spring celebrations of the rebirth of life, as old certainly as the worship of Ishtar. Some Christian practices connected with the day, such as the giving of eggs, sprang from Persian sources. In the Mazdean religion the egg symbolized the world for which Ormazd and Ahriman would contend until Judgment Day; for Christians the egg symbolized the Resurrection, and they colored it red as an allusion to the blood Christ shed for their redemption.

If Easter was eastern in origin, Christmas was western. As previously noted, the date, December 25, was the birth date of Mithra; the customs that came to be connected with the day, such as giving gifts, especially dolls and cakes, lighting candles, and singing, were Roman. The Romans also gave gifts at the New Year. By the fourth century this celebration of the Incarnation had become the greatest festival of the Latin church. In 376 the festival was introduced in Constantinople, in 380 in Antioch, and in 430 in Alexandria.

The four Sundays preceding Christmas were kept as vigils, or watches. The feast of the Epiphany, commemorating the visit of the three wise men to Christ, was celebrated on January 6. Apparently it was first observed by the disciples of Basilides the Gnostic; the church did not adopt it until the fourth century. In some congregations the feast marked the birthday of Christ. Candlemas originally commemorated Christ's entrance into the Temple; in the Armenian church it still retains this significance. The date, February 2, was fixed at the end of a forty-day period beginning at Christmas. The identification of the day with the Purification of the Virgin Mary in the Latin church, although not established until the eighth century, followed a very old tradition. The celebration originally arose at Jerusalem.

4. *The Veneration of the Saints.* Closely connected with the formation of the Christian religious calendar was the development of the worship of saints, for it gave rise to many holidays. In time, indeed, almost every day in the year was set aside for the commemoration of some saint. At first, as previously noted, the term "saint" was applied to all believers. But in the second century it came to be applied to those who exhibited remarkable piety, particularly the martyrs; later it was applied to great ascetics and officials who had rendered noteworthy service to the church. The veneration of the saints arose from the belief that after death the soul lingered near the body; thus the graves of the martyrs, regarded as sacred places, became the sites of chapels and churches.

A prayer addressed to the saints, who were believed to live in the presence of God, was thought to win their intercession in favor of the worshiper. Miracles occurred, it was believed, as a result of successful intervention.

Augustine, who defined the place of the veneration of the saints in Christian worship, drew a clear distinction between the worship of God and the cults of the saints. These cults took the place of the ancient popular cults of heroes and minor deities; in fact, the shrines and festivals of these cults were generally absorbed into Christianity. A notable example of this absorption is All Saints' Day—Halloween is the vigil of All Saints' Day—which arose when a Roman temple, dedicated to Jupiter and minor deities of all sorts, was transformed into a shrine of the Virgin Mary and all the saints. The rise of the cult of the Virgin also illustrates this process. As early as the second century the Virgin Mary was the subject of special veneration; in the fourth and fifth centuries, during the theological controversies, she emerged as the leader among the Christian figures below the Trinity. As the Mother of God her power of intercession with the Son was believed to be very great. Prayers to her indicate that she was thought of very much as the traditional Mother Goddesses—Ishtar, Isis, Anahita, Tellus, and Cybele—had been. Commonly she was addressed, as they had been, with the title "Queen of Heaven." The worship of angels was common, especially in Asia Minor, until prohibited in the fourth century.

The veneration of relics arose along with the worship of saints. From the middle of the second century the bodies of martyrs were regarded as possessing special powers. In some churches their bodies were preserved unburied; in order that their powers might be widely available the bodies were divided up and distributed among the congregations. Theodosius prohibited this practice, and the Latin church long resisted it. Cyril of Jerusalem developed the theological theory of the power of relics; the Greek church fathers generally approved of their veneration.

The worship of saints and the veneration of relics were associated with the use of sacramentals, *i.e.*, objects, gestures, and prayers regarded as having special efficacy in warding off daimons.[1] Among the sacramentals may be enumerated holy water, images of saints, the crucifix, and the sign of the cross. In popular belief

---

[1] See article "Sacramentals" in *The Catholic Encyclopaedia:* "One of the most remarkable effects of sacramentals is the virtue to drive away evil spirits whose mysterious and baleful operations affect sometimes the physical activity of men. To combat this occult power the Church has recourse to exorcism and sacramentals."

the practices were substituted for the ancient worship of idols, magic, divination, astrology, dream interpretation, and oracles, against which the church set its face. Opposition to these pagan practices did not rest, however, on the belief that they were false, but on the belief that they were the work of evil powers. Theodosius, the great imperial partisan of orthodoxy, who legislated against these pagan practices, did not authorize the punishment of persons who used magic to cure disease or to protect growing fields. The monks, whose influence among the laity was at its height in the fourth and fifth centuries, played a great part in the assimilation of these pagan practices into Christian worship.

As a whole, Christian worship may be seen to have been a vast complex of acts, some public and formal and others individual and incidental, designed to win supernatural aid and to resist supernatural attack; except as they served the soul in quest of an eternal spiritual life, they had neither meaning nor significance. Actually, however, these acts wove the faith into daily life throughout the year. In every crisis of individual life the church assumed responsibility; at the performance of every significant social event, the church presided. Worship was not merely an attitude of mind; it was a way of life. Ritual and orderly living were *one* again, as they had been under the ancient-oriental urban cultures.

Christian Moral Doctrine.

"Man is made for God, and only for God," said Augustine, "that he may possess Him here below through faith, and possess Him hereafter in eternal glory. He seeks in vain for rest in the fruition of any other object." To this end all conduct tended. Good conduct contributed to the ultimate union with God; evil conduct made less likely or impossible that union. Morality, therefore, like every other element of the Christian religious system, had meaning only in supernatural terms. The great obstacle to union with God was moral evil, or sin. Fundamentally sin was revolt against God— the willful refusal to love Him and obey His commandments. Morality, by contrast, was the love of God and obedience to His commandments. Two conceptions are basic, therefore, to Christian morality: (1) sin and (2) the moral law.

1. *The Christian Conception of Sin.* Sin existed with God's knowledge but not by His creation. When angels and men were endowed with free will, they could choose to love God or self. The angels who chose to love self became the daimons, the tempters of men. When Adam disobeyed God's command, he doomed the

human race to a life of sin. The Fall was the decisive event in the moral evolution of mankind, for from its corrupting influence no human being escaped except by God's grace. Moral conduct in this world was, therefore, a miraculous occurrence because it was possible only as the result of supernatural intervention. As originally created, the world was not evil; as constituted by the daimons and men, it was completely corrupt, lacked all saving virtue, and opposed all that was godly. Christians, who, because of their faith, had begun the climb back to God, lived *in* the world but were not *of* it. To use it in the achievement of their otherworldly goal was allowed; to enjoy it for itself was sinful.

Christians saw sin as having two sources: (1) temptation, *i.e.*, the promptings of daimons, and (2) the impulses of man's lower nature. Lower nature was to be understood as those attributes of man other than the Godlike qualities, rationality and free will. Neither temptation nor lower impulse was operative, however, except as it overcame the will. Moral freedom was the distinctive quality of man, and sin, with all its consequences, was of his own choosing. God stood ready to support the man who chose to live purely, but the choice was strictly the man's.

Sin, it was believed, consisted of two kinds of acts: (1) willful transgressions of the moral law and (2) incidental manifestations of the lower nature. The first, known as mortal sins, were pride, avarice, intemperance, lust, sloth, or failure to do good works, envy, and anger. Crimes such as idolatry, murder, adultery, and apostasy were mortal sins. Because they deprived the soul of immortal grace, they entailed the penalty of eternal damnation. Origen described them as bringing punishments that burned like wood. Venial sins were committed by every man in his ordinary daily conduct. They were the incidental failures to conform to the moral law which occurred in the harsh word, the broken promise, the lustful glance, and the forgotten prayer. Whereas the mortal sins involved the willful setting of self before God, the venial sins involved only the forgetting of God in the presence of self. The venial sins occurred because man was morally weak, not because he was corrupt. Origen described them as burning like stubble. Sins were recognized as being committed against the different persons of the Trinity. Sins against the Father were committed because of moral weakness, against the Son because of ignorance, and against the Holy Spirit because of malice. For this last sin there was no forgiveness because it involved either the willful refusal to accept the truth or the fixed determination not to repent. To fail to heed

the promptings of the Holy Spirit was not only the supreme
assertion of self-love but also the supreme refusal of God's grace.

By sin man was morally enslaved; only by the willed love of
God was a pure life possible, and its goal was immortality.

We are fallen creatures, and our spiritual life on earth is warfare.
Sin in our enemy, and while of our own strength we cannot avoid sin, with
God's grace we can. . . . Left to ourselves, we fall, by keeping close to
God and continually seeking his help we can stand and struggle against
sin, and if faithful in the battle we must wage shall be crowned in heaven.[1]

The Christian's awareness of sin gave reality to his fear of hell and
hope of heaven.

2. *The Christian Moral Law.* If man willed the evil, God
willed the good. The moral law arose from God's creative action. It
neither existed in nature nor opposed nature; it was above nature.
Man knew it only by revelation. Christians recognized the moral
law as having two parts: (1) the "old law" as revealed by Moses
and (2) the "new law" as revealed by Christ. Obedience to the
Mosaic law assured that man committed no moral wrong. Obedience to Christ's law assured that man loved God. The new law set
no new moral precepts, only new moral obligations. Chief among
these were the acceptance of the revealed truth, the observance
of the divinely established sacraments, and the acceptance of the
church as the interpreter of the moral law.

Augustine explained that the purpose of the moral law was to
direct all conduct toward the goal of union with God, and that
such conduct expressed itself in two ways: (1) in contemplative
purity of heart and (2) in active brotherly love. On one side purity
of heart involved the suppression of self-love which led to mortal
sin; on the other side it produced meekness, humility, and obedience. Concretely it took two forms: (1) self-denial, which evidenced
the breaking of the individual will, and (2) abject acceptance of
ecclesiastical rule. From the first arose asceticism; from the second
flowed priestly supremacy. Both manifestations of purity of heart
were believed to produce the merit that made the individual
worthy of receiving the saving grace. The pious heart was the
foundation of individual morality. Love of neighbor and love of
enemy originally inspired individual acts of kindness; as organized
under priestly control, such love became the consciousness of the
church's mission, for the love of man meant not ministration to his
earthly need but the direction of his will toward his supernatural
goal. Good works were the worldly forms that the service of this

[1] See article "Sin" in *The Catholic Encyclopaedia.*

supernatural purpose took. They increased the merit won by the pious heart.

Like the pagan philosophies, the Christian religious system embodied a catalogue of virtues which, if practiced, would produce the good life. These virtues were of three orders: (1) theological, (2) moral, and (3) religious. The theological virtues were faith, hope, and charity. Faith—a duty to God and the church—bound man to accept every revealed truth. Hope was confidence in God's goodness and an eager awaiting of His saving grace. Charity insured obedience to the commandments to love God and neighbor. Infidelity, apostasy, and heresy flowed from lack of faith. Despair or overconfidence arose from lack of hope. Every mortal sin was likely to be committed from lack of charity. The theological virtues were necessary for obedience to the moral law. The moral virtues were prudence, temperance, fortitude, and justice. They were regarded as natural manifestations of the love of God. Ambrose adapted them from Plato to the Christian way of life. The religious virtues took form in active participation in the life of the church— in obedience, in the profession of faith, in praying, and in strict performance of vows and duties. Actions such as sacrilege and blasphemy, which tended to dishonor God, had origin in the failure to practice the religious virtues. The Christian virtues emphasized *duty* as contrasted with *right;* the individual was urged to seek aggressively the glorification of God in the immolation of self:

Come, then, soldier of Christ, take to heart these small lessons from human affairs and consider eternal blessings. Set before thyself a life without house, city, or possessions. Be free, released from all worldly cares. Let not love of woman enchain thee, nor solicitude of child. For in the divine warfare this cannot be. "For the weapons of our warfare are not of the flesh, but mighty before God."[1]

The Christian Saintly Ideal.

Christianity is a religion of personal striving for spiritual perfection. It is an ethical religion because moral actions contribute to the attainment of this perfection. It is a theistic religion because God is conceived as a person caring for the spiritual welfare of every human being. Its ideal is the saint, whose distinguishing attribute is the love of God.[2] The saint has no interest in the world. Completely holy, he does not sin. He submits patiently to bodily suffering, poverty, and persecution. He envies neither the rich

[1] W. L. Clarke, *The Ascetic Works of Saint Basil* (1925), p. 56, The Macmillan Company, New York.
[2] See F. W. Halweck, *A Biographical Dictionary of the Saints* (1924).

nor the powerful. He forgives those who injure him and loves those who declare their enmity to him. He is kind to all men, particularly to the weak, the poor, and the afflicted. He avoids contention, anger, and violence. He is meek, gentle, patient, and magnanimous. He is chaste. In the face of pain and evil he is courageous and long-suffering. He is obedient to authority and respectful to the law. In brotherly love he manifests his love of God. Repudiation of the world is the mark of moral worth but not the goal of spiritual striving. This goal is attained only when the saint, infused with the saving grace, is sanctified, *i.e.*, when he becomes incapable of all else but the love of God. The way to this goal is beset with temptation, but with eyes fixed on eternal things the saint struggles on, certain that because he loves God, God's love makes his attainment of perfection possible. The rule of love is the supreme Christian law.

For the few, sainthood is possible in this world; for all the faithful it is the reward of heaven. In this world sainthood is a miracle of God's mercy; in the next world it is the full realization of God's purpose for men.

THE CHRISTIAN INTELLECTUAL SYSTEM

The religious system sketched in the preceding pages was the expression of the attitude toward life which underlay the shift in values that occurred in Hellenistic and Roman times; as the chief intellectual product of this change, it embodied not only the Christian outlook upon life but also the main forms of knowledge which were important in terms of this outlook. However expressed —"spirituality," "moral perfection," "eternal things," "the supernatural," or "God"—the leading motif of the system was the hope of otherworldly release from evil. As an ideological structure the system described the mode of this release, the manner of its achievement, and its forms. For Christians all other kinds of intellectual enterprise and learning were subverted to the rendering of this motif: "Theology is the queen of the sciences."

But there were lesser products of this shift important for the development of learning and education. Clustered about religious beliefs, they completed the intellectual system of Christian culture.

THE INTELLECTUAL METHOD OF CHRISTIAN CULTURE.

Chief among these products was a way of thinking which, worked into the various fields of learning and art, gave them distinctive Christian qualities.

An intellectual method consists of a selection of materials from experience, an interpretation of these materials in terms of a number of basic assumptions, and the integration of these interpretations in a coherent body of ideas and values. When the psychological processes involved in such selection, interpretation, and integration are recognized, the procedures constitute a formal intellectual method; when each of the procedures is examined and evaluated with reference to a possible contribution to error, they become a critical intellectual method. When these procedures remain unrecognized, they constitute an intellectual method the existence of which is unknown to the men who use it. In primitive and ancient-oriental cultures intellectual methods were completely lacking in formality. In the early Asiatic urban cultures there was only slight recognition of intellectual procedures. Greek culture produced the first somewhat critical intellectual method. The Christian intellectual method was formal but not critical.

1. *Revelation as the Source of Truth.* At its heart was revelation, *i.e.*, the transmission of truth from God to man. The modes of revelation were several. Moses heard God speaking from the burning bush. The Hebrew Prophets spoke with divine inspiration. The entire life of Jesus was a revelation. Paul saw Jesus in a trance. John had visions. The early Christians "spoke with tongues." These examples indicate that extraordinary physical events, emotional fervor, trances, visions, and various psychological promptings were regarded as the experiential manifestation of revelation.

Orthodox Christians held that, with the Apostolic tradition, revealed knowledge became complete, although they believed that the Holy Spirit continually prompted men to have faith and guided the bishops when they assembled in a council to interpret the divine law. Together the revelations to the Hebrews and the revelations through Jesus formed a *sacred tradition;* as embodied in Scripture, it dominated all Christian thinking. "It is not permitted," declared Leo I, "to depart even in one word from the doctrine of the Evangelists and the Apostles, nor to think otherwise concerning the Holy Scriptures, than the blessed Apostles learned and taught." Clement of Alexandria held that nothing in Scripture contradicted human reason. "The authority of Scripture," said Augustine, "is higher than all effort of human intelligence." "The Gospels," affirmed Basil, "need no dreams to add to their credit." The Church Fathers generally agreed that knowledge other than that embodied in the sacred tradition was of little or no use, if not actually dangerous, to men. For men, then, the chief intellectual act was faith; and credulity, as evidence of the willingness to believe, was praised as an intellectual virtue. The chief function of reason was to explain what appeared to be contradictions between revealed knowledge and experience. In the cases of certain scriptural truths, such as the doctrine of the Trinity, faith accepted them as divine mysteries too subtle for human intelligence to understand. The validity of revelation was proved rationally, it was held, by the fulfillment of the Hebrew prophecies in the life of Jesus. The miracles accompanying the revelations were regarded as testimonials of their divine source. In other words, every revelation was evidence of a succeeding revelation, and, as the fulfillment of a prophecy, a proof of an antecedent revelation. "Thus it is manifest that each link in the chain of revelation carries with it a triple evidence of its divinity."[1]

2. *Allegory.* Because revelation was not to be understood without interpretation, the chief procedures of the Christian intellectual method were aids to the discovery of the meaning of Scripture.[2] As previously noted, the Antiochene and Alexandrine schools produced rival methods of interpretation. The Antiochene school favored a literal interpretation, supported by historical exposition. This method, it would seem, should have produced an accurate rendering of scriptural meaning, but because of the obscurity of language, the obvious contradictions, and the confused symbolism of the sacred texts it merely promoted the growth of a somewhat incoherent, though rigid, construction of the faith. The Alexandrine allegorical method gave freedom from mere verbalism and opened the way for the fusion of philosophy and faith.

The chief impulses to the development of Christian allegory came from the need to interpret the Old Testament against the Jews, who made it the support of the "old law" of Moses as opposed to the "new law" of Jesus, and to save the New Testament from Gnostic distortions. Origen laid down the formal basis of Christian allegorical method; among its leading expositors in the west was Cassian, who introduced Egyptian monastic law into Gaul. He held that four meanings were to be found in a Biblical

[1] James Conway, editor, *Handbook of the Christian Religion for the Use of Advanced Students and the Educated Laity,* trans. from the German of Rev. W. Wilmers, imprimatur Archbishop of New York (3d ed., 1891), p. 52.

[2] See Edwin Hatch, *The Influence of Greek Ideas and Usages upon the Christian Church* (1890), Lecture III, "Greek and Christian Exegesis," on the Christian use of allegory.

verse: (1) the obvious or historical meaning, (2) a moral significance, (3) a prophetic declaration, and (4) a revelation about life
in the other world. Augustine fixed allegory in Christian thinking
by embodying in his influential work on preaching and education,
On Christian Doctrine, the seven rules of Tichonius (fl. *ca.* 400), an
African Christian, who wrote a textbook on the method. His rules
indicated the meanings to be ascribed to certain references and
usages throughout the sacred texts. Under the influence of the
allegorical method every letter and word of a historical document
and every object and event of nature became the symbol of hidden
meaning. And meaning, however symbolized, merely made more
clear or more complete the understanding of the divine plan.[1] The
most enthusiastic Christian allegorists held that the actual scriptural texts were shadows of the "eternal Gospel" kept in heaven.

3. *Authority.* When faced with a diversity of interpretations
of Scripture, Christians fell back upon authority as the final arbiter
between truth and error. At first this authority was exercised
by the bishop over his congregation; later it became the function
of the bishops assembled in council. Theology taught that the
assembled bishops spoke with the guidance of the Holy Spirit, and
consequently, to refuse to believe what they pronounced as truth
was to commit the unpardonable sin. Behind the faith also was
tradition, which, witnessed by the bishops, was no less valid than
Scripture. Scripture and tradition, interpreted by the bishops, were
the living truth. Thus ecclesiastical officials came to exercise an
ultimate jurisdiction over Christian thinking. By virtue of its
predication of revealed truth, Christian thinking necessarily became authoritarian, for obviously revelation, unsupported, could
be superseded by new revelation or demolished by reasoning from
contrary assumptions. Against both, only authority could prevail—
an authority which at first threatened the unbeliever with otherworldly damnation but soon found ways to punish him with
earthly pain.

[1] E. M. Pickman, *The Mind of Latin Christendom* (1937), pp. 112–114: "By the year
400, therefore, this tendency to explain everything symbolically was running riot throughout the Roman Empire. There seemed no end to its possibilities, nothing that it could not
explain. Numbers, herbs, animals, precious stones, qualities of density, shape, and colour,
words and names—all these were henceforth interesting and real only in so far as they were
significant of something else. And natural events which were in any way unusual or variable,
such as storms, floods, droughts, plagues, heavenly conjunctions, eclipses, and comets,
were each observed only in order to learn of what they were a premonition, of what they
were a consequence—always as symbols. . . . Thus the ancient world, pagan and Christian
alike, collapsed in an orgy of symbolism." By permission of the Oxford University Press,
New York.

4. *Mysticism*.   Within the faith Christians recognized a mode of experience that gave a direct knowledge of God; to this mode is generally given the name "mysticism."[1] It rests upon the assumption that man, disregarding sensory experience, can have an inward or intuitive experience of spiritual reality; this assumption embraces the belief that the soul, a part of spiritual reality, can by itself know that reality. Insofar as Christianity or any other religion seeks to bring the soul into union with God, conceived as pure spirituality, it is mystical. Outward concomitants of mystical experience are quietism, asceticism, and ecstasy. Quietism is the avoiding of all physical action and material interests in order to attain experience of spiritual reality. Asceticism is mortification of the flesh and contempt of the material world in order to achieve the purity of soul necessary to know spiritual reality. Ecstasy is the happiness that comes with the attainment of mystical knowledge of spiritual reality. The state of blessedness into which Christians entered in heaven was believed to be ecstatic. Christian mystics emphasized the love of God as the mood surest to lead to spiritual knowledge and bliss.

Mysticism was implicit in the teachings of Jesus. Paul made it explicit in Christianity, and from the first the church recognized it as a normal manifestation of the faith. Probably the members of the earliest congregations were seeking mystical experience; the power of suggestion within such groups was undoubtedly very great. Christ, of course, was the object of their love. The development of mysticism as a formal element in Christianity was stimulated by Gnosticism and nurtured by Neoplatonism. Irenaeus taught that, since the "image of God" is a part of man, man can attain to likeness to God. Clement of Alexandria developed the theory of asceticism as a means of moral purification; through "mental prayer" he sought to live in harmony with God. Origen saw the soul passing beyond all things of earth and heaven to a vision of the ideal as it exists in God. Ambrose deplored the duties of worldly life, even those of brotherly charity, which called him back from the divine experience of self-annihilation in love of God. Dionysius (fl. *ca.* 500), whose works on the celestial and ecclesiastical hierarchies explained the stages of approach to God, described the manner of attaining the mystical goal: "By laying aside all mental energies and by all-pure contemplation the soul shares in the super-essential light, in which all knowledge pre-

[1] Dom Chapman Butler, *Western Mysticism* (1922); Margaret Smith, *An Introduction to a History of Mysticism* (1930).

exists, and enters into a union, above thought, above states of consciousness, above knowledge." Augustine developed the psychology of mystical experience. Through the "eye" of the soul and the "ear" of the mind, he said, God spoke to man with truth itself; thus the soul was "illuminated" with divine light—the wisdom of God. By purification the soul approached its goal: the tumults of the flesh were hushed, the images of the earth were stilled, and the soul, by loss of self-consciousness, passed beyond itself, to be ravished and absorbed and enwrapped in the inward joys of a vision of "That which Is." Between the soul and God there were no barriers which faith and love, infused with purity, could not surmount.

If the Christian saint attained the mystical goal on earth, the ordinary Christian within the church won it in the other world. The church, indeed, existed only to lead all men to the mystical goal—union with God. As previously noted, the mode of this union was the beatific vision.

The Christian intellectual method rested exclusively upon subjective experience; except as occurrences in the physical world were understood as revelation, miracle, or symbol of divinity, they were disregarded. The basic assumption of the method was the existence of truth, having origin in God and known to man through revelation; both the truth and the revelation were regarded as supernatural. The validity of this assumption was proved rationally by arguing that revelation was self-proving. The content of truth, as a body of ideas, was embodied in Scripture; inferential reasoning was valid only within the limits of scriptural propositions. Intellectual effort which conflicted with or questioned these propositions was checked by ecclesiastical officials, acting, it was assumed, under divine guidance. The Christian intellectual method was orientated toward spiritual reality; man's task was not to advance knowledge of the world but to accept a knowledge of God. God gave him full and free opportunity to do so, and in the performance of this task man succeeded best not by rational but by nonrational procedures.

The Place of Literate Learning in Christian Culture.

As a religion of revealed truth embodied in a book, Christianity had need from the first for literate learning, and there can be little doubt that the reading of Scripture was generally encouraged until the fifth century. John Chrysostom denounced as error the idea that only priests and monks should read Scripture. In this connection it should be noted that the spread of literacy in the towns in Hellenistic and Roman times was a significant factor in the rise of Christianity, for it created the public within which the Gospels circulated. Only with the differentiation of the priest class, the rise of the monks, the decay of a knowledge of Greek in the west, and the elaboration of the allegorical method of interpretation did the reading of Scripture pass from the body of the faithful to their leaders.[1]

1. *The Rise of Christian Schools.* Because most of the early Christians came from the lower classes, they did little to promote schools. The Holy Spirit gave the understanding of Scripture necessary for salvation, and nothing else mattered. Early in the second century, however, when converts became numerous, the need for instruction in the faith led to the establishment of a kind of education. The period of this instruction was known as the *catechumenate*. For sometime before baptism, usually three years, converts received oral instruction by the catechetical method, *i.e.*, by question and answer; this method of instruction was derived from the Jews, who probably acquired it from the Egyptians. Although the converts passed through three grades—they were classified as (1) *inquirers*, those who had indicated a desire for instruction, (2) *hearers*, those who had prayers said over them but were excluded from the mass, and (3) *competentes*, those who received doctrinal and liturgical training—instruction was not formalized, and no body of teachers was developed. Just before baptism the convert was taught the Creed. Selected Bible stories and prayers, particularly the Lord's Prayer, were the chief materials of an education whose purpose was strictly religious: to arouse pious feelings, to strengthen conviction, to warn against dangers to faith, and to prepare for the external life—in other words, to teach faith and morals. This form of Christian education was at its height during the great conversions of the fourth and fifth centuries; it died out after the introduction of infant baptism.

The conversion of members of the pagan educated classes led to a widening of the Christian outlook toward literate learning. Justin Martyr taught Christianity as a philosophy, and Clement of Alexandria regarded it as such. The schools of Alexandria, Antioch, and other cities sprang from this root. Although known as catechetical schools, they were actually Christian colleges on the model

---

[1] On the place of literate learning in Christian culture see P. J. Marique, *History of Christian Education* (3 vols., 1934); H. O. Taylor, *The Classical Heritage of the Middle Ages* (1925); E. K. Rand, *Founders of the Middle Ages* (1928); H. R. Patch, *The Tradition of Boethius* (1935); and T. R. Glover, *Life and Letters in the Fourth Century* (1901).

of the pagan philosophical schools. They gave instruction in pagan learning as well as in Christian doctrine. The influences which promoted their growth also stimulated scholarship, so that in the third century Christian learning took on the pattern of pagan intellectual life. By the fourth century many Christians were teachers of rhetoric, but few became teachers in the state-supported elementary schools where pagan traditions were taught. Fourth-century Christian scholars were the equals of their pagan contemporaries in every field of learning; Origen, Jerome, and Augustine compare favorably with the scholars of any age.

2. *The Christian Theory of Education.* But the Christian attitude toward learning was limited by the religious outlook. It is probably best revealed in Augustine's work *On Christian Doctrine*, which was written for the purpose of improving the understanding of Scripture by clarifying the manner of its interpretation. Astrology and divination were rejected as superstitious. A knowledge of signs, such as the alphabet, weights and measures, coins, and differences of clothing distinguishing the sexes was useful. History and the natural sciences were useful as aids to an understanding of God's work. A knowledge of the crafts contributed to the understanding of scriptural figures of speech. Vocabularies of Hebrew and other languages were necessary. Augustine was careful to note the difficulties likely to arise in the use of logic: "As, then, valid conclusions may be drawn not only from true but from false propositions, the laws of valid reasoning may be easily learnt, outside the pale of the Church. But the truth of propositions must be inquired into in the sacred books of the Church." "It is one thing," he said, "to know the laws of inference, another to know the truth of opinion." Since true propositions were to be found only in Scripture, all inferential reasoning was confined to the elaboration of revealed truth. Correct inferences, like mathematical propositions, actually had origin in God; men merely discovered them. The effect of this outlook on pagan learning was to suppress its few critical elements and to conscript its literary, historical, scientific, and philosophical elements for the service of the faith. Augustine showed a healthy skepticism toward many tales of natural wonder which most of his successors failed to preserve; for them, credulity was a virtue.

John Chrysostom was probably, next to Augustine, the greatest Christian educator. He believed that the Christian should extract the honey from pagan poetry and philosophy. In a work known as *The Golden Book* he stated the goal and outlined a method of

Christian education. "Make a Champion for Christ," he said. "I do not speak it that thou should celibate him (a young boy), send him to the desert, and make him a monk; I say not so; I wish it, indeed, and would, with all my heart, that every man could receive it; but since that may seem a burden too great for him to support, I do not compel. Bring up a Champion for Christ, and while he remains in this world instruct him from his cradle." Mothers, he held, were the natural educators of children, and religious training was the essential element in education. Chrysostom looked upon the child's mind as "a city, a city newly built and furnished, a city full of new inhabitants, and yet wholly unexperienced" and dependent upon the teacher as a "lawgiver." The eyes, ears, tongue, and nose were gates to the city which should be barred with the words of God. The child should hear no old wives' tales, no stories about emperors, and no chatter of domestics. Bible stories, particularly the history of Joseph, he should hear often. He should be given no sweet-smelling ointments, wear no soft garments, and never go to the theater. To guard him against desire for the daughters of men, he should be taught to look upon the beauties of nature—the stars and the meadows—and to read good books. His obedience was to be encouraged by promises of a fair wife and a rich office. Above all he should be caused to go frequently to church. By such method he was prepared to be a "citizen of heaven."

Two conceptions of learning found places in monasticism. From Cassiodorus, by way of Jerome and Augustine, came a monastic learning which used pagan as well as Christian materials. Thus the trivium and quadrivium were perpetuated, and the copying of manuscripts became a common employment, especially for young monks; it was looked upon as a means of defense against the Devil. This substitution of mental for physical labor was a notable service to learning because it, more than any other innovation, made the monasteries centers of a kind of intellectual life. Cassian introduced into western monasticism many Egyptian practices; among these was a kind of instruction, based entirely on Christian materials, designed to lead men to God. It had three phases: (1) the inculcation of faith in order to break human pride and instill complete obedience, (2) the renunciation of desire in a violent effort to acquire real virtue, and (3) the joyous exhibition of positive love of others. Ascetic practices were important in each of these phases, for they were regarded as means to purification and as evidences of spirituality. Monastic learning nurtured intellectual growth;

asceticism aimed at spiritual development. Augustine's remark "He who is mature in faith, hope, and love needs Scripture no longer" suggests that the first sought the same end as the second. Benedict (*ca.* 480–543) succeeded in combining the two conceptions in the rule which spread over the west.[1] Eastern monasticism was more ascetic and less intellectual than Western. Monastic learning sought not the advancement of knowledge but the promotion of spiritual growth.

3. *The Main Forms of Christian Literate Learning.* A summary view of the works mentioned in the discussion of the development of Christian theology reveals the main forms of Christian literate learning, all of which, it should be remembered, were based on the sacred writings. In point of time the first type was apologetics, *i.e.*, works of defense against the Gnostics and pagans. *The City of God* was the greatest of all apologies. Closely related to this type were polemical works directed against persecution and heretics. In *The Deaths of Persecutors* Lactantius described the horrible ends of the emperors who persecuted the Christians. Tertullian launched savage attacks against the Marcionites, whose leader he described as "fouler than any Scythian." Dogmatic works, which as time went on bulked larger and larger, stated the principles of faith and supported them with arguments as subtle as those of pagan philosophy. Didactic works, which took various literary forms and utilized materials from science and history as well as philosophy, declared the principles of both faith and morals. Notable among didactic works were *The Banquet of the Ten Virgins*, a dialogue on the virtue of virginity by Methodius (*ca.* 260–312), bishop of Olympus, and *The Morals*, a book of apothegms in which Basil outlined the Christian way of life. Homilies or sermons became the most common of all Christian literary forms; they were the Christian form of oratory. After the suppression of the practice of "speaking with tongues," bishops alone possessed the right to preach; priests spoke only with their permission. John Chrysostom was the greatest orator of the Greek church, Ambrose of the Latin. It became the common practice to devote a separate discourse to each book of the Bible; the virtues also were favorite topics. Exegesis, *i.e.*, the exposition of the sacred writings, became the most erudite form of Christian learning. The study of the texts, as

[1] E. M. Pickman, *The Mind of Latin Christendom* (1937) p. 483: "It was out of Cassian even more than out of Augustine, that the future grew. For the future lay with the monks; and the rule of life for the Middle Ages was, through Benedict, Cassiodorus, and Pope Gregory, the *Rule* of Cassian." By permission of the Oxford University Press, New York.

carried on by Origen and Jerome, was incidental to exegesis as a whole; it was more an expounding of the meaning of Scripture than a determining of correct reading. The texts were accepted as found. Hippolytus of Rome (d. *ca.* 230), who wrote in Greek, seems to have been the first author to undertake an exposition of the whole of Scripture. Hagiology is a modern branch of Christian learning dealing with the lives of the saints.

The development of these types of learning was correlative with the rise of a learned class whose intellectual methods and literary interests were characteristic of Christian culture; the elaboration of these types of learning established the leadership of this class over the common Christians who lost contact even with the Gospels, the simple statement of the faith. From the fifth century, when the decay of pagan elementary schools and changes in the vernaculars constantly widened the gap between the masses and the educated classes, the intellectual monopoly of the priest class was further fortified by the fixing of its learning in languages no longer spoken by the people. As a result Christian literate learning became not only a closed area of intellectual activity but also a means of control over the common Christians and a decoration of the priestly hierarchy; in fact, Christian literate learning was probably less accessible to common Christians than pagan literate learning was to common pagans. The doctrine that faith opened the door to saving knowledge closed the door to the diffusion, if not the pursuit, of worldly learning.

4. *The Great Manuscripts of the Bible.* A technical change highly important for the future of literate learning came with the development of Christianity, namely, the substitution of the *codex*, a bound book, for the traditional roll. Although this form of book was known by the Greeks, it was little used by them or their Hellenistic successors. The Romans of the last century before Christ used the codex for keeping commercial accounts and legal records. Its pages, which were made of vellum, a very thin material prepared from calf or lamb gut, could be cleaned and used over and over again. When sewed together the pages formed a volume. A number of volumes bound together was a codex. The codex was used for literary purposes in the first century, but became popular only in the fourth century, when Christianity spread widely. The Christians found the codex both cheaper and more convenient than the traditional roll when the reading of Scripture became common in large congregations. The codex was cheap enough to permit manufacture at a price not beyond what the lower-class

congregations could pay. The practice of binding the codex in boards arose because it was necessary to press the leaves in order to keep them from rolling. Highly decorated board covers have survived from the fourth century.

The effect of the adoption of the codex upon the transmission of classical learning was considerable. Many classical works were lost because they were never transferred from the roll to the codex, and most of the longer works were shortened when they were copied. The arrangement of the contents of the rolls was sometimes altered, and the beginning and ends of the rolls were frequently lost because they were on those parts most likely to wear out. Because the roll was difficult to use, learned men long retained the habit of memorizing passages of books; this habit declined with the coming of the codex, which was easier to cite and quote directly than the roll. The adoption of the codex by the Christians combined with their unfriendly attitude toward much of classical learning to cause the loss of great numbers of works.[1]

Among the oldest codices known are the important surviving manuscripts of the Bible. The Codex Vaticanus, dating from shortly before the middle of the fourth century, contains most of both the Old and the New Testaments; its rendering of the New Testament books seems to follow the original texts more closely than any other manuscript. The Codex Sinaiticus, also dating from the fourth century, contains the oldest complete New Testament—the books as Origen knew them. The Codex Alexandrinus and the Codex Ephraemi, dating from the fifth century, are incomplete. The former was the first Greek text of Scripture known to modern scholars, the second is a Syriac text. The sixth-century Codex Bezae seems to be a free rendering of a second-century version. In the third century the New Testament writings were grouped according to subjects—gospels, acts, epistles, and revelation, and in the fourth century its books were divided into chapters and the chapters into verses. Punctuation marks, which first appeared in Greek manuscripts of Roman times, came into general use among Christian copyists. The New Testament, of course, was their favorite work; over twelve thousand copies—four thousand in Greek and eight thousand in Latin—are known to have been

---

[1] See F. W. Hall, *A Companion to Classical Texts* (1913); W. Schubart, *Das Buch bei den Griechen und Römern* (1907); T. Birt, *Das antike Buchwesen* (1882). On the early Christian use of the bound book see F. C. Burkitt, "The Gospels and Their Oldest Manuscripts," *Antiquity*, Vol. 4 (1930), pp. 12–21. On the new material about the texts of the Bible see Sir Frederick Kenyon, *The Bible and Archaeology* (1940), especially Chap. IX, "The Papyri," and Chap. X, "Other Manuscripts."

From H. and K. LAKE, *Codex Sinaiticus, The New Testament* (1922). *By permission of the Clarendon Press, Oxford*

CODEX SINAITICUS

This is a page from the Gospel of Mark of the Codex Sinaiticus, the most complete early Bible. It is dated in the fourth century. The manuscript, discovered in 1844, contains a great part of the Septuagint and all of the New Testament, including Barnabas and a part of Hermas, which are regarded as apochryphal.

made between the fourth century and 1500. Altogether they contain some 150,000 textual variations. After the fifth century, books, because of their cost, were practically confined to monasteries.

PHILOSOPHY IN CHRISTIAN CULTURE.

In Greek culture philosophy had been an attempt to answer fundamental questions about the nature of the universe and man independently of traditional beliefs; above all it was an effort to "think out" the answers. Originally the Christians had deplored the activities of the philosophers because they obscured morals and excited heretical opinions. After Clement of Alexandria, however, Christian theologicans adopted increasingly both the conclusions and the methods of the philosophers. Augustine reorientated philosophy in terms of Christian assumptions; for him it was a "diligent inquiry into things human and divine in so far as such inquiry was conducive to blessedness of life." Philosophy, he said, was inferior to Christian truth because it could not direct man to salvation. Thus philosophy, like all other froms of learning, became a handmaiden of theology.

1. *Christian Theology Considered as a Philosophical System.* As a matter of fact Christian truth embodied answers to the questions the philosophers had raised. "What exists?" "God, conceived as spiritual reality," the Christians answered. "How does change occur?" "According to God's will." "How can man know?" "By God's revelation." "How can man tell right from wrong?" "By the revealed moral law." And to the religious questions which displaced these issues as the social and cultural changes of Hellenistic and Roman times progressed, they also gave answers. "How can man know God?" "Through faith." "How can man gain spiritual aid?" "In Christ." "How can man win eternal salvation?" "Through the Church." Above all, the Christians gave an answer to the perplexing question: "Why does evil exist in a universe created by God, when God is the supreme good?" The answer was embodied in those conceptions summarized in the doctrine of the fall of man.

That the exposition of these answers was greatly influenced by philosophical ideas is clear from even a cursory examination. From Plato, whom Augustine praised highly, came the conception of God as spiritual reality. From him also came the doctrine of "forms," rendered by Augustine as "exemplars," which explained knowledge as existing first in the divine mind. From Aristotle came the doctrine of "essences" as the material embodiments of the "forms" that exist in the divine mind. From him also came the concept "substance" that supported the doctrine of the Trinity. The doctrine of the Logos provided the explanation of the mode of divine action in the universe and among men. In the Stoic doctrine of the "natural law" were found the grounds of moral order as it exists among sinful men rather than as it exists among saints. From Neoplatonism came the contrast of "spiritual" with "material" existence, and also the conception of the progression of spiritual reality through the three modes of the Trinity. By adapting these philosophical conceptions to their faith, the Christians appropriated the highest achievements of rational thought of the culture which they inherited; they transcended these conceptions by infusing them with a faith in God as a person who loves men. Thus in fact they raised philosophic idealism to religious theism. For this reason Christianity may be seen as the end product of the philosophical as well as of the religious movements of Greek and Roman times.

From the point of view of philosophy the central point in early Christian thought was the existence of God, for, unless God existed as Christians believed, their thought was false. Thus they were at pains to prove His existence. Their chief reliance for this proof was, as previously noted, on the inner consistency of the revelations, but they also resorted to inferential reasoning. Among the reasonable arguments offered were: (1) the necessity of a creator, (2) the evidence of design and purpose in the universe, and (3) the common consent of mankind. To these, which he supported with great force, Augustine added the contention that "those root-verities which serve as criterions for our knowledge and conduct" are "adumbrations of the necessary and immutable essence of God";[1] in other words, the nature of thought is itself the supreme proof of the existence of God.

2. *The Christian Theory of Human Nature.* In adapting philosophy to their religious beliefs the Christians necessarily dealt with problems of psychology, and among their intellectual achievements none was greater than their doctrine of the soul. That the soul exists as a substantial spiritual entity separate from the body was an idea far too old and universal to be peculiarly Christian; nor were the ideas that the soul survives after death and faces a final judgment exclusively Christian. Doubts, never settled, existed among the Church Fathers on the point of the soul's origin: Was it generated from parent souls as bodies were developed? Was

[1] Maurice de Wulf, *History of Medieval Philosophy* (1909), p. 92.

each soul specially created by God? The Greek church held to the latter view; in the Latin church there was disagreement. Augustine taught that the body was endowed with a soul in the second month of the prenatal period. Following Aristotle, he separated the functions of the soul into two divisions, the irrational and the rational. The irrational functions were concerned with vital activities and organic impulses; the rational ones included memory, reasoning, imagination, and understanding. Augustine regarded memory as fundamental to learning because, following Plato, he believed that all learning was reminiscing. "Go not forth," he said, "withdraw into yourself; in the inward parts of man dwelleth truth." The soul's activities were sevenfold: (1) to infuse the organism with life, sometimes called the "breath of God"; (2) to perceive by means of the senses—of which there were six, the Stoic "common sense" being added to the five physiological senses; (3) to reason, *i.e.*, to make inferences from experience; (4) to meditate, *i.e.*, to contemplate inward experience; (5) to purify itself by meditating on divine truth; (6) to aspire to spiritual perfection; and (7) to envision the truth. As a special function of the soul the will was superior to both its rational and its irrational aspects, and faith, as the will to believe, was supreme over both reason and impulse. Understanding was that comprehension of truth which faith gave; only through faith and understanding were the highest activities of the soul possible.

The physiological processes of the soul's activities were also explained. The six senses gave true pictures of the natural world. The brain was the center of memory and reason. The nerves were filled with air, which, heated in the liver, rose to the brain, which, in turn, sent it out to the sense organs in acts of perception and to the limbs in acts of will. Sleep was understood as the "image of death." Dreams were regarded as messages, some from God and some from the daimons. Insanity was believed to be a form of daimonic possession; the ecstasy of the vision of divine truth was said to be akin to madness.

The most complete Christian exposition of the nature of man was produced by Nemesius (fl. *ca.* 350), bishop of Emesa in Syria; although concerned with proving the dogmas of the incorporeality and the immateriality of the soul, he dealt with both physiological and psychological topics. The work is a notable example of the blending of pagan and Christian ideas which gave Christian culture its enduring patterns. Behind this blending was the assumption, which the Christian theologians of the fourth and fifth centuries found more and more reason to accept, that all truth is a unity. The usefulness of this assumption to a dogmatic religion in an age of cultural reorientation is self-evident.

SCIENCE IN CHRISTIAN CULTURE.

The Christians were indifferent to the natural world, not hostile to it; it was God's work and, as such, was good. Man had a right to use it during the short period of his earthly preparation for eternal life, but he had little or no time to investigate laboriously a world which was doomed to ultimate destruction. Its marvels, of course, were evidences of the divine, but this was better known through revelation and miracles. "Why argue about the elements of heaven?" asked Ambrose.[1]

1. *The Christian Use of Pagan Science.* The Christians did not hesitate, however, to use the scientific knowledge at hand in explaining the ways of God with men. "God created nothing without an ethical or didactic reason," said Augustine. In the following quotation from the great theologian, the Christian use of pagan science is well exemplified:

If the salamander lives in fire, as close observers of nature have recorded, and if certain famous mountains in Sicily from immemorial ages up till the present time and beyond it have been seething with flames and yet still remain entire, we have before us convincing evidence that everything which burns is not consumed. The soul shows that not everything which can feel pain can also die; so why do sceptics require from us further examples: We can prove to them that the bodies of men condemned to everlasting punishment may retain their soul in the fire, and may continue to burn without being consumed, and may feel pain without perishing.[2]

Further exemplification is to be found in observations on birds which, it seems, Ambrose may have copied from Basil:

With what spontaneity, free from constraint, do the cranes mount their watchful guards by night! We see their sentinels, each one at his post, and while the rest of the flock take their repose, they come and go with eye alert, in order to ward off any ambuscade. . . . When once their time of

---

[1] On science in Christian culture see W. C. Dampier Dampier-Whetham, *A History of Science and Its Relation with Philosophy and Religion* (1929), Chap. II, "The Middle Ages"; Lynn Thorndike, *A History of Magic and Experimental Science* (4 vols., 1934); Charles Singer, *From Magic to Science* (1928); T. A. Lacy, *Nature, Miracle, and Sin: A study of St. Augustine's conception of the natural order* (1916); A. S. Pease, "Medical Allusions in the Works of St. Jerome," *Harvard Studies in Classical Philology*, Vol. 25 (1924), pp. 73–86.

[2] Quoted in F. A. Wright, *Fathers of the Church* (1928), p. 313. By permission of George Routledge & Sons, Ltd., London, and Kegan Paul, Trench, Trubner & Co., Ltd., London.

watch is accomplished, they go to sleep, after uttering a shrill cry to awaken those whose turn has come. The latter willingly accept their turn, and without making excuse and with no sluggishness (as happens with us), fulfil their task with a similar zeal and sentiments of duty. With them there is no desertion to fear because their devotion is natural to them. The watch is well kept because their will is free. . . . With men, on the contrary, what a bad grace they show when it falls upon them to undertake weary vigils! With what annoyance does each one accept the perilous post in the camp assigned to him by his chief! In spite of the punishment promised for sluggishness, as a rule carelessness takes possession of him. For bearing in mind that there is nothing so easy as not to offer difficulties, the necessity which imposes a duty on the unwilling is perforce accompanied by disgust. . . .

Let men learn to love their children with the affection of the crows for their little ones. When the latter fly, they follow them with uneasy attention, fearing lest their feebleness may cause them to fall. They procure for them their means of subsistence and for quite a long time make it their business to nourish them. With us, on the contrary, women are in a hurry to wean the children they love, or, if they be rich, they scorn to suckle them. As for poor women, they get rid of theirs, they expose them, and when they are found, refuse to take them back. The rich, from fear of seeing their fortune divided up between many heirs, use murderous juices to kill the children within the womb of the mother. They take away their life even before they have given it to them. . . .

And the turtle dove! When the death of her mate has rendered her a widow, it is said that she conceives a distaste for the nuptial bond and for the very word marriage, inasmuch as her first love has given her the sorrow of seeing the death of the one she cherished. . . . She, therefore, refuses to contract a fresh union and to break the bond which united her to the one she loved. For him alone she reserves her tenderness, for him alone she retains the name of spouse. Learn from this, ye women, the beauty of widowhood, since this is held in esteem even among the birds.[1]

This use of science was not original with the Christians; they took it over from the Hellenized Jews, such as Philo, and certain Greek writers, who as early as the first century were producing moralistic interpretations of geographical and zoological phenomena. The sources of much of the information which found its way into Christian writings were a work known as the *Physiologus*, probably compiled from many writings in Egypt during the second century, and, above all, Pliny's *Natural History*.

2. *The Christian View of the Physical Universe.* In adapting pagan scientific knowledge to their religious interests the Christian

[1] Quoted in P. de Labriolle, *The Life and Times of St. Ambrose* (1928), pp. 172–174. By permission of B. Herder Book Co., St. Louis.

theologians necessarily made selections from it and, as a result, shaped and perpetuated a certain view of nature. The outcome of this process as regards man has been outlined in the discussion of the soul in the preceding section. Syncretism blended the Babylonian view of the heavens as a vault with the Ptolemaic conception of concentric spheres. Above the earth were at least two heavens. In the first were the planets and stars, believed by some to be spiritual beings and by others to be the homes of angels. Above the stars somewhere was the abode of God. Comets were said to be balls of fire thrown from the right hand of God. Origen considered them the portent of the fall of empires. Tertullian held that eclipses were signs of God's wrath. In repudiating the conception of the antipodes, the Christians reverted from the view of the earth as a sphere to the older view of it as a flat plain. They took over from the Jews the belief that Jerusalem was at its center. Jerome held that the scarred surface of the earth was evidence of God's wrath. Tertullian held that the fossils of animals and plants had been made at the time of the Flood. The only geographical works produced by the Christians of late Roman times were itineraries from various parts of the Mediterranean lands to Palestine. The earth held its traditional position at the center of the universe.

The Christians looked upon mathematics as an interesting form of mental exercise. Concentration of attention upon the welfare of the soul led them to neglect the study of physiology, anatomy, and medicine. Under the influence of late pagan scholarship they perpetuated the worst rather than the best of the Greek and Hellenistic works in these fields. For the traditional magical therapeutics they substituted practices conformable to their theology, such as making the sign of the cross or praying to a saint or uttering the name of Christ or His mother. They were inclined to wait for miraculous cures in cases of serious illness. Asceticism led to a wide disregard of the elementary sanitary practices of the Greeks and Romans. The Christians, it is interesting to note, also rejected veterinary medicine on the grounds that animals have no souls; medicine could not be the same for animals as for men.[1] Augustine praised technological advances as evidences of the capacities of the rational mind, only to conclude that, with such capacities, it could not have fallen into sin "had not an exceeding great sin been found in the first man from whom the rest have sprung."

3. *The Christian Theory of Creation.*   The most serious Christian break with pagan science was the acceptance of the Hebrew

[1] See Emmanuel Leclainche, *Histoire de la médecine vétérinaire* (1936).

doctrine of the creation of the world out of nothing in six days. The difficulties that arose from this acceptance were so numerous that a special kind of works dealing with them, known from the six days of creation as "Hexaemeron," became common. Basil in the east and Ambrose in the west produced the greatest of these; Augustine's defense of the Mosaic account of creation was the culmination of the argument against pagan objections. The usual answer to these objections was given by Ambrose: "If, in the creation of the world, there are certain matters which seem to us hard to understand, and inaccessible to our intelligence, such as, for example, the creation of the serpent and other venomous animals, we must not rashly condemn them. We are only men and cannot grasp the motive which determined the creation of each being. Let us not be hasty in criticizing what we cannot understand, when it is a question of Divine Scripture." Augustine faced the difficulties squarely. He was ready to admit, in fact to argue, that the six days of creation were not like the "days" normally known by men; also he developed a theory of "potential creation" which allowed for the formation of animals and plants through time. His thinking along these lines was so complete that modern apologists, confronted with the theory of the evolution of species, have hardly improved upon it. Indeed, it may well be argued that Augustine's view of nature (quite like Aristotle's) as an *ordered whole* has been elaborated but not displaced by modern science. That he recognized nature as an ordered whole did not mean, however, that he felt it was worth investigating; for him the only fit subjects for study were God and the soul.

In view of their attitude toward nature it is not surprising that early Christian scholars produced no scientific works. But less to be commended even than this lack of scientific curiosity was the easy and endless repetition they gave to the worst elements in Greek and Hellenistic science. The Christians placed no new obstacles in the way of the development of natural science; in giving ideological form to the attitude toward life which emerged in Hellenistic and Roman times they did not, of course, develop a field of learning obscured by that attitude. Natural science died in the hands of the pagan philosophers and rhetoricians; Christian theologians found no reason to resurrect it.

HISTORY IN CHRISTIAN CULTURE.

The acceptance of the Hebrew doctrine of creation necessitated a Christian account of the human career which would discover in events the work of Providence.

1. *Sacred and Profane History.* The theme of this account was found in the Old Testament, but Christians, being Gentiles, were compelled to correlate it with non-Jewish history. Thus they set alongside of sacred history a profane history. The earliest Christian history of the world was written by Julius Africanus at the end of the third century; it outlined the movement of events from Adam to Christ, a period of about five thousand years, and declared that the earth was to endure for only about five hundred years more. Origen set pagan history into the Christian scheme of world events by arguing that its occurrences had also been decreed by God. The correlation of sacred and profane history was accomplished by Eusebius (*ca.* 266–340), also to be noted as the greatest historian of the church, in the *Chronological Canons;* in this work, which was based on Greek researches of the second century B.C., Eusebius set down in parallel columns—sacred history on the left and profane history on the right, with dates in the middle—the chronology of Babylonian, Greek, Roman, and Jewish history.[1] Inasmuch as these chronologies were based on different dating points, their correlation was mainly a work of mathematics. Eusebius took a somewhat shorter view of sacred history than that outlined by Julius Africanus. Jerome translated the *Chronological Canons* into Latin. Their completeness, together with the fact that Christian scholars cared little for investigation of human affairs, made them the model of historical works in Christian culture. A Christian chronological system was invented in 527 by Dionysius Exiguus, a Scythian monk living in Rome; from him came the practice of dating events from the birth of Christ.

The classic Christian rendering of profane history, *Seven Books against the Pagans*, was composed by Orosius (fl. *ca.* 415), a Spanish Christian moved to the task by Augustine; Orosius recognized that he knew less history than theology.[2] The work was a refutation of the charge that the sacking of Rome by the Vandals was due to the spread of Christianity. Its central theme was a delineation of the miseries, catastrophes, crimes, and cruelties of pagan times; these evils flowed from original sin. Through a succession of four

[1] On Eusebius see F. J. Foakes-Jackson, *Eusebius Pamphili, Bishop of Caesarea in Palestine and First Christian historian: A study of the man and his writings* (1933); R. A. Lacqueur, *Eusebius als Historiker seiner Zeit* (1929); Alfred Schöne, *Die Weltchronik des Eusebius in ihrer bearbeitung durch Hieronymus* (1900); Kirsopp Lake, *Eusebius, The Ecclesiastical History* (2 vols., 1926–1932).

[2] I. W. Raymond, *Seven Books against the Pagans: The apology of Paulus Orosius* (1936). On the Christian interpretation of history see J. T. Shotwell, *The History of History* (1939).

empires—Babylon, Macedonia, Carthage, and Rome—God had prepared the way for the triumph of the church; after its founding human affairs had been less rather than more miserable. To support this contention Orosius pointed out that the volcano Etna was less active and that locusts consumed less than in former times. The invasions of the Teutons were merciful warnings of future disasters that would befall men unless they turned to the church, and with the advent of the Antichrist miseries even worse than those of pagan times would afflict mankind. The division of the work into seven books reflected Augustine's belief that the number 7 had mystical significance.

2. *The Christian Theory of History.* The Christian view of history was given a theological setting by Augustine in *The City of God.* For him all history was merely the working out of the supernatural process of human redemption; politics, war, law, the arts, and learning moved with the divine plan, and prophecy was the guide to its movement. In developing this argument Augustine gave to Christian culture a philosophy of history, something which, except for the Stoic speculation about the golden, silver, and iron ages, Hellenic and Greco-Roman culture had lacked. A philosophy of history may be said to have three elements: (1) an ordering of events through time as regards their significance, (2) a causal force or process which determines the occurrence of event, and (3) a direction of movement, *i.e.,* a movement from the past through the present into the future. For Augustine the ordering of events moved from creation to the Fall, to the Flood, to the coming of Christ; the causal force was God's purpose; the direction of movement was from the rise of the church to the culmination of history in the final conflict between the Antichrist and Christ and the ultimate reward of the saints by immortal life in the presence of God. The human career was but an interlude, a short one at that, in eternity. What revelation declared, events proved: God and men moved together toward the appointed end. This interpretation of history was, of course, strictly teleological, for final purpose rather than prior condition or present circumstance determined the course of human events.

3. *The Origin of Church History.* Eusebius is known from his greatest work, the *Ecclesiastical History,* as the "father of church history."[1] This work, generally lacking in style, is a truly monumental compilation of materials about the eastern church. His *Life of Constantine,* written to glorify the first Christian emperor,

[1] J. E. L. Oulton, *Eusebius, The Ecclesiastical History* (2 vols., 1932).

is the chief source of information about the council of Nicaea. Eusebius knew of scandals in the church but preferred to denounce rather than to narrate them. Socrates of Constantinople (*ca.* 380–450) wrote a continuation of the *Ecclesiastical History*, and Sozomen (*ca.* 400–443) produced a new history largely based on it. These works compare favorably with the products of contemporary pagan historians. They were written in Greek; the Roman Christians showed little interest in the history of the faith.

THE RANGE OF CHRISTIAN LEARNING.

Ranging from earth to heaven and from creation to the "eternal Sabbath," plumbing the depths of the human soul, and ascending the divine heights, the Christian mind dwelt only on things spiritual and eternal; its chief product was a rationalized view of supernature, orientated about a theory of moral perfection. Faith and credulity were its chief instruments; reason was disciplined to serve faith, and scholarship was incidental to its labor. Only slowly did Christians accept scholarship as a worthy activity and then merely for priests and monks. In fact, the whole body of Christian learning was priestly—serving a priestly purpose and adorning a priestly class. Christianity fused its religious teachings with the low intellectual tradition which shaped the mentality of the masses; in sharing faith with their priestly leaders the masses accepted that intolerance which served the priestly interest, and in the name of this interest their priestly leaders could confuse fanaticism with faith. Actually there was nothing in the Christian view of life opposed to the growth of secular learning except that it might disturb the priestly leadership; this, rather than the faith itself, was the root of Christian intolerance and obscurantism.

CHRISTIAN LITERATURE

Because of their religious interest the Christians cared little for literary pursuits as such. Clement, Origen, and Tertullian condemned rhetoric and denounced the reading of the pagan poets. Yet, as time went on, largely because formal education remained pagan, the Christian theologians and scholars came to cast their thought in pagan literary forms. Their apologetic, didactic, and dogmatic works were modeled on philosophical treatises. Their sermons were influenced by pagan oratory. The evil of this development was the fixing in Christian writing of literary forms already decayed or ossified. Thus the worst practices of the Asianic style of rhetoric passed into Christian literature and also a low literary ethics, which permitted copying and repetition without end. Only in their motifs, which, of course, were drawn mainly from the Bible, did Christian writings differ greatly from their pagan prototypes.[1]

THE ASSIMILATION OF BIBLICAL MATERIALS INTO WESTERN FOLKLORE.

At the base of all Christian literature were the Hebrew sacred writings and the Gospels, which combined religious feeling and poetic imagery with doctrinal materials. As works of men with diverse educational experience, who kept contact with the masses, they were simple in style but rich in literary forms and in human, as opposed to intellectual, interest. Dialogues, tales, and poems, were inextricably mingled. This diversity explained in part their success, for they provided for the common folk among whom the faith spread not only testimonials of the faith but also emotional stimulation. As the elaboration of Christian literate learning progressed, the verbal rendering of Biblical materials became more and more the single literary contact of believers with their faith, with the result that the materials were assimilated into folklore. In the reorientation of the Western cultural tradition this assimilation of Christian materials into the low intellectual tradition was fully as important as the amalgamation of Christian doctrines with the high intellectual tradition.

THE ADAPTATION OF PAGAN LITERARY FORMS IN CHRISTIAN LITERATURE.

Christian contact with pagan literature produced, besides the theological treatise and the sermon, three literary forms: (1) the hymn, (2) the epic poem, and (3) the romantic tale, or "saint's life"; each, of course, had pagan prototypes.

---

[1] On Christian literature see G. L. Hurst, *An Outline History of Christian Literature* (n.d.); W. Herbert, *History and Literature of Christianity from Tertullian to Boethius* (1924); P. de Labriolle, *Histoire de la littérature chrétienne* (1920); Adolf von Harnack, *Geschichte der Altchristlichen Literatur* (2 vols. in 4, 1893–1904); Berthold Altaner, *Patrologie* (1938); Otto Bardenhewer, *Geschichte der altkirchlichen Literatur* (5 vols., 1913–1932).

Selections from Christian authors are found in H. M. Gwatkin, *Selections from Early Christian Writers Illustrative of Church History to the Time of Constantine* (1902); F. A. Wright, *Fathers of the Church* (1928).

The collected writings of early Christian authors are found in English translation in J. B. Lightfoot, *The Apostolic Fathers* (5 vols., 1885–1890); A. Roberts and J. Donaldson, *The Ante-Nicene Fathers: Translations of the Writings of the Fathers down to A.D. 325* (10 vols., 1899); Philip Schaff, editor, *The Nicene and Post-Nicene Fathers* (14 vols., 1889–1890); Philip Schaff and Henry Wace, editors, *The Nicene and Post-Nicene Fathers of the Christian Church* (2d series, 14 vols., 1890–1900).

1. *The Hymn.* The hymn was a Greek song honoring a god or a hero, and its mood varied from sorrow to elation. The psalm was a Hebrew poem in praise of Yahweh. The Christian hymn developed from both sources, probably in imitation of Gnostic paeans. During the conflict of the heresies, the hymn became a medium of propaganda. Athanasius rebuked Arius for rendering sacred themes in popular song. In Constantinople the Arians, who were denied meeting places, gathered in porticoes of public buildings to shout in song their belief in the unity of God. John Chrysostom organized nightly processions of the orthodox, who, bearing candles and crosses, replied with hymns to the Trinity. When riots broke out between the rival songsters, the Arians were forbidden the right to sing. This use of the hymns led the council of Laodicea in 363 to adopt a rule against the singing of poems composed by private persons. The adoption of this rule was a significant step toward making the singing of hymns an exclusive function of the priests; by the fifth century the congregations sang only according to liturgical rule. Because they were popular rather than liturgical, little remains of the early hymns of the Christian faithful. The earliest Christian hymn comes from Clement of Alexandria.

In the fourth century Christians adapted pagan poetic forms to the writing of hymns. An early example of this adaptation is found in the hymn, or dramatic poem, set into the dialogue of Methodius, *The Banquet of the Ten Virgins*, from which the following selection is quoted:

> *Verse:* I forget my own country, O Lord, through desire of
> Thy grace. I forget, also, the company of virgins,
> my fellows, the desire even of mother and kindred,
> for Thou, O Christ, art all things to me.
> *Chorus:* I keep myself for thee, O Bridegroom,
> and holding a lighted torch I go to meet Thee.

Synesius (fl. *ca.* 400), bishop of Ptolemaïs in Cyrenaica, wrote the first Christian hymns in Greek verse, Hilary of Poitiers the first in Latin verse. Ambrose, who founded the musical liturgy of the Latin church, produced a great number of Latin hymns in a variety of meters. His orthodoxy was rendered as follows:

> To Christ and to the Father now,
> And to the Holy Spirit equally,
> We pray for every favoring gift
> One God supreme, a Trinity.

Prudentius (b. *ca.* 348), known as the "first Christian poet," composed two groups of hymns, *The Cathemerinon*, or "Daily Round," and *The Peristephanon*, or "Martyrs' Crowns"; both comprised lyrics in classical meters, the former consisting of twelve poems celebrating the "mystical moments" of the Christian's day and the latter of fourteen poems honoring the Spanish, African, and Roman martyrs. The martyr is portrayed as a soldier of Christ—argumentative before judges, undaunted by tormentors, and fearless before daimons. The following verses suggest the style and mood of Prudentius:

> Night, clouds and darkness, get you gone!
> Depart, confusions of the earth!
> Light comes; the sky so dark and wan
> Brightens—it is the Savior's birth.
>
> * * * * *
>
> How many are the dreams of dread
> Which by thy light are swept apart!
> Thou, Saviour of the sainted dead,
> Shine with calm lustre in the heart.

Less elegant but not less pious in thought is the following verse from the alphabetical hymn—one verse for each of the twenty-three letters in the Latin alphabet—of Caelius Sedulius (fl. *ca.* 450):

> Upon the fourth day Lazarus
> Revived, though all malodorous
> And freed from the enchaining ground
> Himself, his own survivor found.

Of all the Christian hymns none is more famous tnan the one opening "Te Deum laudamus" ("We praise Thee, O God"), written sometime in this early period of Christian poetry; its author is now thought to have been Nicetas (*ca.* 335–414), bishop of Ramesiana in Dacia.[1]

The use of music in worship flowed from both Hebrew and pagan sources into Christianity. Popular singing by the congregation was universal among the early Christians. Tertullian opposed the marriage of a Christian and a pagan on the grounds that they could not sing together. Thus vocal music became the traditional form of Christian music and in the fourth century was developed into a stately and melodious part of the liturgy. Ignatius adapted the pagan chorus to Christian worship, originating the

[1] See S. W. Duffield, *The Latin Hymn-Writers and Their Hymns* (1889).

type of music known as antiphonal, in which two choirs sing with or against each other. He conceived of them as earthly forms of the heavenly choirs around the throne of God. Ambrose created the first system of church music and established schools to train singers. He was opposed to the popular hymnology reflecting the coarse musical tastes of the street. John Chrysostom deplored all music expressing desire or passion. Jerome declared that girls should not know the purpose of the lyre and the cythara. All noisy instruments, such as the flute, cymbals, and trumpet, popular in the Roman theater and circus, were condemned.

2. *The Epic.* The Christian epic was a poetic treatment of sacred history, the events of which lent themselves easily to an epic rendering. Late in the fourth century Apollinaris, bishop of Laodicea, presented the Old Testament in Homeric verse and the New Testament as a Platonic dialogue. The *Psychomachia* of Prudentius described in fine allegory the holy war of the virtues and the vices. In one of their battles Luxury is depicted as hurling corrupting violets and rose leaves, but the Virtues, triumphant, march back to camp singing like the ancient Israelites. In *The Deeds of Spiritual History* Avitus (*ca.* 460–523), described the Fall with a fine feeling for tragedy; Eve, he said, was guilty of setting men at making hypotheses about things of which they knew nothing. Dracontius (fl. *ca.* 500), somewhat more imaginative than his predecessors, drew a moving picture of the discovery by Adam and Eve of nightfall and daybreak.

> As slow the sun set, they in awe looked on,
> Thinking its light was never to return.
> Their hearts were solaced as th' effulgent moon
> Broke through the shadows and a radiant host
> Of stars they counted in the cloudless sky.
> But when the Day-star, rising from the deep,
> Shook his bright mane and called the new-born light
> Flushed with the sun, to ride above the stars,
> They warmed their souls with yesterday's delight;
> Knowing the daily change, they calmed their dread
> And cheered night's shadows with the hope of dawn.[1]

The literary merit of these epics was slight; they were important because through them Christian motifs became themes for poetic treatment. Such great poems as Dante's *Divine Comedy* and

---

[1] Quoted in E. K. Rand, *Founders of the Middle Ages* (1928), p. 202. Reprinted by permission of the President and Fellows of Harvard College.

Milton's *Paradise Lost* and *Paradise Regained* were fruits of the tree that grew from these beginnings.

3. *The Literary Rendering of the Christian Saintly Ideal.* Just as the Christian view of the human career furnished literary motifs, so did the Christian ideal of individual life receive a literary rendering. It gave rise to a body of writings known as the *Lives of the Saints.* The pagan roots from which these writings sprang were the legends of heroes and the Hellenistic tales of adventure and romance. In Christian hands such legends and tales were combined in a biography, largely fictional, which recorded the pious deeds of the soldiers of Christ. The *Life of St. Anthony* by Athanasius set the pattern of these biographies; Jerome's efforts reveal the full adaptation of the pagan forms to Christian uses. In the *Life of St. Malchus* Jerome narrated a hermit's adventures with desert nomads, who, having captured him, compelled him to marry against his will and then sold him and his bride into slavery. His bride, a Christian maid, it turned out, married him in name only. When a lion killed their master, they fled on his camels and, after an exciting chase, escaped their pursuers. They then founded a monastery in the desert, Malchus leading the monks and his wife the nuns, and lived piously ever after. The tale is "an exhortation to chaste living at any cost."

The original sources of the *Lives of the Saints* were accounts of the trials of the martyrs; after the end of the persecutions the lives of hermits and monks, the greatest exponents of asceticism, became popular. The miraculous element was always in the foreground of these biographies. St. Martin of Tours (d. *ca.* 397), whose life by Sulpicius Severus (*ca.* 355–420) is a model of the combination of legend, fiction, and piety of this type of Christian literature, was credited with having performed 206 miracles. Eusebius, the historian, made a collection of the lives of saints, and Prudentius rendered the lives of several saints in verse. The lives were the source from which developed that branch of Christian literate learning now known as hagiology; its purpose is not to discover the objective facts of the lives of the saints but to explain and interpret their pious works.

Although unique in Christian literature, the autobiographical *Confessions of Saint Augustine*, which describes his struggle for faith, reveals better than any other work the soul-searching which the pursuit of the saintly ideal inspired:

Be not vain, O my soul, nor become deaf in the ear of thine heart with the tumult of thy vanity. Harken thou too. The Word itself calleth thee to return: and there is the place of thy rest undisturbed, where love is not forsaken, if itself forsaketh not. . . . Let the restless and the unrighteous depart and flee from Thee; yet thou seest them, and dividest the darkness, and behold, all things with them are fair, but they themselves are foul. . . . And being thence admonished to return to myself, I entered with Thy guidance into my inmost self, and I was enabled to do so, for Thou wert my Helper. And I entered and beheld with the eye of my soul (such as it was), above the same eye of my soul, above my mind, the Light Unchangeable. . . . O eternal Truth, and true Charity, and beloved Eternity. Thou art my God, and to Thee do I sigh night and day. . . . For many and great are those infirmities of mine, many they are, and great; but Thy medicine is greater. . . . He, Thine only Son, "in Whom are hid all the treasures of wisdom and knowledge" hath redeemed me with His Blood. "Let not the proud speak evil of me"; because I think upon the price of my Redemption, and eat and drink and communicate it; and being "poor," I desire to be gratified from Him amongst those who "eat and are satisfied. And they shall praise the Lord that seek Him."

From Augustine there flowed into Christian culture not only a full assertion of ecclesiastical power but also a personal yearning which lifted the individual above ritual to devotion. In this devotion endured that vivid personal faith which had moved the first Christians to construct the vision of the crucified Christ risen from the grave and to set for themselves the saintly ideal. No ecclesiastical rule has ever long suppressed these personal elements in Christianity, and from them has arisen over and over again the renewal of faith. In God, personifying suffering humanity, Western men have ever found the aspiration to achieve not Godhood but manhood.

CHRISTIAN ART

The general qualities of Christian art were derived from pagan art of the late imperial period, which, as previously noted, brought the decay of the Hellenic style and a progressive orientalization of techniques and materials.[1] Two tendencies in Christian art, evident even in the earliest remains, contributed further to these developments: didactic purpose and symbolism. Under the didactic influence representation was concerned chiefly with the teaching of the faith. The use of symbolical figures and objects led to the disregard of naturalism and to their combination in patterns having meaning in religious but not in aesthetic terms. Since Christianity inherited from Judaism a hostility to the plastic arts, a new factor for decay was introduced into sculpture, so that in the artistic sense it may

[1] See pp. 1020 ff.

be said to have disappeared. The Christian abhorrence of nudity and of comedy also stimulated changes in artistic tastes. The effect of these developments was to complete the submergence of the Hellenic style and its elaborations in a new art which sacrificed form to religious feeling; indeed, if the representation of nature, as evident to the senses, or beauty, conceived as an abstract reality, is the function of art, the statement that there was no art in early Christianity may be regarded as true.[1]

THE ADAPTATION OF THE PAGAN ARTS TO CHRISTIAN USES.

But the arts survived in Christianity and of course underwent a development. The earliest Christian art remains have been found in the catacombs, of Rome and other cities. Chief among them are frescoes and inscriptions. During this phase of development the Christians had no public art; their art was personal or, at least, congregational, and different congregations created somewhat different styles. Since the Christians were drawn mainly from the working classes they brought to the artistic expression of their faith the skills and techniques of the crafts; thus the decorative arts—woodcarving, metalworking, jewelry making, cloisonné manufacture (elaborated from an Iranian source), and embroidering—were more important than the monumental classical arts. When Constantine made Christianity the state cult, it became, of course, the beneficiary of imperial favor, and immediately its public artistic expression was greatly elaborated, particularly in architecture. The controversy over images in the fifth century brought, with the victory of the orthodox parties in the Greek and Roman churches, the complete adaptation of the arts to the service of Christianity. The emperors took the lead in introducing images into the churches, where, it was soon discovered, they would serve as the "Bible of the poor." The completion of the conversions, with the consequent admission into the congregations of large numbers of persons long familiar with the use of images and ritualistic objects, also contributed something to this adaptation.

[1] On Christian art see C. R. Morey, *Christian Art* (1935); Josef Strzygowski, *Origins of Christian Church Art: New facts and principles of research* (1923); Josef Strzygowski, *L'ancien art chrétien de Syrie* . . . (1936); G. M. Bevan, *Early Christians of Rome: Their words and pictures* (1927); M. I. Rostovtzeff, "Early Christian and Judaean Art in Mesopotamia," *Proceedings of the British Academy*, Vol. 19 (1935), pp. 321 *ff.*; A. N. Didron, *Christian Iconography, or the History of Christian Art in the Middle Ages* (2 vols., 1891).

On the archaeological remains of early Christian art see Orazio Marucchi *Manual of Christian Archaeology* (trans. from 4th Italian ed., 1935); O. M. Dalton, *Early Christian Art: A survey of the monuments* (1925); F. X. Zimmermann, *Die Kirchen Roms* (1935); Joseph Wilpert, *Erlebnisse und Ergebnisse im dienst der Christlichen archäologie* (1930); Sisto Scaglia, *Les catacombes de saint Calixte* . . . (1909).

The Motifs of Christian Art.

If the style of Christian art was derived mainly from oriental elements in late pagan art, its motifs were mainly its own. The first motifs of the Christian arts were, as a matter of fact, very old symbolical forms, such as the anchor and ship, the lamb, the dove, the fish, Elijah's ascent into heaven, Christ's ascension, and Adam and Eve in the Garden. These events, it will be noted, were interpreted as prophecies of New Testament teachings or occurrences. Another type of Christian picture developed from a second-century Alexandrian book illustrating the Hebrew conquest of the Holy Land. In this book, which set the patterns of Christian artistic treatment of physical nature and architecture, the Jewish conquerors were pictured as Roman soldiers marching down long vistas among rocky hills, which, overhung with dark and foreboding skies, were studded here and there with massive and richly adorned Hellenistic buildings.

In contrast to the harsh moods of the Old Testament motifs was the gentle and peaceful treatment of New Testament themes. The Three Wise Men, the Virgin and Child, the Twelve Apostles, Peter and Paul, and certain of the miracles—for example, the multiplication of the loaves and fishes and the raising of Lazarus— early became popular. Scenes from the critical period of the life of Jesus were not generally portrayed until the third century. The infant Jesus provided the earliest opportunity for naturalistic treatment of a Christian theme. In the rendering of these New Testament motifs nature was depicted as mild and bountiful; favorite scenes were those of figures picking flowers, cutting corn and binding sheaves, harvesting grapes, and gathering olives. Skies were calm or, if stormy, were brightened by supernatural light coming from above. In the fourth century these motifs, together with pictures of priestly processions, saints, and martyrs, became common in the churches, either as wall decorations or on rolls which were hung around the altar, where the members of the congregations could be visually educated in the faith. Mosaics as well as frescoes were common forms of wall decorations.

2. *The Christ Image.* The most important Christian art motif—the Christ image—developed slowly. There is no evidence in the early remains of Christian art that any authentic representation of Jesus survived. At first Christ was depicted symbolically as a lamb, or a fish, or a dove. The earliest human figure associated with Christ was the Good Shepherd, derived, some

From J. WILPERT, *Die Malereien der Katakomben
Roms* (1893). *By courtesy of Messrs. Herder & Co.*

THE VIRGIN AND CHILD

This picture, dating from the second half of the third century, is among the earliest known
Christian treatments of the Madonna motif, whose source was the ancient peasant beliefs
about death and resurrection.

scholars believe, from the classical representation of Orpheus, who charmed animals with his music. About the year 200 Christ was depicted in Egypt as a beardless youth with short hair; a similar treatment, probably derived from Egyptian sources, is found in the Roman catacombs. The Gnostics first represented Christ with a crown. Sculptured images of Christ were set up by the emperors Alexander Severus, who included such a figure among the several statues of his domestic chapel, and Constantine, who placed one in the forum of Constantinople. Under imperial influence Christ came to be represented as a king, majestic and serene, reigning with His Apostles over men and His enemies. In depicting the Apostles, each nation drew on its own traditions; thus Egypt rendered them standing like priests, Asia Minor seated like philosophers, and Rome holding an author's roll like Vergil. In the fourth century Asia Minor and Italy added the beard to the Christ image. An apocryphal description, which pictured Jesus as a slender man with dark hair parted in the middle, a fair forehead, a faultless nose and mouth, and a reddish beard, was a strong influence in the final shaping of the Christ image. By the sixth century pictures of Christ as the Savior or as the sufferer on the cross were common in both churches and homes. The earliest picture of the Crucifixion, showing Christ wearing a loincloth and with a lance wound in the left side, dates from the fifth century. Representations of the suffering Christ were rare even at this time. Some students find the Christ image similar to the image of Asklepios, the Greek healing god, but there is no evidence that it was derived from this source. The Christ image took form as Christian culture was consolidated, and each nation contributed, according to its ideals and virtues, to the shaping.

The Christ image was the supreme achievement of Christian art.[1] Whether it represented the suffering Lord or the calm Savior it expressed the emotion of the uprooted and cruelly exploited Mediterranean masses—their terror or their hope—in a form whose humanity cut through all doctrine and ritual to fix, not as a reply to doubt but as yearning and aspiration, the meaning of their faith. By accurately rendering this living faith, Christian art created its own beauty.

THE BEGINNINGS OF CHRISTIAN ARCHITECTURE.

Originally the Christians met in private homes, and their first buildings were probably houses willed to the congregations by

[1] See p. 1231.

members. Early Christian meeting places had, therefore, no distinguishing form; as meeting places, however, they were known
as basilicas.

The special developments that created the Christian church
as an architectural type took place in Syria, Persia, and Armenia.
Probably a Christian church architecture existed first in Syria,
where in the second century the arch and the column were used
together in Christian buildings. The barrel-vaulted roof originated
in Mesopotamia or Iran. The dome on a square base appeared first
in Iran and Bactria. The dome was first set on squinches, or arches
across the corners of squares, in Armenia. The dome and the
barrel-vaulted roof were combined in Iran. From these elements
square, circular, and octagonal churches having a central dome,
an apse, and a portico were developed; in Armenia they were combined in the cruciform structure, which passed immediately to
the Greek church. In Rome influences from Constantinople and
Armenia carried by migrating Goths and eastern craftsmen met
influences from Mesopotamia and Syria and joined with native
tendencies. The original Latin church was long, with a gabled
timber roof. Under eastern influence this structure was changed
into a style characterized by the nave, *i.e.*, a long central hall,
divided from the main walls by rows of columns, supporting arches,
and aisles. At one end was an apse, usually semicircular, enclosing
the altar and at the other end a porch sheltering the entrance.
About 500, in northern Italy, where imperial influence was strong,
the outline of the basic Christian architectural pattern—the elon-
gated cruciform style with dome, barrel-vaulted roof, nave, apse,
aisles, and portico—appeared.

Closely connected with the emergence of this type of structure
was the evolution of new decorative treatments; like the structure,
they first appeared in Syria, whence they spread chiefly by imperial
influence. Many of the imperial architects after Alexander Severus
had been trained, it seems, in Syria. The distinctive element in
these arts was the use of colored marble panels, terra cottas,
colored glass mosaics, bas-reliefs, and paintings to cover the interior
of a structure almost completely. Sculpture was employed mainly
in embellishing columns and arches; cornices, recessed and balanced
open spaces, and plain columns practically disappeared. Both
geometrical and plant motifs were used in designs covering ordinary
surfaces. Prominent spaces in the apses were filled with mosaics
and paintings of Biblical motifs, for example, Jesus with the
Apostles and Christ as the King of Heaven. Notable in these paint-

Ewing Galloway

SANTA SOPHIA

Santa Sophia—one of the most famous monuments of Christianity during the age of its consolidation in the Western cultural tradition—is remarkable not only for its domes but also
for the penetration of the domes with windows, from which come beautiful lighting effects.

ings was the use of the gold background, the stiff but stately human figure, and two-dimensional representation. In spaces between arches along the nave, processions of saints, Christ's miracles, and other sacred scenes were depicted. These trends culminated in the "composed interior," *i.e.*, the balanced and rhythmical arrangement of scenes, spaces, colors, and movements so as to give unity to an interior; such compositions were oriented about the altar, which, following classical precedence, was more richly adorned than any other part of the structure. This interior was a symbolical environment for the faith which had its chief expression in the sacrament of the Eucharist; in terms of the faith the arts in Christianity were truly functional.

Christian church building began in the third century and, with Constantine, developed rapidly. The old church of St. Peter in Rome, replaced by the present church of St. Peter in the sixteenth century, was begun in 324; it followed closely the plan of the Roman house. Constantine began Christian building in Jerusalem and Constantinople. The most notable examples of early Christian architecture date from the reign of Theodosius I; they are in Ravenna, his imperial seat in the west. They are decorated with fine mosaics of colored glass and marble depicting sacred history and gospel events. Perhaps the most remarkable early Christian building, if not the greatest Christian structure ever raised, is Santa Sophia in Istanbul. It was built by Justinian on the site of an earlier church dedicated by Constantine to the "Divine Wisdom." The first two attempts to construct the great half dome which crowns the structure failed; as indicated by the illustration the feature of the building, besides the use of domes as supports for the central dome, is the penetration of the bases of the domes by windows. Forty windows, admitting light to the interior, circle the base of the great dome.

As a final comment on art in Christian culture it should be noted that the Christians repudiated the free pursuit of aesthetic values; for them there was no "art for art's sake"—only art for the glorification of God and the edification of the faithful.

THE CHRISTIAN SOCIAL OUTLOOK

In the transformation of the early Christian communities, whose members looked toward a quick destruction of the existing social order, into the universal church, organized as a priestly hierarchy, allied to the state, and prepared for an indefinitely long earthly career, occurred a profound adjustment of Christianity to the "world," *i.e.*, the traditional social order of urban cultures. As understood by the Christians this order was the product of sin, and adjustment to it was made mainly by means of theories which explained the political state, coercive law, civil disobedience, tyrannous rulers, poverty, social inequality, and injustice as results of the Fall. Since this adjustment involved the acceptance of these institutions and conditions, there was actually no Christian social order and no Christian program of social reorganization. Practically, however, because the evolution of the Christian priest class introduced a new element into Greco-Roman society, modifications in the exercise of power, the allocation of prestige, and the distribution of wealth were made, but, except as changes arose in the course of the advent of this new social group, few were the changes wrought in society by Christian influences.[1] The adjustment necessarily involved a sublimation of the saintly ideal, for obviously the attainment of moral perfection in a corrupt world was not generally possible; thus, although not abandoned, the ideal became the goal of the few who received miraculous aid in their quest. For priests and laity alike, a lower goal of moral striving was set, consisting, on the one hand, of a patient bearing of the "cross," as the pains and distresses of earthly life were figuratively designated, and, on the other hand, of the performance of the religious duties which, through the church, bound up earthly with supernatural life.

From this adjustment flowed the attitudes which constituted the Christian outlook upon society; society, itself, it must be remembered, was the traditional order of urban cultures.[2]

---

[1] For a discussion of the various aspects of the adjustment between Christianity and pagan life see C. J. Cadoux, *The Early Church and the World: A history of the Christian attitude to pagan society and the state down to the time of Constantine* (1925); Shirley J. Case, *The Social Triumph of the Ancient Church* (1933).

[2] On the social outlook and social influence of Christianity see O. Cone, *Rich and Poor in the New Testament* (1922); H. H. Scullard, *Early Christian Ethics in the West from Clement to Ambrose* (1907); A. J. Carlyle, *The Influence of Christianity upon Social and Political Ideas* (1911); W. E. Lecky, *History of European Morals from Augustus to Charlemagne* (2 vols., 1929); Thomas C. Hall, *History of Ethics within Organized Christianity* (1910); Shirley J. Case, *The Social Triumph of the Ancient Church* (1933); Adriano Tilgher, *Work: What it has meant to men through the ages* (ca. 1930); V. Bartlett, *Property: Its duties and rights* (1913); W. J. Ashley, *An Introduction to English Economic History and Theory* (1925); G. O'Brien, *An Essay on Medieval Economic Teachings* (1920); W. F. Cobb, "The Fathers on Property," *Economic Review*, Vol. 5 (1895), pp. 191 *ff.* The most important work on the social principles of the Christian Churches is Ernst Troeltsch, *The Social Teachings of the Christian Churches* (2 vols., 1931); for the points covered in this chapter see pp. 39–200.

CHURCH AND STATE.

From the first the Christians regarded the church and the state as separate bodies, and this dualism was never given up. Until Constantine the church was at war with the Roman state; after him the two bodies shared authority over society, but questions as to their relation remained to be settled. The political elements of Christian culture were defined in answers given to these questions.

The church, which claimed to be supernatural both in origin and in function, recognized no degrees of political status and no distinctions of race and nationality and asserted the duty of each man to accept it as soon as he was aware of its existence. Its members were one body—*populus catholicus*—united in Christ, and all men—the whole human race—were morally obligated to enter it. As a supernatural association its rule came from God; as an earthly organization its rule was performed by the bishops, the successors of the Apostles. Practically, therefore, the church functioned as a governing body in society through the leaders of the priest class, which its evolution had created; that individual leaders disagreed as regards their respective jurisdiction and prestige in no way weakened the claim to power of the bishops as a group.

The state was a "remedy for sin." Because of the Fall, the preservation of order among corrupt men became necessary, and all human institutions—marriage, property, slavery, law, and government—served this purpose. The state was the organization of these institutions through coercive power, the exercise of which was the rightful check to avarice, violence, inequality, and immorality. The state, therefore, had its origin in divine purpose, and to it was rightfully due the obedience of all men. Its power, however, was defined and limited by God, not by the men whom it existed to rule. Practically, this conception of the state was a recognition of the authority of the Roman emperor in all matters not the concern of the bishops as religious leaders. In fact, Christians came to conceive of the universal church and the Roman state as correlative bodies, exercising a divinely appointed function.

The effect of these conceptions of the church and the state was to divide jurisdiction over society between the bishops as the heads of the church and the emperor as the head of the state, but the line of division was never clear. The struggle between ecclesiastical functionaries and secular rulers became, therefore, the distinctive political conflict of Christian culture.

1. *The Theory of Ecclesiastical Independence.* Under Constantine the bishops accepted imperial participation in affairs of the church because intervention was implicit in the recognition which made Christianity the state cult. But as time went on they increasingly resisted political interference in ecclesiastical affairs, and ultimately they declared the supremacy of the church over the state. Ambrose, the great bishop of Milan, set precedents for ecclesiastical supremacy by refusing to obey the order of Theodosius I to rebuild a Jewish synagogue that Christians had destroyed and by compelling the same emperor to do penance publicly for a massacre at Thessalonica.[1] In the contention aroused by these incidents Ambrose claimed for the church the right to decide all issues affecting the relation of the church and the state and asserted the freedom of the church from interference by the state. God's bishop, he held, was superior to the emperor, who, from the religious point of view, was only a layman. Ambrose, it should be noted, was concerned with an assertion of the power not of the Roman papacy but of the church as a whole. The full theory of church supremacy over the state was declared by Pope Gelasius in a letter to the emperor Anastasius I (*ca.* 491–518):

> There are indeed two powers, O august emperor, by which the world is chiefly governed: the holy authority of the bishops and the royal power. Between them the weight of the bishops is the heavier, because at the divine Judgement they must render an account of even the kings of men.

In line with this theory the church argued that the use of coercive power by the state was justified only when the state was directed by the church or served the church; in effect, therefore, the state ought to be the slave of the church. In theological terms this position was impregnable because clearly the authority of the bishops, divinely appointed by God, was superior to an authority whose existence was rooted in sin. In this theory, however, there was no claim that the bishops should be secular rulers; as yet their functions were strictly religious.

2. *Force in the Service of the Church.* The social realization of this relation of the church and the state was threefold: (1) in the establishment of the priests as a privileged class,[2] (2) in the organization of the priests under a self-determined law enforced by their own agents,[3] and (3) in the use of coercive power by the state

[1] See J. R. Palanque, *Saint Ambroise et l'Empire romaine: Contribution à l'histoire des rapports de l'église et de l'état à la fin du quatrième siècle* (1933).

[2] See p. 1072.

[3] See p. 1206.

against the enemies of the church. The third of these developments was decisive because through it the episcopate became the beneficiary of the coercive power which is the ultimate basis of the supremacy held by any ascendant social group.

When in the fourth century the power of the state was placed at the service of the church, the suppression of five different enemies of the church followed quickly: (1) the pagans, (2) the Jews, (3) rival religious bodies like the Manichaeans, (4) heretics, and (5) schismatics, *i.e.*, those who divided the church. As previously noted, Theodosius I began the legal suppression of paganism; his son and successor, Theodosius II, gave general intolerance a basis in the compilation of law known as the Theodosian Code. Only in 416, when pagans were excluded from the highest offices of the state, did the complete suppression of pagan worship become imperial policy. Constantine began the Christian persecution of the Jews in an edict of 315 which forbade them to convert their slaves to Judaism; the tendency of subsequent imperial anti-Jewish legislation was to reduce them to a status of social inferiority, which status became for the church the main argument for their further suppression. In 339 Jews were forbidden to keep Christian slaves and the marriage of a Jew and a Christian became a punishable offense. The council of Laodicea forbade Christians to rest on the Jewish Sabbath. In 377 Christians who were converted to Judaism were deprived of their property. A concentrated effort to drive the Jews from the Holy Land was made early in the sixth century.

In the late fourth and the early fifth century Manichaeism spread widely among scholars and teachers and among the people through the influence of a work now known as *The Apocryphal Acts of the Apostles;* Augustine, who was for years a Manichaean, is an example of the scholars who responded to its appeal. The first energetic measures against this rival were taken at Rome by Leo I, who had the aid of the state. Valentinian III (*ca.* 425–454) ordered the banishment of the Manichaeans; early in the sixth century the death penalty was imposed on them. The Montanist group, which, although an offshoot of Christianity, became a rival religious body, was so persecuted in the fifth century that congregations burnt themselves to death in their churches. A fierce persecution was also loosed against the heretical Donatists, whose doctrine of the priesthood was so dangerous to the orthodox hierarchy; indeed, gains made by the Donatists after Julian restored their churches to them threatened the overthrow of the hierarchy. They converted runaway slaves and poor men, whose cry "Glory be to God" as they courted martyrdom in civil strife, was more to be feared, it is said, than the roar of a lion. In the year 348 many Donatist leaders were put to death and their worship was proscribed. In 412 all Donatists were fined; two years later they were deprived of civil rights; and in the next year they were forbidden to hold meetings under penalty of death.

The last popular movement against the orthodox episcopate came to an end with the destruction of the Donatists. The Arians, Novatians, and Nestorians were suppressed by measures only a little less severe than those taken against the Donatists. The schism in the church which sprang from the decision of the Council of Chalcedon evoked from the emperor Marcian (*ca.* 450–457) the prohibition of all discussion of matters of faith and an order against the supporters of Eutyches which deprived them of priests and books.

The diverse measures noted in the preceding discussion constituted a well-rounded repressive program: (1) disbarment from public office, (2) refusal of admission to the army, (3) denial of the right to make bequests, (4) exclusion from the building industry, (5) prohibition against holding public meetings, (6) imposition of fines, (7) confiscation of property, (8) censorship, (9) banishment, (10) torture, and (11) the death penalty. The proscription of books began with an edict of Constantine against the possession of the works of Arius and Porphyry. In 399 a council at Alexandria forbade the possession of the works of Origen. Leo I ordered the destruction of a whole list of books and imposed the extreme penalty upon anyone who read or owned them. In 499 Pope Gelasius issued a prohibition against the public reading of certain works which is commonly recognized as the first papal *Index Expurgatorius*. The death penalty for heresy was first employed in 385 against the Spanish bishop Priscillian and six members of his Manichaean-like congregation; convicted of practicing magic, they were tortured and beheaded. A council of bishops, one alone objecting, approved the execution; Ambrose protested against it. A Biblical justification for the death penalty was found by Jerome in Deuteronomy, Chapter 13, verses 6–9.[1] Actually, let it be

---

[1] "If thy brother, . . . or thy son, or thy daughter, or the wife of thy bosom, or thy friend . . . entice thee secretly, saying, Let us go and serve other gods, which thou hast not known, thou, nor thy fathers; . . . Thou shalt not consent unto him, nor hearken unto him; neither shall thine eye pity him . . . : But thou shalt surely kill him. . . . "

noted, the church neither punished nor executed anyone. It only discovered and denounced its enemies; the state suppressed them.

Before Constantine the orthodox Christians could denounce and excommunicate, but not physically punish, heretics. The temper of their denunciation is clear in the names applied to the Gnostics by the apologists, for example, "servants of the Devil," "beasts in human shape," "pirates," "robbers," and "dealers in deadly poison." Opponents of Arius likened the heretics to the hydra, which produced new serpents as rapidly as old ones were lopped off. The nobility of persecution was proclaimed by Nestorius, who asserted that the prince who purges the earth of heretics wins heaven. It remained, however, for Augustine, during the struggle with the Donatists, to produce the doctrine which became for the church the justification of persecution, namely, that the effort to win heretics back to the faith by violence was actually a labor of love, for it was meant only to save them from everlasting damnation. Bound up with this doctrine were two other ideas which had long justified intolerance: (1) attacks on the recognized God of the state were a threat to public order and prosperity, and (2) the preaching of gods other than those of the state cult was a conspiracy with evil powers to disrupt the established order. Neither of these ideas was Christian in origin, but in the struggle to make the orthodox faith supreme Christians found reason to preserve them. Behind all these theories was the claim of the Christians that they alone possessed the truth—a divinely established truth which all men were morally obligated to accept. Clearly the enforcement of the performance of duty that was rewarded with eternal life could not be evil. So the church argued, and so the state acted.

In the end, therefore, coercive violence found a place in Christian culture, as in other cultures, in the service of the ideal which that culture embodied; the repudiation of the original Christian doctrine of passive obedience which this involved was only one aspect of the adjustment that transformed a popular faith into an ecclesiastical regime.

Except as the rise of the Christian priest class altered somewhat the jurisdiction of the state in religious affairs, the triumph of Christianity brought few political changes. In accepting the imperial regime it adopted monarchy and aristocracy as political forms. Even more important was the fact that it sheltered them under new sanctions. Obedience to the "powers that be" was a religious duty. If a ruler was bad it was a punishment for sin, and the true remedy was to turn away from sin. Rulers, of course, were responsible before God but not before the people; their powers were limited by divine and natural law, not by popular will. If, as Augustine held, the state was only a "robber band" when it did not protect the religion of the true God, the essential distinction between a good and a bad ruler was the faithfulness with which the power of the state was placed at the service of the church; of this faithfulness the bishops, not the people, were the judges. Only in the council of bishops, which acted as an eccelsiastical legislature, did Christianity introduce a political innovation, and its importance was far in the future. Certainly democracy, as understood in the modern Western world, owes little to the ecclesiastical regime through which Christianity was organized in the Western cultural tradition.

3. *The Development of Law: Canon Law.* In the exercise of their respective powers the church and the state functioned through law. The church was the exclusive interpreter of the divine law, which all men and, consequently, all rulers were bound to accept. In governing its own affairs the church created a new body of law— the canon law, or *jus canonicum*—defining religious obligations and ecclesiastical relations. The state functioned through human, or positive, law, by which all secular institutions were regulated. Behind positive law, however, was a natural law. As developed by Christians from Stoic sources, the natural law was the rule of conduct prescribed in human nature by God and as such was knowable by reason. For the Stoic primitive age, when men lived under natural law, the Christians substituted the period of innocence before the Fall. Among the basic elements of the natural law, taken over from the Stoic philosophers and the jurisconsults, were the rights of self-preservation, of nourishment, and of living in society and the principle of the equality of men. After the Fall, because of corruption, positive law became necessary as a means of preserving order; consequently positive law was subject to change from time to time. Thus the church, although it assumed the stability of the social order, recognized the possibility of change in secular institutions; in effect, this meant that alterations in positive law which were not dangerous to its position could be accepted by the church. But when the bishops became wealthy and powerful, their interests were so closely identified with secular institutions that their maintenance easily became identified with the protection of the church as a religious organization.

The positive law of Christian culture was, of course, the law of the Roman state. Three considerations are involved in evaluating the influence of Christianity on the last phase of the evolution of Roman law. After the third century legal development turned from the philosophical elaboration of principles to the making of incidental commentaries and codifying. Under the Christian Roman Empire imperial decree became the single source of new legislation. The final product of the tendencies was the great codification of the Roman law carried out under Justinian.

Scholars, although they commonly recognize the softening effects of Christianity on the civil law, are not agreed on the extent to which Christian influences actually modified the law as a whole. Constantine, who first legislated for the interests of Christians, undertook to make the world safe for Christianity and to create a world fit for Christians to live in,[1] or, in other words, Christianity inspired the always hazardous enterprise of reforming morals by legislation. The private fortunes of judges were made liable for damages caused by the judges' neglect or bad faith, and women and orphans were given the right to accuse them of wrongdoing. Women were no longer forced to endure public trials. The exposure of newborn infants was prohibited. Anyone who took an exposed infant could keep it. The Antonine policy of giving state aid to poor children was revived. Landlords lost the right to separate parents from their children among their dependent peasants. Masters were not permitted to part husbands and wives among their slaves. If a couple begot a child out of wedlock, the child became legitimate if they married. Divorce was prohibited except on statutory grounds. A wife could obtain a divorce if the husband was found guilty of assassination, poisoning, or grave robbing; a husband, if the wife was judged guilty of adultery, procuring, or poisoning. If a wife repudiated her husband for any other cause, she was liable to transportation and the loss of her dowry; if a man abandoned his wife for any cause other than those recognized as causes for divorce, he could be forced to restore his wife's dowry and was forbidden to remarry. This legislation perpetuated the traditional double standard of morals. On the whole, the family was strengthened as a legal unit, but the position of the paterfamilias was weakened. New laws against seduction, rape, and adultery carried the death penalty. Elopement was classified as rape. It is worth noting that the violators of barmaids in inns were not subject to these laws. The legal protection of slaves was not significantly

[1] See C. N. Cochrane, *Christianity and Classical Culture* (1940), pp. 197 *ff*.

extended, although manumission was encouraged. The responsibility for recording manumissions was vested in the Christian clergy. Urban workers were encouraged to form guilds; in this connection it should be said that some Christian congregations were organized as collegia. The power of patrons over clients was limited somewhat. Punishments that outraged Christian feeling, such as crucifixion and branding on the face (regarded as an insult to the image of God), were abolished. Branding on other parts of the body was allowed. The punishment for blasphemy was a fine of one-half of one's goods. These gains may be set against the harsh penalties that came with legalized intolerance.

The social and economic changes which transferred legal powers from the imperial bureaucracy to the new landlords weakened the force of imperial law by supplanting it with local customs which varied from place to place; from this development Christian landowners, as well as pagan, drew an increased power over the masses and, inasmuch as Christianity did not recognize as evil the economic exploitation of man by man, found reason to exercise it for their own profit. Social and economic trends, not Christianity, brought most of the changes that occurred in the positive law under the Christian Roman emperors.

Until the third century the church exercised no control over its communicants except that which arose from the power to exclude them from the sacraments, but, because of the belief in eternal damnation, this control was very real. In the fourth century, however, the councils began to formulate canons, *i.e.*, rules, for the government of priests and communicants. Among the early canons was a refusal of communion to soldiers who threw away their arms in wartime. The Council of Nicaea issued the first canons for the whole church; they dealt with the marriage of priests, the practice of usury by priests, and baptism. In the west papal decrees, sometimes sent out as letters but more often issued in reply to questions, became part of the canon law. The first commentary on the law of the church was written by John Scholasticus of Antioch about 550. In the west no uniform body of canon law appeared until the eighth century.

The original trends of ecclesiastical law may be seen in the canons issued by the Council of Chalcedon. Great attention was given to the position and activities of priests and monks. Priests were forbidden to deal in ecclesiastical offices for money, to exercise the military art, to hold public office, to engage in secular traffic except for widows, orphans, and needy persons, to have their names on the religious registers of different cities, and to belong to secret societies. They were not to be transferred from one city to another except in case of dire need. Monks were forbidden to interfere in ecclesiastical affairs. No monastery was to be erected in a diocese without the consent of the bishop, but property once set aside for monastic use was not to be diverted to other uses. A slave was not to be admitted to a monastery without the consent of his master. Regulations for the conduct of church government placed monasteries and rural parishes under the control of the bishops, ordered bishops to hold a synod once a year, and provided for the administration of the property of the church by a special curator. Complaints against bishops and priests were not to be heard until the name of the accuser was known; the lawsuits of priests were to be tried before a bishop or a synod. New bishops were to be ordained within three months after election. The poor and needy, when traveling from town to town, were required to carry letters of introduction. The canon law also dealt with family life, notably the degrees of blood relation within which marriage was permitted, divorce, and the rights of orphans and widows, and such secular matters as oaths, usury, prices, and contracts. But the most important parts of the canon law were concerned with religious crimes, such as perjury, blasphemy, sacrilege, sorcery, and sins which required disciplinary action. At first the church claimed jurisdiction only over the members of the priestly hierarchy, but in time authority over the members of the congregations was claimed and partially made good. Punishments such as banishment, imprisonment, and chastisement were inflicted on both the clergy and laity; physical punishments destroying life, mutilating the body, or causing loss of blood were prohibited.

SOCIAL CLASSES IN CHRISTIAN CULTURE.

Christianity infused the Stoic conceptions of mankind, brotherhood, and the natural equality of men with religious feeling; before God and the altar there were no distinctions of race, nationality, and class, for humanity was one family, beloved of the almighty Father. The introduction of egalitarian sacramentalism was clear gain so far as it went, for it broke the traditional class structure with a democratic rift, but the effect was limited, for it had little or no significance for worldly affairs. Worldly social relations remained as they had been.

1. *The Christian Theory of Class Relations.* The Christians not only accepted the existence of the class structure but found a

new justification for it. Whereas the pagans justified the existence
of classes by a theory of psychological differences[1] or by the
practical circumstance of defeat in war, Christians found an
explanation conformable to their theology.[2] Origen taught that
inequalities of birth and fortune reflected the depths of sin into
which men had sunk. Augustine also held that social classes
originated in sin. John Chrysostom preached that the servility of
woman to man, man to master, and all men to the state was rooted
in moral corruption and, because of this origin, was permanent.
The differentiation of the priest class as a privileged order is complete proof of the Christian acceptance of the existence of social
classes; the energy of many bishops in seeking offices and honors, in
amassing wealth, and in adopting such trappings of aristocracy as
bodyguards, magnificent residences, rich dress and food, and
corrupt morals, emphasized the acceptance. The conversion of the
office-holding and wealth-possessing classes of the Roman state,
when accompanied by the Christian acceptance of public service
and the teaching that the possession of wealth was no bar to
heaven, ensured the persistence of their social attitudes. The final
adaptation of the conception of natural equality among men to
these attitudes was made in the teaching that differences of social
status were merely outward conditions that had no meaning for
the achievement of those moral qualities which distinguished the
Christian; accepting his social status, whatever it might be, the
Christian undertook to dignify it by the attainment of virtue.
These attitudes toward social classes expressed the subversion of
objective circumstances to subjective qualities pervading all
Christian culture.

2. *The Survival of Slavery*. In this subversion was implicit
not only the survival of slavery but also its approval. Paul sent the
slave back to his master with an admonition to obedience. Basil
asserted that, as a matter of morality, the bondservant must obey
his master according to the flesh to the glory of God with all good
will, in all things in which the commandment of God is not broken.
Slavery was tolerable, argued Ambrose, because it was better that
the weak and foolish man who cannot govern and control himself
serve and be in subjection to one who is more prudent, that he may
receive good counsel and not stumble through his rashness and

---

[1] See p. 590.

[2] See A. J. Carlyle, *The Influence of Christianity upon Social and Political Ideas* (1911),
pp. 41-42. The Roman lawyer held that the servile condition existed because the victor
in war chose to keep alive and not to slay defeated enemies.

folly. It was also tolerable, the great bishop said, because it positively afforded a unique opportunity for the practice of the virtues of humility, forgiveness, modesty, obedience, and patience. Like the other Church Fathers he admonished the slave to obedience and the master to kindness, but he denounced those who encouraged slaves to revolt. Just as the adaptation of the church to the world through the acquisition of wealth and power led to the prohibition of the Mass to soldiers who deserted and to the assertion of the doctrine that the possession of wealth is no bar to heaven, so it led to the pronouncement of anathema against those who, under the pretext of religion, excited slaves to despise their masters or to revolt against them. "Work steadily and obey meekly" was the Christian commandment to the slave. In fact, if a slave who had been manumitted became haughty to his former master, he could be returned to the servile status.

3. *Heresy and Class Struggles.* By accepting the class structure of society Christians found themselves entangled in class antagonisms and conflicts. In fact, after the church became identified with the state, the heretical movements were social and economic, quite as much as they were doctrinal, in origin and direction. The Donatist movement found its chief support among rebellious slaves and impoverished peasants. The Egyptian church arose in the course of the struggle of the fellahin against foreign and aristocratic landlords. Throughout Syria and Asia Minor the growth of monasticism was a social as well as a religious movement, and the monks played important roles in politics. A somewhat similar situation existed in the area of the Greek church. The subjection of the monasteries to the control of the bishops in the fifth century was primarily a move to quiet the social agitations that flowed from them. In the west, because the Teutons took over political power, monasticism was both a refuge from disorder and a defense of the ecclesiastical regime against heathenism; in both cases it performed a social as well as a religious service.[1]

---

[1] See James Westfall Thompson, *Economic and Social History of the Middle Ages* (300–1300) (1928), pp. 81–82: "The dogmatic and theological controversies set free the centrifugal and nationalistic forces in the oriental countries of the Empire. The union of the State with the orthodox Church brought this opposition to a head. Arianism, Monophysitism, Donatism became vehicles of popular expression of nationalism in the countries concerned, popular protests against heavy taxation, the great landed proprietorships of Latin masters, administrative abuses, partiality or unjust exemptions and immunities enjoyed by the privileged orthodox and ruling class who were as exploitive as British nabobs in India in the eighteenth century. The clergy, more than the aristocracy, were hated by the masses in these countries, although the Church and the State were hand in glove. For the Church was the greatest landed proprietor, whose acres were tilled by servile peasants or actual

In the light of this relation between religion and politics it is important to recognize that when a social order is explained and justified by a theological system, discontent and conflict within that social order necessarily find ideological expression in criticism of orthodox teachings. It was not accident, therefore, that, from the time of the consolidation of Christianity—in a privileged priestly order, in an alliance with the state, and in dogma—to the revolt against the church at the end of the Middle Ages, heresy and social revolt went hand in hand.

CHRISTIAN ECONOMIC ATTITUDES.

The Christians carried the subversion of material values into that area of life which modern men designate "economic"; in other words, they viewed property, wealth, work, and poverty chiefly as they contributed to the spiritual development of the individual. Consequently they neither recognized the social functions of property and work nor concerned themselves with the social problems of wealth and poverty. In the background of their attitudes toward economic institutions and practices were, it must always be remembered, the cruel exploitation and profligate consumption of the Roman economy, as well as the ancient failure to recognize the relation of economic factors to other aspects of life.

1. *The Christian Theories of Private Property and the Pursuit of Economic Gain.* The Christians believed that private property, like other secular institutions, was rooted in sin. By divine law the earth was the Lord's. By natural law it belonged to all men. Only by positive law did property become the private possession of the individual. "By human right," said Augustine, "one says 'This estate is mine, this servant is mine, this house is mine.' " And the possessor erred if he thought he had acquired it by his own efforts. Wealth, according to Ambrose, was the "gift of God." "My own, sayest thou?" asked the great bishop. "What is it? From what secret places has thou brought it into the world? When thou entered into the light, when thou camest from thy mother's womb, what wealth didst thou bring with thee?" To the evils of wealth and poverty the Christians opposed the "communism of love," which called for the sacrifice of private possession to the love of neighbor. These attitudes involved not the abolition of private

slaves. When the historian perceives that these heresies were motivated by a sense of economic injustice and social wrong, that they had in them the seeds of an agrarian revolution, he discovers a new interest in them and understands their popularity and their power with the masses." By permission of D. Appleton-Century Company, New York.

property, but considerations of the ways of its acquisition and its use.

Ambrose drew in sharp lines a picture of the vanity that was the pursuit of wealth.

Is it not a vain thing to gather riches? Surely to seek for perishable things is vain enough. Even when you have gathered them, how do you know that you will be allowed to retain possession of them? Is it not vain for the merchant to journey night and day, that he may be able to increase his heaps of treasure? Is it not vain for him to gather merchandise and be disquieted about its price, for fear lest he might have to sell for less than he gave? Is it not vain for him to watch the markets everywhere, and provoke men, through envy of his vaunted business, to rob him; or again to suffer shipwreck, because in his pursuit of gain he will not brook delay and wait for the coming of fair weather? And is he not disquieted in vain who with great toil amasses wealth, though he knows not to what heir he will leave it? Often all the avaricious toiler has accumulated at great pains is scattered abroad by his spendthrift heir with reckless prodigality. Why, then, do you vainly occupy yourself with spinning, as it were, webs of useless wealth, which are as worthless and unprofitable as the webs of spiders?[1]

In no less sharp lines he drew the picture of the evils that flowed from the possession of wealth. It contaminated the possessor because it weakened the soul's desire for virtue. It blotted out the image of God and substituted the image of the world of men. It was a sickness which prevented the soul from attaining the state of blessedness. Avarice was a capital vice because from it flowed a multitude of sins—injustice, contention, and lying—and covetousness was a denial of the love of neighbor which was the earthly manifestation of the love of God. Wealth, indeed, was the root of evil.

But the existence of wealth and its production as the necessary basis of life the Christians accepted. Their problem was to produce, acquire, and use it in ways not dangerous to their souls.

2. *The Christian Obligation to Work.* The Christians preached not only the duty to work but also the obligation to do good work. The duty to work originated after the Fall in the condemnation of men to live by the sweat of their brows. "He who will not work," said Paul, "shall not eat." The obligation to do good work was an aspect of the obligation to perform the duties that belonged to

[1] H. F. Dudden, *The Life and Times of St. Ambrose* (2 vols., 1935), Vol. 2, pp. 546–547. By permission of the Oxford University Press, New York. See also L. M. Zucker, *Ambrose, Book of Tobit [On Usury]* (1933).

one's social status; for the worker—slave, serf, or freeman, peasant or craftsman—this meant, of course, that he should be skillful and industrious insofar as he was capable. In these attitudes there was no appreciation of the value of work as a creative activity of the individual or as a factor in the achievement of the well-being of society. Its values were chiefly moral and disciplinary; John Chrysostom, who described them eloquently, also praised work's physical benefits:

. . . Whilst lying on their beds, they [the rich] are frequently without sleep through the whole night; and though they devise many schemes, they do not obtain such pleasure. But the poor man when released from his daily labours, having limbs completely tired, falls almost before he can lie down into a slumber that is sound, and sweet, and genuine, enjoying this reward, which is not a small one, of his fair day's toils. Since therefore the poor man sleeps, and drinks, and eats with more pleasure than the rich man, what further value is left to riches, now deprived of the one advantage they seem to have over poverty?

* * * * *

Let us not then despise labour; let us not despise work; for before the kingdom of Heaven, we receive the greatest recompense from thence, deriving pleasure from that circumstance; and not pleasure only, but what is greater than pleasure, the purest health. For in addition to their want of relish, many diseases also attack the rich; but the poor are freed from the hands of the physicians; and if at times they do fall into a sickness, they recover themselves quickly, being far removed from all effeminacy, and having robust constitutions. Poverty, to those who bear it wisely, is a great possession, a treasure that cannot be taken away. . . [1]

The disciplinary value of labor arose largely in the effects of fatigue upon the bodily impulses which turned men to sin; it was described as a "purifying of the soul."

3. *Callings Dangerous to the Welfare of the Soul.* The Christians, however, were careful to distinguish between kinds of work that nourished virtues and those that were likely to be sinful. Originally they prohibited converts from working at many occupations which served the pagan cults. After the triumph of Christianity this prohibition lapsed, except against callings that were superstitious in character, such as those of the astrologer and magician. Manual labor at the crafts was regarded as least dangerous to the welfare of the soul, and agricultural labor only a little more so. Retail trade, if carried on only to gain a livelihood, was

[1] Philip Schaff, editor, *The Nicene and Post-Nicene Fathers of the Christian Church* (14 vol. 1889–1890) Vol. 9, pp. 352–353. The Christian Literature Company.

recognized as a suitable employment. It was, however, a dangerous calling. "The merchant," said Jerome, "can please God only with difficulty." John Chrysostom was explicit about the circumstances which made trading unlawful:

> Whoever buyeth a thing, not that he may sell it whole or unchanged, but that it may be a material for fashioning something, he is no merchant. But the man who buyeth in order that he may gain by selling it again unchanged as he bought it, that man is of the buyers and sellers who are cast forth from God's Temple.[1]

Trade, therefore, was suspect, and the wholesale trade especially so. In fact, all large-scale enterprise was regarded as having origin in avarice. Speculation was a sin. Usury—the business of lending money for profit—was bitterly denounced, not only because of its avaricious tendency but because loans, usually made for purposes of consumption, were regarded as an exploitation of the poor and needy, whom the rule of love called men to succor. The councils promulgated canons against the practice, particularly by the different ranks of the clergy. The general tenor of this legislation was to define all charges upon lent money as usury and to declare its reception a form of theft. This attitude is well expressed in the following quotation from Basil, the founder of eastern monasticism:

> Listen, you rich men, to the kind of advice I am giving to the poor because of your inhumanity. Far better endure under their dire straits than undergo troubles that are bred of usury! But if you were obedient to the Lord, what need of these words? What is the advice of the Master? Lend to those from whom ye do not hope to receive. [Luke VI, 34, 35.] And what kind of a loan is this, it is asked, from which all idea of the expectation of repayment is withdrawn? Consider the force of the expression, and you will be amazed at the loving kindness of the legislator. When you mean to supply the need of a poor man for the Lord's sake, the transaction is at once a gift and a loan. Because there is no expectation of a return, it is a gift. Yet because of the munificence of the Master, Who repays on the recipient's behalf, it is a loan. "He that hath pity on the poor lendeth to the Lord." [Prov. xix, 17.] Do you not wish the Master of the universe to be responsible for your repayment? If any wealthy man in the town promises you repayment on behalf of others, do you admit his suretyship? But you do not accept God, Who more than repays on behalf of the poor. Give the money lying useless, without weighing it with increase, and both shall be benefited. To you will accrue the security of its safe keeping. The recipients will have the advantage of its use. And if

[1] Quoted in G. G. Coulton, *The Medieval Scene* (1930), p. 141. The Cambridge University Press, London.

it is increase which you seek, be satisfied with that which is given by the Lord. He will pay the interest for the poor. Await the loving-kindness of Him Who is in truth most kind.

What you are taking involves the last extremity of inhumanity. You are making your profit out of misfortune; you are levying a tax upon tears. You are strangling the naked. You are dealing blows on the starving. There is no pity anywhere, no sense of your kinship to the hungry. . . . There are such people as twelve-per-cent men and ten-per-cent men: I shudder to mention their names. They are exactors by the month, like the demons who produce epilepsy, attacking the poor as the changes of the moon come round.[1]

4. *The Christian Uses of Wealth: Almsgiving.* During the first and second centuries Christian spokesmen generally railed at the rich; when, however, the well to do entered the congregations they softened their criticism. Clement of Alexandria explained in the work *Can a Rich Man Be Saved?* that not the possession of wealth but its love was damning.

An instrument, if you use it with artistic skill, is a thing of art; but if you are lacking in skill, it reaps the benefit of your unmusical nature, though not itself responsible. Wealth too is an instrument of the same kind. You can use it rightly; it ministers to righteousness. But if one use it wrongly, it is found to be a means of wrong. For its nature is to minister, not to rule. . . . So let a man do away, not with his possessions, but rather with the passions of his soul, which do not consent to the better use of what he has; in order that, by becoming noble and good, he may be able to use these possessions also in a noble manner.[2]

Augustine concurred in this view. Jesus asked that men live from day to day, trusting the Lord to provide; the Church Fathers asked only that the rich, having property, live as if they had it not. Cyprian exhorted the rich, "Give alms of thy substance, and turn not away thy face from any poor men. So shall it be, that neither the face of God be turned away from thee." "Let the rich man minister aid to the poor man," said Clement of Alexandria, "and let the poor man thank God that He has given him one through whom his wants may be supplied." Ambrose asserted that alms-giving is the antidote to the poisonous effects of wealth but warned that unrighteous gains cannot be made righteous by charity. John Chrysostom welcomed the thronging of beggars at the doors of the church because they gave the rich Christian a chance to cleanse his

[1] Philip Schaff and Henry Wace, editors. *The Nicene and Post-Nicene Fathers* . . . (2d series), Vol. 8, pp. xlviii–xlix.

[2] G. W. Butterworth, *Clement of Alexandria* (1919), p. 299, from "The Rich Man's Salvation."

conscience before he entered. The rich man, so the Church Fathers taught, was only a steward of the "gift of God," and the poor man was God's pensioner. Under these doctrines the church justified completely the possession of great wealth. In 415 a council condemned as heretical a doctrine of Pelagius that the rich can be saved only if they renounce their property.

5. *The Idealization of Poverty.* The acceptance of the possession and use of wealth under these doctrines did not bring, however, the acceptance of the pursuit of wealth as a just goal of life. "Mad and raging" avarice remained a capital vice. Man should work only to obtain enough for subsistence; all beyond this minimum, which was recognized as varying from country to country, should be given away. Poverty was certainly a condition not to be feared. "Hunger," said Tertullian, "can have no terror for him who is ready to die for Christ." "Give ear, ye poor," cried Ambrose, "for your life is precious, and if your flesh is mortal, your soul shall never die." "Remember Lazarus," pleaded John Chrysostom, "who had to buffet disease, and poverty, and desolateness, and those other innumerable trials; and after that so high degree of virtue! Remember the Apostles, who lived in hunger, and in thirst, and nakedness; the prophets, the patriarchs, the just men, and you will find all these not among the rich or luxurious, but amongst the poor, the afflicted, and the distressed." "And if any one were to offer thee sovereignty, and political power, and wealth, and luxury, and then having set against them poverty," the golden-mouthed bishop continued, "were to give thee thy choice to take which thou wouldst, thou wouldst straightway seize upon poverty, if indeed thou knewest the beauty thereof." He called all men to see the beauty of a soul voluntarily poor:

Wouldest thou see the beauty of this soul? Wouldest thou acquaint thyself with the riches of poverty? He commands not men, but he commands evil spirits. He stands not at a king's side, but he hath taken his stand near to God. He is the comrade, not of men, but of angels. He hath not chests, two, or three, or twenty, but such an abundance as to account the whole world nothing. He hath not a treasure, but heaven. He needs not slaves, or rather hath his passions for slaves, hath for slaves the motives that rule over kings. . . . And royalty, and gold, and all such things, he laughs at, as at children's toys; and like hoops and dice, and heads, and balls, so doth he count all these to be contemptible. For he hath an adorning, which they who play with these cannot even see.[1]

[1] Philip Schaff, editor, *The Nicene and Post-Nicene Fathers* . . . , Vol. 10, pp. 295–296.

Involuntary poverty was the natural habitat of the virtues. Voluntary poverty was the highest cultivation they could receive on earth. The abolition of poverty was not to be talked of:

How many do I hear say, Let there be no poverty. Therefor let us stop the mouths of those who murmur at such things. For it is blasphemy to utter such complaints. To such then, let us say, Let there be no meanness of spirit. For poverty brings innumerable good things into our state of life, and without poverty riches would be unprofitable. Hence we should accuse neither the one nor the other of these; for poverty and riches are both alike weapons which will tend to virtue, if we are willing. . . . And thou, then,—art thou rich? Display much bountifulness. Has thou become poor? Shew much endurance and patience! For neither is wealth an evil, nor poverty in itself; but these things, either of them, become so according to the free choice of those who make use of them.[1]

CHRISTIAN ASCETICISM.

Closely related to the idealization of poverty was the conscious denial of worldly interests through spiritual exercises. To these exercises the Christians gave the name "asceticism"; originally this word referred to the bodily exercises of Greek athletes. Inasmuch as the Christians set up a sharp distinction between the body and the soul, between the flesh and the spirit, asceticism necessarily involved repression of bodily impulses, if not a neglect of bodily needs. Through eastern influences, which emphasized the punishment of the body as a means of purifying the soul, there crept into Christian asceticism not only a harsh repression of bodily impulses and needs but also an aggressive cultivation of bodily infirmities. From Christianity itself came the denial of worldly interests. From Cynicism came the repudiation of all refinements of bodily satisfactions. From Manichaeism came the conscious effort to be dirty, loathsome, diseased, and tortured.

On the whole, Christian asceticism was not as excessive as Eastern asceticism. Perhaps its temper is suggested by the following quotation from Jerome:

You bathe daily; another regards such over-niceness as defilement. You surfeit yourself in wild fowl and pride yourself on eating sturgeon; I, on the contrary, fill my belly with beans. You find pleasures in troops of laughing girls; I prefer Paula and Melanium who weep. You covet what belongs to others; they disdain what is their own. You like wines flavored with honey; they drink cold water, more delicious still. You

[1] Philip Schaff, editor, *The Nicene and Post-Nicene Fathers* . . . , Vol. 9, p. 442.

count as lost what you cannot have, eat up, and devour at the moment; they believe in the Scriptures, and look for things to come. And if they are wrong, and if the resurrection of the body on which they rely is a foolish delusion, what does it matter to you? We, on our side, look with disfavor on such a life as yours. You can fatten yourself on your good things as much as you please; I, for my part prefer paleness and emaciation. You suppose men like me are unhappy; we regard you as more unhappy still. Thus we reciprocate each other's thoughts and appear to each other mutually insane.[1]

Monasticism, of course, was an institutionalization of asceticism; the rules of Basil and Benedict saved it from excess. In the fourth and fifth centuries the favorite self-mortifying practice among monks was to remain sleepless as long as possible in the belief that in this process the soul was released from the body. The monks performed severe physical labor as a means of repressing bodily impulses to sin. For lay Christians the substitution of love of the church for love of the world was the chief form of self-denial; the fasts on Wednesday and Friday, and the austerities of Lent were adequate gestures to ascetic living.

But much harsher modes of ascetic living were practiced by individuals, particularly after eastern influences became strong in the fourth century. Two modes became popular at that time. In one the individual lived in a tiny cell or tomb, often so small that lying down was impossible. Of this type of ascetic the two virgins Alexandra and Elizabeth became famous. Alexandra, a beautiful young woman, who feared that she had aroused the amorous desires of a young man, shut herself in a tomb outside Alexandria and remained there twelve years. All but one hour each day she spent in prayer and meditation; the one hour was spent in spinning. It is reported of Elizabeth that she wore a single garment winter and summer, ate no bread or oil, never took a bath, and frequently fasted for forty days. For three years she kept her mind's eye fixed on God without once raising her bodily eye to heaven. She achieved a great reputation as a miracle worker, and after her death dust from her tomb was believed to cure all sorts of diseases. Those who took up the second mode of ascetic living were known as *stylites*, or pillar saints. The founder of this group was Simeon (*ca.* 388–459), a Syrian, who spent thirty-six years of his life on top of a pillar. Originally the pillar was only nine feet tall but as time went on it was built up, or a higher pillar was substituted, for his last abode

[1] Philip Schaff and Henry Wace, editors, *The Nicene and Post-Nicene Fathers* . . . (2d series), Vol. 6, pp. 59–60.

From René Dussaud, Paul Deschamps, *et* Henri Seyrig, *La Syrie antique et médiévale Illustrée (Libraire Orientaliste Paul Geuthner, Paris,* 1931)

THE CONVENT OF ST. SIMEON STYLITES

This structure was built around the famous column of St. Simeon. It is one of the finest examples of early Christian art in Syria, where, during and after the fourth, fifth, and sixth centuries, the rich cities built many churches.

was on top of a pillar fifty feet in height. At the top of the column, which could be ascended by a ladder, was a platform, perhaps with a railing, so small that Simeon could stand, sit, and kneel but not lie down. He was exposed constantly to the elements. During Lent he fasted and yet maintained himself erect; at first he tied himself to a prop, but late in life he needed no artificial support. His whole life was believed to be a miracle.

Voluntary poverty and ascetic living were valued not for themselves but for the spiritual harvest they produced. The Christian saint, it must be understood, never mistook material circumstance for spiritual reality.

Christian Attitudes toward Family Life.

If in the background of the Christians' economic attitudes were the cruel exploitation of labor, the luxury of the rich, and the low productivity of the traditional urban economy, in the background of their attitudes toward sex, marriage, and the family were the licentiousness, the degrading perversions, and the polygamy and the concubinage of aristocratic society, the sensual rites of the fertility cults, and the age-old ignorance of sex, both as a physiological process and as a psychological factor in life. Their attitudes were in part a reaction to these conditions and in part an expression of the submission of the flesh to the spirit which pervaded their entire outlook on life. Above all else they were at war with carnal sin. In developing their attitudes they drew heavily upon the teachings which declared sex, particularly in the female form, to be the root of sin and shame. This idea, of course, was much older than Hebrew culture. Although its earliest literary expression was in the Babylonian epic of creation, which portrayed Tiamat as the leader of the evil daimons, the idea was undoubtedly deep in preliterate thought, because among primitive peoples the belief that women are unclean is almost universal. If earlier beliefs affected the Christian conception of the role of sex in life, other beliefs lay behind the practices they condemned. The forthright, indeed joyful, acceptance of sex as the mode of nature's productivity was at the base of the fertility cults which influenced deeply the sex life of the pagan masses. Sexual expression was a normal part of the rites of the Eleusinian, Orphic, and other mysteries, and sex experience was understood as the mode of union with the spirit in certain mystical sects. Valentinus, the Gnostic, seems to have taught this doctrine. In this connection it is proper to recall that the Christians spoke of Christ as the "Heavenly Bridegroom", and of salvation as a "spiritual marriage." This metaphor was carried through the hymn in *The Banquet of the Ten Virgins* noted above in the discussion of Christian literature.

1. *Monogamous Marriage.* Monogamous marriage, conceived as a spiritual union, which the Christians substituted for the polygamous marriage sanctioned by Hebrew law, was the sole condition under which the sexual act was lawful. Concubinage, prostitution, adultery, and divorce were sinful, and the second marriage, originally condemned, was approved grudgingly. Within the marriage bond the sexual act, except for the procreation of children, was a venial sin. The proper attitude even then, so Augustine said, was one of regret.

Love your wives then, but love them chastely. In your intercourse with them keep yourselves within the bounds necessary for the procreation of children. And in as much as you cannot otherwise have them, descend to it with regret. For this necessity is the punishment of that Adam from whom we are sprung. Let us not make a pride of our punishment.[1]

Just as the rich were asked to live as if they were not rich, so men were called upon to live as if they did not have wives. Since there was no marriage in heaven, it was well that men should begin before death to be what they were to be after they were resurrected.

2. *The Praise of Virginity.* The Christians called for sexual purity at all times. Before marriage chastity was to be complete. After marriage continence was to be the rule. The widowed who chose to forego a second marriage was more virtuous than the married, and the virgin was superior to either. The Church Fathers outdid themselves in the praise of virginity, especially Ambrose and Jerome, as the following quotations indicate:

The marriage bond is not then to be shunned as though it were sinful, but rather declined as being a galling burden. For the law binds the wife to bear children in labour and in sorrow, and in subjection to her husband, for that he is lord over her. So, then, the married woman, but not the widow, is subject to labour and pain in bringing forth children, and she only that is married, not she that is a virgin, is under the power of her husband. The virgin is free from all these things. . . . [2]

Some people may be eunuchs from necessity; I am one of free will. [Math. XIX, 11, 12] . . . I praise wedlock, I praise marriage, but it is because they give me virgins.[3]

Jerome climaxed his praise with the assertion that the virgin conferred on her mother the high privilege of being "the mother-in-law of God." He was particularly explicit about the protection that should be given the female virgin's "angelic virtue":

A girl should associate only with girls, she should know nothing of boys and should dread even playing with them. She should never hear an unclean word, and if amid the bustle of the household she should chance to hear one, she should not understand it. Her mother's nod should be to her as much a command as a spoken injunction. . . . She should not appear in public too freely or too frequently attend crowded churches. All her pleasure should be in her chamber. She must never look at young men or turn her eyes upon curled fops; and the wanton songs

---

[1] Philip Schaff, editor, *The Nicene and Post-Nicene Fathers* . . . , Vol. 6, p. 254.
[2] Philip Schaff and Henry Wace, editors, *The Nicene and Post-Nicene Fathers* . . . (2d series), Vol. 10, p. 405.
[3] *Ibid.*, Vol. 6, pp. 29–30.

of sweet voiced girls which wound the soul through the ears must be kept from her.[1]

As regards the use of the bath, I know that some are content with saying that a Christian virgin should not bathe along with eunuchs or with married women, with the former because they are still men at all events in mind or with the latter because women with child offer a revolting spectacle. For myself, however, I wholly disapprove of baths for a virgin of full age. Such an one should blush and feel overcome at the idea of seeing herself undressed. By vigils and fasts she mortifies her body and brings it into subjection. By a cold chastity she seeks to put out the flame of lust and to quench the hot desires of youth. And by a deliberate squalor she makes haste to spoil her natural good looks. Why, then, should she add fuel to a sleeping fire by taking baths.[2]

In this quotation may be seen the attitude which until recent decades forbade not only the diffusion of knowledge of sexual relations but also the scientific investigation of sex; it fixed as morality the age-old ignorance of sex.

3. *The Place of Woman in Christian Culture.* The view that woman is "weak, wicked, and fickle" was rendered in Christianity with great emphasis. By virtue of the circumstances of woman's creation she was regarded as inferior and subject to man, and sin with all its consequences—hard labor, shame, and death—had entered the world as a result of her deceit. She had been the chosen tool of the devil and the chief calamity of man, and so she remained! Only as a virgin could she rise to spirituality; if married, only by childbearing was she saved from complete worldliness. The husband was "head" of the wife; her obligation was to do his will in all things. To remain silent, to wear modest apparel, to shun adornment, to abhor cosmetics, to conceal her charm and beauty were the forms of behavior best suited to her nature; for her to reflect on her nature was shameful. Even in prayer she should not uncover her head. Outside of the family circle she could participate in no activities other than the worship and good works of the church. Such participation, however, was an extension of the field of activity permitted to woman by the Hebrew and pagan traditions. Within the family circle she was, it should be remembered, an important producer of economic goods and services. To the drudgery and perpetual childbearing of the traditional lot of woman, Christianity added at least a renewed emphasis on the repression of those natural impulses which made her attractive

[1] *Ibid.*, p. 259.
[2] *Ibid.*, p. 194.

and companionable. Except as companions in ascetic living, Christianity found no praiseworthy relation for the sexes. The married man was spiritually purer when away from than when with his wife.

4. *The Survival of the Patriarchal Family.* By virtue of doctrine and social inheritance from Hebrew and pagan sources, family organization under Christianity was a strict patriarchate. The husband and father was both legal and spiritual head of the family. The rule of love modified in practice the rights of overlordship which law and moral precept granted him. That its influence was great among the peasant-village masses may be doubted, for their ancient mores were too tenacious to be altered by doctrines which they did not understand. For them Christianity meant the introduction of priestly influence into family life; at just this point, in fact, priestly influence had its chief extension. Marriage, conceived as a sacrament, was within the legal jurisdiction of the church, and the family, conceived as a spiritual unit, was the natural field of priestly control. The effect of priestly influence was, it may be believed, almost wholly good. Violence in family relations, except as a form of chastisement for children, was condemned. Religious teaching was added to affection as a stimulus to mutual helpfulness. Sexual purity, especially after marriage, was probably greatly increased. And the family became the center of the religious education through which the children were brought into the church; filial duty and obedience to the church were united in a single emotional fixation. The social foundation of the sovereignty of the church over the masses was laid in this function of the family. Women, it must be remembered, had been from the first a significant factor in the growth of Christianity, and under priestly influence in the family they became the bedrock of its ecclesiastical structure.

On the whole, however, family life went on under Christianity much as it had in the pagan world. The prohibitions of child exposure and abortion abated these ancient evils, but the economic conditions and the lack of knowledge of child care, which caused high infant mortality, remained, so that many of those children whose lives were saved by the prohibitions suffered death or physical deformity from natural causes. The gain in these respects, it may be believed, was moral, not physical. The woman bore still the ancient burdens of drudgery and fecundity. The man possessed still his legal overlordship. No important changes in child care and training, in the customs of courtship and marriage, in the mores that shaped domestic life, and in the property rights of the members of families flowed from Christian teachings and priestly influence. With the decay of the Roman aristocracy the worst features of pagan domestic life disappeared; with the decline of the cities the traditional family life of peasant villagers displaced the disorganized family life of impoverished urban workers. Most of the gains in family stability had origin in these social changes rather than in religious teachings. A new religious feeling was woven into the traditional patriarchal family; otherwise it remained virtually unaltered.

THE SOCIAL WORK OF THE CHRISTIAN CHURCH.

It is difficult to evaluate the social work of Christianity because the emotions attached to the faith, when disturbed by assertions that do not glorify the church, thwart a reasoned judgment or deny its findings. Clearly the claim that "all true civilization" roots in Christianity is an overstatement, as is the assertion that every good act, no matter by whom performed, is a Christian act. Such views are as wrong as those which see Christianity as the "opiate of the poor" and the chief obstacle to the advancement of secular well-being. Somewhere between these extremes is a more nearly correct position which can be discovered only if present social developments and issues are disregarded.[1]

The evaluation of the social services of Christianity must be made in terms of the conditions under which it arose and the circumstances which, as its priestly leaders won power, modified ethical teachings in favor of ecclesiastical interests. The teaching of a doctrine of moral perfection is not quite identical with the amelioration of suffering and the abatement of cruelties; particularly is this seen to be true when it is realized that the teaching declared suffering a primary condition for the attainment of moral perfection. Some of the present difficulty in evaluating Christianity's social achievements certainly has origin in the fact that many Western men now doubt this relation between poverty and moral achievement.

1. *The Christian Treatment of the Poor and Afflicted.* From the social point of view the positive element in the teachings of Jesus was the orientation of suffering in spiritual terms; suffering men moved to the center of God's interest, and as objects of God's love they became the rightful recipients of men's care. From the first,

[1] See *The Catholic Encyclopaedia*, article "Priesthood," IV, "What the Catholic Priesthood has done for civilization"; G. Uhlhorn, *Christian Charity in the Ancient Church* (1883).

therefore, the poor, the widowed, the orphaned, the disabled, the sick, and the infirm received kindly treatment among Christians. Originally this treatment was merely an aspect of that sharing of goods and sympathy which accompanied the expectation of the immediate Second Coming. As this expectancy faded and the congregations grew, the care of the needy became an activity of the several churches. Each church developed its own methods, but in general, it may be conjectured, they followed the practices of the Roman collegia. The congregations, it may be believed, were for a long time more or less self-supporting bodies of workers to which the unemployed looked for aid in time of need.[1] Funds for charitable work were raised in different ways. Each month the members of the congregations brought gifts of money and produce to the church, and from time to time special collections, known as oblations, were made at the performance of the Eucharist. The month of December, when the gladiatorial combats were held, became the special period for gifts to the poor. The amounts of the gifts were left to the conscience of the individual, but gifts from sources regarded as impure were rejected. These funds were distributed by the bishops, usually with the aid of the deacons. Lists of recipients were kept, but no investigation was made when allotments were determined. Widows and orphans were the favored recipients. Supplementary aid was given to large families if earnings were insufficient. The sick, the disabled, the aged, and needy mothers were cared for, probably at first in private homes and later in hospitals. Paupers were given Christian burial. The "sick at heart" were comforted by visits. Brethren condemned to the mines for their beliefs were given special foods.

In the fourth century the administration of charity, like every other work of the church, passed from the control of the congregations into the hands of the ecclesiastical authorities. Behind this

[1] Adolf von Harnack, *The Mission and Expansion of Christianity in the First Three Centuries* (2 vols. 1908), Vol. I, p. 176: " . . . It is beyond question, therefore, that a Christian brother could demand work from the church, and that the church had to furnish him with work. What bound the members together, then, was not merely the duty of supporting one another—that was simply the *ultima ratio;* it was the fact that they formed a guild of workers, in the sense that the churches had to provide work for a brother whenever he required it. This fact seems to me of great importance, from the social standpoint. The churches were also labour unions. The case attested by Cyprian proves that there is far more here than a merely rhetorical maxim. The church did prove in this way a refuge for people in distress, who were prepared to work. Its attractive power was consequently intensified, and from the economic standpoint we must attach very high value to a union which provided work for those who were able to work, and at the same time kept hunger from those who were unfit for any labour." By permission of G. P. Putnam's Sons, New York.

development were, on the one hand, the growth of the power of the priest class and, on the other hand, the increase of distress, notably in the great cities. The Christian bishop succeeded the Roman noble as the distributor of aid to the poor and needy; he entrusted the administration of relief to special officers, known as stewards. Pagans as well as Christians received aid. At the same time institutional relief for the sick, the orphaned, and the aged was provided in hospitals, which were modeled on the centers of the cult of Asklepios or the Roman public hospitals. The church also became a refuge for those accused of crime and for the poor; legislation to prevent the abuse of this privilege by slaves and debtors was passed late in the fourth century. A change in the financial support of charity accompanied these developments. Gifts were now placed on the altar as offerings to God, and the bishops distributed them in the name of God. In other words, the rich offered their wealth to God, and God gave it to the needy. When the economic position of the priest class was consolidated,[1] the claim of the poor to one-fourth of all ecclesiastical revenues was recognized. At the same time the congregational support of hospitals was revived, with the result that their numbers increased rapidly throughout the late fourth and the fifth century.

In view of the harsh pagan attitudes toward the poor and the weak, the human sympathy manifested in these services to the poor and the afflicted was more significant than the services, for it was fundamental in the shift of values which transformed pagan into Christian culture. That this sympathy was orientated in supernatural terms and not in institutional terms is evidence of the fact that common men, as carriers of the low intellectual tradition, were able to think only in terms of the daimonic universe.

2. *The Christian Treatment of Slaves.* The changes in the status of the slave in the fourth and fifth centuries were largely due to the economic and social developments by which serfdom displaced slavery as the chief form of labor control. Christians accepted serfdom with less objection than slavery because its customs—the ways of the peasant village—were less cruel than those of slavery—the harsh practices of urban cultures. Christians approved manumission as a charitable work, but so had the Romans under Stoic influence. Under Constantine the only public act permitted on the Sabbath was the manumission of a slave. The Christians protested against selling children into slavery on account of the debts of their parents and opposed the enslavement

[1] See p. 1074.

of children who had been exposed by their parents. But no church council ventured to abolish the practices. In fact, many of the serfs acquired by the church in the fifth century were children saved from death by exposure. Great concern was shown by Christians for female slaves because of the danger to chastity involved in their condition. Laws were passed forbidding the sale of a female slave by a procurer except to a Christian master and permitting ecclesiastical officials to emancipate women handed over to prostitution. Great pressure was brought to bear against the treatment of the female slaves of the stage, especially the musicians, who commonly combined prostitution with their artistic profession. Probably the most significant modification of the servile status brought about by Christianity was the recognition of the sacredness of the slave's marriage and family life; this modification, it should be recognized, came not from social idealism but as a by-product of the doctrine that marriage is a sacrament.

Slaves owned by a Christian master were not free to become Christians without his consent; nor could they take a church office without his permission. Slaves and serfs who entered a monastery were not liberated from all obligations to their masters. As previously noted, the Council of Chalcedon forbade monasteries to admit slaves and serfs without the approval of their masters. Christianity neither modified the legal status of the slave nor altered his working conditions; as a form of labor control the ancient institution of slavery was not touched. Christianity's contribution to the amelioration of the lot of the slave was the result almost entirely of the desire for sexual purity and the abatement of cruelties that sprang from the doctrine that love triumphs over all worldly circumstances.

3. *The Abatement of Cruelties.*   Greco-Roman culture accepted physical violence as a normal element of human life; Christianity set its face against the cruelties this acceptance involved. Chief among the cruelties abated by Christian influence were those of the arena and the stage. Constantine attempted to prohibit the practice of the gladiatorial profession, and the church denied communion to those attached to it and other occupations connected with the games. The first Christian emperor also forbade the sending of criminals into the arena. Animal combats and chariot racing, which became the great sport of the hippodrome in Constantinople, continued long after the gladiatorial spectacle had ceased. Closely connected with the prohibition against sending criminals into the arena were reforms in the treatment of prisoners.

Constantine forbade the imposition of capital punishment except when the accused person confessed or when there was sworn testimony as to his guilt. He also abolished the practice of scourging persons when they were arrested. Even more humane than these acts was the order requiring that prisoners must be kept in quarters open to light and air. In 340 the mingling of the sexes in the prisons was prohibited. Mutilation as a form of punishment, although opposed by the Christians, did not entirely disappear. The mutilation of a slave gave him freedom. The castration of males in order to obtain docile servants was abolished. The effect of these reforms was to remove much of the suffering among common men that did not have direct origin in the severity of labor and poverty.[1]

THE CHRISTIAN SOCIAL IDEAL.

As a personal religion Christianity taught an ideal of the moral perfection of the individual; it did not produce a conception of an ideal social order. Moral perfection and social justice were believed to flow from a strict adherence to revealed truth as organized in individual behavior. Thus the feeling of common humanity inherited from the Stoics became merely a feeling of the unity of mankind under God as realized through the church; so also altruism, charity, and love were conceived as having subjective value for individuals rather than objective value in social amelioration. Even the good works necessary in the scheme of salvation were not understood as having any social purpose.

Dreadfully prominent in the ethical ideals of this age [of the Church Fathers] is the separation between "good works" and social purpose. Obedience of the most slavish kind is exalted as a virtue *per se*. A monk waters a stick for years at the behest of his superior merely to test obedience, and hard work at useless tasks is constantly praised. This unnatural separation of virtue from its social meaning results in actual brutality. A monk is praised for burning love letters from home unread, lest they distract him from his prayers. A brother refuses the simplest act of assistance to his brother on the basis of his "being dead" to the world. A husband deserts a loving wife, to "save his soul," and although it is evident that Cassianus is not quite sure of his ground, yet he praises the husband's conduct, while making half-hearted excuse for marriage. The ideal is a false suppression of natural and legitimate human desires, and results, of course, in all kinds of questionable conduct. Above all,

[1] For a summary of the effect of Christianity on cruel practices, see Charles Loring Brace, *Gesta Christi, or a History of Humane Progress under Christianity* (1882).

the *gratia castitatis* [the love that punishes] is, of course, most especially praised, and most questionable means of testing and proving it are suggested.[1]

The social results of Christian teachings, even in terms of the feelings that life is sacred, violence is abhorrent, and greed is sinful, were, therefore, the by-products of the pursuit of an ideal of individual purity, which, when pressed to extremes, not only obscured the social good but added to social evil. Indeed, it may be argued that Christianity, because of its doctrine that virtue is subjective and individual and that the social world has origin in sin, was peculiarly denied the opportunity to develop a social ideal.

The concrete effects of this denial were evident in (1) the acceptance of the existing social order and (2) the failure to develop any program of social reorganization.[2] These effects were, of course, merely two aspects of the same thing, namely, the belief that individual sin and virtue are the supreme realities in terms of which the relation of men and God is organized. The social fact— the organization of men with men—was only incidental to this relation. Politically, this acceptance and failure meant the continuation of aristocratic government. Socially, it meant the perpetuation of the traditional class structure with all its inequalities and exploitation. Economically, it meant the endurance of poverty in the presence of riches without striving to increase wealth or to alter its distribution. "For the poor always ye have with you." Except in the minimum amounts necessary to subsistence, economic satisfactions, although they were not evil in themselves, were not to be sought after. For the individual these

[1] Thomas C. Hall, *History of Ethics within Organized Christianity* (1910), pp. 247–248. By permission of Charles Scribner's Sons, New York.

[2] K. S. Latourette, *The Expansion of Christianity* (2 vols, 1937), Vol. I, pp. 244–245: "Even had the heads of the Church wished to bring in a fully Christian society, they would have been estopped by the alliance with the state. It was with the aid of the government that the majority of the once pagan population came into the Church. That government was conservative. Probably one of the motives of the Emperors in supporting the new faith was the hope of gaining the assistance of the Church in the preservation of the existing order against the impending disintegration. . . .

"The monastic movement, roughly coinciding as it did with the great influx into the Church, also tended to prevent the emergence of any plan for the remaking of civilization. The monastic ideal drew its devotees out of normal society into communities built upon what it esteemed Christian principles. Attracting as it did a large proportion of the most ardent Christians, it tended to distract attention from any effort to bring all of society up to its own exacting standards. Indeed it despaired of doing so and acquiesced in a division between those who wished to attain perfectly to the Gospel rule and those who admittedly had given over any effort to carry out more than a portion of its precepts." By permission of Harpers & Brothers, New York.

things together brought the acceptance of the position he occupied in society as his proper status. The attempt to alter this status was regarded as evil; the effort should be to glorify it by exhibiting Christian virtues—humility, obedience, modesty, honesty, industriousness, and competence. However, if social changes occurred, altering institutions, the individual was not bound to resist them. In other words, the Christian was not obligated to resist any more than he was to promote social change. His only duty, as an individual and as a member of society, was to lead a Christian life. Inasmuch as traditionalism pervaded the existing social order, this seeming freedom from conservatism amounted actually to a profound social inertia.

It is important in this connection to recognize that Christianity taught its adherents, as far as possible, to shun the "world," *i.e.*, the aims and behavior of secular society. The result of this teaching was the giving of a unique position in the social order to the Christian priest class; as organized in the divinely established church, it was merely a worldly projection of the spiritual kingdom. This theory of the social position of the Christian priest class, it is not difficult to understand, removed the priesthood from consideration as a secular phenomenon, for obviously the theory meant the independence of the Christian priest class and the subservience of the individual Christian to it. For individual priests there was a life of virtue, which exemplified the ideal life to the congregations; for the priest class as a whole there were prestige, power, and wealth in which the church, as the organization of the divine will among men, was glorified. Like other dominant social classes, the Christian priest class assumed for its members those responsibilities, and enforced upon them those obligations, which ensured its position. And, like other dominant social classes, it fused these responsibilities in an ideal which identified the general welfare with the maintenance of its position. By setting an otherworldly goal for men Christianity did not achieve separation from the "world"; it merely subverted the "world" to those of its elements whose supremacy was served by the seeking of the other world. And to bear the cross of this world was necessary to attain the otherworldly goal. The unity of men under the Christian priest class, suffering the pains and obligations of whatever social order existed among them in order to enjoy the glory of the next world, was the Christian social ideal.

In the moral freedom of the individual there was the means of escape from sin, and this escape took form in a spiritual regeneration of the individual, not in a reorganization of his relations with other men. In the interplay of human and divine wills, society, although a conditioning factor, was actually unimportant; to live with God required only the realization of virtue in an individual behavior which, while having good effects, might or might not leave society unchanged. In either case the results were irrelevant to the achievement of the true goal.

THE SIGNIFICANCE OF THE CHRISTIAN CONSOLIDATION OF THE WESTERN CULTURAL TRADITION

In Christian patterns the Western cultural tradition was consolidated, without significant change, for a thousand years. Through these patterns many of the achievements of the ancient-oriental and Mediterranean lands were transmitted to medieval and modern European peoples. In them also was a structure of life into which these peoples moved and within which their creative energies were constrained. To a remarkable degree Christianity, by setting before men an otherworldly future, became in fact a living past. The indirect effects of Christianity were to strengthen the forces of social and intellectual conservatism.

As emphasized in the preceding pages, the primary social result of the development of Christianity was the reconstitution of a priest class in Western society. Most of the institutional changes brought about by this development were merely alterations in the social controls by which the older powerful social classes had ruled; in some cases old controls were displaced by new ones, but in many more cases they were merely adapted to the service of the new powerful class. Although this class accepted the existence of other classes and also the existence of nations, it superimposed on them "Christendom"—the fellowship in Christ into which all men might enter. Unity under the Christian priests was not only an ideal but also a fact in the Western world. Men of all classes and nations shared a common life under God. They served in a universal organization. They associated freely with one another. They looked forward to a common destiny. And suffering they understood as a common trial. Christianity embodied a solution of the ancient problem of social and cultural differences among men. In the suffering Christ glorified was sublimated distressed humanity. The symbol synthesized the social values which common men, because they had suffered and realized that they must continue to suffer, aspired to achieve. That the goal of the aspira-

From C. C. Dobson, *The Face of Christ* (1933). *By the courtesy of the Morehouse-Gorham Co., New York*

JESUS

When an individual becomes a culture symbol, his features and expression, if unknown as is the case with Jesus, are inventions which depict not his personal traits but the attitudes and emotions of those to whom he has supreme significance. In this portrait of Jesus, which has been described as "the divinest and most human" of all representations in the Roman catacombs, is expressed the suffering of common men and their sympathy for one another which together formed the sociopsychological core of the Christian orientation of the Western cultural tradition. The absence of the nimbus indicates an early date, perhaps the late second or early third century, for the picture; at least one representation of Jesus is believed to antedate this picture.

tion was set in the supernatural world in no way made less real the values which defined it.

The distinctive intellectual achievement of Christianity was closely related to this social result: it was the reintegration of the low and high intellectual traditions of the Western world. If there was, at the heart of Christianity, a reasoned theology which men learned in the philosophies and literatures of Western culture could accept, around the heart were popular beliefs in the daimonic universe which made easy a faith in Christianity's teachings of God's ways with men. In Christ, the personal savior, the supernatural world came nearer to men than it had ever been in popular beliefs. For in Him were synthesized the emotional fixations of common men as they suffered in urban cultures. Thus there were lost many ancient superstitions that had origin in different relations between men and nature, and in their place prevailed beliefs that reflected the emotional reactions having origin in the relations of men with men in urban society. In fact, the reintegration of the low and high intellectual traditions of Western culture was far more the result of reactions to the social conditions of urban culture than the product of reasoned arguments, for under these conditions learning had been brought to serve intellectually the emotions to which they gave rise. In the suffering Christ the emotions of common men as organized in the traditional urban social structure were interpreted in terms of the daimonic universe. Common men, illiterate and distressed, had no other terms than these for understanding or wishing about their lot. From the high intellectual tradition of Western culture, as shaped by the Greek philosophers, came the rational and systematizing methods which elaborated this understanding and wishing into a firm intellectual structure. But what the learned proved by reason, the unlearned understood by faith. In faith all men were intellectually united.

Implicit in Christianity were conceptions of the freedom of the individual, of his moral responsibility, and of the sacredness of his life. From the point of view of the traditional urban culture, these conceptions were revolutionary, if applied in secular affairs. For Christians, however, they had mainly religious meaning and value, so that only in casual ways did they operate to ameliorate the injustices and inequalities of the traditional social structure. By virtue of their presence, however, Christianity was not inherently bound to the maintenance of this order.

There is nothing in Christianity, let it be emphasized, which, by its character, sets Christians against either social or intellectual progress, if such progress is understood to mean the amelioration of worldly existence by means of the advancement and application of knowledge. But Christianity developed under historical circumstances which made it the heir of the two primitive obstacles to such advancement, namely, (1) the lack of recognition that individual life is organized in social interaction controlled through institutions and (2) the disregard of the role that factual information as applied in technology plays in human life. In fact, it may be argued that Christianity, by making central in its view of life the ideas that man can have a direct relation with God and that revelation is the source of all necessary knowledge, buttressed these obstacles. But, if this was the case, it is still true that, if social institutions change and worldly knowledge increases, these central teachings can exist. Indeed, if the freedom of the individual, his moral responsibility, and the sacredness of his life were to be realized in terms of institutional changes and served by increasing worldly knowledge, these central teachings could still exist. Not because Western men have been Christians but because they, like other men, have failed to understand the roles of social control and scientific knowledge in life, have they remained afflicted with ancient distresses. Perhaps to work out the conceptions of personal freedom, moral responsibility, and the sacredness of human life for humanity, with or without allegiance to the Christian priest class, in terms of an understanding of these roles would be to achieve the Kingdom of God as common men—the historic revealers of Christianity—can know it.

Conclusion

THE RISE AND DECLINE OF THE TRADITIONAL URBAN CULTURES OF ASIA AND EUROPE

Chapter XX

STRUCTURE AND PROCESS IN CULTURAL DEVELOPMENT

≪-≪-≫-≫

As the scientific understanding of phenomena has developed, they have come more and more to be dealt with in terms of two general concepts: (1) "structure" and (2) "process."

The concept "structure" predicates that a phenomenon consists of identifiable parts organized in functional relations; *i.e.*, the parts work together as a whole. For example, the science of chemistry recognizes the *elements*, which, having fundamental form as atoms, enter into the various physical substances. In different combinations these physical substances compose, in turn, all forms of inorganic and organic matter. In a similar way the science of biology knows one of these substances, the living substance *protoplasm*, which exists as *cells*. Specialized in various ways cells form different kinds of tissues, and these, in turn, become organs which together constitute an organism. And organisms form two grand divisions, plant and animal, each of which has thousands of species and varieties related to one another in various ways. The cell is a biochemical structure. The tissue is a cellular structure. The organ is a structure of tissues. And the plant and animal kingdoms are structures of organisms. In each instance the part is a whole, and the whole is a part. Where this relation appears not to exist may be taken as indicating a limit of man's knowledge rather than as an end of the relation. Therefore, it may be held that within the boundaries of observation, all phenomena enter into a structure of one kind or another.

The concept "process" predicates that a structure under the play of external forces and through its own energy undergoes action or acts so that change affects it. The science of chemistry knows occurrences among substances which are designated "reactions." Combustion and oxidation, for example, occur as various substances enter into combination with oxygen. Some enter so rapidly that the result is an explosion; others make a fire—quick or slow; and still others proceed in such a way that they are recognizable mainly in the formation of different substances—in popular speech, ashes. The science of biology recognizes *metabolism* as the fundamental biochemical process which, occurring in cells, builds up and breaks down the living substance protoplasm. Reproduction, nutrition, growth, disintegration, and death are aspects of this basic process of organic life. By processes, therefore, structures are broken down and built up, and all structures may be conceived as having existence in terms of some process.

Together the concepts "structure" and "process" may be seen as exhibiting the static and dynamic aspects of phenomena. In some phenomena the static aspect may appear more significant, while in others the dynamic aspect may seem decisive; actually they should be viewed together, each as a manifestation of the other. Structure, however enduring, exists in terms of process, and process, no matter how slowly or rapidly it operates, always moves through structure. Structure and process are correlative, not opposing, aspects of phenomena.

To study human affairs in terms of the concepts "structure" and "process" would seem, therefore, to be the scientific way to an understanding of them.

CULTURAL TRADITIONS: THE OBJECTIVE CONTENT OF HISTORY

In the foregoing pages the development of cultural traditions from the beginnings of culture as recognizable in the sparse data of prehistoric archaeology to the opening of the sixth century of the Christian era has been sketched. By that century the cultural traditions which, except as elaborated by new peoples or as disturbed by recent movements, still organize human life had been consolidated. Their patterns had been fixed in enduring structures.

The Social Organization of Cultural Traditions.

Even in the period of emergence from subhuman form the distinctive characteristic of the human species, it is reasonably conjectured, was a capacity for socially organized behavior; with the development of speech and, later, of other symbols this capacity functioned not only in terms of going experience but also in terms of accumulated experience transmitted from the past. By this capacity, which was active through the social process—interaction, cooperation, conflict, and assimilation—culture was created and then developed through time, becoming a cultural tradition:

Man is a traditional animal. The capacity for handing on tradition is carried to a far higher pitch in man than in any other vertebrate. The evolution of the brain seems to have been largely directed to increasing this capacity. . . . The individual element in each of us is minute compared with the traditional.[1]

The vast machinery of culture is maintained, regulated and preserved by the body of traditional lore. This is made possible by language, which allows man to formulate general rules and condense them into concepts. Thus to systems of action there correspond systems of thought.[2]

Tradition makes the man, by circumscribing his behavior within certain bounds; but it is equally true that man makes traditions.[3]

Culture is a determinant of human behavior, and culture as a dynamic reality is also subject to determination. There exist scientific laws of culture.[4]

Since the development of cultural traditions, although always carried in the social process, occurred through time, it was the outcome of a process peculiar to itself. This process is, of course, the interplay of factors influencing human social development; among these factors, besides those having origin in physical nature and the biological qualities of the human species, were those which had origin in culture. In other words the social process gave the capacity for culture, while culture, in turn, affected the social process. Thus culture and cultural development are above all else the phenomena to be studied in history.

Culture is a thing *sui generis* which can be explained only in terms of itself. This is not mysticism but sound scientific method. . . . Culture, it seems, is a matter of exceedingly slow growth until a certain "threshold" is passed, when it darts forward, gathering momentum at an unexpected rate. . . . A given culture is, in a measure, at least a unique phenomenon. In so far as this is true it must defy general treatment, and the explanation of a cultural phenomenon will consist in referring it back to the particular circumstance that preceded it. . . . The field of culture, then, is not a region of complete lawlessness. Like causes produce like effects here as elsewhere, though the complex conditions with which

[1] A. M. Hocart, *The Progress of Man: A short history of his evolution, his customs and his works* (1933), p. 33. By permission of Methuen & Co., Ltd., London.

[2] B. Malinowski, "Culture as a Determinant of Behavior," *The Scientific Monthly*, Vol. 43 (1936), p. 447.

[3] V. Gordon Childe, *Man Makes Himself* (1936), p. 270. C. A. Watts & Co., Ltd., London.

[4] B. Malinowski, "Culture as a Determinant of Behavior," *The Scientific Monthly*, Vol. 43 (1936), p. 440.

we are grappling require unusual caution in definitely correlating phenomena. . . . It is not so difficult as might at first appear to harmonize the principle that a cultural phenomenon is explicable only by a unique combination of antecedent circumstances with the principle that like phenomena are the product of like antecedents. The essential point is that in either case we have past history as the determinant.[1]

The significance for the study of history of the fact that cultural development occurs in a social process is that both populations and individuals may be understood as carriers of a cultural tradition which influences them just as they in turn influence it.

Society, culture, and the individual constitute a configuration whose elements are in constant interaction. A society and a culture are always paired and extend through time as parallel elements in a single continuum. Neither one of them can exist without the other. The individuals who compose the society and express the culture enter this continuum through birth and pass out of it through death. They are themselves continuums, but they extend over a much briefer time interval than the social-cultural continuum of which they temporarily form a part. We might liken this longer continuum to a rope twisted from the short strands of individual lives. A cross section of a rope taken at any point in its length would reveal its component strands in particular positions with relation to each other and to the rope as a whole. Similarly, a cross section of the social-cultural continuum, taken at any point in time, will reveal the individuals who compose the society in particular relations to each other and to the society and culture as a whole. These relationships will never be identical for any two individuals, or even for the same individual at any two points of time, but here, just as in the case of the behavior from which culture traits are abstracted, there are recognizable modes in the variational ranges. In other words, each society is organized according to a particular system and every individual in it can be placed with relation to this system. Such systems undergo changes through time and may be markedly different at different points in the social continuum, but they usually change slowly enough to provide a comparatively stable frame for the orientation of individuals. Thus a society's system of organization may change profoundly in the course of a thousand years, but it usually does not change much in the time covered by a single life span.[2]

This aspect of cultural development is likely to prevent individuals from recognizing persisting patterns in their behavior and thought which, viewed historically, may be described as one of several

[1] R. H. Lowie, *Culture & Ethnology* (1929), p. 66 *et passim*. By permission of Peter Smith, Publisher, New York.

[2] Ralph Linton, "Psychology and Anthropology," *Journal of Social Philosophy*, Vol. 5 (1940), pp. 121–122.

sociocultural types.[1] This difficulty is particularly great for Western men because many elements of their cultural tradition assert the uniqueness of the individual with peculiar intensity. For example, the Greek concept "rational mind" and the Christian concept "conscience" obscure the social organization of individual behavior, the former in regard to sources of beliefs and methods of thinking and the latter in regard to norms of right and wrong and the making of ethical judgments. It is essential to a correct understanding of the individual to recognize that his mentality—indeed, his intelligence—is a product of cultural development in a social process.

"We" undeniably live in a world where intelligence is the property of human beings who are born, live through a common life-cycle and die—both as biological units and as minds. And they are certainly born completely ignorant, without minds, and acquire knowledge and intelligence by a process about which the developed intelligence knows and can say a good deal. Under the conditions of the only world we know anything about, knowledge and intelligence are completely "unthinkable" apart from a continuing and developing social process of learning. This necessarily involves for the learner intercommunication with other selves, including large numbers of selves who know (have learned) vastly more about himself and all of whom live in and react to a world of not-self, about which they habitually intercommunicate. Thus our knowledge of the world and our knowledge of one another and of "mind" in general form inseparable bodies of knowledge which must be studied in relation to one another, if we are to know anything about any of them, or to talk sense about them. All are to be accounted for "genetically" in terms of a twofold historical evolution, in the individual and in the race.[2]

From this point of view cultural traditions may be understood as organizations of behavior (or, subjectively, of mentality) shaped in a process which, arising partly in culture itself, moves through time in social interaction. Thus although each cultural tradition has a distinctive development, it also has structure comparable with those of similar traditions, and the processes and structures

[1] Anonymous, "An Analysis of Jewish Culture," *International Journal of Ethics*, Vol. 47 (1936–1937), p. 430: "The fact that we are normally almost completely unconscious of our cultural settings does not in the least detract from the importance of their influence. Indeed, our unawareness may even enhance it. Since it is characteristic of cultures that they seem to those who live within them to be the normal and natural, the right and only way of life, and the personality type one's own culture creates to be like basic human nature, other cultures and their corresponding cultural type seem not only strange but somehow wrong. One does not normally see the peculiarities of one's own cultural type of personality because they seem the rock-bottom fundamentals of human nature everywhere."

[2] Frank H. Knight, "What Is Truth in Economics," *Journal of Political Economy*, Vol. 48 (1940), p. 14.

alike are to be studied in history. The concept "culture" gives the continuity of history new meaning and significance both for individuals and for populations.

THE COURSE OF CULTURAL DEVELOPMENT.

Because there were always different human groups, it seems clear that there were from earliest times several, if not many, cultural traditions, and as the experience of these groups was diversified and as it accumulated, their capacities for carrying cultural traditions increased. Indeed, as the groups were enlarged or as social interaction within them was intensified, the type of cultural traditions they could carry changed.

As indicated by the accompanying chart, showing the general course of cultural development, after the evolution of the biosocial bases of culture, the earliest human groups carried hunting cultures. This designation—"hunting culture"—suggests one of the characteristics which distinguish types of cultural traditions from one another, namely, the integration of the group with the physical environment. In terms of this integration the activities which bring subsistence to the members of the group go on. At least two other characteristics, only to be known for the early hunting cultures by inferences from artifacts, distinguish cultural traditions as to type: the organization of relations among members within the group and the interpretation of experience carried by the group. In the early hunting cultures the social relations were summated in the *camp-site community* and the interpretation of experience in the concept "daimonic universe" and its corollaries. The integration with the physical environment gave rise to specialized activities which entered into social relations and also to much of the experience that was interpreted. In turn the community organized these specializations and the interpretation in enduring patterns. And the interpretation provided an orientation of behavior and thought which, on the one hand, explained the going mode of life and, on the other hand, provided emotional adjustments to it.

A cultural tradition has, therefore, three major elements: (1) the technological, (2) the institutional, and (3) the intellectual; and each is related to the others both as cause and as effect. This relation exists because each of these elements develops only within the social process, from which individuals receive the organization of their behavior and to which they give new elements through interaction with other individuals.

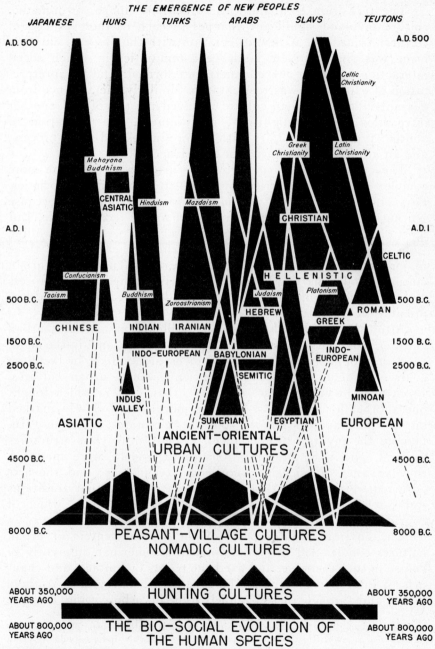

This chart, reading upward, indicates the interrelations of the cultures which contributed to the formation of the great Asiatic and European cultural traditions.

The transition from hunting to peasant-village, or nomadic, culture involved significant changes in each of these aspects of cultural traditions. A new integration with the physical environment was shaped. New kinds of communities in which social interaction flowed in new channels were formed. And the interpretation of experience was reorientated. Similarly the advance from peasant-village to urban culture involved the rise of still another integration with the physical environment, the formation of another type of community with a more intensified social process, and an altered interpretation of experience.

The cultural traditions carried by urban societies were more complex than those carried by camp-site and village societies. Part of this complexity was more apparent than real, because writing made possible the formation of a new record of life. But most of it had origin in the intensified social process of urban life, from which issued many innovations, affecting each of the three major aspects of cultural traditions.[1] The original patterns of urban cultural traditions as shaped by this intensified social process and the innovations it produced were developed in the ancient-oriental urban cultures.

After the middle of the second millennium B.C. new urban cultures arose in the Eastern and Western worlds, and, in the main, their developments ran parallel courses, not unlike, in fact, the courses of development of the ancient-oriental urban cultures. From peasant-village bases emerged urban centers which fought one another for supremacy in areas more or less clearly marked out by geographical factors, and the victorious cities, in turn, became the pivots of imperialism. Concurrently class structures evolved, and new interpretations of experience were made. A slow advance of scientific knowledge, technology, and the arts occurred at the same time; also, literate intellectual traditions were set off from the oral learning of preliterate times, which of course persisted among the great part of the population.

The environmental aspects of the several centers of urban cultures conditioned these developments somewhat differently of course in each instance, and fixed the points of contacts and channels of intercourse between the several urban centers. At these points and through these channels went on a borrowing, in some

---

[1] Karl Kekoni, "The Problem of the City: The fundamental problem of human geography," *The Scientific Monthly*, Vol. 45 (1937), p. 547: "Science and art, philosophy and higher religion may be regarded as the natural products of city life. The city existed before the state which was created by it."

instances great and in others slight, so that each urban culture owed a debt to the others for specific materials and, on occasion, for stimulus that meant new growth.

The accompanying map shows the centers of the European and Asiatic urban cultures and their areas as they were in the fifth century A.D. Within each area there were many local differences, but the dominant tradition gave overall organization to life. In the s veral cultures similarities of patterns composed a unity which, because of its pervasiveness, can be recognized as the *traditional civilization* of the Eastern and Western worlds, *i.e.*, the general organization of life which embodied what men had made of man since the beginning of cultural development in primordial times. Because this unity existed not only in the structure of these cultural traditions but also in the processes of their development, an analysis of them is relevant not only to an exposition of the unity of the traditional civilization of the Eastern and Western worlds but also to the scientific understanding of human behavior and mentality.

The central concept which emerges from the consideration of ancient cultural developments is, therefore, "urban culture" or, viewed historically, "urban cultural tradition," and the remarks in this chapter are concerned mainly with the exposition of these concepts.

THE STRUCTURE OF THE URBAN CULTURAL TRADITIONS OF ASIA AND EUROPE

As previously noted, the chief elements of a culture are (1) the technological, or the integration of the carrying group with its environment, (2) the institutional, or the organization of social relations with the carrying group, and (3) the intellectual, or the interpretation of the experience of the carrying group. Inasmuch as a culture exists only in a social process, it is necessary also to direct attention to the dynamic factors which affect the development of urban culture. They operate mainly in the relations between the carrying group and external urban and nonurban communities. It appears, therefore, that an urban culture has a life in time, moving from emergence through certain identifiable phases toward a final disintegration or reorientation. In this movement changes in the elements of the culture may be understood as occurring in relation to the sequence of social developments and, in turn, as affecting the sequence. This interrelation between the development of the elements of an urban culture and its social movement is so close that they should always be seen together.

Environment, Technology, and the Production of Wealth.

The early urban cultures of Asia and Europe, like their primitive and ancient-oriental predecessors, were based on integrations of men with nature in terms of the principle of the selective use of the environment. In the first instance, therefore, natural factors—topography, climate, soil, flora, and fauna—conditioned the integrations, and in the second instance technology gave them form by determining the use of resources. The integrations took form in modes of wealth production and, over a period of time, in fluctuations of wealth production. Inasmuch as the natural factors seem to have changed little from time to time and technological innovations, although significant, did not involve a genuinely new relation with nature, the integrations developed without disorganizing their fundamental pattern. The development of the integrations was conditioned, of course, by the intellectual elements of the several cultural traditions, so that in fact, although the integrations between men and their environments had objective forms in economic activities that produced wealth and levels of living that arose in the distribution and consumption of wealth, they also embodied the fundamental psychological reactions of men to their environments.

1. *The Modes of Wealth Production.* The modes of wealth production of the Asiatic and European urban cultures were developed more by the shaping of neolithic and ancient-oriental techniques into new patterns than by technological innovations. The diffusion of ancient-oriental techniques went on steadily, though unevenly, throughout the period of the development of the several cultural traditions.

Everywhere the application of human labor to land was the chief source of wealth. Everywhere men struggled to bring more land under cultivation—to win soil for tillage from the forests, the grasslands, the swamps, and the tangled growths of the river valleys. Among all the labors of men, none has been so severe and so long-continuing as that which transforms the wilderness into the well-kept countryside. Everywhere men of the urban cultures planted, tilled, and harvested. Everywhere they found well-being in nature's bounty and poverty in her niggardliness. Everywhere crop failure was the cruelest disaster they knew, for it denied them the fruits of their labor and left them helpless and hopeless.

In each urban culture the integration between man and nature was a complex of practices which had a wide basis in both history and geography. Although environment conditioned the integration in each culture area, men had made it, and they alone preserved and elaborated it.

In the Mediterranean Basin, field agriculture, based on the cereals and the traction plow and combined with husbandry and the keeping of vineyards and orchards, prevailed, but it was confined generally to scattered valleys and plains, limited in area and, because of variations in soil, suited to different crops. Because the subtropical seasonal movement gave rise to several growing seasons, it also contributed to the diversification of crops. In many localities mixed terrain and mingled grasslands and forests made grain growing and cattle keeping separate industries. Except in Syria and north Africa, where irrigation was extensively used, and in Egypt, watered always by the Nile, Mediterranean agriculture depended on rainfall. On the whole the agriculture of the Mediterranean lands was more diversified and less intensive than that of other urban culture areas; this was more true of the northern parts, where forests, plains, valleys, and upland pastures were mingled, than of the southern parts bordering the tropical deserts.

On the Plateau of Iran and in central Asia, except for well-tilled spots in southwestern Persia and Bactria, agriculture was mostly confined to small watered areas, and husbandry was largely pastoral. Although the cereals were grown, the intensive cultivation of vegetables and fruits was the common industry. Irrigation, managed more by hand than by reservoirs and ditches, was a necessity. Spring and fall were the main growing seasons, for the winter was too cold and the summer too hot. Mesopotamia preserved its ancient agriculture as long as its irrigation system remained efficient.

Indian agriculture began in the jungle and, in spite of the fact that the early Aryas were grain growers and cattle keepers, it retained many hoe-culture characteristics. The field cultivation of wheat and millet moved from the northwest to the east and south. Pastoral agriculture was widely spread through the northwest and along the Himalayan foothills. Rice tillage dominated the Gangetic plain. In the heavy forested areas of the Deccan gardens were probably more numerous than fields. The monsoon climate was the decisive factor in Indian agriculture. When rainfall was plentiful, great heat caused rank growth; when the precipitation was scanty, it destroyed growth. And in either case the result was that hard labor was required to win even a bare subsistence.

Chinese agriculture originated on the loess soils of the Huang valley, which, because they were easy to spade, early gave rise to an intensive cultivation. The rich flora of China provided a variety of crops unknown elsewhere, but they were suited more to garden tillage than to field agriculture. Except millet and rice, the cereals came late to China, and the traction plow later still. Husbandry and field agriculture of the Western pattern never became fully developed. However, water control gave wide support to the intensive cultivation of rice. The cyclonic climate of north China brought variable temperatures and uncertain rainfall in all seasons of the year. Drought and dust storms were common in summer; with them came sometimes the locusts of the northern grasslands. Spring floods caused by the melting of snow on the central Asiatic mountains were as dangerous to crops and men as the summer droughts. As agriculture spread toward the coasts and through the Yangtze valley, where the monsoon climate prevailed, it became, if possible, more intensive. Rice, the leading crop, was grown in small fields, and the bamboo replaced the forests which were cut away to make more room for gardens and fields. Hand irrigation and the use of human excrement as fertilizer were elements of the intensive cultivation characteristic of China. In no other urban culture was the integration of man with nature in terms of plants so complex as in China.

Labor applied to land gave foodstuffs and also the most widely used raw materials—wood, fibers, and leather—from which were made the consumption goods that raised the level of living above bare subsistence. The central problem of wealth production was, therefore, an organization of land usage ensuring continuous production in an amount sufficient to maintain an economic surplus that would support cities.

Although the importance of minerals and metals in the traditional Eastern and Western cultures can hardly be overstated, it should be recognized that the means of working them were cumbersome, *i.e.*, required a great amount of labor to achieve a low productivity. Mines were only shallow pits or narrow shafts from which extended a web of narrower underground passages. The largest mines, like the Roman silver mines of northern Spain, were opened by inclined passages which penetrated almost a mile underground. In the Mediterranean Basin, where mining reached its highest development, hoisting contrivances of pulleys and ropes were used, but the ores were frequently carried out in sacks by men who climbed ladders or steep stairs in the walls of shafts. In pit mines, some of which are known to have existed in China, the ores were sometimes lifted out in buckets suspended from long poles that worked as levers. Timbering, draining, and ventilating, alike expensive and laborious, set limits to underground workings, but the tools—the mallet, the chisel, the pick, and the spade—made progress to these limits relatively slow. Mining was drudgery of the severest kind; indeed, it was so destructive of labor that everywhere man power was recruited from criminals and war captives and held in a slavery from which there was almost no escape but death.

Iron, copper, lead, and silver were most plentiful in the Mediterranean lands. Iran had a supply of iron sufficient to support an export trade. Alluvial deposits at the foot of the Himalayan ranges gave India gold and precious gems. Iron was more plentiful in northern than in southern India. China was not rich in either the common or the precious metals, although in the imperial age gold from central Asia and iron from Shantung became common.

The working of metals, once the ores were obtained, was limited, first, by the weight of the materials and, second, by the difficulty of producing the degrees of heat necessary for successful manufacture. Neither of these difficulties was overcome in any of the traditional urban cultures of the Eastern and Western worlds; however, the metals were so important both to the production of wealth and to the exercise of power that slight changes in supplies or small improvements in their manufacture had far-reaching effects.

Like the ancient-oriental urban cultures, each of the traditional Asiatic and European cultures began with the use of copper, turned to bronze, and finally displaced both with iron, at least for industrial and military purposes. This development occurred most rapidly in the Mediterranean lands, probably owing to their proximity to the ancient-oriental urban culture area, and least rapidly in China. If the Mediterranean lands led in the quantity production of metals, the Asiatic lands were most skillful in tooling them. After agriculture, mining and metalworking were the most important industries in urban cultures, because they gave, in improved tools, a greater productivity of labor and, in improved weapons, the high concentration of power necessary to organize labor for greater enterprises.

A progressive elaboration of the craft industries went forward in each of the Asiatic and European cultures, and each developed special skills in them. The Mediterranean lands led all others in the building industries. The use of hard stone superseded the use of soft stone and brick first in Syria and western Iran. It spread mainly westward, while the Mesopotamian and Iranian use of brick and colored tile spread eastward. Distinctive textiles were produced by each urban culture area—woolens and linens by the Mediterranean lands, cottons by India, and silks by China. In Iran the rug was the unique specialization. Colorful printed materials were produced in China and India; rich fabrics of mixed materials were woven in Syria. India and Iran developed the best dyes, the Mediterranean lands, except Syria, the poorest. The pottery craft lost artistic importance in the urban cultures as metalworking advanced; however, the use of common grades undoubtedly spread everywhere. By Han times the Chinese were the leaders in the pottery industry, a development probably connected with the slow advance of their metal industries. The diffusion of the glass industry from Syria into all of the Asiatic and European urban culture areas was a notable achievement.

As in the ancient-oriental urban cultures, the craft industries were carried on at two levels of skill. A few workers produced goods and articles of exceptionally fine quality for a luxury trade, while a large number of workers turned out crude wares, mainly for their own consumption. Everywhere the peasants seem to have supplied most of their own craft products. This class aspect of the crafts tended to limit the production of wealth, for it restricted the output of quality products to the amount necessary to satisfy the demand of a very small part of the population.

2. *The Fluctuations of Wealth Production.* The result of the modes of producing wealth noted in the preceding paragraphs was the formation of the economic surpluses upon which the traditional Asiatic and European urban cultures were based. The productivity of labor was never sufficiently great to maintain these surpluses at high levels; they always remained small and subject to fluctuation. The factors which caused the fluctuation of wealth production seem to have been everywhere the same.

Soil, it should be noted, does not produce wealth automatically; it must be cleared, tilled, watered, and conserved. And many circumstances affect these operations, some to increase and others to decrease yields. In the traditional Asiatic and European urban cultures agricultural production was increased from time to time in at least three ways: (1) by bringing new areas under cultivation, (2) by introducing new methods of tillage and the care of live stock, and (3) by developing new crops.

New lands were brought under cultivation mainly by clearing forests and by controlling water. Everywhere the tillage that gave rise to the original economic surpluses of the European and Asiatic urban cultures began in areas relatively easy to clear—in the oases and park lands of Iran, in the park lands and on the small open plains around the Mediterranean coasts, on the grasslands of the upper Indus valley and in the park lands of the upper Gangetic plain, and on the almost treeless loess soils of the lower Huang valley. The decisive event in the spread of tillage from these to adjacent areas was the introduction of iron tools which made easier the clearing of forests. The control of water was even more difficult than the clearing of land, because it called for the organization of large enterprises involving great numbers of laborers and high engineering skill. Whereas clearing added new lands to the tilled areas, water control preserved old areas and, in many instances, increased their productivity.

With the expansion of the areas under tillage commonly went the introduction of new agricultural methods and new crops, or, at least, the diffusion of old methods and crops. Probably the most important factor in the development of urban culture in India and China was the cultivation of rice on wet lands; the use of the water buffalo as a draft animal was an innovation which contributed considerably to the spread of this type of tillage. In the Mediterranean lands the diffusion of the grape and the olive was almost as important as the spread of rice tillage in India and China. An improved whetstone which made easier the sharpening of sickles apparently played some part in the increase of cereal production in the Mediterranean lands. The introduction of the Roman barn in Gaul and Britain raised productivity by improving their husbandry; similarly the diffusion of the Roman cart contributed to the spread of field agriculture. On the central Asiatic grasslands the adaptation of the horse to riding greatly extended the area through which nomads could move and led to the increase of the herds they kept.

Ordered wealth production in urban cultures was everywhere evidenced in the well-kept countryside. Even at the height of the traditional urban cultures of Asia and Europe, such areas were relatively small. In China they included the greater parts of the central Huang, Han, Hwai, and Yangtze valleys and bits of the coastal plains. In central Asia and Iran they were confined to a few river valleys and scattered oases. In India probably only the upper Indus valley and the Jumna-Ganges Doab, and the fringes of the lower Gangetic plain were so developed. The largest of such areas was in southwestern Asia; it included the entire Fertile Crescent, almost all of Asia Minor and a large part of Armenia. In the Mediterranean lands, besides the ancient Nile valley, the well-kept countryside was found only in the chief peninsulas and on narrow areas along the coasts of northern Africa and southern Gaul. In northern Gaul, the Rhineland, and Britain it was restricted to soils unfavorable for forests; it did not extend to the wet lands of the coasts and river valleys.

Only by continuous labor were these areas maintained, let alone extended, for several factors tended either to bring about their reversion to a wild state or to destroy their productivity.

Irregularities of temperature and precipitation were year-to-year hazards which might at any time cut yields. Crop failures, normal occurrences everywhere, were probably less numerous in the Mediterranean than in Asiatic lands. Freezes, frosts, and excessive moisture early in the growing season, rather than flood and summer drought, were dangerous in the European coastal areas of the Mediterranean Basin. North China was likely to be affected by both the spring and the summer hazards. Northwestern India knew drought and central India excessive rainfall. Local droughts were widely recurrent in Iran. At best agricultural production was uncertain everywhere, and famine, local rather than general, was normal. A series of bad years anywhere was likely to reduce population and decrease the tilled areas.

As an urban culture was extended throughout the geographical area to which its modes of wealth production were suited, a circumstance that tended to decrease the production of wealth began to appear. This circumstance, once regarded as a decline of rainfall, is probably now better understood as a disturbance by human action of the balance of natural factors in a region.[1] "Rainfall is not so much the determining factor as is the balance between rainfall and evaporation." The deforestation of China and the Mediterranean lands was a primary interference with this balance, and the erosion which occurred as water drained away more swiftly destroyed the soil. A loss of soil fertility accompanied this destruction, and methods of tillage everywhere except in China were not

[1] For a popular discussion of this balance, known scientifically as the "hydrologic cycle," see Stuart Chase, *Rich Land Poor Land* (1936), pp. 69 ff.

of the kind to preserve it. When these conditions developed about the original urban centers, the economic problem they brought was met, first, by organizing an improved transportation system so that the products of outlying areas could be more easily obtained and, second, by shifting nonagricultural industries to the outlying areas, where food was plentiful. In the end the center of administration and cultural energy also moved. Leading examples of this phenomenon are the Roman and Chinese empires. The shift of the capital from Rome to Constantinople was due partly to a need to bring the political center of the empire nearer to the center of wealth production, and the transition from the Earlier, or Western, Han to the Later, or Eastern, Han had a similar underlying cause. The movement of the seats of power in Iran and India may have been the result of a comparable circumstance.

Other forms of wealth production also tended to reach a peak output and then recede. Mining, for example, approached a limit set by existing technological equipment so that the supplies of ore, it is said, were "worked out." In industries carried on with slave labor, productivity depended on a continuous supply of man power. But the supply of man power, which usually increased as imperial expansion progressed, tended to decrease as imperial expansion slowed down. If slaves from peoples not yet at the level of urban culture were introduced, the quality of the product declined, because such slaves did not possess the skills of their predecessors.

During the early periods of the development of the Asiatic and European urban cultures the production of wealth gradually increased, chiefly by a slow expansion over new lands. The decisive factor in the growth of their economic surpluses was the adaptation of iron to various industrial uses. Apparently the height of the several cultures coincided with the period when the widened areas—politically, they were the great empires—were first fully exploited with iron tools. Also slaves were most abundant at this time. But few improvements of tools and implements followed the introduction of iron, so that, although output was increased, little change occurred in the basic modes of wealth production. Everywhere, therefore, the technological basis of wealth production, whose improvement alone could have ensured the continued increase of the economic surplus—or, in the face of resources becoming more difficult to work, maintained it—remained fundamentally unchanged. Expansion of wealth production followed by contraction was, therefore, the normal economic movement in the traditional urban cultures of Asia and Europe.

Although based on complex technological integrations with their respective environments, the traditional urban cultures of Asia and Europe never possessed large and secure economic surpluses. Productivity was low. Labor was arduous. The bulk of the wealth consisted of raw materials and crudely manufactured products. From year to year output was uncertain. And when productivity declined, because technological advance failed to offset the factors that tended to lessen production, the decrease of the economic surpluses was swift. Above all the power of natural factors over economic life remained almost absolute.

CITIES, SOCIAL STRUCTURE, AND INSTITUTIONS.

As in the ancient-oriental urban cultures the social organization of the traditional Asiatic and European urban cultures developed as small urban groups emerged within the large rural populations. The fundamental social line in these cultures was the country-city line, not merely because the city drew economic support from the country but, more, because the social processes of the two were different. Among the greatly preponderant rural population life was organized in the village community, where social isolation and the uniformity of custom were primary aspects of life. Few left the village, and fewer returned to it. New specializations appeared so infrequently that they did not disturb either economic, social, or intellectual stereotypes. The patterns of behavior and thought received from the past were unquestioned. Probably only physical disaster and war ever stirred the village world. Its inertia was everywhere proverbial. Among the small urban population, however, there was a more active social process. It knew widened contacts with the world, received new commodities, transitory rumors, and vague reports, developed new specializations, and entered into various excitements. Whereas the village confined energies to established routines, the city turned them into uncertain projects. Thus between the peasant-village masses and the small urban population stood a difference not only of economic function but also of level of cultural attainment. So, although the cities were never secure against the shrinkage of the wealth that supported them, they dominated the social order both through institutions and as centers of creative effort. To them new things came, and from them new things issued. The village held fast to the old.

1. *The Ruling Classes in the Asiatic and European Urban Cultures*. Each of the Asiatic and European urban cultures devel-

oped class structures which, however differing in detail from one another, duplicated the fundamental pattern of the ancient-oriental social pyramids. This similarity was due to the fact that implicit in urban cultures was a differentiation of groups in terms of the production and utilization of the economic surplus. Political and intellectual factors sharpened the differentiation.

At the summit of the urban social pyramids were secular aristocracies whose members combined the possession of wealth with the exercise of power, and made each serve the other. Usually these aristocracies were made up of several grades. At the head stood the members of the ruling houses. Beneath them was the high nobility—the Roman senators, the Iranian warrior-nobles, the Indian princes, and the Chinese noble-officials. Associated with the high nobility was at least one lower order of privileged persons, such as the Roman knights, the Persian knights, the Indian land-lords, and the Chinese provincial officials. Everywhere these privileged groups, very few in number, were identified with the civil and military establishments and, in some places, with the ecclesiastical. Military prowess or the purchase of office ordinarily gave entrance to the aristocracy, and birth, if not by right at least by opportunity that came with family status, perpetuated the possession of the status. Differences in manners, dress, etiquette, education, and occupation set off the aristocratic orders from one another and from the masses. Controversy and conflict between the aristocratic orders was more or less continuous in each of the Asiatic and European cultures.

The priestly groups of these cultures offer many comparisons and contrasts. They held privileged positions because their members possessed the learning which was believed to be necessary for human welfare, either in this world or in the next. They functioned on the principle that knowledge is power, regardless of what kind of knowledge it may be. Everywhere the antecedents of the privileged intellectual classes were the priests of ancient cults. If these classes had not developed directly from the early priesthoods, they had acquired positions originally held by them, and the fact that their learning might be different from that of the antecedent groups did not prevent succession to their position. In fact, the tendency to specialize social functions implicit in urban cultures made for a clearer differentiation of the priestly group than had been known in village communities, and when the urban cultures were consolidated this group became everywhere a sharply defined social class.

A brief summary will indicate the positions the privileged intellectual groups held in the several Asiatic and European urban cultures. The Indian Brahmans were a dispersed but socially and culturally dominant group whose power rested in a knowledge of rituals. The Iranian Magi were a closed priesthood administering a state religion; as such they served the state and received support from it. The Confucian literati, recruited by examination rather than by birth or political preferment, were not only the official servants of the imperial regime but also the arbiters of social standards; their monopoly of learning was practically complete. The Jewish rabbis, having no state to serve, maintained control over a scattered people through religious learning. In Greece and Rome the priestly groups were too closely identified with the secular ruling classes to develop independent power; nor did they possess a monopoly of literate learning. However, with the rise of Christianity a new priest class was formed in Western culture which was shaped, it seems, by many Egyptian precedents and established as a privileged group mainly by the winning of the position of the pagan priests. Like the Indian Brahman, the Christian priest's social position rested on a knowledge of ritual, and like the Iranian Magi he became the member of a closed hierarchy, controlling its own membership and organization. The monastic establishments of Indian, Chinese, and Christian cultures were merely specialized divisions of their respective priestly groups.

Inasmuch as the several priest classes were the intellectual leaders in their respective cultures, their social attitudes were highly significant in the outlooks of the cultures. In the main the priest classes agreed on propositions like the following:

1. Long ago there was a just and righteous age.
2. Existing institutions, although imperfect, are sacred because they are derived from this ancient age.
3. Loyalty and obedience are the essential duties of the people.
4. The higher social classes possess moral and spiritual qualities or attainments superior to those of the common people.
5. An act which injures the position of the privileged intellectual class is dangerous to social well-being.
6. Repudiation of the teachings of the privileged intellectual group is a crime.
7. This crime should be punished in this world and will be punished in the next.

The secular aristocracies and the masses commonly accepted these views, the former partly from interest and partly from belief and the latter because tradition asserted and confirmed them. The effect of such beliefs was usually to make the well-being of common men a condition to be gained in the other world only through their performance in this world of duties which actually assured the priests and princes of whatever well-being there was attainable in this world. In this connection, it should be noted that the members of the priestly groups were by no means agreed that the possession of wealth was morally desirable; however, they did not hesitate to obtain power either by moral example or, if occasion demanded, by the use of force. Also it should be recalled that the aristocratic orders and priestly groups were often rivals for supreme power, although they commonly found ways to share it.

Besides these two privileged orders, the social pyramids consisted of three main groups: (1) the tillers of the soil, (2) the traders and merchant-manufacturers, and (3) the urban workers. The position of these groups will be made clear in the following discussion of economic and political institutions.

2. *Economic Institutions in the Asiatic and European Urban Cultures.* Since the economic institutions of urban cultures had origin in the circumstances connected with the formation, distribution, and maintenance of the economic surpluses, they were bound up with the differentiation of the social classes and the maintenance of their respective positions.

Because the basis of the production of wealth was land, the fundamental economic institutions everywhere fixed rights of use and ownership in the soil and its products. In the background of these institutions were the early villages, which on the one hand made the use of land a source of private rights in the soil and on the other hand created, because of common need, some communal controls over its use. From this source there flowed into the traditional Asiatic and European cultures practices such as (1) the periodic allotment of fields to families and (2) rights of common use in pasture and waste lands—which conditioned the right of private property in land.

As the control of urban groups over land was established the village system of land tenure was modified in several ways. The differentiation of the ruling classes from the working groups brought elaborations of the system of obligations and services. When new lands were cleared private rights or new obligations and services were commonly established. The introduction of money was decisive in the development of the right of private ownership, for with its use land could be readily bought, sold, pledged, and mortgaged. Above all it could be cultivated for a profit. Thus the introduction of money was a prelude to the growth of large-scale farming wherever cities provided a market for foodstuffs. And conquest usually was followed by the establishment of new land-owners, military in origin, who, in order to enjoy the full benefit of victory, necessarily organized permanent control over the land and its workers.

In the course of these developments the village system, although it did not completely disappear anywhere, was submerged in a system of mixed rights of land. The ownership of land was sometimes vested in the sovereign but more commonly it was shared by the aristocratic and priestly groups. In the feudal system of land tenure, usual in aristocratic orders, the possession of land was made dependent upon the performance of service by the holder to an overlord. Lands held by priests or priestly groups were not usually subject to these obligations, but they could rarely be transferred to other holders. In these systems of mixed tenure the tillers of the soil might be in one of four different positions, namely, that of (1) the free man, owing military service or a fixed rent, (2) the tenant, having temporary rights of use in return for a payment of a rent in kind or the performance of service, or both, (3) the serf, bound to the land but having rights of use as well as obligations to the lord, and (4) the slave, who tilled the soil but had no rights in it or its products. A system of mixed tenure gave rise usually to an estate, or domanial, organization of land use.

In Iran, India, Greece, and Rome, where the early Indo-European peoples still at the tribal level of social organization conquered lands, the members of the tribes became generally free peasants; the Ch'in conquerors of the western Chou seem also to have won private rights in land. But, as time went on, these private rights were assimilated into (1) the surviving village system or (2) a domanial system. If opportunity for farming for profit by selling surpluses in a market was not at hand, the private rights tended to lapse into the village system. This seems to have occurred in India and Iran. If opportunity for high profits was at hand, large-scale farming developed, with the great landholders squeezing the free peasants from their holdings. This circumstance occurred at one time or another in Palestine, Greece, Rome, India, and China. When new lands were steadily made available by conquest, both great landowners and small freeholders tended to multiply. Something like this accompanied the early development of the Roman and Chinese empires. If slave labor was abundant when high profits were to be made, the great slave-worked estate appeared. When agricultural productivity declined, several important changes in land tenure occurred. Thus, as in the Roman and Chinese empires when economic decay began, slaves were raised to the status of serfs in order to stimulate production, free peasants who found it difficult to make a living on their holdings sank to this status, and urban workers, forced to abandon their callings in the cities, accepted it in order to obtain subsistence. Payments in kind and work replaced money dues, and the landowners, no longer able to count on regular profits, organized their estates as self-sufficient households, producing not only foodstuffs but also craft wares. In Iran and India, where low productivity never permitted the full development of farming for a profit, the domanial system became very early the general form of economic organization of land use.

Except in times and places highly favorable for farming for profit, neither the right of private property in land nor the use of slave labor in agriculture was fully developed. Usually the land was held by aristocratic or priestly owners having obligations to a political or an ecclesiastical establishment, with the tillers of the soil—as serfs—retaining vestiges of the ancient village rights in the land. When and where agricultural productivity remained low or became so, the feudal system of land tenure prevailed. But whatever system of tenure existed, it functioned to give those who held rights of ownership in the land the surplus which the tillers of the soil produced.

Because the traditional Asiatic and European cultures possessed little capital goods except land, the basis for a complex organization of industrial enterprise did not exist. The simple tools of the crafts made universal their practice in small units. Only when cities or foreign countries provided markets for textiles, pottery, and metal-wares did larger enterprises employing, sometimes as many as several hundred workers, appear. These enterprises were commonly directed by merchants or the heads of state. Royal factories appeared in all the cultures, and the merchant-manufacturers were generally forced to share their profits with the state, through either taxes or licenses or a state participation in management. In Mauryan India, Han China, Sassanian Persia, the Hellenistic kingdoms, and imperial Rome the state, *i.e.*, the politically organized ruling class, kept industrial enterprise mainly in its hands. The state monopolies were established more as a means of raising revenue, directing labor, and controlling prices than as a way of organizing capital, and except in mining, metalworking, and textile making the state enterprises were principally of the kind known as public works—the building of walls, roads, aqueducts, canals, embankments, palaces, and temples. Such enterprises were conducted as state undertakings, partly because only the state could finance them and partly because the necessary labor force could be commanded only by political authority. Large-scale private enterprises were possible only when slave labor was very cheap, for only then could such enterprises invade the market normally served by small local producers.

Three types of commerce developed in the traditional Asiatic and European urban cultures: (1) a local trade in agricultural and craft products, (2) an interregional trade in raw materials and food-stuffs, and (3) a trade, mainly in luxury goods, with other urban culture areas. The local trade was in the hands of peasants, shop-keepers, and hawkers. The interregional trade was carried on by merchants, who purchased both the surplus foodstuffs and the craft products of the estates and sold them in neighboring cities, chiefly to shopkeepers. The trade between urban centers and out-lying raw material areas was commonly organized under state supervision. The long-distance trade was in the hands of merchants, who met at certain points to deal with one another; sometimes they maintained agents in several cities. Partnerships and joint-stock associations developed mainly in the interregional trade and the mining enterprises closely connected with it. Partnerships seem to have been common in the Mediterranean lands and India. Joint-stock enterprises, without limited liability, appeared in the Hellenistic kingdoms and spread throughout the Mediterranean lands and, possibly, to India, where they seem to have existed under the Guptas. In China merchants' associations operated under state control in both trade and industry.

Closely connected with the development of trade was the growth of organized means of transport on both land and sea. The Achaemenian Persians set the model which was followed in developing the road systems of the Mediterranean lands, south-western Asia, and India. The first purpose of these roads was military, but soon they came to serve commerce as well. In China the road system was developed partly to facilitate the transporta-tion of agricultural products to cities and partly to aid in the clearing of land. On the long overland routes of central Asia there was almost no through traffic; rather there were transfer points at which traders and caravans met. From the eastern Mediterranean ports to the great cities of China the chief forms of transport were the camel caravan and the donkey pack train. Carts were means of local transportation everywhere; heavy wagons were used only in the West. Navigation became well organized in the Mediterranean Basin, in the Red Sea and the Indian Ocean, and around southeastern Asia. On the Mediterranean Sea there were both free merchant ships and state-owned fleets. The Red Sea-Indian Ocean traffic was developed by private merchants sailing in a fleet. The coastwise navigation around southeastern Asia was, it seems, exclusively private venturing. Whereas the Hellenistic kingdoms and the Roman Empire gave the Mediterranean Sea well-built ports, a freedom from piracy, and continuous navigation, China built a system of internal waterways which contributed greatly to her wealth and unification.

The mechanism of exchange—credit, loans, interest, and investment—was considerably developed in the traditional Asiatic and European urban cultures, especially as the use of money spread. Besides facilitating exchange and giving the right of private property a new significance, money economy brought problems which gave the Asiatic and European urban cultures common characteristics. Among these problems were (1) the standard of value, (2) the unification of minting, (3) the fluctuation of prices, and (4) the liquidation of debts. In each urban culture the experience of fixing monetary value by law was tried disastrously. As a means of giving coins a fixed value, centralized minting under government control was adopted. The fluctuation of prices, having origin in the manipulation of coinage, the variations in the supply of precious metal, and the abundance or scarcity of commodities, became so serious that price fixing was resorted to in China, India, the Hellenistic kingdoms, and Rome. The problem of debt tended to give rise to political problems, because it led commonly to the transformation of free peasants into landless laborers. Among urban workers debt often culminated in enslavement.

The scarcity of wealth, the great uncertainty of profit, and the menace of political disorder or confiscation gave a great value to capital, a fact which was evident in the yearly rate of interest. In the Hellenistic kingdoms and under the Roman Republic the interest rate was relatively low, from 6 to 12 per cent; under the Roman Empire, after the first Christian century, it constantly advanced until it reached the high rate of 30 per cent. In India 25 per cent was not uncommon. In China, where capital loans were made mostly to peasants in the form of seeds and food, the rate was always excessive. Petty moneylenders preyed on the poor in India, Iran, and the Mediterranean lands, and attempts to regulate their profits were nowhere successful.

The traders and merchant-enterprisers who carried on large-scale enterprises in manufacturing and mining, long-distance trade, organized transportation, and moneylending were few in number in the early Asiatic and European urban cultures. Sometimes they acquired great wealth, but their possessions, whether large or small, were always insecure because of arbitrary government action, insurrection, and uncertainty of trade. The small traders were especially likely to suffer from political disorder. Because the large merchants, on account of their wealth, were useful allies of the ruling group, they enjoyed a somewhat greater security. But they gained political power only as they became identified with the aristocratic orders. However, they made economic power, especially through loan capital and usury, the means of an exploitation of the economically weak, just as the possessors of political power made force the means of an exploitation of the politically weak. The almost universal condemnation by the ethical teachers of the traditional Asiatic and European urban cultures of economic greed reflects partly their aversion to the pursuit of profit as such and partly their dislike of the disturbance of tradition to which its pursuit gave rise. Only for very short times in the Greek cities were the traders sufficiently prominent to make economic individualism significant either as a social or as a cultural force.

Originally the need for subsistence caused men to work; with the formation of economic surpluses, the desire of their possessors to maintain them led to the creation of systems of administration of labor which would ensure continuous production of the forms of wealth determined by the possessors of the economic surpluses. Thus, as cities developed, the free peasants and herdsmen of the neolithic communities passed under religious and, later, legal controls which either compelled them to work or deprived them of part of the product of their labor. Among the general devices to accomplish one or the other of these purposes were dues, taxes, forced labor, rent, usury, serfdom, and slavery. Slavery was the master device, for under it men were forced to work but the product was transferred to those who exercised power over them. These devices, embodied in law, combined to establish the social status of workers.

Slavery was most common in domestic service. The labor forces of those enterprises, whether state or private, which were operated in an export market commonly consisted of slaves. Enterprises employing large numbers of slaves at the crafts were well known in the Mediterranean lands, India, and China. Everywhere mining was a slave-worked industry, as was also the building of roads, walls, harbors, embankments, and canals. As previously noted, slavery prevailed in agriculture when and where farming for a profit was possible.

Serfs, sometimes recruited from the peasants, manned the state monopolies. When the capacity to produce began to decline, both free and slave labor seem to have given way to serfdom; in other words the principle of the hereditary occupation, *i.e.*, the binding of workers to the callings of their fathers, was introduced when it became necessary to preserve a labor force in kinds of production in which output was decreasing.

Free laborers were always numerous in both agriculture and the craft industries. They were subject to taxation and, on occasion, forced labor. Also they were sometimes beset by conditions which either left them unemployed or forced them to accept very low wages. When they fell into debt, the almost certain result was enslavement. As slavery spread into agriculture many free peasants were driven into the cities, where they swelled the ranks of the unemployed. The free worker was always in a precarious economic position.

Whereas the free peasants generally remained unorganized except under village custom, craft workers commonly formed guilds. These associations existed in China, India, southwestern Asia, and the Mediterranean lands. In China they were bound up with the family and the village. In India they were usually attached to temples. Indian merchants sometimes held the workers' guilds in an almost tributary position. In the Mediterranean lands workers' guilds seemed to have had more religious than economic functions, at least during the period of the Roman Empire; when the cities of the Mediterranean lands decayed, especially in the west, these organizations tended to disappear. The principle of hereditary employment, which held the son to the occupation of the father, probably developed in the guilds.

The controls over labor, it should be remembered, were religious as well as political. Originally the religious controls over peasants were organized in the rituals of the seasonal festivals and integrated in a yearly routine by religious calendars. With the development of cities the religious controls became less applicable to all forms of labor but more explicit where they did apply. In China peasants who violated the imperial commands to plow, plant, and harvest lost their burial rights. In India caste rules defined the obligation to work and made disobedience a religious crime. In southwestern Asia and the Mediterranean Basin the many religions emphasized, to different degrees it is true, the duty of workers to perform the obligations of their position in society. Christianity taught that the worker was bound not only to labor but also to do good work. No religion or philosophy in the traditional Asiatic or European cultures taught that the lot of the worker should be ameliorated beyond security of subsistence, and few declared the dignity of labor. The universal assertion of the workers' duty to labor was the correlative of controls which, while compelling them to work, denied them the right to alter the controls. These controls were supported by social attitudes which stigmatized workers so that those who received their products felt justified in using the force necessary to command their obedience.

In just what proportions the free craftsmen, serfs, and slaves combined to form the urban working class cannot be determined; in any case the proportions seem to have changed during the several phases of the development of urban cultures. The free craftsmen were probably most numerous during the early imperial phase because wealth was then flowing generally into local markets. Certainly slaves were most numerous at the crest of the imperial phase, when the enslavement of conquered peoples was at its height. Serfdom became general whenever economic decline set in. The urban working groups, much larger in number than the privileged classes, were far smaller in number than the rural working groups.

It should be emphasized that the modes of control over labor of the early Asiatic and European urban cultures made possible the conduct of enterprises too great in size for individuals to undertake, and these enterprises probably greatly increased production; thus the administration of labor, as well as the exertions of workers, was a significant factor in maintaining and increasing the economic surpluses. One may be sure, though, that management got its full reward, for regardless of the increase of production workers everywhere seldom received more than subsistence.

Aside from the environmental, technological, and political factors which led to the decline of productivity, the movements of the precious metals among the several urban culture areas seem to have contributed to a growing economic stagnation in the

Mediterranean Basin, Iran, and India, especially after the second Christian century.[1]

In the Mediterranean Basin, Rome and Italy drew wealth by political means from the entire empire, but much of its gold passed quickly to the more highly industrialized areas of Asia Minor, Syria, and Mesopotamia. There a flow of wealth by trade moved constantly to and from Iran, central Asia, India, and China. For a time northwestern Iran and central Asia drew high profits from this trade; when economic decline in the Mediterranean lands lessened the flow of wealth, they quickly fell back into their relatively impoverished condition, and the central Asiatic center of wealth and power shifted to southwestern Iran—Persia. The flow of the precious metals into and out of China was never great enough to disturb the fundamental basis of its economy, although gold first became plentiful there in the first century B.C., when trade with the West opened up. The movement of precious metal into India from the West, however, was considerable for a very long period. In fact, after the formation of the Achaemenian Persian empire, except for the brief period of Alexander's campaigns, it was not seriously interrupted. This movement seems slowly to have depleted the capital resources of the West and, as a result, hastened the reversion to a self-sufficient economy.

But the flow of precious metal to India did not stimulate an economic expansion. The reasons for this failure were undoubtedly to be found in the fundamental quality of Indian culture. Brahman, Buddhist, and Jain ideals not only opposed the profit motive but ennobled poverty. The scarcity of raw materials made new enterprise difficult to develop. The profits of the trade in luxury goods concentrated industrial activity in their production. The princely tradition of hoarding gold and gems and of consuming wealth in ostentatious display defined the chief use of the economic surplus. The caste system denied to merchants, peasants, and laborers the full social benefits of the successful pursuit of gain. And the Hindu tabu on going to sea undoubtedly restricted enterprise. Thus Indian culture did not make the flow of precious metal from the West the stimulus to economic expansion. As the West lost its fluid capital, India acquired it, only to hoard it. The peculiar orientation of Indian culture was a factor in the growing economic stagnation of Asiatic and European cultures.

[1] For a note on gold in the Mediterranean Basin see W. B. Sedgwick, "The Gold Supply in Ancient and Medieval Times and Its Influence in History," *Greece & Rome*, Vol. 5 (1935), pp. 148–154.

Fundamentally, however, this stagnation was rooted in the interaction between imperialism and technology—an interaction which, having carried wealth production to a peak, could not maintain it—and the peculiar religious condition of India intensified the stagnation in Rome and Iran. Under these circumstances the centers of wealth production supported mainly by a concentration of flow of precious metals declined, and those supported by natural advantages of soil and water or of a concentration of trade routes regained prominence. It is also probable that a recovery of mining in the Balkans, Armenia, and Pontus contributed to the rise of the eastern Mediterranean area to economic prominence in the fourth century. But nowhere did economic activity again reach the level of the first two Christian centuries.

3. *Political Institutions of Asiatic and European Urban Cultures.* Regardless of the original social organizations of the founders of the traditional Asiatic and European urban cultures, these cultures moved through political evolutions which brought them to one end: the oriental monarchy. Among Indo-European peoples, except the Iranians, the course passed through a republican phase (tribal republics are known to have existed in ancient India); among other peoples it moved through a feudal phase. This difference is probably best understood as an outcome of the fact that the Indo-European peoples began the development of their urban cultures as conquering tribes, with the result that the aroused in-group feeling tended to preserve an equality among the members of the tribes. The Iranians moved quickly to an oriental monarchy under the influence of the ancient-oriental imperial regimes which they succeeded; and the Greeks and the Indians received its elements from them. Insofar as the Roman state became an oriental monarchy not by its own internal development but by diffusion, the Egyptian Ptolemaic regime, probably the most systematic of all oriental monarchies, was the chief source of borrowed materials. In Palestine, where conquest destroyed the political regime, the ecclesiastical elements of the oriental monarchy developed into a priestly state, which lacked the bureaucratic and military aspects of the political regimes of other urban cultures. The Chinese feudal regime reflected a low development of urban life; to obtain the surplus produced by peasant villagers it was necessary to disperse the conquerors rather than to concentrate them, as in the city-states of the Mediterranean lands. Feudalism was an institutional device to preserve the unity of a ruling class whose possession of wealth could be organized only on a local basis.

However, when an increase of wealth followed the introduction of iron tools, large-scale irrigation, and the traction plow, the Chinese feudal regime gave way to the centralized and absolute state. Behind the oriental monarchies everywhere stood (1) innovations in armaments and military organization which deprived local groups of military importance and (2) a means of transportation which permitted not only the use of military force in a wide area but also the drawing of wealth from a wide area to support it. Political centralization became possible only as power and wealth developed forms that made their concentration practicable.

Inasmuch as the several oriental monarchies have been described in some detail, here it is necessary only to note their common characteristics: (1) The state was believed to have divine foundation, and the worship of its gods was necessary to its power and prosperity. (2) The head of the state, a king or emperor, was absolute in power and responsible only to his gods. If he did not claim to be a god, he was certain to claim that he had been divinely appointed or that he ruled with the guidance of heaven. (3) The functions of government were performed by a body of advisers and officials. The highest rank formed a "court," which was usually dominated by the king's relatives, or favorites, frequently female, or by eunuchs, priests, or military commanders, and sometimes mere adventurers. Except when they sought personal advantage, these figures ruled in the interest of the sovereign, which, indeed, they conceived as a class matter, not a personal one. (4) Quarrels among rivals in the court often disorganized administration or caused a change of rulers. But a change of ruler seldom meant any alteration in the structure or the policy of government. Provincial rulers, although they represented the supreme authority, were generally more or less independent. Their administrations were duplicates on a small scale of the central regime. And the district governments were smaller replicas of the same model. Through this administrative structure were scattered magistrates, inspectors, clerks, and police, who really governed; except to do the bidding of those above, they had no political duty. (5) The military, fiscal, and judicial functions were not clearly defined; the legislative function, however, was the prerogative of the supreme ruler. (6) When foreign peoples were conquered they were usually treated with great severity. Orderly imperial government evolved from military rule set up to wring wealth from the vanquished. In its simplest form, like the Iranian, it was content to take the wealth and allow local institutions to remain; at best, as in the Roman Empire, it brought the vanquished under the law of the conqueror.

The law commonly had two aspects. The masses followed the ancient customs of their village communities; except as it defined and enforced obligations, the law of the ruling group meant little to them. A harsh criminal code stood guard over the interests of the ruling group. The village law usually dealt with the family, the inheritance of property, and ordinary debts. Only the Romans developed a rational system of law embodying a conception of universal justice. But it, like less coherent legal systems, recognized rights and duties as aspects of socioeconomic status. Chief among the rights of the subject (usually the only significant one) was the right of appeal to the supreme ruler. This appeal, even when acted on by a benevolent sovereign, could not relieve the population of its normal burdens; it could only relieve an individual of an arbitrary punishment or exaction.

Above all, it should be understood that the masses possessed neither civil liberties nor political rights. In fact, conceptions of such liberties and rights were unknown in fully developed oriental monarchies. Arbitrary power was not responsible for its actions. The sole political instrument in the hands of the population was resort to violence, and insurrections were recurrent in all the traditional Asiatic and European urban cultures. Only because the interest of the ruling group was served best by a condition of life which made possible the continuous performance by the population of those acts which maintained the ruling group was arbitrary irresponsibility modified by benevolence. Not by right but by benevolence was the population permitted to lead the orderly life that served the interest of the rulers.

Of special importance, in view of the political helplessness of the masses, was the fusing of civil, military, and ecclesiastical authority which ruled them. Alongside the civil bureaucracy stood the military and religious establishments, each working in its own way to control those from whom it drew support. Thus law, force, and religion mingled sanctions to establish a rule which the best sentiments of the masses—obedience, loyalty, and piety—bade them accept. The social basis of this fusion of authority was, of course, the ruling classes, whose positions gave them the functions that left the masses politically inert.

4. *The Regimented Social Order of the Asiatic and European Urban Cultures.* If the class structures, economic institutions, governmental regimes, and legal systems of the traditional Asiatic and European urban cultures are brought together in one focus, they are seen as forming regimented social orders. What is the essential element in regimentation? It is the use of power—

economic, political, military, and intellectual power, alone or in combination—by one group to transfer, under law, the wealth of another group to itself. Inasmuch as the production of wealth is dynamic, this transfer had to be organized in controls over production and distribution that functioned through time. These controls fixed different positions in regard to the ownership and use of wealth, as well as in regard to the labor which contributed to its production. They also differentiated among these positions in terms of the exercise of political power. And they embodied intellectual judgments which justified the several positions they established and differentiated. Their combined effect was to create an order in which a few groups were functionally distinct and in which individuals were able to move from one group to another only with the greatest difficulty. The general principle was: Birth fixes status, and status determines function, right, and duty. When religious significance was attached to differences of status so established, the order became a caste system; ordinarily it was a legal regime, in which a few individuals changed position from time to time, but in which the great part of the population was held fast in a few sharply defined positions.

In a regimented social order those who held power—always few in proportion to the mass—made and enforced the controls, and this power they obtained and held by force or by propaganda, or by both. At this point in regimented social orders the military and priestly groups usually found a basis for cooperation. With political power, law was made. In law, claims that gave the possession of wealth produced by others were established. With military force, when less violent methods were insufficient, the claims were executed. With the wealth thus obtained, the power that established and enforced controls was supported. The cycle of regimentation was complete: he who possessed power obtained wealth, and with wealth he organized power; obversely, he who was without power worked to produce wealth, and the fact that he worked was a reason to deny him political power. The intellectual groups who shared power and wealth with the aristocracies made learning the means of release from labor and found in learning reasons why those who worked could not or should not acquire learning, power, or wealth.

TRADITION, LEARNING, AND IDEOLOGY.

The intellectual structure of the traditional Asiatic and European urban groups began to develop with the use of writing. From oral traditions stemmed literate traditions embodied in a few books and many commentaries upon them. Around these core traditions clustered bodies of speculative and literary learning. And beyond them were diffused beliefs, which, having spread among the illiterate masses, bound these masses, at least loosely, to the core traditions. Inasmuch as the core traditions and the bodies of speculative and literary learning attached to them were carried by small groups possessing a knowledge of writing, they constituted the *high intellectual traditions* of these cultures, while the elements of the core traditions diffused among the illiterate masses and the persisting primitive beliefs of the masses formed the *low intellectual traditions*. It is worth noting that there was some movement of ideas between these two traditions in each of the traditional Asiatic and European cultures, and that in some circumstances it was probably considerable.

In Indian, Greek, and Chinese cultures there were attempts to discover a basis for intellectual validity other than tradition reinforced by purported revelation or purported revelation developed as tradition. Each of these attempts—the Buddhist, the Socratic, and the Moist—undertook to establish validity by human reason operating with a system of logic. But they survived in traditions which made them, insofar as they were used at all, instruments for giving coherence to systems of thought based not upon reason but upon tradition as rendered in authoritative works. Thus Buddhistic logic became secondary to the Buddhist canon, even for Buddhism, and gave rise to the system of reasoning which some of the Hindus used to establish the meaning of the Vedic texts. From the Socratic innovation stemmed the Aristotelian logic, which became the rationalizing instrument of the Christian tradition. And the Moist logic survived only in the Confucian use of history to confirm tradition. After contact with Greek culture the Hebrew high intellectual tradition borrowed the Aristotelian logic and used it as the Christian tradition did. The Iranians never attempted a logical integration of Zoroastrianism. Of each of the traditional Asiatic and European cultures it may be said, therefore, that intellectual method did not develop in a way to weaken the traditionally received concepts and modes of thought.

A summary view of the general elements of the high and low intellectual traditions of these cultures supports this conclusion.

1. *The High Intellectual Traditions of the Traditional Asiatic and European Urban Cultures.* As was pointed out in the discussion of the high intellectual traditions of the ancient-oriental urban cultures, such traditions embodied four kinds of learning: (1)

liturgical, (2) meditative, (3) decorative, and (4) operational. These forms of learning constituted the high intellectual traditions now under survey, although each type of learning had a somewhat different position in each culture.

Liturgical learning, *i.e.*, the learning necessary for the conduct of public worship, was easily of first importance in each high intellectual tradition, except the Greek. But in Christian culture, into which the Greek high intellectual tradition was assimilated, it outweighed all other forms. Liturgical learning consisted of a knowledge not only of rituals but also of the beliefs which they expressed and the objectives which they served. From one point of view it may be regarded as the "social magic" of each culture, for in terms of it well-being, however defined, was believed to be achieved.

As each culture moved toward consolidation, its meditative learning grew more important and, once liturgical learning was authoritatively rendered, became the leading form of individual intellectual enterprise. The monastic regimes of the several cultures were institutions for the pursuit (or practice) of meditative learning, and, next to the ecclesiastical establishments, they were the most important intellectual institutions of the several cultures. The emphasis on meditative learning was entirely upon the subjective content of life, which, as evidenced by the works of the prophets, poets, and philosophers of these cultures, was the stuff of creative imagination, and from it they produced, as was inevitable in the nature of the case, little that was more than systematized revery. Meditative learning built "air castles" and filled them with "daydreams," sometimes romantic, sometimes horrible, and sometimes just diffuse and dull. It nourished the "higher things of life." In the most extreme form it begot a cessation of all physical action—in fact, its distortion—on the theory that inactivity is conducive to the experience of spiritual reality.

The decorative learning of each culture was specialized to serve the prestige of the ascendant class, for its chief purpose was to distinguish this class intellectually from all others. In its simplest form, as among the Iranians and Chinese, decorative learning consisted mainly of a knowledge of ranks, etiquette, and the military exercises necessary to the maintenance of the class interest. In its most complete form, as among the Greeks, Romans, and Indians, it added to these materials literary accomplishment and familiarity with philosophy. To refinement of manners were added literary graces and an intellectual interest in "higher things." But neither manners nor grace nor elevated interest was allowed to sacrifice class interest to an ethical principle. From decorative learning issued ultimately in every culture its "humanities," "belles-lettres," and "fine arts," from which, together with its "classics," its "gentlemen and scholars" were made. Insofar as these forms of learning remained materials of class distinction, their significant elements—intellectual orderliness, aesthetic standards, and individual refinement—were adulterated with social prejudices; disentangled from these prejudices they were materials useful in whatever amelioration of common life could be organized. Their possessors seldom undertook to disentangle them.

The operational learning in the high intellectual traditions of the Asiatic and European urban cultures was hardly greater in amount than that carried in the high intellectual traditions of the ancient-oriental cultures. As in these cultures it had two main parts, social and scientific, *i.e.*, it consisted of the learning by which men controlled men and the learning by which they manipulated nature for their own ends. The social element consisted of moral dogma, theories of political and economic judgments, and law. The moral dogma, having a religious orientation, was closely bound up with liturgical learning. Political and economic judgments gave support to the oriental monarchy and a regimented social order. Law was important in all high intellectual traditions, but in various forms. In the Iranian, Indian, and Hebrew high intellectual traditions religious law was the core of functional learning. In the Christian high intellectual tradition moral dogma was uppermost, although a religious law grew within it and a secular law stood alongside it. The Chinese did not disentangle either religious or secular law from liturgical learning. Little need be said about the sciences in these high cultural traditions. They were mainly small bodies of theory and smaller bodies of fact. Mathematics was easily the leading science in each culture, probably because, since it was subjective and deductive, it was nourished by the general outlook of the several cultures. Those sciences whose development required the systematic gathering and classifying of facts about natural phenomena very early ceased to develop at all, except as, incidental to war and trade, new facts were thrown together and attracted the attention of individuals who assimilated them into the existing body of similar facts. Indeed, it is not incorrect to see the natural sciences growing almost entirely by this uncertain process. If a knowledge of literary skills is regarded as a part of operational learning, as well as a chief element of decorative learning, it seems that they were used little in any service that ameliorated the conditions of life or advanced the procedures which might enrich it. However, as instruments of social interaction literary learning contributed significantly to the development of the modes of interaction, and these modes became, in turn, important factors in shaping thought. Unfortunately, under the influence of liturgical, meditative, and decorative learning literary skill was often subverted to the service of formalism, jargon, expression without thought, and even magical gibberish.

When the foregoing types of learning are viewed together as an intellectual structure, they may be seen as embodying a number of elements which combined in one way or another to establish authoritative knowledge:

1. *Sacred Books.* At the core of the intellectual systems of the traditional Asiatic and European urban cultures were "sacred books"—the Hebrew Pentateuch, the Iranian Zend-Avesta, the Indian Vedas, the Buddhist Canon, the Chinese Classics, and the Christian Old and New Testaments. The Homeric poems held a somewhat similar position in Greek culture; among the Romans an oral legal tradition, supported by the Twelve Tables, was the core of the only learning they ever could call their own. The sources of the learning embodied in these works were oral traditions, commonly believed to have been divinely inspired or revealed; for this reason their written renderings were regarded as having supreme intellectual authority. Several of the oral traditions which the sacred books embodied persisted long after their carriers had acquired a knowledge of writing.

2. *Methods of Interpreting Texts.* Once these oral traditions were given a written rendering, enduring form combined with religious sanctions and age to harden their authority, and, as a result, further intellectual activity began with their meanings. But their meanings had to be ascertained. To do this several methods of interpretation were developed in the various cultures: (1) literal rendering, *i.e.*, the texts mean exactly what they say, (2) self-revelation, *i.e.*, the texts have the power to make their meanings known, (3) spiritual meditation, *i.e.*, the meaning of the texts becomes known when the seeker attains a certain spiritual condition, and (4) allegorical interpretation, *i.e.*, the texts are symbols whose meaning can be known only after careful study. In applying these methods the need to have exact language promoted the development of grammar, philology, and etymology, while the need to have information about divine and human activities relevant to the meanings led to historical study and antiquarian research. In Indian and Greek culture the development of the study of words and modes of their use produced grammar and

logic; in Chinese, Hebrew, and, later, Christian culture history, or, at least, antiquarian research, appeared.

Closely related to methods of ascertaining the meanings of sacred texts was the belief that there were ways to go beyond the texts to the divine source of knowledge; among these ways were mystical experience, meditation, physical enervation culminating in stupor, trance, vision, ecstatic feeling, dream, and oracle. Sometimes knowledge obtained by these methods was believed to supersede the established tradition; more often it was regarded as either confirming or elaborating the established tradition. When knowledge so obtained was believed to supersede the established tradition, it was commonly embodied in a new sacred work. Intellectual history knows several transitory sacred works, as well as the long-lived ones.

In each culture interpreters of the sacred texts used these various methods (in one combination or another), and controversies among them were normal occurrences. These controversies usually reflected some kind of social issue; similarly, heresies were identified with social or political movements against established regimes. To preserve a recognized interpretation of sacred texts authoritative spokesmen were sometimes established, as in the Iranian, Indian, Hebrew, and Christian cultures.

3. *The Elaboration of Knowledge from Texts.* The elaboration of the meanings found in the sacred texts became the usual intellectual activity of those possessing a knowledge of the texts. Sometimes, as with Hebrew learning, the elaboration included science, philosophy, law, and literature —in fact, every intellectual interest. Among the Indians science, philosophy, and law were believed to stem from the Vedas; after the fixing of the Buddhist Canon, speculation gave several fields of learning a Buddhist rendering. As Chinese Confucianism absorbed the yin and yang dynamics and the Taoist "way," it also assimilated all forms of learning. As far as is now known, the Avestan tradition mingled legal and scientific with religious learning. The Greeks pursued learning beyond the limits of their poetic tradition, but the results survived mainly in the Christian tradition, in which all forms of learning were adapted to the religious core. The Roman legal tradition, finally rendered in the Justinian Code, was also adapted to the Christian tradition.

Analysis of the elaboration of knowledge from the sacred texts indicates that each contained elements similar to those of the others: (1) a broad concept of the universe, (2) a theory of health and disease, (3) an interpretation of history, (4) a view of human nature, and (5) a theory of social relations. The details of these elements, however variable from culture to culture, do not obscure their underlying similarities.

4. *An Educational Practice.* Inasmuch as the sacred texts were the basis of knowledge, educational practice began with a study of them, often the memorizing of them. Their authority tended to establish "classics" as the authoritative basis of knowledge in other fields, so that

the study of words rather than the investigation of phenomena came to constitute all education. The adaptation of intellectual method to a learning almost exclusively verbal in content gave rise to systems of logic which made possible the spinning of vast webs of propositions regarded as having validity but not checked against any body of facts. The tendency was to fit facts into deduced propositions rather than to induce propositions from facts. Thus the educational practices of the traditional Asiatic and European urban cultures became an "arid scholasticism." If education began with the memorizing of sacred texts, its completion was an examination of proficiency in terms of knowledge elaborated from them. The Chinese examination, the Indian debate, Hindu and Buddhist alike, and the Hebrew and the Christian colloquies between masters and pupil were varieties of the testing of students' mastery of an approved body of learning.[1]

5. *An Over-all Intellectual Orientation.* Behind the sacred texts and the learning elaborated from them were concepts which, when brought together in a coherent body of thought, are commonly designated a "theology," *i.e.*, the intellectual content of a religion. Inasmuch as these concepts—"spirit," "soul," "life beyond the grave," and "other world," among others—were originally corollaries of the primitive concept "daimonic universe," a theology was, in fact, merely a rendering of primitive beliefs. Although the social and intellectual forces of urban cultures gave theologies a coherence and an abstraction lacking in the mythologies of preliterate peoples, they did not alter the fundamental concepts from which the theologies were developed.

The theologies of the respective cultures were the inclusive interpretations of experience which explained supreme reality, man's relation to supreme reality, man's relation to man in terms of his relation to supreme reality, and man's place in nature as nature existed under supreme reality. In other words the theologies were those orientations of experience in terms of which men understood themselves. Needless to say the orientations, although elaborated from the same primitive concepts, were not valid from one culture to another.

6. *Systems of Speculative Thought.* Amplifying these over-all orientations were various systems of speculative thought which served to bridge the gaps between phenomena, *i.e.*, going experience, and the static concepts of the theologies. These systems—monism, dualism, materialism, atomism, idealism, and realism—were not equally well developed in all the high intellectual traditions. In the Indian and Greek they were the most diversely elaborated; in the Iranian the least. The Chinese owed a debt to the Indians for their philosophy, and the Hebrews to the Greeks. The Christians assimilated Greek idealism and Greek dualism

---

[1] For a brief survey of educational practices in early urban cultures see H. L. Smith, R. S. McElhinney, and G. R. Steele, *The Old World Historical Background of Religious and Moral Education* (1934, Bureau of Cooperative Research, Indiana University).

into their theology. The dominant philosophy in each culture, however, worked out in detail, was teleological.

As noted in the foregoing chapters the speculative philosophies dealt with practical questions. How is the world organized? Does change occur, and how? How can man know anything? What is the good life? How can man follow this way of life? Insofar as these questions were given systematic answers, the speculative elements of the several high intellectual traditions were advances in abstract thinking over their traditionally perpetuated concepts, but in no instance did the new abstractions displace these concepts. Rather, in every case they were assimilated into those concepts in the over-all orientations. The result was that in each culture, although several views of phenomena existed, they were organized in the prevailing overall interpretations; these views were evident in the various schools of orthodoxy which arose. On the whole, however, those philosophies which declared the unimportance, if not the unreality, of the phenomenal world, were more in accord with the underlying concepts of the overall orientations than those, such as materialism, which made difficult the rendering of these underlying concepts. Similarly dualism, an easier derivative from primitive beliefs than monism, existed more widely.

Although the high intellectual traditions of the early Asiatic and European urban cultures were alike both in their fundamental forms and in the relation of these forms to one another, they were pervaded by differences in attitude toward life. These differences, it seems reasonably clear, had origin mainly in the general social experience which entered into the several cultures; in other words, the experience of the masses was the source of the unique feeling for life of each high intellectual tradition. Among the Chinese this feeling flowed from a peasant-village life never greatly disturbed; on the one hand it declared the enduring rule of custom and on the other hand declared the power of Heaven. The Iranians, conquerors of diverse peoples, projected the battle feelings—the hatred of the enemy, *i.e.*, evil, and the joy of victory, *i.e.*, triumphant right— into a universal struggle. The Jews, having suffered recurrent political frustration, asserted a universal moral ascendancy—an imperialism of righteousness. The Greeks, who made a hard environment, both physical and social, yield to varied efforts, proclaimed human reason to be the master of the universe. The Romans, having conquered many peoples and then fought one another over the spoils, accepted the Greek reason as the master of the universe, providing it was orderly and sober; the Greeks were not so certain about the qualities human reason must have in order to claim the universe for its own—that it was human was enough. The Christians, drawn from the uprooted and dispossessed masses of the Mediterranean lands, identified suffering with Deity and claimed for the individual, as the individual, in the other world what this world had denied him, namely, peace, joy, and worth. Although not so poignant in the other cultures as in the Christian, this feeling arose everywhere from the disorganization of mass life that imperialism brought and found expression in a religion of salvation. The unity of the early Asiatic and European intellectual developments is finally evident in the Savior-Gods they produced—Christ, the Messiah, Mithra, Krishna, Amitabha, and Omito-Fo—who, through the faith of the individual in divine compassion, came to offer men an otherworldly state which is best understood as a compensation for the distresses of worldly life.

2. *The Low Intellectual Tradition of the Traditional Asiatic and European Urban Cultures.*   Although the artifacts and documents of the early Asiatic and European urban cultures give somewhat more information about the illiterate mases than do the materials of the ancient-oriental urban cultures, the mentality of these masses must still be inferred from the circumstances of their social formation and their status in the several cultures. As illiterates it may be assumed that these masses carried a primitive mentality, shaped partly in hunting cultures and partly in peasant-village cultures.[1] With this mentality were blended elements developed under the various conditions of life that characterized urban cultures. As was the case with the high intellectual tradition, it may

---

[1] There are very few studies which bear on the materials here considered under the designation "low intellectual tradition." This paucity of studies is due partly to lack of materials and partly to the fact that the intellectual interests supported by the "high intellectual tradition" have not considered common men worthy of investigation. A study which clearly recognizes the distinction developed here between the "low" and "high" intellectual traditions is Solomon Gandz, "The Dawn of Literature," *Osiris*, Vol. 7 (1939), pp. 263–522. In the words of the author it "attempts to deal with the civilization of the savages, with the literature of illiterates and preliterates"; the author also recognizes that "the relics of primitive mentality" are so numerous and rampant in our civilization that it is hard to rise above them. Two articles which bear on the extremely important problem of the intellectual phenomenon of passing from the "low" to the "high" intellectual level are Bathscombe Gunn, "The Religion of the Poor in Ancient Egypt," *The Journal of Egyptian Archaeology*, Vol. 3 (1916), pp. 81–94, and Dora Zuntz, "Two Styles of Coptic Painting," *The Journal of Egyptian Archaeology*, Vol. 21 (1935), pp. 63–67. Miss Zuntz observes of the fact of the "low" and "high" intellectual traditions: "Similarly, and because of these social conditions, culture and civilization were sharply divided into two: the foreign Hellenic or Hellenized layer, cosmopolitan, educated in classical learning and philosophy and art, and the illiterate lower stratum, full of gloomy nationalistic hatred and a narrow, passionate religiosity." Mr. Gunn notes that in Egyptian hymns, probably composed by artisans, of the period 1350–1200 B.C., the folk faith became momentarily articulate; its chief content was a religious hope for mercy in a world in which good and bad are not clearly known.

be assumed that the details of the low intellectual traditions were everywhere different but their basic elements were more or less alike. In the following remarks, which, in the nature of the case, are mainly conjectural, the circumstances in hunting, peasant-village, and urban cultures which probably gave enduring elements to the mentality of the masses of urban cultures are noted.

1. *A Considerable Body of Factual Information.* The body of factual information had been built up mainly by technological developments and was organized almost exclusively in the technological procedures of daily life. In the shift from hunting to peasant-village civilization it had been considerably increased. It was somewhat specialized as a result of the division of labor which appeared in the early cities. But among the peasant-village masses it had an almost unchanging content. In the main it consisted of a limited acquaintance with the weather, the different seasons, the growing habits of various cultivated plants, the life routines of the several domesticated animals, the simple processes of combustion and fermentation, a few uses of a rather large number of natural substances and materials, and the reactions of plants, animals, and men to some common external situations.

Except as this knowledge was carried in technological skills which were passed from generation to generation of laborers, it had no existence; at the same time, however, it was the actual basis of economic production and consequently the chief factor in the maintenance of the economic surpluses upon which all urban cultures rested. No one recognized its importance, for the original neglect of factual information by primitive men persisted among the carriers of both the low and the high intellectual traditions. Furthermore, it was everywhere bound up with ritualistic practices and superstitious beliefs.

2. *The Belief in the Efficacy of Violence.* Under the circumstances which everywhere surrounded them, it was inevitable that early men should find in physical violence the essential means of survival. Against fang and claw and tine they opposed crude weapons, and physical strength and courage more than knowledge or skill or strategy determined the outcome of the clashes. Of course, knowledge, skill, and strategy entered to a slight degree into the behavior of hunting men, but they were probably unaware of the significance of these aspects of mentality for the successful culmination of their struggles. For always these aspects of mentality were submerged by the fierce emotions that surged during the pursuit of game and the "kill." Thus the resort to violence was given a primary role in behavior.

Under the conditions of life which prevailed, emotional expression tended to be violent. Against physical opposition strength alone was at hand as the means of overcoming resistance. And in social relations the application of force provided a simple and effective solution of disturbing problems. For by its successful applications antagonists were either destroyed or reduced to conditions which made them no longer dangerous. That such a victory had psychological consequences which promoted further resort to violence only seemed to justify the conclusion that the supreme moral dereliction is to become weak or to fail to keep ready for any emergency in which the use of force may be necessary.

Thus in the earliest mental structure of mankind the resort to violence received both the sanction of necessity and the approval of moral judgment; among all the psychological types received into later cultures from primordial human experience, the "killer"—his forms have been legion—is the one most rigidly set in basic emotional fixations.

3. *The Superstitious Attitude.* The superstitious attitude is a state of mind in which every object in the environment is thought of as a person; in other words, a subjective distinction is not made between objects and individuals. From this point of view the universe is seen to be a vast complex of intangible and uncanny forces which act as if they were persons. They cannot be dealt with by means of physical manipulations based upon factual knowledge obtained by the observation of nature, but must be treated as persons, *i.e.*, dealt with in terms of interest, desire, love, hate, and vanity. What happens to man as he goes about the affairs of daily life is a matter of "luck." The unseen spirits determine this luck, good or bad, and there is no rational explanation of how or why luck "breaks" good or bad.

In the face of universal uncertainty (which was quite as much a primary aspect of hunting life as violence) man can do little for himself, but show his dependence upon the overworld of uncanny beings. He can fear, or supplicate, or worship, or stand in awe of the spirits, but he can never disdain, or neglect, or thwart them. To do so is to invite dire disaster. The heart of the superstitious attitude is a feeling of dependence upon beings believed to be more powerful than man; that this attitude has been a significant element in all traditional religions is too well known for comment here.

4. *The Patriotic Fervor.* As a gregarious species it is highly probable that the evolution of the human race was achieved more through social than through individual development; *i.e.*, individual development always occurred within a definite field of interaction with other individuals; and each individual within the field of interaction felt the other individuals who made it up to be an entity—a group. On the one hand the individual found personal survival chiefly through the survival of his group; on the other hand the group protected itself by destroying those individuals who endangered its existence. Between this hammer and anvil was forged the powerful feeling of in-group loyalty.

Under its spell the individual lost all sense of fairness, forgot all rational judgment, and, deeply stirred by emotion, rushed headlong into action with no regard to consequences whatever. But this action was tremendously satisfying, for in it self was identified with society; in other words, the individual felt that he was serving a high social purpose. That the individual desire for this satisfaction is a powerful factor in motivating behavior has too long been lost sight of by those expounders of social philosophies who place self-interest at the heart of individual conduct. To an extreme degree the patriotic fervor obstructs all rational conduct; as an enduring emotional fixation it orientates individual behavior about social purposes.

That this orientation was always uppermost in primitive life when conflict broke out between rival groups unfortunately obscured the fact that service to the in-group can take many forms other than military; in this circumstance was fixed the original conjunction of patriotism and the resort to violence.

5. *The Sentimental Mood.* In hunting life the way of experiencing the environment was different from the way in which modern urban dwellers experience it. This was true both as regards the attention given to specific objects and as regards the responses to be made to them. The hunter lived always on the *qui vive;* every movement, sound, and visual image was assimilated at once into a moving picture of events which at any instant might call for violent action. The uncertainty of the "kill" and the necessity for its successful outcome, both as a matter of immediate survival and as a matter of winning subsistence, pressed sensations, emotions, and physical responses into situations toward which the individual had no perspective; and the necessity for taking violent action kept emotions always near the surface of consciousness.

The gross effect of this way of life was to fix in man's earliest mentality the habit of attending to experience always in terms of immediate and concrete situations into which were infused emotions of varying degrees of intensity. As an enduring aspect of the psychology of preliterate men, this way of attending to experience may be called the "sentimental mood." It always sought to know the edge of an experience, *i.e.*, to sense its uniqueness as opposed to its general aspects. It built an understanding of the world in terms of diversified emotional reactions rather than in terms of abstractions generalized from logically considered items of experience. And it lacked any significant sense of the duration of time, for the pressing concern with immediate situations completely obscured the fact of continuity in human behavior. The sentimental mood nourished an intellectual empiricism of the crudest sort. Under its spell men were drunk with the keen brew of experience spiked with emotions of their own distillation.

6. *The Idea "Work."* Only with the invention of cultivation and the crafts did men come to expend their physical energies in a regular sequence of acts continued over relatively long periods of time, *i.e.*, in *work*. The inefficiency of the means of production made such exertions arduous and fatiguing, but the returns from them gave a security of life which compensated for their arduousness. As settled communities

became dependent upon these efforts for continued existence, group pressures were evolved which directed the energies of individuals into such channels. Thus the individual was required to "work"; there was no other way to live.

Since the emotional excitement which accompanied the exertions of the hunt were obliterated in the monotonous routines of the new occupations, new emotional excitements of a communal character were organized, for example, house-raisings, housewarmings, harvest festivals, and the like. All of those aspects of work—long hours, excessive fatigue, unsanitary conditions, child labor, and women's employment at heavy tasks—which only lately have been recognized as evils, were common-places of peasant-village life. And those persons who could not endure them were looked upon as weaklings. Peasant villagers invented hard labor, and for them it was an expected and moralized element of daily life.

7. *The Idea "Property."* The idea "property" was closely bound up with the idea "work." The possession of a bit of land, a few animals, and the simple tools of the field and shop meant life, independence, and security to peasant villagers. They knew nothing of employment in the modern sense of the word. To win the ownership of land was their chief economic concern beyond obtaining a subsistence; to live independently by working their own land was the highest social achievement they en-visioned. And everywhere in the world peasant villagers have found some way to institutionalize this economic aim and social idea. Usually they have established some sort of parcelization of land, either in the actual ownership of small plots or in the sharing of numerous rights in variously sized fields.

Once entrenched in a system of such rights of possession, peasant villagers have shown most enduring power to thwart change and, in fact, have only given way under the pressure of economic circumstances which destroyed the security customarily afforded by the ownership of land. The peasant villager's hunger for land has been the greatest single motive working for the extension of the institution of private property over the earth. That other men have made the institution something quite different from what it was originally is a fact which peasant villagers have seldom learned.

When the ideas "work" and "property" were fused with the mental traits socially inherited from hunting ancestors, the peasant-village mentality was given an enduring form. That the essential traits of hunting mentality persisted in the peasant-village mind is amply evidenced in the crude outbursts of violence, the crass superstitions, the heated patriotism, and the gross sentimentality which have everywhere featured peasant-village life. At the same time peasant villagers developed an economic "hardness"; above all other men they were the formulators and practical apostles of the morality of thrift. But thrift did not mean saving in order to begin to speculate, nor even to accumulate wealth for its own sake. Rather it meant the gaining of an economic security that was well defined by custom, the winning of whatever opportunities for cultural and political activities the village offered, and the achievement of that type of prestige which peasant villagers most respected.

8. *The Ethics of Neighborliness.* "Rugged individualism" was deeply embedded in peasant-village mentality, but that sense of communal life which the "village"—a small, compact group of perennial gossips—nourished prevented its crude release in pure economic self-aggrandizement. This sense of communal life took form in a well-defined ethical code: the ethics of neighborliness.

The root of this ethics, like that of every other ethics, was in the sensitivity of the individual to group pressures, or rather to the pressures exerted by other individuals acting in the name of the group. But since the group, or rather the conception of the group in terms of which individuals act, varies under different historical circumstances, the definitions of right and wrong also vary both in time and in place. Thus although such virtues as kindness, mutual sympathy and regard, family affection, respect for elders, integrity, duty, loyalty, and charity may have absolute meanings as abstractions, they never exist actually except in the behavior of individuals who are acting under pressures applied by others in the name of a group. For this reason it is all-important to realize that these virtues as defined by the communal sense of peasant villagers embodied a peculiar content.

In addition to the patriotic and economic attitudes referred to in the preceding paragraphs, the distinctive element which entered into the definition of these virtues was derived from the fact that the peasants lived in permanent and intimate face-to-face relations. In this close and continuous living together personal feeling was always present in the relations of individuals, and sentiment was the strongest bond among them. Thus were shaped those ethical concepts "neighbor" and "neighborliness" which are distinctive, in that personal contact and sentiment are united in them.

Under these concepts kindness, charity, mutual aid, sympathy, honesty, integrity, duty, and loyalty were qualities of behavior expressed in direct contacts with others. The "good neighbor" acted directly and with feeling; he was no unknown and distant benefactor. This was particularly true in all circumstances which called for aid and sympathy; they were given in the form that was immediately necessary and with the display of sentiment that made them most acceptable. Since under similar circumstances they were returned in the same way, there was generated between neighbors a feeling of equality that was vitalized with emotion and understanding. In the peculiar forms which they had in the ethics of neighborliness, all the social virtues were uniquely personal in their manifestations; action and feeling were combined in a conduct which was fully known to those whom it touched.

The significance of this achievement of the peasant-village mind can hardly be overestimated, for it established among the masses of all urban cultures many social relations in which, in spite of superstitions, crudities of taste, low standards of living, and outbursts of violence, sound sentiments and right actions were uppermost. The peasant-village masses always had a correct understanding of the social *good* when it was realizable in terms of direct personal relation. Unfortunately, since they always expected wrong action to be exhibited (as was right action) in the immediate behavior of persons, they were never able to understand injustice that was wrought impersonally through the institutions of the early urban cultures. It is a leading tragedy of history that the virtues of the peasant-village masses were so psychologically defined that they made easy the rule of exploiters.

9. *The Subservient Manner.* Upon these elements of the mentality of the masses of urban cultures was superimposed the psychological projection of the traditional polity, *i.e.*, a complex of social prejudices which, by stigmatizing labor, justified the suppression of the masses; under this suppression they became abject and subservient in manner.

At the root of the class structure of urban culture was the superstitious attitude which explained all occurrences for the peasant-village masses. Because they could understand nothing except as an act of the spirits, they regarded the work by which the economic surplus was maintained as a religious duty. But conditions of urban economic organization disrupted their original notion of the relation of property and work. Property no longer meant the possession of the means of production which the owner, through his work, could make the means of his subsistence and security; rather it meant the right to receive continuously a portion of the economic surplus which others produced. By this distortion the right of property was made to serve not the security of the worker but his exploitation, and rigidly defined in law this distortion was made effective by force.

In the alliance of the priest class and the military class religious duty, legal right, and force were fused, and the original peasant-village attitude of acquiescence to the overworld of spirits was elaborated into a subservient manner toward earthly superiors. As the masses became servile, the priestly and military classes became lordly and arrogant. They looked upon labor as degrading and explained the refinements of life which their exploitation of the masses made possible as the result of their own superior mental and moral qualities. To the subservience of the exploited masses they opposed a patronizing insolence and declared the masses fit for no better lot than working to support their betters. They suppressed the resistance of the masses by a ferocity which, while maintaining their domination, only made the masses more brutal. Urban cultures taught both the power-holding groups and the powerless masses the utility of the resort to violence for political purposes.

It is necessary to understand that these elements of the low intellectual tradition were shaped by preliterate men under routines of daily life which continued unbroken until the development of machine technology and industrial urban life. In fact, until these developments began to shape a new routine of daily life the masses preserved the mentality of their preliterate ancestors, which, although passed from parent to offspring by word of mouth, was more perfectly transmitted in the behavior that each generation of workers acquired from its predecessors. The low intellectual tradition was the product of thousands of centuries in the wilderness and hundreds of centuries on the soil. When the rise of cities in ancient-oriental times gave social definition to the masses of urban cultures, they possessed the mentality carried in this tradition, and in the succeeding urban cultures of Asia and Europe, at least until very recent times, nothing happened to modify it in any significant manner.

In traditional urban cultures no institutions except religious ones existed for the instruction of the masses, and the priestly ministrants of religious institutions, not because of evil intention but because of the mentality carried in the high intellectual tradition, maintained the mass mentality which served so well the possessing and ruling classes. In view of the fact that this mentality of the masses has been always and is now the first circumstance affecting any effort, either their own or reformers', to alter or improve the lot of common men, its significance can hardly be overemphasized.

3. *The Bases of Social Conservatism.* A development more important in history never occurred than the differentiation of the low and high intellectual traditions, for in these traditions psychological fixations and social structure were correlated. Such a relation, in which a social structure perpetuates the psychological fixations and the psychological fixations support the social structure, constitutes an ideology; because its function is to bind individuals from generation to generation into an enduring organization of life, its elements always form the bases of social conservatism. The ideology embodied in the high and low intellectual traditions was historically evolved both for those who controlled and for those who were controlled. Neither had ever known any other social position than that in which it found itself, and neither was able to think that it would ever occupy any other position.

Analysis of this ideology, which was carried in both the low and the high intellectual traditions, indicates that its elements were grounded in a conformity between the psychological reaction of the masses to their own conditions of life and the social institutions which organized their lives. In other words the social institutions of urban cultures persisted because the masses were psychologically conditioned to accept them and no other ones.

1. *The Principle of Hierarchy.* At the heart of all traditional urban cultures was a structure of controls binding the social classes into a solidarity that held in-group interest to the fore amidst the other interests to which urban cultures had given birth. This solidarity was organized under the principle of hierarchy. It defined individual worth in terms of social status and declared that superior worth was the correlative of superior status. At the same time it identified in-group interest with the maintenance of the socially superior class. As a result of this correlation, authority—the right and power to enforce the social controls necessary to maintain the in-group interest—functioned without responsibility except to itself.

When applied in the organization of collective enterprises—governments, cults, armies, corporations, and guilds—this principle reduced collective action to regimentation, for cooperation was possible only as social inferiors acted under the direction of superiors. This meant that every effort at freedom of action by persons having an inferior social status had the characteristic of insubordination; furthermore it meant, as those exercising authority declared, that they were too honorable to abuse it while those who questioned any exercise of authority were proved by the mere act of questioning to be morally perverse, if not actually corrupt.

Thus the principle of hierarchy organized the supremacy of the group over the individual in a solidarity which set against innovation the most powerful social motives—the interest of the in-group, the prejudices of the classes, and the moral aspirations of individuals. In this manner social conservatism originally seemed to embrace every interest having a rightful claim to any service whatsoever.

2. *The Doctrine of Acquiescence.* The doctrine of acquiescence had its roots in the belief in man's dependence upon beings (or forces) beyond his power to control. Whatever distresses affected him were conditions imposed by such beings or forces, and he was helpless. For him there could be only suffering and patient endurance, and virtue consisted in acquiescing to whatever was. As distorted under the social controls imposed in urban cultures, this doctrine became for the masses the practice of subserviency. The consequence of this doctrine was to keep the masses docile and inert; it prevented them, except when driven to desperation, from taking any action against those who exercised controls over them. The doctrine of acquiescence was the corollary of the principle of hierarchy.

3. *The Disregard of Factual Knowledge.* The hunter's need for action obscured the fact that he always acted in terms of a body of knowledge

and that whatever skills he developed embodied this knowledge. His superstitious attitude also prevented the realization that knowledge entered into his behavior as a determining factor, for under its spell he saw the outcome of his acts as depending upon the favor or disfavor of spiritual beings. The patriotic fervor obscured knowledge in group excitement. And the sentimental mood made experience only the point of departure for feeling. As elaborated by the literate few, liturgical, meditative, and decorative learning failed to attend to observed experience of the physical and social worlds in a systematic manner.

In all these ways the role of a knowledge of the objective world in human affairs was obscured, and men followed the uninformed paths of necessity, worship, in-group loyalty, and sentiment; thus they made ignorance, motivated by emotions, the essential guide to action. There is no more significant fact in all history than the failure of preliterate men and their intellectual heirs to understand the role of factual knowledge in the shaping of human life.

4. *The Pursuit of the Unique.*   The extreme significance of the startling sound or image or movement to hunting men provided the psychological base for the belief that the unique object, event, or personality was more important than the familiar, commonplace, and general ones. In pursuing the unique men sought "thrill" rather than knowledge. That priestly observation of phenomena which sought in them the signs of supernatural intention intensified this original tendency to consider the unique more meaningful than the commonplace. And the sentimental mood as rendered in literary productions worked generally in the same direction. Thus hunting, peasant-village, and early urban men failed in just that decisive manner which made inevitable the prevalence and persistence of false principles of action, for, in always seeking the distinctive in experience, they necessarily disregarded those general aspects of the world which are the true manifestations of whatever orderliness it embodies.[1]

5. *The Confusion of Social Phenomena with the Overworld of Spiritual Beings.*   By virtue of the fact that social phenomena exist through psychological interstimulation and interaction, they are intangible and immaterial. They are, moreover, the most pressing of all phenomena with which men have to deal, for, in fact, men exist as men only in and through them. But primitive men never recognized interstimulation and interaction as social phenomena; for them such phenomena were the very substance of the spiritual overworld. In fact, primitive men probably developed the conception of such an overworld by projecting into every

[1] Franz Boas and others, *General Anthropology* (1938), p. 141: "In primitive culture people speak about actual experience. They do not discuss what is virtue, good, evil, beauty; the demands of their daily life, like that of our uneducated classes, do not extend beyond the virtues shown on definite occasions by definite persons, good or evil deeds of their fellow tribesmen, and the beauty of a man or of a woman, or of an object. They do not talk about abstract ideas." Houghton Mifflin Company, Boston.

aspect of their environment the attributes of personality which they experienced but did not identify in relation with their fellows. Proof of this failure of early men to identify social phenomena as such exists in the fact that languages lack words for them; in fact, contemporary sociologists and social psychologists have to deal generally with social phenomena by means of metaphors. Thus they speak of "social force," "impact," "pressure," "dynamics," "statics," "controls," etc.—terms derived, of course, from mechanics. A further manifestation of the traditional confusion of social phenomena with the spiritual order is found in the habitual discussion of such personality attributes as love, kindness, humility, honesty, duty, gratitude, honor, loyalty, courage, etc., as if they were spiritual qualities or to be acquired or kept only through the guidance of a spiritual being primarily concerned with moral behavior.

This confusion of social phenomena with the order of spiritual beings prevented any consideration of social phenomena as such; the best that the literate carriers of the high intellectual tradition could do with them was to orientate them about ethical principles existing, it was claimed, by divine sanctions, while the masses necessarily undertook every social action essentially as a religious action. In all traditional urban cultures significant social opinion always found expression as religious thought, and all social movements which had support among the masses were essentially religious movements.

Under the foregoing social fixations "truth" and "right" were identified with those institutions which maintained the unequal distribution of wealth and the concentrated exercise of power of urban cultures. For the possessors of wealth and the wielders of power, class prejudice functioned in ideas which justified their position and conduct. For the masses these fixations attached their emotions to the social controls under which they were exploited. Thus the masses were unable to lift the burden of their distresses, and the ruling classes discovered no reason to ease the burden, even if they had known how to do it.

The masses, whose interests could be served only by liberation and amelioration, were without the means of action because their mentality, shaped in the low intellectual tradition, contained no materials which could be made the basis of the social controls that might achieve liberation and amelioration. For them action was possible only under the anger or despair generated by misery— leading directly to blind violence—or under the emotional drive of religious inspiration—ending only in a new acquiescence in the poverty imposed by inadequate technology. Furthermore, action of these sorts, since it broke the only social regime the masses knew, became abruptly an irritant even to them, so that the "return to the good old ways" was the only means of restoring emotional equilibrium. In all traditional urban cultures movements of social reform always arose and were carried out under the spell of emotional excitement; when this excitement subsided the masses reverted to old habits, for in them was release from the mental effort which the creation of new social controls necessitated. For the masses, therefore, social conservatism was social habit which would endure as long as they inherited and preserved the low intellectual tradition.

Until the psychological conformity between the mentality of the peasant-village masses and the social structure of urban cultures was broken by the evolution of new psychological materials bearing upon these masses, there was no possibility of the development of a civilization different in pattern from the traditional urban culture. Thus, although the cultural traditions of the Western and Eastern worlds evolved in peculiar ways, they retained the basic pattern of their early urban cultures, for they rested continually upon the mentality of the peasant-village masses. The differences among these cultural traditions arose chiefly as the literate carriers of the various high intellectual traditions gave distinctive elaborations to the elements of this peasant-village mentality. The unity of all traditional urban cultures, Western and Eastern alike, rested upon mental patterns which their peasant-village masses transmitted from generation to generation; their diversity arose as the literate few originated and elaborated the complexes that endured chiefly in liturgical, meditative, and decorative learning.

The objective expressions of the ideology of the traditional urban cultures were persisting sociocultural types. Chief among them was the peasant, held fast in the village milieu, whose labor on the land created the economic surplus that supported the other types; these other types were products of the urban social process and embodiments of the social controls and culture complexes which defined the several social classes. Thus priests, military aristocrats, common soldiers, merchants, craftsmen, and slaves, although differing in the details of their behavior in the various traditional urban cultures, composed a social structure which rested on the basic type, the peasant. Each of these sociocultural types embodied, along with the social controls and culture complexes which distinguished it, the prevailing ideology, which bound them together into an almost rigid structure, enduring from generation to generation. Thus the specialization of new sociocultural types, occurring in the urban social process, only contributed to the refinement of a tradition which, because it received and preserved the chief materials of the primitive mentality, in either the low or the high intellectual tradition, remained fundamentally primitive in outlook. Only class interests, which affected social attitudes as well as social institutions, introduced materials into the urban cultural traditions that were not distinctly primitive; writing, unfortunately, served more to solidify both the primitive and the class elements of traditional civilization than it did to generate forces that might have dissipated the pervasive social conservatism.

To condemn the possessing and ruling classes of early urban cultures for having invented social conservatism as a defense for their material interests is to misread history, because, as a matter of fact, social conservatism was implicit in both the low and the high intellectual tradition as derived from preliterate mentality. Furthermore, the technological basis of early urban cultures was not adequate for the production of an economic surplus sufficiently great to support a regime different from that organized in the urban social pyramid. The principle of hierarchy and the doctrine of acquiescence were merely the psychological projections of this basic economic fact. But the obstacles to technological advance, as well as the frustrations of altruistic intentions, had origin in the disregard of factual knowledge, the pursuit of the unique, and the confusion of social phenomena with the overworld of spiritual beings, which the literate few, without conscious intention, of course, made the central motifs in liturgical, meditative, and decorative learning. Condemnation can with justice be laid upon the few literates of traditional urban cultures because they made learning at once the justification and the servant of exploitation. In their defense it may be pleaded that, in contributing something to the advancement of knowledge and the broadening of ethical principles, they invented the means of liberation and amelioration. So they did; however, they not only misunderstood the means but also resisted its utilization. They can be forgiven the resistance, for they had interests at stake, but not the misunderstanding, for to be ignorant while claiming to be wise is the greatest of crimes for literate intellectuals.

THE DYNAMICS OF URBAN CULTURAL DEVELOPMENT

Although the social process within which culture has its being is always concrete, in varying degrees of intensity, within a given aggregate of living individuals, it preserves an orientation toward a past and projects itself somewhat into the future. Human life, it has been well said, is distinguished by a "flow of duration," *i.e.*, the past persists through the present into the future. For this reason events occur in the social process in recognizable sequences, and from this fact issues the unique characteristic of cultural development: its process is historical. In other words, factors arising because of the persistence of psychological materials, as organized in the social process, are fundamental in cultural development. Thus, as indicated in the preceding chapters, cultures are seen to exist as organized traditions deeply set in time.

But this is not the only aspect of the process of cultural development having origin in the fact that human social life has flow. A second aspect arises from the circumstance that between a culture, *i.e.*, a society in action, and an environment there is a constant interaction. The environment, it should be understood, is both physical and social, for out-groups must be considered elements in the environment of an in-group. This had special significance when, under the conditions of emergence of the first urban cultures, the out-groups were hunting, nomadic, or peasant-village groups. In this interaction, depending on the types of culture groups in contact, certain forces affecting cultural development arose and, as a result, gave it a varied movement. In camp-site, peasant-village, and nomadic cultures the variations probably reflected mostly environmental factors. But in urban cultures the interaction became so complex that factors shaped within the urban social process were sufficiently powerful to give rise to variations. The early urban cultures, it may therefore be held, had a dynamics evolved within their own structures. External factors might disturb the operation of this dynamics in many ways, but only in extreme forms did they disrupt its movement. Thus, as indicated by the histories outlined in the preceding chapters, the cultural traditions passed through similar courses of development. Even in the Mediterranean Basin, where many local cultures came into contact, the course was not fundamentally different from that followed in Iran, India, and China; the dissimilarity between developments in the Mediterranean lands and those of other urban culture areas is less evident if they are seen together, instead of being viewed separately as the products of local regions.

The Phases of Urban Cultural Development.

In the light of the history of the ancient-oriental and the traditional Asiatic and European urban cultures the phases of urban cultural development appears to be as sketched below.

Certain general tendencies of the development may be noted before its phases are indicated. The specialization of social classes within the urban culture group occurred in a relatively clear order. Economic, social, political, and intellectual aspects of urban cultural development were in the main correlative; each changed as the others changed and each contributed to the development of the others. Interaction between an urban cultural group and out-groups followed a sequence more or less parallel to the order of specialization of urban social classes within the culture group. Lastly, the degree of integration of urban cultures varied with the interaction set up by these external and internal movements; in other words, at certain points in the development of urban cultures the patterns were loosely formed, while at others they were far more rigid. Indeed, the phases of urban cultural development are merely aspects of the movement which was generally characterized by the interaction of these general tendencies. Individuals were responsible for innovations in these various phases of development, but whatever they achieved was relevant to the cultural situation within which they worked and its significance was relevant to the social organization it was given in the culture as a whole.

1. *The Emergence of an Urban Culture.* An urban culture emerged when production gave rise to an accumulation of wealth which permitted a more permanent specialization of social functions than was possible in communities living near or at the subsistence level. Production which gave rise to an economic surplus commonly rested on field agriculture, as in Mesopotamia, Egypt, the Mediterranean lands, Iran, and India. In China the loess soils made possible an intensive hoe culture which sustained an economic surplus.

The primary social specialization was the drawing of an urban group, originally very small, from the rural population, *i.e.*, the peasant villagers. Within this urban population two specializations occurred, resulting in: (1) a power holding group and (2) an industrial group. The power-holding group consisted of persons who served both as priests and as secular officials. As priests they maintained the orientation toward the daimonic universe upon whose favor everyone believed well-being to depend. As secular officials they drew wealth from the rural population and organized its uses. Some of this wealth gave them a level of consumption above that of the tillers of the soil, but most of it was undoubtedly invested in useful enterprises—in erecting temples (the most useful of all activities, considering the universal belief in dependence upon daimonic powers for well-being), in constructing defensive works, and in making ditches and dikes for the control of water serviceable in the production of wealth. These activities varied, of course, with the physical environments.

In carrying on these activities the power-holding group commanded both capital and labor. They directed the labor of the craftsmen withdrawn from agriculture and managed whatever exchange of commodities was carried on between the cities and also between the cities and the out-groups. Usually they could call upon the entire working population to build defensive works and participate in defensive military action. At first offensive military action was very infrequent and was carried on by small forces. As consumers the members of the administrative group created a demand which could not be satisfied merely by agricultural, *i.e.*, primary, production. Since this demand could be met only by new industrial goods or foreign articles, it set in motion economic activities which promoted a deepening integration with both the social and the physical environment. The use of power by the administrative group in the direction of the various communal enterprises gave rise to a quest for further power. Together these economic and social demands were primary factors in further urban cultural development.

At the base of intellectual development in an urban culture was the primitive orientation of life in the daimonic universe. The emergence of the city and its social specializations did not in the least alter this orientation but led to a reshaping of the daimonic powers believed to have significance for human life. The chief alteration was the elevation of a few spiritual beings to greater power and their close identification with the continued well-being of the city. In the name of these beings the urban priestly group elaborated the ceremonials, *i.e.*, the social magic, under which life was believed to be served by them. The emergence of these spiritual beings did not disturb the belief in the other daimons important in every aspect of life.

The decisive fact in the intellectual development of an urban culture was the invention or borrowing of writing. In almost every instance writing was first used as an instrument of administration, *i.e.*, for recording economic obligations, and only later as a means of fixing the fundamental orientation of the urban culture group. Usually the oral tradition in which was perpetuated this fundamental orientation persisted long after writing was known; through this tradition, usually by means of a calendar of religious ceremonies, the urban culture group was bound up with the seasonal routine of its physical environment. When this orientation was embodied in writing, the high and low intellectual traditions were formed. Both, it must not be forgotten, stemmed from the mentality of preliterate men. The former was developed by those who learned writing, *i.e.*, the literate; the latter was perpetuated by those who never learned writing, *i.e.*, the illiterate. Whatever contributions writing made to intellectual advancement were originally organized in these traditions.

Since the productivity of the rural population was low, only a very small part of the population could be withdrawn from primary production for secondary pursuits, with the result that the emergence of an urban culture was very slow. The effect of this almost imperceptible movement was to preserve for a long period of time a system of customary and ritualistic social controls.

2. *Social Specialization and Integration within an Urban Culture.* From this beginning an urban culture passed into a phase characterized by relatively rapid social specialization and by elaboration of culture patterns. The point of departure of this phase of urban cultural development was an increase of wealth having origin in the bringing of new lands under cultivation and in the higher productivity, both agricultural and industrial, that arose as a result of the improvement of tools. Originally this improvement was made with copper; at later times similar improvements came with the introduction of bronze and iron.

With the increase of wealth the activities of the power-holding group, although it preserved the priestly function, were extended over a wider and, at the same time, better integrated area. The extended activities took the form of a managed quest for raw materials (usually metals and timber) not available in sufficient quantities in the original culture area; the better integration was achieved by the organization of a secular administration (contrasting with control under religious ceremonials) and the emergence of law, by which the relations of the newly specialized groups were defined.

These specializations distinguished but did not separate the secular-military and priestly sections of the power-holding group. The urban craftsmen increased in number as trade expanded with the quest for raw materials. On the land a better organization of labor was achieved by a threefold economic differentiation which set off: (1) the owners of the soil, *i.e.*, those who held land in order to obtain its products, (2) tenants, *i.e.*, those who held land only in order to work it, and (3) serfs, *i.e.*, those who were bound to the land in order that it might be worked. Because wealth production on the land increased, a larger number of workers could be withdrawn from agriculture, with the result that the administrative group could recruit an ever larger body of laborers and set them to work as it saw fit. The institutionalization of this socioeconomic development was slavery. In most urban cultures the enslaved workers were from out-groups, *i.e.*, were war captives. Correlative with these new modes of labor control on the land and in urban industries was the establishment of a system of diverse property rights.

As the extended activities of the urban power-holding group touched various out-groups, wars became more frequent; such conflicts commonly ended with the victory of the urban forces, because they possessed superior arms. Also their conclusion threw into the hands of the victors the movable wealth of the defeated peoples and the captives, who became part of the urban labor force. Thus the urban culture group discovered the "sweets" of imperialism. An internal circumstance tending to cause war also appeared with the increase of wealth: the cities multiplied in number and became rivals for wealth and power.

The economic demands of the power-holding group gave rise to a permanent body of skilled workers producing luxury goods and a tiny corps of men who knew and used writing, *i.e.*, scribes. Also, these demands promoted a widened trade in raw materials and luxury goods, so that traders and transport workers increased in numbers. The rise of warfare led to the formation of a soldiery. Because of their association with the power-holding group, these new social elements—skilled workers, scribes, traders, and soldiers—were urban groups and felt themselves to be set apart from the peasant-village masses. The better integration of administrative controls gave increased power to those who exercised control, and this circumstance stimulated a greater exercise of power. Probably these several developments combined to give a strong accent to the wealth-holding and power-exercising motives, which shaped the leading characteristics of the next phase of urban cultural developments.

The intellectual developments accompanying these specializations were: (1) the adaptation of writing to literary as well as liturgical and administrative uses, (2) the literary statement of the outlook pervading the fundamental orientation of the urban culture group, and (3) the fixing of writing as an intellectual characteristic of the wealth-holding and power-exercising group. These developments gave a fixed form to the high intellectual tradition, although its elements were not clearly distinguished from one another. The traditional conception of the daimonic universe was elaborated into a formal hierarchy of spiritual beings. No feeling of internal disharmony entered into these renderings of the fundamental orientation of the urban culture group; right and justice still existed in their traditional forms.

3. *The Internal Crisis of an Urban Culture.* The heightened economic and political motives of the urban administrative groups made them rivals for the control of the whole urban area, which, it is important to realize, they continued to expand by bringing new lands under cultivation. From the rivalry of these groups, usually several in number, issued a bitter struggle which ended only when one among them gained a more or less complete ascendancy.

Under the stress of warfare the power-holding classes of victorious urban culture groups were impelled to apply systematically the wealth-producing techniques and the power-creating methods which had emerged in the preceding phase of urban cultural development. The wealth-producing techniques, commonly better tools and a more efficient organization of labor use, gave rise to the wealth which supported the struggle for ascendancy and, throughout the period of conflict, promoted an increase of wealth, especially when the areas under control became larger as a victor took the land, movable wealth, and labor force of a defeated rival.

The systematic application of wealth-producing techniques and the successful use of power had direct effects in wider social specializations. The number of slaves constantly increased, and a large body of urban craftsmen, producing not luxury goods but arms, appeared. The introduction of systematic management into agriculture increased primary production, so that the population grew and a somewhat larger part of it was withdrawn into secondary pursuits. Since the increase of wealth, especially in movable forms, made easier its exchange, the rudiments of money economy appeared; this innovation facilitated not only the diversification of the modes of holding and using wealth but also the intensification of the social movement and specialization. On the one hand, the trading group expanded and its members, accumulating wealth, became useful to the power-exercising group. On the other hand, the changes in agricultural production drove many tillers of the soil from the land, transforming them into landless laborers, who either fell into slavery or became soldiers in the growing military establishment.

In this phase of urban cultural development contacts with out-groups multiplied rapidly. In order to obtain raw materials, especially metals, military activity in out-group areas increased. Several developments accompanied this activity. Organized expeditions were sent out to obtain the desired commodities. A few semipermanent settlements were established in these areas. Urban cultural materials were diffused among the out-group peoples. Resistance to the military activities of the urban group caused a relatively rapid advance of military organization and techniques within the out-groups. As their mastery of warfare increased, they made counterraids into the urban culture areas; also they made more or less continuous warfare on one another. Punitive expeditions against them, when successful, obtained large numbers of captives who became slaves; thus a non-native labor force grew rapidly within the urban culture group. During periods of intense struggle between cities, out-groups sometimes won domination of an urban area or a part of it, but the small number of the invaders resulted either in their quick absorption or in their expulsion. The effect of this interaction between the urban culture groups and the out-groups was to intensify the imperialistic motive, so that any lull in the internal struggle of the urban social groups was likely to bring urban aggression against the out-groups.

In the course of these developments the priestly section of the power-holding group lost ground to the expanded secular-military section, but, because the secular-military section and the various divisions of the producing population retained the traditional orientation to the daimonic universe, the priestly section continued to perform its historic function of maintaining the proper relation between the urban culture group and the overworld of spirits. The secular-military section, it must be emphasized, believed that its power was due to the favor of certain of the spiritual beings. The shift in position of the two sections of the power-holding group had intellectual reactions. The priestly section elaborated rituals whenever possible, so that formalism more and more characterized religious worship. The fundamental tradition was reorientated with emphasis on those elements which showed the dominance of the secular-military section; if the leading figures of the supernatural hierarchy were not changed, their characteristics were modified so that they exercised a greater power over the daimonic hosts. On the whole the orders of the supernatural hierarchy were more sharply defined.

But far more important than these intellectual reactions to the advance of the secular-military section to first place among the urban groups were the repercussions caused by the social dislocations brought about by the new modes of wealth production, the increased importance of military action, and the shift in position of the two sections of the power-wielding group. These developments disturbed the traditional orientation of the urban culture group in several ways. (1) The uprooting of large sections of the producing population disorganized the customs under which their members had long lived. (2) The heightened emphasis on the economic motive among the members of the secular-military section of the power-wielding group subjected these uprooted individuals to an intensified exploitation. (3) The increased social specialization created new relations to which customs did not apply. (4) The dropping of the priestly section of the power-holding group to a secondary position weakened the traditional intellectual leadership. (5) The emergence of new social specializations created different points of view from which to interpret experience. (6) The growth of the urban population brought more and more individuals under the play of new stimuli, so that intellectual innovation on a widened scale was possible. The effect of these developments was to create a milieu in which, first, a sense of loss of security or a feeling that the time was out of joint prevailed and, second, an effort to discover a new basis for right social and individual conduct was made. The religio-philosophical reorientations which gave lasting intellectual content to each of the great urban cultural traditions occurred under some combinations of the foregoing circumstances.

4. *The Imperial Ascendancy of an Urban Culture.* As the secular-military section improved its position within the urban culture group, it carried further the reorganization of wealth-producing techniques and the use of military power to obtain wealth. The former dislocated still more the various socioeconomic divisions within the urban culture group, while the latter touched various out-groups. The outcome of these activities was a crisis having both an internal and an external aspect. The out-groups, sometimes aggressive on their own part, resisted conquest, and the in-group divisions, uprooted by war and economic change, made a final attempt to recover and hold their positions. But the rising secular-military section, having mastered the new wealth-producing and power-creating procedures (they were in the main organizational, not technological), beat down both antagonists; with victory it became the organizer of a centralized regime resting on military force, and the city ruled by this regime stood forth as an ascendant power in the urban culture area.

In the course of the imperial conflict new men, who had acquired great wealth or performed significant military action, rose to prominence, and along with them came some men who played decisive parts in the internal struggle. But commonly the men important in one area of action were also prominent in the other. Because these struggles killed off many members of the old secular-military section, the rise of the new men gave the dominant section when it won power a somewhat different composition than it had had originally. The effect of this change was to weaken its traditions so that its members were free to act in new ways. The dislocation of other socioeconomic groups affected their members in somewhat the same manner and with a similar result. These circumstances made the early period of imperial ascendancy a time of cultural innovation. Along with the reconstitution of the dominant secular-military section occurred a sharp differentiation of the original priestly section; as it lost power its functions became more and more exclusively religious and increasingly formal. However, it retained a position secondary only to the dominant secular-military section, which made participation in the religious ceremonies performed by the priest section the symbol of in-group unity. Thus the union of the secular-military and priestly sections of the urban ruling group was preserved in the new regime.

The results of the organization of this regime were immediate and far-reaching. They gave distinctive characteristics to the phase of imperial ascendancy of an urban culture.

Rapid imperial action soon carried the rule of the dominant regime not only over the neighboring out-groups but also over others heretofore outside the area of direct urban cultural influences. The limits of this expansion were fixed by a number of factors, such as (1) the reaching of areas within which local productivity was so low that little wealth was available for immediate confiscation or continuous exploitation, (2) the making of contact with another imperial urban culture able to resist further advance, and (3) the establishment of commercial relations with urban culture areas too far away to be reached by military expeditions. The mode of transport also limited the area within which wealth could be efficiently collected and carried to the center of imperial power. Finally it may be noted that the area of imperial urban expansion normally coincided with the environmental region to which its techniques of agricultural production were adapted.

The political integration of this increased area of urban control was achieved by simple methods. Provincial rulers responsible to the central regime were appointed. Military forces were provided to support them. And methods of taxation were devised to draw revenue from the orderly economic production which the conqueror's peace made possible. Incidental variations in these political forms were introduced in order to increase their efficiency but not to alter their function, which was, of course, to wring wealth out of the conquered people. Such a far-flung political regime seemed irresistible in power.

The economic correlatives of imperial ascendancy gave the regime wealth seemingly as great as its power. War captives created a maximum labor force of slaves owned partly by the regime itself and partly by the individual members of the group which manned the regime. Confiscations of movable wealth in conquered areas and permanent taxes levied upon them raised the flow of wealth to the central regime to a high point. The application of systematized methods of production to new lands and resources carried current productivity to a crest. Commerce, both domestic and foreign, flowed in an increasing stream. And orderly government—the conqueror's peace—gave stability to the high level of prosperity. The cessation of warfare permitted the spending of much of this increased wealth in nonmilitary ways. Part of it went to pay the costs of peacetime administration, which, as time went on, tended to become more elaborate and consequently more expensive. Advancement in the administrative hierarchy, rather than military achievement, became the way to wealth. Another part of the wealth supported private luxury among the dominant group. And another part of it paid for buildings which gave an outward aspect of magnificance to the regime. Owing to the increased turnover of wealth caused by these modes of expenditure, there was a diffusion of wealth among a considerable part of the urban population. But little of the increased wealth was invested in new productive enterprises. The dominant secular-military section knew how to obtain wealth from production which already existed; it did not know how to create new capacity to produce. Its forte was organization, not invention. Its economic type was the *rentier*, not the *entrepreneur*.

Significant social developments accompanied these political and economic changes. Outwardly the social order seemed stable because the dominant group was so firmly established, but actually movements significant for future change got under way and increased in strength as time went on. The first of these had origin in the growth of cities where mixed populations were thrown together in increasing numbers; the imperial phase of urban culture quickly developed a cosmopolitan aspect. The introduction of large numbers of slaves, mainly members of out-groups, in both agriculture and industry slowly changed the basic population. A part of the native population went with the armies and, as a result, was dispersed throughout the area of imperial control. Another part of it, crowded from the land, went to the cities, where it competed with foreign labor for low-paid jobs. A third part migrated to the provinces, where it settled on new lands or found employment in the administrative hierarchy. A fourth part, probably the largest, remained on the land but changed its socioeconomic status as institutional controls changed. Only the urban population, a very small part of the whole population, and the original population of the urban culture area were affected by these movements; the great bulk of the population of the whole imperial area was, as always, culturally inert in the villages.

The intellectual concomitants of these political, economic, and social developments were decisive in the evolution of an urban culture. Literacy spread beyond the power-holding groups in the cities, and literary activity became diversified. Spokesmen for the dominant secular-military section wove poetry and history into splendid literary monuments of its ascendancy; the literary expressions preserved the historic orientation of the urban social groups. The loosening of tradition opened the way for literary treatment of many aspects of life, and literary forms were elaborated. Members of the secular-military section dealt with sensual pleasure and momentary aspects of life in refined language. At the same time out-group materials became prominent in intellectual life; they were mainly of three kinds: (1) factual information about new lands, (2) religious beliefs, and (3) philosophical ideas. Because all these types of materials were torn away from their original cultural traditions, they were free to enter into new combinations, and soon they did. The new factual information provided a basis for restatements of scientific learning. The religious and philosophical ideas combined with those from (1) the historic orientation of the urban culture group and (2) the ethical philosophies persisting from the earlier phase of internal specialization; the result was not new thinking but the mingling of ideas from these several sources in new patterns. Needless to say, frequently these patterns were quite unlike the traditional orientation of the urban culture group. At this time the gap between the low and the high intellectual traditions was widest. However, new influences, having origin mainly in the emotional reactions of dislocated groups to their circumstances of life, began to work the varied patterns together. Among these groups the mixed urban population was most important, for social intercourse organized its reaction into a pervasive influence. At the heart of this reaction was an intense longing for a new life; inasmuch as this new life seemed impossible to achieve on earth, it became an otherworldly goal. Because the members of this population had lost their cultural identity, they had an individual, not a social, conception of the achievement of this goal. When the members of the dominant secular-military section sensed this new feeling, they came quickly to the opinion that society was decaying. Thus the enthusiasm of the early imperial age was displaced by a pessimism which, welling up from the social depths of the mixed urban population, soon engulfed all intellectual activity.

5. *The Decline of an Urban Culture.* The outward prosperity and power of the imperial phase of urban cultural development masked circumstances which, in the course of time, brought a relatively swift decline. In the main these circumstances had three sources: (1) the imperial regime itself, (2) a changing basic population, and (3) rising out-groups.

The primary forces of decline flowed from the imperial regime itself because, having been organized to obtain a maximum of wealth and power from existing techniques, it was bound, over a period of time, to bring diminished returns. Evidences of this trend commonly appeared early in the imperial phase. The exploitation of resources in the original urban culture area slowed down because the cost of production became higher than in new areas where fresh resources existed or where for a time the new organization of production increased the output from previously little-worked resources. At the same time that conquest came to its limits the supply of slaves dwindled, and a labor shortage began to develop. This was most noticeable in the original urban culture area, where the secular-military section had first fully applied its method of organizing production. A further difficulty arose because, as production in the central urban area decreased, the continuous transportation of wealth (bulky in form, of course, because it consisted mostly of the products of fields and mines) from outlying areas became necessary, and the facilities of transport were hardly adequate for the task. Thus at the time when the need for stabilized private incomes and state revenues was greatest because the luxury level of living of the secular-military section was accepted as customary and the administration of the empire was well organized, economic difficulties began to appear; they were soon evident in the adoption of financial expedients and ultimately paramount in a severe financial crisis.

The change in the basic population was the direct result of imperial activity. On the one hand, as previously noted, the original population of the urban culture area was dispersed by economic changes which removed a large part of it from the land, by military enterprises which either killed it or left it unfit for orderly economic activities, and by migration to outlying areas in the course of the performance of imperial administrative duties. At the same time new population elements were planted in the central parts of the empire. In the cities these elements were mixed, including slaves from many lands, traders, provincial migrants, and uprooted citizens; on the land they consisted mainly of slaves. The effects of this change were manifold, especially in the intellectual field.

Three effects followed the dispersion of the original urban population. In the first place, because the secular-military section was advantageously placed in the imperial regime, its members had opportunity for intellectual pursuits, but, because the original urban population was progressively dispersed, the carriers of the traditional orientation of the urban culture became fewer. These conditions were reflected in the drawing together of the elements of the high intellectual tradition of the urban culture, mainly in compilations rather than in original renderings. In the second place, as materials from out-group sources became more widely diffused, they found their way into intellectual products, which, as a result, diverged considerably from the traditional orientation of the urban culture. In the third place, largely because of the mingling of out-group materials with traditional literary forms, modes of expression as well as forms of thought began to change. From the point of view of the original intellectual renderings of the urban cultural tradition, each of these developments seemed to mark a decline.

As the new mixed population displaced the original base of the urban culture, the high and the low intellectual traditions diverged further, until, in the end, individuals emerging from the low intellectual tradition carried both emotional and intellectual materials which prevented them from becoming carriers of the historic high intellectual tradition. Their literary products reflected their origins, *i.e.*, the uprooted masses, and, as a result, embodied the emotions of the masses and asserted the interests of the masses in combinations of materials from the urban culture and from out-group sources. Between these products and those of the original carriers of the urban high intellectual tradition, into which the pessimistic mood and out-group materials seeped, there was some affinity. Thus the new mixed population of the urban culture found intellectual leaders, who, because the masses, mainly illiterate, carried a number of low intellectual traditions, were necessarily orientated toward the daimonic universe at the religious rather than the philosophic level; the result was a resurgence of superstition.

In this circumstance the priestly elements of society found new opportunities. If the original priestly section of the power-holding group remained attached to the dominant secular-military section—as in Rome—it was not in a position to recover leadership of the masses; if, on the contrary, it stood apart from the secular-military group—especially if it had kept contact with the peasant-village masses as in Iran, India, and China—it was likely to take up its original role. Under the first condition new priestly elements arose among the masses, especially in the cities, where out-group materials entered into a religious syncretism.

Since nothing in the development affecting an urban culture disintegrated the fundamental orientation toward the daimonic universe, the belief that well-being depended on the favor of the overworld of spirits remained as strong as ever. But economic distress and political disorder caused uncertainty as to the prevailing orientation and promoted the quest for a new orientation that would restore well-being. This factor combined with those noted in the preceding paragraph to promote religious change. The over-all effect of these several circumstances was to make religious thinking almost the sole intellectual activity.

Commonly these internal factors contributing to the decline of an urban culture were obscured behind more spectacular occurrences, namely, invasion by out-groups. But invasion was itself, in large part, a result of the development of urban culture. Before active invasion began, the labor shortage in the urban culture area led to the admission of a considerable out-group population, usually as settlers in decayed agricultural areas. These settlers were another element in the changing basic population. In this connection it is worth noting that these out-group settlers were probably not able to take from the land a yield as high as had been obtained by the organization of labor originally set up by the dominant secular-military section. But they did check the further decline of agricultural production. Among the out-groups beyond the rule of the urban culture empire, contacts with the urban culture area promoted cultural advance, first by trade, which stimulated economic activity, and second by a diffusion of modes of military, economic, and political organization, as well as consumption tastes and some intellectual materials. Because the contacts between out-groups and the urban culture groups were in terms of imperial activities, the out-groups necessarily tended to develop from these materials an improved military organization. Thus while the urban culture group slowly lost strength, the out-groups slowly gained strength.

Invasion of the urban culture area by the out-groups was the result of these developments; in fact, the admission of out-group settlers made invasion relatively easy. To meet invasion, the secular-military section of the urban culture tightened economic controls in order to obtain a larger proportion of the decreasing wealth and organized armies of the new mixed peoples. The heavier taxation disorganized further economic production, the city populations declined, and insurrections broke out in the country; rigid political control was the only device the still dominant secular-military section knew how to apply in these circumstances. At the same time in the fighting with out-group invaders, members of the secular-military section were killed off, while from the new armies of mixed peoples arose new men, who, in the course of time, began to mix with the remnant of the old secular-military section. Also, in the confusion of warfare, members of the out-group invaders won power in some areas and, as fighters, were accepted into the changing secular-military section.

From this mingling of peoples emerged a new social structure composed of three elements: (1) a secular-military order developed as indicated above, (2) a revived priestly order possessing almost a complete monopoly of learning and having the loyalty of the masses whose emotional reactions to life it expressed, and (3) the new basic population, mainly peasant-village, for economic decline and warfare had greatly decreased the number of urban dwellers. The priestly monopoly of learning had origin in the fact that the reconstituted secular-military order, composed of new men either from the mixed population or from the out-group invaders, had never been carriers of the high intellectual tradition of the urban culture.

This social structure rested on a less productive agriculture than that which had existed in the imperial phase of urban cultural development. Land and resources, worked by laborers having lower skills because they came from a lower cultural level, gave diminishing returns. The new administrative groups retained the modes of extracting income from land, industry, and labor, as developed during the economic crisis of the urban culture, and so obtained as great a share as possible of this decreased wealth. With the decline of cities, trade tended to disappear. Since the chief source of wealth was labor applied to land, wealth had to be consumed mainly where it was produced. This drew wealth holders and power wielders into the country, and central authority over them became weak. Thus a political and a military decentralization followed the economic decentralization in spite of the fact that the central regime was in theory more absolute than in any other phase of cultural development.

If economic factors played a significant role in the decline of urban cultures, it must be recognized that social and intellectual conditions lay back of them. The high point of economic prosperity of an urban culture was the result of a combination of labor supply, availability of resources, and organization of production, which, because it was the result of temporary circumstances, could not long be maintained, even if the leaders of the urban culture had known that it needed to be; as the disintegration of this combination occurred, a decline of production necessarily accompanied it. Except for short periods of time the ancient-oriental and traditional Asiatic and European urban cultures did not know an increasing productivity based on technological advances; without such advances, once the available resources were brought into production, diminished output was bound to occur.

Why was technological advance so slow?

The answer to this question seems to inhere in the social and intellectual elements of these cultures. In the first place, the power-wielding groups, priestly and secular-military, were able to organize labor in order to obtain a high output with whatever technological means were at hand, but their social and intellectual outlook prevented them from making technological innovations. They despised labor and looked to daimonic powers for prosperity. And the philosophers, even the greatest of them, added to these intellectual obstructions to technological advance certain others, such, for example, as the ideas that the phenomenal world is unreal, that contact with matter is corrupting, that interference with nature is evil, and that knowledge is to be obtained only by meditation or direct experience of spiritual reality. A development of thought which ultimately arrived at an ascetic ideal of life as a means of moral purification or spiritual experience could not promote a technological advance any more than it could cause that infinite multiplication of human wants which, according to classical political economy, is the certain source of continuous economic expansion; such thinking could not conceive of physical exertion as productive labor or of the consumption of its products as an individual or a social good. Combined with the intellectual developments, which everywhere moved along these lines, was the failure to gather factual information about nature; without such investigation the intellectual materials for technological advance were not at hand. Both the positive and negative aspects of intellectual developments in the traditional Asiatic and European urban cultures worked against technological advance.[1]

Among the masses who possessed the technological skills upon which production rested, the two factors most likely to further technological development did not exist. First, because they were not normally allowed to share in any larger production which resulted from their labor, they had no incentive to increase output. Second, because so little wealth was left in their hands, they did not form a market, the supplying of which would have made possible the making of a profit, with the result that the possessors of capital were not stimulated to find ways to increase production.[2] On the other hand, the concentration of wealth in the possession of the secular-military or priestly sections, whose demand was for luxury goods, caused the organization of the skilled production of small quantities of fine wares and the quest for rare commodities by a far-flung commerce.

The fundamental causes of decline in the ancient-oriental and traditional Asiatic and European urban cultures were in the functions and correlative intellectual outlooks of their power-wielding groups. Politically, their modes of organization led to a regimenta-

[1] On the intellectual outlook of these cultures see Fritz Graebner, *Das Weltbild der Primitiven* (1924), pp. 109–130. See also William Salant, "Science and Society in Ancient Rome," *The Scientific Monthly*, Vol. 47 (1938), pp. 525–535; Gina Lombroso-Ferrero, "Le Mécanisme dans l'antiquité," *Revue du mois*, Vol. 21 (1920), pp. 459 *ff.*; Feng Yu-lan, "Why China Has No Science," *The International Journal of Ethics*, Vol. 32 (1922), pp. 237–264.

[2] On this point see M. I. Rostovtzeff, "The Hellenistic World and Its Economic Development," *American Historical Review*, Vol. 41 (1936), p. 252: "The chief reason, to my mind, was the character of the market. It very seldom happened in the evolution of the Ancient World that the market for goods was expanding and its buying power steadily increasing. . . . When it did happen—in the Fifth and Fourth Centuries B.C. in Greece, in the early Hellenistic Period, in the early Roman empire—ancient technique and capitalistic organization made rapid progress. But this firmness and growth of the market never lasted long."

tion of the social order. Economically, their development of production and distribution reached a high point of prosperity from which decline was inevitable. Socially, their political and economic actions brought about changes in the actual composition of the power-holding groups and, also, in the basic population, which made difficult the carrying of the traditional elements of the urban culture. Intellectually, they carried originally and elaborated, as time went on, methods of thinking and ideas which obstructed the intellectual developments—namely, the growth of natural science and technological innovation—which alone could have prevented decline. And in decline they were themselves destroyed. That the masses, whose exploitation they had organized and, as a result, whose traditional modes of life they had disturbed, necessarily contributed to a cultural reorganization at a level of accomplishment below that which the power-holding groups had for a time attained, was only incidental to their own failure. The significant question posed by these considerations is not "Will not a culture decay if it spreads to the masses?" but "Can men educated in the traditional literate learning of these cultures ever lead men to a secure and enriched life?"

VARIABLE FACTORS IN CULTURAL DEVELOPMENT

Throughout the development and decline of an urban culture various factors work together, one affecting the other, in a moving complex. A superficial analysis indicates that these factors have three sources: (1) in the physical environment, (2) in the original nature of man, and (3) in culture as developed and organized in the social process. A more careful analysis indicates that, at least for urban cultural development, the most important forces flow from the third source. Before indicating these forces, brief final comments on the roles of the physical environment and the original nature of man in cultural development are pertinent.

Over the period of the rise of the ancient-oriental and the traditional Asiatic and European urban cultures no changes in the physical environments of the several cultures great enough to have influenced significantly the direction of cultural development seem to have occurred; as previously noted, present archaeological evidence does not support the view that a decline of rainfall was an important factor in the decay of the Roman Empire, in breaking the contact between the Chinese empire and Western lands, or in the movement of nomadic peoples into the urban culture areas. From the point of view of present knowledge it appears that effects once interpreted in this manner were, perhaps, the outcome of man's own action as a geological agent; in other words, his economic activities so disturbed the hydrologic cycle that the original relation between precipitation and evaporation was altered, with adverse results for himself. If the physical environments of the several urban culture areas remained unchanged during the periods of urban cultural development, it would seem that these environments were constant factors, giving a general pattern to the integration of men with nature and, through this integration affecting their whole culture, rather than from time to time providing stimuli to action which accounted for phases of cultural development. Although the physical environments of the several urban culture areas set the fundamental natural conditions under which cultural development could go on and gave a variety of details to cultural forms, the movement of cultural development was little affected by them.

Similarly, there are no demonstrable biological developments, either racial or individual, which account for the course of cultural development.[1] Even if such developments occurred, their existence cannot now be proved, for obviously there are no ways to measure the biological capacities of men long since dead. The common mode of argument on this point is to indicate certain cultural achievements, if they are admired, as the products of high biological quality and certain others, if they are condemned, as the results of low biological quality, and to declare, then, that the approved cultural achievements were the products of high biological quality and the condemned ones were the results of low biological quality. Such argument merely runs in a circle: cultural achievement indicates biological quality, and biological quality, thus recognized, in turn explains the cultural achievement.

Until biological knowledge reaches a stage making possible the establishment of a direct connection between combinations of genes and chromosomes (accepting the prevailing theory of biological heredity) and specific cultural achievements, argument for the biological factor as a decisive influence in cultural development must remain weak. The historian can hardly be expected to

---

[1] R. H. Lowie, *Culture & Ethnology* (1929), pp. 35–36: "That no essential organic change has taken place in the human race during the historic period is universally admitted without question by biologists, physical anthropologists, and brain specialists. Accordingly, when we concentrate our attention on a definite people and follow their fortunes during historic times, we are dealing with a genuine constant from the racial point of view. It requires no very great acquaintance with history to note startling cultural diversity correlated with this stability of organic endowment." Peter Smith, New York.

find an explanation for the change from a culture which recognized the Roman senator as the approved type to a culture which made the Christian saint the admired type in a modification of the original nature of the Mediterranean peoples during the relatively short period of four centuries. Even if such a change occurred, how can it be known now? In sharper terms it can be said with reference to a more recent cultural development, namely, the technological innovations summated in the designation "industrial revolution," that the proponents of the biological factor as a decisive cultural influence ought to be able to demonstrate that throughout the early eighteenth century, mainly in central England, combinations of genes and chromosomes were formed which functioned toward the end of that century in remarkable mechanical inventiveness. These assertions are meant to suggest that the argument for the biological factor as a decisive influence in the movement of cultural development disregards the fact that the cultural achievements of any given time period apparently have a pattern. It can hardly be argued that the men of Greece in the fourth and fifth centuries B.C. were impelled by specific biological impulses to produce "philosophy," the "drama," and "classical art," while men of the fourth and fifth Christian centuries from all Mediterranean lands were moved by specific biological impulses to the types of activities summated in the designation "Church Father."

To argue this way does not imply that cultural development has no biological base; it does mean to suggest, however, that this base, insofar as it is knowable for any period in the past, was common to all cultural developments and gave them only a broad organization, not specific movement. The biological base of cultural development functions, it seems, in two ways: (1) to maintain the social process and (2) to provide motives which can be organized into various patterns of action within the social process.

When attention is directed toward the social process, through which culture originates and develops, the factors affecting the course of cultural development may be seen as having been shaped in this process and as operating through it. In the following paragraphs some of the factors having this origin and action are noted.

1. *Communication.* At any given time the means of communication fixes both a range and a rate of social interaction; in other words, it organizes intercourse among individuals in space and time. Speech gave rise to an intensive interaction within face-to-face contact groups. Writing made possible intercourse over

wide geographic areas and the accumulation of experience through long periods of time. As the means of transport developed, the area of intercourse was widened, and the rapidity of the exchange of experience was increased. In this connection it should be noted that geographical factors long affected the social process by establishing the lines of communication. On land the use of the ox, the ass, the horse, and the camel each in turn affected both the transmission of experience from individual to individual and the transportation of goods from place to place. The development of roads had a similar significance. On the sea the ship, as it was improved, brought separated populations ever closer together. These developments, in turn, influenced economic, political, and intellectual activities among the populations affected. From the point of view of the formation of cultural traditions, it seems clear that each of the great cultural traditions developed in a geographic area within which these ways of communication and transportation permitted general social intercourse and, consequently, a pervasive organization of experience: the cultural tradition, of course, was this organization of experience.

Because the modes of social interaction at any given time establish the field of intercourse within which individuals can organize experience, they are particularly important for the growth of culture. On the one hand they bring more persons into relation with one another, and on the other hand they provide them with new experience. Such developments increase the opportunity for individual abilities to function in creative activity. Thus the number of potential innovators is multiplied, and the materials in terms of which innovation is possible are amplified. The functioning of individual abilities, it should be understood, is relevant to social and cultural opportunities for achievement, and they cannot accomplish things not possible in terms of these opportunities.

2. *The Production of Wealth.* Just as the development of the means of communication affected the organization of the social process, so other technological innovations shaped the integration of human life with the physical environment. This integration had four objective aspects: (1) specialized economic activities, *i.e.*, occupations, (2) certain commodities, (3) the amounts of these commodities, and (4) the particular locations of these commodities which required their transportation before consumption could take place. On the one hand, therefore, the production of wealth involved forms of labor, and on the other hand, kinds and amounts of commodities, and, as technological innovations were made, both

changed. As tools developed from stone to copper, from copper to bronze, and from bronze to iron, both work and wealth were altered; improvements in agricultural methods had similar results. Work changed as regards the division of labor and the ratio of energy expended to the output obtained, while wealth entered into various modes of subsistence, different types of enterprise, diversified forms of power, elaborations of the luxury level of consumption, and varieties of leisure activities. These specializations gave changing characteristics to every urban culture.

More significant still, the forms of work and wealth established the economic surplus, and, as they changed forms, it varied. It is important to note that such variations emerged not only in the social specializations commonly designated as "social classes," but also in the diversification of the modes in which human energy could be released. And cultural development was especially affected by this diversification. Thus, in fact, arose the characteristic military, artistic, literary, and intellectual pursuits in urban cultures. Furthermore, when for any reason a decrease of an economic surplus occurred, these activities tended to decline, for less energy was available to be spent on them. An increase or a decrease of productivity, it is important to note, was a decisive factor affecting cultural development because each had immediate consequences for the release of individual energy and ability. Also it may be observed that the *lebensraum, i.e.,* the area of land and water which a culture group regarded as necessary for its life, was usually defined technologically, not physiographically; changes in transportation, in the means of production, and in the means of violence altered the conception of this area, and, more important still, as technological advances gave use to hitherto unexploited resources and created demands for raw materials not supplied within the established area of the group, a new conception of it formed. And the group always found in its tradition some justification for claiming the area which the new conditions of wealth getting and power exercising made it desirable to possess.

3. *The Forms of Power.* By "power" is meant the capacity of some men to control other men, usually for purposes determined by those who exercise the power. Originally power undoubtedly sprang from the group's domination of its members, and the individuals who wielded it claimed to act as servants of the group. This social basis of power never disappeared, and most power-wielding groups have found it necessary to maintain their position by finding some justification for it that the masses would accept.

Because competition for power is always as active as competition for wealth, if not more so, the individuals who wield power change from time to time; such changes normally occur as the bases of power change.

The form of power in any culture has a basis (1) in the instruments of violence, (2) in the means of commanding wealth, and (3) in the modes of inculcating social acceptance. A power-wielding group maintains its position only by an effective use of these sources of power. When any cultural change occurs that reduces the capacity of an established power-wielding group to use these sources of power, its position is jeopardized, and a new power-wielding group may displace it.

In the early phase of the development of an urban culture, priests, who, according to common belief, gained the favor of the supernatural beings that aided men, held power over men as a concomitant of the capacity to command or placate spirits. The power of priests resided in the acceptance of their position by the masses at the primitive level of mentality. In time, however, a group having command of the means of violence gained power; its position was established by technological changes which permitted some persons to have means of violence—weapons—that the body of the population did not have. Normally such a military group did not completely displace the priest class; indeed, it usually found the priest class useful in gaining the social acceptance of its position in terms of the same belief that had originally supported the priest class. The introduction of each of the metals—copper, bronze, and iron—and of the horse led to changes within the military group, and those parts of it which obtained possession of the most efficient means of violence won power. The earliest knightly order arose because the horse, the chariot, and bronze weapons were so expensive that only a few could possess them. When the introduction of iron weapons coincided with an increased capacity to produce wealth (given by iron tools), relatively large armies of common soldiers appeared, and knightly orders disappeared or were assimilated into new forces. An advantage in arms, although important in winning power, was seldom lasting; it was significant especially when it gave a command over wealth, which made possible the continuous maintenance of power. For this reason technological innovations which changed the production of wealth were also important in the organization of power. For ages the ordinary tools of the peasants were weapons sufficiently dangerous to make it possible for them to resist those who sought to control them by violence. But when the crafts developed, especially metallurgy, means of producing wealth and means of using violence came into existence over which the peasants had no command; under this circumstance they passed almost completely under the domination of the groups controlling these new sources of power. But even then attitudes of mind more than the disparity of arms held the peasants under the control of aristocratic and priestly rulers. The efforts of the rulers of the early Asiatic and European urban cultures to control the iron industry and the breeding of horses indicates the relation which these activities had to the maintenance of power. Similarly the rise of long-distance trade, which on the one hand gave large profits and on the other hand required military protection, supported the growth of merchant groups which the kings found reason to serve and control.

Through law, supported by the means of violence in the possession of the power-wielding group, economic obligations were enforced on the powerless. Slavery and serfdom, dues and taxes, rent and usury were devices by which those who wielded power, or those who enjoyed their favor, legally obtained wealth from those upon whom power was exercised. Changes in the means of producing wealth commonly resulted only in changing the devices by which wealth was taken from those who produced it, not in the advance of a new group to power. This circumstance does not mean, however, that, when the means of production are greatly altered, a group able to command wealth in a new way may not arise. Economic regimentation under power, not the possession of power by those who produced wealth or obtained possession of it by economic methods, was the normal fact in the traditional urban cultures of Asia and Europe.

Inasmuch as the great body of the populations of urban cultures remained illiterate, the social acceptance of the power-wielding groups was normally maintained by means of the union of church and state. Two developments sometimes disturbed this acceptance: (1) the spread of literate learning among persons not possessing power and (2) the formation of associations among bodies of workers who, as a result, could agitate political issues. The first circumstance almost always promoted a literary criticism of the existing order, usually by the raising of ethical questions. The second circumstance generally found expression in a religious movement having some economic or social objective. In either case the established power-wielding group was likely to resort to censorship, coercion, and suppression. The best means of maintaining social acceptance was to leave the masses at the level of primitive mentality so that they recognized the gods of the power-wielding group as the guardians of heaven. Thus their acquiescence in this world was the assurance of their entrance into a joyous life in the next; the correlative of this doctrine was the threat of eternal punishment—in every hell the worst punishments were inflicted upon those who disobeyed or injured their superiors—for rebels. An established power-wielding group almost always held fast to the most firmly fixed religious elements of their cultural tradition. A movement against an established power-wielding group was commonly bound up with some heresy. And a group that won power made certain that its position was justified by some element of the religious tradition. In the traditional Asiatic and European urban cultures the secularization of intellectual life was always an aspect of the liberation of the masses.

4. *The Differentiation of Special-interest Aggregates.* Within an in-group various differentiations of social function arise from time to time. In the main these differentiations reflect the advancement of knowledge and its application in technology. Each specialized body of knowledge is likely to have a social projection in a profession. Each technological innovation is likely to have a social projection in an occupation. Each way of obtaining wealth—by magic, labor, force, or exchange—commonly gives rise to a specialized body of wealth holders. And each specialization tends to create modes of social control by which it is protected from the exercise of power by other specializations and by which it can exercise power over other specializations. Usually several such specializations and the respective modes of social control combine to establish the social structure of the in-group.

When a special-interest aggregate is able to maintain a control over the admission of new members it becomes a social class; when its members act together, more or less as a unit, in advancing their common interests and in opposing other interests, it is a special-interest aggregate. Normally such special-interest aggregates are also prestige groups, inasmuch as their members are regarded as inferior or superior to individuals who are not members of them. Thus special-interest aggregates may be seen as distinguished by a mode of action (commonly technological, economic, religious, military, or political, but sometimes a combination of them), the possession of wealth, the exercise of power, and the acquisition of prestige. At any given time, therefore, the structure of an in-group is a social projection of the main elements of its culture.

Between the special-interest aggregates of an in-group and its culture there is constant interaction. Each special-interest aggregate, if it wins power, undertakes to adapt the elements of the culture to the service of its interests. As innovations occur the positions of special-interest aggregates are favorably or adversely affected in some respect. The most significant effects of this sort are those which alter the way in which wealth is acquired or the way in which power is exercised. For example, if wealth is acquired mainly by an exercise of force upon a producing population, a change in production, such as the introduction of large-scale water control, which cannot be created or managed by force, necessitates an adjustment of interests among specialized groups; also if a development of military technology occurs which permits a concentration of power or, on the contrary, favors a dispersion of force, a similar adjustment occurs.

It has been emphasized in recent thought that these adjustments—"class conflicts," they are called—are the decisive movements in history, affecting all other developments more than they are affected by them. The role of special-interest aggregates in cultural change has been emphasized throughout this book. But at few points in time does it appear that the "class conflict" occurred between the ruling class and the exploited masses. Far more frequently new special-interest aggregates arose which contested with the established ruling class for power over the masses. In other words, the class struggles most common throughout history have not been the conflicts between the exploiters and the exploited, but the strife between rival groups for the control of the exploited. Because these new special-interest aggregates represent new social specializations, which in turn are the results of innovation in military or industrial technology or in modes of organizing the production of wealth, it is quite as correct to see class conflicts as products of cultural change as it is to see cultural change as a result of class conflicts.

Furthermore, it should be realized that the capacity of a special-interest aggregate to win and exercise power may increase or disintegrate as the bases of power are altered by cultural developments. Priests lost power because their mode of action became less significant as secular knowledge advanced. Military groups exercising power changed as new weapons were introduced; also they lost importance whenever it became possible to acquire wealth by exchange as well as by coercion. The role of management of production and exchange in altering the position of a military aristocracy was fully evident in the controversy over social policy in the Chinese Han empire. Craft workers and peasants never obtained power, largely because, since they were diversified in function by the division of labor, they never possessed a basis for common action. And slaves were freed mainly as changing modes of production reduced their productivity in comparison with that of free laborers. The status of peasants changed from freedom to serfdom first as the modes of organizing power over wide areas developed; recovery of the free status, once it was lost, was always more the result of changes in economic conditions and organization than of insurrection. History affords no example of the peasant-village masses using force successfully in a movement to ameliorate their lot.

From the adjustment of special-interest aggregates to one another, partly in conflict but more in the cultural circumstances affecting their respective positions, emerges the administrative or control group in a population. The modes of action of a control group are relative not only to its dominant interest but also to the means of violence, the methods of wealth production, and the prestige-giving elements of the cultural tradition carried by the population over which it exercises power. The means of violence determines the way it exhibits power to those it controls and upon whom it exercises power when its position is threatened. The methods of production establish the form of economic regimentation imposed on the subject population. And the prestige-giving elements of the cultural tradition shape its propaganda. The conservatism of a special-interest aggregate once it has adapted these elements of a culture to its service normally blinds its members to innovations which are likely to affect its position; they continue to hold fast to old ways of realizing their interests when, because the means of violence, or the methods of production, or the elements of propaganda have changed, new modes of action are necessary. New special-interest aggregates usually rise to power when cultural changes have weakened the power of the ruling class or have created a new basis of power which the ruling class cannot or does not use.

It appears, therefore, that social classes and class struggles develop with culture quite as much as culture develops with them.

5. *The Type of Community Organization.*   Within any field of social intercourse, regardless of the means of communication, there are points at which interaction concentrates; these points are the typical communities which the culture of a group organizes. The

original community was, it seems, the hunting pack. Much later it became the more or less impermanent camp, and later the village. Finally, it became the city, which, on account of differences of relations between its dominant special-interest aggregate and the basic population, had various forms—the *temple* city, the *fortress* city, the *capital* city, the *port* city, and in very recent times the *industrial* city. In each of these types of community the flow of social stimuli is channelled by the social specializations through which the existing body of knowledge functions, and the modes of social control through which power is exercised are organized in relatively clear patterns, with the result that individual mentalities are shaped relative to these channels and patterns. Thus the communities organized by a culture are its essential carriers, for individuals who live in them receive and transmit through their localized social processes the patterns they possess.

As the focus of social interaction, the community is important not only as the carrier of a culture but also as the milieu of innovation, for in it individuals release their energies in terms of going experience, and such release is the only source of departures from past experience as organized in culture. Since the community is the decisive factor in the shaping and directing of individual mentality, it is the social matrix of a cultural tradition and the means of its continuous elaboration. If innovations are sufficiently powerful in their effects to alter the type of community, the community will reorganize individual mentalities, which, in turn, bring cultural innovations in terms of the patterns of the new community. Since special-interest aggregates are integrated in the community, its overall influence is a modifying factor in their action.

Because the type of community organizes the fundamental mentality carried in a culture, it may be said to give leading characteristics to the cultural tradition.

6. *The Reorientation of Experience and Tradition.* Between going experience and transmitted interpretations of past experience there is always some interplay in which occur (1) an assimilation of new experience into tradition and (2) a reorientation of tradition in terms of new experience. When interpretations of past experience are transmitted orally, new experience is likely to be assimilated into tradition without much contention. But when they are transmitted in writing, which makes them far more rigid, the assimilation of new experience may be difficult; in fact, it probably can occur only through the considerable intellectual controversy which commonly accompanies an adjustment of special-interest

aggregates. A reorientation of tradition always involves both intellectual and social disturbance, for it necessitates altering social controls and the justifications for them.

Two broad classes of experience generally give rise to new interpretations: (1) widened observation of the natural world and (2) a change in social conditions bringing to many individuals altered circumstances of living.

Throughout the period under survey in this book the first was almost completely the product of occupations, travel and commerce, and war, for in none of the urban cultures studied was a systematic investigation of natural phenomena undertaken. The second occurred mainly as a by-product of technological innovation, the development of social controls, the organization of a money economy, and the spread of imperial action. In the development of knowledge of the natural world in the traditional Asiatic and European urban culture three transitions can be recognized: (1) from a disorganized daimonism to a formal hierarchy of spiritual beings, (2) from a formal hierarchy of spiritual beings to the astrological integration of spiritual forces with natural phenomena, and (3) from the astrological integration of spiritual forces with natural phenomena to the postulation of metaphysical principles or substances which give unity to nature. No one of these transitions was complete, so that beliefs about nature at any time were a medley of daimonistic, religious, astrological, and metaphysical notions. In the interpretation of social phenomena the movement was (1) from the customary definition of right and wrong to the concept "law" and (2) from the concept "law" to the philosophical definition of the good life. Commonly a movement in one of the categories affected that in the other. And the formation of the urban community may be seen as having given rise to the abstract thinking which culminated in both natural and moral philosophy. In the Greek, Indian, and Chinese cultural traditions the supreme outcome of the advance of abstract thinking was an attempt to formulate the methods by which experience can be validly interpreted—in other words, the creation of intellectual methods, of which the most important was logic. The combined effect of these movements was the embodiment of various interpretations of experience in systems of thought that bound together physical nature, social nature (*i.e.*, morality), and supernature as parts of a single whole. Such, indeed, were the religions that became the enduring intellectual forms in the several cultural traditions.

Because a cultural tradition is historically evolved, it includes interpretations of experience from different periods in time and from different geographical areas, and as individuals acquire the traditions, they may set these interpretations against one another or use them in various ways in dealing with going experience. Thus, for example, in the Hebrew cultural tradition one might set the concept "righteousness" against the concept "law," and in the Western cultural tradition one might appeal to Greek learning as contrasted with the learning of the Church Fathers. Indeed, within Christianity itself one might set "primitive" against "ecclesiastical" belief and organization. The significance of such stresses in a cultural tradition is that they become, as experience changes, materials in terms of which new experiences may be assimilated into tradition. In this assimilation, which is actually achieved by special-interest aggregates, although individuals project it through innovations, those elements of the cultural tradition which serve this or that special interest are emphasized or suppressed. Thus when the Christian priestly group rose to power certain elements of the Greco-Roman culture were abandoned while others were accepted; similarly the ascendancy of the Indian Brahmans and Confucian literati was achieved by an assimilation of certain primitive beliefs into their respective traditional beliefs which permitted them to retain intellectual contact with the peasant-village masses.

Not the least important aspect of cultural development at any time is, therefore, the competition of special-interest aggregates for the sanction of tradition; this takes form in an effort by one aggregate to cause other groups—through their acceptance of tradition—to identify the interest of the assertive aggregate with tradition. The method commonly used is to select from the various elements of tradition the one most in line with the special interest and to establish by interpretation that this aspect is the basic element of the tradition. From this point of view every "class struggle" involves a reinterpretation of the cultural tradition or of some part of it. Cultural change does not go on merely in terms of new experience; it always involves the mergence of new experience with tradition through an identification of meaning with some element of past experience. For this reason a Utopia is generally described as a restoration of a circumstance that once prevailed in an ideal past.

One recurring situation in the development of urban cultures which had great significance for both the assimilation of experience into tradition and the reorientation of tradition was the movement of a group of individuals from illiteracy to literacy; such a movement meant, of course, passing from the low to the high intellectual tradition. But it did not mean the loss of the predications of thinking carried in the low intellectual tradition. Rather it meant a renewed importance for them in the high intellectual tradition. Therefore, the first result of the winning of literacy by a new group was in many instances some kind of religious development in which mythological and emotional elements, as contrasted with metaphysical and rational elements, were uppermost. If the group winning literacy also became a power-wielding special-interest aggregate, it was likely to achieve a reorientation of tradition in terms of its interest and the intellectual outlook correlative with it. This type of development points to the fact that intellectual advance as well as economic gain plays an important part in the action of special-interest aggregates.

7. *Diffusion through Contacts with Out-groups.* Because there are different social groups carrying different cultural traditions, interaction among these groups is a factor in the growth of their respective cultural traditions. The passing of cultural materials from one group to another is known as "diffusion." This phenomenon is exemplified in many phases of the development of the Western and Eastern cultural traditions; among the leading examples may be mentioned the "wedding of the East and the West" in Hellenistic times and the spread of Buddhism in China.

Diffusion is the normal result of travel, commerce, and above all imperialism. Innovations in communication and transport immediately result in diffusion, and the elaboration of military technology and imperial action is likely to give it greater speed. Among its more significant aspects are: (1) the spread of technological procedures which affect the production of wealth, (2) the mingling of ideas and beliefs which, as a result, enter into new interpretations of experience, and (3) an increase in the body of factual knowledge possessed by a culture. Indeed, until the rise of scientific investigation the increase of factual information by diffusion was the most important mode of the advancement of knowledge.

Since diffusion occurred commonly under circumstances which aroused the in-group-out-group antipathy, it often brought a reaction against foreign cultural materials, especially by special-interest aggregates who were able to make the assertion of in-group loyalty advance their interest. Such an assertion was frequently successful against special-interest aggregates whose members were identifiable with out-group modes of living. Thus, in fact, diffusion frequently played a part in the competition of special-interest aggregates for the sanction of tradition. But regardless of such a development, diffusion went on and played a part in cultural change in a broader way than the adjustment of special interests. As noted above, it was the common means of advancing knowledge, with the result that there flowed from it continually various results having origin in the application and interpretation of new knowledge.

8. *The Basic Routines of Mass Life.* It is important to realize that in any culture the routines of mass life are well established and that associated with them are certain emotional accents which are repeated as the routines are repeated; thus hunting and peasant-village life may be clearly viewed as embodying fundamentally different routines, and in contrast with them there may be seen the more complex routines of urban life. Every social specialization may be understood as having origin in the development of at least one but more commonly several routines which characterize the behavior of those who follow its way. Here it is emphasized that, regardless of the number of social specializations developed, there always remained the great mass of a culture group which carried the relatively simple routines of the culture. After the rise of urban culture the basic routines were organized in the life of the peasant-village masses. This life was patterned not only by occupations in close association with climate, soil, flora, and fauna, but also by the simple social interaction of the relatively isolated village community and the controls enforced by power-wielding groups. In terms of this complex of routines, the peasant-village masses, it may be held, developed emotional reactions which, because the masses were numerous, pervaded the culture. Indeed, it seems that these routines and emotional accents gave stability and tone to cultural traditions as a whole, while innovations developed and organized in urban life gave it only a distinctive core. This social fact was projected in all cultures as the low and the high intellectual traditions.

Any disturbance of the basic routines of mass life, it may be understood, was likely to cause far-reaching cultural changes. But such disturbances were infrequent and commonly not long-enduring. After the shift from hunting to agriculture and husbandry, the basic routines, as far as occupation was concerned, remained stable; indeed, the rise of cities did not alter them, for it only produced a number of social specializations which were confined to a small part of the population. And so in all urban cultures the masses remained peasant villagers. Besides the natural calamities which brought famine, the chief disturbances in mass life, after the rise of cities, were war and debt, and these commonly ended in enslavement. Debt, of course, became peculiarly disturbing after the introduction of money. War was most distressing in the phase of imperial expansion. The outcome of these disturbances was, as has been said before, the "uprooting" of the masses. This uprooting should be understood as involving the separation of many common men by violence from their traditional geographical homes, the disorganization of their customary modes of life, and their mingling, under harsh social controls, with multitudes of others similarly detached from their traditional cultures; in fine, the masses were torn loose from their local cultural traditions and, because many different individuals were brought together in new ways, were thrown into a chaotic process of diffusion.

Two important results flowed from this uprooting: (1) a pervasive negative emotional reaction to life, commonly sublimated in an enthusiastic quest for an otherworldly salvation and (2) a stripping of the local details from a culture, leaving only the more general or universal characteristics. Each of the great Asiatic and European urban cultures showed these effects in some way as imperialism took its course.

Stability and change in the basic routines of mass life should be recognized as decisive factors in cultural development. As long as these routines remain stable, cultural development occurs mainly as the elaboration of the elements of the persisting tradition and moves in a direction set by the basic routines, as they affect the rejecting and accepting of innovations. However, when the basic routines of mass life are altered, the fundamental orientation of the culture is disturbed and, as a result, every element of the culture undergoes change. This phenomenon occurs because the human species evolved in the social process, selection always taking place in terms of an integration of individuals in group life rather than in terms of the direct adjustment of individuals to the environment. For individuals the integration with the group and adjustment to the environment through the cultural tradition constitute a total orientation which has its objective forms in the basic routines of mass life. It follows, therefore, that the disturbance of these routines must involve the reorganization of individual behavior at the level of selection that governs the survival of the group, and no individual can escape completely such a reorganization. When the fundamental routines of mass life change, the primordial law of human evolution, namely, social selection that contributes to the survival of the species, operates rigorously. This circumstance intensifies the sense of in-group loyalty and directs the energies of the in-group toward the organization of those ways of life which, because they embody the new routines of mass life, promote survival. Under its influence, also, individuals identify themselves with the group in terms of new purposes which, because they serve group survival, give the individual a satisfying orientation to his world. Together these effects reestablish the social norms of selecting and rejecting innovations so that cultural development again moves in a well-defined direction.[1]

THE INTERACTION OF THE VARIABLE FACTORS IN CULTURAL DEVELOPMENT.

The foregoing factors in cultural development (which, it should be understood, arise because social changes promote cultural

[1] It may be suggested that the circumstances affecting cultural development in the twentieth century are of this kind and quality. See V. Gordon Childe, "A Prehistorian's Interpretation of Diffusion," in *Independence, Convergence, and Borrowing in Institutions, Thought, and Art* (1937), pp. 15–16: "The new cities [in ancient-oriental times] exceed the old neolithic hamlets and chalcolithic townships as much as modern industrial cities exceed medieval burghs and market-towns. The whole scale of human life has been transformed. The Urban Revolution is first discernible in the valleys of the Nile, the Tigris-Euphrates, and the Indus. There it was consummated round about 3000 B.C. Yet on closer inspection the Urban Revolution turns out to be a long and complex process just like the Industrial Revolution to which it may legitimately be compared. The harnessing by man of non-human motive power through the soil, the yoke, the wheel, and the metallurgy of copper and bronze take the part of the steam engine and the power loom, coal and iron in the modern counterpart." (Reprinted by permission of the President and Fellows of Harvard College.) Then, as now, the life of the masses was cast in new routines because the communal and occupational organization of their lives changed; now, the modes of the recasting of the life of the masses are more diversified than then and, indeed, affect directly a greater part of the population.

Because the present age is witnessing cultural development in these fundamental terms the drawing of parallels between occurrences now and at most times in the past is likely to be confusing rather than enlightening. What is needed today is an understanding of historical development as *process*, so that events and movements may be recognized as having relation to one another and to the underlying factors causing and directing cultural change.

Preliminary considerations about the reorganization of mass life in recent times and its possible significance for cultural development may be found in Ralph Turner, "The Industrial City: Center of Cultural Change," in Caroline Ware, editor, *The Cultural Interpretation of History* (1940); Ralph Turner, "The Cultural Significance of the Early English Industrial Town," in *Studies in British History*, University of Iowa Press, 1941; Ralph Turner, "The Cultural Setting of American Agricultural Problems," in *The Agricultural Year Book*, 1940; Ralph Turner, "Culture, Change and Confusion," in *Public Opinion Quarterly*, Vol. 4 (1940), pp. 579–600.

innovations, and cultural innovations cause social changes) may and sometimes do occur simultaneously. But each may act with a variable force in the social process, not only because it is strong or weak by itself but also because the other factors may be strong or weak.

Communication may be extended without affecting the form of power, although such an extension is likely to alter the area within which power may be exercised. Wealth production may increase or decrease without affecting communication or diffusion, but it is almost certain to influence community organization, social specialization, and the exercise of power. Special-interest aggregates may shift positions without disturbing the fundamental types of community organization. Currents of diffusion may run in new channels without reacting upon special-interest aggregates. Factual information may increase without entering into new social specializations or new forms of power; however, by entering into new interpretations of experience it may bring special-interest aggregates to assert their interest in new ways and by entering into new technological procedures it may alter the modes of producing wealth and exercising power. The disturbance of the basic routines of mass life is most likely to alter interpretation of experience in such a manner that the positions of all special-interest aggregates are modified. The significant matter is that at any time some combination of these variable factors establishes the circumstances of individual and social action; just how they enter into the combination and flow into action can be determined only by investigation.

From the point of view expressed in the preceding paragraph it appears that there is no one interpretation of history, *i.e.*, the movement of events is not to be explained by one directing force or leading purpose. Rather, in every situation there is a complex of factors, having origin in the application of past human experience to the service of present life, which can be known only by analysis and can be evaluated only by synthesis. However, it appears also that these factors are not unknowable in themselves, nor are the tendencies they give rise to without knowable effect or direction; the problem of the interpretation of history becomes, then, like any other scientific problem, that of discovering in data the modes and tendencies of action and interaction. Above all it should be emphasized that, whatever these modes and tendencies may be, they function through human thinking and feeling, which, although originating in individuals, are organized through the social process in culture. Culture stands at the beginning and at the end of all historical action.

SOME DEMOGRAPHIC ASPECTS OF URBAN CULTURAL DEVELOPMENT

Although there is little evidence about the populations that carried the urban cultures discussed in the preceding chapters, there are a few facts which point to some of the demographic conditions which prevailed. And these facts suggest that the foregoing variable factors in cultural development were also important in creating these conditions. In other words, just as people make culture, so culture makes people; indeed, an urban culture seems to unmake and remake its carrying population.

In the first place, it may be believed, the population increased and decreased as the production of wealth rose and fell. With each advance in productivity which added to the economic surplus, part of the new wealth went to the power wielders and wealth holders, while another part became the support of a larger population. There is little reason to believe that any part of it went to raise the standard of living of the masses. In Egypt, it seems, the number of fellahin followed closely the yearly crop yield, for when the year was lean a larger number of the newborn infants died and when the year was fat a larger proportion survived. The formation and multiplication of cities may be considered as evidence of both increased production of wealth and growth of population. In this connection it should be noted that the cities, except those favorably situated for drawing foodstuffs from wide areas by water, were small; in fact, it was almost impossible to provision a town having a hundred thousand people without special transportation advantages.[1] Thus both the total population and, in proportion, the urban population remained small. There is little reason to believe that the urban population formed more than 10 or 15 per cent of the total population, and in most instances it was probably less than 10 per cent. Moreover, when production decreased, a contraction of the population ensued. The evidence suggests that the economic crisis which came with imperial expansion was accompanied and followed by a decline of population. In the first century the population of the Roman Empire, it has been estimated, was between 70 and 75 millions; by the end of the third century it had fallen to about 50 millions. The decrease occurred almost entirely in the second half of the third century. A similar course seems to

[1] See G. Fererro, *The Greatness and Decline of Rome* (5 vols., 1909), Vol. 2, p. 323.

have been followed in China. Throughout early Han times the population increased, until it reached, in 105, a maximum of over 53 millions; by 146, however, it had dropped to 47½ millions and after that date it appears to have continued a very slow decline for about four centuries. Nothing is known about the movement of population growth in other urban culture areas.[1]

Only the most general surmises can be made about birth and death rates and the composition of the several populations. If the circumstances known in recent times may be considered as nearly normal for peasant villagers, it is a fair guess that the birth and infant mortality rates were high in comparison with those of Western industrial nations. It may be assumed, too, that the proportion of females who were married was large and that excessive childbearing brought them to an early senility. At forty a woman was a hag. The age of marriage for both males and females was low—between ten and twenty years. Life expectancy at birth was probably no greater than it was at the end of the eighteenth century, when, in European rural areas, it was about thirty years. In the first century B.C. life expectancy in Rome has been estimated at between twenty and twenty-five years,[2] a figure comparable with those for eighteenth-century European cities. In the Roman provinces, especially those of northern Africa, where sunlight was continuous the year round, life expectancy may have been almost twice as long as in the Mediterranean cities. A low life expectancy was correlative, of course, with a high death rate, especially among the young. Among persons who attained the age of fifty the death rate was probably no higher than now. With low life expectancy it followed that the proportion of aged persons was low and the percentage of the young was high. There is no way of estimating what these proportions were, except to guess that they were not greatly different from those found among contemporary primitive peoples and nations composed mainly of peasant villagers.[3]

[1] See Ernst Stein, *Geschichte des spätrömischen Reiches* (284–476 n.C.) (1928), p. 3; and C. P. Fitzgerald, "Historical Evidence for the Growth of the Chinese Population," *The Sociological Review*, Vol. 28 (1936), pp. 133–148.

[2] W. R. MacDonnell, "On the Expectation of Life in Ancient Rome, and in the Provinces of Hispania, and Lusitania, and Africa," *Biometrika*, Vol. 9 (1913), p. 366.

[3] Among contemporary primitive peoples the percentage of the young (boys under eighteen and girls under sixteen years) falls just above or below fifty per cent of the entire population, and the children twelve years and under are between twenty-five and thirty-three per cent. (See Ludwik Krzywicki, *Primitive Society and Its Vital Statistics* [1934], pp. 250 ff.) In 1820 the population of the United States was divided by age groups as follows: 57.9 per cent twenty years and under, 39.7 per cent twenty to sixty-five years, and 2.5 per cent sixty-five years and over; in 1930 the percentages for these respective age groups were 38.8, 55.8, and 5.4. In the following table the age groupings of Eastern agrarian and Western

Poverty, war, famine, and disease were the universal destroyers of population. Poverty, rooted in low productivity, was intensified by the fact that labor was drudgery, a body-destroying exertion of energy necessitated by the fact that almost all mechanical power used in production was human in origin. The rise of systems of enforced labor increased the destructive effects of drudgery. War not only killed people off but left a trail of devastation and enslavement behind; from one point of view, it was a method of concentrating enough capital and labor to raise production to a level sufficient to maintain an urban culture. War played an essential economic function in the development of urban cultures. Famine was the direct result of the natural disasters, drought, floods, and visitations of pests; it should be realized, however, that its effects were not uniform throughout a population, for the poor always suffered more than the well to do.[1]

The role of disease in history is little known, for only hints of its action are given in the records. The dread of disease was universal, and the methods of treating it were ineffective, except for a few sanitary practices developed in each of the urban cultures. Ancient men suffered from many of the ailments of modern men; above all, they were the prey of the epidemic and the endemic diseases now so recently brought under control. Epidemics were known in the

industrial nations are given:

	China (1929–1931)	India (1931)	England and Wales (1927)	United States (1930)
Under 10 years	25.0	28.5	16.9	19.6
10–19 years	19.3	20.7	17.7	19.2
20–29 years	17.0	18.1	16.7	16.9
30–39 years	13.8	13.9	14.3	14.9
40–49 years	11.4	9.3	13.2	12.3
50 years and over	13.5	9.5	21.2	17.1

See Frank W. Notestein, "A Demographic Study of 38,256 Rural Families in China," *The Milbank Quarterly*, Vol. 16 (1938), p. 63.

[1] See K. S. Gapp, "The Universal Famine under Claudius," *Harvard Theological Review*, Vol. 28 (1935), p. 261: "In the ancient world, as in the modern, famine was always a class famine. Since the poor and improvident never had large reserves either of money or of food, they suffered immediately upon any considerable rise in the cost of living. The rich, on the other hand, had large reserves both of money and of hoarded grain and rarely, if ever, experienced hunger during a famine. Thus, while all classes of society suffered serious economic discomfort during a shortage of grain, the actual hunger and starvation were restricted to the lower classes. As a famine became more severe, the distress mounted higher and higher in the social structure."

Mediterranean Basin continuously after the Persian invasions of Greece, and after the second century the plague was a constant menace. The endemic diseases are more difficult to trace than the plagues, for they worked quietly to destroy or enervate a population. There is reason to believe that malaria was prevalent in Greece in the fourth century B.C. and throughout the Mediterranean Basin after the second century B.C. The Second Punic War was an important factor in its spread. After the second century it, like the plague, seems to have grown more destructive. Although the ravages of disease in Iran, India, and China can rarely be dated, their occurrence can be inferred from references in literature and religious texts. Floods, famines, and wars everywhere brought disease in their wake.

Of special significance in connection with the role of disease in the early urban cultures is the fact that the cities became cesspools of infection; this was the direct outcome of poor sanitation and inadequate medical knowledge. As early as Cicero's time, Rome was regarded as especially unhealthy.[1] Part of the idealization of country life which pervaded the aristocratic and learned circles of the early urban cultures had origin in the greater healthfulness of rural areas. Any concentration of persons, an army as well as a city, was likely to be struck by an infection. The fear of social contacts as a cause of illness was well expressed in the Sumerian belief, previously noted, that the fever daimon lived at the crossroads. The disease hazard which accompanied the expansion of urban culture is indicated by the fact that in the second century the plague spread from the Black Sea to China, taking forty years for the journey. Indeed, a culture area became a disease area, and diseases were diffused as well as culture traits.[2]

---

[1] See Ludwig Friedländer, *Roman Life and Manners under the Early Roman Empire* (n.d.), pp. 27–29.

[2] Karl Sudhoff, "The Hygienic Idea and Its Manifestations in World History," *Annals of Medical History*, Vol. I (1917), pp. 111–117: In Egypt *Osteoarthritis deformans* afflicted both sexes with such frequency as to stagger all power of imagination. Arnold C. Klebs, "The History of Infection," *Annals of Medical History*, Vol. I (1917), pp. 159–173: The Babylonians knew eighteen kinds of lice, and the fly was the symbol of Nergal, the god of destruction, who commanded fourteen demons. See also Joseph L. Miller, "Some Diseases of Ancient Man," *Annals of Medical History*, Vol. I (n.s. 1929), pp. 394–402; David A. Stewart, "Disease and History," *Annals of Medical History*, Vol. 7 (n.s. 1935), pp. 351–371; Alfred C. Reed, "The Medicine of History," *The Scientific Monthly*, Vol. 44 (1937), pp. 249–256; and *Isis*, Vol. 22 (1934–1935), p. 319. W. H. S. Jones, in *Malaria and Greek History* (1909) and *Malaria: A neglected factor in the history of Greece and Rome* (1907), develops the thesis that malaria was an important factor in the decline of Mediterranean urban culture. See also Hans Zinsser, *Rats, Lice and History* (1935), a popular discussion of the plague, malaria, and typhus fever.

In the unmaking and remaking of the population carrying an urban cultural tradition at least two fundamental factors were operative: (1) birth rate differentials among the social groups and (2) movements of peoples within a culture area.

In general available evidence indicates that the power-wielding, wealth-holding, and learned groups of an urban culture possessed a lower reproductive capacity than the working groups, especially the peasant villagers. Furthermore, it appears that over a period of time this capacity fell so low that the ratio of the groups to the total populations was not maintained, so that, if social controls remained effective, the power-holding group grew constantly smaller. However, as a compensation for the loss of numbers in the power-wielding group, some way of ascent from lower groups, usually through the performance of military service or the acquisition of wealth was opened. To this process has been given the designation "demographic metabolism." Its effects were far-reaching:

. . . It explains the disappearance of celebrated families and the need of infusing new blood into the nobility; it tends to accentuate the concentration of wealth; one of its results is that the hereditary physical and intellectual characteristics—no less than those relating to culture, religion, language, traditionally handed down in family lineage—tends to spread from the lower strata of society to the whole population, sometimes transforming its racial composition, ideals, and habits, and always keeping the governing classes in close touch with the mass of the people.[1]

Three circumstances contributed generally to the change of the basic population carrying an urban cultural tradition.

First, because the cities were "centers of extinction," there was a constant movement to them of persons born in other places; in the main these persons came from the native peasantry, but over a period of time there was bound to be an admixture of foreign strains, so that the urban population slowly became "mongrelized." Inasmuch as the new persons who rose into the ruling group commonly came from the urban population, they were likely to

---

[1] Corrado Gini and others, *Population* (1930), p. 19. By permission of the University of Chicago Press, Chicago. For a discussion of matters noted in this section see especially pp. 1–140, "The Cyclical Rise and Fall of Population." On the fact of differential fertility see Raymond Pearl, *The Natural History of Population* (1939), p. 181. On the relation of differential fertility to cultural change see J. Rumney, "The Problem of Differential Fertility," *Population* (Nov., 1935), pp. 3–21; especially pp. 20–21: "Indeed, no student must neglect the metabolism of population changes and the social changes in culture, religion, language, and politics. . . . In differential fertility a valuable clue is obtained for tracing the ever-recurrent disturbances in law and custom, and the new equilibrium that consequently arises."

From ROBBIN FEDDEN, *The Land of Egypt* (1939). *B. T. Batsford, Ltd., London. Photograph by A. Costa*

SAND AND TIME

These ghostly ruins testify to both the grandeur and the decay of the traditional urban cultures. When men fail, nature has no healing power that checks the disintegration of a culture. The crises that destroy an urban culture result from the acts of those individuals or that group of individuals exercising power and directing policy. When an urban culture disintegrates, the ruling classes perish: common men alone survive.

carry the mixture of strains to it; on the other hand, as the ruling class held fast to its native origin, it was likely to turn toward the country, maintaining estates and admiring the past, while the urban population produced its own leaders, who ultimately contested with the original ruling class for supremacy. Economic factors had only a secondary effect on the emergence of this kind of a situation.

Second, during the phase of imperial expansion, its centrifugal force carried the native population away from the center of the culture area as soldiers, traders, and administrators. And imperial success, insofar as it required their settlement outside the original culture area, led relatively quickly to their submergence in the foreign population. As evidenced by the Macedonians and Greeks and the Romans, the common soldiers married foreign women and begot mixed offspring. Traders did likewise. And the administrators, as members of the ruling class, disappeared entirely, natives of the conquered lands filling their places as servants of the imperial power. At the same time the centripetal forces of imperialism introduced large numbers of foreigners into the original culture area and added a mixture in the rural areas to the fusion of peoples already under way in the cities. Competition between native and foreign labor commonly brought the natives to practice infanticide in order to maintain a favorable position in the labor market, but it also resulted in an ultimate replacement of the native by the foreign population. The effect of this circumstance was to widen the social gap between the ruling class and the basic population; indeed, at the very crest of their power urban ruling classes rested on a population base no longer adequate to support them, either biologically or socially.

Third, when the economic peak of the imperial concentration of wealth was passed, the shortage of labor required the further admission of foreigners, commonly as settlers on the land, so that the basic population was further mixed. It was in this phase of imperialism, too, that epidemic and endemic diseases were most destructive, and inasmuch as their ravages contributed to depopulation, they also caused the introduction of new settlers into wasted areas. Throughout these developments the flow from country to city continued, so that the mongrelization of the population increased, but its effects were no longer limited to the urban part of the population.

The cumulative effects of these three movements within a population carrying an urban cultural tradition was the disintegration of the original culture group and its social structure, and its replacement by a new mongrelized population and a new social structure with a power-wielding group produced by those factors of social specialization giving power and wealth in the phase of imperial decline. Commonly this group, rising from the mongrelized population of the cities, consisted of new military leaders and the priests of a religion which, at best, was a reorientation of the early religious elements of the urban cultural tradition.

In terms such as those outlined in the two preceding paragraphs, the history of the early Asiatic and European urban cultures can be seen in a new light. Scholars commonly speak of "Rome" as if it endured as a population from the eighth century before Christ to the fifth century after Christ. As a matter of fact it seems that throughout this long period there were at least three distinct populations evolved: (1) the patrician-plebeian population of the early Roman Republic, (2) a population fused from the mixed population of Rome and the Italic peoples and led by the "new nobility" that emerged in the Punic Wars and carried Rome to imperial ascendancy, and (3) a population blended from the Mediterranean stocks in the imperial cities and increased by the introduction of slaves and, later, of Germans into the rural areas.[1] This last population was the base of the Christian Roman Empire, and, in the eastern Mediterranean area, where the Germanic element was negligible, of the Byzantine Empire. In China at least two population changes appear to have occurred. The period of "warring states," from which the Ch'in emerged triumphant seems to have altered the basic peasant population of the Wei and Huang valleys, and the period of Han imperialism introduced northern, western, and southern peoples from lands outside the original Chinese urban culture area. The mixture of these peoples with the antecedent population was an aspect of the reshaping of the Chinese cultural tradition after the fall of the Han Dynasty. Whereas the Chinese peasantry has never been entirely uprooted, it has absorbed conquerors and migrants in sufficient numbers to

[1] On population changes in the Mediterranean Basin see A. Landry, "Quelque aperçus concernant la dépopulation dans l'antiquité greco-romaine," *Revue Historique*, Vol. 177 (1936), pp. 1–36. On changes in the Roman ruling classes in the empire see M. I. Rostovtzeff, *A History of the Ancient World*, Vol. 2, *Rome* (1933), p. 293; also Tenney Frank, editor, *An Economic Survey of Ancient Rome* (5 vols., 1933–1940), Vol. 5, *Rome and Italy* (1940), p. 23; George La Piana, "Foreign Groups in Rome during the First Centuries of the Empire," *Harvard Theological Review*, Vol. 20 (1927), p. 223: "Rome, the denationalized capital of the great empire, came to be ruled by the offspring of races which originally had come to the city to serve."

have changed somewhat its composition from time to time. In India the triumph of Hinduism was probably accompanied by a mixing of peoples in the Ganges valley, in which migrants from the Deccan and the Himalayan foothills played an important part.

These population tendencies also suggest the fate of many of the peoples whose disappearance history records. The Phoenicians, for example, are not known after the first century B.C., when the full effects of Roman imperialism first fell upon the small Asiatic peoples; the Hebrews survived these effects only because their cultural tradition made possible the creation of a religious communal life within a foreign political organization. The Greeks were assimilated into the population that became the base of the Byzantine Empire. Because a ruling class rather than a nation is commonly meant when a designation is given to a culture, the disappearance of a nation may not mean the disintegration of a population. Thus, for example, the term "Persian," used sparingly in this work, is applied correctly only to a small ruling group which exercised power over the basic population of Iran. The fall of the Achaemenian Persian Empire before the Greeks and Macedonians involved only the disintegration of this ruling group. The Greeks and Macedonians, in turn, disappeared in Iran in the second and the first century B.C. Indeed, there is little reason to believe that the conquerors of Iran at any time ever displaced the basic peasant and pastoral population. However, in Mesopotamia and Bactria, which were the centers of urban culture upon which Iranian imperialism rested from time to time, there is reason to believe that the same population changes occurred that took place in other centers of urban culture. The coming of the Huns, Teutons, Turks, Arabs, and Berbers into the areas of the traditional urban cultures of Europe and Asia completed a mixing of peoples from which emerged carriers of reorientations of their great traditions.

INDEX

i